BARRON'S
BUSINESS
TRAVELERS

RUSSIAN
FOR THE
BUSINESS
TRAVELER

by
Shane R. DeBeer, Esq.

D1121244

BARRON'S

All inquiries should be addressed to:
Barron's Educational Series, Inc.
250 Wireless Boulevard
Hauppauge, New York 11788

Library of Congress Catalog Card No. 93-31834

International Standard Book No. 0-8120-1784-6

Library of Congress Cataloging-in-Publication Data

DeBeer, Shane R.
    Russian for the business traveler/Shane R. DeBeer.
    p. cm. –– (Bilingual business guides)
    ISBN 0-8120-1784-6
    1. Business – Dictionaries – Russian. 2. Russian language – Dictionaries – English. 3. Business – Dictionaries. 4. English languages – Dictionaries – Russian. 5. Business travel – Russia (Federation) – Guidebooks. I. Title.
    II. Series: Barron's bilingual business guides.
HF1002.D36 1994   93-31834
650′.03 –– dc20   CIP

CONTENTS

I. INTRODUCTION

Many observers in the business press in the 1980s commented on the "globalization" of national economies and of business in general. Few at the time could have predicted just how truly global business would become with the collapse of the iron curtain and the transformation of the Soviet Union into more than a dozen separate nations. Even armed with a knowledge of the language in the relatively similar cultures of the West, businesspeople abroad often find it difficult to negotiate the idiosyncratic terminology and customs of the business world in a foreign country. This problem is compounded when doing business in the former Soviet Union, where the businessperson often must present new ideas to representatives of new (or newly legalized) entities in newly independent nations. Communication under these circumstances is both enormously challenging and critically important.

Now there is a solution — Barron's *Russian for the Business Traveler*. Here is the essential pocket reference for all international business travelers to the Newly Independent States. Whether your business is trade or energy extraction, sales or manufacturing, this comprehensive guide will put the right words in your mouth and the best expressions in your correspondence. It is a book you'll carry with you on every trip and take to every meeting. But it is also the reference you'll keep on your desk at the office. This is *the* business dictionary for people who conduct business in Russian.

This book is one of a new series of business dictionaries. We welcome your comments on additional phrases that could be included in future editions.

Conventions and Nomenclature

Since the collapse of the Soviet Union in 1991, there has been widespread uncertainty and inconsistency regarding the names of the successor nations and of the region as a whole. A brief review of the "name game" is therefore required, not only to explain the conventions used in this book, but to ensure that you refer to the regions you visit by their proper names.

The former Soviet Union consisted of fifteen republics: fourteen of these republics were called Soviet Socialist Republics (SSRs); the largest republic, Russia, was called a Soviet Federated Socialist Republic. The reason for this distinction is that the Russian Soviet Federated Socialist Republic (RSFSR) subsumed within its borders numerous autonomous republics and autonomous okrugs inhabited by non-Russian peoples, such as Tatars, Chechens, and others.

Today, the fourteen non-Russian republics are independent nations, known by native language versions of their Soviet names without SSR. Thus, the former Ukrainian Soviet Socialist Republic is now Ukraine, the former Moldavian Soviet Socialist Republic is now Moldova, and so forth. The RSFSR, by contrast, is now called the Russian Federation, reflecting the continued existence of numerous non-Russian autonomous regions within its borders. Recently, however, the Russian government officially adopted the name Russia as a coequal name to the Russian Federation, so that technically both names are correct. For the sake of simplicity, this book refers to the country as the Russian Federation and uses the adjective *Russian* to signify only the people and language the world knows as Russian.

When referring to the fifteen nations of the former Soviet Union as a whole, this book uses the term *Newly Independent States* (NIS). The reader is also likely to be familiar with the term *Commonwealth of Independent States* (CIS) used to refer to the former Soviet Union. This term actually denotes a voluntary organization of several of the governments of former Soviet republics, but does not include all fifteen nations. For that reason, NIS was chosen as the more accurate and inclusive term.

Scope of this Guide

This business guide is intended to assist businesspeople wherever Russian is spoken — even where it is no longer the official language. The complex linguistic and ethnic makeup of the NIS is discussed briefly in Section IV. Suffice it to note here that Russian remains the *lingua franca* of the NIS. Although it is beyond the scope of this book to provide exhaustive information on the dozens of other languages spoken in the NIS, Section VI includes a list of all NIS official representatives as well as other helpful organizations in the United States for the traveler who wishes to pursue the language and culture of non-Russians in the NIS in greater depth.

How to Use this Guide

This guide is intended to serve both as a Baedeker and a business dictionary. Before your trip to the NIS you should read Section IV, "Doing Business," all the way through. Next, refer to the listings in Section VI, in order to contact the government agencies and foreign representatives who can provide you with specifics you may need for your trip. Depending on your familiarity with the Russian language, you may want to get an early start by reviewing the alphabet and pronunciation Guide in Section II and the basic words and phrases in Section IV. Finally, refer to Section V "Key Words and Phrases" to learn the terminology of your particular industry, and to Section VII, "Business Dictionary" as needed for the general terminology of finance, freight, law, and international trade. Pronunciation is included in both sections V and VII.

II. ALPHABET AND PRONUNCIATION GUIDE

The Russian language is written in the Cyrillic alphabet, named for the Greek missionary St. Cyrill, who, along with St. Methodius, introduced writing to the Slavic peoples in the 9th Century AD. This explains the similarity of the Russian alphabet to the Greek alphabet.

Here is the Russian alphabet in its entirety:

LETTER	NAME OF LETTER	LETTER	NAME OF LETTER
А, а	ah	Р, р	err
Б, б	beh	С, с	ess
В, в	veh	Т, т	teh
Г, г	geh	У, у	oo
Д, д	deh	Ф, ф	eff
Е, е	ye	Х, х	kha
Ё, ё	yo	Ц, ц	tse
Ж, ж	zhe	Ч, ч	cha
З, з	ze	Ш, ш	sha
И, и	ee	Щ, щ	shcha
Й, й	ee KRAT-ka-ye	ъ	TVYOR-dy znak
К, к	ke	Ы, ы	ye-RIH
Л, л	ell	ь	MYA-khy znak
М, м	em	Э, э	eh a-ba-ROT-na-ye
Н, н	en		
О, о	oh	Ю, ю	yu
П, п	peh	Я, я	ya

Russian spelling is very nearly phonetic, with a few exceptions. The phonetic transcriptions in this book are English approximations of the Russian sounds and should be read as you would normally read them in English. Capitalized letters indicate stressed syllables and should be pronounced with more emphasis than that given lowercase syllables in the same word.

This book assumes some familiarity with the Russian language, but the following review of the basic pronunciation rules may be helpful.

RUSSIAN LETTER	ENGLISH SOUND	EXAMPLE
	Vowels:	
а	between the **a** in bat and the **ea** in heart	так (tahk)
е	like the **ye** in yes	нет (nyet)
ё	like the **yo** in yolk	идёт (ee-DYOT)
и	like the **ee** in beet	мир (meer)
й	like the **y** in toy	бой (boy)
о (stressed)	like the **o** in boat	слово (SLOH-va)
(unstressed)	like Russian a	молоко (ma-la-KOH)
у	like the **oo** in root	ум (oom)
ы	between the **i** in sit and the **ee** in tree	вы (viy)
э	like the **e** in bet	это (EH-ta)
ю	like the word **"you"**	юг (yoog)
я	like the **ya** in yacht	ясно (YAS-na)
	Diphthongs	
ай	like **ig** in sign	май (m-IGH)
яй	like **yi** in yikes	негодяй (ne-ga-DYAY)
ой	like the **oy** in toy	бой (boy)
ей	like the **ya** in Yale	пей (pyay)
ый	like the **i** in sit and the **y** in toy	красный (KRAHS-niy)
уй	like **uoy** in buoy	буржуй (boor-ZHUY)
юй	like the preceding, beginning with a **y**	плюй (pl-YOOY)
	Consonants	
б	like **b** in bat	брат (braht)
в	like **v** in vest	валовой (va-la-VOY)
г	like **g** in get	город (GOH-rad)
д	like **d** in dog	дело (DYE-la)
ж	like **s** in measure	жиро (zhee-ROH)
к	like **k** in key	как (kahk)
л	like **l** in lane	лето (LYE-ta)
м	like **m** in made	метро (me-TRO)
н	like **n** in net	нет (nyet)
п	like **p** in pass	паспорт (PAHS-part)
р	like **r** in red (slightly trilled)	русский (ROO-skee)
с	like **s** in sit	сад (sahd)
т	like **t** in ten	так (tahk)
ф	like **f** in forest	флот (flot)
х	like **ch** in Bach	хорошо (kha-ra-SHOH)
ц	like **ts** in tsetse	цена (tse-NAH)

RUSSIAN LETTER	ENGLISH SOUND	EXAMPLE
ч	like **ch** in check	член (chlen)
ш	like **sh** in shoe	шапка (SHAHP-ka)
щ	like **sh** followed close by **ch** in "plushchair"	щи (shchee)

Other Letters

ъ	"hard sign," denotes that a compound word beginning with e, ё, ю or я should be clearly enunciated	подъём (pad-YOM)
ь	"soft sign," softens the sound of the preceding consonant	боль (bol')

This section provides the basic units of reference required to calculate and analyze in Russian, including numbers, days of the week, months, seasons, time, weights and measures, temperature and climate, travel-times, communications codes, telex usage, time zones, holidays, and currencies.

Numbers	*Числа (chees-LAH)*
Cardinal Numbers	**Количественные числительные (ka-LEE-chest-ven-nee-ye chees-LEE-tel-nee-ye)**
0	ноль (nol)
1	один (a-DEEN)
2	два (dva)
3	три (tree)
4	четыре (che-TEE-re)
5	пять (pyat)
6	шесть (shest)
7	семь (sem)
8	восемь (VO-sem)
9	девять (DEV-yat)
10	десять (DES-yat)
11	одиннадцать (a-DEE-nad-tsat)
12	двенадцать (dve-NAD-tsat)
13	тринадцать (tre-NAD-tsat)
14	четырнадцать (che-TEER-nad-tsat)
15	пятнадцать (pyat-NAD-tsat)
16	шестнадцать (shest-NAD-tsat)
17	семнадцать (sem-NAD-tsat)
18	восемнадцать (va-sem-NAD-tsat)
19	девятнадцать (de-vyat-NAD-tsat)
20	двадцать (DVAHD-tsat)
21	двадцать один (DVAHD-tsat a-DEEN)
22	двадцать два (DVAHD-tsat dva)
23	двадцать три (DVAHD-tsat tree)
24	двадцать четыре (DVAHD-tsat che-TEE-re)
25	двадцать пять (DVAHD-tsat pyat)
26	двадцать шесть (DVAHD-tsat shest)
27	двадцать семь (DVAHD-tsat sem)
28	двадцать восемь (DVAHD-tsat VO-sem)
29	двадцать девять (DVAHD-tsat DEV-yat)
30	тридцать (TREED-tsat)
31	тридцать один (TREED-tsat a-DEEN)
40	сорок (SO-rak)
41	сорок один (SO-rak a-DEEN)
50	пятьдесят (pyat-de-SYAT)

60	шестьдесят (shest-de-SYAT)
70	семьдесят (SEM-de-syat)
80	восемьдесят (VO-sem-de-syat)
90	девяносто (de-vya-NOH-sta)
100	сто (sto)
101	сто один (sto a-DEEN)
102	сто два (sto dva)
200	двести (DVE-stee)
300	триста (TREE-sta)
400	четыреста (che-TEE-re-sta)
500	пятьсот (pyat-SOT)
600	шестьсот (shest-SOT)
700	семьсот (sem-SOT)
800	восемьсот (VO-sem-SOT)
900	девятьсот (de-vyat-SOT)
1,000	тысяча (TEE-syach-ya)
2,000	две тысячи (dve TEE-syach-ee)
3,000	три тысячи (tree TEE-syach-ee)
4,000	четыре тысячи (che-TEE-re TEE-syach-ee)
5,000	пять тысяч (pyat TEE-syach)
6,000	шесть тысяч (shest TEE-syach)
7,000	семь тысяч (sem TEE-syach)
8,000	восемь тысяч (VO-sem TEE-syach)
9,000	девять тысяч (DEV-yat TEE-syach)
10,000	десять тысяч (DES-yat TEE-syach)
20,000	двадцать тысяч (DVAHD-tsat TEE-syach)
30,000	тридцать тысяч (TREED-tsat TEE-syach)
40,000	сорок тысяч (SO-rak TEE-syach)
50,000	пятьдесят тысяч (pyat-de-SYAT TEE-syach)
60,000	шестьдесят тысяч (shest-de-syat TEE-syach)
70,000	семьдесят тысяч (SEM-de-syat TEE-syach)
80,000	восемьдесят тысяч (VO-sem-de-syat TEE-syach)
90,000	девяносто тысяч (de-vya-NOH-sta TEE-syach)
100,000	сто тысяч (STO TEE-syach)
200,000	двести тысяч (DVE-stee TEE-syach)
300,000	триста тысяч (TREE-sta TEE-syach)
400,000	четыреста тысяч (che-TEE-re-sta TEE-syach)
500,000	пятьсот тысяч (pyat-SOT TEE-syach)
600,000	шестьсот тысяч (shest-SOT TEE-syach)
700,000	семьсот тысяч (sem-SOT TEE-syach)
800,000	восемьсот тысяч (VO-sem-SOT TEE-syach)
900,000	девятьсот тысяч (de-vyat-SOT TEE-syach)
1,000,000	миллион (mee-lee-ON)
2,000,000	два миллиона (dva mee-lee-ON-a)
10,000,000	десять миллионов (DES-yat mee-lee-ON-ov)
100,000,000	сто миллионов (sto mee-lee-ON-ov)
1,000,000,000	миллиард (mee-lee-ARD)

Examples	Примеры (pree-MER-ee)
540	пятьсот сорок (pyat-SOT SǪ-rak)
1,540	тысяча пятьсот сорок (TEE-syach-a pyat-SOT SO-rak)
11,540	одиннадцать тысяч пятьсот сорок (a-DEEN-nad-tsat TEE-syach pyat-SOT SO-rak)
611,540	шестьсот одиннадцать тысяч пятьсот сорок (shest-SOT a-DEEN-nad-tsat TEE-syach pyat-SOT SO-rak)
1,611,540	миллион шестьсот одиннадцать тысяч пятьсот сорок (mee-lee-ON shest-SOT a-DEEN-nad-tsat TEE-syach pyat-SOT SO-rak)

Years	Годы (GOH-dee)
1900	тысяча девятисотый год (TEE-syach-a dev-yat-SOT-ee god)
1993	тысяча девятьсот девяносто третий год (TEE-syach-a de-vyat-SOT de-vya-NO-sta TRE-tee god)
1994	тысяча девятьсот девяносто четвёртый год (TEE-syach-a de-vyat-SOT de-vya-NOH-sta chet-VYOR-tee god)
1995	тысяча девятьсот девяносто пятый год (TEE-syach-a de-vyat-SOT de-vya-NOH-sta PYA-tee god)
2000	двухтысячный год (dvookh-TEE-syach-nee god)

Ordinal Numbers	Порядковые числительные (par-YAD-ka-vee-ye chees-LEE-tel-nee-ye)
first	первый (PER-vee)
second	второй (fta-ROY)
third	третий (TRE-tee)
fourth	четвертый (chet-VYOR-tee)
fifth	пятый (PYA-tee)
sixth	шестой (shes-TOY)
seventh	седьмой (sed-MOY)
eighth	восьмой (vas-MOY)
ninth	девятый (de-VYA-tee)
tenth	десятый (de-SYA-tee)
the first day	первый день (PER-vee den)
for the second time	во второй раз (vo fta-ROY raz)
once	однажды (ad-NAZH-dee)
twice	дважды (DVAZH-dee)
a half	половина (pa-la-VEE-na)
a quarter	четверть (CHET-vert)
three quarters	три четверти (tree CHET-ver-tee)
a third	одна треть (ad-NAH tret)
two thirds	две трети (dve TRET-ee)
a cup of___	чашка ____(CHASH-ka ___)

a kilo of___	кило_____(KEE-lo___)
a liter of___	литр_____(LEE-ter___)
a little bit of___	немного_____(ne-MNOH-ga___)
a small piece of__	кусок _____(koo-SOK)
a bunch of___	куча _____ (KOO-cha)
a pair of___	пара_____(PAH-ra___)
enough of___	достаточно_____(da-STA-tach-na___)
too much of___	слишком_____(SLEESH-kam)

Days of the Week
Дни недели (Dnee ne-DYE-lee)

Today is _____	Сегодня___(se-VOD-nya___)
• Monday	• понедельник (pa-ne-DEL-neek)
• Tuesday	• вторник (FTOR-neek)
• Wednesday	• среда (sre-DAH)
• Thursday	• четверг (CHET-verg)
• Friday	• пятница (PYAT-nee-tsa)
• Saturday	• суббота (soo-BO-tah)
• Sunday	• воскресенье (vas-kre-SEN-ye)
yesterday	вчера (fche-RAH)
the day before yesterday	позавчера (PO-za-fche-ra)
tomorrow	завтра (ZAHF-tra)
the day after tomorrow	послезавтра (POS-le-zahf-tra)
in the morning	утром (OO-trom)
afternoon	днём (dnyom)
evening	вечером (VE-che-rom)
tonight	сегодня вечером (se-VOD-nya VE-che-rom)
this afternoon	сегодня днём (se-VOD-nya dnyom)
every day	каждый день (KAHZH-dee den)

Months
Месяцы (MES-ya-tsee)

January	январь (yan-VAHR)
February	февраль (fe-VRAHL)
March	март (mart)
April	апрель (a-PREL)
May	май (ma-ee)
June	июнь (ee-YOON)
July	июль (ee-YOOL)
August	август (AHF-goost)
September	сентябрь (sen-TYA-ber)
October	октябрь (ak-TYA-ber)
November	ноябрь (na-YA-ber)
December	декабрь (de-KA-ber)
What is today's date?	Какое сегодня число? (ka-KOY-ye se-VOD nya chee-SLOH)
Today is May 3.	Сегодня третье мая. (se-VOD-nya TRET-ye MA-ya)

monthly	ежемесячно (e-zhe-MES-yach-na)
this month	этот месяц, в этом месяце (EH-tot MES-yats, FEH-tom MES-ya-tse)
next month	следующий месяц, в следующем месяце (SLED-oo-yoo-shchee MES-yats, FSLED-oo-yoo-shchem MES-ya-tse)
last month	прошлый месяц, в прошлом месяце (PROH-shlee MES-yats, FPROH-shlam MES-ya-tse)

The Four Seasons — *Времена года (vre-me-NAH GOH-da)*

spring	весна (ves-NA)
summer	лето (LYEH-ta)
autumn	осень (O-syen)
winter	зима (zee-MAH)
in the fall	осенью (O-syen-yoo)
during the spring	весной (ves-NOY)
every summer	каждое лето (KAHZH-da-ye LYEH-ta)
in the summer	летом (LYEH-tam)
in the winter	зимой (zee-MOY)

Time — *Время (VREM-ya)*

What time is it?	Который час? (ka-TOR-ee chas) *or* Сколько времени (SKOHL-ka VREH-me-nee)
• hour	час (chas)
• minute	минута (mee-NOO-ta)
• second	секунда (se-KOON-da)
• half an hour	полчаса (pal-cha-SA)
• an hour and a half	полтора часа (pal-ta-RA cha-SA)
twenty after twelve	двадцать минут первого (дня - PM or ночи - AM) (DVAHD-tsat mee-NOOT PER va-va {dnya/NOH-chee})
twelve-twenty	двенадцать двадцать (dve-NAHD-tsat DVAHD-tsat)
one-thirty	половина второго (pa-la-VEE-na fta-ROH-va)
half an hour (30 minutes)	полчаса (тридцать минут) (pal-cha-SA {TREED-tsat mee-NOOT})
eight to three (2:52)	без восьми три (bez vas-MEE tree)
five to seven (6:55)	без пяти семь (bez pya-TEE syem)
nine after four (4:09)	девять минут пятого (DYE-vyat me-NOOT PYAH-ta-va)
a quarter after three (3:15)	четверть четвертого (CHEHT-vert chet-VYOR-ta-va)
What time shall we meet?	В котором часу мы встретимся? (fka-TOR-am cha-SOO mee FSTRE-teem-sya)
We'll eat at eight (o'clock).	Мы будем есть в восемь (часов). (mee-BOOD-em yest FOH-sem {cha-SOV})

Weights and Measures

U.S. UNIT	METRIC EQUIVALENT
mile	1.609 kilometers
yard	0.914 meters
foot	30.480 centimeters
inch	2.540 centimeters
square mile	2.590 square kilometers
acre	0.405 hectares
square yard	0.836 square meters
square foot	0.093 square meters
square inch	6.451 square centimeters
cubic yard	0.764 cubic meters
cubic foot	0.028 cubic meters
cubic inch	16.387 cubic centimeters
short ton	0.907 metric tons
long ton	1.016 metric tons
short hundredweight	45.359 kilograms
long hundredweight	50.802 kilograms
pound	0.453 kilograms
ounce	28.349 grams
gallon	3.785 liters
quart	0.946 liters
pint	0.473 liters
fluid ounce	29.573 milliliters
bushel	35.238 liters
peck	8.809 liters
quart	1.101 liters
pint	0.550

Temperature and Climate

DEGREES CELSIUS	DEGREES FAHRENHEIT
-5	23
0	32
5	41
10	50
15	59
20	68
25	77
30	86
35	95
40	104

AVERAGE TEMPERATURES FOR MAJOR CITIES IN FAHRENHEIT				
	JAN	*APR*	*SEPT*	*DEC*
Kiev	21	44	56	26
Moscow	14	39	51	19
St. Petersburg	18	37	51	22

hot	жаркий (ZHAR-kee)
sunny	солнечный (SOL-nech-nee)
warm	тепло (tye-PLOH)
cool	прохладно (pra-KHLAD-na)
windy	ветрено (VE-tre-na)
snowing	идёт снег (ee-DYOT sneg)
raining	идёт дождь (ee-DYOT dozhd)

Travel Times

Approximate Flying Times to Key Russian Cities*

	Moscow	St. Petersburg	Vladivostok
New York	9 hrs	10 hrs	n/a
Chicago	11 hrs	12 hrs	n/a
Los Angeles	n/a	n/a	16 hrs
San Francisco	11 hrs	12 hrs	15 hrs
Seattle	n/a	n/a	13 hrs
Anchorage	n/a	n/a	9 hrs
Montreal	10 hrs	12 hrs	n/a
Toronto	13 hrs	14 hrs	n/a
London	4 hrs	4 hrs	n/a
Sydney	21 hrs	22 hrs	n/a
Tokyo**	10 hrs	11 hrs	4 hrs

Average Flying Times between Major Russian/NIS Cities *
From Moscow to:

Chelyabinsk	2 hours
Ekaterinburg	2 hours
Kazan	1 hour
Khabarovsk	7 hours
Kiev	2 hours
Krasnoyarsk	5 hours
Magadan	8 hours
Nizhny Novgorod	1 hour
Novosibirsk	4 hours
Omsk	3 hours
Perm	2 hours

---

* includes required layovers
** via Niigata, Japan, includes bullet train transit from Tokyo

Petropavlovsk - Kamchatsky	9 hours
Rostov-on-Don	1 hour
St. Petersburg	1 hour, 20 minutes
Samara	1 hour
Ufa	2 hours
Vladivostok	7 hours
Volgograd	1 hour
From St. Petersburg to:	
Chelyabinsk	5 hours
Ekaterinburg	5 hours
Kazan	2 hours, 30 minutes
Khabarovsk	17 hours
Kiev	3 hours
Krasnoyarsk	9 hours
Magadan	20 hours, 30 minutes
Moscow	1 hour, 25 minutes
Nizhny Novgorod	1 hour, 45 minutes
Novosibirsk	8 hours
Omsk	6 hours, 30 minutes
Perm	3 hours
Petropavlovsk - Kamchatsky	24 hours
Rostov-on-Don	2 hours, 30 minutes
Samara	3 hours, 15 minutes
Ufa	4 hours, 30 minutes
Vladivostok	19 hours
Volgograd	2 hours, 20 minutes

Telephones

The domestic telephone network in the NIS remains overburdened and technologically backward, despite agreement by government and business alike on the need for improvement. Every aspect of telephone service in the NIS is a challenge: it is difficult and time-consuming to have a telephone line installed or repaired; no official telephone directories are published (though private directories are available); and even local circuits are frequently busy. At this writing, the only reliable telephone service in the NIS is provided by private satellite link services. U.S. satellite link services include AT&T, which can be reached in Moscow at (095) 284-3399.

Satellite access codes differ from the domestic country and city codes listed here.

City Codes for the Major Cities of the Russian Federation

Chelyabinsk	3512	Magadan	41322
Ekaterinburg	3432	Moscow	095
Kazan	8432	Nizhny Novgorod	8312
Khabarovsk	4212	Novosibirsk	3832
Krasnoyarsk	3912	Omsk	3812

Perm	3422	Samara	8462
Petropavlovsk-		Stavropol	865
Kamchatsky	41522	Ufa	3472
Rostov-on-Don	8632	Vladivostok	4232
St. Petersburg	812	Volvograd	8422

City Codes for Other NIS Cities

Alma Ata	3272	Odessa	0482
Ashkhabad	3632	Riga	2
Baku	8922	Tallinn	2
Bishkek	3312	Tartu	34
Chisinau	2	Tashkent	3712
Dushanbe	3772	Tblisi	8832
Kharkiv	057(2)*	Vilnius	2
Kiev	044	Yerevan	885(2)*
Minsk	017(2)*		

International Country Codes (NIS Nations in Bold)

Afghanistan	93	Hong Kong	852
Algeria	213	Hungary	36
Andorra	33	Iceland	354
Argentina	54	India	91
Armenia	**7**	Iran	98
Australia	61	Ireland	353
Austria	43	Israel	972
Azerbaijan	**7**	Italy	39
Belarus	**7**	Japan	81
Belgium	32	**Kazakhstan**	**7**
Bosnia-Herzegovina	38	Kuwait	965
Brazil	55	**Kyrgyzstan**	**7**
Bulgaria	359	**Latvia**	**371**
Canada	1	Liechtenstein	41
Chile	56	**Lithuania**	**370**
China (PRC)	86	Luxembourg	352
Colombia	57	Macedonia	38
Croatia	38	Malta	356
Cuba	53	Mexico	52
Czech Republic	42	**Moldova**	**373**
Denmark	45	Monaco	33
Egypt	20	Mongolia	976
Estonia	**372**	Morocco	212
Finland	358	Netherlands	31
France	33	New Zealand	64
Georgia	**7**	Norway	47
Germany	49	Pakistan	92
Gibraltar	350	Philippines	63
Greece	30	Poland	48

---

* additional digits may be required for telephone numbers having six or fewer digits

Portugal	351	**Tajikistan**	**7**
Rumania	40	Thailand	255
Russian Federation	**7**	Tunisia	216
Saudi Arabia	966	Turkey	90
Singapore	65	**Turkmenistan**	**7**
Slovakia	42	**Ukraine**	**7**
South Africa	27	United Kingdom	44
South Korea	82	**Uzbekistan**	**7**
Spain	34	USA	1
Sri Lanka	94	Venezuela	58
Sweden	46	Vietnam	84
Switzerland	41	Yugoslavia (Serbia)	38
Taiwan	886		

Telex Usage

The most reliable form of communication with the NIS (in remote areas sometimes the only reliable form of communication) remains the telex. The country prefix for the entire NIS is **871**. Cyrillic-lettered telexes are used for internal transmissions within the NIS; however, all external telex traffic uses the Latin alphabet. If your party does not speak English, you may choose to telex him or her in Russian. To do so, use the following standard system of transliteration.

Russian Letter	Latin Alphabet Transliteration	Russian Letter	Latin Alphabet Transliteration
А	A	Р	R
Б	B	С	S
В	V	Т	T
Г	G	У	U
Е	E	Х	KH
Ё	E	Ц	C
Ж	ZH	Ч	CH
З	Z	Ш	SH
И	I	Щ	SHCH
Й	J	Ъ	–
К	K	Ы	Y
Л	L	Ь	–
М	M	Э	E
Н	N	Ю	IU
О	O	Я	IA
П	P		

Postal Service

Domestic mail service in the NIS is unreliable, and there is a real and continuing problem with the theft of packages that appear to contain something valuable. Any important mail should be sent by private courier. The following courier services are reliable, although service in the NIS may differ from stateside service. Next Day Federal Express service, for example, may take two to three days.

Airborne Express
c/o RUSCP-RGW Express Limited
9/1 Arkhipova Ul., 2nd floor
101000 Moscow
Tel. (095)262-9515
     (703)823-2303 in U.S.
NOTES: Transit time four business
   days, hand delivered to 160 major
   cities in the NIS, five business
   days for dutiable shipments

Delta Airlines
Krasnopresnenskaya nab. 12,
   11th floor
Tel: (253)2658/2659
     (800)638-7333 in U.S.
Telex: 413089
NOTES: Small packages to Moscow
   only; recipient must clear packages

DHL Courier Service
c/o Soyuzvneshtrans, 3
Pochtovaya pl.
252076 Kiev
Tel: (36-1)157-6992
     (800)225-5345 in U.S.
c/o Soyuzvneshtrans, 7
Primorski bl.
270026 Odessa
Tel: (36-1)157-6992
     (800)225-5345 in U.S.
NOTES: Cities served include Alma
   Ata, Baku, Kiev, St. Petersburg,
   Moscow, Odessa, Tblisi, and
   Vladivostok

Federal Express
Sovincenter, 3rd Entrance, 1st Floor
Krasnopresnenskaya nab. 12
123610 Moscow
Tel: (095)253-1641
     (800)247-4747 in U.S.
Fax: (095)253-1066
NOTES: Cities served include
   Kazan, Moscow, Nizhny
   Novgorod, St. Petersburg, and
   Zhukovsky

United Parcel Service
UPA/Sovtransavto
Bolshaya Ochakovskaya 15A
119361 Moscow
Tel: (095)430-6398
     (800)457-4022
Telex:(064)612251
NOTES: Cities served include
   Khabarovsk, Magadan, Moscow,
   Nakhodka, St. Petersburg, and
   Vladivostok

United States Postal Service
Express Mail International
(contact local U.S. Post Office)
NOTES: All major cities are served;
   the list is constantly expanding

Time Zones

The NIS spans eleven time zones, although the international operator generally quotes only Moscow time. Moscow is one hour ahead of central European time (three hours ahead of Greenwich Mean Time) and also in the earliest time band of the NIS. The Russian Federation adds one hour for daylight saving time from April 1 to October 1. Fortunately, most of the major cities in the NIS are within a few hours of Moscow time, as the following list indicates.

If it's Tuesday, noon, in Moscow:

Alma Ata	3 P.M. Tuesday	Bishkek	3 P.M. " "
Anadyr	10 P.M. " "	Chelyabinsk	2 P.M. " "
Ashkhbad	2 P.M. " "	Dushanbe	3 P.M. " "
Baku	1 P.M. " "	Ekaterinburg	2 P.M. " "

Irkutsk	5 P.M. " "	Petropavlovsk-	
Kharkiv	12 P.M. " "	Kamchatsky	9 P.M. " "
Kiev	12 P.M. " "	St. Petersburg	12 P.M. " "
Magadan	8 P.M ." "	Samara	1 P.M. " "
Minsk	12 P.M. " "	Tallinn	12 P.M. " "
Nizhny Novgorod	12 P.M. " "	Ufa	2 P.M. " "
Novosibirsk	4 P.M. " "	Yakutsk	6 P.M. " "
Omsk	3 P.M. " "	Yerevan	1 P.M. " "
Perm	2 P.M. " "	Vladivostok	7 P.M. " "

While elsewhere in the world:

Honolulu	10 P.M. Monday
London	9 A.M. Tuesday
Los Angeles	1 A.M. Tuesday
New York	4 A.M. Tuesday
Tokyo	5 P.M. Tuesday

Major Holidays (Russian Federation)

January 1	New Year's Day
January 7	Russian Orthodox Christmas
March 8	International Women's Day
May 1	Labor and Spring Day
May 8-9	Victory Day (WWII)
June 12	Independence Day

Currencies of the World (NIS Currencies in Bold)

Afghanistan	Afghan
Algeria	Dinar
Argentina	Astral
Andorra	French Franc
Armenia	**Dram**
Australia	Australian Dollar
Austria	Schilling
Azerbaijan	**Azerbaijani Manat**
Belarus	**Russian Ruble**
Belgium	Belgian Franc
Bosnia-Herzegovina	Dinar
Brazil	Cruzado
Bulgaria	Lev
Canada	Canadian Dollar
Chile	Peso
China (PRC)	Yuan
Colombia	Colon
Croatia	Croatian Dinar
Cuba	Cuban Peso
Czech Republic	Kronor
Denmark	Danish Krone
Egypt	Egyptian Pound

Estonia	**Kroon**
Finland	Markka
France	French Franc
Georgia	**Russian Ruble (coupon)**
Germany	Deutsche Mark (DM)
Gibraltar	Pound
Greece	Drachma
Hong Kong	HK Dollar
Hungary	Forint
Iceland	Krone
India	Indian Rupee
Iran	Rial
Ireland	Punt (Irish Pound)
Israel	Shekel
Italy	Italian Lira
Japan	Yen
Kazakhstan	**Tenge**
Kuwait	Kuwaiti Dinar
Kyrgyzstan	**Som**
Latvia	**Lat**
Liechtenstein	Swiss Franc
Lithuania	**Lit**
Luxembourg	Luxembourg Franc
Macedonia	Dinar
Malta	Maltese Lira
Mexico	Mexican Peso
Moldova	**Leu**
Monaco	French Franc
Netherlands	Guilder
New Zealand	New Zealand Dollar
Mongolia	Tugrik
Norway	Norwegian Krone
Pakistan	Pakistani Rupee
Philippines	Philippine Peso
Poland	Zloty
Portugal	Escudo
Rumania	Lei
Russian Federation	**Russian Ruble**
Saudi Arabia	Riyal
Singapore	Singapore Dollar
Slovakia	Czech Kronor
South Africa (RSA)	Rand
South Korea (ROK)	Won
Spain	Peseta
Sri Lanka	Sri Lankan Rupee
Sweden	Swedish Krone
Switzerland	Swiss Franc
Taiwan	Dollar (Yuan)
Tajikistan	**Russian Ruble**
Thailand	Baht

Tunisia	Dinar
Turkey	Turkish Lira
Turkmenistan	**Turkmenistan Manat**
Ukraine	**Karbovanets**
United Kingdom	Pound Sterling
United States	Dollar
Uzbekistan	**Som-Coupon**
Venezuela	Bolivar
Vietnam	Dong
Yugoslavia (Serbia)	Dinar

IV. DOING BUSINESS

Doing business with another culture and in another language can be a difficult and mystifying experience. Customs and procedures may be quite different from what is perceived as the normal way of conducting oneself in a business setting.

In this section, some of the customs and habits, as well as basic economic aspects of the various nations where Russian is spoken, are outlined in order to assist you in effectively conducting business in these areas. The NIS, however, spans an enormous amount of territory, both geographic and cultural. As a result, differences in customs and conditions can be dramatic. Moreover, the entire region is undergoing political and economic change of historic proportions, which involves the customs and even the languages. This dictionary was written with the aim of preparing businesspeople to adapt and succeed in this fast-changing environment.

Your first stop in considering a business venture in the NIS should be the U.S. government. The Department of Commerce offers a business information service for the NIS, with data on trade and investment opportunities, and financing alternatives, as well as trade statistics. Information can be obtained from the U.S. Department of Commerce, International Trade Administration, Business Information Service for the Newly Independent States, Room H-7413, Washington, D.C. 20230 or through a 24-hour fax delivery system at (202) 482-3145.

Language

The Russian language is the native tongue of about 150 million people and is spoken as a second tongue by another 100 million people. Thus, despite certain ethnic and linguistic tensions, Russian is the *lingua franca* of the NIS and is bound to remain so for the foreseeable future. Russian is part of the Slavic group of Indo-European languages, which also includes Bulgarian, Belorussian, Czech, Polish, Serbo-Croatian, and Ukrainian. It is distantly related to English, which belongs to the Germanic group of Indo-European languages.

Russian is a highly inflected language; changing word endings are used to denote part of speech, tense, and so on. Russian is also a flexible language and, like English, has absorbed many foreign words over the centuries. For example, the Russian word for money, деньги (DYEN-gee), derives from the Mongol dialect of Genghis Khan and the Russian word for chess, шахматы (SHAKH-ma-tee), derives from old Persian. Many technical and legal terms derive from French, German, and, increasingly, English.

The Soviet Union, and the Russian Empire before it, expanded over a vast stretch of territory, conquering and absorbing numerous non-Russian peoples over a span of many centuries. In that context it should not be surprising that the last census taken in the Soviet Union counted well over 100 spoken languages, although most were spoken by fewer than 500,000 people. Although Russian is directly related to Belorussian (10 million speakers) and Ukrainian (30 million speakers), it is wholly unrelated to the vast majority of other non-Slavic languages recorded in the census. However, as a result of a long-standing policy of Russification under the Soviets, most non-Russian adults in the NIS speak Russian, although many prefer not to. Often, Russian is the only foreign language spoken by non-Russians in the NIS, whose native tongues are little known to the outside world or even to other nationalities within the NIS. As a result, business between between non-Russians is conducted in Russian: if an Uzbek and a Lithuanian needs to communicate they speak Russian.

The most popular foreign language studied in the NIS today is English. Regionally, Turkish is very popular in Central Asia, and German is popular throughout the European parts of the NIS. Many people in Ukraine, Belarus and Lithuania speak Polish; Finnish is closely related to Estonian and is widely understood in Estonia, just as Rumanian is in Moldova.

Business Customs

Russian Federation, Belarus, and Ukraine

There is already a noticeable gap in business styles between the older and younger generations in the Slavic nations of the NIS, but a few generalizations are applicable. Russians tend to be formal in their business relations, and first impressions are very important. Older Russians are likely to believe in a hierarchy and to regulate their relations accordingly, although most Russians tend to open up and become more friendly as the business relationship progresses. Russians are often compared to Americans in this respect. Russians shake hands frequently and firmly and customarily exchange small gifts with new business associates. Like most westerners, Russians expect to be looked in the eye when spoken to, and consider lack of eye contact a sign of dishonesty. Russians expect promptness and a professional appearance, especially from westerners.

The Russian Federation remains a nation of smokers, and you may expect to be exposed to secondhand smoke frequently. If you do smoke, you should ask permission before smoking and offer your cigarettes to others. This habit seems to be on the decline among younger people, but remains much more prevalent throughout the NIS than in the West.

Western businesspeople as far back as Marco Polo have remarked on the Russian capacity for and love of strong drink; vodka still sells quite well in the Russian Federation, but attitudes have changed somewhat. Alcoholism is a serious health problem throughout the NIS and especially in the Slavic regions, and the more indulgent and philosophical attitudes toward heavy drinking have given way to more western attitudes toward drink. It is thus no longer advisable to give alcoholic beverages as gifts, nor is it seen as an insult to decline to drink alcohol with one's Russian host, as might once have been the case.

Russian retains an old-fashioned system of names, which may be confusing to usually less formal westerners. New business associates should be addressed by Mr. (Господин, pronounced "ga-spa-DEEN") or Ms. (Госпожа, pronounced "ga-spa-ZHA") and their last names. The once common address Comrade (товарищ, pronounced "ta-VA-reeshch") is strictly out, as it technically refers to membership in the Communist party. Mr. or Ms. should also be used to attract the attention of strangers, but not service personnel (use "waiter," "porter," etc. for service personnel). Once you have become acquainted with your Russian business associate, you may address him or her by name and patronymic (middle name, based on one's father's first name). Women's last names generally add an a to the male form of the last name, and female patronymics are formed differently as well.

For example, assume that you are meeting Mr. and Mrs. Ivanov. Mr. Ivanov's full name is Matvei Petrovich Ivanov; from his patronymic (Petrovich), you know that his father's name is Petr. You would originally address Mr. Ivanov as Господин Иванов (Mr. Ivanov, pronounced "ga-spa-DEEN ee-VAHN-off"), and perhaps later as Матвей Петрович (Matvei Petrovich, pronounced "mat-VEY pe-TROH-vich"), which is an address of moderate formality, but not so familiar as using a first name. Many Slavs, in the American fashion, will move quickly to a first name basis, but this step should not be expected. Similarly, assume that Mr. Ivanov's wife's full name is Anna Borisovna Ivanova. Notice that her last name ends in an a, unlike Mr. Ivanov's, although it is essentially the same name. You know from her patronymic that Mrs. Ivanova's father's name is Boris. You would initially address her as Госпожа Иванова (Mrs. Ivanova, pronounced "ga-spa-ZHA ee-VAHN-a-va"), and perhaps later as Анна Борисовна (Anna Borisovna, pronounced "AHN-na ba-REES-av-na").

If you become intimate with Russians you will find that the language has an impressive array of diminutive, affectionate versions of first names. For example, Sergei may be called Seriyozha, Seryozhechka, Seryozhka, Seryozhik, Seryozhenka and others.

In Ukraine, nationalism has become an increasingly important issue. Ukraine has a sizable Russian population, which constitutes the majority population in the Crimea, and a near majority in the Donetsk mining and industrial regions. Western Ukraine was formerly predominantly Roman Catholic and greatly influenced by Poland; these influences are now reasserting themselves, hence there is greater nationalism in the western region of Ukraine as well as Russian separatism in Crimea.

Central Asia

Geographically, Central Asia refers to Kazakhstan, Kyrgyzstan, Tajikistan, Turkmenistan, and Uzbekistan; culturally this area also includes Azerbaijan, which is located at the foot of the Caucasus Mountains. These lands — but not these nation-states — have a very long history and many old customs. In Kazakhstan and Kyrgyzstan, as in Mongolia and parts of China, there still live nomads who sleep in tents of skins, called yurts, and keep sheep or horses for their livelihood. In Central Asia, the majority of people are Muslim, but, with the possible exception of Tajikistan, fundamentalism has made little progress. Central Asians are very formal and quite hospitable in the Asian tradition. Although you may expect a different attitude toward alcohol consumption among Muslims than among Russians, alcohol is much more tolerated here than in other predominantly Muslim cultures. In fact, you may well be offered — and expected to drink — koumiss, a traditional drink made of fermented mare's milk.

Central Asians have a hierarchical society, and you should always address the superior of any group of people with whom you are dealing.

Similarly, the senior person in your group should establish his or her position when initiating contact. Most of Central Asian society remains quite traditional, which for many western women, especially businesswomen, means chauvinistic. Women should dress conservatively, and in particular should avoid pantsuits and low-cut necklines. Family relations are important in Central Asia, and the wise businessperson will ascertain what, if any, family relations exist between the parties with whom he or she is dealing. As with Russians, a firm handshake and eye contact are expected, and the lack of either may be construed as a sign of dishonesty or indecisiveness. Be sure to give your Central Asian hosts small gifts and graciously to accept gifts offered.

The Baltic States

The Baltic states, Estonia, Latvia and Lithuania, were independent nations prior to World War II, when the Soviets invaded as a "peacekeeping" force pursuant to the prewar peace treaty between Stalin and Hitler. Although all three nations had once been part of the Russian Empire (and other empires before it), they were nonetheless the most independent-minded and least Sovietized of the Soviet republics. Indeed, the Foresters, an armed resistance group opposing Soviet rule, held out in Estonia into the 1960s. The Baltic republics were also the most economically developed and remained so under communism.

Estonia is the most developed of the three, with significant dairy, chemical, and industrial capacity. The Estonian language is closely related to Finnish (and almost no other language), and Estonians receive and understand television and radio broadcasts from Finland. Finland has made great inroads in investment in and joint ventures with Estonia. Estonians were primarily Protestant (Lutheran) Christian before the Soviet era, and, like the Eastern Lander of Germany, are now returning to that faith. Estonia has no significant energy resources, except for shale oil, which is abundant. Ethnic Estonians constitute about 60 percent of the population; the remainder is primarily Russian (30+%), but also comprises Ukrainian, Belorussian, and other NIS nationalities. The non-Estonian population is concentrated in the cities (Tallinn, Narva, Kohtla-Jarva) and is primarily employed in heavy industry and defense-related production. There is some tension between Estonia and the Russian Federation over the voting and language rights of Russians living in Estonia. You should be aware of this situation as it affects the work force.

Businesspeople will find that Estonians are much like Scandinavians — reserved and formal. It takes time to get to know them, and they are not likely to warm up or open up in the first series of meetings.

Latvia has experienced the most Russification of any Soviet republic, and ethnic Latvians today account for just over 50 percent of the population. As in Estonia, a variety of other nationalities are represented in Latvia, including predominantly Russians, but also Ukrainians, Belorussians, other Baltic nationalities, and Caucasian nationalities. The capital city, Riga, is a major Baltic seaport, and Latvia has a diversified industrial and agricultural base, although it is now suffering from a steep decline in defense production. The Latvian language is unrelated to Russian, but is noticeably similar to Lithuanian. Russian is widely spoken in Latvia where, given the demographics, the government has been less successful than in Estonia in promoting the official use of the native language. Latvia was predominantly Roman Catholic before being absorbed into the Soviet Union. Latvians are pragmatic and somewhat more easygoing and less formal than Estonians.

Lithuania is the largest of the Baltic states and the most ethnically homogenous — about 80 percent of the population is ethnic Lithuanian. Lithuania's *Sajudis* movement was one of the first and most aggressive nationalist movements seeking to leave the Soviet Union, and blood was shed more than once before the failed coup attempt solidified Lithuania's independence. in 1991 Today, Lithuania has a relatively conservative (in NIS terms) government, which is not instituting economic reforms as rapidly as its Baltic neighbors. Many Lithuanians speak Polish or are ethnically Polish, and there is a lively and growing trade relationship between Lithuania and Poland, which were once allied as an important empire opposed to the Russians. Lithuanians, like Poles, are strongly Roman Catholic, and tend to be a bit more excitable than are the more sober Estonians or the pragmatic Latvians.

The Caucasus Region

The Caucasus Mountains straddle three nations: Armenia, Georgia, and Azerbaijan. Only Armenia and Georgia can really be characterized as "Caucasian" in the cultural sense. Azerbaijan, a predominantly Muslim nation whose inhabitants speak a language (Azeri) related to Farsi (spoken in Iran), is better classified as a Central Asian nation. Georgia is predominantly Orthodox Christian (Georgian rite, akin to Greek Orthodox), with a long history and a distinct culture. Georgians have been called Mediterranean in outlook and are considered expressive and emotional. In Soviet times, Georgians were often informally criticized as wheeler-dealers, but it must be remembered that ordinary free enterprise was, at the time, a criminal offense. In fact, Georgia does have a long-standing mercantile tradition, which will likely become valuable to the newly independent country in the future. It is interesting to note that the most famous Georgian of all, however, was the greatest enemy of capitalism of his time: Joseph Dzhugashvili, better known to the rest of the world as Joseph Stalin. Georgia has faced several economic setbacks since independence, not the least of which is a low-intensity struggle over certain northern, mountainous territories inhabited by minority peoples. In particular, the Black Sea resort town Sukhumi has suffered significant damage as a result of this conflict.

Armenians are renowned businesspeople worldwide, as the diaspora has succeeded as far afield as California and Canada. Like Georgians, Armenians are predominantly Orthodox Christian with a long-standing trade and mercantile tradition, a long history, and an ancient culture. Armenia has few energy resources, but has an important agricultural base. Armenia has been involved in a debilitating dispute with Azerbaijan over the fate of an enclave of Armenians living within the Azerbaijani borders in a region called Nagorno-Karabakh. Because Armenia is landlocked, and in part because of the struggle with Azerbaijan, Armenia faces a difficult economic outlook, and production has slowed dramatically.

General Government Policy and Economic Situation

Russian Federation

At 6.6 million square miles (17.07 million square kilometers), the Russian Federation is the largest country on earth, with nearly twice the territory of the United States. It comprises 51 percent of the total NIS population (148.5 million), 73.9 percent of which is urbanized. Ethnically, Russians make up 81.5 percent of the population, followed by Tatars, 3.8 percent, Ukrainians, 3 percent, and Others, 11.7 percent. Eighty-six percent of the population speak Russian as a first language. Other languages spoken include Tatar, Ukrainian, and various Altaic and Finno-Ugric dialects and even Korean and Yiddish. Religion does not have a place in the lives of most Russians, although some people are returning to traditional Russian Orthodoxy and both American-style evangelism and what might be called new age mysticism are attracting followers.

Russia's political and economic upheavals since the Gorbachev era have captured the world's headlines often. In October 1993, President Boris Yeltsin disbanded the recalcitrant Soviet era Parliament, whose supporters eventually engaged in civil disturbances in a violent showdown with the president. After the surrender of the parliamentary leaders, a new Russian Federation contitution was adopted by referendum, establishing a strong presidency and a bicameral legislature consisting of a lower house called the State Duma and an upper house called the Federal Assembly.

The Russian Federation encompasses sixteen autonomous republics and fifteen lesser autonomous territories (okrugs), generally based on ethnicity. Many autonomous jurisdictions challenge the central government's control over natural resources, creating difficult jurisdictional issues to be resolved in the new constitution, not to mention frustrating conflicts for western businesspeople seeking to acquire natural resource concessions or production rights.

In 1992 total exports were estimated, in U.S. dollars, at 35.4 billion and total imports were estimated at $37.1 billion with a resulting trade deficit of $2.7 billion. Contrary to historical trends, the western nations (including the EEC and the Scandinavian nations, notably Finland) and, increasingly, Japan and the United States accounted for nearly 70 percent of foreign trade in 1992. This statistic tracks the precipitous decline in production and the trade deficit as traditional markets in the former Eastern bloc (and other NIS nations) demand hard currency for their exports and seek higher-quality imports. This trend is expected to slow as production is rationalized and traditional trade links are re-established under new conditions, but the western export market will remain strong.

Trade Fairs and Exhibits

Moscow

Russia Travel Show	Travel and Tourism Mid-February to Mid-March
Technology '94	New Technology Late March
International Computer Forum	Computers and peripheral devices Annually, Early June.

Machinexpo	Mid-June.
Health Industry	Medical Products and Services
	Mid-June
AutoService	Late June
Moscow International	Motor vehicles
Motor Show	Late August
Moscow Aerospace	Aerospace technology
	Annualy, Early September

St. Petersburg

Baltika	Consumer Goods (furniture, clothes, appliances)
	Annually, end of June.
Hospital	Medical Technology
	Annually. Swiss sponsored.
Inrybprom	Commercial Fishing Equipment and Processing
	Every 5 years, next one is in 1995.
Lesobumaga	Forest Product and Paper mill Equipment
Neva	Ship Building
	Every 1-2 years, Summer.
Russian Farmer	Food Production and Processing
	Annually, end of August.

Major Periodicals

Newspapers
Chas Pik ("Rush Hour") (St. Petersburg)
Ekonomika i Zhizn
Finansovaya Gazeta
Izvestia
Kommersant
Moscow News (English)
Nezavisimaya Gazeta (Moscow)
Rossiiskaya Gazeta

Magazines
Delovie Liudi

Passports

All permanent U.S. residents must carry a valid passport in order to travel to, from, and within the Russian Federation or any of the other Newly Independent States. Application should be made by mail or in person at least eight and preferably twelve weeks in advance to (1) a U.S. Passport Agency office (these are located in most major cities in the United States); (2) a designated U.S. post office; or (3) a state or federal courthouse. You many also consult your travel agent or international airline office. Any of these offices will let you know what documents you need and the proper procedures to follow. Requirements for citizens and noncitizens differ somewhat. No international travel tickets will be issued by an airline or travel agent to persons without valid passports.

Visas

All NIS nations require foreign visitors to obtain visas. In the United States, you should obtain an application form through the Consular Office of the embassy (or nearest consulate) of the NIS nation to be visited. (see Section VI)

Along with the completed application form, you must submit a copy of the inside pages of your valid passport; three passport-sized photos, signed on the back; a fee, ranging from $50 to $100; and an *official invitation from your proposed NIS host.* Your host may be a business organization or an individual, but if the stated purpose of your visit is to conduct business, you must be invited by an organization; individuals may only invite foreigners as tourists or personal visitors.

You should request an invitation of your NIS host well in advance, and provide him or her with all passport data, dates of your stay, point of entry, and cities to be visited. To expedite the process, your host may fax or telex the invitation directly to the embassy or consulate through which you applied. It is also possible to request 24-hour processing from some NIS embassy consular divisions for additional fees. You might consider sending a self-addressed, prepaid express air bill along with your visa application to speed the process.

If you expect to travel frequently to the NIS, you may consider applying for a multientry visa. For this type of visa, you must meet the same requirements already detailed, with the exception that your NIS host must apply to the appropriate Ministry of Foreign Affairs in the NIS, which will then issue the invitation instead of your host. This process is more easily accomplished when you are at your NIS destination.

It is rare for valid visa requests to be refused, and you should immediately explore any problem with the Consular Office through which you applied. Usually, a refusal is based on a procedural problem — your passport will expire within 60 days of your stay, your host organization is not registered, and so on. You may petition the Consular Office, but the U.S. Department of State has no jurisdiction over this process.

Finally, it is good practice to make copies of all important documents and to keep the copies in a separate piece of luggage. This precaution will greatly reduce your difficulties in replacing them.

Immunizations

No immunizations or inoculations are presently required by the U.S. Department of State for U.S. citizens and permanent residents visiting the Russian Federation or the other NIS nations. However, the Centers for Disease Control in Atlanta recommends that visitors to the NIS have their tetanus and diphtheria vaccinations updated. Also, visitors to Siberia and the Russian Far East during the summer months should be aware that tick-borne encephalitis has been reported there recently; when outdoors long pants and long-sleeved shirts should be worn.

Customs and Currency Regulations

Customs procedures have improved dramatically since the Soviet period, when printed matter or consumer electronics frequently were confiscated for political reasons and visitors suffered inexplicable delays both entering and leaving. Today, a few simple precautions should enable a painless passage through customs.

Depending on the airline, you may or may not be provided with a customs declaration form before your arrival. You may want to prepare a list of all valuables in your luggage, including money, art, consumer electronics, tapes, and business samples, and their respective values to expedite filling in the customs declaration form when you receive it. It is best to err on the side of caution, as luggage is more frequently checked when leaving and duties for undocumented goods can be steep. Written material is no longer confiscated for political reasons, but sexually explicit materials may be confiscated as pornography. Computers may be taken in freely, but must be declared. If you intend to give a computer away as a gift, be prepared to pay the duty on it when leaving. Be sure to bring prescriptions and permits for any medicine and to obtain documentation from the supplier or agent for any trade samples that you bring back from the NIS.

Be particularly conservative about what you take home from the NIS. Recently, there has been a flood of valuable icons and precious metals leaving the NIS, and the authorities have become zealous about such exports as a result. Even obvious fakes or derivative works may be confiscated by young customs officers who are not likely to be discriminating art appraisers. If you do want to bring home an authentic work of art, you should obtain a permit from the Ministry of Culture, which may take from three to six weeks. Luxury goods such as vodka, caviar, perfume, samovars, and tea sets may generally be exported without restrictions if you have a receipt showing that they were purchased for hard currency. Nonretail goods, such as privately canned caviar, mushrooms, smoked fish, and so on, are limited in export quantity.

Finally, common sense is especially important in the NIS. Narcotics and firearms cannot be imported to or exported from the NIS, and contact with them should be avoided during your stay. Penalties are especially harsh, and there is little your government will be able to do to assist you if you are caught in a violation.

Travelers' Checks and Credit Cards

Although travelers' checks and credit cards have not yet fully penetrated the countryside, the large and growing hard currency sector readily accepts major credit cards, and, to a lesser degree, travelers' checks. Travelers' checks are recommended for travelers to the NIS because, unlike in Western Europe, the traveler need not lose on the exchange rate, but may spend the hard currency of their own nations. Thus, an American may buy travelers' checks at home and spend them as dollars in Moscow hard currency stores, just as a German can spend travelers' checks denominated in deutsche marks in hard currency stores in Kiev; neither need exchange them for another hard currency. You may find that prices are quoted in hard currency rubles, which is simply an artificial number for purposes of setting an exchange rate. Take careful notice of this rate to be sure that you are not being overcharged.

Foreign Exchange

Formerly, visitors to the Soviet Union were required to follow strict and inconvenient rules concerning currency exchange and possession; it was technically illegal, for example, to carry even a single ruble note out of the country as a souvenir. Today, there are few restrictions on the ruble, which nevertheless remains a soft currency. Hard currencies, such as the dollar and most Western European currencies, are readily accepted in an increasing number of venues throughout the NIS, particularly in urban areas. Rubles may be purchased at the airport, at the banks listed in this guide, and at the numerous exchange offices found in most cities. Given the expected rate of inflation of the Russian ruble for the foreseeable future, it is not advisable to exchange or hold large amounts; the only strong NIS currency as of now is the Estonian Kroon.

Travel Tips

The traditional advice to travelers is that, having packed and planned, the traveler should "take half the luggage and twice the money." The first part of the advice is not strictly accurate in the NIS where, despite vast improvements in selection and variety owing to the opening of trade and the development of a hard currency sector, many items are not available or are prohibitively expensive. It is especially important to take along such items as electrical converters (the NIS uses 220 volts and 50 hertz), surge protectors, extra disks or supplies if you are bringing a computer, and any medications you may need. For example, many travelers are warned about drinking the water in St. Petersburg, which can cause a mild bacterial dysentery. If you will be spending significant time in St. Petersburg, you should ask your physician to prescribe a remedy in case this problem develops.

Unfortunately, the second part of the advice is quite applicable to the NIS. Although there are bargains to be found in the ruble sector, high quality western goods, services, and accommodations are simply in short supply relative to the demand in the NIS, and the newly freed prices reflect this situation. Moscow is an expensive city, comparable not to Paris or Chicago, but to Tokyo or certain Third World capitals. Although prices are less elsewhere in the NIS, the traveler should be prepared for an expensive trip.

Jet Lag

Although a variety of diets and sleeping patterns have been suggested to ward off the physical and mental sluggishness attendant to international travel, no one regimen works for everyone. Ideally, business travelers should begin to shift to the work and sleep patterns of the destination's time zone even before boarding the plane. A few facts are known about jet lag: excessive alcohol consumption and caffeine consumption close to the time of arrival exacerbate it, and exposure to natural daylight on arrival eases it. If possible, set your watch to your destination time, and, with an alarm or the assistance of the airplane cabin crew, awake at your normal hour on destination time, stretch your legs, move about the cabin, and open the window shade.

Even if you are not aware of it, jet lag affects your reflexes and mental acuity. If possible, avoid important meetings or decisions for the first day after arrival, and try to get outside as much as possible, in order to naturally reset your circadian rhythms.

Shopping

The NIS has never been a shopper's paradise, although interesting items and bargains do exist. High quality western goods are available in hard currency shops, but they are generally more expensive and offered in less variety than you are likely to find at home. In the ruble economy, a flood of inexpensive goods from China, Southeast Asia and Eastern Europe has enveloped the shops, probably to the benefit of the beleaguered NIS shopper on a fixed budget. If you read Russian or another NIS language, you will be well rewarded by shopping for books, especially at the Букинист (boo-kee-NEEST), or secondhand bookshop. Many of the better quality souvenirs, such as lacquer boxes and painted eggs, are available for hard currency, but might be found for rubles with a bit of poking around.

Electrical Appliances

If you are taking any electrical equipment that is not battery-operated, you will need a two round-pin plug adapter, a 220 volt/50hertz converter, and a state-of-the-art surge protector, especially for delicate computer equipment. Electrical current surges of 20 to 30 volts are not uncommon. The NIS uses the PAL format for VCRs. American videos must be converted to the PAL format if you wish to use them on Russian equipment. Major U.S. cities with sizable populations of Indians, Russians, or Poles have video outlets that convert to PAL for under $100 per cassette.

Clothing Sizes

As noted in the section on shopping, quality can vary greatly, both in private and state-owned stores. The western legal precept *caveat emptor* is especially applicable in the NIS. The following are rough approximations of Russian clothing sizes:

	American	Russian
For Women		
Dresses/suits	10/12/14...	32/34/36...
Shoes	6/7/8...	36/37/38.5...
Stockings	8/8.5/9...	0/1/2...
For Men		
Suits/Coats	36/38/40...	46/48/50...
Shirts	15/16/17...	38/41/43...
Shoes	5/6/7...	38/39/41

Tipping/Gifts

Until recently, tipping was officially discouraged in the former Soviet Union, but this attitude from the communist era has now been wholly eradicated. For waiters and other service personnel, a 10 to 15 percent tip is standard. Any doorman or maid who does personal favors (obtains sundry items, gives advice) should be shown appreciation with a gift, not money. You should take a stock of small, quality gifts for those people you meet professionally: pens, cigarette lighters, wallets, pocket knives, perfume. Anything with a well-known or corporate logo will be especially appreciated (for example Disney, Calvin Klein, etc.)

Taxis

Taxis are plentiful in Moscow, but they can be difficult to hail and their drivers difficult to negotiate with. As a result of the many devaluations and currency redemptions, the taxi's meter will be incomprehensible, and a complicated conversion mechanism will be required to determine the fare in rubles. This is not likely to be a problem, however, as the driver will likely insist on hard currency from a western businessperson. Avoid gypsy (unmarked) cabs; although many are simply hard-pressed people moonlighting to get by, more than a few incidents of robbery and kidnapping have been connected with gypsy cabs in recent years. On that note, you should arrange travel to and from the airport in advance, and avoid cabs there altogether, as your clothing and luggage may prove to be too much of a temptation to crime.

Crime

Crime is on the rise throughout the NIS, in part because of difficult economic conditions and in part because of the disintegration of central authority. At the same time, this problem should be kept in perspective: if you are coming from a major city in the United States, you will probably not find Moscow or St. Petersburg any worse in terms of personal safety. You should be aware that conspicuously dressed (or simply well-dressed) westerners are a target for muggings, and you should not be on the streets alone at night in the major urban areas. Another common crime is "gassing" on trains and overnight boats; the criminal drugs the victims in the coupe or cabin and removes their valuables as they sleep. Finally, both prostitution and Mickey Finn scams are on the rise and may be encountered even in expensive hotels. The business traveler should be alert, not alarmed; commonsense precautions, such as wearing money belts underneath your clothing, being aware of your surroundings, and soliciting the advice of your NIS hosts as to safe areas, should greatly minimize the possibility of being a victim.

If you are victimized, do not resist. Many criminal gangs and even individuals in the NIS are well armed. Report the incident immediately, not only to the local police (милиция, pronounced "mee-LEE-tsee-ya"), but to your hotel, your NIS host, and to your embassy or consulate.

Driving

In the NIS nations, people drive on the right-hand side of the road, and, at least theoretically, drivers in the NIS are subject to traffic rules and procedures familiar to American drivers. However, driving conditions in the NIS are very different from those in the United States and Western Europe: road conditions are poor outside the major cities, where large potholes and abruptly disintegrating shoulders are common. Within the major cities, and especially in Moscow, signs are small, and Muscovites in particular have a well-earned reputation as aggressive drivers. (The stereotype of Russian passivity seems wholly unfounded after a drive around Moscow's Ring Road.) It is advisable to map your route in advance of getting behind the wheel, as easily missed turn-offs and poorly marked one-way streets are a certainty.

Business travelers planning to do any driving in the NIS should obtain an International driver's license before departing. International drivers' licenses are issued to anyone with a valid domestic driver's license and are inscribed in five languages, including Russian. In the United States, an international driver's license may be obtained in most states in one day from the local Department of Motor Vehicles for a fee ranging from $10 to $25. Traffic violation fines in the Russian Federation may be assessed on the spot, and the G.A.I. (traffic police) officer has broad discretion in enforcement.

**Drivers should
recognize these
written signs:**

Guarded railroad crossing	Железнодорожный переезд со шлагбаумом
Yield	Уступите дорогу
Stop	Стоп
Right of way	Преимущество перед встречным движением
Dangerous intersection ahead	Приближение к опасному участку
Gasoline (petrol) ahead	Автозаправочная станция
Parking	Стоянка
No vehicles allowed	Движение транспорта запрещено
Dangerous curve	Опасный поворот
Pedestrian crossing	Пешеходный переход
Oncoming traffic has right of way	Встречный транспорт имеет преимущество
No bicycles allowed	Движение велосипедов запрещено
No parking allowed	Стоянка запрещена
No entry	Въезд запрещен
No left turn	Левый поворот запрещён
No U-turn	Разворот запрещён
No passing	Обгон запрещён
Border crossing (customs)	Таможня
Traffic signal ahead	Приближение к светофору
Speed limit	Ограничение скорости
Traffic circle (roundabout) ahead	Въезд на перекрёсток с круговым движением
Minimum speed limit	Ограничение минимальной скорости
All traffic turns left	Движение налево
End of no passing zone	Конец зоны "Обгон запрещён"
One-way street	Одностороннее движение
Detour	Объезд
Danger ahead	Опасность
Entrance to expressway	Въезд на автомагистраль
Expressway ends	Конец автомагистрали

**And the following symbolic road signs are also
found in the NIS (following two pages):**

Two-Way Traffic

Maximum Speed
Limit

Minimum Speed
Limit

No Passing

No Vehicles

Traffic Goes
This Way

One-Way Traffic

Caution

Main Road

End of Restriction

Bicycles Only

Filling Station

Pedestrians Only

No Entry

No Parking

Traffic Circle

Keep Right

Keep Left

No Through Road

Intersection

Dangerous Hill

Motor Vehicles Only

Dangerous Curve

Falling Rocks

Intersection with
Secondary Road

Road Narrows

Yield

Uneven Road

Hospital

Parking

Expressway
(Motorway)

BASIC WORDS AND EXPRESSIONS

Yes.	Да. (dah)
No.	Нет. (nyet)
Maybe.	Может быть. (MO-zhet byt)
Please.	Пожалуйста. (pa-ZHA-loo-sta)
Thank you very much.	Большое спасибо. (bol-SHOH-ye spa-SEE-ba)
Excuse me. I'm sorry.	Извините. (iz-vee-NEE-te)
Just a second.	Минуточку. (mee-NOO-tach-koo)
It doesn't matter.	Это не важно. (EH-ta ne VAZH-na)
That'll be fine.	Хорошо. (kha-ra-SHOH)
Good morning.	Доброе утро. (DOH-bra-ye OO-tra)
Good afternoon.	Добрый день. (DOH-bry den)
Good evening.	Добрый вечер. (DOH-bry VE-cher)
Good night.	Спокойной ночи. (spa-KOY-nay NOH-chi)
Good-bye!	До свидания. (da svee-DAN-ya)
How are you? (How do you do?)	Как вы поживаете? (kak vee pa-zhee-VAH ye-te)
How are things?	Как дела? (kak de-LAH)
Fine, thank you. And you?	А Вы? (a VEE) Спасибо, хорошо. (spa-SEE-ba, kha-ra-SHOH)
See you later.	Пока. (pa-KAH)
See you soon.	До скорой встречи. (da SKOH-ray VSTRECH-chee)
Do you speak English?	Вы говорите по-английски? (vee ga-va-REE-te pa-an-GLEE-sky)
I don't speak Russian.	Я не говорю по-русски. (ya ne ga-va-RYOO pa-ROO-skee)
Do you understand?	Вы понимаете? (vee pa-nee-MAH-ye-te)
I (don't) understand.	Я не понимаю. (ya ne pa-nee-MAH-yoo)
What was that you said?	Что Вы сказали? (shtoh vee ska-ZAH-lee)
I speak little Russian.	Я говорю немного по-русски. (ya ga-va-RYOO ne-MNOH-ga pa-ROO-skee)
Does anyone here speak English?	Говорит ли кто-нибудь здесь по-английски? (ga-va-REET lee KTON-nee-boot zdyes pa an-GLEE-skee)
Please write it down.	Напишите это пожалуйста. (na-pee-SHEE-te EH-ta pa-ZHA-loo-sta)
Please speak more slowly.	Говорите, пожалуйста, помедленнее. (ga-va-REE-te, pa-ZHA-loo-sta pa-med-len-YE-ye)
Please repeat.	Повторите, пожалуйста. (pav-ta-REE-te pa-ZHA-loo-sta)
What does that mean?	Что это значит? (shtoh EH-ta ZNAH-cheet)
How do you say that in Russian	Как это сказать по-русски? (kak EH-ta ska-ZAT pa-ROO-skee)
What's your name?	Как Вас зовут? (kak vahs za-VOOT)
(The) gentleman, Mr.	Господин. (ga-spa-DEEN)
(The) lady, Mrs.	Госпожа. (ga-spa-ZHA)
(The) young lady, Miss.	Госпожа. (ga-spa-ZHA)

Here's my address and telephone number.	Вот мой адрес и номер телефона. (Vot moy AH-dres ee NOH-mer te-le-FOH-na)
Where are you staying?	Где Вы остановились? (gdye vee a-stan-a-VEE-lees)
Where can I reach you?	Где Вас можно найти? (gdye vahs MOHZH-na nay-TEE)
I'll pick you up at your house (hotel).	Я зайду за Вами домой (в гостиницу). (ya zay-DOO za VAH-mee da-MOY {fga-STEE-nee-tsoo})
Nice to have met you.	Очень приятно было познакомиться. (OH-chen pree-YAHT-na BEE-la pa-zna-KOH-meet-sya)

Common Questions and Phrases

Where is ___?	Где ___? (gdye ___)
When?	Когда? (kag-DAH)
How?	Как? (kak)
How much does that cost?	Сколько это стоит? (SKOL-ka EH-ta STOH-eet)
Who?	Кто? (ktoh)
Why?	Почему? (pa-che-MOO)
Which?	Какой, какая? (kah-KOY, kah-KAH-ya)
Here is ___.	Вот ___. (vot ___)
There is ___.	Там ___. (tam ___)
That is ___.	Это ___. (EH-ta ___)
It is ___.	Это ___. EH-ta ___)
My name is ___.	Меня зовут ___. (men-YAH za-VOOT ___)
I am an American. (m/f)	Я американец/американка. (ya ah-mer-ee-KAHN nets/ah-mer-ee-KAHN-ka)
I'm staying at ___. (m/f)	Я остановился/остановилась в ___. (ya a-stan-a-VEEL-sy/a-stan-a-VEE- las v___)
Here is my passport.	Вот мой паспорт. (vot moy PAHS-part)
I'm on a business trip.	Я в командировке. (ya fka-man-dee-ROHV-ke)
I'm just passing through.	Я здесь проездом. (ya zdyes pra-YEZ-dam)
I'll be staying ___.	Я пробуду здесь ___. (ya pra-BOO-doo zdyes___)
• a few days	несколько дней (NE-skal-ka dnyey)
• few weeks	несколько недель (NE-skal-ka ne-DYEL)
• a month	месяц (MESH-syats)
I have nothing to declare.	Мне нечего декларировать (mnye NEH-che-va de-kla-REE-ro-vat)

Useful Nouns

address	адрес (AH-dres)
amount	сумма (SOOM-ma)
appointment	встреча (VSTREH-cha)
bill	счёт (schyoht)
business	бизнес (BEEZ-nes)
car	машина (ma-SHEE-na)
cashier	кассир (kas-SEER)
check	чек (chek)
city	город (GOH-rad)
customs	таможня (ta-MOZH-nya)
date	дата (DAH-ta)
document	документ (da-koo-MYENT)
elevator	лифт (leeft)
fight	борьба (bar-BAH)
friend	друг (droog)
hanger	вешалка (VEH-shal-ka)
key	ключ (klyooch)
list	список (SPEE-sak)
maid	горничная (GOR-neech-na-ya)
mail	почта (POHCH-ta)
magazine	журнал (zhoor-NAHL)
manager	управляющий (менеджер) (oo-prav-LYAH-yoo-shchee {MEH-ned-zher})
map	карта (KAHR-ta)
mistake	ошибка (a-SHEEP-ka)
money	деньги (DYEN-gee)
name (object)	название (naz-VAH-nee-ye)
name (person)	имя (EEM-ya)
newspaper	газета (ga-ZYE-ta)
office	офис (OH-fees)
package	посылка, пакет (pa-SIL-ka, pa-KET)
paper	бумага (boo-MAH-ga)
passport	паспорт (PAHS-part)
pen	ручка (ROOCH-ka)
pencil	карандаш (ka-ran-DAHSH)
porter	носильщик (na-SEEL-shcheek)
post office	почта (почтовое отделение) (POHCH-ta {pach-TOH-vo-ye at-de-LYE-nee-ye})
postage	плата за почту (PLAH-ta za POHCH-too)
price	цена (tse-NAH)
raincoat	плащ (plahshch)
reservation	предварительный заказ (pred-va-REE-tel-nee za-KAZ)
restroom	туалет (too-a-LYET)
restaurant	ресторан (re-sta-RAN)
road	дорога (da-ROH-ga)
room	комната (KOHM-na-ta)

shirt	рубашка (roo-BAHSH-ka)
shoes	туфли (TOO-flee)
shower	душ (doosh)
store	магазин (ma-ga-ZEEN)
street	улица (OO-lee-tsa)
suit	костюм (ka-STYOOM)
suitcase	чемодан (che-ma-DAHN)
taxi	такси (tak-SEE)
telegram	телеграмма (te-le-GRAHM-ma)
telephone	телефон (te-le-FOHN)
terminal	вокзал, станция (vak-ZAHL, STAHN-tsee-ya)
ticket	билет (bee-LYET)
time	время (VREHM-ya)
tip	чаевые (cha-ya-VEE-ye)
train	поезд (POH-yezd)
trip	поездка (pa-YEZD-ka)
umbrella	зонтик (ZOHN-teek)
waiter(tress)	официант(ка) (a-feef-tsee-AHNT/a-fee-tsee-AHNT-ka)
watch	часы (cha-SEE)
water	вода (va-DAH)

Useful Verbs (infinitive forms)

In Russian, verbs have two "aspects," imperfective and perfective. In very rough terms, the aspect indicates whether the action described by the verb is continuous or incomplete in nature (imperfective), or finite or complete (or to be completed), in nature (perfective). In this section, the verbs are given in both imperfective and perfective infinitive forms, respectively. Some verbs, because they are intrinsically — or at least grammatically — "imperfective" by nature (strictly processes), have only imperfective forms. These imperfective-only verbs are designated by an asterisk (*). In some cases, an English verb will have only the specific meaning embodied in one or another aspect of the Russian word. In those cases, the single applicable Russian verb is designated by two asterisks (**).

accept	принимать/принять (pree-nee-MAHT/pree-NYAT)
answer	отвечать/ответить (at-ve-CHAHT/at-VEH-teet)
arrive	приезжать/приехать (pree-ye-ZHAHT/pree-YE-khat)
ask	спрашивать/спросить (spra-shee-VAHT/spra-SEET)
assist	помогать/помочь (pa-ma-GAHT/pa-MOCH)
be	быть (beet)*
begin	начинать/начать (na-chee-NAHT/na-CHAHT)
bring (on foot)	приносить/принести (pree-na-SEET/pree-nes-TEE)

bring (by vehicle)	привозить/привезти (pree-va-ZEET/pree-vez-TEE)
buy	покупать/купить (pa-koo-PAHT/koo-PEET)
call	звонить/позвонить (zva-NEET/pa-zva-NEET)
carry	носить/нести (na-SEET/nes-TEE)
change	менять/изменить (men-YAHT/eez-me-NEET)
close	закрывать/закрыть (za-kree-VAHT/za-KREET)
come	приходить/прийти (pree-kha-DEET/pree-TEE)
confirm	подтверждать/подтвердить (pad-tverzh-DAHT/pad-tver-DEET)
continue	продолжать/продолжить (pra-dal-ZHAHT/pra-dal-ZHEET))
cost	стоить (sta-EET)*
deliver	поставлять/поставить (pa-stav-LYAHT/pa-STAH-veet)
direct	руководить (roo-ka-va-DEET)*
do	делать/сделать (DYE-lat/SDYE-lat)
eat	есть/съесть (yest/syest)
end	кончать/кончить (kan-CHAHT/KON-cheet)
enter	входить/войти (vkha-DEET/vay-TEE)
examine	осматривать/осмотреть (a-SMAH-tree-vat/a-sma-TRET)
exchange	обменивать/обменять (ab-MYEN-ee-vat/ab-mi-NYAT)
feel	чувствовать/почувствовать (CHOOVST-va-vat/pa-CHOOST-va-vat)
finish	кончать/кончить (kan-CHAHT/KON-cheet)
fix	ремонтировать/отремонтировать (re-man-TEE-ra-vat/at-re-man-TEE-ra-vat)
follow	следовать/последовать (SLED-a-vat/pa-SLED-a-vat)
forget	забывать/забыть (za-bee-VAT/za-BEET)
forward	отсылать/отослать (at-see-LAHT/at-a-SLAT)
get (obtain)	доставать/достать (da-sta-VAHT/da-STAHT)
get (receive)	получать/получить (pa-loo-CHAT-pa-loo-CHEET)
give	давать/дать (da-VAHT/dat)
go (by foot)	ходить/идти (kha-DEET/eet-TEE)
go (by vehicle)	ездить/ехать (YEZ-deet/YEKH-at)
hear	слышать/услышать (SLEE-shat)/oo-SLEE-shat)
help	помогать/помочь (pa-ma-GAHT/pa-MOCH)
keep	хранить (khra-NEET)*
know	знать (znat)*
learn	учиться/выучиться (oo-CHEET-sya/VEE-oo-cheet-sya)
leave (by foot)	уходить/уйти (oo-kha-DEET/wee-TEE)
leave (by vehicle)	уезжать/уехать (oo-ye-ZHAHT/oo-YEKH-at)

like	нравиться/понравиться (NRAH-veet-sya/pa-NRAH-veet-sya)
listen	слушать/послушать (SLOO-shat/pa-SLOO-shat)
look at	смотреть/посмотреть на (sma-TRET/pa-sma-TRET na)
lose	терять/потерять (ter-YAHT/pa-ter-YAHT)
make	производить/произвести (pra-eez-va-DEET/pra-eez-ves-TEE)
mean	значить (ZNAH-cheet)*
meet (by appointment)	встречать/встретить (fstre-CHANT/FSTRE-teet)
meet (get accquainted)	знакомиться/познакомиться (zna-KOM-eet-sya/pa-zna-KOM-eet-sya)
miss (not attend)	пропускать/пропустить (pra-poo-SKAHT/pra-poo-STEET)
miss (feel an absence)	проскучать/скучать (pra-skoo-CHAHT/skoo-CHAHT)
need	нуждаться (noozh-DAHT-sya)*
open	открывать/открыть (at-kree-VAHT/at-KREET)
order	заказывать/заказать (za-KAH-zee-vat/za-ka-ZAHT)
park	парковаться/запарковаться (za-par-ka-VAHT-sya/par-ka-VAHT-sya)
pay	платить/заплатить (pla-TEET/za-pla-TEET)
prefer	предпочитать/предпочесть (pred-pa-chee-TAHT/pred-pa-CHEST)
prepare	готовить/подготовить (ga-TO-veet/pad-ga-TO-veet)
present	представлять/представить (pred-stav-LYAHT/pred-STAH-veet)
prove	доказывать/доказать (da-KAH-zee-vat/da-ka-ZAHT)
pull	тянуть/потянуть (tya-NOOT/pa-tya-NOOT)
purchase	покупать/купить (pa-koo-PAHT/koo-PEET)
put	ставить/поставить (STAH-veet/pa-STAH-veet))
read	читать/прочитать (chee-TAHT/pra-chee-TAHT)
receive	получать/получить (pa-loo-CHANT/pa-loo-CHEET)
recommend	рекомендовать/порекомендовать (re-ka-men-da-VAHT/pa-re-ka-men-da-VAHT)
remain	оставаться/остаться (a-sta-VAHT-sya/a-STAHT-sya)
repair	ремонтировать/отремонтировать (re-man-TEE-ra-vat/at-re-man-TEE-ra-vat)

repeat	повторять/повторить (pav-tar-YAT/pav-ta-REET)
return	возвращаться/вернуться (vaz-vra-SHCHAHT-sya/ver-NOOT-sya)
run	бегать/побежать (BYEH-gat/pa-be-ZHAT)
say	сказать (ska-ZAHT)**
see	видеть/увидеть (VEE-det/oo-VEE-det)
send	посылать/послать (pa-see-LAHT/pa-SLAHT)
show	показывать/показать (pa-KAH-zee-vat/pa-ka-ZAHT)
sit	сидеть/посидеть (see-DYET/pa-see-DYET)
speak	говорить (ga-va-REET)**
stand	стоять/постоять (sta-YAHT/pa-sta-YAHT)
start	начинать/начать (na-chee-NAHT/na-CHANT)
stop	останавливать/остановить (a-sta-NAHV-lee-vat/a-sta-na-VEET)
take	брать/взять (brat/vzyat)
talk	разговаривать (raz-ga-VAR-ee-vat)**
tell	рассказывать/рассказать (ras-SKAH-zee-vat/ras-ska-ZAHT)
think	думать/подумать (DOO-mat/pa-DOO-mat)
use	использовать (ees-POL-za-vat)*
visit	посещать/посетить (pa-se-SHCHAHT/pa-se-TEET)
wait	ждать/подождать (zhdat/pa-da-ZHDAT)
walk (take a walk)	гулять/погулять (goo-LYAT/pa-goo-LYAT)
walk (go by foot)	ходить/идти пешком (kha-DEET/eet-TEE pesh-KOM)
want	хотеть/захотеть (kha-TYET/za-kha-TET)
wear	носить/нести (na-SEET/nes-TEE)
work	работать/поработать (ra-BO-tat/pa-ra-BO-tat)
write	писать/написать (pee-SAT/na-pee-SAT)

Useful Adjectives and Adverbs

above/below	вверху/внизу (ver-KHOO/fnee-ZOO)
ahead/behind	впереди/позади (fpe-re-DEE/pa-za-DEE)
best/worst	лучший/худший (LOOCH-shee/KHOOD-shee)
big/small	большой/маленький (bal-SHOY/MA-len-kee)
early/late	рано/поздно (RAH-na/POZD-na)
easy/difficult	легко/трудно (lekh-KO/TROOD-na)
few/many	мало/много (MAH-la/MNOH-ga)
first/last	первый/последний (PER-vee/pa-SLED-nee)
full/empty	полный/пустой (POL-nee/poo-STOY)
good/bad	хороший/плохой (kha-ROH-shee/pla-KHOY)
hot/cold	горячий/холодный (gar-YAH-chee/kha-LOD-nee)
high/low	высокий/низкий (vee-SOH-kee/NEEZ-kee)
large/small	большой/маленький (bal-SHOY/MA-len-kee)
more/less	больше/меньше (BOL-she/MEN-she)

old/new	старый/новый (STA-ree/NO-vee)
open/shut	открытый/закрытый (at-KREE-tee/za-KREE-tee)
right/wrong	правильный/ошибочный (PRAH-veel-nee/a-SHEE-bach-nee)
slow/fast	медленно/быстро (MYED-len-na/BEE-stra)
thin/thick	толстый/тонкий (TOL-stee/TON-kee)
wide/narrow	широкий/узкий (shee-ROH-kee/OOZ-kee)

Other Useful Words

across	через (CHE-rez)
after	после (POS-le)
again	опять (a-PYAT)
all	все (fsye)
almost	почти (pach-TEE)
also	также (TAHK-zhe)
always	всегда (fseg-DAH)
among	среди (sre-DEE)
and	и (ee)
another	другой (droo-GOY)
around	вокруг (va-KROOG)
away	оттуда (at-TOO-da)
back	обратно (a-BRAHT-na)
because	потому что (pa-ta-MOO shto)
before	перед тем, как (PER-ed tem, kak)
behind	позади (pa-za-DEE)
between	между (MEZH-doo)
both	оба (O-ba)
but	но (no)
down	внизу (fnee-ZOO)
each	каждый (KAHZH-dee)
enough	достаточно (da-STAH-tach-na)
every	каждый (KAHZH-dee)
except	кроме (KRO-me)
few	немного (ne-MNOH-ga)
for	для (dlya)
from	из (eez)
however	однако (ad-NAH-ka)
if	если (YES-lee)
in	в (v)
instead	вместо (VMES-ta)
into	в (v)
maybe	может быть (MO-zhet beet)
more	больше (BOL-she)
much	много (MNOH-ga)
next to	рядом (RYAD-am)
not	не (ne)
now	сейчас (sey-CHAHS)

often	часто (CHAH-sta)
only	только (TOL-ka)
or	или (EE-lee)
other	другой (droo-GOY)
perhaps	может быть (MO-zhet beet)
same	тот же (TOT-zhe)
since	с тех пор, как (stekh por, kak)
some	некоторые (NEH-ka-ta-ree-ye)
still	ещё (yesh-SHOH)
that	тот (tot)
these	эти (EH-tee)
this	этот (EH-tot)

Directions   **Направления (na-prav-LEN-ee-ya)**

Which way do I go?	В каком направлении мне идти? (fka-KOM na-prav-LEN-ee-mnye eet-TEE?)
• straight ahead	• прямо (PRYA-ma)
• north	• на север (na SE-ver)
• south	• на юг (na YOOG)
• east	• на восток (na va-STOK)
• west	• на запад (na ZAH-pad)
• left	• налево (na LE-va)
• right	• направо (na PRA-va)
Is this the road to ___?	Это дорога в ___? (EH-ta da-ROH-ga v)
Am I on the right road now?	Правильно ли я иду? (PRA-veel-na lee ya ee-DOO?)
Can you show it to me on the map?	Не могли бы Вы показать путь по карте? (ne ma-GLEE bee vee pa-ka-ZAHT poot pa KAR-te?)
Please show it to me on the map.	Покажите мне, пожалуйста, на этой карте. (pa-ka-ZHEE-te mnye, pa-ZHA-loo-sta, na EH-tay KAR-te)

Arrival/Hotel   **Прибытие/Отель (pree-BEE-tee-ye/a-TEL)**

My name is ___.	Меня зовут ___. (men-YA za-VOOT ___.)
Here is my passport.	Вот мой паспорт. (vot moy PAHS-part)
I'm on a business trip.	Я в командировке. (ya fko-man-dee-ROHV-ke)
I'm just passing through.	Я здесь проездом. (ya zdes pra-YEZ-dam)
I'll be staying ___	Я остановлюсь на ___ (y a-sta-na-VLYOOS na ___)
• a few days	• несколько дней (NE-skal-ka dnyey)
• a few weeks	• несколько недель (NE-skal-ka ne-DEL)
• a month	• месяц (MES-yats)
I have nothing to declare.	Мне нечего декларировать. (mnye NE-che-va de-kla-REE-ro-vat)

I'm looking for the ____ hotel.	Я ищу отель. (ya EE-shchoo a-TEL____)
Where is the taxi stand?	Где стоянка такси? (gdye sta-YAN-ka tak-SEE)
Please call a taxi for me.	Вызовите мне, пожалуйста, такси. (VEE-za-vee-te mnye, pa-ZHA-loo-sta, tak-SEE)
I (don't) have a reservation.	У меня нет брони. (oo men-YA nyet BRON-ee)
I'd like a single (double) room for tonight.	Я бы хотел отдельный номер (номер на двоих) на эти сутки. (ya bee kha-TEL at-DEL-nee NOH-mer {NOH-mer na dva-EEKH} na EH-tee SOOT-kee)
Is breakfast included in the price of the room?	Включается ли завтрак в стоимость номера? (fklyu-CHA-yet-sya lee ZAHF-trak FSTOH-ee-most NOH-me-ra)
Where is the elevator?	Где лифт? (gdye leeft)
Please wake me tomorrow at ___ o'clock.	Пожалуйста, разбудите меня завтра в ___ часов. (pa-ZHA-loo-sta, raz-boo-DEE-te men-YA ZAHF-tra ___ cha-SOV)
Are there any letters (messages) for me?	Нет ли писем (сообщений) для меня? (nyet lee PEE-sem {sa-ab-SHCHEN-ee} dlya men-YA)
May I leave this in your safe?	Можно ли оставить это Вам на хранение? (MOZH-na lee a-STAH-veet EH-ta vam na khra-NEN-ee-ye)
Please send someone up for the bags.	Пришлите, пожалуйста, носильщика за багаж. (pree-SHLEE-te, pa-ZHA-loo-sta, na-SEEL-shchee-ka za ba-ga-ZHOM)
Please prepare my bill.	Приготовьте, пожалуйста, мой счёт. (pree-ga-TOHV-te, pa-ZHA-loo-sta, moy schyot)

Transportation   *Транспорт (TRANS-part)*

Street car	трамвай (tram-VAY)
Trolley	троллейбус (tral-LEY-boos)
Bus	автобус (af-TO-boos)
Suburban commuter train of Russian Rail	электричка (e-lek-TREECH-ka)
Subway	метро (me-TROH)
• the men's room	• мужской туалет (Moozh-SKOY too-a-LYET)
• the ladies' room	• женский (дамский) туалет (ZHEN-skee {DAM-skee}to-a-LYET)
• the bus stop	• остановка автобуса (a-sta-NOHV-ka af-TO-boos-a)
• the nearest subway station	• ближайшая станция метро (blee-ZHAY-sha-ya STAHN-tsee-ya me-TROH)

Where can I buy a ticket?	Где можно купить билет? (gdye MOZH-na koo-PEET bee-LYET)
Do I have to change trains?	Должен/должна ли я пересаживаться на другой поезд? (DOL-zhen/dolzh-NA lee ya pe-re-SAHZH-ee-vat-sya nadroo-GOY PO-yezd)*
Drive me to the hotel.	Отвезите меня в гостиницу. (at-ve-ZEE-te men-YA fga-STEE-nee-tsa)
• railroad station	• вокзал (vak-ZAL)
• airport	• аэропорт (aer-a-PORT)
Let me off at the next corner.	Остановитесь пожалуйста у следующего поворота. (a-sta-na-VEE-tes pa-ZHA-loo-sta oo SLED-oo-yoo-shche-va pa-va-RO-ta)
Please wait for me.	Подождите меня, пожалуйста. (pa-dazh-DEE-te men-YA, pa-ZHA-loo-sta)
Please tell me the arrival and departure time again.	Повторите мне, пожалуйста, время прибытия и отправления (pav-ta-REE-te mnye, pa-ZHA-loo-sta, VREM-ya pree-BEE-tee-ya ee at-prav-LEN-ee-ya)
I want a seat next to the window in the (non) smoking section.	Я хочу место у окна в {не}курящей секции. (ya kha-CHOO MYES-ta oo ak-NA f{nye}-koo-RYA-shchey SEK-tsee)
When do I have to check in?	Когда мне нужно проходить регистрацию? (kag-DA mnye NOOZH-na pra-kha-DEET re-gee-STRA-tsee-yoo)
May I take this with me as carry-on luggage?	Могу ли я взять это с собой в качестве ручной клади? (ma-GOO lee ya vzyat EH-ta sa-BOY FKA-chest-ve rooch-NOY KLAH-dee)
Is there a car rental office nearby?	Есть ли здесь прокат автомобилей? (yest lee zdyes pra-KAT af-ta-ma-BEE-lyey)
What sort of cars do you have available?	Какие у Вас есть автомобили напрокат? (ka KEE-ye oo vas yest af-ta-BEE-lee na-pra-KAT)
How much does it cost per ___?	Сколько стоит аренда автомобиля ___? (SKOL-ka STO-eet a-REN-da af-ta-ma-BEE-lya)
• day	• на день (na den)
• week	• на неделю (na ne-DYE-lyoo)
• month	• на месяц (na MES-yats)
• kilometer	• за километр (za kee-lo-METR)
How much is the insurance?	Сколько стоит страховка? (SKOL-ka STO-eet stra-KHOV-ka)
Do I have to pay for gas?	Должен/должна ли я платить за бензин? (DOL-zhen/dolzh-NA lee ya plat-teet za ben-ZEEN)*

Do I have to leave a deposit?	Должен/должна ли я оставить залог? (DOL-zhen/dolzh-NA lee ya a-STAH-veet za-LOG)*
I want to rent the car here and leave it in St. Petersburg.	Я хочу арендовать машину здесь, а вернуть её в Санкт-Петербурге. (ya kha-CHOO a-ren-da-VAHT ma-SHEE-noo zdyes, ah ver-NOOT ye-YO fsankt-pe-ter-BOORG)
Is there an additional charge for that?	Оплачивается ли это дополнительно? (a-PLA-chee-va-yet-sya lee EH-ta da-pal-NEE-tel-na)
Here is my driver's license.	Вот мои водительские права (vot ma-EE va-DEE-tel-skee-ye pra-VAH)
Where is the nearest gas station with service?	Где здесь ближайшая автозаправочная станция с техобслуживанием? (gdye zdyes blee-ZHAY-sha-ya af-ta-za-PRAH-vach-na-ya STAHN-tsee-ya stekh-ab-SLOOZH-ee-va-nee-em)
Fill it up, please.	Заправьте её, пожалуйста (za-PRAHV-te ye-YO, pa-ZHA-loo-sta)

Leisure Time   *Свободное время (sva-BOHD-na-ye VREM-ya)*

I'd like to visit an interesting night-club tonight.	Хотелось бы посетить интересный ночной клуб сегодня. (kha-TE-las bee pa-se-TEET in-te-RES-nee nach-NOY kloob se-VOHD-nya)
Is a reservation necessary?	Нужно ли резервировать предварительно? (NOOZH-na lee rezer-VEE-ra-vat pred-va-REE-tel-na)
I'd like a good table.	Я хочу хороший столик. (ya kha-CHOO kha-ROH-shee STOO-leek)
Where is the checkroom?	Где гардероб? (gdye gar-de-ROB)
May I smoke?	Можно закурить? (MOZH-na za-koo-REET)
Where can I buy English newspapers?	Где можно купить английские газеты? (gdye MOZH-na koo PEET an-GLEE-skee-ye ga-ZYE-tee)
I'm looking for ___.	Я ищу ___ (ya EE-shchoo___)
• a tennis court	• теннисную площадку (TEN-nees-noo-yoo plo SHCHAD-koo)
• a golf course	• поле для игры в гольф (PO-le dlya ee GREE fgolf)
Where can I find a swimming pool?	Где находится ближайший бассейн? (gdye na-KHO-deet-sya blee-ZHAY-shee bas-SEYN)

* masculine/feminine forms of verb given respectively.

Restaurants **Рестораны** *(res-ta-RA-nee)*

breakfast	завтрак (ZAHF-trak)
lunch	обед (a-BYED)
dinner	ужин (OO-zhin)
spoon	ложка (LOZH-ka)
fork	вилка (VEEL-ka)
knife	нож (NOHZ)
glass	стакан (sta-KAN)
plate	тарелка (tar-YEL-ka)
chair	стул (stool)
ashtray	пепельница (PE-pel-nee-tsa)
napkin	салфетка (sal-FYET-ka)

Is there a good, not too expensive, Russian restaurant around here?	Есть ли здесь хороший не слишком дорогой русский ресторан? (yest lee zdyes kha-ROH shee ne SLEESH-kam da-ra-GOY ROO-skee re-sta-RAN)
Waiter!	Официант! (af-fee-tsee-AHNT)
Waitress!	Официантка! (af-fee-tsee-AHNT-ka)
Do you have a table for me?	У вас есть свободный стол для меня? (oo vas yest sva-BOD-nee stol dlya men-YA)
May we see the menu, please?	Покажите, пожалуйста, меню (pa-ka-ZHEE-te, pa-ZHA-loo-sta, men-YOO)
What do you recommend?	Что Вы посоветуете? (shto vee pa-sa-VYE-too-ye-te)
May I take a look at the wine list please?	Можно взглянуть на перечень вин? (MOZH na vzglya-NOOT na pe-RE-chen veen)
Beer, please.	Пиво, пожалуйста. (PEE-va, pa-ZHA-loo-sta)
Where can I wash my hands?	Где я могу вымыть руки? (gdye ya man-GOO VEE-meet ROO-kee)
The check, please.	Чек, пожалуйста. (check, pa-ZHA-loo-sta)

Shopping **Покупки** *(pa-KOOP-kee)*

I must do some shopping today.	Я должен/должна кое-что купить сегодня. (ya DOL-zhen/dolzh-NA KOY-ye-shto koo-PEET se-VOHD-nya)*
I'm looking for ___.	Я ищу ___. (ya EE-shchoo ___)
• a department store	• универмаг (oo-nee-ver-MAG)
• a camera shop	• фотомагазин (fa-ta-ma-ga-ZEEN)
• a book store	• книжный магазин (KNEEZH-nee ma-ga-ZEEN)
• a china shop	• магазин, где продается фарфор. (ma-ga-ZEEN, gdye pra-da-YOT-sya far-FOR)
How much does that cost?	Сколько это стоит? (SKOL-ka EH-ta STO-eet)

---

* masculine/feminine forms of verb given respectively.

Will you accept this credit card?	Вы принимаете кредитные карточки? (Vee pree-nee-MAY-e-te kre-DEET-nee-ye KAR-tach-kee)

Medical Care **Медицинская помощь** (*me-dee-TSEEN-ska-ya PO-mashch*)

I don't feel well.	Я себя плохо чувствую. (ya se-BYA PLO-kha CHOOVST-voo-yoo)
I think I'm sick.	Я думаю, что я болен/больна. (ya DOO-ma-yoo, shto ya BO-len/bol-NA)
I need a doctor.	Мне нужен доктор (врач). (mnye NOOZH-en DOK-tar {vrach})
Is there a doctor here who speaks English?	Есть ли здесь врач, говорящий по английски?. (yest lee zdyes vrach ga-var-YASHCH-ee pa-an-GLEE-skee)
I've had this pain since yesterday.	Я чувствую эту боль со вчерашнего дня. (ya CHOOVST-voo-yoo EH-too bol sa fche-RASH-ne-va dnya)
I am a diabetic and take insulin.	Я диабетик и принимаю инсулин. (ya dee-a-BET-eek ee pree-nee-MA-yoo een-soo-LEEN)
I have heart trouble.	Я сердечник. (ya ser-DECH-neek)
Unfortunately, I must go to the dentist.	К сожалению, мне надо пойти к зубному врачу. (k sa-zha-LEN-ee-yoo, mnye NA-da pay-TEE k zoob-NO-moo vra-CHOO)
Do you know a good one?	Вы знаете хорошего врача? (Vee ZNA-ye-te kha-ROH-she-va vra-CHA)
Where can I find the nearest (all-night) pharmacy?	Где можно найти ближайшую дежурную (круглосуточную) аптеку? (gdye MOZH-na nay-TEE blee-ZHAY-shoo-yoo de-ZHOOR-noo-yoo {kroog-la-SOO-tach-noo-yoo} ap-TEK-oo)
I'm looking for something for___.	Мне нужно что-нибудь от ___. (mnye NOOZH-na SHTO-nee-bood ot ___)

- a cold
- constipation
- a cough
- a fever
- diarrhea
- a hangover
- indigestion

- a headache
- insomnia

- насморка (NAS-mar-ka)
- запора (za-POR-a)
- кашля (KASH-lya)
- температуры (tem-pe-ra-TOO-ree)
- паноса (pah-NOS-a)
- похмелья (pakh-MEL-ya)
- расстройства желудка (ras-STROYST-va zhe-LOOD-ka)

- головной боли (ga-lav-NOY BO-lee)
- бессонницы (bes-SON-nee-tsee)

Telephones **Телефоны** (*te-le-FON-ee*)

I'm looking for___.	Я ищу ___ (ya ee-SHCHOO ___

• a telephone booth	• телефонную будку (телефон) (te-le-FON-noo-yoo BOOD-koo {te-le-FON})
• a telephone directory	• телефонный справочник (te-le-FON-nee SPRA-vach-neek)
May I use your phone?	Можно воспользоваться Вашим телефоном? (MOZH-na vas-POL-za-vat-sya VASH-eem te-le-FON-om)
Here is the number.	Вот этот номер. (vot EH-tot NO-mer)
Can you help me?	Не могли бы Вы помочь мне? (ne ma-GLEE bee vee pa-MOCH mnye)
It's a local call.	Это местный разговор (звонок) (EH-ta MEST-nee raz-ga-VOR {zva-NOK})
• a long-distance call	• междугородный разговор (звонок) (mezh-doo-ga-ROHD-nee raz-ga-VOR {zva-NOK})
• a person-to-person call	• личный разговор (звонок) (LEECH-nee raz-ga-VOR {zva-NOK})
• a collect call	• разговор за счет вызываемого абонента (raz ga-VOR za schyot vee-zee-VA-ye-ma-va a-ba-NENT-a)
Can you dial direct?	Есть ли автоматическая связь? (yest lee af-ta-ma-TEE-che-ska-ya svyaz)
May I speak to Mr. (Mrs., Miss)___?	Могу я поговорить с господином (госпожой) ___? (ma-GOO ya pa-ga-va-REET sgas-pa-DEEN-am {sgas-pa-ZHOY}___)
Speak louder (more slowly).	Говорите громче (медленнее). (ga-va-REE-te GROM-che {med-len-YE-ye})
Don't hang up.	Не вешайте трубку. (ne ve-SHAY-te TROOP-koo)
I'll call again later.	Я позвоню еще раз позже. (ya pa-zva-NYOO ye-SHCHYO raz POZH-zhe)
I'd like to leave a message.	Я хочу оставить сообщение. (ya kha-CHOO a-STAH-veet sa-ab-SHCHE-nee-ye)
Where is the post office?	Где находится почта? (gdye na-KHO-deet-sya POCH-ta)
Where can I find a mailbox?	Где я могу найти почтовый ящик? (gdye ya ma-GOO nay-TEE pach-TO-vee YA-shcheek)
Where is the stamp window?	Где можно купить почтовые марки? (gdye MOZH-na koo-PEET pach-TO-vee-ye MAR-kee)
Where can I send a telegram?	Откуда я могу послать телеграмму? (at-KOO-da ya ma-GOO pa-SLAT te-le-GRAM-moo)
I want to send it collect.	Я хочу послать её за счёт получателя. (ya kha-CHOO pa-SLAT ye-YO za schyot pa-loo-CHA-tel-ya)
At what time will it arrive?	Когда она дойдёт? (kag-DA a-NA day-DYOT)

V. KEY WORDS AND PHRASES

The business and legal dictionary that forms Section VII of *Russian for the Business Traveler* is a compendium of some 3,000 words that you are likely to use or encounter as you conduct business abroad. It will greatly facilitate fact-finding about the business possibilities that interest you, and will help guide you through negotiations as well as reading documents. To supplement the dictionary, we have added a special feature — groupings of key terms common to twelve industries. As you explore any of these industries, you'll want to have *Russian for the Business Traveler* at your fingertips to help make sure you don't misunderstand or overlook an aspect that could have a material effect on the outcome of your business decision. The industries covered in the vocabulary lists are the following:

- aerospace
- agriculture
- chemicals
- computers
- electronics
- forest products
- iron and steel
- leather goods
- motor vehicles
- oil and gas
- pharmaceuticals
- printing and publishing

AEROSPACE

The key NIS states for aerospace development are Russia, Kazakhstan, and Ukraine, although all the NIS states now have airlines and need a vast array of equipment. Aeroflot, in terms of miles flown, was the largest airline in the world prior to the breakup of the Soviet Union. Particularly important segments of this industry include the modernization of the air traffic control system and satellite support, both of which promise to be fertile ground for commercial ventures.

English to Russian

aerodynamic balance	аэродинамические весы	*(AH-e-ra-dee-na-MEE-ches-kee-ye ve-SEE)*
aerodynamics	аэродинамика	*(AH-e-ra-dee-NAH-mee-ka)*
aeronautics	аэронавтика	*(AH-e-ra-NAHF-tee-ka)*
after-burner	форсажная камера	*(far-SAHZH-na-ya KAH-me-ra)*
air force	военно-воздушные силы (ВВС)	*(va-YEN-na-vaz-DOOSH-nee-ye SEE-lee) [VEH-VEH-ES])*
air navigation	аэронавигация	*(AH-e-ra-na-vee-GAH-tsee-ya)*
airplane	самолёт	*(sa-ma-LYOT)*
airport	аэропорт	*(AH-e-ra-POHRT*
altitude	высота	*(vee-sa-TAH)*
auto-pilot	автопилот	*(AHF-ta-pee-LOT)*
aviation	авиация	*(a-vee-AH-tsee-ya)*
avionics	авиаэлектроника	*(AH-vee-a-e-lek-TROH-nee-ka)*
ballistic	баллистический	*(bal-lee-STEE-ches-kee)*
boost-glide aircraft	ракетоплан	*(ra-ke-ta-PLAHN)*
bulkhead	шпангоут	*(shpan-GOH-oot)*
cockpit	кабина лётчика	*(ka-BEE-na LYOT-chee-ka)*
combat thrust booster	ускоритель маневра	*(oos-ka-REE-tel ma-NYOV-ra)*
commercial aviation	гражданская авиация	*(grazh-DAHN-ska-ya a-vee-AH-tsee-ya)*
cosmodrome	космодром	*(kas-ma-DROM)*
count-down	отсчёт времени	*(at-SHCHYOT VREH-me-nee)*

crash	авария	*(a-VAH-ree-ya)*
defense conversion	конверсия (оборонная)	*(kan-VEHR-see-ya a-ba-RON-na-ya)*
directional beacon	направленный радиомаяк	*(nap-RAHV-len-nee RAH-dee-a-ma-YAHK)*
Doppler effect	эффект Допплера	*(ef-FEKT DOP-ple-ra)*
dual rotor helicopter	двухвинтовой вертолёт	*(dvookh-vin-ta-VOY ver-ta-LYOT)*
early warning radar	радиолокализационная станция (РЛС) дальнего обнаружения	*(RAH-dee-a-la-ka-tsee-ON-na-ya STAHN-tsee-ya (EHR-EL-ES) DAHL-ne-va ab-na-roo-ZHEH-nee-ya)*
flight computer	навигационный вычислитель	*(na-vee-ga-tsee-ON-nee vee-chee-SLEE-tel)*
fuselage	фюзеляж	*(fyoo-ze-LYAHSH)*
hangar	ангар	*(an-GAHR)*
helicopter	вертолёт	*(ver-ta-LYOT)*
hydraulic booster	гидроусилитель	*(GHEED-ra-oo-see-LEE-tel)*
in-line booster	последовательно расположенный ускоритель	*(pas-LEH-da-va-tel-na ras-pa-LOH-zhen-nee oos-ka-REE-tel)*
jet plane	реактивный самолёт	*(re-ak-TEEV-nee sa-ma-LYOT)*
jet fighter	реактивный истребитель	*(re-ak-TEEV-nee ees-tre-BEE-tel)*
jet fuel	топливо для реактивных самолётов	*(TOP-lee-va dla re-ak-TEEV-nikh sa-ma-LYOH-taf)*
landing gear	шасси	*(shas-SEE)*
launch pad	пусковой стол	*(poos-ka-VOY stol)*
launcher	пусковая установка	*(poos-ka-VAH-ya oos-ta-NOF-ka)*
lift	подъёмная сила	*(pad-YOM-na-ya SEE-la)*
liquid fuel	жидкое топливо	*(ZHIT-ka-ye TOP-lee-va)*
mach speed	сверхзвуковая скорость (сверх Маха)	*(SVEHRKH-zvoo-ka-VAH-ya SKOH-rast (sverkh MAH-kha)*
Mig fighter	истребитель «МиГ»	*(ees-tre-BEE-tel meeg)*

mobile launcher	передвижная пусковая обстановка	*(pe-re-dveezh-NAH-ya poos-ka-VAH-ya oos-ta-NOF-ka)*
orbit	орбита	*(ar-BEE-ta)*
orbital refueling base	орбитальная заправочная станция	*(ar-bee-TAHL-na-ya zap-RAH-vach-na-ya STAHN-tsee-ya)*
probe	космический зонд	*(kas-MEE-ches-kee zont)*
re-entry	вход в плотные слои атмосфера	*(fkhot FPLOT-nee-ye sla-EE at-mas-FEH-ree)*
recoverable booster	ускоритель многократного действия	*(oos-ka-REE-tel mna-ga-KRAHT-na-va DEY-stvee-ya)*
rocket	ракета	*(ra-KEH-ta)*
satellite	спутник	*(SPOOT-neek)*
solid fuel	твёрдое топливо	*(TVYOHR-da-ya TOP-lee-va)*
space walk	передвижение в открытом космосе	*(pe-re-dvee-ZHEH-nee-ye vat-KREE-tam KOS-ma-se)*
space shuttle	многоразовый воздушно-космический аппарат (МВКА)	*(mna-ga-RAH-za-vee vaz-DOOSH-na-kas-MEE-ches-kee a-pa-RAHT; EM-VEH-KAH-AH)*
space	космос	*(KOS-mas)*
space station	орбитальная станция (ОС)	*(ar-bee-TAHL-na-ya STAHN-tsee-ya; OH-ES)*
space-plane	воздушно-космический самолёт	*(vaz-DOOSH-na-kas-MEE-ches-kee sa-ma-LYOT*
space-suit	космический скафандр	*(kas-MEE-ches-kee ska-FAHNDR)*
spacecraft	космический аппарат (КА)	*(kas-MEE-ches-kee a-pa-RAHT; KAH-AH)*
supersonics	аэродинамика сверхзвуковых скоростей	*(AH-eh-ra-dee-NAH-mee-ka sverkh-zvoo-ka-VIKH ska-ra-STEY)*
thermal lift	подъёмная сила восходящих потоков воздуха	*(pad-YOM-na-ay SEE-la vas-kha-DYAH-shcheekh pa-TOH-kaf VOZ-doo-kha*
turbine	турбина	*(toor-BEE-na)*

turbo-jet	турбо-реактивный двигатель	*(TOOHR-ba-re-ak-TEEV-nee DVEE-ga-tel)*
turbulence	турбулентность	*(toor-boo-LENT-nast)*
wing	крыло	*(kree-LOH)*
zero gravity	невесомость	*(ne-ve-SOH-mast)*

Russian to English

авария	*(a-VAH-ree-ya)*	crash
авиация	*(a-vee-AH-tsee-ya)*	aviation
авиаэлектроника	*(AH-vee-a-e-lek-TROH-nee-ka)*	avionics
автопилот	*(AHF-ta-pee-LOT)*	auto-pilot
ангар	*(an-GAHR)*	hangar
аэродинамика	*(AH-e-ra-dee-NAH-mee-ka)*	aerodynamics
аэродинамика сверхзвуковых скоростей	*(AH-e-ra-dee-NAH-mee-ka sverkh-zvoo-ka-VIKH ska-ra-STEY)*	supersonics
аэродинамические весы	*(AH-e-ra-dee-na-MEE-ches-kee-ye ve-SEE)*	aerodynamic balance
аэронавигация	*(AH-e-ra-na-vee-GAH-tsee-ya)*	air navigation
аэронавтика	*(AH-e-ra-NAHF-tee-ka)*	aeronautics
аэропорт	*(AH-e-ra-POHRT)*	airport
баллистический	*(bal-lee-STEE-ches-kee)*	ballistic
вертолёт	*(ver-ta-LYOT)*	helicopter
военно-воздушные силы (ВВС)	*(va-YEN-na-vaz-DOOSH-nee-ye SEE-lee (VEH-VEH-ES)*	air force
воздушно-космический самолёт	*(vaz-DOOSH-na-kas-MEE-ches-kee sa-ma-LYOT)*	space-plane
вход в плотные слои атмосферы	*(fkhot FPLOT-nee-ye sla-EE at-mas-FEH-ree)*	re-entry
высота	*(vee-sa-TAH)*	altitude
гидроусилитель	*(GHEED-ra-oo-see-LEE-tel)*	hydraulic booster
гражданская авиация	*(grazh-DAHN-ska-ya a-vee-AH-tsee-ya)*	commercial aviation

двухвинтовой вертолёт	(dvookh-vin-ta-VOY ver-ta-LYOT)	dual rotor helicopter
жидкое топливо	(ZHIT-ka-ye TOP-lee-va)	liquid fuel
истребитель «МиГ»	(ees-tre-BEE-tel meeg)	Mig fighter
кабина лётчика	(ka-BEE-na LYOT-chee-ka)	cockpit
конверсия (оборонная)	(kan-VEHR-see-ya [a-ba-ROH-na-ya])	defense conversion
космический аппарат (КА)	(kas-MEE-ches-kee a-pa-RAHT [KAH-AH])	spacecraft
космический зонд	(kas-MEE-ches-kee zont)	probe
космический скафандр	(kas-MEE-ches-kee ska-FAHNDR)	space-suit
космодром	(kas-ma-DROM)	cosmodrome
космос	(KOS-mas)	space
крыло	(kree-LOH)	wing
многоразовый воздушно-косми-ческий аппарат (МВКА)	(mna-ga-RAH-za-vee vaz-DOOSH-na-kas-MEE-ches-kee a-pa-RAHT) [EM-VEH-KAH-AH]	space shuttle
навигационный вычислитель	(na-vee-ga-tsee-ON-nee vee-chee-SLEE-tel)	flight computer
направленный радиомаяк	(nap-RAHV-len-nee RAH-dee-a-ma-YAHK)	directional beacon
невесомость	(ne-ve-SOH-mast)	zero gravity
орбита	(ar-BEE-ta)	orbit
орбитальная заправочная станция	(ar-bee-TAHL-na-ya zap-RAH-vach-na-ya STAHN-tsee-ya)	orbital refueling base
орбитальная станция (ОС)	(ar-bee-TAHL-na-ya STAHN-tsee-ya [OH-ES])	space station
отсчёт времени	(at-SHCHYOT VREH-me-nee)	count-down
передвижение в открытом космосе	(pe-re-dvee-ZHE-nee-ye vat-KREE-tam KOS-ma-se)	space walk
передвижная пусковая установка	(pe-re-dveezh-NAH-ya poos-ka-VAH-ya oos-ta-NOF-ka)	mobile launcher

подъёмная сила	*(pad-YOM-na-ya SEE-la)*	lift
подъёмная сила восходящих потоков воздуха	*(pad-YOM-na-ya SEE-la vas-kha-DYAH-shcheekh pa-TOH-kaf VOZ-doo-kha)*	thermal lift
последовательно расположенный ускоритель	*(pas-LEH-da-va-tel-na ras-pa-LOH-zhen-nee oos-ka-REE-tel)*	in-line booster
пусковая установка	*(poos-ka-VAH-ya oos-ta-NOF-ka)*	launcher
пусковой стол	*(poos-ka-VOY stol)*	launch pad
радиолокацион-ная станция (РЛС) дальнего обнаружения	*(RAH-dee-a-la-ka-tsee-ON-na-ya STAHN-tsee-ya [EHR-EL-ES] DAHL-ne-va ab-na-roo-ZHEH-nee-ya)*	early warning radar
ракета	*(ra-KEH-ta)*	rocket
ракетоплан	*(ra-ke-ta-PLAHN)*	boost-glide aircraft
реактивный истребитель	*(re-ak-TEEV-nee ees-tre-BEE-tel)*	jet fighter
реактивный самолёт	*(re-ak-TEEV-nee sa-ma-LYOT)*	jet plane
самолёт	*(sa-ma-LYOT)*	airplane
сверхзвуковая скорость (сверх Маха)	*(SVEHRKH-zvoo-ka-VAH-ya SKOH-rast [sverkh MAH-kha])*	mach speed
спутник	*(SPOOT-neek)*	satellite
твёрдое топливо	*(TVYOHR-da-ye TOP-lee-va)*	solid fuel
топливо для реактивных самолётов	*(TOP-lee-va dla re-ak-TEEV-nikh sa-ma-LYOH-taf)*	jet fuel
турбина	*(toor-BEE-na)*	turbine
турбо-реактивный двигатель	*(TOOHR-ba-re-ak-TEEV-nee DVEE-ga-tel)*	turbo-jet
турбулентность	*(toor-boo-LENT-nast)*	turbulence
ускоритель маневра	*(oos-ka-REE-tel ma-NYOV-ra)*	combat thrust booster
ускоритель многократного действия	*(oos-ka-REE-tel mna-ga-KRAHT-na-va DEY-stvee-ya)*	recoverable booster

форсажная камера	*(far-SAHZH-na-ya KAM-me-ra)*	after-burner
фюзеляж	*(fyoo-ze-LYAHSH)*	fuselage
шасси	*(shas-SEE)*	landing gear
шпангоут	*(shpan-GOH-oot)*	bulkhead
эффект Допплера	*(ef-FEKT DOP-ple-ra)*	Doppler effect

AGRICULTURE

The Russian Empire was a major agricultural exporter before the revolution, particularly from the "black earth" region of Ukraine. Today, the agricultural sector throughout the NIS faces serious challenges in renovating the infrastructure, converting to more environmentally benign processes, and improving yields. However, most analysts believe that agricultural production will respond dramatically to investment and new technology.

English to Russian

acidic (soil)	кислая почва	*(KEES-la-ya POCH-va)*
acre	акр	*(ahkr)*
aeration	аэрация	*(a-eh-RAH-tsee-ya)*
agricultural engineering	агротехника	*(ag-ra-TEKH-nee-ka)*
alfalfa	люцерна	*(lyoo-TSEHR-na)*
alkaline (soil)	щелочная почва	*(shche-lach-NAH-ya POCH-va)*
aphid	тля	*(tlyah)*
apiary	пасека	*(PAH-se-ka)*
apple	яблоко	*(YAHB-la-ka)*
arable land	пахотная земля	*(PAH-khat-na-ya zem-LYAH)*
autumn	осень	*(OH-sen)*
badger	барсук	*(bar-SOOK))*
barley	ячмень	*(yach-MEN)*
barn	сарай	*(sa-RAHY)*
bean	фасоль	*(fa-SOL)*
beet	свёкла	*(SVYOK-la)*
beet sugar	свекловичный сахар	*(svek-la-VEECH-nee SAH-khar)*
beetle	жук	*(zhook)*
botulism	ботулизм	*(ba-too-LEEZM)*
brand (on cattle)	тавро	*(tav-ROH)*
bread	хлеб	*(khlep)*
breeding	выведение	*(vee-ve-DEH-nee-ye)*
breeding stock	племенной скот	*(ple-men-NOY skot)*
bull	бык	*(bik)*

butter	масло	*(MAHS-la)*
cabbage	капуста	*(ka-POOS-ta)*
calf	телёнок	*(te-LYOH-nak)*
canning	консервирование	*(kan-ser-VEE-ra-va-nee-ye)*
carrot	морковь	*(mar-KOF)*
cattle	скот	*(skot)*
chicken	курица	*(KOO-ree-tsa)*
clover	клевер	*(KLEH-ver)*
collective farm	колхоз	*(kal-KHOS)*
colt	жеребёнок	*(zhe-re-BYOH-nak)*
combine harvester	уборочная машина	*(oo-BOH-rach-na-ya ma-SHEE-na)*
cooperative	кооператив	*(ka-a-pe-ra-TEEF)*
corn	кукуруза	*(koo-koo-ROO-za)*
cotton	хлопок	*(KHLOH-pak)*
country house	дача	*(DAH-cha)*
cow	корова	*(ka-ROH-va)*
crop-dusting	опыление посевов	*(a-pee-LEH-nee-ye pa-SEH-vaf)*
crows	ворона	*(va-ROH-na)*
cucumber	огурец	*(a-goo-RETS)*
dairy farm	молочная ферма	*(ma-LOCH-na-ya FEHR-ma)*
drip irrigation	капельное орошение	*(KAH-pel-na-ye a-ra-SHEH-nee-ye)*
drought	засуха	*(ZAH-soo-kha)*
duck	утка	*(OOT-ka)*
egg	яйцо	*(YAHY-tso)*
embryo	эмбрион	*(em-bree-OHN)*
ewe	овца	*(af-TSAH)*
fallow-field	поле под паром	*(POH-le pod PAHR-am)*
farm	хутор	*(KHOO-tar)*
farm labor	батрак	*(bat-RAHK)*
farmer	фермер	*(FEHR-mer)*
feed	корм	*(kohrm)*

fertilizer	удобрение	(oo-da-BREH-nee-ye)
field	поле	(POH-le)
fishery	рыбный промысел	(RIB-nee PROH-mee-sel)
flock	стая	(STAH-ya)
fowl	птица	(PTEE-tsa)
frost	мороз	(ma-ROZ)
fruit	фрукты	(FROOK-tee)
goose	гусь	(goos)
goat (f)	коза	(ka-ZAH)
goat (m)	козёл	(ka-ZYOL)
gophers	гофры	(GOF-ree)
grain	зерно	(zer-NOH)
granary	зернохранилище	(zer-na-khra-NEE-lee-shche)
grazing land	выпас	(VEE-pas)
grass	трава	(tra-VAH)
grasshopper	кузнечик	(kooz-NEH-chek)
green house	теплица	(tep-LEE-tsa)
ground water	грунтовая вода	(groon-TOH-va-ya va-DAH)
harvest	урожай	(oo-ra-ZHAHY)
hay	сено	(SEH-na)
hectare	гектар	(ghek-TAHR
hen	курица	(KOO-ree-tsa)
herbs	кухонные травы	(koo-KHON-nee-ye TRAH-vee)
herbicide	гербицид	(gher-bee-TSEED)
herd	стадо	(STAH-da)
hops	хмель	(khmel)
hormones	гормоны	(gar-MOH-nee)
horse	лошадь	(LOH-shat)
hydroponics	гидропоника	(gheed-ra-POH-nee-ka)
insecticide	инсектицид	(een-sek-tee-TSIT)
insects	насекомые	(na-se-KOH-mee-ye)
irrigate (v)	орошать	(a-ra-SHAHT)
lamb	ягнёнок	(yag-NYOH-nak)

land reform	земельная реформа	*(ze-MEL-na-ya re-FOHR-ma)*
lettuce	салат	*(sa-LAHT)*
locust (insect)	саранча	*(sa-ran-CHAH)*
lot	удел	*(oo-DYEL)*
manure	навоз	*(na-VOS)*
mare	кобыла	*(ka-BEE-la)*
mice	мыши	*(MEE-shee)*
milk	молоко	*(ma-la-KOH)*
milking machine	доильная машина	*(da-EEL-na-ya ma-SHEE-na)*
mushroom	гриб	*(greeb)*
orchard farming	садоводство	*(sa-da-VOT-stva)*
pasteurizer	пастеризатор	*(pas-te-ree-ZAH-tar)*
peach	персик	*(PEHR-seek)*
pear	груша	*(GROO-sha)*
plant (v)	сеять	*(SEH-yat)*
plant	растение	*(ras-TEH-nee-ye)*
plough	плуг	*(plook)*
plum	слива	*(SLEE-va)*
pollination	опыление	*(a-pee-LEH-nee-ye)*
potato	картофель	*(kar-TOH-fel)*
pond	пруд	*(proot)*
private farm	частный хутор	*(CHAHS-nee)*
radish	редиска	*(re-DEES-ka)*
ram	баран	*(ba-RAHN)*
rats	крысы	*(KREE-see)*
reaper	жатвенная машина	*(ZHAHT-ven-na-ya ma-SHEE-na)*
rooster	петух	*(pe-TOOKH)*
rural	деревенский	*(de-re-VEN-skee)*
rust (plant disease)	ржавчина	*(RZHAHF-chee-na)*
rye	рожь	*(rozh)*
scythe	коса	*(ka-SAH)*
seeder	сеялка	*(SEH-yal-ka)*

seeds	семена	*(se-me-NAH)*
sheep	баран	*(ba-RAHN)*
sickle	серп	*(sehrp)*
silo	силос зерновой	*(SEE-las zehr-na-VOY)*
slaughter house	скотобойня	*(ska-ta-BOY-nya)*
sow	свиноматка	*(svee-na-MAHT-ka)*
soybeans	соевые бобы	*(SOH-ye-vee-ye ba-BEE)*
spring	весна	*(ves-NAH)*
spring wheat	яровая пшеница	*(ya-ra-VAH-ya pshe-NEE-tsa)*
stable	стоило	*(STOY-la)*
starlings	скворцы	*(skvar-TSEE)*
subsidy	субсидия	*(soop-SEE-dee-ya)*
summer	лето	*(LEH-ta)*
swine	свинья	*(sveen-YAH)*
thresher	молотильщик	*(ma-la-TEEL-shcheek)*
tomato	помидор	*(pa-mee-DOHR)*
tractor	трактор	*(TRAHK-tar)*
truck farming	промышленное огородничество	*(pra-MISH-len-na-ye a-ga-ROD-nee-chest-va)*
urea	мочевина	*(ma-che-VEE-na)*
vegetables	овощи	*(OH-va-shchee)*
veterinarian	ветеринар	*(ve-te-ree-NAHR)*
village	село	*(se-LOH)*
viticulture	виноградство	*(vee-na-GRAH-dar-stva)*
weeds	сорняки	*(sar-nya-KEE)*
well	колодец	*(ka-LOH-dets)*
wheat	пшеница	*(pshe-NEE-tsa)*
wind-break	защитная лесополоса	*(za-SHCHEET-na-ya LEH-sa-pa-la-SAH)*
windmill	ветряная мельница	*(vet-rya-NAH-ya MEL-nee-tsa)*
winter	зима	*(zee-MAH)*
winter wheat	озимая пшеница	*(a-ZEE-ma-ya pshe-NEE-tsa)*
worm	червь	*(chehrf)*

Russian to English

агротехника	*(ag-ra-TEKH-nee-ka)*	agricultural engineering
акр	*(ahkr)*	acre
аэрация	*(a-eh-RAH-tsee-ya)*	aeration
баран	*(ba-RAHN)*	ram, sheep
барсук	*(bar-SOOK)*	badger
батрак	*(bat-RAHK)*	farm labor
ботулизм	*(ba-too-LEEZM)*	botulism
бык	*(bik)*	bull
весна	*(ves-NAH)*	spring
ветеринар	*(ve-te-ree-NAHR)*	veterinarian
ветряная мельница	*(vet-rya-NAH-ya MEL-nee-tsa)*	windmill
виноградство	*(vee-na-GRAH-dar-stva)*	viticulture
ворона	*(va-ROH-na)*	crows
выведение	*(vee-ve-DEH-nee-ye)*	breeding
выпас	*(VEE-pas)*	grazing land
гектар	*(ghek-TAHR)*	hectare
гербицид	*(gher-bee-TSEED)*	herbicide
гидропоника	*(gheed-ra-POH-nee-ka)*	hydroponics
гормоны	*(gar-MOH-nee)*	hormones
гофры	*(GOF-ree)*	gophers
гриб	*(greeb)*	mushroom
грунтовая вода	*(groon-TOH-va-ya va-DAH)*	ground water
груша	*(GROO-sha)*	pear
гусь	*(goos)*	goose
дача	*(DAH-cha)*	country house
деревенский	*(de-re-VEN-skee)*	rural
доильная машина	*(da-EEL-na-ya ma-SHEE-na)*	milking machine
жатвенная машина	*(ZHAHT-ven-na-ya ma-SHEE-na)*	reaper
жеребёнок	*(zhe-re-BYOH-nak)*	colt
жук	*(zhook)*	beetle
засуха	*(ZAH-soo-kha)*	drought

защитная лесополоса	*(za-SHCHEET-na-ya LEH-sa-pa-la-SAH)*	wind-break
земельная реформа	*(ze-MEL-na-ya re-FOHR-ma)*	land reform
зерно	*(zer-NOH)*	grain
зернохранилище	*(zer-na-khra-NEE-lee-shche)*	granary
зима	*(zee-MAH)*	winter
инсектицид	*(een-sek-tee-TSIT)*	insecticide
капельное орошение	*(KAH-pel-na-ye a-ra-SHEH-nee-ye)*	drip irrigation
капуста	*(ka-POOS-ta)*	cabbage
картофель	*(kar-TOH-fel)*	potato
кислая почва	*(KEES-la-ya POCH-va)*	acidic (soil)
клевер	*(KLEH-ver)*	clover
кобыла	*(ka-BEE-la)*	mare
коза	*(ka-ZAH)*	goat (f)
козёл	*(ka-ZYOL)*	goat (m)
колодец	*(ka-LOH-dets)*	well
колхоз	*(kal-KHOS)*	collective farm
консервирование	*(kan-ser-VEE-ra-va-nee-ye)*	canning
кооператив	*(ka-a-pe-ra-TEEF)*	cooperative
корм	*(kohrm)*	feed
корова	*(ka-ROH-va)*	cow
коса	*(ka-SAH)*	scythe
крысы	*(KREE-see)*	rats
кузнечик	*(kooz-NEH-cheek)*	grasshopper
кукуруза	*(koo-koo-ROO-za)*	corn
курица	*(KOO-ree-tsa)*	hen, chicken
кухонные травы	*(koo-KHON-nee-ye TRAH-vee)*	herbs
лето	*(LEH-ta)*	summer
лошадь	*(LOH-shat)*	horse
люцерна	*(lyoo-TSEHR-na)*	alfalfa
масло	*(MAHS-la)*	butter
молоко	*(ma-la-KOH)*	milk

молотильщик	(ma-la-TEEL-shcheek)	thresher
молочная ферма	(ma-LOCH-na-ya FEHR-ma)	dairy farm
морковь	(mar-KOF)	carrot
мороз	(ma-ROZ)	frost
мочевина	(ma-che-VEE-na)	urea
мыши	(MEE-shee)	mice
навоз	(na-VOS)	manure
насекомые	(na-se-KOH-mee-ye)	insects
овощи	(OH-va-shchee)	vegetables
овца	(af-TSAH)	ewe
огурец	(a-goo-RETS)	cucumber
озимая пшеница	(a-ZEE-ma-ya pshe-NEE-tsa)	winter wheat
опыление	(a-pee-LEH-nee-ye)	pollination
опыление посевов	(a-pee-LEH-nee-ye pa-SEH-vaf)	crop-dusting
орошать	(a-ra-SHAHT)	irrigate (v)
осень	(OH-sen)	autumn
поле под паром	(POH-le pod PAHR-am)	fallow-field
пасека	(PAH-se-ka)	apiary
пастеризатор	(pas-te-ree-ZAH-tar)	pasteurizer
пахотная земля	(PAH-khot-na-ya zem-LYAH)	arable land
персик	(PEHR-seek)	peach
петух	(pe-TOOKH)	rooster
племенной скот	(ple-men-NOY skot)	breeding stock
плуг	(plook)	plough
поле	(POH-le)	field
помидор	(pa-mee-DOHR)	tomato
промышленное огородничество	(pra-MISH-len-na-ye a-ga-ROD-nee-chest-va)	truck farming
пруд	(proot)	pond
птица	(PTEE-tsa)	fowl
пшеница	(pshe-NEE-tsa)	wheat
растение	(ras-TEH-nee-ye)	plant

редиска	*(re-DEES-ka)*	radish
ржавчина	*(RZHAHF-chee-na)*	rust (plant disease)
рожь	*(rozh)* *	rye
рыбный промысел	*(RIB-nee PROH-mee-sel)*	fishery
садоводство	*(sa-da-VOT-stva)*	orchard farming
салат	*(sa-LAHT)*	lettuce
сарай	*(sa-RAHY)*	barn
саранча	*(sa-ran-CHAH)*	locust (insect)
свекловичный сахар	*(SVYOK-la-VEECH-nee SAH-khar)*	beet sugar
свёкла	*(SVYOK-la)*	beet
свиноматка	*(svee-na-MAHT-ka)*	sow
свинья	*(sveen-YAH)*	swine
село	*(se-LOH)*	village
семена	*(se-me-NAH)*	seeds
сено	*(SEH-na)*	hay
серп	*(sehrp)*	sickle
сеялка	*(SEH-yal-ka)*	seeder
сеять	*(SEH-yat)*	plant (v)
силос зерновой	*(SEE-las zehr-na-VOY)*	silo
скворцы	*(skvar-TSEE)*	starlings
скот	*(skot)*	cattle
скотобойня	*(ska-ta-BOY-nya)*	slaughter house
слива	*(SLEE-va)*	plum
соевые бобы	*(SOH-ye-vee-ye ba-BEE)*	soybeans
сорняки	*(sar-nya-KEE)*	weed
стадо	*(STAH-da)*	herd
стая	*(STAH-ya)*	flock
стойло	*(STOY-la)*	stable
субсидия	*(soop-SEE-dee-ya)*	subsidy
тавро	*(tav-ROH)*	brand (on cattle)
телёнок	*(te-LYOH-nak)*	calf
теплица	*(tep-LEE-tsa)*	green house
тля	*(tlyah)*	aphid

трава	*(tra-VAH)*	grass
трактор	*(TRAHK-tar)*	tractor
уборочная машина	*(oo-BOH-rach-na-ya ma-SHEE-na)*	combine harvester
удел	*(oo-DYEL)*	lot
удобрение	*(oo-da-BREH-nee-ye)*	fertilizer
урожай	*(oo-ra-ZHAHY)*	harvest
утка	*(OOT-ka)*	duck
фасоль	*(fa-SOL)*	bean
фермер	*(FEHR-mer)*	farmer
фрукты	*(FROOK-tee)*	fruit
хлеб	*(khlep)*	bread
хлопок	*(KHLOH-pak)*	cotton
хмель	*(khmel)*	hops
хутор	*(KHOO-tar)*	farm
частный хутор	*(CHAHS-nee KHOO-tar)*	private farm
червь	*(chehrf)*	worm
щелочная почва	*(shche-lach-NAH-ya POCH-va)*	alkaline (soil)
эмбрион	*(em-bree-OHN)*	embryo
яблоко	*(YAHB-la-ka)*	apple
ягнёнок	*(yag-NYOH-nak)*	lamb
яйцо	*(YAHY-tso)*	egg
яровая пшеница	*(ya-ra-VAH-ya pshe-NEE-tsa)*	spring wheat
ячмень	*(yach-MEN)*	barley

CHEMICALS

Despite steadily falling production since the mid-1980s, Russia, together with the other European NIS states, continues to maintain one of the largest chemical industries in the world. Sub-sectors with strong potential for joint venture and export activity include inorganic chemicals, nitrogen-function compounds, and carboxylic acids.

English to Russian

acetic acid	уксусная кислота	*(OOK-soos-na-ya kees-la-TAH)*
acid	кислота	*(kees-la-TAH)*
ammonia	аммиак	*(am-mee-AHK)*
analysis	анализ	*(a-NAH-lees)*
analytic chemistry	аналитическая химия	*(a-na-lee-TEE-ches-ka-ya KHEE-mee-ya)*
atom	атом	*(AH-tam)*
atomic	атомный	*(AH-tam-nee)*
base	основание	*(as-na-VAH-nee-ye)*
benzene	бензол	*(ben-ZOL)*
biochemistry	биохимия	*(bee-a-KHEE-mee-ya)*
biologist	биолог	*(bee-OH-lak)*
biology	биология	*(bee-a-LOH-ghee-ya)*
carbon	углерод	*(oog-le-ROT)*
catalyst	катализатор	*(ka-ta-lee-ZAH-tar)*
chemical	химический продукт	*(khee-MEE-ches-kee pra-DOOKT)*
chemistry	химия	*(KHEE-mee-ya)*
chloride	хлорид	*(khla-REET)*
chloroform	хлороформ	*(khla-ra-FOHRM)*
component	компонент	*(kam-pa-NENT)*
composition	композиция	*(kam-pa-ZEE-tsee-ya)*
compound	химическое соединение	*(khee-MEE-ches-ka-ye sa-ye-dee-NEH-nee-ye)*
concentration	концентрирование	*(kan-tsen-TREE-ra-va-nee-ye)*
cracking	растрескивание	*(ras-TRES-kee-va-nee-ye)*
crystallization	кристаллизация	*(krees-tal-lee-ZAH-tsee-ya)*

degree (general)	степень	(STEH-pen)
degree (temperature)	градус	(GRAH-doos)
density	плотность	(PLOT-nast)
dosage	дозировка	(da-zee-ROF-ka)
electrolysis	электролиз	(eh-lek-TROH-lis)
electron	электрон	(e-lek-TRON)
element	элемент	(e-le-MENT)
engineer	инженер	(een-zhe-NEHR)
enzyme	фермент	(fer-MENT)
ethane	этан	(e-TAHN)
ether	простой эфир	(pra-STOY e-FEEHR)
evaporation	испарение	(ees-pa-REH-nee-ye)
experiment	эксперимент	(eks-pe-ree-MENT)
experimental	экспериментальный	(eks-pe-ree-men-TAHL-nee)
formula	формула	(FOHR-moo-la)
homogeneity	гомогенность	(ga-ma-GHEN-nast)
hydrocarbon	углеводород	(oog-le-va-da-ROT)
hydrochloric acid	соляная кислота	(sa-LYAH-na-ya kees-la-TAH)
hydrolysis	гидролиз	(gheed-ROH-lees)
impurity	примесь	(PREE-mes)
inorganic chemistry	неорганическая химия	(ne-ar-ga-NEE-ches-ka-ya KHEE-mee-ya)
isotope	изотоп	(ee-za-TOP)
laboratory	лаборатория	(la-ba-ra-TOH-ree-ya)
mole	грамм-молекула	(GRAHM-ma-LEH-koo-la)
natural gas	природный газ	(pree-ROD-nee gahs)
nitric acid	азотная кислота	(a-ZOT-na-ya kees-la-TAH)
organic chemistry	органическая химия	(ar-ga-NEE-ches-ka-ya KHEE-mee-ya)
petroleum	нефть	(neft)
phosphate	соль фосфорной кислоты	(sol FOS-far-nay kees-la-TEE)
polymer	полимер	(pa-lee-MEHR)
product	продукт	(pra-DOOKT)

purification	очистка	(a-CHEEST-ka)
reactant	реагент	(re-a-GHENT)
reduction (chemical)	восстановление	(vas-sta-nav-LEH-nee-ye)
refine (v)	очищать	(a-chee-SHCHAHT)
refinery	нефтеочистительный завод	(NEF-te-a-chees-TEE-tel-nee za-VOT)
research	исследование	(ees-SLEH-da-va-nee-ye)
salt	соль	(sol)
saponification	омыление	(a-mee-LEH-nee-ye)
solubility	растворимость	(ras-tva-REE-mast)
solute	растворенное вещество	(ras-tva-RYON-na-ye ve-shche-STVOH)
solution	раствор	(ras-TVOHR)
solvent	растворитель	(ras-tva-REE-tel)
sulfuric acid	серная кислота	(SEHR-na-ya KEES-la-tah)
test tube	пробирка	(pra-BEEHR-ka)
titration	титрование	(tee-tra-VAH-nee-ye)
yield (v) (give into)	подаваться	(pa-da-VAHT-sa)

Russian to English

азотная кислота	(a-ZOT-na-ya kees-la-TAH)	nitric acid
аммиак	(am-mee-AHK)	ammonia
анализ	(a-NAH-lees)	analysis
аналитическая химия	(a-na-lee-TEE-ches-ka-ya KHEE-mee-ya)	analytic chemistry
атом	(AH-tam)	atom
атомный	(AH-tam-nee)	atomic
бензол	(ben-ZOL)	benzene
биолог	(bee-OH-lak)	biologist
биология	(bee-a-LOH-ghee-ya)	biology
биохимия	(bee-a-KHEE-mee-ya)	biochemistry
восстановление	(vas-sta-nav-LEH-nee-ye)	reduction (chemical)
гидролиз	(gheed-ROH-lees)	hydrolysis
гомогенность	(ga-ma-GHEN-nast)	homogeneity

градус	(GRAH-doos)	degree (temperature)
градм-молекула	(GRAHM-ma-LEH-koo-la)	mole
дозировка	(da-zee-ROF-ka)	dosage
изотоп	(ee-za-TOP)	isotope
инженер	(een-zhe-NEHR)	engineer
испарение	(ees-pa-REH-nee-ye)	evaporation
исследование	(ees-SLEH-da-va-nee-ye)	research
катализатор	(ka-ta-lee-ZAH-tar)	catalyst
кислота	(kees-la-TAH)	acid
композиция	(kam-pa-ZEE-tsee-ya)	composition
компонент	(kam-pa-NENT)	component
концентрирование	(kan-tsen-TREE-ra-va-nee-ye)	concentration
кристаллизация	(krees-tal-lee-ZAH-tsee-ya)	crystallization
лаборатория	(la-ba-ra-TOH-ree-ya)	laboratory
неорганическая химия	(ne-ar-ga-NEE-ches-ka-ya KHEE-mee-ya)	inorganic chemistry
нефтеочисти-тельный завод	(NEF-te-a-chees-TEE-tel-nee za-VOT)	refinery
нефть	(neft)	petroleum
омыление	(a-mee-LEH-nee-ye)	saponification
органическая химия	(ar-ga-NEE-ches-ka-ya KHEE-mee-ya)	organic chemistry
основание	(as-na-VAH-nee-ye)	base
очистка	(a-CHEEST-ka)	purification
очищать	(a-chee-SHCHAHT)	refine (v)
плотность	(PLOT-nast)	density
подаваться	(pa-da-VAHT-sa)	yield (v) (give into)
полимер	(pa-lee-MEHR)	polymer
примесь	(PREE-mes)	impurity
природный газ	(pree-ROD-nee gahs)	natural gas
пробирка	(pra-BEEHR-ka)	test tube
продукт	(pra-DOOKT)	product
простой эфир	(pra-STOY e-FEEHR)	ether
раствор	(ras-TVOHR)	solution

растворённое вещество	*(ras-tva-RYON-na-ye ve-shche-STVOH)*	solute
растворимость	*(ras-tva-REE-mast)*	solubility
растворитель	*(ras-tva-REE-tel)*	solvent
растрескивание	*(ras-TRES-kee-va-nee-ye)*	cracking
реагент	*(re-a-GHENT)*	reactant
серная кислота	*(SEHR-na-ya KEES-la-tah)*	sulfuric acid
соль	*(sol)*	salt
соль фосфорной кислоты	*(sol FOS-far-nay kees-la-TEE)*	phosphate
соляная кислота	*(sa-LYAH-na-ya kees-la-TAH)*	hydrochloric acid
степень	*(STEH-pen)*	degree (general)
титрование	*(tee-tra-VAH-nee-ye)*	titration
углеводород	*(oog-le-va-da-ROT)*	hydrocarbon
углерод	*(oog-le-ROT)*	carbon
уксусная кислота	*(OOK-soos-na-ya kees-la-TAH)*	acetic acid
фермент	*(fer-MENT)*	enzyme
формула	*(FOHR-moo-la)*	formula
химический продукт	*(khee-MEE-ches-kee pra-DOOKT)*	chemical
химическое соединение	*(khee-MEE-ches-ka-ye sa-ye-dee-NEH-nee-ye)*	compound
химия	*(KHEE-mee-ya)*	chemistry
хлорид	*(khla-REET)*	chloride
хлороформ	*(khla-ra-FOHRM)*	chloroform
эксперимент	*(eks-pe-ree-MENT)*	experiment
эксперимен- тальный	*(eks-pe-ree-men-TAHL-nee)*	experimental
электролиз	*(eh-lek-TROH-lis)*	electrolysis
электрон	*(e-lek-TRON)*	electron
элемент	*(e-le-MENT)*	element
этан	*(e-TAHN)*	ethane

COMPUTERS

Although the NIS inherited a great deal of computer design and programming talent from the former Soviet Union, most analysts agree that computer technology and software will be one of the first service-based industries in which the major NIS states will become competitive, notwithstanding the ongoing "brain drain" of programmers and designers to the west. Meanwhile, there is enormous demand for all types of business computers, from main-frames to networks of PCs.

English to Russian

address	адрес	*(AHD-res)*
Apple	компания «Эппл»	*(kam-PAH-nee-ya "Apple")*
array	массив	*(mas-SEEF)*
artificial intelligence	искусственный интеллект	*(ees-KOOS-tven-nee een-tel-LEKT)*
backup (system)	резервное устройство	*(re-ZEHRV-na-ye oos-TROY-stva)*
backward compatible	совместимый назад	*(sav-mes-TEE-mee na-ZAHT)*
batched jobs	пакетные задания	*(pa-KET-nee-ye za-DAH-nee-ya)*
bit	бит	*(beet)*
byte	байт	*(bahyt)*
cable	кабель	*(KAH-bel)*
character	знак/символ	*(znahk)/(SEEM-val)*
chip	микросхема	*(meek-ra-SKHEH-ma)*
client	клиент	*(klee-YENT)*
column	колонка	*(ka-LON-ka)*
compiler	компилятор	*(kam-PEE-lya-tar)*
computer program	программа	*(pra-GRAHM-ma)*
computer	ЭВМ/компьютер	*(eh-veh-EM/kam-PYOO-ter)*
connect (into network)	подключать	*(pad-klyu-CHAHT)*
CPU	центральный процессор	*(tsen-TRAHL-nee pra-TSES-sar)*
crunching (data)	сжатие	*(SZHAH-tee-ye)*
data	данные	*(DAHN-nee-ye)*
database	база данных	*(BAH-za DAHN-nikh)*

DEC	компания «ДЭК»	*(kam-PAH-nee-ya dek)*
desktop publishing	настольные издательские средства	*(nas-TOL-nee-ye eez-DAH-tel-skee-ye SRETST-va)*
dial	номеронабиратель	*(NOH-me-ra-na-bee-RAH-tel)*
disk	диск	*(deesk)*
disk (floppy)	гибкий диск	*(GHEEP-kee deesk)*
disk (hard)	жёсткий диск	*(ZHOST-kee deesk)*
disk (laser)	лазерный диск	*(LAH-zehr-nee deesk)*
disk drive (hard)	дисковод для гибких дисков	*(dees-ka-VOT dla GHEEP-keekh DEES-kaf)*
disk drive (floppy)	дисковод для жёстких дисков	*(dees-ka-VOT dla ZHOST-keekh DEES-kaf)*
disk space	пространство на диске	*(pra-STRAHN-stva na-DEES-ke)*
document	документ	*(da-koo-MENT)*
error message	сообщение об ошибке	*(sa-ap-SHCHEH-nee-ye a-ba-SHIP-ke)*
field (data)	поле данных	*(POH-le DAHN-nikh)*
field (display)	поле индикации	*(POH-le een-dee-KAH-tsee-ee)*
field (input)	область ввода	*(OB-last VVOH-da)*
file	файл	*(fahyl)*
font	комплект шрифта	*(kam-PLEKT SHREEF-ta)*
hardware	аппаратные средства	*(a-pa-RAHT-nee-ye SRET-stva)*
IBM	компания «ИБМ»	*(kam-PAH-nee-ya AHY-BEE-EM)*
IBM compatible	ИБМ-совместимый	*(AHY-BEE-EM-sav-me-STEE-mee)*
icon	образ	*(OO-bras)*
index	индекс	*(EEN-deks)*
integrated circuit (IC)	интегральная схема (ИС)	*(een-te-GRAHL-na-ya SKHEH-ma)*
Intel	компания «Интел»	*(kam-PAH-nee-ya EEN-tel)*
Intel-based	Интеловский	*(EEN-te-lof-skee)*
job	задание	*(za-DAH-nee-ye)*
key	клавиша	*(KLAH-vee-sha)*

keyboard	клавиатура	*(kla-vee-a-TOO-ra)*
kilobyte	килобайт	*(kee-la-BAHYT)*
LAN (local area network)	локальная сеть	*(la-KAHL-na-ya set)*
laptop	портативная ЭВМ	*(par-ta-TEEF-na-ya eh-veh-EM)*
local	локальный	*(la-KAHL-nee)*
mainframe	универсальная ЭВМ	*(oo-nee-vehr-SAHL-na-ya eh-veh-EM)*
manual	справочное руководство	*(SPRAH-vach-na-ye roo-ka-VOT-stva)*
megabyte	мегабайт	*(me-ga-BAHYT)*
memory	запоминающее устройство (ЗУ)	*(za-pa-mee-NAH-yoo-shche-ye oos-TROY-stva (ZEH-OO)*
memory resident	находящийся постоянно в ЗУ	*(na-kha-DYAH-shcheey-sa pas-ta-YAHN-na VZEH-OO)*
menu-driven	управляемый в режиме меню	*(oop-rav-LYAH-ye-mee vre-ZHEE-me me-NYOO)*
microcomputer	микроЭВМ	*(MEEK-ra-eh-veh-EM)*
minicomputer	миниЭВМ	*(MEE-nee-eh-veh-EM)*
modem	модем	*(ma-DEM)*
monitor	монитор	*(ma-nee-TOHR)*
mother board	объединительная плата	*(ab-ye-dee-NEE-tel-na-ya PLAH-ta)*
mouse	манипулятор «мышь»	*(ma-nee-poo-LYAH-tar mish)*
multi-user	многоабонентский	*(MNOH-ga-a-ba-NENT-skee)*
null	нуль	*(nool)*
optical character recognition	оптическое распознание символов	*(ap-TEE-ches-ka-ye ras-pa-zna-VAH-nee-ye SEEM-va-laf)*
OS	ОС	*(os)*
PC	персональная ЭВМ	*(per-sa-NAHL-na-ya eh-veh-EM)*
peripheral	периферийное устройство	*(pe-ree-fe-REEY-na-ye oos-TROYST-va)*

port	порт	*(port)*
portable	мобильный	*(ma-BEEL-nee)*
printer	принтер	*(PREEN-tehr)*
processor	процессор	*(pra-TSES-sar)*
programming	программирование	*(pra-gram-MEE-ra-va-nee-ye)*
query	запрос	*(zap-ROS)*
random access memory (RAM)	ЗУ с произвольным порядком выборки	*(ZEH-OO spra-eez-VOL-nim pa-RYAHT-kam VEE-bar-kee)*
range	диапазон	*(dee-a-pa-ZON)*
reboot (v)	повторять начальную загрузку	*(paf-ta-RYAHT na-CHAHL-noo-yoo za-GROOS-koo)*
record	запись	*(ZAH-pees)*
relational data base	реляционная база данных	*(re-la-tsee-ON-na-ya BAH-za DAHN-nikh)*
ROM	постоянное запоминающее устройство (ПЗУ)	*(pas-ta-YAHN-na-ye za-pa-mee-NAH-yoo-shche-ye oos-TROYST-va)*
row	строка	*(stra-KAH)*
run-time	период прогона	*(pe-REE-at pra-GOH-na)*
save	сохранять	*(sakh-ra-NYAHT)*
scanner	сканнер	*(SKAHN-nehr)*
screen	экран	*(ek-RAHN)*
serial	серийный	*(se-REEY-nee)*
server	сервер	*(SER-ver)*
software	программное обеспечение/ «совтвер»	*(pra-GRAHM-na-ye a-bes-pe-CHEH-nee-ye/saft-VEHR)*
space-bar	клавиша пробела	*(KLAH-vee-sha pra-BEH-la)*
spreadsheet	динамическая электронная таблица	*(dee-na-MEE-ches-ka-ya e-lek-TRON-na-ya tab-LEE-tsa)*
system crash	полный отказ системы	*(POL-nee at-KAHS sees-TEH-mee)*
table	таблица	*(tab-LEE-tsa)*
tape	лента	*(LEN-ta)*

trouble-shooter	щуп для поиска неисправностей	*(shchoop dla POH-ees-ka ne-ees-PRAHV-na-stey)*
uncrunching (data)	развёртывание (сжатого файла)	*(RAHZ-vyor-tee-va-nee-ye SZHAH-ta-va FAHY-la)*
Univac	система «Юнивак»ю	*(sees-TEH-ma oo-nee-VAHK)*
user	пользователь	*(POL-za-va-tel)*
window-based	основанный на применении окон	*(as-NOH-van-nee na-pree-me-NEH-nee-ee OH-kan)*
word-processing	текстообработка	*(teks-ta-ab-ra-BOT-ka)*
workstation	рабочая станция	*(ra-BOH-cha-ya STAHN-tsee-ya)*
write-protected адрес	защищённый от записи	*(za-shchee-SHCHYON-nee ad-ZAH-pee-see)*

Russian to English

адрес	*(AHD-res)*	address
аппаратные средства	*(a-pa-RAHT-nee-ye SRET-stva)*	hardware
база данных	*(BAH-za DAHN-nikh)*	database
байт	*(bahyt)*	byte
бит	*(beet)*	bit
гибкий диск	*(GHEEP-kee deesk)*	disk (floppy)
данные	*(DAHN-nee-ye)*	data
диапазон	*(dee-a-pa-ZON)*	range
динамическая электронная таблица	*(dee-na-MEE-ches-ka-ya e-lek-TRON-na-ya tab-LEE-tsa)*	spreadsheet
диск	*(deesk)*	disk
дисковод для гибких дисков	*(dees-ka-VOT dla GHEEP-keekh DEES-kaf)*	disk drive (floppy)
дисковод для жёстких дисков	*(dees-ka-VOT dla ZHOST-keekh DEES-kaf)*	disk drive (hard)
документ	*(da-koo-MENT)*	document
жёсткий диск	*(ZHOST-kee deesk)*	disk (hard)
задание	*(za-DAH-nee-ye)*	job
запись	*(ZAH-pees)*	record

запоминающее устройство (ЗУ)	*(za-pa-mee-NAH-yoo-shche-ye oos-TROY-stva [ZEH-OO])*	memory
запрос	*(zap-ROS)*	query
защищённый от записи	*(za-shchee-SHCHYON-nee ad-ZAH-pee-see)*	write-protected
знак	*(znahk)*	character
ЗУ с произволь- ным порядком выборки	*(ZEH-OO spra-eez-VOL-nim pa-RYAHT-kam VEE-bar-kee)*	random access memory (RAM)
ИБМ- совместимый	*(AHY-BEE-EM-sav-me-STEE-mee)*	IBM compatible
индекс	*(EEN-deks)*	index
интегральная схема (ИС)	*(een-te-GRAHL-na-ya SKHEH-ma [EES])*	integrated circuit (IC)
Интеловский	*(EEN-te-lof-skee)*	Intel-based
искусственный интеллект	*(ees-KOOS-tven-nee een-tel-LEKT)*	artificial intelligence
кабель	*(KAH-bel)*	cable
килобайт	*(kee-la-BAHYT)*	kilobyte
клавиатура	*(kla-vee-a-TOO-ra)*	keyboard
клавиша	*(KLAH-vee-sha)*	key
клавиша пробела	*(KLAH-vee-sha pra-BEH-la)*	space-bar
клиент	*(klee-YENT)*	client
колонка	*(ka-LON-ka)*	column
компания «Интел»	*(kam-PAH-nee-ya EEN-tel)*	Intel
компания «ИБМ»	*(kam-PAH-nee-ya "AHY-BEE-EM")*	IBM
компания «Эппл»	*(kam-PAH-nee-ya "Apple")*	Apple
компания «ДЭК»	*(kam-PAH-nee-ya dek)*	DEC
компилятор	*(kam-PEE-lya-tar)*	compiler
компьютер	*(kam-PYOO-ter)*	computer
лазерный диск	*(LAH-zehr-nee deesk)*	disk (laser)
лента	*(LEN-ta)*	tape
локальная сеть	*(la-KAHL-na-ya set)*	LAN (local area network)
локальный	*(la-KAHL-nee)*	local

манипулятор «мышь»	*(ma-nee-poo-LYAH-tar mish)*	mouse
массив	*(mas-SEEF)*	array
мегабайт	*(me-ga-BAHYT)*	megabyte
микросхема	*(meek-ra-SKHEH-ma)*	chip
микроЭВМ	*(MEEK-ra-eh-veh-EM)*	microcomputer
миниЭВМ	*(MEE-nee-eh-veh-EM)*	minicomputer
многоабонентский	*(MNOH-ga-a-ba-NENT-skee)*	multi-user
мобильный	*(ma-BEEL-nee)*	portable
модем	*(ma-DEM)*	modem
монитор	*(ma-nee-TOHR)*	monitor
настольные издательские средства	*(nas-TOL-nee-ye eez-DAH-tel-skee-ye SRETST-va)*	desktop publishing
находящийся постоянно в ЗУ	*(na-kha-DYAH-shcheey-sa pas-ta-YAHN-na VZEH-OO)*	memory resident
номеронабиратель	*(NOH-me-ra-na-bee-RAH-tel)*	dial
нуль	*(nool)*	null
область ввода	*(OB-last VVOH-da)*	field (input)
образ	*(OO-braz)*	icon
объединительная плата	*(ab-ye-dee-NEH-nee-tel-na-ya PLAH-ta)*	mother board
оптическое распознавание символов	*(ap-TEE-ches-ka-ye ras-pa-zna-VAH-nee-ye SEEM-va-laf)*	optical character recognition
ОС	*(os)*	OS
основанный на применении окон	*(as-NOH-van-nee na pree-me-NEH-nee-ee OH-kan)*	window-based
пакетные задания	*(pa-KET-nee-ye za-DAH-nee-ya)*	batched jobs
период прогона	*(pe-REE-at pra-GOH-na)*	run-time
периферийное устройство	*(pe-ree-fe-REEY-na-ye oos-TROYST-va)*	peripheral
персональная ЭВМ	*(per-sa-NAHL-na-ya eh-veh-EM)*	PC

повторять начальную загрузку	*(paf-ta-RYAHT na-CHAHL-noo-yoo za-GROOS-koo)*	reboot (v)
подключать	*(pad-klyu-CHAHT)*	connect (into network)
поле данных	*(POH-le DAHN-nikh)*	field (data)
поле индикации	*(POH-le een-dee-KAH-tsee-ee)*	field (display)
полный отказ системы	*(POL-nee at-KAHS sees-TEH-mee)*	system crash
пользователь	*(POL-za-va-tel)*	user
порт	*(port)*	port
портативная ЭВМ	*(par-ta-TEEF-na-ya eh-ve-EM)*	laptop
постоянное запоминающее устройство (ПЗУ)	*(pas-ta-YAHN-na-ye za-pa-mee-NAH-yoo-shche-ye oos-TROYST-va)*	ROM
принтер	*(PREEN-tehr)*	printer
программа	*(pra-GRAHM-ma)*	computer program
программирование	*(pra-gra-MEE-ra-va-nee-ye)*	programming
программное обеспечение, «совтвер»	*(pra-GRAHM-na-ye a-bes-pe-CHEH-nee-ye, saft-VEHR)*	software
пространство на диске	*(pra-STRAHN-stva na DEES-ke)*	disk space
процессор	*(pra-TSES-sar)*	processor
рабочая станция	*(ra-BOH-cha-ya STAHN-tsee-ya)*	workstation
развёртывание (сжатого файла)	*(RAHZ-vyor-tee-va-nee-ye [ZHZHAH-ta-va FAHY-la])*	uncrunching (data)
резервное устройство	*(re-ZEHRV-na-ye oos-TROY-stva)*	backup
реляционная база данных	*(re-la-tsee-ON-na-ya BAH-za DAHN-nikh)*	relational data base
сервер	*(SER-ver)*	server
серийный	*(se-REEY-nee)*	serial
сжатие	*(SZHAH-tee-ye)*	crunching (data)
символ	*(SEEM-val)*	character

система «Юнивак»	*(sees-TEH-ma oo-nee-VAHK)*	Univac
сканнер	*(SKAHN-nehr)*	scanner
совместимый назад	*(sav-mes-TEE-mee na-ZAHT)*	backward compatible
сообщение об ошибке	*(sa-ap-SHCHEH-nee-ye a-ba-SHIP-ke)*	error message
сохранять	*(sakh-ra-NYAHT)*	save
справочное руководство	*(SPRAH-vach-na-ye roo-ka-VOT-stva)*	manual
строка	*(stra-KAH)*	row
таблица	*(tab-LEE-tsa)*	table
текстообработка	*(teks-ta-ab-ra-BOT-ka)*	word-processing
универсальная ЭВМ	*(oo-nee-vehr-SAHL-na-ya eh-veh-EM)*	mainframe
управляемый в режиме меню	*(oop-rav-LYAH-ye-mee vre-ZHEE-me me-NYOO)*	menu-driven
файл	*(fahyl)*	file
центральный процессор	*(tsen-TRAHL-nee pra-TSES-sar)*	CPU
щуп для поиска неисправностей	*(shchoop dla POH-ees-ka ne-ees-PRAHV-na-stey)*	trouble-shooter
ЭВМ компьютер	*(eh-veh-EM, kam-PYOO-ter)*	IBM computer
экран	*(ek-RAHN)*	screen

ELECTRONICS

There is a great demand for western electronic equipment of all kinds throughout the NIS, in addition to consumer electronics, that are already imported in growing quantities. Modernizing and converting industries will continue to have an enormous appetite for high-technology items such as integrated circuits and television and CD components which the domestic industry is not presently able to satisfy in sufficient quantity or quality.

English to Russian

alternating current	переменный ток	*(pe-re-MEN-nee tok)*
amplifier	усилитель	*(oo-see-LEE-tel)*
amplitude modula-tion (AM)	амплитудная модуляция	*(am-plee-TOOD-na-ya ma-doo-LYAH-tsee-ya)*
beam	луч	*(looch)*
binary code	двоичный код	*(dva-EECH-nee KOT)*
broadcasting	радиовещание	*(RAH-dee-a-ve-SHCHAH-nee-ye)*
cable television	кабельное телевидение	*(KAH-bel-na-ye te-le-VEE-de-nee-ye)*
capacitor	конденсатор	*(kan-den-SAH-tar)*
cassette	кассета	*(kas-SEH-ta)*
cathode	катод	*(ka-TOT)*
CD-ROM	неперезаписываемый компактный звукодиск	*(ne-pe-re-za-PEE-see-va-ye-mee kam-PAHKT-nee zvoo-ka-DEESK)*
channel	канал	*(ka-NAHL)*
circuit	схема	*(SKHEH-ma)*
coaxial cable	коаксиальный кабель	*(ka-ak-SEEL-nee KAH-bel)*
compact disk	компактный звукодиск	*(kam-PAHKT-nee zvoo-ka-DEESK)*
computer	ЭВМ	*(eh-veh-EM)*
condenser	конденсатор	*(kan-den-SAH-tar)*
current	ток	*(tok)*
diode	диод	*(dee-OT)*
direct current	постоянный ток	*(pas-ta-YAHN-nee tok)*
electricity	электричество	*(e-lek-TREE-chest-va)*
electrode	электрод	*(e-lek-TROT)*

electron	электрон	*(e-lek-TRON)*
electronic	электронный	*(e-lek-TRON-nee)*
electrostatic	электростатический	*(e-lek-tra-sta-TEE-ches-kee)*
filter	фильтр	*(feeltr)*
frequency	частота	*(chas-ta-TAH)*
frequency modulation (FM)	частотная модуляция	*(chas-TOT-na-ya ma-doo-LYAH-tsee-ya)*
high fidelity	с высокой точностью воспроизведения	*(SVEE-so-kay TOCH-nast-yoo vas-pra-eez-ve-DEH-nee-ya)*
induction	индукция	*(een-DOOK-tsee-ya)*
insulator	изолятор	*(ee-so-LYAH-tar)*
integrated circuit	интегральная схема (ИС)	*(een-te-GRAHL-na-ya SKHEH-ma (EE-ES)*
kilowatt	киловатт	*(kee-la-VAHT)*
laser	лазер	*(LAH-zehr)*
LED display	светодиодный индикатор	*(sve-ta-dee-OD-nee een-dee-KAH-tar*
microphone	микрофон	*(meek-ra-FON)*
microwave	микроволновый	*(meek-ra-val-NOH-vee)*
optical	оптический	*(ap-TEE-ches-kee)*
oscillator	осциллятор	*(as-tsil-LYAH-tar)*
panel	щит	*(shcheet)*
parallel circuit	параллельная схема	*(pa-ral-LEL-na-ya SKHEH-ma)*
power	энергия	*(e-NEHR-ghee-ya)*
printed circuit	печатная схема	*(pe-CHANT-na-ya SKHEH-ma)*
receiver	приёмник	*(pree-YOM-neek*
resistance	сопротивление	*(sap-ra-teev-LEH-nee-ye)*
resonance	резонанс	*(re-za-NAHNS)*
scanning	развёртка	*(raz-VYOHRT-ka)*
screen	экран	*(ek-RAHN)*
semiconductor	полупроводник	*(POH-loo-pra-vad-NEEK)*
short waves	короткие волны	*(ka-ROT-kee-ye VOL-nee)*
silicon	кремний	*(KREM-nee)*

sound	звук	*(zvook)*
speaker	акустическая система	*(a-koos-TEE-ches-ka-ya sees-TEH-ma)*
stereophonic	стереофонический	*(ste-re-a-fa-NEE-ches-kee)*
switch	переключатель	*(pe-re-kloo-CHAH-tel)*
tape recorder	магнитофон	*(mag-nee-ta-FON)*
telecommunica-tions	телесвязь	*(TEH-le-SVYAHS)*
tone	тон	*(ton)*
transformer	трансформатор	*(trans-far-MAH-tar)*
transistor	транзистор	*(tran-ZEES-tar)*
transmitter	передатчик	*(pe-re-DAHT-cheek)*
videocassette player	видеомагнитофон	*(VEE-de-a-mag-nee-ta-FON)*
voltage	напряжение	*(na-pre-ZHEH-nee-ye)*
wave	волна	*(val-NAH)*
wire	проволока	*(PROH-va-la-ka)*

Russian to English

акустическая система	*(a-koos-TEE-ches-ka-ya sees-TEH-ma)*	speaker
амплитудная модуляция	*(am-plee-TOOD-na-ya ma-doo-LYAH-tsee-ya)*	amplitude modulation (AM)
видеомагнитофон	*(VEE-de-a-mag-nee-ta-FON)*	videocassette player
волна	*(val-NAH)*	wave
двоичный код	*(dva-EECH-nee KOT)*	binary code
диод	*(dee-OT)*	diode
звук	*(zvook)*	sound
изолятор	*(ee-so-LYAH-tar)*	insulator
индукция	*(een-DOOK-tsee-ya)*	nduction
интегральная схема (ИС)	*(een-te-GRAHL-na-ya SKHEH-ma [EES])*	integrated circuit
кабельное телевидение	*(KAH-bel-na-ye te-le-VEE-de-nee-ye)*	cable television
канал	*(ka-NAHL)*	channel

кассета	*(kas-SEH-ta)*	cassette
катод	*(ka-TOT)*	cathode
киловатт	*(kee-la-VAHT)*	kilowatt
коаксиальный кабель	*(ka-ak-SEEL-nee KAH-bel)*	coaxial cable
компактный звукодиск	*(kam-PAHKT-nee zvoo-ka-DEESK)*	compact disk
конденсатор	*(kan-den-SAH-tar)*	capacitor, condenser
короткие волны	*(ka-ROT-kee-ye VOL-nee)*	short waves
кремний	*(KREM-nee)*	silicon
лазер	*(LAH-zehr)*	laser
луч	*(looch)*	beam
магнитофон	*(mag-nee-ta-FON)*	tape recorder
микроволновый	*(meek-ra-val-NOH-vee)*	microwave
микрофон	*(meek-ra-FON)*	microphone
напряжение	*(na-pre-ZHEH-nee-ye)*	voltage
неперезаписывае-мый компакт-ный звукодиск	*(ne-pe-re-za-PEE-see-va-ye-mee kam-PAHKT-nee zvoo-ka-DEESK)*	CD-ROM
оптический	*(ap-TEE-ches-kee)*	optical
осциллятор	*(as-tsil-LYAH-tar)*	oscillator
параллельная схема	*(pa-ral-LEL-na-ya SKHEH-ma)*	parallel circuit
передатчик	*(pe-re-DAHT-cheek)*	transmitter
переключатель	*(pe-re-kloo-CHAH-tel)*	switch
переменный ток	*(pe-re-MEHN-nee tok)*	alternating current
печатная схема	*(pe-CHAHT-na-ya SKHEH-ma)*	printed circuit
полупроводник	*(POH-loo-pra-vad-NEEK)*	semiconductor
постоянный ток	*(pas-ta-YAHN-nee tok)*	direct current
приёмник	*(pree-YOM-neek)*	receiver
проволока	*(PROH-va-la-ka)*	wire
радиовещание	*(RAH-dee-a-ve-SHCHAH-nee-ye)*	broadcasting
развёртка	*(raz-VYOHRT-ka)*	scanning
резонанс	*(re-za-NAHNS)*	resonance

с высокой точно-стью воспроиз-ведение	*(SVEE-so-kay TOCH-nast-yoo vas-pra-eez-ve-DEH-nee-ye)*	high fidelity
светодиодный индикатор	*(sve-ta-dee-OD-nee een-dee-KAH-tar)*	LED display
сопротивление	*(sap-ra-teev-LEH-nee-ye)*	resistance
стереофонический	*(ste-re-a-fa-NEE-ches-kee)*	stereophonic
схема	*(SKHEH-ma)*	circuit
телесвязь	*(TEH-le-SVYAHS)*	telecommunications
ток	*(tok)*	current
тон	*(ton)*	tone
транзистор	*(tran-ZEES-tar)*	transistor
трансформатор	*(trans-far-MAH-tar)*	transformer
усилитель	*(oo-see-LEE-tel)*	amplifier
фильтр	*(feeltr)*	filter
частота	*(chas-ta-TAH)*	frequency
частотная модуляция	*(chas-TOT-na-ya ma-doo-LYAH-tsee-ya)*	frequency modulation (FM)
щит	*(shcheet)*	panel
ЭВМ	*(eh-veh-EM)*	computer
экран	*(ek-RAHN)*	screen
электричество	*(e-lek-TREE-chest-va)*	electricity
электрод	*(e-lek-TROT)*	electrode
электрон	*(e-lek-TRON)*	electron
электронный	*(e-lek-TRON-nee)*	electronic
электростати-ческий	*(e-lek-tra-sta-TEE-ches-kee)*	electrostatic
энергия	*(e-NEHR-ghee-ya)*	power

FOREST PRODUCTS

Russia has the greatest amount of forest acreage in the world, and supports a large wood and paper industry that generates significant hard currency earnings. Notwithstanding the scale, however, there is a serious shortage of all grades of paper, and the need for new equipment, wood processing and paper mill components, will grow dramatically.

English to Russian

accumulation	накопление	*(na-ka-PLEH-nee-ye)*
acid-tolerant	кислотоустойчивый	*(kees-LOH-ta-oos-TOY-che-vee)*
air-seasoned	воздушно-сухой	*(vaz-DOOSH-na-soo-KHOY)*
alder	ольха	*(al-KHAH)*
alkalization	засоление	*(za-sa-LEH-nee-ye)*
anaerobe	анаэробный микроорганизм	*(a-na-e-ROB-nee meek-ra-ar-ga-NEEZM)*
analysis of forest ecosystem	анализ экосистемы леса	*(a-NAH-lees e-ka-sees-TEH-mee LEH-sa)*
ash (tree)	ясень	*(YAH-sen)*
ash (residue)	зола	*(za-LAH)*
balsa	бальза заячья	*(BAHL-za ZAH-yach-ya)*
bark	кора	*(ka-RAH)*
barker	окорочный станок	*(OH-ka-rach-nee sta-NOK)*
beam	балка	*(BAHL-ka)*
beech	бук	*(book)*
beetle	жук	*(zhook)*
bilberry	черника	*(cher-NEE-ka)*
birch	берёза	*(be-RYOH-za)*
blade	пильное полотно	*(PEEL-na-ye pa-lat-NOH)*
blueberry	голубика	*(ga-loo-BEE-ka)*
board foot	досковой фут	*(das-ka-VOY foot)*
board	доска	*(das-KAH)*
cambium	камбий	*(KAHM-bee)*
cedar	кедр	*(KEDR)*
cellulose	целлюлоза	*(tse-lyoo-LOH-za)*

clear-cutting	вырубаемый сплошной рубкой	*(vee-roo-BAH-ye-tee SPLAHSH-noy ROOP-kay)*
cloudberry	морошка	*(ma-ROSH-ka)*
conifer	хвойное дерево	*(KHVOY-na-ye DEH-re-va)*
cordwood	лесоматериал в кордах	*(LEH-sa-ma-te-ree-AHL FKOHR-dakh)*
cutting angle	угол резания	*(OO-gal REH-za-nee-ya)*
elm	вяз	*(vyas)*
erosion	эрозия	*(e-ROH-zee-ya)*
fir	пихта	*(PEEKH-ta)*
fire-break	противопожарная полоса	*(pra-tee-va-pa-ZHAHR-na-ya pa-la-SAH)*
float	лесосплав	*(le-sa-SPLAHF)*
forest	лес	*(les)*
forest fire	лесной пожар	*(les-NOY pa-ZHAHR)*
furniture	мебель	*(MEH-bel)*
hand-tooled	обработанный вручную	*(ab-ra-BOH-tan-nee vrooch-NOO-yoo)*
hardwood	древесина лиственных пород	*(dre-ve-SEE-na LEEST-ven-nikh pa-ROT)*
harvestable	годный на сводку	*(GOD-nee nas-VOT-koo)*
hatched larvae	вылупившиеся личинки	*(VEE-loo-peef-shee-ye-sa lee-CHEEN-kee)*
hornbeam	граб	*(grahp)*
jenny	подвижной кран	*(pad-veezh-NOY krahn)*
kiln	печь	*(pech)*
knot	сучок	*(soo-CHOK)*
lacquer	лак	*(lahk)*
larch	лиственница	*(LEEST-ven-nee-tsa)*
leaf	лист	*(leest)*
leaf-eating insects	листоеды	*(lees-ta-YEH-dee)*
lichen	лишайник	*(lee-SHAHY-neek)*
lime (linden tree)	липа	*(LEE-pa)*
lime (soil)	известь	*(EEZ-vest)*
lingonberry	брусника	*(broos-NEE-ka)*

management-vol- ume inventory	изучение запаса, прироста и отпада насаждений	*(ee-zoo-CHEH-nee-ye za-PAH-sa, pree-ROS-ta ee at-PAH-da na-sazh-DEH-neey)*
maple	клён	*(klyon)*
milling allowance	допуск на обработку	*(DOH-poosk na-ab-ra-BOT-koo)*
oak	дуб	*(doop)*
owl	сова	*(sa-VAH)*
pallet	паллет	*(PAHL-let)*
paper mill	бумажная фабрика	*(boo-MAHZH-na-ya FAHB-ree-ka)*
particle board	древесностружечная плита (ДСП)	*(dre-VES-na-STROO-zhech-na-ya plee-TAH [DEH-ES-PEH])*
pine	сосна	*(sas-NAH)*
plywood	фанера	*(fa-NEH-ra)*
production length	стандартная длина заготовки	*(stan-DAHRT-na-ya dlee-NAH za-ga-TOF-kee)*
pulp	волокнистый полуфабрикат	*(va-lak-NEES-tee poh-loo-fab-ree-KAHT*
reforestation	лесовосстановление	*(LEH-sa-vas-sta-nav-LEH-nee-ye)*
saw	пила	*(pee-LAH)*
saw-mill	лесопильный	*(le-sa-PEEL-nee)*
sawdust	опилки	*(a-PEEL-kee)*
seedling	сеянец	*(SEH-ya-nets)*
spruce	ель	*(yel)*
timberland	лесная площадь	*(les-NAH-ya PLOH-shchat)*
tree ring analysis	анализ годичных слоев	*(aNAH-lees ga-DEECH-nikh sla-YOF)*
tree	дерево	*(DEH-re-va)*
tree gene bank	лесосеменная плантация	*(LEH-sa-se-men-NAH-ya plan-TAH-tsee-ya)*
wood	древесина	*(dre-ve-SEE-na)*

Russian to English

анализ годичных слоев	*(a-NAH-lees ga-DEECH-nikh sla-YOF)*	tree ring analysis
анализ экосистемы леса	*(a-NAH-lees e-ka-sees-TEH-mee LEH-sa)*	analysis of forest ecosystem
анаэробный микроорганизм	*(a-na-e-ROB-nee meek-ra-ar-ga-NEEZM)*	anaerobe
балка	*(BAHL-ka)*	beam
бальза заячья	*(BAHL-za ZAH-yach-ya)*	balsa
берёза	*(be-RYOH-za)*	birch
брусника	*(broos-NEE-ka)*	lingonberry
бук	*(book)*	beech
бумажная фабрика	*(boo-MAHZH-na-ya FAHB-ree-ka)*	paper mill
воздушно-сухой	*(vaz-DOOSH-na-soo-KHOY)*	air-seasoned
волокнистый полуфабрикат	*(va-lak-NEES-tee poh-loo-fab-ree-KAHT)*	pulp
вылупившиеся личинки	*(VEE-loo-peef-shee-ye-sa lee-CHEEN-kee)*	hatched larvae
вырубаемый сплошной рубкой	*(vee-roo-BAH-ye-mee SPLAHSH-noy ROOP-kay)*	clear-cutting
вяз	*(vyas)*	elm
годный на сводку	*(GOD-nee nas-VOT-koo)*	harvestable
голубика	*(ga-loo-BEE-ka)*	blueberry
граб	*(grahp)*	hornbeam
дерево	*(DEH-re-va)*	tree
допуск на обработку	*(DOH-poosk na-ab-ra-BOT-koo)*	milling allowance
доска	*(das-KAH)*	board
досковой фут	*(das-ka-VOY foot)*	board foot
древесина	*(dre-ve-SEE-na)*	wood
древесина лиственных пород	*(dre-ve-SEE-na LEEST-ven-nikh pa-ROT)*	hardwood
древесностружечная плита (ДСП)	*(dre-VES-na-STROO-zhech-na-ya plee-TAH [DEH-ES-PEH])*	particle board

дуб	*(doop)*	oak
ель	*(yel)*	spruce
жук	*(zhook)*	beetle
засоление	*(za-sa-LEH-nee-ye)*	alkalization
зола	*(za-LAH)*	ash (residue)
известь	*(EEZ-vest)*	lime (soil)
изучение запаса, прироста и отпада насаждений	*(ee-zoo-CHEH-nee-ye za-PAH-sa, pree-ROS-ta ee at-PAH-da na-sazh-DEH-neey)*	management-volume inventory
камбий	*(KAHM-bee)*	cambium
кедр	*(kedr)*	cedar
кислотоустой-чивый	*(kees-LOH-ta-oos-TOY-che-vee)*	acid-tolerant
клён	*(klyon)*	maple
кора	*(ka-RAH)*	bark
лак	*(lahk)*	lacquer
лес	*(les)*	forest
лесная площадь	*(les-NAH-ya PLOH-shchat)*	timberland
лесной пожар	*(les-NOY pa-ZHAHR)*	forest fire
лесовосстановлен-ие	*(LEH-sa-vas-sta-nav-LEH-nee-ye)*	reforestation
лесоматериал в кордах	*(LEH-sa-ma-te-ree-AHL FKOHR-dakh)*	cordwood
лесопильный	*(le-sa-PEEL-nee)*	saw-mill
лесосеменная плантация	*(LEH-sa-se-men-NAH-ya plan-TAH-tsee-ya)*	tree gene bank
лесосплав	*(le-sa-SPLAHF)*	float
липа	*(LEE-pa)*	lime (linden tree)
лист	*(leest)*	leaf
лиственница	*(LEEST-ven-nee-tsa)*	larch
листоеды	*(lees-ta-YEH-dee)*	leaf-eating insects
лишайник	*(lee-SHAHY-neek)*	lichen
мебель	*(MEH-bel)*	furniture
морошка	*(ma-ROSH-ka)*	cloudberry
накопление	*(na-ka-PLEH-nee-ye)*	accumulation

обработанный вручную	(ab-ra-BOH-tan-nee vrooch-NOO-yoo)	hand-tooled
окорочный станок	(OH-ka-rach-nee sta-NOK)	barker
ольха	(al-KHAH)	alder
опилки	(a-PEEL-kee)	sawdust
паллет	(PAHL-let)	pallet
печь	(pech)	kiln
пила	(pee-LAH)	saw
пильное полотно	(PEEL-na-ye pa-lat-NOH)	blade
пихта	(PEEKH-ta)	fir
подвижной кран	(pad-veezh-NOY krahn)	jenny
противопожарная полоса	(pra-tee-va-pa-ZHAHR-na-ya pa-la-SAH)	fire-break
сеянец	(SEH-ya-nets)	seedling
сова	(sa-VAH)	owl
сосна	(sas-NAH)	pine
стандартная длина заготовки	(stan-DAHRT-na-ya dlee-NAH za-ga-TOF-kee)	production length
сучок	(soo-CHOK)	knot
угол резания	(OO-gal REH-za-nee-ya)	cutting angle
фанера	(fa-NEH-ra)	plywood
хвойное дерево	(KHVOY-na-ye DEH-re-va)	conifer
целлюлоза	(tse-lyoo-LOH-za)	cellulose
черника	(cher-NEE-ka)	bilberry
эрозия	(e-ROH-zee-ya)	erosion
ясень	(YAH-sen)	ash (tree)

IRON AND STEEL

This industry was favored under the communist regimes, as being an indicator of development and a bulwark of military production. As a result, Russia today is the world's second largest producer of crude steel, second to Japan. Throughout the NIS, steel-producing capacity is greater than local demand that, in combination with low labor costs, creates opportunity for joint ventures and low-cost production.

English to Russian

alloy steel	легированная сталь	*(le-GHEE-ra-van-na-ya stahl)*
aluminum	алюминий	*(a-lyoo-MEE-neey)*
annealing	отжиг	*(OT-zhik)*
billets	сутунки	*(soo-TOON-kee)*
blast furnace	домна	*(DOM-na)*
carbon steel	углеродистая сталь	*(oog-le-ROH-dees-ta-ya stahl)*
cast iron	чугун	*(choo-GOON)*
chromium	хром	*(khrom)*
coil	змеевик	*(zme-ye-VEEK)*
cold rolling	холодная прокатка	*(kha-LOD-na-ya pra-KAHT-ka)*
continuous mill	непрерывный прокатный стан	*(ne-pre-RIV-nee pra-KAHT-nee stahn)*
conveyor	конвейер	*(kan-VEH-yehr)*
conveyor belt	конвейерная лента	*(kan-VEH-yehr-na-ya LEN-ta)*
copper	медь	*(met)*
crucible	тигель	*(TEE-ghel)*
cupola	вагранка	*(va-GRAHN-ka)*
electric arc furnace	электродуговая печь	*(e-LEK-tra-doo-ga-VAH-ya pech)*
electrolytic process	электролитический процесс	*(e-lek-tra-lee-TEE-ches-kee pra-TSES)*
ferroalloys	ферросплавы	*(fehr-ra-SPLAH-vee)*
ferromanganese	ферромарганец	*(fehr-ra-MAHR-ga-nets)*
ferronickel	ферроникель	*(fehr-ra-NEE-kel)*

finished products	конечные продукты	*(ka-NECH-nee-ye pra-DOOK-tee)*
finishing mill	чистовой прокатный стан	*(chees-ta-VOY pra-KAHT-nee stahn)*
foundry	литейный завод	*(lee-TEY-nee za-VOT)*
furnace	печь	*(pech)*
galvanizing	гальванизация	*(gal-va-nee-ZAH-tsee-ya)*
grinding	шлифование	*(shlee-fa-VAH-nee-ye)*
heat	теплота	*(tep-la-TAH)*
hot rolling	горячая прокатка	*(ga-RYAH-cha-ya pra-KAHT-ka)*
induction furnace	индукционная печь	*(een-dook-tsee-ON-na-ya pech)*
ingot mold	изложница	*(eez-LOZH-nee-tsa)*
ingots	слитки	*(SLEET-kee)*
iron ore	железная руда	*(zhe-LEZ-na-ya roo-DAH)*
limestone	известняк	*(eez-ves-NYAHK)*
malleability	ковкость	*(KOF-kast)*
manganese ore	марганцевая руда	*(MAHR-gan-tse-va-ya roo-DAH)*
molybdenum	молибден	*(ma-leeb-DEN)*
nickel	никель	*(NEE-kel)*
nitrogen	азот	*(a-ZOT)*
ore	руда	*(roo-DAH)*
pickling	травление	*(trav-LEH-nee-ye)*
pig iron	чушковый чугун	*(CHOOSH-ka-vee choo-GOON)*
plate	толстый лист	*(TOL-stee leest)*
powder	порошок	*(pa-ra-SHOK)*
pressure	давление	*(dav-LEH-nee-ye)*
process	процесс	*(pra-TSES)*
refractories	огнеупорные материалы	*(ag-ne-oo-POHR-nee-ye ma-te-ree-YAH-lee)*
rod	стержень	*(STEHR-zhen)*
rolling mill	прокатный стан	*(pra-KAHT-nee stahn)*
scale	окалина	*(a-KAH-lee-na)*

scrap	(металлический) лом	*([me-tal-LEE-ches-kee] lom)*
sheet	лист	*(leest)*
slabs	плоская заготовка	*(PLOS-ka-ya za-ga-TOF-ka)*
specialty steels	специальные стали	*(spe-tsee-AHL-nee-ye STAH-lee)*
stainless steel	нержавеющая сталь	*(ne-rzha-VEH-yoo-shcha-ya stahl)*
steel mill	сталеплавильный завод	*(sta-le-pla-VEEL-nee za-VOT)*
structural shapes	профили	*(PROH-fee-lee)*
super alloys	жаропрочный сплав	*(zha-ra-PROCH-nee splahf)*
titanium	титан	*(tee-TAHN)*
toughness	вязкость	*(VYAHS-kast)*
tungsten	вольфрам	*(val-FRAHM)*
vacuum melting furnace	вакуумированная плавильная печь	*(va-koo-oo-MEE-ra-van-na-ya pla-VEEL-na-ya pech)*
vanadium	ванадий	*(va-NAH-deey)*
wire	проволока	*(PROH-va-la-ka)*

Russian to English

азот	*(a-ZOT)*	nitrogen
алюминий	*(a-lyoo-MEE-neey)*	aluminum
вагранка	*(va-GRAHN-ka)*	cupola
вакуумированная плавильная печь	*(va-koo-oo-MEE-ra-van-na-ya pla-VEEL-na-ya pech)*	vacuum melting furnace
ванадий	*(va-NAH-deey)*	vanadium
вольфрам	*(val-FRAHM)*	tungsten
вязкость	*(VYAHS-kast)*	toughness
гальванизация	*(gal-va-nee-ZAH-tsee-ya)*	galvanizing
горячая прокатка	*(ga-RYAH-cha-ya pra-KAHT-ka)*	hot rolling
давление	*(dav-LEH-nee-ye)*	pressure
домна	*(DOM-na)*	blast furnace
жаропрочный сплав	*(zha-ra-PROCH-nee splahf)*	super alloys

железная руда	*(zhe-LEZ-na-ya roo-DAH)*	iron ore
змеевик	*(zme-ye-VEEK)*	coil
известняк	*(eez-ves-NYAHK)*	limestone
изложница	*(eez-LOZH-nee-tsa)*	ingot mold
индукционная печь	*(een-dook-tsee-ON-na-ya pech)*	induction furnace
ковкость	*(KOF-kast)*	malleability
конвейер	*(kan-VEH-yehr)*	conveyor
конвейерная лента	*(kan-VEH-yehr-na-ya LEN-ta)*	conveyor belt
конечные продукты	*(ka-NECH-nee-ye pra-DOOK-tee)*	finished products
легированная сталь	*(le-GHEE-ra-van-na-ya stahl)*	alloy steel
лист	*(leest)*	sheet
литейный завод	*(lee-TEY-nee za-VOT)*	foundry
лом (металлический)	*(lom [me-tal-LEE-ches-kee])*	scrap
марганцевая руда	*(MAHR-ga-tse-va-ya roo-DAH)*	manganese ore
медь	*(met)*	copper
молибден	*(ma-leeb-DEN)*	molybdenum
непрерывный прокатный стан	*(ne-pre-RIV-nee pra-KAHT-nee stahn)*	continuous mill
нержавеющая сталь	*(ne-rzha-VEH-yoo-shcha-ya stahl)*	stainless steel
никель	*(NEE-kel)*	nickel
огнеупорные материалы	*(ag-ne-oo-POHR-nee-ye ma-te-ree-YAH-lee)*	refractories
окалина	*(a-KAH-lee-na)*	scale
отжиг	*(OT-zhik)*	annealing
печь	*(pech)*	furnace
плоская заготовка	*(PLOS-ka-ya za-ga-TOF-ka)*	slabs
порошок	*(pa-ra-SHOK)*	powder
проволока	*(PROH-va-la-ka)*	wire
прокатный стан	*(pra-KAHT-nee stahn)*	rolling mill
профили	*(PROH-fee-lee)*	structural shapes

процесс	(pra-TSES)	process
руда	(roo-DAH)	ore
слитки	(SLEET-kee)	ingots
специальные стали	(spe-tsee-AHL-nee-ye STAH-lee)	specialty steels
сталеплавильный завод	(sta-le-pla-VEEL-nee za-VOT)	steel mill
стержень	(STEHR-zhen)	rod
сутунки	(soo-TOON-kee)	billets
теплота	(tep-la-TAH)	heat
тигель	(TEE-ghel)	crucible
титан	(tee-TAHN)	titanium
толстый лист	(TOL-stee leest)	plate
травление	(trav-LEH-nee-ye)	pickling
углеродистая сталь	(oog-le-ROH-dees-ta-ya stahl)	carbon steel
ферромарганец	(fehr-ra-MAHR-ga-nets)	ferromanganese
ферроникель	(fehr-ra-NEE-kel)	ferronickel
ферросплавы	(fehr-ra-SPLAH-vee)	ferroalloys
холодная прокатка	(kha-LOD-na-ya pra-KAHT-ka)	cold rolling
хром	(khrom)	chromium
чистовой прокатный стан	(chees-ta-VOY pra-KAHT-nee stahn)	finishing mill
чугун	(choo-GOON)	cast iron
чушковый чугун	(CHOOSH-ka-vee choo-GOON)	pig iron
шлифование	(shlee-fa-VAH-nee-ye)	grinding
электродуговая печь	(e-LEK-tra-doo-ga-VAH-ya pech)	electric arc furnace
электролитичес-кий процесс	(e-lek-tra-lee-TEE-ches-kee pra-TSES)	electrolytic process

LEATHER GOODS

As with agriculture, the NIS governments have put large amounts of resources behind the support of this industry. Russian furs are world-famous and continue to be abundant, and the domestic leather and related goods industries cannot presently supply domestic demand. Although there have been increasing imports from China, South-East Asia, and even South America, increased production of hides and low-cost labor bode well for this industry.

English to Russian

ankle boots	ботинки	*(ba-TEEN-kee)*
astrakhan	каракуль	*(ka-RAH-kool)*
attaché case	кожаный ручной чемоданчик/атташе	*(KOH-zha-nee rooch-NOY che-ma-DAHN-cheek [at-ta-SHEH])*
beaver	бобёр	*(ba-BYOR)*
belt	пояс	*(POH-yas)*
billfold	бумажник	*(boo-MAHZH-neek)*
blotter	бювар	*(byoo-VAHR)*
boots	сапоги	*(sa-pa-GHEE)*
briefcase	атташе (кэйс)	*(at-ta-SHEH [kehys])*
calfskin	телячья кожа	*(te-LYAHCH-ya KOH-zha)*
card case	футляр для визиток	*(foot-LYAHR dla vee-ZEE-tak)*
cigarette case	портсигар	*(part-see-GAHR)*
cowhide	воловья кожа	*(va-LOH-vya KOH-zha)*
dye (v)	красить	*(KRAH-seet)*
eyeglass case	футляр для очков	*(foot-LYAHR dla ach-KOF)*
fitch	хорьковый мех	*(khar-KOH-vee mekh)*
fox	лисий мех	*(LEE-see mekh)*
gloves	перчатки	*(per-CHAHT-kee)*
handbag	дамская сумка	*(DAHM-ska-ya SOOM-ka)*
holster	кобура	*(ka-boo-RAH)*
key case	футляр для ключей	*(foot-LYAHR dla kloo-CHEY)*
kidskin	шевро	*(shev-ROH)*
lamb	мерлушка	*(mer-LOOSH-ka)*
leather	кожа	*(KOH-zha)*

leather goods	кожевенный товар	*(ka-ZHEH-ven-nee ta-VAHR)*
leather jacket	кожаная куртка	*(KOH-zha-na-ya KOOHRT-ka)*
lizard (skin)	кожа из ящерицы	*(KOH-zha YAH-shche-ree-tsee)*
lynx	рысь	*(ris)*
makeup case	коробка для косметики/ косметичка	*(ka-ROP-ka dla kas-MEH-tee-kee/kas-me-TEECH-ka)*
marmot	сурок	*(soo-ROK)*
mink	норковый	*(NOHR-ka-vee)*
Morocco leather	сафьян	*(saf-YAHN)*
nutria	нутрия	*(NOOT-ree-ya)*
opossum	опоссум	*(a-POS-soom)*
ostrich (skin)	страусовая кожа	*(STRAH-oo-sa-va-ya KOH-zha)*
otter	выдра	*(VID-ra)*
passport case	футляр для паспорта	*(foot-LYAHR dla PAHS-par-ta)*
patent leather	лакированная кожа/лак	*(la-kee-ROH-van-na-ya KOH-zha/lak)*
pigskin	свиная кожа	*(svee-NAH-ya KOH-zha)*
pocketbook	записная книжка	*(za-pees-NAH-ya KNEEZH-ka)*
portfolio	портфель	*(part-FEL)*
purse	сумочка	*(SOO-mach-ka)*
rabbit	кролик	*(KROH-leek)*
raccoon	енот	*(ye-NOT)*
repair shop	сапожная мастерская	*(sa-POZH-na-ya mas-ter-SKAH-ya)*
sable	соболь	*(SOH-bal)*
saddle	седло	*(sed-LOH)*
saddler	шорник	*(SHOHR-neek)*
scissor case	футляр для ножниц	*(foot-LYAHR dla NOZH-neets)*
sealskin	тюленья шкура	*(tyoo-LEN-ya SHKOO-ra)*
sewing kit	швейный комплект	*(SHVEY-nee kamp-LEKT)*

slippers	туфли/тапочки	*(TOOF-lee/TAH-pach-kee)*
snakeskin	змеиная кожа	*(zme-EE-na-ya KOH-zha)*
suede	замша	*(ZAHM-sha)*
suede jacket	замшевая куртка	*(ZAHM-she-va-ya KOOHRT-ka)*
suitcase	чемодан	*(che-ma-DAHN)*
tan (v)	дубить	*(doo-BEET)*
tanner	дубильщик	*(doo-BEEL-shcheek)*
tannery	кожевенный завод	*(ka-ZHEH-ven-nee za-VOT)*
tannin (tannin)	танин	*(ta-NEEN)*
tote bag	мешок	*(me-SHOK)*
trunk	сундук	*(soon-DOOK)*
watch band	ремешок для часов	*(re-me-SHOK dla cha-SOF)*
whip	плётка	*(PLYOT-ka)*

Russian to English

атташе (кэйс)	*(at-ta-SHEH [kehys])*	briefcase
бобёр	*(ba-BYOR)*	beaver
ботинки	*(ba-TEEN-kee)*	ankle boots
бумажник	*(boo-MAHZH-neek)*	billfold
бювар	*(byoo-VAHR)*	blotter
воловья кожа	*(va-LOH-vya KOH-zha)*	cowhide
выдра	*(VID-ra)*	otter
дамская сумка	*(DAHM-ska-ya SOOM-ka)*	handbag
дубильщик	*(doo-BEEL-shcheek)*	tanner
дубить	*(doo-BEET)*	tan (v)
енот	*(ye-NOT)*	raccoon
замша	*(ZAHM-sha)*	suede
замшевая куртка	*(ZAHM-she-va-ya KOOHRT-ka)*	suede jacket
записная книжка	*(za-pees-NAH-ya KNEEZH-ka)*	pocketbook
змеиная кожа	*(zme-EE-na-ya KOH-zha)*	snakeskin
каракуль	*(ka-RAH-kool)*	astrakhan

кобура	(ka-boo-RAH)	holster
кожа	(KOH-zha)	leather
кожа из ящерицы	(KOH-zha YAH-shche-ree-tsee)	lizard (skin)
кожаная куртка	(KOH-zha-na-ya KOOHRT-ka)	leather jacket
кожаный ручной чемоданчик	(KOH-zha-nee rooch-NOY che-ma-DAHN-cheek)	attachO case
кожевенный завод	(ka-ZHEH-ven-nee za-VOT)	tannery
кожевенный товар	(ka-ZHEH-ven-nee ta-VAHR)	leather goods
коробка для косметики	(ka-ROP-ka dla kas-MEH-tee-kee)	makeup case
красить	(KRAH-seet)	dye (v)
кролик	(KROH-leek)	rabbit
лак	(lak)	patent leather
лакированная кожа	(la-kee-ROH-van-na-ya KOH-zha)	patent leather
лисий мех	(LEE-see mekh)	fox
мерлушка	(mer-LOOSH-ka)	lamb
мешок	(me-SHOK)	tote bag
норковый	(NOHR-ka-vee)	mink
нутрия	(NOOT-ree-ya)	nutria
опоссум	(a-POS-soom)	opossum
перчатки	(per-CHAHT-kee)	gloves
плётка	(PLYOT-ka)	whip
портсигар	(part-see-GAHR)	cigarette case
портфель	(part-FEL)	portfolio
пояс	(POH-yas)	belt
ремешок для часов	(re-me-SHOK dla cha-SOF)	watch band
рысь	(ris)	lynx
сапоги	(sa-pa-GHEE)	boots
сапожная мастерская	(sa-POZH-na-ya mas-ter-SKAH-ya)	repair shop
сафьян	(saf-YAHN)	Morocco leather

свиная кожа	*(svee-NAH-ya KOH-zha)*	pigskin
седло	*(sed-LOH)*	saddle
соболь	*(SOH-bal)*	sable
страусовая кожа	*(STRAH-oo-sa-va-ya KOH-zha)*	ostrich (skin)
сумочка	*(SOO-mach-ka)*	purse
сундук	*(soon-DOOK)*	trunk
сурок	*(soo-RHOK)*	marmot
танин	*(ta-NEEN)*	tannin (tannin)
тапочки	*(TAH-pach-kee)*	slippers
телячья кожа	*(te-LYAHCH-ya KOH-zha)*	calfskin
туфли	*(TOOF-lee)*	slippers, shoes
тюленья шкура	*(tyoo-LEN-ya SHKOO-ra)*	sealskin
футляр для визиток	*(foot-LYAHR dla vee-ZEE-tak)*	card case
футляр для ключей	*(foot-LYAHR dla kloo-CHEY)*	key case
футляр для ножниц	*(foot-LYAHR dla NOZH-neets)*	scissor case
футляр для очков	*(foot-LYAHR dla ach-KOF)*	eyeglass case
футляр для паспорта	*(foot-LYAHR dla PAHS-par-ta)*	passport case
хорьковый мех	*(khar-KOH-vee mekh)*	fitch
чемодан	*(che-ma-DAHN)*	suitcase
швейный комплект	*(SHVEY-nee kamp-LEKT)*	sewing kit
шевро	*(shev-ROH)*	kidskin
шорник	*(SHOHR-neek)*	saddler

	MOTOR VEHICLES	

Although Russia is a major producer of automobiles, the present designs are not yet competitive in the world market, even when pitted against other Eastern European models. As a result, there has been a remarkable flow of imported automobiles. Domestic demand for automobiles is so great, however, that there remains strong demand for domestically-produced automobiles within the NIS, as well. Lower cost trucks and large agricultural vehicles are also promising sub-sectors, both domestically and for export.

English to Russian

air filter	воздушный фильтр	*(vaz-DOOSH-nee feeltr)*
alternator	синхронный генератор	*(seen-KHRON-nee ghe-ne-RAH-tar)*
assembly line	конвейер	*(kan-VEH-yehr)*
automatic gearshift	автоматическая коробка передач	*(af-ta-ma-TEE-ches-ka-ya ka-ROP-ka pe-re-DAHCH)*
automobile	автомобиль	*(af-ta-ma-BEEL)*
battery fluid	аккумуляторная жидкость	*(ak-koo-moo-LYAH-tar-na-ya ZHIT-kast)*
battery	аккумулятор	*(ak-koo-moo-LYAH-tar)*
bearings	подшипник	*(pat-SHIP-neek)*
block	блок	*(blok)*
body	кузов	*(KOO-zaf)*
brake	тормоз	*(TOHR-mas)*
brake pedal	тормозная педаль	*(tar-maz-NAH-ya pe-DAHL)*
bumper	буфер	*(BOO-fer)*
camshaft	кулачковый вал	*(koo-lach-KOH-vee val)*
car	автомобиль	*(af-ta-ma-BEEL)*
carburetor	карбюратор	*(kar-byoo-RAH-tar)*
chassis	шасси	*(shas-SEE)*
clutch	сцепление	*(stse-PLEH-nee-ye)*
clutch pedal	педаль сцепления	*(pe-DAHL stse-PLEH-nee-ya)*
connecting rod	соединительная тяга	*(sa-ye-dee-NEE-tel-na-ya TYAH-ga)*
convertible	автомобиль с откидным верхом	*(af-ta-ma-BEEL sat-keed-NIM VEHR-kham)*

crankshaft	коленчатый вал	*(ka-LEN-cha-tee val)*
cylinder head gasket	прокладка головки цилиндра	*(prak-LAHT-ka ga-LOF-kee tsee-LEEN-dra)*
cylinder head	головка цилиндра	*(ga-LOF-ka tsee-LEEN-dra)*
defroster	обогреватель	*(a-ba-gre-VAH-tel)*
designer	конструктор	*(kan-STROOK-tar)*
disc brake	дисковый тормоз	*(DEES-ka-vee TOHR-mas)*
displacement	рабочий объём	*(ra-BOH-chee ab-YOM)*
distributor	распределитель	*(ras-pre-de-LEE-tel)*
driver	водитель	*(va-DEE-tel)*
engine	двигатель	*(DVEE-ga-tel)*
exhaust	выхлоп	*(VIKH-lap)*
fan	вентилятор	*(ven-tee-LYAH-tar)*
fender	крыло	*(kree-LOH)*
four-cylinder engine	четырёхтактный двигатель	*(che-tee-RYOKH-TAHKT-nee DVEE-ga-tel)*
front-wheel drive	передний привод	*(pe-RED-nee PREE-vat)*
fuel pump	бензиновый насос	*(ben-ZEE-na-vee na-SOS)*
gas consumption	расход горючего	*(ras-KHOT ga-RYOO-che-va)*
gasoline	бензин	*(ben-ZEEN)*
gasoline tank	газгольдер	*(gaz-GOL-der)*
gearshift	коробка передач	*(ka-ROP-ka pe-re-DAHCH)*
generator	генератор	*(ghe-ne-RAH-tar)*
grille	решётка	*(re-SHOT-ka)*
horsepower	лошадиная сила	*(la-sha-DEE-na-ya SEE-la)*
ignition	зажигание	*(za-zhee-GAH-nee-ye)*
injector	инжектор	*(een-ZHEK-tar)*
lubrication	смазывание	*(SMAH-zee-va-nee-ye)*
mileage	расстояние в милях на галлон топлива	*(ras-sta-YAH-nee-ye VMEE-lyakh na gal-LON TOP-lee-va)*
odometer	одометр	*(a-DOH-metr)*
paint	краска	*(KRAHS-ka)*
pinion	шестерня	*(shes-ter-NYAH)*

piston	поршень	*(POHR-shen)*
power steering	рулевое управление с усилителем	*(roo-le-VOH-ye oop-rav-LEH-nee-ye soo-see-LEE-te-lem)*
radial tire	радиальная шина	*(ra-dee-AHL-na-ya SHEE-na)*
radiator	радиатор	*(ra-dee-AH-tar)*
rear axle	задний мост/задняя ось	*(ZAHD-nee most/ZAHD-nya-ya os)*
rings	кольца	*(KOL-tsa)*
seat	сиденье	*(see-DEN-ye)*
shaft	вал	*(vahl)*
shock absorber	амортизатор	*(a-mar-tee-ZAH-tar)*
six-cylinder engine	шеститактный двигатель	*(shes-tee-TAHKT-nee DVEE-ga-tel)*
spare tire	запасная шина	*(za-pas-NAH-ya SHEE-na)*
spark plug	запальная свеча	*(za-PAHL-na-ya sve-CHAH)*
speedometer	спидометр	*(spee-DOH-metr)*
spring	рессоры	*(res-SOH-ree)*
starter	стартер	*(star-TYOHR)*
steering column	колонка руля	*(ka-LON-ka roo-LYAH)*
steering	рулевое управление	*(roo-le-VOH-ye oop-rav-LEH-nee-ye)*
steering wheel	руль	*(rool)*
suspension	подвеска	*(pad-VES-ka)*
tire	шина	*(SHEE-na)*
torque	крутящий момент	*(kroo-TYAH-shchee ma-MENT)*
V8 engine	двигатель с восемью клапанами	*(DVEE-ga-tel sva-se-MYOO KLAH-pa-na-mee)*
valve	клапан	*(KLAH-pan)*
water pump	водяной насос	*(va-dya-NOY na-SOS)*
wheel	колесо	*(ka-le-SOH)*
windshield	ветровое стекло	*(vet-ra-VOH-ye stek-LOH)*

Russian to English

автоматическая коробка передач	*(af-ta-ma-TEE-ches-ka-ya ka-ROP-ka pe-re-DAHCH)*	automatic gearshift
автомобиль	*(af-ta-ma-BEEL)*	automobile, car
автомобиль с откидным верхом	*(af-ta-ma-BEEL sat-keed-NIM VEHR-kham)*	convertible
аккумулятор	*(ak-koo-moo-LYAH-tar)*	battery
аккумуляторная жидкость	*(ak-koo-moo-LYAH-tar-na-ya ZHIT-kast)*	battery fluid
амортизатор	*(a-mar-tee-ZAH-tar)*	shock absorber
бензин	*(ben-ZEEN)*	gasoline
бензиновый насос	*(ben-ZEE-na-vee na-SOS)*	fuel pump
блок	*(blok)*	block
буфер	*(BOO-fer)*	bumper
вал	*(vahl)*	shaft
вентилятор	*(ven-tee-LYAH-tar)*	fan
ветровое стекло	*(vet-ra-VOH-ye stek-LOH)*	windshield
водитель	*(va-DEE-tel)*	driver
водяной насос	*(va-dya-NOY na-SOS)*	water pump
воздушный фильтр	*(vaz-DOOSH-nee feeltr)*	air filter
выхлоп	*(VIKH-lap)*	exhaust
газгольдер	*(gaz-GOL-der)*	gasoline tank
генератор	*(ghe-ne-RAH-tar)*	generator
головка цилиндра	*(ga-LOF-ka tsee-LEEN-dra)*	cylinder head
двигатель	*(DVEE-ga-tel)*	engine
двигатель с восемью клапанами	*(DVEE-ga-tel sva-se-MYOO KLAH-pa-na-mee)*	V8 engine
дисковый тормоз	*(DEES-ka-vee TOHR-mas)*	disc brake
задний мост	*(ZAHD-nee most)*	rear axle
задняя ось	*(ZAHD-nya-ya os)*	rear axle
зажигание	*(za-zhee-GAH-nee-ye)*	ignition
запальная свеча	*(za-PAHL-na-ya sve-CHAH)*	spark plug

запасная шина	(za-pas-NAH-ya SHEE-na)	spare tire
инжектор	(een-ZHEK-tar)	injector
карбюратор	(kar-byoo-RAH-tar)	carburetor
клапан	(KLAH-pan)	valve
коленчатый вал	(ka-LEN-cha-tee val)	crankshaft
колесо	(ka-le-SOH)	wheel
колонка руля	(ka-LON-ka roo-LYAH)	steering column
кольца	(KOL-tsa)	rings
конвейер	(kan-VEH-yehr)	assembly line
конструктор	(kan-STROOK-tar)	designer
коробка передач	(ka-ROP-ka pe-re-DAHCH)	gearshift
краска	(KRAHS-ka)	paint
крутящий момент	(kroo-TYAH-shchee ma-MENT)	torque
крыло	(kree-LOH)	fender
кузов	(KOO-zaf)	body
кулачковый вал	(koo-lach-KOH-vee val)	camshaft
лошадиная сила	(la-sha-DEE-na-ya SEE-la)	horsepower
обогреватель	(a-ba-gre-VAH-tel)	defroster
одометр	(a-DOH-metr)	odometer
педаль сцепления	(pe-DAHL stse-PLEH-nee-ya)	clutch pedal
передний привод	(pe-RED-nee PREE-vat)	front-wheel drive
подвеска	(pad-VES-ka)	suspension
подшипник	(pat-SHIP-neek)	bearings
поршень	(POHR-shen)	piston
прокладка головки цилиндра	(prak-LAHT-ka ga-LOF-kee tsee-LEEN-dra)	cylinder head gasket
рабочий объём	(ra-BOH-chee ab-YOM)	displacement
радиальная шина	(ra-dee-AHL-na-ya SHEE-na)	radial tire
радиатор	(ra-dee-AH-tar)	radiator
распределитель	(ras-pre-de-LEE-tel)	distributor

расстояние в милях на галлон топлива	*(ras-sta-YAH-nee-ye VMEE-lyakh na gal-LON TOP-lee-va)*	mileage
расход горючего	*(ras-KHOT ga-RYOO-che-va)*	gas consumption
рессоры	*(res-SOH-ree)*	spring
решётка	*(re-SHOT-ka)*	grille
рулевое управление	*(roo-le-VOH-ye oop-rav-LEH-nee-ye)*	steering
рулевое управление с усилителем	*(roo-le-VOH-ye oop-rav-LEH-nee-ye soo-see-LEE-te-lem)*	power steering
руль	*(rool)*	steering wheel
сиденье	*(see-DEN-ye)*	seat
синхронный генератор	*(seen-KHRON-nee ghe-ne-RAH-tar)*	alternator
смазывание	*(SMAH-zee-va-nee-ye)*	lubrication
соединительная тяга	*(sa-ye-dee-NEE-tel-na-ya TYAH-ga)*	connecting rod
спидометр	*(spee-DOH-metr)*	speedometer
стартер	*(star-TYOHR)*	starter
сцепление	*(stse-PLEH-nee-ye)*	clutch
тормоз	*(TOHR-mas)*	brake
тормозная педаль	*(tar-maz-NAH-ya pe-DAHL)*	brake pedal
четырёхтактный двигатель	*(chee-tee-RYOKH-TAHKT-nee DVEE-ga-tel)*	four-cylinder engine
шасси	*(shas-SEE)*	chassis
шестерня	*(shes-ter-NYAH)*	pinion
шеститактный двигатель	*(shes-tee-TAHKT-nee DVEE-ga-tel)*	six-cylinder engine
шина	*(SHEE-na)*	tire

OIL AND GAS

Russia is the world's largest producer of natural gas and the third-largest producer of oil, pumping more than 7.9 million barrels per day in 1992. Russia's oil and gas sector could potentially produce much more, except for equipment failures and technical problems. Besides vast new fields discovered in Siberia and off-shore of the Sakhalin Island, Azerbaijan, Kazakhstan and Uzbekistan all have major untapped reserves. As the bureaucratic and jurisdictional difficulties are worked out, this sector should prove to be a major export generator, a market for western equipment and expertise, and an important stimulus to the rest of the NIS economies.

English to Russian

above-ground retorting	наземная перегонка	*(na-ZEM-na-ya pe-re-GON-ka)*
acid spoil	кислые отходы	*(KEES-lee-ye at-KHOH-dee)*
acidification	подкисление	*(pat-kee-SLEH-nee-ye)*
active gas	активный газ (подземного газохранилища)	*(ak-TEEV-nee gahs [pad-ZEM-na-va ga-za-khra-NEE-lee-shcha])*
active reserves	активные запасы	*(ak-TEEV-nee-ye za-PAH-see)*
additions to reserves	прирост запасов	*(pree-ROST za-PAH-saf)*
appraisal well	оценочная скважина	*(a-TSEH-nach-na-ya SKVAH-zhee-na)*
ash content	зольность	*(ZOL-nast)*
asphalt	асфальт	*(as-FAHLT)*
average productivity per unit vol.	средняя удельная продуктивность	*(SRED-nya-ya oo-DEL-na-ya pra-dook-TEEV-nast)*
barrel	баррель	*(BAHR-rel)*
base price	базовая контрактная цена (на природный газ)	*(BAH-za-va-ya kan-TRAHKT-na-ya tse-NAH [na pree-ROD-nee gahs])*
below ground value	стоимость подготовки запасов	*(STOH-ee-mast pad-ga-TOF-kee za-PAH-saf)*
benchmark price (of crude)	базисная цена на "эталонную" нефть	*(BAH-zees-na-ya tse-NAH na e-ta-LON-noo-yoo neft)*
bitumen	битум	*(bee-TOOM)*
blue gas	водяной газ	*(va-dya-NOY gahs)*

British Thermal Unit (BTU)	Британская Тепловая Единица (БТЕ)	*(bree-TAHN-ska-ya tep-la-VAH-ya e-dee-NEE-tsa [BEH-TEH-YEH])*
bunker oil	жидкое бункерное топливо	*(ZHIT-ka-ye BOON-ker-na-ye TOP-lee-va)*
by-product	побочный продукт	*(pa-BOCH-nee pra-DOOKT)*
casinghead gas	нефтяной газ	*(nef-ta-NOY gaz)*
coal gas	угольный газ	*(OO-gal-nee gahs)*
coal gasification	газификация угля	*(ga-zee-fee-KAH-tsee-ya oog-LYAH)*
coal oil	угольная нефть	*(OO-gal-na-ya neft)*
combustible gas	горючий газ	*(ga-RYOO-chee gahs)*
combustible shale	горючий сланец	*(ga-RYOO-chee SLAH-nets)*
commercially exploitable reserves	рентабельно извлекаемые запасы	*(ren-TAH-bel-na eez-vle-KAH-ye-mee-ye za-PAH-see)*
condensate	конденсат	*(kan-den-SAHT)*
contract crude oil	контрактная нефть	*(kan-TRAHKT-na-ya neft)*
contract oil market	рынок долгосрочных сделок (на купле-продаже нефти)	*(REE-nak dal-ga-SROCH-nikh ZDEH-lak [na KOOP-le pra-DAH-zhe NEF-tee])*
cost recovery	возмещение издержек (добычи)	*(vaz-me-SHCHEH-nee-ye eez-DEHR-zhek [da-BEE-chee])*
crude oil	(сырая) нефть	*([SEE-ra-ya] neft)*
dead oil	"мёртвая" (неподвижная) нефть	*(MYOHRT-va-ya [ne-pad-VEEZH-na-ya] neft)*
delivered cost	цена с включением расходов по доставке	*(tse-NAH sfklyoo-CHEH-nee-yem ras-KHOH-daf pa das-TAHF-ke)*
demonstrated resources	подтверждённые ресурсы	*(pat-tverzh-DYON-nee-ye re-SOOHR-see)*
deposit	месторождение	*(mes-ta-razh-DEH-nee-ye)*
desliming	обеспыливание	*(a-bes-PEE-lee-va-nee-ye)*
developed field	освоенное месторождение	*(as-VOH-yen-na-ye mes-ta-razh-DEH-nee-ye)*
developed drilling	эксплуатационное бурение	*(eks-ploo-a-ta-tsee-ON-na-ye boo-REH-nee-ye)*

development well	эксплуатационная скважина	*(eks-ploo-a-ta-tsee-ON-na-ya SKVAH-zhee-na)*
devonian shale	девонский сланец	*(de-VON-skee SLAH-nets)*
diesel fuel	дизельное топливо	*(DEE-zel-na-ye TOP-lee-va)*
differential rent	дифференциальная рента	*(deef-fe-ren-tsee-AHL-na-ya REHN-ta)*
discovery bonus	"бонус" за открытие	*(BOH-noos za at-KREE-tee-ye)*
domestic gas	отечественный газ	*(a-TEH-chest-ven-nee gahs)*
dry hole	непродуктивная ("сухая") скважина	*(ne-pra-dook-TEEV-na-ya [soo-KHAH-ya] SKVAH-zhee-na)*
dump gas	сбросовый газ	*(ZBROH-sa-vee gahs)*
dung	кизяк	*(kee-ZYAHK)*
economic life	период рентабельной разработки месторождения	*(pe-REE-at ren-TAH-bel-nay raz-ra-BOT-kee mes-ta-razh-DEH-nee-ya)*
emergency petroleum reserves	чрезвычайные запасы жидкого топлива	*(chrez-vee-CHAHY-nee-ye za-PAH-see ZHIT-ka-va TOP-lee-va)*
energy return ratio	коэффициент энергоотдачи	*(ka-ef-fee-tsee-ENT e-NEHR-ga-ad-DAH-chee)*
energy resources	источники энергии	*(ees-TOCH-nee-kee e-NEHR-ghee-ee)*
enhanced oil recovery	повышенное извлечение нефти	*(pa-VEE-shen-na-ye eez-vle-CHEH-nee-ye NEF-tee)*
equity crude oil	"собственная" нефть	*(SOP-stven-na-ya neft)*
ethanol	этанол	*(e-ta-NOL)*
ex-gasifier price	цена франко-газогенератора	*(tse-NAH FRAHN-ka GAH-za-ghe-ne-RAH-ta-ra)*
exploratory costs	затраты на проведение поиска-разведочных работ	*(za-TRAH-tee na pra-ve-DEH-nee-ye POH-ees-ka-va-raz-VEH-dach-nikh ra-BOT)*
exploratory well	поиска-разведочная скважина	*(POH-ees-ka-va-raz-VEH-dach-na-ya SKVAH-zhee-na)*
extraction ratio	коэффициент извлечения	*(ka-ef-fee-tsee-ENT eez-vle-CHEH-nee-ya)*

extra-heavy oil	"сверхтяжелая" нефть	*(sverkh-tya-ZHOH-la-ya neft)*
farm-out	договор о субаренде (продуктивного участка)	*(da-ga-VOHR a-soob-a-REHN-de [pra-dook-TEEV-na-va oo-CHAHST-ka])*
feed materials	сырьевые материалы	*(sihr-ye-VEE-ye ma-te-ree-YAH-lee)*
field	месторождение	*(mes-ta-razh-DEH-nee-ye)*
final oil recovery	конечная нефтеотдача	*(ka-NECH-na-ya NEF-te-ad-DAH-cha)*
fixed-commitment contract	контракт с "твердым обязательством"	*(kan-TRAHKT STVYOHR-dim a-bya-ZAH-tel-stvam)*
fixed frame rig/platform	стационарная буровая установка/платформа	*(sta-tsee-a-NAHR-na-ya boo-ra-VAH-ya oos-ta-NOF-ka/plat-FOHR-ma)*
fixed-rate royalty	фиксированное "роялти"	*(fee-KSEE-ra-van-na-ye ROH-yal-tee)*
fossil fuels	горючие полезные ископаемые	*(ga-ryoo-chee-ye pa-LEZ-nee-ye ees-ka-PAH-ye-mee-ye)*
free gas	свободный газ (газ чисто газовых залежей)	*(sva-BOD-nee gahs [gahs CHEES-ta GAH-za-vikh ZAH-le-zhey])*
fuel cycle	топливный цикл	*(TOP-leev-nee tsikl)*
fuel gas	топливный газ	*(TOP-leev-nee gahs)*
fuel oil	котельное топливо/мазут	*(ka-TEL-na-ye TOP-lee-va/ma-ZOOT)*
fuel oil parity	мазутный паритет (цен на газ)	*(ma-ZOOT-nee pa-ree-TET [tsen na gahs])*
gas company	газовая компания	*(GAH-za-va-ya kam-PAH-nee-ya)*
gas condensate	газовый конденсат	*(GAH-za-vee kan-den-SAHT)*
gas oil	газойль	*(ga-ZOYL)*
gas pool	газовая залежь	*(GAH-za-va-ya ZAH-lesh)*
gas well	газовая скважина	*(GAH-za-va-ya SKVAH-zhee-na)*
gas hydrate deposit	газогидратная залежь	*(GAH-za-gheed-RAHT-na-ya ZAH-lesh)*

gasohol	газохол	*(ga-za-KHOL)*
gasoline	бензин	*(ben-ZEEN)*
geopressured gas	газ зон геодавлений	*(gahz zon ghe-a-dav-LEH-neey)*
guaranteed gas supplies	гарантированные поставки газа	*(ga-ran-TEE-ra-van-nee-ye pas-TAHF-kee GAH-za)*
guaranteed royalty	гарантированное "роялти"	*(ga-ran-TEE-ra-van-na-ye ROH-yal-tee)*
hard energy	централизованная энергия	*(tsen-tra-lee-ZOH-van-na-ya e-NEHR-ghee-ya)*
high-BTU gas	высококалорийный газ	*(vee-SOH-ka-ka-la-REEY-nee gahs)*
hydrocarbon fuel	углеводородное топливо	*(oog-le-va-da-ROD-na-ye TOP-lee-va)*
hydrocarbon liquids	жидкие углеводороды (ЖУВ)	*(ZHIT-kee-ye oog-le-va-da-ROH-dee [zhoof])*
hydrocarbon prospects	перспективы нефтегазоносности	*(per-spek-TEE-vee NEF-te-GAH-za-NOS-na-stee)*
industrial direct heating	прямое промышленное использование топлива	*(pre-MOH-ye pra-MISH-len-na-ye ees-pol-za-va-nee-ye TOP-lee-va)*
industrial gas	промышленный природный газ	*(pra-MISH-len-nee pree-ROD-nee gahs)*
inferred reserves	подразумеваемые запасы	*(pad-ra-zoo-me-VAH-ye-mee-ye za-PAH-see)*
initial reserves	начальные разведанные запасы	*(na-CHAHL-nee-ye raz-VEH-dan-nee-ye za-PAH-see)*
International Energy Agency	Международное Энергетическое Агентство	*(mezh-doo-na-ROD-na-ye e-ner-ghe-TEE-ches-ka-ye a-GHENT-stva)*
International Gas Union	Международный Газовый Союз	*(mezh-doo-na-ROD-nee GAH-za-vee sa-YOOS)*
International Geological Congress	Международный Геологический Конгресс	*(mezh-doo-na-ROD-nee ghe-a-la-GHEE-ches-kee kan-GRES)*
lean gas	тощий газ	*(TOH-shchee gahs)*
lease bonus	арендный бонус	*(a-REND-nee BOH-noos)*
light (crude) oil	легкая нефть	*(LYOKH-ka-ya neft)*
liquified gases	сжиженные газы	*(ZHZHEE-zhen-nee-ye GAH-zee)*

liquified natural gas	сжиженный природный газ	*(SZHZHEE-zhen-nee pree-ROD-nee gahs)*
liquified natural gas carrier	танкер-метановоз	*(TAHN-ker me-ta-na-VOS)*
low-BTU gas	низкокалорийный газ	*(NEES-ka-ka-la-REEY-nee gahs)*
marginal costs	предельные издержки производства	*(pre-DEL-nee-ye eez-DEHRSH-kee pra-eez-VOT-stva)*
marginal field	"маржинальное" (экономически граничное) месторождение	*(mar-ZHEE-nal-na-ye [e-ka-na-MEE-ches-kee gra-NEECH-na-ye] mes-ta-RAHZ-dee-nee-ye)*
marginal producer well	"маржинальная" (экономически граничная) скважина	*(mar-ZHEE-nal-na-ya [e-ka-na-MEE-ches-kee gra-NEECH-na-ya] SKVAH-zhee-na)*
marginal reserve	"маржинальные" (экономически граничные) запасы	*(mar-ZHEE-nal-nee-ye [e-ka-na-MEE-ches-kee gra-NEECH-nee-ye] za-PAH-see)*
marker (crude) oil	"эталонная" нефть	*(e-ta-LON-na-ya neft)*
marketable gas	товарный газ	*(ta-VAHR-nee gahs)*
marsh gas	болотный газ	*(ba-LOT-nee gahs)*
mixed fuel	смешанное топливо	*(SMEH-shan-na-ye TOP-lee-va)*
multi-national oil company	транснациональная нефтяная компания	*(TRAHNS-na-tsee-a-NAHL-na-ya nef-tee-NAH-ya kam-PAH-nee-ya)*
natural gas	природный газ	*(pree-ROD-nee gahs)*
net refinery output	чистое производство нефтепродуктов	*(CHEES-ta-ye pra-eez-VOT-stva NEF-te-pra-DOOK-taf)*
new field wildcat	поисковая скважина на новое месторождение	*(pa-ees-KOH-va-ya SKVAH-zhee-na na NOH-va-ye mes-ta-razh-DEH-nee-ye)*
new pool test	поисковая скважина на новую залежь (новый горизонт)	*(pa-ees-KOH-va-ya SKVAH-zhee-na na NOH-voo-yoo ZAH-lesh [NOH-vee ga-ree-ZONT])*
non-recoverable reserve	неизвлекаемые запасы	*(ne-eez-vle-KAH-ye-mee-ye za-PAH-see)*

obligatory (oil) stocks	обязательные товарные запасы (жидкого топлива)	*(a-bee-ZAH-tel-nee-ye ta-VAHR-nee-ye za-PAH-see {ZHEED-ka-va-TOHP-lee-va])*
oil	нефть	*(neft)*
oil bitumen	нефтяной (технический) битум	*(nef-tee-NOY [tekh-NEE-ches-kee] bee-TOOM)*
oil bonus	натуральный (нефтяной) бонус	*(na-too-RAHL-nee [nef-tee-NOY] BOH-noos)*
oil (stocks) afloat/at sea	"нефть на плову"	*(neft na pla-VOO)*
oil well	нефтяная скважина	*(nef-tee-NAH-ya SKVAH-zhee-na)*
oil yield	выход нефти (сланцевой смолы)	*(VEE-khat NEF-tee [SLAHN-tse-vahy sma-LEE])*
oil-well gas	газ нефтяных скважин	*(gahs nef-tee-NIKH SKVAH-zhin)*
Organization of Petroleum Exporting Countries (OPEC)	Организация Стран Экспортеров Нефти (ОПЕК)	*(ar-ga-nee-ZAH-tsee-ya strahn eks-par-TYOH-raf NEF-tee [oh-PEK])*
parity crude	"паритетный" (базисный) сорт	*(pa-ree-TET-nee [BAH-zees-nee] sort)*
participation crude	"нефть партнёра"	*(neft part-NYOH-ra)*
petro dollars	"нефтяные доллары"	*(nef-tee-NEE-ye DOL-la-ree)*
petroleum	нефть и газ	*(neft ee gahs)*
petroliferous	нефтегазоносный	*(nef-te-ga-za-NOS-nee)*
pipe line fill	"наполнение трубопровода"	*(na-pal-NEH-nee-ye troo-ba-pra-VOH-da)*
preferential crude	"преференциальная" (льготная) нефть	*(pre-fe-ren-tsee-AHL-na-ya [LGOT-na-ya] neft)*
primary reserves	запасы/извлекаемые первичными методами разработки месторождения	*(za-PAH-see/eez-vle-KAH-ye-mee-ye per-VEECH-nee-mee MEH-ta-da-mee raz-ra-BOT-kee mes-ta-razh-DEH-nee-ya)*
process gas	технологический газ	*(tekh-na-la-GHEE-ches-kee gahs)*
producer gas	генераторный газ	*(ghe-ne-RAH-tar-nee gahs)*

production life	период эксплуатации месторождения	*(pe-REE-at eks-ploo-a-TAH-tsee-ee mes-ta-razh-DEH-nee-ya)*
pump price	цена франко-бензоколонки	*(tse-NAH FRAHN-ka-ben-za-ka-LON-kee)*
raw gas	неочищенный газ	*(ne-a-CHEE-shchen-nee gahs)*
recoverable reserves	извлекаемые запасы	*(eez-vle-KAH-ye-mee-ye za-PAH-see)*
refinery feed stock	нефтезаводское сырье	*(NEF-te-za-vat-SKOH-ye sihr-YOH)*
refinery fuel	нефтезаводское топливо	*(NEF-te-za-vat-SKOH-ye TOP-lee-va)*
secondary (crude) oil	вторичная нефть	*(fta-REECH-na-ya neft)*
secondary fuel	вторичное топливо	*(fta-REECH-na-ye TOP-lee-va)*
secondary reserves	вторичные запасы	*(fta-REECH-nee-ye za-PAH-see)*
security oil stocks	сверхнормативные коммерческие запасы (жидкого топлива)	*(SVEHRKH-nar-ma-TEEV-nee-ye kam-MEHR-ches-kee-ye za-PAH-see [ZHIT-ka-va TOP-lee-va])*
separated gas	сепарированный газ	*(se-pa-REE-ra-van-nee ghas)*
service contract	подрядный контракт	*(pad-RYAHD-nee kan-TRAHKT)*
the "Seven Sisters"	"Семь Сестёр"(монополии участники нефтяного картеля)	*(sem ses-TYOHR [ma-na-POH-lee-ee oo-CHAHST-nee-kee nef-tee-NOH-va kar-TEH-la])*
shale oil	сланцевая нефть	*(SLAHN-tse-va-ya neft)*
signature bonus	первоначальный бонус	*(per-va-na-CHAHL-nee BOH-noos)*
sludge gas	отстойный газ	*(at-STOY-nee gahs)*
sour crude oil	кислая (высокосернистая) нефть	*(KEES-la-ya [vee-SOH-ka-ser-NEES-ta-ya] neft)*
sour gas	кислый (высоко-сернистый) газ	*(KEES-lee [vee-SOH-ka-ser-NEES-tee] gahs)*
spot market	рынок "спот"(наличного товара)	*(REE-nak [na-LEECH-na-va ta-VAH-ra])*

spot price	цена рынка "спот"	*(tse-NAH RIN-ka spot)*
stock-tank oil	резервуарная нефть	*(re-zer-voo-AHR-na-ya neft)*
storage facility	хранилище	*(khra-NEE-lee-shche)*
strategic reserves	стратегические запасы	*(stra-te-GHEE-ches-kee-ye za-PAH-see)*
stripper (well)	малодебитная скважина	*(MAH-la-DEH-beet-na-ya SKVAH-zhee-na)*
substitute fuel	заменяющее топливо	*(za-me-NYAH-yoo-shche-ye TOP-lee-va)*
success ratio	коэффициент результативности	*(ka-ef-fee-tsee-ENT re-zool-ta-TEEV-na-stee)*
sweet crude	сладкая (малосернистая) нефть	*(SLAHT-ka-ya [MAH-la-ser-NEES-ta-ya] neft)*
sweet gas	сладкий (малосернистый) газ	*(SLAHT-kee [MAH-la-ser-NEES-tee] gahs)*
synthetic crude (oil)	синтетическая нефть	*(seen-te-TEE-ches-ka-ya neft)*
synthetic liquid fuels (SLF)	синтетические жидкие топлива	*(seen-te-TEE-ches-kee-ye ZHIT-kee-ye TOP-lee-va)*
synthetic natural gas (SNG)	синтетический природный газ	*(seen-te-TEE-ches-kee pree-ROD-nee gahs)*
tertiary (crude) oil	третичная нефть	*(tre-TEECH-na-ya neft)*
tertiary (oil) inventory	третичные товарные запасы	*(tre-TEECH-nee-ye ta-VAHR-nee-ye za-PAH-see)*
tertiary reserves	третичные запасы	*(tre-TEECH-nee-ye za-PAH-see)*
tight gas	газ в плотных породах	*(gahs FPLOT-nikh pa-ROH-dakh)*
town gas	коммунальный газ	*(kam-moo-NAHL-nee gahs)*
true in situ recovery of shale oil (TIS)	обычная внутрипластовая перегонка (горючих сланцев)	*(a-BICH-na-ya vnoot-ree-plas-ta-VAH-ya pe-re-GON-ka [ga-RYOO-cheekh SLAHN-tsef])*
ultimate recoverable reserves	максимальные извлекаемые запасы	*(mak-see-MAHL-nee-ye eez-vle-KAH-ye-mee-ye za-PAH-see)*
undeveloped proved reserves	неосвоенные доказанные запасы	*(ne-as-VOH-yen-nee-ye da-KAH-zan-nee-ye za-PAH-see)*

undiscovered potential resources	неоткрытые ресурсы	*(ne-at-KREE-tee-ye re-SOOHR-see)*
undrilled proved reserves	неразбуренные доказанные запасы	*(ne-raz-BOO-ren-nee-ye da-KAH-zan-nee-ye za-PAH-see)*
Unit Energy cost	удельные энергетические затраты	*(oo-DEL-nee-ye e-ner-ghe-TEE-ches-kee-ye zat-RAH-tee)*
"unpumpables"	перерабатываемая нефть	*(pe-re-ra-BAH-tee-va-ye-ma-ya neft)*
useable commercial inventories	коммерческие запасы	*(kam-MEHR-ches-kee-ye za-PAH-see)*
value of a field	оценочная стоимость (запасов) месторождения	*(a-TSEH-nach-na-ya STOH-ee-mast [za-PAH-saf) mes-tarazh-DEH-nee-ya])*
well	скважина	*(SKVAH-zhee-na)*
well density	плотность бурения	*(PLOT-nast boo-REH-nee-ya)*
well permit	лицензия на бурение скважины	*(lee-TSEN-zee-ya na boo-REH-nee-ye SKVAH-zhee-nee)*
well tangibles	амортизируемые расходы на строительство скважин	*(a-mar-tee-ZEE-roo-ye-mee-ye ras-KHOH-dee na stra-EE-tel-stva SKVAH-zhin)*
well head price	цена франко-скважины	*(tse-NAH FRAHN-ka-SKVAH-zhee-nee)*
well head value	выручка на устье скважины	*(VEE-rooch-ka na OOST-ye SKVAH-zhee-nee)*
wild cat	поисковая скважина	*(pa-ees-KOH-va-ya SKVAH-zhee-na)*
wild cat drilling	поисковое бурение	*(pa-ees-KOH-va-ye boo-REH-nee-ye)*
working interest	деятельное долевое участие на основе аренды	*(DEH-ya-tel-na-ye da-le-VOH-ye oo-CHAHS-tee-ye na as-NOH-ve a-REN-dee)*

Russian to English

активные запасы	*(ak-TEEV-nee-ye za-PAH-see)*	active reserves

активный газ (подземного газохранилища)	(ak-TEEV-nee gahs [pad-ZEM-na-va ga-za-khra-NEE-lee-shcha])	active gas
амортизируемые расходы на строительство скважин	(a-mar-tee-ZEE-roo-ye-mee-ye ras-KHOH-dee na stra-EE-tel-stva SKVAH-zhin)	well tangibles
арендный бонус	(a-REND-nee BOH-noos)	lease bonus
асфальт	(as-FAHLT)	asphalt
базисная цена на «эталонную» нефть	(BAH-zees-na-ya tse-NAH na e-ta-LON-noo-yoo neft)	benchmark price (of crude oil)
базовая контрактная цена (на природный газ)	(BAH-za-va-ya kan-TRAHKT-na-ya tse-NAH [na pree-ROD-nee gahs])	base price
баррель	(BAHR-rel)	barrel
бензин	(ben-ZEEN)	gasoline
битум	(bee-TOOM)	bitumen
болотный газ	(ba-LOT-nee gahs)	marsh gas
«бонус» за открытие	(BOH-noos za at-KREE-tee-ye)	discovery bonus
Британская Тепловая Единица (БТЕ)	(bree-TAHN-ska-ya tep-la-VAH-ya e-dee-NEE-tsa [BEH-TEH-YEH])	British Thermal Unit (BTU)
водяной газ	(va-dya-NOY gahs)	blue gas
возмещение издержек (добычи)	(vaz-me-SHCHEH-nee-ye eez-DEHR-zhek [da-BEE-chee])	cost recovery
вторичная нефть	(fta-REECH-na-ya neft)	secondary (crude) oil
вторичное топливо	(fta-REECH-na-ye TOP-lee-va)	secondary fuel
вторичные запасы	(fta-REECH-nee-ye za-PAH-see)	secondary reserves
выручка на устье скважины	(VEE-rooch-ka na OOST-ye SKVAH-zhee-nee)	well head value
высококалорий-ный газ	(vee-SOH-ka-ka-la-REEY-nee gahs)	high-BTU gas
выход нефти (сланцевой смолы)	(VEE-khat NEF-tee [SLAHN-tse-vahy sma-LEE])	oil yield

газ нефтяных скважин	*(gahs nef-tee-NIKH SKVAH-zhin)*	oil-well gas
газ зон геодавлений	*(gahs zon ghe-a-dav-LEH-neey)*	geopressured gas
газ в плотных породах	*(gahs FPLOT-nikh pa-ROH-dakh)*	tight gas
газификация угля	*(ga-zee-fee-KAH-tsee-ya oog-LYAH)*	coal gasification
газовая залежь	*(GAH-za-va-ya ZAH-lesh)*	gas pool
газовая скважина	*(GAH-za-va-ya SKVAH-zhee-na)*	gas well
газовая компания	*(GAH-za-va-ya kam-PAH-nee-ya)*	gas company
газовый конденсат	*(GAH-za-vee kan-den-SAHT)*	gas condensate
газогидратная залежь	*(GAH-za-gheed-RAHT-na-ya ZAH-lesh)*	gas hydrate deposit
газойль	*(ga-ZOYL)*	gas oil
газохол	*(ga-za-KHOL)*	gasohol
гарантированное «роялти»	*(ga-ran-TEE-ra-van-na-ye ROH-yal-tee)*	guaranteed royalty
гарантированные поставки газа	*(ga-ran-TEE-ra-van-nee-ye pas-TAHF-kee GAH-za)*	guaranteed gas supplies
генераторный газ	*(ghe-ne-RAH-tar-nee gahs)*	producer gas
горючие полезные ископаемые	*(ga-RYOO-chee-ye pa-LEZ-nee-ye ees-ka-PAH-ye-mee-ye)*	fossil fuels
горючий газ	*(ga-RYOO-chee gahs)*	combustible gas
горючий сланец	*(ga-RYOO-chee SLAH-nets)*	combustible shale
девонский сланец	*(de-VON-skee SLAH-nets)*	devonian shale
деятельное долевое участие на основе аренды	*(DEH-ya-tel-na-ye da-le-VOH-ye oo-CHAHS-tee-ye na as-NOH-ve a-REN-dee)*	working interest
дизельное топливо	*(DEE-zel-na-ye TOP-lee-va)*	diesel fuel
дифференциаль-ная рента	*(deef-fe-ren-tsee-AHL-na-ya REHN-ta)*	differential rent

договор о субаренде (продуктивного участка)	(da-ga-VOHR a-soob-a-REHN-de [pra-dook-TEEV-na-va oo-CHAHST-ka])	farm-out
жидкие углеводороды (ЖУВ)	(ZHIT-kee-ye oog-le-va-da-ROH-dee [zhoof])	hydrocarbon liquids
жидкое бункерное топливо	(ZHIT-ka-ye BOON-ker-na-ye TOP-lee-va)	bunker oil
заменяющее топливо	(za-me-NYAH-yoo-shchee-ye TOP-lee-va)	substitute fuel
запасы, извлекаемые первичными методами разработки месторождения	(za-PAH-see eez-vle-KAH-ye-mee-ye per-VEECH-nee-mee MEH-ta-da-mee raz-ra-BOT-kee mes-ta-razh-DEH-nee-ya)	primary reserves
затраты на проведение поисково-разведочных работ	(za-TRAH-tee na pra-ve-DEH-nee-ye POH-ees-ka-va-raz-VEH-dach-nikh ra-BOT)	exploratory costs
зольность	(ZOL-nast)	ash content
извлекаемые запасы	(eez-vle-KAH-ye-mee-ye za-PAH-see)	recoverable reserves
источники энергии	(ees-TOCH-nee-kee e-NEHR-ghee-ee)	energy resources
кизяк	(kee-ZYAHK)	dung
кислая (высокосернистая) нефть	(KEES-la-ya [vee-SOH-ka-ser-NEES-ta-ya] neft)	sour crude oil
кислые отходы	(KEES-lee-ye at-KHOH-dee)	acid spoil
кислый (высокосернистый) газ	(KEES-lee [vee-SOH-ka-ser-NEES-tee] gahs)	sour gas
коммерческие запасы	(kam-MEHR-ches-kee-ye za-PAH-see)	useable commercial inventories
коммунальный газ	(kam-moo-NAHL-nee gahs)	town gas
конденсат	(kan-den-SAHT)	condensate
конечная нефтеотдача	(ka-NECH-na-ya NEF-te-at-DAH-cha)	final oil recovery

контракт с «твердым обязательством»	*(kan-TRAHKT STVYOHR-dim a-bya-ZAH-tel-stvam)*	fixed-commitment contract
контрактная нефть	*(kan-TRAHKT-na-ya neft)*	contract crude oil
котельное топливо	*(ka-TEL-na-ye TOP-lee-va)*	fuel oil
коэффициент извлечения	*(ka-ef-fee-tsee-ENT eez-vle-CHEH-nee-ya)*	extraction ratio
коэффициент результативности	*(ka-ef-fee-tsee-ENT re-zool-ta-TEEV-na-stee)*	success ratio
коэффициент энергоотдачи	*(ka-ef-fee-tsee-ENT e-NEHR-ga-ad-DAH-chee)*	energy return ratio
легкая нефть	*(LYOKH-ka-ya neft)*	light (crude) oil
лицензия на бурение скважины	*(lee-TSEN-zee-ya na boo-REH-nee-ye SKVAH-zhee-nee)*	well permit
мазут	*(ma-ZOOT)*	fuel oil
мазутный паритет (цен на газ)	*(ma-ZOOT-nee pa-ree-TET [tsen na gahs])*	fuel oil parity
максимальные извлекаемые запасы	*(mak-see-MAHL-nee-ye eez-vle-KAH-ye-mee-ye za-PAH-see)*	ultimate recoverable reserves
малодебитная скважина	*(MAH-la DEH-beet-na-ya SKVAH-zhee-na)*	stripper (well)
«маржинальная» (экономически граничная) скважина	*(mar-ZHEE-nal-na-ya [e-ka-na-MEE-ches-kee gra-NEECH-na-ya] SKVAH-zhee-na)*	marginal producer well
«маржинальное» (экономически граничное) месторождение	*(mar-ZHEE-nal-na-ye [e-ka-na-MEE-ches-kee gra-NEECH-na-ye] mes-ta-razh-DEH-nee-ye)*	marginal field
«маржинальные» (экономически граничные) запасы	*(mar-ZHEE-nal-na-ye [e-ka-na-MEE-ches-kee gra-NEECH-nee-ye] za-PAH-see)*	marginal reserve
Международное Энергетическое Агентство	*(mezh-doo-na-ROD-na-ye e-ner-ghe-TEE-ches-ka-ye a-GHENT-stva)*	International Energy Agency
Международный Газовый Союз	*(mezh-doo-na-ROD-nee GAH-za-vee sa-YOOS)*	International Gas Union

Международный Геологический Конгресс	(mezh-doo-na-ROD-nee ghe-a-la-GHEE-ches-kee kan-GRES)	International Geological Congress
месторождение	(mes-ta-razh-DEH-nee-ye)	field, deposit
«мёртвая» (неподвижная) нефть	(MYOHRT-va-ya [ne-pad-VEEZH-na-ya] neft)	dead oil
наземная перегонка	(na-ZEM-na-ya pe-re-GON-ka)	above-ground retorting
«наполнение трубопровода»	(na-pal-NEH-nee-ye troo-ba-pra-VOH-da)	pipe line fill
натуральный (нефтяной) бонус	(na-too-RAHL-nee [nef-tee-NOY] BOH-noos)	oil bonus
начальные разведанные запасы	(na-CHAHL-nee-ye raz-VEH-dan-nee-ye za-PAH-see)	initial reserves
неизвлекаемые запасы	(ne-eez-vle-KAH-ye-mee-ye za-PAH-see)	non-recoverable reserve
неосвоенные доказанные запасы	(ne-as-VOH-yen-nee-ye da-KAH-zan-nee-ye za-PAH-see)	undeveloped proved reserves
неоткрытые ресурсы	(ne-at-KREE-tee-ye re-SOOHR-see)	undiscovered potential resources
неочищенный газ	(ne-a-CHEE-shchen-nee gahs)	raw gas
непродуктивная ("сухая") скважина	(ne-pra-dook-TEEV-na-ya [soo-KHAN-ya] SKVAH-zhee-na)	dry hole
неразбуренные доказанные запасы	(ne-raz-BOO-ren-nee-ye da-KAH-san-nee-ye za-PAH-see)	undrilled proved reserves
нефтегазоносный	(nef-te-ga-za-NOS-nee)	petroliferous
нефтезаводское сырьё	(NEF-te-za-vat-SKOH-ye sihr-YOH)	refinery feed stock
нефтезаводское топливо	(NEF-te-za-vat-SKOH-ye TOP-lee-va)	refinery fuel
нефть (сырая)	(neft [SEE-ra-ya])	crude oil
нефть	(neft)	oil
нефть и газ	(neft ee gahs)	petroleum
«нефть партнёра»	(neft part-NYOH-ra)	participation crude

«нефть на пплову»	*(neft na pla-VOO)*	oil (stocks) afloat/at sea
нефтяная скважина	*(nef-tee-NAH-ya SKVAH-zhee-na)*	oil well
нефтяной (технический) битум	*(nef-tee-NOY [tekh-NEE-ches-kee] bee-TOOM)*	oil bitumen
нефтяной газ	*(nef-tee-NOY gaz)*	casinghead gas
«нефтяные доллары»	*(nef-tee-NEE-ye DOL-la-ree)*	petro dollars
низкокалорийный газ	*(NEES-ka-ka-lo-REEY-nee gahs)*	low-BTU gas
обеспыливание	*(a-bes-PEE-le-va-nee-ye)*	desliming
обычная внутрипластовая перегонка (горючих сланцев)	*(a-BICH-na-ya vnoot-ree-plas-ta-VAH-ya pe-re-GON-ka [ga-RYOO-cheekh SLAHN-tsef])*	true in situ recovery of shale oil (TIS)
обязательные товарные запасы (жидкого топлива)	*(a-bee-ZAH-tel-nee-ye ta-VAHR-nee-ye za-PAH-see [ZHEED-ka-va- TOHP-lee-va])*	obligatory (oil) stocks
Организация Стран Экспортеров Нефти (ОПЕК)	*(ar-ga-nee-ZAH-tsee-ya strahn eks-par-TYOH-raf NEF-tee [oh-PEK])*	Organization of Petroleum Exporting Countries (OPEC)
освоенное месторождение	*(as-VOH-yen-na-ye mes-ta-razh-DEH-nee-ye)*	developed field
отечественный газ	*(a-TEH-chest-ven-nee gahs)*	domestic gas
отстойный газ	*(at-STOY-nee gahs)*	sludge gas
оценочная стоимость (запасов) месторождения	*(a-TSEN-nach-na-ya STOH-ee-mast [za-PAH-saf] mes-ta-razh-DEH-nee-ya)*	value of a field
оценочная скважина	*(a-TSEN-nach-na-ya SKVAH-zhee-na)*	appraisal well
«паритетный» (базисный) сорт	*(pa-ree-TET-nee [BAH-zees-nee] sort)*	parity crude
первоначальный бонус	*(per-va-na-CHAHL-nee BOH-noos)*	signature bonus
перерабатываемая нефть	*(pe-re-ra-BAH-tee-va-ye-ma-ya neft)*	"unpumpables"
период рентабельной разработки месторождения	*(pe-REE-at ren-TAH-bel-nay raz-ra-BOT-kee mes-ta-razh-DEH-nee-ya)*	economic life

период эксплуатации месторождения	*(pe-REE-at eks-ploo-a-TAH-tsee-ye mes-ta-razh-DEH-nee-ya)*	production life
перспективы нефтегазонос- ности	*(per-spek-TEE-ve NEF-te-GAH-za-NOS-na-stee)*	hydrocarbon prospects
плотность бурения	*(PLOT-nast boo-REH-nee-ya)*	well density
побочный продукт	*(pa-BOCH-nee praxDOOKT)*	by-product
повышенное извлечение нефти	*(pa-VEE-shen-na-ye eez-vle-CHEH-nee-ye NEF-tee)*	enhanced oil recovery
подкисление	*(pat-kee-SLEH-nee-ye)*	acidification
подразумеваемые запасы	*(pad-ra-zoo-me-VAH-ye-mee-ye za-PAH-see)*	inferred reserves
подрядный контракт	*(pad-RYAHD-nee kan-TRAHKT)*	service contract
подтвержденные ресурсы	*(pat-tverzh-DYON-nee-ye re-SOOHR-see)*	demonstrated resources
поисково- разведочная скважина	*(pa-ees-KOH-va-raz-VEH-dach-na-ya SKVAH-zhee-na)*	exploratory well
поисковая скважина на новое месторождение	*(pa-ees-KOH-va-ya SKVAH-zhee-na na NOH-va-ye mes-ta-razh-DEH-nee-ye)*	new field wildcat
поисковая сква- жина на новую залежь (новый горизонт)	*(pa-ees-KOH-va-ya SKVAH-zhee-na na NOH-voo-yoo ZAH-lesh [NOH-vee ga-ree-ZONT])*	new pool test
поисковая скважина	*(pa-ees-KOH-va-ya SKVAH-zhee-na)*	wildcat
поисковое бурение	*(pa-ees-KOH-va-ye boo-REH-nee-ye)*	wildcat drilling
предельные издержки производства	*(pre-DEHL-nee-ye eez-DEHRSH-kee pra-eez-VOT-stva)*	marginal costs
«преференциаль- ная» (льготная) нефть	*(pre-fe-ren-tsee-AHL-na-ya [LGOT-na-ya] neft)*	preferential crude
природный газ	*(pree-ROD-nee gahs)*	natural gas
прирост запасов	*(pree-ROST za-PAH-saf)*	additions to reserves

промышленный природный газ	*(pra-MISH-len-nee pree-ROD-nee gahs)*	industrial gas
прямое промышленное использование топлива	*(pre-MOH-ye pra-MISH-len-na-ye ees-POL-za-va-nee-ye TOP-lee-va)*	industrial direct heating
резервуарная нефть	*(re-zer-voo-AHR-na-ya neft)*	stock-tank oil
рентабельно извлекаемые запасы	*(ren-TAH-bel-na eez-vle-KAH-ye-mee-ye za-PAH-see)*	commercially exploitable reserves
рынок долгосрочных сделок (на купле-продаже нефти)	*(REE-nak dal-ga-SROCH-nikh ZDEM-lak [na KOOP-le pra-DAH-zhe NEF-tee])*	contract oil market
рынок «спот» (наличного товара)	*(REE-nak spot [na-LEECH-na-va- ta-VAH-ra])*	spot market
сбросовый газ	*(ZBROH-sa-vee gahs)*	dump gas
сверхнормативные коммерческие запасы (жидкого топлива)	*(SVEHRKH-nar-ma-TEEV-nee-ye kam-MEHR-ches-kee-ye za-PAH-see [ZHIT-ka-va TOP-lee-va])*	security oil stocks
«сверхтяжелая» нефть	*(sverkh-tya-ZHOH-la-ya neft)*	extra-heavy oil
свободный газ (газ чисто газовых залежей)	*(sva-BOD-nee gahs [gahs CHEES-ta GAH-za-vikh ZAH-le-zhey])*	free gas
«Семь Сестёр» (участники нефтяного картеля)	*(sem ses-TYOHR [ma-na-POH-lee-ee oo-CHAHST-nee-ke nef-tee-NOH-va kar-TEH-la])*	the "Seven Sisters"
сепарированный газ	*(se-pa-REE-ra-van-nee gahs)*	separated gas
сжиженные газы	*(SZHEE-zhen-nee-ye GAH-zee)*	liquified gases
сжиженный природный газ	*(ZHZHEE-zhen-nee pree-ROD-nee gahs)*	liquified natural gas
синтетическая нефть	*(seen-te-TEE-ches-ka-ya neft)*	synthetic crude (oil)
синтетические жидкие топлива	*(seen-te-TEE-ches-kee-ye ZHIT-kee-ye TOP-lee-va)*	synthetic liquid fuels (SLF)

синтетический природный газ	*(seen-te-TEE-ches-kee pree-ROD-nee gahs)*	synthetic natural gas (SNG)
скважина	*(SKVAH-zhee-na)*	well
сладкая (малосернистая) нефть	*(SLAHT-ka-ya [MAH-la-ser-NEES-ta-ya] neft)*	sweet crude
сладкий (малосернистый) газ	*(SLAHT-kee [MAH-la-ser-NEES-tee] gahs)*	sweet gas
сланцевая нефть	*(SLAHN-tsee-va-ya neft)*	shale oil
смешанное топливо	*(SMEH-shan-na-ye TOP-lee-va)*	mixed fuel
«собственная» нефть	*(SOP-stven-na-ya neft)*	equity crude oil
средняя удельная продуктивность	*(SRED-nya-ya oo-DEL-na-ya pra-dook-TEEV-nast)*	average productivity per unit vol.
стационарная буровая установка/ платформа	*(sta-tsee-a-NAHR-na-ya boo-ra-VAH-ya oos-ta-NOF-ka/plat-FOHR-ma)*	fixed frame rig/platform
стоимость подготовки запасов	*(STOH-ee-mast pad-ga-TOF-kee za-PAH-saf)*	below ground value
стратегические запасы	*(stra-te-GHEE-ches-kee-ye za-PAH-see)*	strategic reserves
сырьевые материалы	*(sihr-ye-VEE-ye ma-te-ree-YAH-lee)*	feed materials
танкер-метановоз	*(TAHN-ker-me-ta-na-VOS)*	liquified natural gas carrier
технологический газ	*(tekh-na-la-GHEE-ches-kee gahs)*	process gas
товарный газ	*(ta-VAHR-nee gahs)*	marketable gas
топливный газ	*(TOP-leev-nee gahs)*	fuel gas
топливный цикл	*(TOP-leev-nee tsikl)*	fuel cycle
тощий газ	*(TOH-shchee gahs)*	lean gas
транснациональная нефтяная компания	*(TRAHNS-na-tsee-a-NAHL-na-ya nef-tee-NAH-ya kam-PAH-nee-ya)*	multi-national oil company
третичная нефть	*(tre-TEECH-na-ya neft)*	tertiary (crude) oil
третичные запасы	*(tre-TEECH-nee-ye za-PAH-see)*	tertiary reserves
третичные товарные запасы	*(tre-TEECH-nee-ye ta-VAHR-nee-ye za-PAH-see)*	tertiary (oil) inventory

углеводородное топливо	*(oog-le-va-da-ROD-na-ye TOP-lee-va)*	hydrocarbon fuel
угольная нефть	*(OO-gal-na-ya neft)*	coal oil
угольный газ	*(OO-gal-nee gahs)*	coal gas
удельные энергетические затраты	*(oo-DEL-nee-ee e-ner-ghe-TEE-ches-kee-ye zat-RAH-tee)*	Unit Energy cost
фиксированное «роялти»	*(fee-KSEE-ra-van-na-ye ROH-yal-tee)*	fixed-rate royalty
хранилище	*(khra-NEE-le-shchee)*	storage facility
цена франко-бензоколонки	*(tse-NAH FRAHN-ka-ben-za-ka-LON-kee)*	pump price
цена франко-газогенератора	*(tse-NAH FRAHN-ka-GAH-za-ghe-ne-RAH-ta-ra)*	ex-gasifier price
цена франко-скважины	*(tse-NAH FRAHN-ka-SKVAH-zhee-nee)*	well head price
цена рынка «спот»	*(tse-NAH RIN-ka spot)*	spot price
цена с включе-нием расходов по доставке	*(tse-NAH sfklyoo-CHEH-nee-yem ras-KHOH-daf pa das-TAHF-ke)*	delivered cost
централизованная энергия	*(tsen-tra-lee-ZOH-van-na-ya e-NEHR-ghee-ya)*	hard energy
чистое производ-ство нефте-продуктов	*(CHEES-ta-ye pra-eez-VOT-stva NEF-te-pra-DOOK-taf)*	net refinery output
чрезвычайные запасы жидкого топлива	*(chrez-vee-CHAHY-nee-ye za-PAH-see ZHIT-ka-va TOP-lee-va)*	emergency petroleum reserves
эксплуатационная скважина	*(eks-ploo-a-ta-tsee-ON-na-ya SKVAH-zhee-na)*	development well
эксплуатационное бурение	*(eks-ploo-a-ta-tsee-ON-na-ye boo-REH-nee-ye)*	developed drilling
«эталонная» нефть	*(e-ta-LON-na-ya neft)*	marker (crude) oil
этанол	*(e-ta-NOL)*	ethanol

PHARMACEUTICALS

According to the United States Department of Commerce's International Trade Administration, in 1993 out of 3000 different kinds of medicines currently prescribed in the NIS, at least 500 are solely imports, and many more are in short supply. Because of the public health ramifications, the governments of the NIS have placed great priority on revitalizing this sector, which has a strong demand. They are actively seeking foreign investment and joint production arrangements.

English to Russian

AIDS	СПИД	*(speet)*
anaesthetic	анестезирующее средство	*(a-ne-ste-ZEE-roo-yoo-shche-ye SRET-stva)*
analgesic	болеутоляющее (средство)	*(BOH-le-oo-ta-LYAH-yoo-shchee [SRET-stva])*
antacid	антационное средство	*(an-ta-tsee-ON-na-ya SRET-stva)*
anti-inflammatory	противовоспалительный	*(PROH-tee-va-vas-pa-LEE-tel-nee)*
antibiotic	антибиотик	*(an-tee-bee-OH-teek)*
anticoagulant	антикоагулянт	*(an-tee-koh-a-goo-LYAHNT)*
antidepressant	антидепрессант	*(an-tee-de-pres-SAHNT)*
antiseptic	антисептическое средство	*(an-tee-sep-TEE-ches-ka-ye SRET-stva)*
bleed (v)	кровоточить	*(kra-va-ta-CHEET)*
blood	кровь	*(krof)*
botanic	ботаническое средство	*(ba-ta-NEE-ches-ka-ye SRET-stva)*
cancer	рак	*(rahk)*
capsule	желатиновая капсула	*(zhe-la-TEE-na-va-ya KAHP-soo-la)*
compounds	соединения	*(sa-ye-dee-NEH-nee-ya)*
content	содержание	*(sa-der-ZHAH-nee-ye)*
cough (v)	кашлять	*(KAHSH-lyat)*
cough drop	капли от кашля	*(KAHP-lee at KAHSH-lya)*
cough syrup	сироп от кашля	*(see-ROP at KAHSH-lya)*
crude	грубый	*(GROO-bee)*
density	плотность	*(PLOT-nast)*

disease	болезнь	*(ba-LEZN)*
diuretic	мочегонное средство	*(ma-che-GON-na-ye SRET-stva)*
dose	доза	*(DOH-za)*
dressing	повязка	*(pa-VYAHZ-ka)*
drop	капля	*(KAHP-lya)*
drug	лекарственное средство/ лекарство	*(le-KAHR-stven-na-ye SRET-stva/le-KAHR-stva)*
drugstore	аптека	*(ap-TEH-ka)*
eyedrop	глазные капли	*(glaz-NEE-ye KAHP-lee)*
hypertension	гипертензия	*(ghee-per-TEN-zee-ya)*
injection	инъекция	*(een-YEK-tsee-ya)*
iodine	йод	*(yot)*
iron	железо	*(zhe-LEH-za)*
laboratory technician	лаборант	*(la-ba-RAHNT)*
laxative	слабительное средство	*(sla-BEE-tel-na-ye SRET-stva)*
medicine	медицина	*(me-dee-TSEE-na)*
medication	медикамент	*(mee-dee-ka-MENT)*
morphine	морфин	*(mar-FEEN)*
narcotic	наркотик	*(nar-KOH-teek)*
ointment	мазь	*(mas)*
opium	опиум	*(OH-pee-oom)*
organic	органический	*(ar-ga-NEE-ches-kee)*
pellet	пилюля	*(pee-LYOO-lya)*
penicillin	пенициллин	*(pe-nee-tsee-LEEN)*
pharmaceutical	фармацевтический	*(far-ma-tsef-TEE-ches-kee)*
pharmacist	фармацевт	*(far-ma-TSEFT)*
physician	врач	*(vrahch)*
pill	таблетка	*(tab-LET-ka)*
plants	растения	*(ras-TEH-nee-ya)*
prescription	рецепт	*(re-TSEPT)*
purgative	очистительное средство	*(a-chees-TEE-tel-na-ye SRET-stva)*

remedies	лечебные средства	*(le-CHEB-nee-ye SRET-stva)*
salts	соли	*(SOH-lee)*
salve	мазь	*(mahs)*
sedative	седативное средство	*(se-da-TEEV-na-ye SRET-stva)*
serum	сыворотка	*(SEE-va-rat-ka)*
sinus	синус	*(SEE-noos)*
sleeping pill	снотворная таблетка/ снотворное	*(sna-TVOHR-na-ya tab-LET-ka/sna-TVOHR-na-ye)*
sneeze (v)	чихать	*(chee-KHAHT)*
starch	крахмал	*(krakh-MAHL)*
stimulant	стимулятор	*(stee-moo-LAH-tar)*
sulphamide	сульфамид	*(sool-fa-MEET)*
synthesis	синтез	*(SEEN-tes)*
syringe	шприц	*(shpreets)*
tablet	таблетка	*(tab-LET-ka)*
thermometer	термометр	*(ter-MOH-metr)*
toxicology	токсикология	*(tak-see-ka-LOH-ghee-ya)*
toxin	токсин	*(tak-SEEN)*
tranquilizer	транквилизатор	*(trank-vee-lee-ZAH-tar)*
vaccine	вакцина	*(vak-TSEE-na)*
vitamin	витамин	*(vee-ta-MEEN)*
zinc	цинк	*(tsink)*

Russian to English

анестезирующее средство	*(a-ne-stee-ZEE-roo-yoo-shchee-ye SRET-stva)*	anaesthetic
антационное средство	*(an-ta-tsee-ON-na-ya SRET-stva)*	antacid
антибиотик	*(an-tee-bee-OH-teek)*	antibiotic
антидепрессант	*(an-tee-de-pres-SAHNT)*	antidepressant
антикоагулянт	*(an-tee-koh-a-goo-LYAHNT)*	anticoagulant
антисептическое средство	*(an-tee-sep-TEE-ches-ka-ye SRET-stva)*	antiseptic

аптека	*(ap-TEH-ka)*	drugstore
болезнь	*(ba-LEZN)*	disease
болеутоляющее (средство)	*(BOH-le-oo-ta-LYAH-yoo-shchee-ye [SRET-stva])*	analgesic
ботаническое средство	*(ba-ta-NEE-ches-ka-ye SRET-stva)*	botanic
вакцина	*(vak-TSEE-na)*	vaccine
витамин	*(vee-ta-MEEN)*	vitamin
врач	*(vrachch)*	physician
гипертензия	*(ghee-per-TEN-zee-ya)*	hypertension
глазные капли	*(glaz-NEE-ye KAHP-lee)*	eyedrop
грубый	*(GROO-bee)*	crude
доза	*(DOH-za)*	dose
желатиновая капсула	*(zhe-la-TEE-na-va-ya KAHP-soo-la)*	capsule
железо	*(zhe-LEE-za)*	iron
инъекция	*(een-YEK-tsee-ya)*	injection
йод	*(yot)*	iodine
капли от кашля	*(KAHP-lee at KAHSH-lya)*	cough drop
капля	*(KAHP-lya)*	drop
кашлять	*(KAHSH-lyat)*	cough (v)
крахмал	*(krakh-MAHL)*	starch
кровоточить	*(kra-va-ta-CHEET)*	bleed
кровь	*(krof)*	blood
лаборант	*(la-ba-RAHNT)*	laboratory technician
лекарственное средство/ лекарство	*(le-KAHR-stven-na-ye SRET-stva/le-KAHR-stva)*	drug
лечебные средства	*(le-CHEB-nee-ye SRET-stva)*	remedies
мазь	*(mahs)*	ointment, salve
медикамент	*(me-dee-ka-MENT)*	medication
медицина	*(mee-dee-TSEE-na)*	medicine
морфин	*(mar-FEEN)*	morphine
мочегонное средство	*(ma-che-GON-na-ye SRET-stva)*	diuretic

наркотик	*(nar-KOH-teek)*	narcotic
опиум	*(OH-pe-oom)*	opium
органический	*(ar-ga-NEE-ches-kee)*	organic
очистительное средство	*(a-chees-TEE-tel-na-ye SRET-stva)*	purgative
пенициллин	*(pe-nee-tsee-LEEN)*	penicillin
пилюля	*(pee-LYOO-lya)*	pellet
плотность	*(PLOT-nast)*	density
повязка	*(pa-VYAHZ-ka)*	dressing
противовоспали-тельный	*(PROH-tee-va-vas-pa-LEE-tel-nee)*	anti-inflammatory
рак	*(rahk)*	cancer
растения	*(ras-TEH-nee-ya)*	plants
рецепт	*(re-TSEPT)*	prescription
седативное средство	*(se-da-TEEV-na-ye SRET-stva)*	sedative
синтез	*(SEEN-tes)*	synthesis
синус	*(SEE-noos)*	sinus
сироп от кашля	*(see-ROP at KAHSH-lya)*	cough syrup
слабительное средство	*(sla-BEE-tel-na-ye SRET-stva)*	laxative
снотворная таблетка	*(sna-TVOHR-na-ya tab-LET-ka)*	sleeping pill
содержание	*(sa-der-ZHAH-nee-ye)*	content
соединения	*(sa-ye-dee-NEH-nee-ye)*	compounds
соли	*(SOH-lee)*	salts
СПИД	*(speet)*	AIDS
стимулятор	*(stee-moo-LAH-tar)*	stimulant
сульфамид	*(sool-fa-MEET)*	sulphamide
сыворотка	*(SEE-va-rat-ka)*	serum
таблетка	*(tab-LET-ka)*	pill, tablet
термометр	*(ter-MOH-metr)*	thermometer
токсикология	*(tak-see-ka-LOH-ghee-ya)*	toxicology
токсин	*(tak-SEEN)*	toxin
транквилизатор	*(trank-vee-lee-ZAH-tar)*	tranquilizer

фармацевт	*(far-ma-TSEFT)*	pharmacist
фармацевти- ческий	*(far-ma-tsef-TEE-ches-kee)*	pharmaceutical
цинк	*(tsink)*	zinc
чихать	*(chee-KHAHT)*	sneeze (v)
шприц	*(shpreets)*	syringe

PRINTING AND PUBLISHING

Most of the NIS states, and the Soviet Union before them, enjoyed high literacy and expentional demand for newspapers, journals, and books of all kinds. Prior to the advent of "glasnost" under Gorbachev, much of this demand went unsatisfied for political reasons (ideologically correct works were printed to the detriment of the more popular printed matter); today there is greater variety, but demand remains unsatisfied because of critical shortages of paper and printing equipment. As a result, the Russian government has set up a special fund to support printing and publishing operations, and nearly every publisher in the NIS is now actively seeking foreign markets and foreign investment.

English to Russian

art	искусство	*(ees-KOOS-stva)*
binding	переплёт	*(pe-re-PLYOT)*
black and white	чёрно-белый	*(CHOHR-na-BEH-lee)*
bleed	обрезать страницу в край	*(ab-REH-zat stra-NEE-tsoo fkrahy)*
blowup	большое увеличение	*(bal-SHOH-ye oo-ve-lee-CHEH-nee-ye)*
boldface	жирный шрифт	*(ZHIHR-nee shrift)*
book	книга	*(KNEE-ga)*
bookbinder	переплётчик	*(pe-re-PLYOT-cheek)*
bookbinding press	переплётный пресс	*(pe-re-PLYOT-nee press)*
book-end paper	форзацная бумага	*(far-ZAHTS-na-ya boo-MAH-ga)*
brochure	брошюра	*(bra-SHOO-ra)*
capital letter	прописная/заглавная буква	*(pra-pees-NAH-ya/za-glav-NA-ya BOOK-va)*
carbon copy	машинописная копия	*(ma-shee-na-PEES-na-ya KOH-pee-ya)*
chapter	глава	*(gla-VAH)*
circulation	тираж	*(tee-RAHSH)*
coated paper	бумага с покрытием	*(boo-MAH-gaspa-KREE-tee-yem)*
composition	набор	*(na-BOHR)*
color filter	цветофильтр	*(tsve-ta-FEELTR)*
color printing	цветная печать	*(tsvet-NAH-ya pe-CHANT)*
copy (reproduction)	экземпляр	*(ek-zem-PLYAHR)*

copy (v)	копировать	*(ka-PEE-ra-vat)*
copyright	авторское право	*(AHF-tar-ska-ye PRAH-va)*
cover	обложка	*(ab-LOSH-ka)*
crop	подрезать снимок	*(pad-REH-zat SNEEM-ak)*
distribution	распределение	*(ras-pre-de-LEH-nee-ye)*
dummy	макет	*(ma-KET)*
edit (v)	редактировать	*(re-dak-TEE-ra-vat)*
edition	издание	*(eez-DAH-nee-ye)*
editor	редактор	*(re-DAHK-tar)*
embossed paper	тиснёная бумага	*(tees-NYOH-na-ya boo-MAH-ga)*
engrave (v)	делать клишю	*(DEH-lat klee-SHEH)*
font	комплект шрифта	*(kam-PLEKT shreef-TAH)*
foreword	предисловие	*(pre-dees-LOH-vee-ye)*
format	формат	*(far-MAHT)*
four-color	четырёхсветная печать	*(che-tee-ryokh-TSVET-na-ya pe-CHAHT)*
galley proof	корректурная гранка	*(kar-rek-TOOHR-nee-ye GRAHN-kee)*
glossy paper	глянцевая бумага	*(GLYAHN-tse-va-ya boo-MAH-ga)*
hardcover	в жёстком/в твёрдом переплёте	*(VZHOST-kam/FTVYOHR-dam pe-re-PLYOH-te)*
headline	заголовок/заглавие	*(za-ga-LOH-vak/za-GLAH-vee-ye)*
inch	дюйм	*(dyooym)*
ink	чернила	*(cher-NEE-la)*
insert	вкладыш	*(FKLAH-deesh)*
introduction	введение	*(vve-DEH-nee-ye)*
italic	курсив	*(koor-SEEF)*
jacket	суперобложка	*(SOO-per-ab-LOSH-ka)*
justify (v)	выключать (строку)	*(vee-kloo-CHAHT [stra-KOO])*
layout	расположение	*(ras-pa-la-ZHEH-nee-ye)*
letter	буква	*(BOOK-va)*
line	строка	*(stra-KAH)*

line drawing	штриховой оригинал	*(shtree-kha-VOY a-ree-ghee-NAHL)*
lithographic paper	литографская бумага	*(lee-ta-GRAHF-ska-ya boo-MAH-ga)*
lower case	строчная буква	*(strach-NAH-ya BOOK-va)*
matrix	матрица	*(MAH-tree-tsa)*
negative	негатив	*(ne-ga-TEEF)*
newsletter	информационный бюллетень	*(een-far-ma-tsee-ON-nee byoo-le-TEN)*
newspaper	газета	*(ga-ZEH-ta)*
newsprint	газетная бумага	*(ga-ZET-na-ya boo-MAH-ga)*
newsstand	газетный киоск	*(ga-ZET-nee kee-OSK)*
page	страница	*(stra-NEE-tsa)*
page makeup	расположение страницы	*(ras-pa-la-ZHEH-nee-ye stra-NEE-tsee)*
pagination	пагинация	*(pa-ghee-NAH-tsee-ya)*
pamphlet	памфлет	*(pam-FLET)*
paper	бумага	*(boo-MAH-ga)*
paperback	в бумажном переплёте	*(vboo-MAHZH-nam pe-re-PLYOH-te)*
pica	цицеро	*(TSEE-tse-roh)*
pigment	пигмент	*(peeg-MENT)*
plate	стереотип	*(ste-re-a-TEEP)*
positive	позитивный	*(pa-zee-TEEV-nee)*
preface	предисловие	*(pre-dee-SLOH-vee-ye)*
press clipping	газетная вырезка	*(ga-ZET-na-ya VEE-res-ka)*
print run	тираж	*(tee-RAHSH)*
printing	печатания	*(pe-CHAH-ta-nee-ye)*
proofreading	корректурное чтение	*(kar-rek-TOOHR-na-ye CHTEH-nee-ye)*
publisher	издатель	*(eez-DAH-tel)*
publishing house	издательство	*(eez-DAH-tel-stva)*
ream	стопа	*(sta-PAH)*
scanner	сканнер	*(SKAHN-ner)*
sewn cover	тканевый переплёт	*(TKAH-ne-vee pe-re-PLYOT)*

sheet	оттиск	*(OT-teesk)*
size	размер	*(raz-MEHR)*
small capital	капитель	*(ka-pee-TEL)*
spine	переплёт	*(pe-re-PLYOT)*
table of contents	оглавление	*(ag-lav-LEH-nee-ye)*
title	название	*(naz-VAH-nee-ye)*

Russian to English

авторское право	*(AHF-tar-ska-ye PRAH-va)*	copyright
большое увеличение	*(bal-SHOH-ye oo-ve-lee-CHEH-nee-ye)*	blowup
брошюра	*(bra-SHOO-ra)*	brochure
буква	*(BOOK-va)*	letter
бумага	*(boo-MAH-ga)*	paper
бумага с покрытием	*(boo-MAH-ga spa-KREE-tee-yem)*	coated paper
в бумажном переплёте	*(vboo-MAHZH-nam pe-re-PLYOH-te)*	paperback
в жёстком/в твёрдом переплёте	*(VZHOST-kam/FTVOHR-dam pe-re-PLYOH-te)*	hardcover
введение	*(vve-DEH-nee-ye)*	introduction
вкладыш	*(FKLAH-deesh)*	inset
выключать (строку)	*(vee-kloo-CHAHT [stra-KOO])*	justify (v)
газета	*(ga-ZEH-ta)*	newspaper
газетная бумага	*(ga-ZET-na-ya boo-MAH-ga)*	newsprint
газетная вырезка	*(ga-ZET-na-ya VEE-res-ka)*	press clipping
газетный киоск	*(ga-ZET-nee kee-OSK)*	newsstand
глава	*(gla-VAH)*	chapter
глянцевая бумага	*(GLYAHN-tsee-va-ya boo-MAH-ga)*	glossy paper
делать клише	*(DEH-lat klee-SHEH)*	engrave (v)
дюйм	*(dyooym)*	inch
жирный шрифт	*(ZHIR-nee shrift)*	boldface

заголовок/ заглавие	(za-ga-LOH-vak/za-GLAH- vee-ye)	headline
издание	(eez-DAH-nee-ye)	edition
издатель	(eez-DAH-tel)	publisher
издательство	(eez-DAH-tel-stva)	publishing house
информационный бюллетень	(een-far-ma-tsee-ON-nee byoo-le-TEN)	newsletter
искусство	(ees-KOOS-tva)	art
капитель	(ka-pee-TEL)	small capital
книга	(KNEE-ga)	book
комплект шрифта	(kam-PLEKT shreef-TAH)	font
копировать	(ka-PEE-ra-vat)	copy (v)
корректурные гранки	(kar-rek-TOOHR-nee-ye GRAHN-kee)	galley proof
корректурное чтение	(ka-rek=TOOHR-na-ye CHTEH-nee-ye)	proofreading
курсив	(koor-SEEF)	italic
литографская бумага	(lee-ta-GRAHF-ska-ya boo- MAH-ga)	litographic paper
макет	(ma-KET)	dummy
матрица	(MAH-tree-tsa)	matrix
машинописная копия	(ma-shee-na-PEES-na-ya KOH-pee-ya)	carbon copy
набор	(na-BOHR)	composition
название	(naz-VAH-nee-ye)	title
негатив	(ne-ga-TEEF)	negative
обложка	(ab-LOSH-ka)	cover
обрезать страницу в край	(ab-REH-zat stra-NEE-tsoo fkrahy)	bleed
оглавление	(ag-lav-LEH-nee-ye)	table of contents
оттиск	(OT-teesk)	sheet
пагинация	(pa-ghee-NA-tsee-ya)	pagination
памфлет	(pam-FLET)	pamphlet
переплёт	(pe-re-PLYOT)	binding, spine
переплётный пресс	(pe-re-PLYOT-nee press)	bookbinding press
переплётчик	(pe-re-PLYOT-cheek)	bookbinder

печатание	(pe-CHAH-ta-nee-ye)	printing
пигмент	(peeg-MENT)	pigment
подрезать снимок	(pad-REH-zat SHNEE-mak)	crop
позитивный	(pa-zee-TEEV-nee)	positive
предисловие	(pre-dees-LOH-vee-ye)	foreword, preface
прописная/заглав-ная буква	(pra-pees-NAH-ya/za-GLAHV-na-ya BOOK-va)	capital letter
размер	(raz-MEHR)	size
расположение	(ras-pa-la-ZHEH-nee-ye)	layout
расположение страницы	(ras-pa-la-ZHEH-nee-ye stra-NEE-tsee)	page makeup
распределение	(ras-pre-de-LEH-nee-ye)	distribution
редактировать	(re-dak-TEE-ra-vat)	edit (v)
редактор	(re-DAHK-tar)	editor
сканнер	(SKAHN-ner)	scanner
стереотип	(ste-re-a-TEEP)	plate
стопа	(sta-PAH)	ream
страница	(stra-NEE-tsa)	page
строка	(stra-KAH)	line
строчная буква	(strach-NAH-ya BOOK-va)	lower case
суперобложка	(SOO-per-ab-LOSH-ka)	jacket
тираж	(tee-RAHSH)	circulation, print run
тиснёная бумага	(tees-NYOH-na-ya boo-MAH-ga)	embossed paper
тканевый переплёт	(TKAH-nee-vee pe-re-PLYOT)	sewn cover
форзацная бумага	(far-ZAHTS-na-ya boo-MAH-ga)	book-end paper
формат	(far-MAHT)	format
цветная печать	(tsvet-NAH-ya pe-CHAHT)	color printing
цветофильтр	(tsve-ta-FEELTR)	color filter
цицеро	(TSEE-tse-roh)	pica
чернила	(cher-NEE-la)	ink
четырёхцветная печать	(chee-tee-ryokh-TSVET-na-ya pe-CHAHT)	four-color
чёрно-белый	(CHOR-na-BE-lee)	black and white

штриховой оригинал	*(shtree-kha-VOY a-ree-ghee-nahl)*	line drawing
экземпляр	*(ek-zem-PLYAHR)*	copy (reproduction)

COMMON BUSINESS ABBREVIATIONS (English)

a.a.	always afloat
a.a.r.	against all risks
a/c	account
A/C	account current
a.c.v.	actual cash value
a.d.	after date
a.f.b.	air freight bill
agcy.	agency
a.m.t.	air mail transfer
a/o	account of
A.P.	accounts payable
A/P	authority to pay
approx.	approximately
A.R.	accounts receivable
a/r	all risks
A/S, A.S.	account sales
a/s	at sight
at.wt.	atomic weight
av.	average
avdp.	avoirdupois
a/w	actual weight
a.w.b.	air waybill
bal.	balance
bar.	barrel
bbl.	barrel
b/d	brought down
B/E, b/e	bill of exchange
b/f	brought forward
B.H.	bill of health
bk.	bank
bkge.	brokerage
B/L	bill of lading
b/o	brought over
B.P.	bills payable
b.p.	by procuration
B.R.	bills receivable
B/S	balance sheet
b.t.	berth terms
bu.	bushel
B/V	book value
ca.	circa; centaire
C.A.	chartered accountant
c.a.	current account
C.A.D.	cash against documents
C.B.	cash book

C.B.D.	cash before delivery
c.c.	carbon copy
c/d	carried down
c.d.	cum dividend
c/f	carried forward
cf.	compare
c & f	cost and freight
C/H	clearing house
C.H.	custom house
ch. fwd.	charges forward
ch. pd.	charges paid
chq.	check, cheque
c.i.f.	cost, insurance, freight
c.i.f. & c	cost, insurance, freight, and commission
c.i.f. & e	cost, insurance, freight, and exchange
c.i.f. & i	cost, insurance, freight, and interest
c.l.	car load
C/m	call of more
C/N	credit note
c/o	care of
C.O.D.	cash on delivery
comm.	commission
corp.	corporation
C.O.S.	cash on shipment
C.P.	carriage paid
C/P	charter party
c.p.d.	charters pay duties
cpn.	corporation
cr.	credit; creditor
C/T	cable transfer
c.t.l.	constructive total loss
c.t.l.o.	constructive total loss only
cum.	cumulative
cum div.	cum dividend
cum. pref.	cumulative preference
c/w	commercial weight
C.W.O.	cash with order
cwt.	hundredweight
D/A	documents against acceptance; deposit account
DAP	documents against payment
db.	debenture
DCF	discounted cash flow
d/d	days after date; delivered
deb.	debenture
def.	deferred
dept.	department
d.f.	dead freight
dft.	draft
dft/a.	draft attached

dft/c.	clean draft
disc.	discount
div.	dividend
DL	dayletter
DLT	daily letter telegram
D/N	debit note
D/O	delivery order
do.	ditto
doz.	dozen
D/P	documents against payment
dr.	debtor
Dr.	doctor
d/s, d.s.	days after sight
d.w.	deadweight
D/W	dock warrant
dwt.	pennyweight
dz.	dozen
ECU	European Currency Unit
E.E.T.	East European Time
e.g.	for example
encl.	enclosure
end.	endorsement
E. & O.E.	errors and omissions excepted
e.o.m.	end of month
e.o.h.p.	except otherwise herein provided
esp.	especially
Esq.	esquire
est.	established
ex	out
ex cp.	ex coupon
ex div.	ex dividend
ex int.	ex interest
ex h.	ex new (shares)
ex stre.	ex store
ex whf.	ex wharf
f.a.a.	free of all average
f.a.c.	fast as can
f.a.k.	freight all kinds
f.a.q.	fair average quality; free alongside quay
f.a.s.	free alongside ship
f/c	for cash
f.c. & s.	free of capture and seizure
f.c.s.r. & c.c.	free of capture, seizure, riots, and civil commotion
F.D.	free delivery to dock
f.d.	free discharge
ff.	following; folios
f.g.a.	free of general average

f.i.b.	free in bunker
f.i.o.	free in and out
f.i.t.	free in truck
f.o.b.	free on board
f.o.c.	free of charge
f.o.d.	free of damage
fol.	following; folio
f.o.q.	free on quay
f.o.r.	free on rail
f.o.s.	free on steamer
f.o.t.	free on truck(s)
f.o.w.	free on wagons; free on wharf
F.P.	floating policy
f.p.	fully paid
f.p.a.	free of particular average
frt.	freight
frt. pd.	freight paid
frt. ppd.	freight prepaid
frt. fwd.	freight forward
ft.	foot
fwd.	forward
f.x.	foreign exchange
g.a.	general average
g.b.o.	goods in bad order
g.m.b.	good merchantable brank
G.M.T.	Greenwich Mean Time
GNP	gross national product
g.o.b.	good ordinary brank
gr.	gross
GRT	gross register ton
gr. wt.	gross weight
GT	gross tonnage
h.c.	home consumption
hgt.	height
hhd.	hogshead
H.O.	head office
H.P.	hire purchase
HP	horsepower
ht.	height
IDP	integrated data processing
i.e.	that is
I/F	insufficient funds
i.h.p.	indicated horsepower
imp.	import
Inc.	incorporated
incl.	inclusive
ins.	insurance

int.	interest
inv.	invoice
I.O.U.	I owe you
J/A, j.a.	joint account
Jr.	junior
KV	kilovolt
KW	kilowatt
KWh	kilowatt hour
L/C, l.c.	letter of credit
LCD	telegram in the language of the country of destination
LCO	telegram in the language of the country of origin
ldg.	landing; loading
l.t.	long ton
Ltd.	limited
l. tn.	long ton
m.	month
m/a	my account
max.	maximum
M.D.	memorandum of deposit
M/D, m.d.	months after date
memo.	memorandum
Messrs.	plural of Mr.
mfr.	manufacturer
min.	minimum
MLR	minimum lending rate
M.O.	money order
m.o.	my order
mortg.	mortgage
M/P, m.p.	months after payment
M/R	mate's receipt
M/S, m.s.	months' sight
M.T.	mail transfer
M/U	making-up price
n.	name; nominal
n/a	no account
N/A	no advice
n.c.v.	no commercial value
n.d.	no date
n.e.s.	not elsewhere specified
N/F	no funds
NL	night letter
N/N	no noting
N/O	no orders
no.	number
n.o.e.	not otherwise enumerated

n.o.s.	not otherwise stated
nos.	numbers
NPV	no par value
nr.	number
n.r.t.	net register ton
N/S	not sufficient funds
NSF	not sufficient funds
n. wt.	net weight
o/a	on account
OCP	overseas common point
O/D, o/d	on demand; overdraft
o.e.	omissions excepted
o/h	overhead
ono.	or nearest offer
O/o	order of
O.P.	open policy
o.p.	out of print; overproof
O/R, o.r.	owner's risk
ord.	order; ordinary
O.S., o.s	out of stock
OT	overtime
p.	page; per; premium
P.A., p.a.	particular average; per annum
P/A	power of attorney; private account
PAL	phase alternation line
pat. pend.	patent pending
PAYE	pay as you earn
p/c	petty cash
p.c.	percent; price current
pcl.	parcel
pd.	paid
pf.	preferred
pfd.	preferred
pkg.	package
P/L	profit and loss
p.l.	partial loss
P/N	promissory note
P.O.	post office; postal order
P.O.B.	post office box
P.O.O.	post office order
p.o.r.	pay on return
pp.	pages
p & p	postage and packing
p. pro.	per procuration
ppd.	prepaid
ppt.	prompt
pref.	preference
prox.	proximo

P.S.	postscript
pt.	payment
P.T.O., p.t.o.	please turn over
ptly. pd.	partly paid
p.v.	par value
qlty.	quality
qty.	quantity
r. & c.c.	riot and civil commotions
R/D	refer to drawer
R.D.C.	running down clause
re	in regard to
rec.	received; receipt
recd.	received
red.	redeemable
ref.	reference
reg.	registered
retd.	returned
rev.	revenue
R.O.D.	refused on delivery
R.P.	reply paid
r.p.s.	revolutions per second
RSVP	please reply
R.S.W.C.	right side up with care
Ry	railway
s.a.e.	self addressed envelope
S.A.V.	stock at valuation
S/D	sea damaged
S/D, s.d.	sight draft
s.d.	without date
SDR	special drawing rights
sgd.	signed
s. & h. ex	Sundays and holidays excepted
shipt.	shipment
sig.	signature
S/LC, s. & l.c.	sue and labor clause
S/N	shipping note
s.o.	seller's option
s.o.p.	standard operating procedure
spt.	spot
Sr.	senior
S.S., s.s.	steamship
s.t.	short ton
ster.	sterling
St. Ex.	stock exchange
stg.	sterling
s.v.	sub voce

T.A.	telegraphic address
T.B.	trial balance
tel.	telephone
temp.	temporary secretary
T.L., t.l.	total loss
T.L.O.	total loss only
TM	multiple telegram
T.O.	turn over
tr.	transfer
TR	telegram to be called for
T.R., T/R	trust receipt
TT, T.T.	telegraphic transfer (cable)
TX	telex
UGT	urgent
u.s.c.	under separate cover
U/ws	underwriters
v.	volt
val.	value
v.a.t.	value added tax
v.g.	very good
VHF	very high frequency
v.h.r.	very highly recommended
w.	watt
WA	with average
W.B.	way bill
w.c.	without charge
W.E.T.	West European Time
wg.	weight guaranteed
whse.	warehouse
w.o.g.	with other goods
W.P.	weather permitting; without prejudice
w.p.a.	with particular average
W.R.	war risk
W/R, wr.	warehouse receipt
W.W.D.	weather working day
wt.	weight
x.c.	ex coupon
x.d.	ex dividend
x.i.	ex interest
x.n.	ex new shares
y.	year
yd.	yard
yr.	year
yrly.	yearly

VI. LISTINGS

The following listings are provided as a jumping-off point for your business in the NIS. In addition to a comprehensive list of the major commercial banks, this section contains lists of hotels and restaurants; embassies and consulates in the NIS, as well as NIS governmental representatives in the United States; useful U.S. government agencies and NIS-related business associations. One caveat: with the rapid pace of events in the NIS, private addresses and phone numbers may change without warning. If you find that an address or phone number is no longer correct, contact the appropriate commercial office for the correct coordinates. The author would also be grateful for any corrections that can be inserted in future editions.

In order to assist you in comprehending addresses in the NIS, the following list provides the address abbreviations used in listings found in this book along with their translations.

bul.	бульвар (bul-VAR)	Boulevard
d.	дом (dom)	House, Building
dv.	двор (dvor)	Court (yard)
most	мост (mohst)	Bridge
kan.	канал (ka-NAHL)	Canal
kor.	корпус (KOR-poos)	Block (building in a complex)
kv.	квартира (kvar-TEE-ra)	Apartment, Suite
nab.	набережная (NA-be-rezh-na-ya)	Embankment
per.	переулок (pe-re-OO-lak)	Corner
pl.	площадь (PLO-shchad)	Square
pod.	подъезд (pod-YEZD)	Entrance
pr.	проспект (pra-SPEKT)	Avenue
pro.	проезд (pra-YEZD)	Passage
r.	река (re-KAH)	River
sh.	шоссе (shas-SYE)	Highway
ul.	улица (OO-lee-tsa)	Street
vul.	вулюца (VOO-lee-tsa)	Street (Ukrainian)

MAJOR COMMERICAL BANKS

Moscow

AKIB NTP Menatep
Manezhnaya pl. 7
Tel: 202-8556

AVTOBANK
Delegatskaya ul. 11
Tel: 973-3216

BAZIS BANK
sh. Entuziastov 7
Tel: 362-6968

CENTROCREDIT
Pyatnitskaya ul. 31
Tel: 231-7581

CREDIT-MOSCOW
Tverskaya ul. 7
Tel: 201-9067

DIALOGBANK
Staropansky per. 4
Tel: 921-9104
Fax: 923-6556

ELEXBANK
Malyi Sukharevsky per. 12
d. 2
Tel: 208-6703

HELP BANK
Presnensky Val 27
Tel: 166-8019

INKOMBANK
Nametkina ul. 14/1
Tel: 332-0699
Fax: 331-8833

INTERNATIONAL ECONOMIC
COOPERATION BANK
ul. Mashi Poryvaievoi
Tel: 975-3861
         204-7722/7729
Fax: 975-2202

INTERNATIONAL INVESTMENT
BANK
ul. Mashi Poryvaivoi 7
Tel: 975-4008
         204-7311
Fax: 975-2070

MOSCOW BUSINESS BANK
pro. Khudozhestvennovo
Teatra 6
Tel: 292-0709/9873
Fax: 975-2214

MOSCOW INTERREGIONAL
COMMERCIAL BANK
Leningradsky pr. 9
Tel: 250-2195

NGSBANK
Zhitnaya st. 14
Tel: 239-1508

RESURS-BANK
Tretya Parkovaya ul. 24
Tel: 306-7855

STOLICHNY BANK
Pyatnitskaya ul. 72
Tel: 233-5892
Fax: 237-2993

TEKHNOBANK
Bolshaya Gruzinskaya ul. 56
Tel: 254-7935

TELEBANK
Znamenka ul. 13, d. 3
Tel: 291-8706

St. Petersburg

ABI-BANK
Zakharevskaya ul. 25
Tel: 275-4526
         275-5328
Fax: 275-7728

AGROPROMBANK
nab. kan. Griboedova 13
Tel: 312-1054
         311-3474

ASTROBANK
Nevskii pr. 13
Tel: 311-3600
Fax: 311-0825

BALTIISKII BANK
Sadovaya ul. 34
Tel: 310-0580
Fax: 310-9274

BANK ST. PETERSBURG
nab. r. Fontanka 70/72
Tel: 219-8529
Fax: 315-8327

GANZAKOM BANK
Mokhovaya ul. 26
Tel: 273-0521
Fax: 110-7320

INNOVATSIONNII BANK
Chaikovskovo ul. 24
Tel: 279-0004
          279-3002
          234-2689
Fax: 279-0281

LENBANK (State)
nab. r. Fontanka 70/72
Tel: 219-8529

LESOPROMYSHLENNI BANK
Millionnaya ul. 10
Tel: 541-8217
Fax: 541-8393

MARIINSKII BANK
B. Porokhovskaya ul. 52/2
Tel: 224-0440
          227-1927
Fax: 222-4370

NEVSKII KOMMERCHESKII
BANK
Sadovaya ul. 21
Tel: 310-3191

PETROVSKII BANK
Ruzovskaya ul. 8
Tel: 292-5322
Branch: Zakharevskaya ul. 14
Tel: 275-7636

PROMSTROI BANK
Nevskii pr. 38
Tel: 110-4638
          314-8985

RUSSKII TORGOVO PROMYSH-
LEMII BANK
Bolshaya Morskaya ul. 15
Tel: 315-7833
Fax: 311-2135

SEVERNII TORGOVII BANK
Nekrasova ul. 14
Tel: 275-8798
          275-0001

STROIKOM BANK
Bolshaya Morskaya ul. 15
Tel: 315-7833

VITABANK
Bolshaya Morskaya ul. 59
Tel: 311-5193
Fax: 311-8361

VNESHEKONOMBANK (State)
Bolshaya Morskaya ul. 29
Tel: 314-6037
Fax: 312-7817

FOREIGN BANKS WITH REPRESENTATIONAL OFFICES IN MOSCOW

American Banks

Bank of America
Krasnopresnenskaya nab. 12
16th Floor, kv. 1605
Tel: 253-7054/1910

Chase Manhattan
Krasnopresnenskaya nab. 12
17th Floor, kv. 1709
Tel: 253-2865/8377/1499
Fax: 253-2174

You may also choose to contact the international departments of the following banks for information on their services in the NIS.

Amro Bank
Banca Nazionale del Lavora
Banco Exterior de Espana
Banco Hispano Americano
Bank of Naples
Bank of Rome
Bank of Scotland
Banque Nationale de Paris
Banque Paribas
Barclays
Creditanstalt
Credit Lyonnais
Deutsche Bank
Deutsche Genossenschaftsbank
Donau Bank

Dresdner Bank
Generale Bank (Brussels)
Italian Commercial Bank
Lloyds Bank
Midland Montagu
Morgan Grenfell
National Westminster Bank
Ost-West Handelsbank
Skandinavska Emskilda Banken
Societe General
State Bank of India
Swedbank
Union Bank of Finland
Union Bank of Switzerland
WestLB

MAJOR HOTELS

Moscow

Aerostar
Leningradskiy pr. 37
kor. 9
Tel: 151-5624
Telex: 411108
Restaurant

Intourist
ul. Mokhovaya 13
Tel: 292-2871

Marco Polo Presnaya Hotel
Spridonevsky 9
Tel: 202-0381
Telex: 414748

Metropol Hotel
Teatralny pro. 1
Tel: 225-6677
Restaurant

Mezhdunarodnaya Hotel I/II
Krosnopresnenskaya nab. 12
Tel: 253-2761
Telex: 411446
Major credit cards accepted
Restaurant

Novotel Hotel
Sheremetevo II Airport
Tel: 578-9407
Telex: 911620

Olympic Penta Hotel
Olympiyskiy pr. 18/1
Tel: 971-6101
Telex: 411061
Restaurant

President (Oktyabrskaya I)
ul. Dimitrova 24
Tel: 238-7303

Pullman-Iris Hotel
Korovinskoye sh. 10
Tel: 488-8000
Telex: 413656
Restaurant

Savoy
ul. Rozhdestvenka 3
Tel: 928-9169
Telex: 411620
Restaurant

Slavyanskaya-Radisson
Berezhkovskaya nab. 2
Tel: 941-8020

St. Petersburg

Astoria
Bolshaya Morskaya ul. 39
Tel: 210-5020
Restaurant

Grand Hotel Europe
Mikhailovskaya ul. 1/7
Tel: 312-0072
Telex: 121073
Restaurant

Nevsky Palace
pr. Nevsky 57
Tel: 113-1470

Olympia
pr. Morskoi Slavi 1
Tel: 217-4416

Pribaltiyskaya
ul. Korablestroiteley 14
Tel: 356-0263
Telex: 121322
Restaurant

Pulkovskaya Hotel
pl. Pobedy 1
Tel: 264-5109
Telex: 321318
Restaurant

MAJOR RESTAURANTS

Moscow

Arlecchino Restaurant JV
Druzhinnikovskaya ul. 15
Tel: 205-7088
Hard currency only

Baku-Livan-Nasr JV
ul. Tverskaya 24
Tel: 299-8506

Boyarskiy Restaurant
Hotel Metropol, 4th floor
Tel: 927-6089
Hard currency only

Champs Elysees Restaurant
Pullman Iris Hotel
Tel: 488-8000
Hard currency only

DAB Beer Bar
Zolotoe Koltso Hotel
Tel: 248-2696
Hard currency only

Die Bierstube
Olympic Penta Hotel
Tel: 971-6101
Hard currency only

Delhi Restaurant
ul. Krasnopresnenskaya 23b
Tel: 255-0492
Hard currency for alcohol

Evropeiskiy Zal Restaurant
Hotel Metropol
Tel: 927-6039
Hard currency only

Glazur Restaurant
Smolenskiy bul. 12/19
Tel: 248-4438
Hard currency only

Golden Dragon
Mezhdunarodnaya Exhibition Center
Tel: 248-3602

Greek Restaurant
On board the "Aleksander Blok"
Tel: 255-9278
Hard currency only

Guria Cafe
Komsomolskiy pr. 7/3
Tel: 246-0378

Le Cafe Francais
Pullman Iris Hotel
Tel: 488-8000
Hard currency only

Le Chalet Restaurant
Korobeynikov per. 1/2
(Chaika Tennis Club)
Tel: 202-0106
Hard currency only

McDonald's
Bolshaya Bronnaya ul. 29
Tel: 229-1811

Moosh Cafe
ul. Oktyabrskaya 2/4
Tel: 284-3670
Hard currency for alcohol

Pekin Restaurant
ul. Bolshaya Sadovaya 1/17
Tel: 209-1815
Hard currency only

Pescatore Restaurant
pr. Mira 36
Tel: 280-0850
Hard currency only

Pizza Hut Restaurant
Kutuzovskiy pr. 17
Tel: 243-1727
Hard currency for alcohol

Potel et Chabot
Hotel Mezhdunarodnaya
Tel: 253-2760
Hard currency only

Rincon Espanol Restaurant (El)
Hotel Moskva
Tel: 292-2893
Hard currency only

Savoy Restaurant
ul. Rozhdestvenka 3
Tel: 928-0450
Hard currency only

Skazka II Restaurant
Yaroslavskoe sh. 43
Tel: 184-3436

Slalvyanskiy Bazaar Restaurant
ul. 25 Oktyabrya 13
Tel: 921-1872

Sorok Cheterie (44) Cafe
Leningradskoye sh. 44
Tel: 159-9951
Hard currency only

Taiga Cafe
Aerostar Hotel
Tel: 155-5030
Hard currency only

Terrace Bar
Aerostar Hotel
Tel: 155-5030
Hard currency only

Tino Fontana Restaurant
Hotel Mezhdunarodnaya, 3rd Floor
Tel: 253-2241
Hard currency only

Sappora Restaurant
pr. Mira 14
Tel: 207-8253
Hard currency only

U Pirosmani Cafe
Novodevichy pro. 4
Tel: 247-1926
Hard currency for alcohol

Vecherny Siluet Restaurant
Taganskaya pl. 88
Tel: 272-1503
Hard currency only

Vienna Cafe
Olympic Penta Hotel
Tel: 971-6101
Hard currency only

Vltava Cafe
Vasilyevskaya 15/24
Tel: 251-6898

Yakimanka Cafe
Bolshaya Polyanka 2/10, Str. 1
Tel: 238-8888

St. Petersburg

Admiralteyskiy Restaurant
Bolshaya Morskaya ul. 27
Tel: 314-4514

Astoria Restaurant
Astoria Hotel
Bolshaya Morskaya ul. 39
Tel: 210-5838
Hard currency only

Austeria Restaurant
Peter and Paul Fortress
Ioannovskiy Ravelin
Tel: 238-4262

Chaika Restaurant
nab. kan. Griboyedova 14
Tel: 312-4631
Hard currency only

Daddy's Steak Room
Moskovskiy pr. 73
Tel: 298-9552
Hard currency only

Demyanova Ukha Restaurant
pr. Maksima Gorkovo 53
Tel: 232-8090

Diamond Jack
ul. Lenina 32
Tel: 230-8830

Europe Restaurant
Grand Hotel Europe
Tel: 312-0072 (switchboard)
Hard currency only

Fortetskiya Restaurant
Kuybysheva ul. 7
Tel: 233-9468

Imperial Restaurant
Kamenoostrovskiy pr. 53
Tel: 234-1742

Le Bistro Brasserie
Grand Hotel Europe
Tel: 312-0072
Hard currency only

Literaturnoye Cafe
Nevskiy pr. 18
Tel: 312-8536

Melody JV Restaurant
Sverdlovskaya nab. 62
Tel: 227-2676
Hard currency only

Nevskiy 40
Nevskiy pr. 40
Tel: 311-9066
Hard currency only

Nevskiye Zvyozdy Restaurant
ul. Babushkina 91
Tel: 265-5490
Hard currency only

Okhotnichny Klub Restaurant
Gorokhovaya ul. 45
Tel: 310-0770

Pizza-Express JV
Podolskaya ul. 23
Tele.: 292-2666
Hard currency only

Sadkos
Grand Hotel Europe
Tel: 312-0072
Hard currency only

Sankt Peterburg Restaurant
nab. kan. Griboyedova 5
Tele.: 314-4947
Hard currency only

Schwabskiy Domik Restaurant JV
Krasnogvardeyskiy pr. 28/19
Tel: 528-2211
Hard currency only

Troika Restaurant JV
Zagorodny pr. 27
Tel: 113-5376
Hard currency only

U Prichala Restaurant
V.O. Bolshoy pr. 91
Tel: 217-4428

Venice Restaurant
ul. Korablestroiteley 21
Tel: 352-1432
Hard currency only

Trattoria
Grand Hotel Europe
Tel: 312-0072
Hard currency only

Zimny Sad Restaurant
Hotel Astoria
Tel: 210-5838
Hard currency only

U.S. EMBASSIES IN THE NEWLY INDEPENDENT STATES

Armenia

U.S. Embassy - Yerevan
Gen Bagramian 18
Yerevan, Armenia
Tel: (885) 215-1144
        215-1122
        (873)151-2107
Tel./Fax: (885) 215-1122
Mailing Address:
U.S. Embassy Yerevan
U. S. Department of State
Washington, DC 20521-7020

Azerbaijan

U.S. Embassy - Baku
Neftyanikov 77
Baku, Azberbaijan
Tel: (873) 151-2713
        (8922) 921-898
Mailing address:
U.S. Embassy Baku

U.S. Department of State
Washington, DC 20521-7050

Belarus

U.S. Embassy - Minsk
Starovilenskaya 46
Minsk, Belarus
Tel: (017) 231-5000
Fax: (017) 234-7853
Mailing address:
U.S. Embassy Minsk
APE AE 09723

Estonia

U.S. Embassy - Tallinn
Kentmanni 20
200000 Tallinn, Estonia
Tel: (358 49) 303 182
        (873) 150 6775
Fax: (358 49) 306 817
        (873) 150 6776

Georgia

U.S. Embassy - Tbilisi
Antonely 25
Tbilisi, Georgia
Tel: (8832) 989-967/68
    (8832) 744-623
    (873) 151-2723
Fax: (8832) 933-759
Mailing address:
U.S. Embassy Tbilisi
U.S. Department of State
Washington, DC 20521-7060

Kazakhstan

U.S. Embassy - Alma Ata
Seyfullina Building
Alma Ata, Kazakhstan
Tel: (3272) 632-426
    (873) 151-2106
Fax: (3272) 633-883
Mailing address:
U.S. Embassy Alma Ata
U.S. Department of State
Washington, DC 20521-7030

Kyrgyzstan

U.S. Embassy - Bishkek
Erkindik 66
Bishkek, Kyrgyzstan
Tel: (3312) 222-2693 (Hotel
Pishpek)
    (873) 151-2111
Fax: (3312) 223-551
Mailing address:
U.S. Embassy Bishkek
U.S. Department of State
Washington, DC 20521-7040

Latvia

U.S. Embassy - Riga
Raina Blvd. 7
226000 Riga, Latvia
Tel: (358 49) 311-348
    (358 49) 315-830
Fax: (358 49) 314-665
    (871) 150-7503

Mailing address:
American Embassy Riga
U.S. Department of State
Washington, DC 20521-4520

Lithuania

U.S. Embassy - Vilnius
Akmenu 4
2001 Vilnius, Lithuania
Tel: (122) 223-031
    (873) 150-6773
Fax: (122) 222-779
    (873) 150-6774
Mailing address:
American Embassy Vilnius
U.S. Department of State
Washington, DC 20521-4510

Moldova

U.S. Embassy - Chisinau
Strada Alexei Mateevici 102
Chisinau, Moldova
Tel: (3732) 233-772
    (422) 232-896
    (873) 151-2442
Fax: (3732) 233-044
Mailing address:
U.S. Embassy Chisinau
U.S. Department of State
Washington, DC 20521-7080

Tajikistan

U.S. Embassy - Dushanbe
Ainii Str. 39
Dushanbe, Tajikistan
Tel: (3772) 248-233
    (3773) 243-223 (Hotel
Oktyabr'skaya)
    (873) 151-2712
Mailing address:
U.S. Embassy Dushanbe
U.S. Department of State
Washington, DC 20521-7090

Turkmenistan

U.S. Embassy - Ashkhabad
Jubileinaya Hotel
Ashkhabad, Turkmenistan
Tel: (3632) 244-925
    (873) 151-1532
Mailing address:
U.S. Embassy Ashkhabad
U.S. Department of State
Washington, DC 20521-7070

Ukraine

U.S. Embassy - Kiev
Vul. Yuriy Kotsubinskoho 10
Kiev, Ukraine
Tel: (044) 244-7349
    (873) 150-7476
Fax: (044) 244-7350
Telex: (871) 131142
Mailing address:
U.S. Embassy Kiev
U.S. Department of State
Washington, DC 20521-5850

Uzbekistan

U.S. Embassy - Tashkent
Chelendarskaya 55
Tashkent, Uzbekistan
Tel: (3712) 771-407
    (3712) 331-574 (Hotel
    Uzbekistan)
    (873) 151-2441
Mailing address:
U.S. Embassy Tashkent
U.S. Department of State
Washington, DC 20521-7110

U.S. CONSULATES IN THE NIS

St. Petersburg

U.S. Consulate General
Furshtadskaya ul.
   (formerly ul. Petra Lavrova) 15
Tel: 850-4170
Fax: 110-7022
Telex: (871) 64121527
Mailing address:
Box L
APO AE 09723

Vladivostok

American Consulate to Vladivostok
Tel: (4232) 266-734
Fax: (4232) 268-445
Mailing address:
American Consulate of Vladivostok
U. S. Department of State
Washington, DC 20521-5880

OTHER FOREIGNS EMBASSIES IN THE NIS

Moscow

Afghanistan
Sverchkov per. 3/2
Tel: 923-5515
Fax: 924-0478
Telex: 413270

Albania
ul. Mytnaya 3, dv. 23
Tel: 230-1722

Algeria
Krapivenskiy per. 1a
Tel: 200-6642
Telex: 413273

Angola
ul. Olaf Palme 6
Tel: 143-6324
Tel: 143-6335 (Commer. office)

Argentina
ul. Sadovaya-Triumfalnaya 4/10
Tel: 299-0367
Telex: 413259

Armenia
Armianskiy per. 2
Tel: 924-1269

Australia
Kropotkinskiy per. 13
Tel: 246-5012
Fax: 230-2606
Telex: 413474

Austria
Starokonyushenny per. 1
Tel: 201-7317
Tel: 201-7308 (Commer. office)
Fax: 230-2365
Telex: 413398

Azerbaijan
ul. Stanislavskovo 16
Tel: 229-1649

Bangladesh
Zemledelcheskiy per 6
Tel: 246-7900
Fax: 248-3185
Telex: 413196

Belarus
ul. Maroseika 17/6
Tel: 924-7031

Belgium
ul. Malaya Molchanovka 7
Tel: 203-0531
Fax: 291-6005
Telex: 413471

Benin
Uspenskiy per. 4a
Tel: 299-2360
Fax: 200-0226
Telex: 413645

Bolivia
Lopukhinskiy per. 5
Tel: 201-2508
Telex: 413356

Brazil
ul. Gertsena 54
Tel: 290-4022
Telex: 413476

Bulgaria
ul. Mosfilmovskaya 66
Tel: 147-9000
Tel: 147-9007 (Commer. office)

Canada
Staronyshenny per. 23
Tel: 241-5882
Fax: 241-4400
Telex: 413401

Chile
ul. Tunosti 11, kor. 1
Tel: 373-9176
Telex: 413751

China
ul. Druzhby 6
Tel: 143-1540
Tel: 938-2005 (Commer. office)

Colombia
ul. Burdenko 20
Tel: 248-3042
Fax: 248-3025
Telex: 413206

Costa Rica
Rublevskoye sh. 26, kv. 58-59
Tel: 415-4042
Telex: 413963

Cuba
ul. Mosfilmovskaya 40
Tel: 147-4312
Tel: 290-6230 (Commer. office)

Cyprus
ul. Gertsena 51
Tel: 290-2154
Fax: 200-1254
Telex: 4134777

Czech Republic/Slovakia
ul. Yuliusa Fuchika 12/14
Tel: 251-0540
Tel: 250-8403 (Commer. office)

Denmark
per. Ostrovskovo 9
Tel: 201-7860
Tel: 238-6930 (Commer. office)
Fax: 201-7860
Fax: 230-2072 (Commer. office)
Telex: 413378
Telex: 413928 (Ccommer. office)

Ecuador
Gorokhovskiy per. 12
Tel: 261-5544
Telex: 413174

Egypt
Skatertny per. 25
Tel: 291-6283
Tel: 243-0363 (Commer. office)
Fax: 291-4609
Fax: 230-2114 (Commer. office)
Telex: 413276
Telex: 413200 (Commer. office)

Estonia
Kalashny per. 8
Tel: 290-3178

Ethiopia
Orlovo-Davydovskiy per. 6
Tel: 230-2036
Telex: 413980

Finland
Kropotkinskiy per. 15/17
Tel: 246-4027
Fax: 230-2721
Telex: 413405

France
ul. Dimitrova 45
Tel: 236-0003
Tel: 237-8740 (Commer. office)
Telex: 413290
Telex: 413325 (Commer. office)

Georgia
ul. Paliashvili 6
Tel: 290-6902

Germany
ul. Bolshaya Gruzinskaya 17
Tel: 252-5521
Fax: 253-9276
Telex: 413412

Greece
ul. Stanislavskovo 4
Tel: 290-2274
Tel: 290-4753 (Commer. office)
Fax: 200-1252
Telex: 413472

Hungary
ul. Mosfilmovskaya 62
Tel: 148-8611
Tel: 252-0001 (Commer. office)
Fax: 143-4625
Telex: 414428

Iceland
Khlebny per. 28
Tel: 290-4742
Fax: 200-1264
Telex: 413181

India
ul. Obukha 6-8
Tel: 297-0820
Telex: 413409

Indonesia
ul. Novokuznetskaya 12
Tel: 231-9549
Fax: 230-2213
Telex: 413444

Iran
Pokrovskiy bul. 7
Tel: 227-5788
Telex: 413493

Iraq
ul. Pogodinskaya 12
Tel: 246-5506
Tel: 246-4061 (Economic Bureau)
Fax: 230-2922
Telex: 413184

Ireland
Grokholskiy per. 5
Tel: 288-4101
Tel: 280-6500 (Commer. office)
Telex: 413204
Telex: 413512

Israel
ul. Bolshaya Ordynka 56
Tel: 238-1346
Fax: 238-1346

Italy
ul. Vesnina 5
Tel: 241-1533
Tel: 248-3152 (Commer. office)
Fax: 253-9289
Telex: 413453

Japan
Kalashny per. 12
Tel: 291-8500
Telex: 413141

Jordan
per. Sadovskikh 3
Tel: 299-9564
Fax: 299-4354
Telex: 413447

Kazakhstan
Chistoprudny bul. 3a
Tel: 208-9852

Kenya
ul. Bolshaya Ordynka 70
Tel: 237-3462
Fax: 230-2340
Telex: 413495

Kyrgyzstan
ul. Bolshaya Ordynka 64
Tel: 237-4882

Korea (North)
ul. Mosfilmovskaya 72
Tel: 143-6249
Tel: 1436241 (Commer. Office)

Telex: 413272
Telex: 413279 (Commer. Office)

Korea (South)
ul. Gubinka 14
Tel: 937-8-2802

Kuwait
3rd Neopalimovskiy per. 13/5
Tel: 248-5001
Fax: 230-2423
Telex: 413353

Laos
ul. Bolshaya Ordynka 18/1
Tel: 233-2035
Tel: 231-2862 (Commer. Office)
Telex: 413101

Latvia
ul. Chaplygina
Tel: 925-2707

Lebanon
ul. Sadovaya-Samotechnaya 14
Tel: 200-0022
Fax: 200-3222
Telex: 413120

Libya
ul. Mosfilmovskaya 38
Tel: 143-0345
Fax: 143-7644
Telex: 143443

Lithuania
ul. Pisemskovo 10
Tel: 291-2643

Luxembourg
Khruschevskiy per. 3
Tel: 202-2171
Fax: 200-5243
Telex: 413131

Madagascar
Kursovoy per. 5
Tel: 291-0214
Telex: 413370

Malaysia
ul. Mosfilmovskaya 50
Tel: 147-1514
Fax: 147-1526
Telex: 413478

Malta
Koroviy Val 7, kv. 219
Tel: 237-1939
Fax: 237-2158
Telex: 413919

Mauritania
ul. Bolshaya Ordynka 66
Tel: 237-3792
Telex: 413439

Mexico
ul. Shchukina 4
Tel: 201-4848
Fax: 230-2042
Telex: 413125

Moldova
Kuznetsky most 18
Tel: 928-5405

Mongolia
ul. Pisemskovo 11
Tel: 290-6792
Tel: 229-5407 (Commer. Office)

Morocco
per. Ostrovskovo 8
Tel: 201-7395
Fax: 230-2067
Telex: 413446

Mozambique
ul. Gilyarovskovo 20
Tel: 284-4007
Telex: 413369

Myanmar (Burma)
ul. Gertsena 41
Tel: 291-0534
Fax: 291-0163
Telex: 413403

Namibia
ul. Konyushkovskaya 28, kv. 10
Tel: 252-2471
Fax: 253-9610
Telex: 413567

Nepal
2nd Neopalimovskiy per. 14/7
Tel: 244-0215
Telex: 413292

Netherlands
Kalashny per. 6
Tel: 291-2999
Fax: 200-5264
Telex: 413442

New Zealand
ul. Vorovskovo 44
Tel: 290-1277
Fax: 290-4666
Telex: 413187

Nicaragua
ul. Mosfilmovskaya 50, kor. 1
Tel: 938-2701
Telex: 413264

Niger
Kursovoy per. 7/31
Tel: 290-0101
Fax: 200-4251
Telex: 413180

Norway
ul. Voroskovo 7
Tel: 290-3872
Tel: 202-3484 (Commer. Office)
Fax: 200-1221
Telex: 413488
Telex: 413563 (Commer. Office)

Oman
per. Obukha 6
Tel: 928-6418
Fax: 975-2174
Telex: 411432

Pakistan
ul. Sadovaya-Kudrinskaya 17
Tel: 250-3991
Telex: 413194

Palestine
Kropotkinskiy per. 26
Tel: 201-4340
Telex: 413126

Peru
Smolenskiy bul. 22/14, kv. 15
Tel: 248-7738
Tel: 246-6836 (Commer. Office)

Philippines
Karmanitskiy per. 6
Tel: 241-0563
Fax: 230-2534
Telex: 413156

Poland
ul. Klimashkina
Tel: 255-0017
Tel: 254-3421 (Commer. Office)
Fax: 254-2286
Telex: 414362

Portugal
Botanicheskiy per. 1
Tel: 230-2435
Fax: 280-3134
Telex: 413254

Qatar
Koroviy Val 7, kv. 197-8
Tel: 230-1577
Fax: 230-2240
Telex: 413728

Romania
ul. Mosfilmovskaya 64
Tel: 143-0424

Singapore
per. Voyevodina
Tel: 241-3702
Fax: 230-2937
Telex: 413128

Somalia
Spasopeskovskaya pl. 8
Tel: 241-8624
Telex: 413164

Spain
ul. Gertsena 50/8
Tel: 202-2160
Tel: 202-7772 (Commer. Office)
Fax: 200-1230
Fax: 200-1226 (Commer. Office)
Telex: 413220
Telex: 413900 (Commer. Office)

Sri Lanka
ul. Schepkina 24
Tel: 288-1651
Telex: 413140

Sudan
ul. Vorovskovo 9
Tel: 290-3993
Telex: 413448

Sweden
ul. Mosfilmovskaya 60
Tel: 147-9009
Fax: 147-8788
Telex: 413410

Switzerland
per. Stopani 2/5
Tel: 925-5322
Fax: 200-1728
Telex: 413418

Syria
Mansurovskiy per. 4
Tel: 203-1521
Telex: 413145

Tajikistan
Skaterny per. 19
Tel: 290-6102

Tanzania
ul. Pyatnitskaya 33
Tel: 231-8146
Fax: 230-2968
Telex: 413352

Thailand
Eropskinskiy per. 3
Tel: 201-4893
Telex: 413309

Tunisia
ul. Kachalova 28/1
Tel: 291-2858
Telex: 413449

Turkey
Vadkovskiy per. 7/37
Tel: 972-6500
Tel: 972-6500 (Commer. Office)
Fax: 200-2223
Telex: 413731
Telex: 413148 (Commer. Office)

Turkmenia
per. Adsokova 22
Tel: 291-6636

Uganda
per. Sadovskikh 5
Tel: 251-0060
Telex: 413473

Ukraine
ul. Stanislavskovo 18
Tel: 229-2804

United Arab Emirates
ul. Olaf Palme 4
Tel: 147-6286
Telex: 413547

United Kingdom
nab. Morisa Toreza 14
Tel: 231-8511
Tel: 248-2001 (Commer. Office)
Telex: 413341
Telex: 413314 (Commer. Office)

United States of America
Novinsky bul. 19/23
121834 Moscow
Tel: 252-2451
Telex: (871) 413160
Mailing address:
U.S. Embassy Moscow (MOS)
APO AE New York 09862
Commercial Office:
Novinsky bul. 15
Tel: 255-4848; (502) 224-1105
Fax: 230-2101; (502) 224-1106
Telex: (871) 413205

Uruguay
Lomonosovskiy pr. 38
Tel: 143-0401
Fax: 938-2045
Telex: 413238

Uzbekistan
Pogorelskiy per. 12
Tel: 230-0076

Venezuela
ul. Yermolova 13/15
Tel: 299-9621
Fax: 200-0248
Telex: 413119

Vietnam
ul. B. Pirogovskaya 13
Tel: 245-0925
Tel: 250-4852 (Commer. Office)

Yemen
2nd Neopalimovskiy per. 6
Tel: 246-1814
Telex: 413214

Yugoslavia (Serbia)
ul. Mosfilmovskaya 46
Tel: 147-4106
Commercial Office, INA Commerce,
Krasnopresnenskaya nab. 12, office 107
Tel: 253-1253
Fax: 253-1270
Telex: 414451

OTHER FOREIGN CONSULATES IN THE NIS

St. Petersburg

Bulgaria
ul. Ryleeva 27
Tel:	273-6969
	273-4018
	273-7347
Fax:	272-5718

China
V.O. 3rd Line 12
Tel:	218-1721
	213-7953
	218-3492

Czech Republic/ Slovakia
ul. Tverskaya 5
Tel:	271-0459
	271-4615
	271-3065
Fax:	271-4615

Cuba
ul. Ryleeva 37
Tel:	272-5303
	273-7885
Fax:	272-7506

Denmark
Kamennyi Ostrov
Bolshaya Alleya 13
Tel:	234-3755
Fax:	119-3755

Finland
ul. Chaikovskovo 71
Tel:	272-4256
	272-1421
Fax:	272-1421

France
nab. r. Moika 15
Tel:	314-1443
	312-1180
Fax:	311-3225

Germany
Furshtadskaya ul. (formerly
    ul. Petra Lavrova) 39
Tel:	273-5586
	273-5731
Fax:	279-3242

Hungary
ul. Marata 15
Tel:	312-6458
	312-6753
	312-6786
Fax:	312-6432

Italy
Teatral'naya pl. 10
Tel:	312-2896
	312-3217
Fax:	114-3862

Japan
nab. r. Moika 29
Tel: 314-1434
         312-1133
Fax: 311-4891

Mongolia
Leninskii pr. 115
Tel: 153-8051

Netherlands
pr. Engels 101
Tel: 544-4900
Fax: 554-3619

Poland
ul. 5-aya Sovietskaya 14
Tel: 274-4170
Fax: 274-4318

South Africa (RSA)
nab. r. Moika 11
Tel: 110-6367
Fax: 119-0302

Sweden
V.O. 10-Liniya, 11
Tel: 218-3526
         218-3528
         218-3527
Fax: 213-7198

United Kingdom
pl. Proletarskoy Diktatury 5
Tel: 119-6036
Fax: 119-6037

OTHER USEFUL COORDINATES IN THE NIS

Moscow

American Business Club
c/o Dresser Marketing
ul. Lunacharskovo
7 Floor 6, Apt. 16/17
Tel: 202-1229
Telex: 413337 CME SU

British-Soviet Chamber of Commerce
Krasnopresnenskaya nab.,
    Office 1904
Tel: 253-2554,253-7704

Canada-Russia Business Council
Chapayevskiy per. 8
Tel: 157-7619

Finnish-Russian Chamber of
    Commerce
Pokrovskiy bul. 4/17
Tel: 925-9001, 925-9092

Franco-Russian Chamber of
    Commerce
Pokrovskiy bul. 4/17, kv.3
Tel: 297-9092

Hungarian Chamber of Commerce
Tel: 253-2921

Inform VES
Ovchinnikovskaya nab. 18/1
Tel: 220-1606

Inter-Republican Universal
    Trade Exchange
Tel: 208-6681

Italian-Russian Chamber of
    Commerce
ul. Vesnina 7
Tel: 241-5729, 241-6217, 241-6517

Japan-Russia Trade Association
ul. Mytnaya 1
Tel: 237-2465

Ministry of Foreign Economic
    Relations
Smolskaya-Sennaya 32-34, 6th pod.
Tel: 244-1320

Moscow Central Customs
ul. Marinoy Roshchy 12
Tel: 971-1178, 971-1196
Fax: 971-0105

Moscow Chamber of Commerce
ul. Chekhova 13-17
Tel: 299-7612

Russian Agency for International
  Cooperation and Development
Vozdvizhenka ul., 18
Tel: 290-0903
Fax: 975-2253

Russian Chamber of Commerce and
    Industry
ul. Ilyinka 6
Tel: 924-5645, 923-4323
ul. Kuybysheva 6
Tel: 921-0811

Russian Ministry of Foreign
  Economic Relations
Department of Trade and Economic
  Relations with the Americas
32/34 Smolenskaya-Sennaya
Tel: 244-3726

United States Commercial Office
Novinskiy bul. 12-15
Tel: 255-4848

Trade and Economic Council
3 Shevchenko nab.
Tel: 243-5470, 243-5621

St. Petersburg

St. Petersburg Joint Ventures
    Association
ul. Plekhanova 36
Tel. 312-7954
Fax: 315-9470
Telex: 121132 JVLENSU

U.S. Foreign Commercial Service
Hotelship Peterhof
Pier Makarov Embankment
Vasilievsky Ostrov,
Tel: 210-8252
Satellite Fax: 00873-140-1452
Local Fax: 213-6312
Telex: 00583140452

Tallinn

Estonian-American Chamber of Commerce
Toom-Kooli 17
200106 Tallinn
Tel: (358 142) 444 661
Fax: (358 142) 443 656
Telex: (871) 173193

EMBASSIES OF THE NEWLY INDEPENDENT STATES IN THE UNITED STATES

Embassy of Armenia
1660 L Street, NW
Suite 210
Washington, DC 20036
Tel: (202) 628-5766
Fax: 628-5769

Embassy of Belarus
1619 New Hampshire Ave., NW
Washington, DC 20036
Tel: (202) 986-1606
Fax: (202) 638-3058

Embassy of Kyrgyzstan
1511 K St., NW
Washington, DC 20005
Tel: (202) 347-3732
Fax: (202) 347-3718

Embassy of Latvia
4325 17th St., NW
Washington, D.C. 20011
Tel: (202) 726-8213
       (202) 726-6757
Fax: (202) 726-6785
       (202) 829-0644

Embassy of Lithuania
2622 16th St., NW
Washington, D.C. 20009
Tel: (202) 234-5860
       (202) 234-2639
Fax: (202) 328-0466

Embassy of the Russian Federation
1125 16th Street, NW
Washington, DC 20036
Tel: (202) 628-7554
       (202) 347-1347 (press office)
       (202) 737-7915 (Ambassador's
       office)
       (202) 347-0333 (Economic
       office)
Fax: 202) 347-5028

Embassy of Ukraine
3350 M St., NW
Washington, D.C. 20007
Tel: (202) 333-0606
Fax: (202) 333-0817

Consulates

Estonia
Estonian Consulate General
630 5th Avenue
Suite 2415
New York, NY 10111
Tel: (212) 247-1450
Fax: (212) 262-0893

Latvia
Latvian Consul (honorary)
1149 South Broadway Street
Suite 812
Los Angeles, CA 90015
Tel: (213) 765-2251
Fax: (213) 765-2696

Lithuania
Consulate of Lithuania
6500 South Pulaski Road
Chicago, IL 60629
Tel: (312) 582-5478
Fax: (312) 582-0961

Russian Federation
Consular Office of the Russian
   Federation
1825 Phelps Place, NW
Washington, DC 20008
Tel: (202) 939-8907
   (9:30 A.M. - 12:30 P.M.)
Fax: (202) 483-7579

Russian Federation
Consulate of the Russian Federation
2790 Green Street
San Francisco, CA 94123
Tel: (415) 202-9800
Fax: (415) 929-0306

Russian Federation
Consulate of the Russian Federation
9 East 91st Street
New York, NY 10128
Tel: (212) 348-0926
Fax: (212) 831-9162

Russian Federation
Consulate of the Russian Federation
2323 Westin Building
2001 Sixth Avenue
Seattle, WA 98121
Tel: (206) 728-1910
Fax: (206) 728-1871

OTHER USEFUL COORDINATES IN THE UNITED STATES

American-Latvian Association
P. O. Box 4578
Rockville, MD 20849-4578
Tel: (301) 340-1914
       (301) 340-8174
Fax: (301) 762-5438

Belarus Mission to the U.N.
136 East 67th Street
New York, NY 10021
Tel: (212) 535-3420
Fax: (212) 743-4810

Estonian-American Chamber of
    Commerce
269 West 71st St.
New York, NY 10023
Tel: (212) 496-2700
Fax: (212) 724-3393

Estonian-American National Council
243 East 34th Street
New York, NY 10016
Tel: (212) 685-0776
Fax: (212) 683-4418
Washington Office:
P. O. Box 11134
Arlington, VA 22210
Tel: (703) 522-0345
Fax: (703) 243-5978

U.S. Department of Commerce
14th St. and Constitution, NW
Washington, DC 20230
Tel: (202) 482-4655
Fax: (202) 482-2293

International Monetary Fund
1 United Nations Plaza
Room 1140
New York, New York 10017
Tel: (212) 963-6009
Washington Office:
700 19th St., NW
Washington, DC 20431

Lithuanian-American Community
National Office:
2715 East Alagare
Philadelphia, PA 19134
Tel: (215) 739-9353
Fax: (215) 739-6587
Chicago Office:
2713 West 71st Street
Chicago, IL 60629
Tel: (312) 436-0197
Fax: (312) 436-6909

Lithuanian-American Council, Inc.
6500 South Pulaski Road
Chicago, IL 60629
Tel: (312) 735-6677
Fax: (312) 735-8793

Russian Mission to the U.N.
136 East 67th Street
New York, NY 10021
Tel: (212) 861-4900/4
Fax: (212) 628-0252

Russian-American Chamber
731 8th Street, S.E.
Washington, D.C. 20003
Tel: (202)546-3275
Fax: (202)546-4784

Trade Mission of the Russian
  Federation to the U.S.
2001 Connecticut Avenue, NW
Washington, DC 20008
Tel: (202) 232-5988
        (202) 234-7170
Fax: (202) 232-2917

Ukranian Mission to the U.N.
136 East 67th Street
New York, NY 10021
Tel: (212) 535-3418
Fax: (212) 288-5361

US Agency For International
  Development (USAID)
USAID, SA-2
Washington, DC 20523-0029
Tel: (202) 663-2660 or
        1-800-USAID-4-U
Fax: (202) 663-2149

US Department of Agriculture
  (USDA)
USDA, Rm. 4079
Washington, DC 20250-1000
Tel: (202) 720-3573
Fax: (202) 690-0727

US Department of State
2201 C St., NW
Washington, DC 20520
Tel: (202) 647-2626
Fax: (202) 647-2636

US Department of the Treasury
1500 Pennsylvania Ave., NW
Washington, DC 20220
Tel: (202) 622-2130
Fax: (202) 622-2308

US Export/Import Bank (Eximbank)
811 Vermont Ave., NW
Washington, DC 20571
Tel: (202) 566-8190
Fax: (202) 566-7524

US Information Agency (USIA)
301 4th St., SW
Washington, DC 20547
Tel: (202) 619-5057
Fax: (202) 619-6821

US Overseas Private Investment
  Corporation (OPIC)
1100 New York Avenue, NW
Washington, DC 20527
Tel: 202) 336-8423 (Legal Affairs)
        (202) 336-8589 (Insurance)
        (202) 336-8474 (Finance)
        (202) 336-8620 (Investor
          Services)

US Trade and Development Program
  (TDP)
SA-16, Rm. 309
Washington, DC 20523-1602
Tel: (703) 875-4357
Fax: (703) 875-4009

U.S.-Russia Business Council
1701 Pennsylvania Avenue, N.W.
Suite 650
Washington, D.C. 20006
Tel: (202) 956-7670
Fax: (202) 956-7674

Vneshekonombank
527 Madison Avenue
New York, NY 10022
Tel: (212) 421-8660
Fax: (212) 421-8677

	A	

abandon (v)	отказаться от претензий	*(at-ka-ZAH-tsa at pre-TEN-zeey)*
abandon	абандон	*(a-ban-DON)*
abatement (reduction)	уменьшение	*(oo-men-SHEH-NEE-ye)*
abatement (suspension)	аннулирование	*(an-noo-LEE-ra-va-nee-ye)*
ability-to-pay concept	формула кредитоспособности	*(FOHR-moo-la kre-dee-ta-spa-SOB-na-stee)*
above-ground retoring	наземная перегонка	*(na-ZEM-na-ya pe-re-GON-ka)*
above mentioned	вышеупомянутый	*(VEE-she-oo-pa-MYAH-noo-tee)*
above par	выше номинальной цены	*(VEE-she na-mee-NAHL-nay tse-NEE)*
above-the-line	выше нормы	*(VEE-she NOHR-mee)*
above-the-line (short term)	краткосрочно выше нормы	*(krat-ka-SROCH-na VEE-she NOHR-mee)*
absentee owner	собственник, абсентеист	*(SOPST-ven-neek, ap-sen-te-EEST)*
absenteeism	абсентеизм	*(ap-sen-te-EEZM)*
absorb (v)	покрывать/покрыть	*(pa-kree-VAHT/pa-KREET)*
absorb the loss (v)	покрывать/покрыть убыток	*(pa-kree-VAHT/pa-KREET oo-BEE-tak)*
absorption costing	калькуляция стоимости с учётом убытков	*(kal-koo-LYAH-tsee-ya STOH-ee-ma-stee)*
accelerated depreciation	ускоренная амортизация	*(oos-KOH-ren-na-ya a-mar-tee-ZAH-tsee-ya)*
accelerating premium	ускоренная премия	*(oos-KOH-ren-na-ya PREH-mee-ya)*
acceleration clause	оговорка об ускорении	*(a-ga-VOHR-ka ab oos-ka-REH-nee-ee)*
accept (v)	принимать/принять	*(pree-nee-MAHT/pree-NYAHT)*
acceptable quality level	удовлетворительный уровень качества	*(oo-dav-le-tva-REE-tel-nee OO-ra-ven KAH-ches-tva)*

acceptance agreement	договор об акцепте	*(da-ga-VOHR ab ak-TSEP-te)*
acceptance bill	акцептованный вексель	*(ak-tsep-TOH-van-nee VEK-sel)*
acceptance (bill of agreement)	акцепт	*(ak-TSEPT)*
acceptance credit	кредитный	*(kre-DEET-nee)*
acceptance house	банк-акцептант	*(bahnk-ak-tsep-TAHNT)*
acceptance sampling	отбор	*(at-BOR)*
acceptor	акцептант	*(ak-tsep-TAHNT)*
accession rate	ставка присоединения	*(STAHF-ka pree-sa-e-dee-NEH-nee-ya)*
accident damage	аварийное повреждение	*(a-va-REEY-na-ye pav-re-ZHDEH-nee-ye)*
accommodation bill	дружеский акцепт	*(DROO-zhes-kee ak-TSEPT)*
accommodation credit	дружеский кредит	*(DROO-zhes-kee kre-DEET)*
accommodation endorsement	дружеское жиро	*(DROO-zhes-ka-ye zhee-ROH)*
accommodation paper	денежный вексель	*(DEH-nezh-nee VEK-sel)*
accommodation parity	дружественный паритет	*(DROO-zhes-tven-nee pa-ree-TET)*
accommodation platform	согласительная платформа	*(sa-gla-SEE-tel-na-ya plat-FOHR-ma)*
accompanied goods	сопровождающие товары	*(sa-pra-vazh-DAH-yoo-shchee-ye ta-VAH-ree)*
accord and satisfaction	обоюдное согласие и взаимоудовлетворение	*(a-ba-YOOD-na-ye sa-GLAH-see-ye ee vza-EE-ma-oo-dav-let-va-REH-nee-ye)*
account	счёт	*(schyot)*
account balance	баланс текущих расчётов	*(ba-LAHNS tee-KOO-shcheekh ra-SHCHYOH-taf)*
account day	день расчёта	*(den ra-SHCHYOH-ta)*
account executive	исполнитель на счету	*(ees-pal-NEE-tel na shche-TOO)*

account for (v)	предусматривать в смете	*(pree-doos-MAHT-ree-vat v v SMEH-te)*
account number	номер счёта	*(NOH-mer SHCHYOH-ta)*
accountable	ответственный	*(at-VET-stven-nee)*
accountant	бухгалтер	*(bookh-GAHL-ter)*
accountant, chief	главный бухгалтер	*(GLAHV-nee bookh-GAHL-ter)*
accountant (CPA)	высококвалифицирован-ный бухгалтер	*(vee-SOH-ka-kva-lee-fee-TSEE-ra-van-nee bookh-GAHL-ter)*
accounting, cost	калькуляция издержек производства	*(kal-koo-LYAH-tsee-ya eez-DEHR-zhek pra-eez-VOT-stva)*
accounting department	бухгалтерский отдел	*(bookh-GAHL-ter-skee at-DEL)*
accounting, management	оперативный учёт	*(a-pe-ra-TEEV-nee oo-CHYOT)*
accounting method	порядок учёта	*(pa-RYAH-dak oo-CHYOH-ta)*
accounting period	балансовый срок	*(ba-LAHN-sa-vee srok)*
accounting principles	принципы бухгалтерского дела	*(PREEN-tsee-pee bookh-GAHL-ter-ska-va DEH-la)*
accounts payable	счета, подлежащие оплате	*(shche-TAH pad-le-ZHAH-shchee-ye ap-LAH-te)*
accounts receivable	счета дебиторов	*(shche-TAH de-BEE-ta-raf)*
accretion	прирост	*(pree-ROST)*
accrual	нарастание	*(na-ras-TAH-nee-ye)*
accrue	нарастать	*(na-ras-TAHT)*
accrued assets	наросшие активы	*(na-ROSH-shee-ye ak-TEE-vee)*
accrued depreciation	наросшая амортизация	*(na-ROSH-sha-ya a-mar-tee-ZAH-tsee-ya)*
accrued expenses	наросшие расходы	*(na-ROSH-shee-ye ras-KHOH-dee)*
accrued interest	наросшие проценты	*(na-ROSH-shee-ye pra-TSEN-tee)*
accrued revenue	наросший доход	*(na-ROSH-shee da-KHOT)*
accrued taxes	наросшие налоги	*(na-ROSH-shee-ye na-LOH-ghee)*

A

accumulated depreciation	накопленная амортизация	*(na-KOP-len-na-ya a-mar-tee-ZAH-tsee-ya)*
accumulation	накопление	*(na-ka-PLEH-nee-ye)*
acetic acid	уксусная кислота	*(OOK-soos-na-ya kees-la-TAH)*
acid	кислота	*(KEES-la-ta)*
acidic (soil)	кислая почва	*(KEES-la-ya POCH-va)*
acidification	подкисление	*(pat-kee-SLEH-nee-ye)*
acid-test ratio	коэффициент ликвидности	*(ka-ef-fee-tsee-ENT leek-VEED-na-stee)*
acid-tolerant	кислотоустойчивый	*(kees-LOH-ta-oos-TOY-chee-vee)*
acknowledge (v)	признавать/признать	*(preez-na-VAHT/preez-NAHT)*
acknowledgement of payment	подтверждение акцепта	*(pat-tver-ZHDEH-nee-ye ak-TSEP-ta)*
acoustic coupler	акустическая муфта	*(a-koos-TEE-ches-ka-ya MOOF-ta)*
acquire (v)	приобретать/приобрести	*(pree-ab-re-TAHT/pree-ab-re-STEE)*
acquired rights	приобретённые права	*(pree-ab-re-TYON-nee-ye pra-VAH)*
acquisition	приобретение	*(pree-ab-re-TEH-nee-ye)*
acquisition profile	описание приобретения	*(a-pee-SAH-nee-ye pree-ab-re-TEH-nee-ya)*
acre	акр	*(ahkr)*
acreage allotment	земельный участок	*(zee-MEHL-nee oo-CHAHS-tak)*
acronym	акроним	*(ak-ROH-neem)*
across the board	общая	*(OP-shcha-ya)*
act of God	стихийное бедствие	*(stee-KHEEY-na-ye BET-stvee-ye)*
action, legal	правовой акт	*(pra-va-VOY akt)*
active account	действительный счёт	*(dey-STVEE-tel-nee shchot)*
active assets	действительные активы	*(dey-STVEE-tel-nee-ye ak-TEE-vee)*
active debts	действительные долги	*(dey-STVEE-tel-nee-ye dal-GHEE)*

active gas	активный газ (подземного газохранилища)	*(ak-TEEV-nee gahs [pad-ZEM-na-va ga-za-khra-NEE-lee-shcha)*
active reserves	активные запасы	*(ak-TEEV-nee-ye za-PAH-see)*
actual cash value	фактическая стоимость в наличии	*(fak-TEE-ches-ka-ya STOH-ee-mast v na-LEE-chee-ee)*
actual costs	фактические расходы	*(fak-TEE-ches-kee-ye ras-KHOH-dee)*
actual liability	фактическая ответственность	*(fak-TEE-ches-ka-ya at-VET-stven-nast)*
actual total loss	реальный общий убыток	*(re-AHL-nee OP-shchee oo-BEE-tak)*
actuary	актуа́рий	*(ak-too-AH-reey)*
ad valorem duty	адвалорная пошлина	*(ad-va-LOHR-na-ya POSH-lee-na)*
add-on sales	добавочные продажи	*(da-BAH-vach-nee-ye pra-DAH-zhee)*
addendum	адендум	*(a-DEN-doom)*
additions to reserves	прирост запасов	*(pree-ROST za-PAH-saf)*
address	адрес	*(AHD-res)*
adjudge (v)	решать/решить	*(re-SHAT/re-SHEET)*
adjudication	решение	*(re-SHEH-nee-ye)*
adjust (v)	изменять/изменить	*(eez-me-NYAHT/eez-me-NEET)*
adjust (v) correct	исправлять/исправить	*(ees-prav-LYAHT/ees-PRAH-veet)*
adjusted CIF price	исправленная цена СИФ	*(ees-PRAHV-len-na-ya tse-NAH seef)*
adjusted gross income	исправленный валовой доход	*(ees-PRAHV-len-nee va-la-VOY da-KHOT)*
adjusted rate	исправленная ставка	*(ees-PRAHV-len-na-ya STAHF-ka)*
adjusting entry	исправленная статья в балансе	*(ees-PRAHV-len-na-ya sta-TYAH v ba-LAHN-se)*
administration	администрация	*(ad-mee-nee-STRAH-tsee-ya)*
administrative	административный	*(ad-mee-nee-stra-TEEV-nee)*

administrative expenses	административные расходы	*(ad-mee-nee-stra-TEEV-nee-ye ras-KHOH-dee)*
administrator	администратор	*(ad-mee-nee-STRAH-tar)*
advance (v) money	авансировать	*(a-van-SEE-ra-vat)*
advance (v) (promote)	повышать/повысить	*(pa-vee-SHAHT)*
advance freight	аванс фрахта	*(a-VAHNS FRAHKH-ta)*
advance notice	предварительное извещение	*(pred-va-REE-tel-na-ye eez-ve-SHCHEH-nee-ye)*
advance payment	платёж авансом	*(pla-TYOZH a-VAHN-sam)*
advance refunding	предварительное возмещение	*(pred-va-REE-tel-na-ye vaz-me-SHCHEH-nee-ye)*
adverse balance	пассивный баланс	*(pas-SEEV-nee ba-LAHNS)*
advertisement	реклама	*(rek-LAH-ma)*
advertising agency	рекламное агентство	*(rek-LAHM-na-ye a-GHENT-stva)*
advertising budget	рекламный бюджет	*(rek-LAHM-nee byood-ZHET)*
advertising campaign	рекламная кампания	*(rek-LAHM-na-ya kam-PAH-nee-ya)*
advertising expenses	рекламные расходы	*(rek-LAHM-nee-ye ras-KHOH-dee)*
advertising manager	рекламный менеджер	*(rek-LAHM-nee MEH-ned-zhehr)*
advertising media	рекламные средства	*(rek-LAHM-nee-ye SRET-stva)*
advertising rate	ставка платы за рекламу	*(STAHF-ka PLAH-ty za rek-LAH-mee)*
advertising research	исследования по рекламе	*(ees-SLEH-da-va-nee-ya pa rek-LAH-me)*
advice note	авизо	*(a-VEE-za)*
advise (v)	авизовать	*(a-vee-za-VAHT)*
advisory council	совещательный совет	*(sa-ve-SHCHAH-tel-nee sa-VEHT)*
advisory service	совещательное обслуживание	*(sa-ve-SHCHAH-tel-na-ye ap-SLOO-zhee-va-nee-ye)*
aeration	аэрация	*(a-eh-RAH-tsee-ya)*
aerodynamic balance	аэродинамические весы	*(AH-e-ra-dee-na-MEE-ches-kee-ye ve-SEE)*

A

aerodynamics	аэродинамика	*(AH-e-ra-dee-NAH-mee-ka)*
aeronautics	аэронавтика	*(AH-e-ra-NAHF-tee-ka)*
affidavit	письменное показание под присягой	*(PEES-men-na-ye pa-ka-ZAH-nee-ye pat pree-SYAH-gay)*
affiliate	дочерняя компания	*(da-CHEHR-nya-ya kam-PAH-nee-ya)*
affirmative action	утвердительное действие	*(oo-tver-DEE-tel-na-ye DEY-stvee-ye)*
affreightment	фрахтование	*(frakh-ta-VAH-nee-ye)*
afloat (debt-free)	(платежеспособный)	*(pla-te-zhe-spa-SOB-nee)*
afloat (in circulation)	(в обращении)	*(vab-ra-SHCHEH-nee-ee)*
after-burner	форсажная камера	*(far-SAHZH-na-ya KAH-me-ra)*
after-hours trading	круглосуточные биржевые операции	*(kroog-la-SOO-tach-nee-ye beer-zhe-VEE-ye a-pe-RAH-tsee-ee)*
after-sales service	обслуживание после продажи товара	*(ap-SLOO-zhee-va-nee-ye POS-le pra-DAH-zhee ta-VAH-ra)*
after-tax real rate of return	реальный доход после вычета налогов	*(re-AHL-nee da-KHOT POS-le VEE-che-ta na-LOH-gaf)*
against all risks	против всех рисков	*(PROH-teev fsekh REES-kaf)*
agency	агентство	*(a-GHENT-stva)*
agency fee	вознаграждение агентства	*(vaz-na-grazh-DEH-nee-ye a-GHENT-stva)*
agenda	повестка дня	*(pa-VEST-ka dnya)*
agent	агент	*(a-GHENT)*
aggregate demand	общий спрос	*(OP-shchee spros)*
aggregate risk	общий риск	*(OP-shchee reesk)*
aggregate supply	общее предложение	*(OP-shche-ye pred-la-ZHEH-nee-ye)*
agreement	соглашение	*(sa-gla-SHEH-nee-ye)*
agreement (written)	письменное соглашение	*(PEES-men-na-ye sa-gla-SHEH-nee-ye)*
agricultural engineering	агротехника	*(ag-ra-TEKH-nee-ka)*

A

agricultural paper	сельскохозяйственный бюллетень	*(sel-ska-kha-ZYAHY-stven-nee byool-le-TEN)*
agricultural products	сельскохозяйственные товары	*(sel-ska-kha-ZYAHY-stven-nee-ye ta-VAH-ree)*
agriculture	сельское хозяйство	*(SEL-ska-ye kha-ZYAHY-stva)*
AIDS	СПИД	*(speet)*
air express	срочная авиаперевозка	*(SROCH-na-ya AH-vee-a-pe-re-VOS-ka)*
air filter	воздушный фильтр	*(vaz-DOOSH-nee feeltr)*
air force	военно-воздушные силы (ВВС)	*(va-YEN-na-vaz-DOOSH-nee-ye SEE-lee [VEH-VEH-ES])*
air freight	авиафрахт	*(AH-vee-a-FRAHKHT)*
air navigation	аэронавигация	*(AH-e-ra-na-vee-GAH-tsee-ya)*
airplane	самолёт	*(sa-ma-LYOT)*
airport	аэропорт	*(AH-e-ra-POHRT)*
air-seasoned	воздушно-сухой	*(vaz-DOOSH-na-soo-KHOY)*
air shipment	авиаперевозка	*(AH-vee-a-pe-re-VOS-ka)*
alder	ольха	*(al-KHAH)*
alfalfa	люцерна	*(lyoo-TSEHR-na)*
algorithm	алгоритм	*(al-ga-REETM)*
alien corporation	иностранное общество акционеров	*(ee-na-STRAHN-na-ye OP-shche-stva ak-tsee-a-NEH-raf)*
alkaline (soil)	щелочная почва	*(shche-lach-NAH-ya POCH-va)*
alkalization	засоление	*(za-sa-LEH-nee-ye)*
allocation of costs	ассигнование расходов	*(as-see-gna-VAH-nee-ye ras-KHOH-daf)*
allocation of responsibilities	ассигнование ответственностей	*(as-see-gna-VAH-nee-ye at-VET-stven-na-stee)*
allocation, resource	ассигнование ресурсов	*(as-see-gna-VAH-nee-ye re-SOOHR-saf)*
allonge	аллонж	*(al-LONZH)*
allot (v)	распределять/распределить	*(ras-pre-de-LYAHT/ras-pre-dee-LEET)*

allotment	распределение	*(ras-pre-de-LEH-nee-ye)*
allotment letter	договор о распределении	*(da-ga-VOHR a ras-pre-de-LEH-nee-ee)*
allow (v)	разрешать/разрешить	*(raz-re-SHAHT/raz-re-SHEET)*
allowance, depreci-ation	ставка допустимой амортизации	*(STAHF-ka da-poos-TEE-may a-mar-tee-ZAH-tsee-ee)*
allowance (dis-count)	скидка	*(SKEET-ka)*
allowance (sub-sidy)	надбавка	*(nad-BAHF-ka)*
alloy steel	легированная сталь	*(le-GHEE-ra-van-na-ya stahl)*
alongside	вдоль	*(vdol)*
alteration	изменение	*(eez-me-NEH-nee-ye)*
alternating current	переменный ток	*(pe-re-MEN-nee tok)*
alternative order	альтернативный заказ	*(al-ter-na-TEEV-nee za-KAHS)*
alternator	синхронный генератор	*(seen-KHRON-nee ghe-ne-RAH-tar)*
altitude	высота	*(vee-sa-TAH)*
aluminum	алюминий	*(a-lyoo-MEE-neey)*
amalgamation	объединение	*(ab-ye-dee-NEH-nee-ye)*
amend (v)	изменять/изменить	*(eez-me-NYAHT/eez-me-NEET)*
amendment	изменение	*(eez-me-NEH-nee-ye)*
ammonia	аммиак	*(am-mee-AHK)*
amortisation	погашение в рассрочку	*(pa-ga-SHEH-nee-ye vras-SROCH-koo)*
amount	сумма	*(SOOM-ma)*
amount due	причитающаяся сумма	*(pree-chee-TAH-yu-shcha-ya-sya SOOM-ma)*
amplifier	усилитель	*(oo-see-LEE-tel)*
amplitude modula-tion (AM)	амплитудная модуляция	*(am-plee-TOOD-na-ya ma-doo-LYAH-tsee-ya)*
anaerobe	анаэробный микроорганизм	*(a-na-e-ROB-nee meek-ra-ar-ga-NEEZM)*

anaesthetic	анестезирующее средство	*(a-ne-ste-ZEE-roo-yoo-shche-ye SRET-stva)*
analog computer	аналоговая ЭВМ	*(a-NAH-la-ga-va-ya eh-veh-EM)*
analgesic	болеутоляющее	*(BOH-le-oo-ta-LYAH-yoo-shchee)*
analysis	анализ	*(a-NAH-lees)*
analysis, break-even	анализ безубыточности	*(a-NAH-lees be-zoo-BEE-tach-na-stee)*
analysis, competi-tor	анализ соперников	*(a-NAH-lees sa-PEHR-nee-kaf)*
analysis, cost	анализ издержек	*(a-NAH-lees eez-DEHR-zhek)*
analysis, cost-bene-fit	анализ рентабельности	*(a-NAH-lees ren-TAH-bel-na-stee)*
analysis, financial	анализ финансового состояния	*(a-NAH-lees fee-NAHN-sa-va-va sa-sta-YAH-nee-ya)*
analysis, functional	анализ деятельности	*(a-NAH-lees DEH-ya-tel-na-stee)*
analysis, input-out-put	анализ доходов и расходов	*(a-NAH-lees da-KHOH-daf ee ras-KHOH-daf)*
analysis, invest-ment	анализ капиталовложений	*(a-NAH-lees ka-pee-TAH-la-vla-ZHEH-neey)*
analysis, job	анализ работ	*(a-NAH-lees ra-BOT)*
analysis, needs	анализ требований	*(a-NAH-lees TREH-ba-va-neey)*
analysis of forest ecosystem	анализ экосистемы леса	*(a-NAH-lees e-ka-sees-TEH-mee LEH-sa)*
analysis, product	анализ качества продукции	*(a-NAH-lees KAH-ches-tva pra-DOOK-tsee-ye)*
analysis, profitabil-ity	анализ прибыльности	*(a-NAH-lees PREE-bil-na-stee)*
analysis, risk	анализ риска	*(a-NAH-lees REES-ka)*
analysis, sales	анализ доходов от продажи товара	*(a-NAH-lees da-KHOH-daf at pra-DAH-zhee ta-VAH-ra)*
analysis, systems	системный анализ	*(sees-TEM-nee a-NAH-lees)*
analyst	аналитик	*(a-na-LEE-teek)*
analytic chemistry	аналитическая химия	*(a-na-lee-TEE-ches-ka-ya KHEE-mee-ya)*

anchorage dues	якорная пошлина	*(YAH-kar-na-ya POSH-lee-na)*
ancillary operation	вспомогательная деятельность	*(fspa-ma-GAH-tel-na-ya DEH-ya-tel-nast)*
ankle boots	ботинки	*(ba-TEEN-kee)*
annealing	отжиг	*(OT-zhik)*
annual	годовой	*(ga-da-VOY)*
annual accounts	годовые счета	*(ga-da-VEE-ye shche-TAH)*
annual audit	годовая ревизорская проверка/ревизия	*(ga-da-VAH-ya re-vee-ZOHR-ska-ya pra-VEHR-ka)*
annual report	годовой отчёт	*(ga-da-VOY at-CHYOT)*
annuitant	получающий ежегодную ренту	*(pa-loo-CHAH-yoo-shchee ye-zhe-GOD-noo-yoo REN-too)*
annuity	аннуитет (ежегодная рента)	*(ye-zhe-GOD-na-ya REN-ta)*
antacid	антационное средство	*(an-ta-tsee-ON-na-ye SRET-stva)*
anti-dumping duty	антидемпинговая пошлина	*(AHN-tee-DEM-peen-ga-va-ya POSH-lee-na)*
anti-inflammatory	противовоспалительный	*(PROH-tee-va-vas-pa-LEE-tel-nee)*
antibiotic	антибиотик	*(an-tee-bee-OH-teek)*
anticoagulant	антикоагулянт	*(an-tee-koh-a-goo-LYAHNT)*
antidepressant	антидепрессант	*(an-tee-de-pres-SAHNT)*
antiseptic	антисептическое средство	*(an-tee-sep-TEE-ches-ka-ye SRET-stva)*
antitrust laws	антимонопольное законодательство	*(AHN-tee-ma-na-POL-na-ye za-ka-na-DAH-tel-stva)*
aphid	тля	*(tlyah)*
apiary	пасека	*(PAH-se-ka)*
apparel	одежда	*(a-DEZH-da)*
Apple	компания «Аппл»	*(kam-PAH-nee-ya "Apple")*
apple	яблоко	*(YAHB-la-ka)*
application form	анкета	*(an-KEH-ta)*
appointment (engagement)	встреча	*(FSTREH-cha)*

appointment (nom-ination)	назначение	*(na-zna-CHEH-nee-ye)*
appraisal	оценка	*(o-TSEN-ka)*
appraisal well	оценочная скважина	*(a-TSEN-nach-na-ya SKVAH-zhee-na)*
appraise (v)	оценивать/оценить	*(a-TSEH-nee-vat/a-tse-NEET)*
appreciation	вздорожание	*(vzda-ra-ZHAH-nee-ye)*
apprentice	подмастерье	*(pad-mas-TEH-rye)*
appropriation	ассигнование	*(as-seeg-na-VAH-nee-ye)*
approval	одобрение	*(a-da-BREH-nee-ye)*
approve (v)	одобрять/одобрить	*(a-da-BRYAHT/a-da-BREET)*
arable land	пахотная земля	*(PAH-khat-na-ya zem-LYAH)*
arbitrage	арбитраж	*(ar-beet-RAHSH)*
arbitration	арбитраж	*(ar-beet-RAHSH)*
arbitration agree-ment	договор об арбитраже	*(da-ga-VOHR ab ar-beet-RAH-zhe)*
arbitrator	арбитр	*(ar-BEETR)*
area manager	менеджер района	*(MEH-ned-zher ray-OH-na)*
arithmetic mean	среднее арифметическое	*(SRED-nee-ye a-reef-me-TEE-ches-ka-ye)*
armaments	оружие/вооружение	*(a-ROO-zhee-ye)*
array	массив	*(MAS-seef)*
arrears	отставание	*(at-sta-VAH-nee-ye)*
art	искусство	*(ees-KOOS-stva)*
artificial intelli-gence	искусственный интеллект	*(ees-KOOS-tven-nee een-tel-LEKT)*
as per advice	по извещению	*(pa-eez-ve-SHCHEH-nee-yoo)*
ash (residue)	зола	*(za-LAH)*
ash (tree)	ясень	*(YAH-sen)*
ash content	зольность	*(ZOL-nast)*
asphalt	асфальт	*(as-FAHLT)*
as soon as possible	как можно скорее	*(kak MOZH-na ska-REH-ye)*

asked price	запрашиваемая цена	*(za-PRAH-shee-va-ye-ma-ya tse-NAH)*
assay	испытание	*(ees-pee-TAH-nee-ye)*
assay (v)	испытывать/испытать	*(ees-PEE-tee-vat/ees-pee-TAHT)*
assemble (v) (people)	собирать/собрать	*(sa-bee-RAHT/sa-BRAHT)*
assemble (v) (things)	собирать/собрать	*(sa-bee-RAHT)*
assembly	собрание	*(sa-BRAH-nee-ye)*
assembly line	конвейер	*(kan-VEH-yer)*
assess (v)	оценивать/оценить имущество	*(a-TSEH-nee-vat /a-tse-NEET ee-MOO-shche-stva)*
assessed valuation	оценка имущества для обложения налогом	*(a-TSEN-ka ee-MOO-shchest-va dla ab-la-ZHEH-nee-ya na-LOH-gam)*
assessment	оценка	*(a-TSEN-ka)*
asset	актив	*(ak-TEEF)*
asset turnover	оборот активов	*(a-ba-ROT ak-TEE-vaf)*
asset value	стоимость активов	*(STOH-ee-mast ak-TEE-vaf)*
assets, accrued	наросшие активы	*(na-ROSH-shee-ye ak-TEE-vee)*
assets, current	текущие активы	*(te-KOO-shchee-ye ak-TEE-vee)*
assets, fixed	основные средства	*(as-nav-NEE-ye SRET-stva)*
assets, intangible	нематериальные активы	*(ne-ma-ter-YAHL-nee-ye ak-TEE-vee)*
assets, liquid	ликвидные активы	*(leek-VEED-nee-ye ak-TEE-vee)*
assets, net	чистые активы	*(CHEES-tee-ye ak-TEE-vee)*
assets, tangible	материальные активы	*(ma-ter-YAHL-nee-ye ak-TEE-vee)*
assign (v)	ассигновывать/ассигновать	*(as-seeg-NOH-vee-vat/ a-seeg-na-VAHT)*
assignee	правопреемник	*(PRAH-va-pre-YEM-neek)*
assignor	правопередатель	*(PRAH-va-pe-re-DAH-tel)*
assistant	помощник	*(pa-MOSH-neek)*

A

assistant general manager	первый заместитель менеджера	*(PEHR-vee za-mes-TEE-tel MEH-ned-zhe-ra)*
assistant manager	помощник менеджера	*(pa-MOSH-neek MEH-ned-zhe-ra)*
assumption of the liability	принятие ответственности	*(pree-NYAH-tee-ye at-VET-stven-na-stee)*
astrakhan	каракуль	*(ka-RAH-kool)*
at best	в лучшем случае	*(VLOOCH-shem SLOO-cha-ye)*
atom	атом	*(A-tam)*
atomic	атомный	*(AH-tam-nee)*
at par	альпари	*(al-pa-REE)*
at sight	на предъявителя	*(na pred-ya-VEE-te-la)*
at the close	при закрытии	*(pree za-KREE-tee-ee)*
at the market	на рынке	*(na REEN-ke)*
at the opening	при открытии	*(pree at-KREE-tee-ee)*
attach (v) (affix, adhere)	прикреплять/прикрепить	*(pree-krep-LYAHT/pree-kre-PEET)*
attach (v) (seize)	арестовывать/арестовать	*(a-res-TOH-vee-vat/a-res-ta-VAHT)*
attache case	кожаный ручной чемоданчик (кейс)	*(KOH-zha-nee rooch-NOY che-ma-DAHN-cheek keis])*
attachment (con-tract)	приложение	*(pree-la-ZHEH-nee-ye)*
attestation	аттестация	*(a-tes-TAH-tsee-ya)*
attorney	адвокат	*(ad-va-KAHT)*
attorney, power of	доверенность	*(da-VEH-ren-nast)*
attrition	истощение	*(ees-ta-SHCHEH-nee-ye)*
audit (v)	ревизовать	*(re-vee-za-VAHT)*
audit, internal	внутренняя ревизия	*(VNOOT-ren-nya-ya re-VEE-zee-ya)*
audit, outside	внешняя ревизия	*(VNESH-nya-ya re-VEE-zee-ya)*
auditing balance sheet	ревизия баланса	*(re-VEE-zee-ya ba-LAHN-sa)*
auditor	ревизор	*(re-vee-ZOHR)*
autarchy	автаркия	*(af-TAHR-kee-ya)*

authority, to have (v)	иметь полномочие	*(ee-MET pal-na-MOH-chee-ya)*
authorize (v)	уполномочить	*(oo-pal-na-MOH-cheet)*
authorized dealer	уполномоченный представитель фирмы	*(oo-pal-na-MOH-chen-nee pret-sta-VEE-tel FEEHR-mee)*
authorized shares	уполномоченные акции	*(oo-pal-na-MOH-chen-nee-ye AHK-tsee-ee)*
authorized signature	уполномоченная подпись	*(oo-pal-na-MOH-chen-na-ya POT-pees)*
automatic	автоматический	*(af-ta-ma-TEE-ches-kee)*
automatic gearshift	автоматическая коробка передач	*(af-ta-ma-TEE-ches-ka-ya ka-ROP-ka pe-re-DACH)*
automation	автоматизация	*(af-ta-ma-tee-ZAH-tsee-ya)*
automobile	автомобиль	*(af-ta-ma-BEEL)*
autonomous	автономный	*(af-ta-NOM-nee)*
auto-pilot	автопилот	*(AHF-ta-pee-LOT)*
autumn	осень	*(OH-sen)*
average	средний	*(SRED-nee)*
average cost	общая аварийная стоимость	*(OP-shcha-ya a-va-REEY-na-ya STOH-ee-mast)*
average price	средняя цена	*(SRED-nya-ya tse-NAH)*
average productivity per unit vol.	средние издержки на единицу	*(SRED-nee-ye eez-DEHRSH-kee na ye-dee-NEE-tsoo)*
average unit cost	средняя удельная продуктивность	*(SRED-nya-ya oo-DEL-na-ya pra-dook-TEEV-nast)*
aviation	авиация	*(a-vee-AH-tsee-ya)*
avionics	авиаэлектроника	*(AH-vee-a-e-lek-TROH-nee-ka)*

B

back date (n)	пометка задним числом	*(pa-MET-ka ZAD-neem chees-LOM)*
back date (v)	антидатировать	*(an-tee-da-TEE-ra-vat)*
back haul	обратный фрахт	*(ab-RAHT-nee frahkht)*
back order	невыполненный заказ	*(ne-VEE-pal-nen-nee za-KAHS)*

back selling	перепродажа	*(pe-re-pra-DAH-zha)*
back taxes	дополнительный налог	*(da-pal-NEE-tel-nee na-LOK)*
back note	гарантийный вексель	*(ga-ran-TEEY-nee VEK-sel)*
back and filing	аваль и регистрация	*(a-VAHL ee re-ghees-TRAH-tsee-ya)*
backing, support	поддержка	*(pad-DEHRSH-ka)*
back log	невыполненные заказы	*(nee-VEE-pal-nen-nee-ye za-KAH-zee)*
backup bonds	залоговая поддержка	*(za-LOH-ga-va-ya pad-DEHRSH-ka)*
backup (system)	резервное устройство	*(re-ZEHRV-na-ye oos-TROY-stva)*
backwardation	депорт	*(de-POHRT)*
backward compatible	совместимый назад	*(sav-mes-TEE-mee na-ZAHT)*
bad debt	безнадёжная задолженность	*(bez-na-DYOZH-na-ya za-DOL-zhen-nast)*
badgers	барсуки	*(bar-soo-KEE)*
balance	баланс	*(ba-LAHNS)*
balance, bank	банковский баланс	*(BAHN-kaf-skee ba-LAHNS)*
balance, credit	кредитовый баланс	*(kre-DEE-ta-vee ba-LAHNS)*
balance of payments	платёжный баланс	*(pla-TYOZH-nee ba-LAHNS)*
balance ratios	коэффициенты баланса	*(ka-ef-fee-tsee-EN-tee ba-LAHN-sa)*
balance sheet	баланс	*(ba-LAHNS)*
bale	кипа	*(KEE-pa)*
bale cargo	товар в кипах	*(ta-VAHR FKEE-pakh)*
ballast	балласт	*(bal-LAHST)*
ballistic	баллистический	*(bal-lee-STEE-ches-kee)*
balsa	бальза заячья	*(BAHL-za ZAH-yach-ya)*
bank	банк	*(bahnk)*
bank acceptance	банковский акцепт	*(BAHN-kaf-skee ak-TSEPT)*
bank account	счёт в банке	*(shchyot VBAHN-ke)*
bank balance	банковский баланс	*(BAHN-kaf-skee ba-LAHNS)*

bank charges	банковские расходы	*(BAHN-kaf-skee-ye ras-KHOH-dee)*
bank check	банковский чек	*(BAHN-kaf-skee chek)*
bank deposit	банковский вклад	*(BAHN-kaf-skee fklaht)*
bank draft	банковский вексель	*(BAHN-kaf-skee VEK-sel)*
bank examiner	банковский ревизор	*(BAHN-kaf-skee re-vee-ZOHR)*
bank exchange	банковский обмен	*(BAHN-kaf-skee ab-MEN)*
bank holiday	временное закрытие банков	*(VREH-men-na-ye za-KREE-tee-ye BAHN-kaf)*
bank letter of credit	банковский аккредитив	*(BAHN-kaf-skee a-kre-dee-TEEF)*
bank loan	банковская ссуда	*(BAHN-kaf-skay SSOO-da)*
bank money order	банковский ордерный чек	*(BAHN-kaf-skee OHR-der-nee chek*
bank note	банкнота	*(bank-NOH-ta)*
bank rate	банковская ставка	*(BAHN-kaf-ska-ya STAHF-ka)*
bank release	банковское оправдание	*(BAHN-kaf-ska-ye ap-rav-DAH-nee-ye)*
bank statement	банковская ведомость	*(BAHN-kaf-ska-ya VEH-da-mast)*
Bar (legal profession)	адвокатура	*(ad-va-ka-TOO-ra)*
bareboat charter	бэрбоут-чартер	*(behr-BOO-OOT CHAHR-ter)*
bargain	хорошая сделка	*(kha-ROH-sha-ya ZDEL-ka)*
bargain, collective	коллективное соглашение	*(kal-lek-TEEV-na-ye sag-la-SHEH-nee-ye)*
barge transportation	баржа	*(BAHR-zha)*
bark	кора	*(ka-RAH)*
barker	окорочный станок	*(OH-ka-rach-nee sta-NOK)*
barley	ячмень	*(yach-MEN)*
barn	сарай	*(sa-RAHY)*
barratry	баратрия	*(ba-RAHT-ree-ya)*
barrel	баррель	*(BAHR-rel)*
barter	обмен товаров	*(ab-MEHN ta-VAH-raf)*

barter (v)	менять/обменять товары	*(me-NYAHT/ab-me-NYAHT ta-VAH-ree)*
base	основание	*(as-na-VAH-nee-ye)*
base currency	базисная валюта	*(BAH-zees-na-ya va-LYOO-ta)*
base price	базисная цена	*(BAH-zees-na-ya tse-NAH)*
base price	базовая контрактная цена (на природный газ)	*(BAH-za-va-ya kan-TRAHKT-na-ya tse-NAH [na pree-ROD-nee gahs])*
base rate	базисная ставка	*(BAH-zees-na-ya STAHF-ka)*
base year	базисный год	*(BAH-zees-nee got)*
basis point	базисный процент	*(BAH-zees-nee pra-TSENT)*
batch processing	переработка по наделам	*(pe-re-ra-BOT-ka pa na-DEH-lam)*
batch production	производство по наделам	*(pra-eez-VOT-stva pa na-DEH-lam)*
batched jobs	пакетные задания	*(pa-KET-nee-ye za-DAH-nee-ya)*
battery	аккумулятор	*(ak-koo-moo-LYAH-tar)*
battery fluid	аккумуляторная жидкость	*(ak-koo-moo-LYAH-tar-na-ya ZHIT-kast)*
beam	балка	*(BAHL-ka)*
beam	луч	*(looch)*
bean	фасоль	*(fa-SOHL)*
bear	спекулянт/играющий на понижение	*(spe-koo-LYAHNT/eeg-RAH-yoo-shchee na pa-nee-ZHEE-nee-ye)*
bear market	падение на биржевом рынке	*(pa-DEH-nee-ye na beer-zhe-VOM REEN-ke)*
bearer	держатель	*(der-ZHAH-tel)*
bearer bond	облигация на предъявителя	*(ab-lee-GAH-tsee-ya na pred-ya-VEE-te-lya)*
bearer security	акция на предъявителя	*(AHK-tsee-ya na pred-ya-VEE-te-lya)*
bearings	подшипник	*(pat-SHIP-neek)*
beaver	бобр	*(bobr)*
beech	бук	*(book)*
beet	свёкла	*(SVYOK-la)*

binary code

beet sugar	свекловичный сахар	*(svek-la-VEECH-nee SAH-khar)*
beetle	жук	*(zhook)*
bell-shaped curve	кривая в форме колокола	*(kree-VAH-ya FFOHR-me KOH-la-ka-la)*
below ground value	стоимость подготовки запасов	*(STOH-ee-mast pad-ga-TOF-kee za-PAH-saf)*
below par	ниже номинальной цены	*(NEE-zhe na-mee-NAHL-nay tse-NEE)*
below the line	ниже нормы	*(NEE-zhe NOHR-mee)*
belt	пояс	*(POH-yas)*
benchmark price (of crude)	базисная цена на «эталонную» нефть	*(BAH-zees-na-ya tse-NAH na eta-LON-noo-yoo neft)*
beneficiary	бенефициар	*(be-ne-fee-tsee-AHR)*
benzene	бензол	*(ben-ZOL)*
bequest	посмертный дар	*(pa-SMEHRT-nee dar)*
berth terms	оговорка о причале	*(a-ga-VOHR-ka a pree-CHAH-le)*
bid (takeover)	предложение за покупку контрольного пакета акций	*(pred-la-ZHEH-nee-ye za pa-KOOP-ku kant-ROL-na-va pa-KEH-ta AHK-tseey)*
bid and asked	цена покупателя и продавца	*(tse-NAH pa-koo-PAH-te-lya ee pra-daf-TSAH)*
bilberry	черника	*(cher-NEE-ka)*
bill	вексель	*(VEK-sel)*
bill broker	вексельный маклер	*(VEK-sel-nee MAHK-ler)*
bill (currency)	банкнота	*(bank-NOH-ta)*
bill (invoice)	фактура	*(fak-TOO-ra)*
bill of exchange	тратта	*(TRAHT-ta)*
bill of lading	коносамент	*(ka-na-sa-MENT)*
bill of sale	закладная	*(za-klad-NAH-ya)*
bill of sight	временный вексель	*(VREH-men-nee VEK-sel)*
billboard	рекламный стенд	*(rek-LAHM-nee stend)*
billets	сутунки	*(soo-TOON-ke)*
billfold	бумажник	*(boo-MAHZH-neek)*
binary code	двойной код	*(dvay-NOY KOT)*

binder	папка	*(PAHP-ka)*
binding	переплёт	*(pe-re-PLYOT)*
biochemistry	биохимия	*(bee-a-KHEE-mee-ya)*
biologist	биолог	*(bee-OH-lak)*
biology	биология	*(bee-a-LOH-ghee-ya)*
birch	берёза	*(be-RYOH-za)*
bit	бит	*(beet)*
bitumen	битум	*(bee-TOOM)*
black market	чёрный рынок	*(CHOHR-nee REE-nak)*
black and white	чёрно-белый	*(CHOR-na-BEE-lee)*
blade	пильное полотно	*(PEEL-na-ye pa-lat-NOH)*
blanket bond	глобальный бонд	*(gla-BAHL-nee bond)*
blanket insurance	глобальная страховка	*(gla-BAHL-na-ya stra-KHOF-ka)*
blanket order	глобальный заказ	*(gla-BAHL-nee za-KAHS)*
blast furnace	домна	*(DOM-na)*
bleed (v)	истекать кровью/у кого кровотечение	*(ees-te-KAHT KROH-vyoo)*
bleed	обрезать страницу в край	*(ab-REH-zat stra-NEE-tsoo fkrahy)*
block	блок	*(blok)*
blockage of funds	замораживание фондов	*(za-ma-RAH-zhee-va-nee-ye FON-daf)*
blocked currency	блокированная валюта	*(bla-KEE-ra-va-na-ya va-LYOO-ta)*
blood	кровь	*(krof)*
blotter	бювар	*(byoo-VAHR)*
blowup	большое увеличение	*(bal-SHOH-ye oo-ve-lee-CHEH-nee-ye)*
blue-chip stock	первоклассная акция	*(per-va-KLAHS-na-ya AHK-tsee-ya)*
blueberry	голубика	*(ga-loo-BEE-ka)*
blue-collar worker	«синий воротничок» (рабочий)	*(SEE-nee va-rat-nee-CHOK [ra-BOH-chee])*
blue gas	водяной газ	*(va-dya-NOY gahs)*
blueprint	проект/синька	*(pra-YEKT/SEEN-ka)*
board	доска	*(das-KAH)*

board, executive	руководящий комитет	*(roo-ka-va-DYAH-shchee ka-mee-TET)*
board foot	досковой фут	*(das-ka-VOY foot)*
board meeting	совещание директоров	*(sa-ve-SHCHAH-nee-ye dee-rek-ta-ROF)*
board of directors	совет директоров	*(sa-VET dee-rek-ta-ROF)*
board of supervisors	наблюдательный совет	*(na-blyoo-DAH-tel-nee sa-VET)*
boardroom	зал для совещаний	*(zahl dlya sa-ve-SHCHA-neey)*
body	кузов	*(KOO-saf)*
boilerplate	набор стандартных формулировок	*(na-BOHR stan-DAHRT-nikh far-moo-lee-ROH-vak)*
boldface	жирный шрифт	*(ZHIHR-nee shrift)*
bond	бонд/облигация	*(bond/ab-lee-GAH-tsee-ya)*
bond areas	зона таможенного досмотра	*(ZOH-na ta-MOH-zhen-na-va da-SMOT-ra)*
bond issue	выпуск облигаций	*(VEE-poosk ab-lee-GAH-tseey)*
bond power	право выпускать облигации	*(PRAH-va vee-poos-KAHT ab-lee-GAH-tsee-ee)*
bond rating	классификация облигаций	*(klas-see-fee-KAH-tsee-ya ab-lee-GAH-tseey)*
bonded carrier	бондовая транспортная компания	*(BON-da-va-ya TRAHNS-part-na-ya kam-PAH-nee-ya)*
bonded goods	товары/пломбированные таможней	*(ta-VAH-ree/plam-BEE-ra-van-nee-ye ta-MOZH-ney)*
bonded warehouse	таможенный склад	*(ta-MOH-zhen-nee sklaht)*
bonds (and stocks)	ценные бумаги	*(TSEN-nee-ye boo-MAH-ghee)*
bonus (premium)	премия	*(PREH-mee-ya)*
book	книга	*(KNEE-ga)*
bookbinder	переплётчик	*(pe-re-PLYOT-cheek)*
bookbinding press	переплётный пресс	*(pe-re-PLYOT-nee press)*
book-end paper	форзацная бумага	*(far-ZAHTS-na-ya boo-MAH-ga)*

B

B

book inventory	бухгалтерская опись	_(bookh-GAHL-ter-ska-ya OH-pees)_
book value	бухгалтерская стоимость	_(bookh-GAHL-ter-ska-ya STOH-ee-mast)_
book value per share	бухгалтерская стоимость по акции	_(bookh-GAHL-ter-ska-ya STOH-ee-mast pa AHK-tsee-ee)_
bookkeeping	бухгалтерия	_(bookh-gal-TEH-ree-ya)_
boom	бум	_(boom)_
boost-glide aircraft	ракетоплан	_(ra-ke-ta-PLAHN)_
boots	сапоги	_(sa-pa-GHEE)_
border	граница	_(gra-NEE-tsa)_
border tax adjustment	изменение пограничных пошлин	_(eez-me-NEH-nee-ye pa-gra-NEECH-nikh POSH-leen)_
borrow (v)	брать/взять в долг	_(braht/vsyat vdolk)_
botanic	ботаническое средство	_(ba-ta-NEE-ches-ka-ye SRET-stva)_
botulism	ботулизм	_(ba-too-LEEZM)_
boycott	бойкот	_(bay-KOT)_
brake	тормоз	_(TOHR-mas)_
brake pedal	тормозная педаль	_(tar-maz-NAH-ya pe-DAHL)_
brainstorm	мозговой штурм	_(maz-ga-VOY shtoorm)_
branch office	филиал	_(fee-lee-AHL)_
brand	фирменный знак	_(FEEHR-men-nee znahk)_
brand (of cattle)	тавро	_(tav-ROH)_
brand acceptance	принятие фирменного знака	_(pree-NYAH-tee-ye FEEHR-men-na-va ZNAH-ka)_
brand image	рейтинг фирменного знака	_(REY-teenk FEEHR-men-na-va ZNAH-ka)_
brand loyalty	приверженность к данной марке	_(pree-VEHR-zhen-nast GDAHN-nay MAHR-ke)_
brand manager	менеджер данного фирменного знака	_(MEH-ned-zher DAHN-na-va FEEHR-men-na-va ZNAH-ka)_
brand recognition	признание фирменного знака	_(pree-ZNAH-nee-ye FEEHR-men-na-va ZNAH-ka)_
bread	хлеб	_(khlep)_

break-even (v)	достичь предела рентабельности	*(da-STEECH pre-DEH-la ren-TAH-bel-na-stee)*
break-even analysis	анализ безубыточности	*(a-NAH-lees be-zoo-BEE-tach-na-stee)*
break-even point	предел безубыточности	*(pre-DEHL be-zoo-BEE-tach-na-stee)*
breeding	выведение	*(vee-ve-DEH-nee-ye)*
breeding stock	племенной скот	*(ple-men-NOY skot)*
briefcase	атташе (кейс)	*(at-ta-SHEH [kehys])*
British Thermal Unit (BTU)	Британская Тепловая Единица (БТЕ)	*(bree-TAHN-ska-ya tep-la-VAH-ya e-dee-NEE-tsa (BEH-TEH-YEH)*
broadcasting	радиовещание	*(RAH-dee-a-ve-SHCHAH-nee-ye)*
brochure	брошюра	*(bra-SHOO-ra)*
broken stowage	бракераж	*(bra-ke-RAHSH)*
broker	маклер	*(MAHK-ler)*
broker, software	маклер софтвера	*(MAHK-ler saft-VEH-ra)*
budget	бюджет	*(byood-ZHET)*
budget advertising	рекламный бюджет	*(rek-LAHM-nee byood-ZHET)*
budget appropriation	ассигнование	*(as-seeg-na-VAH-nee-ye)*
budget, capital	капитальный бюджет	*(ka-pee-TAHL-nee byood-ZHET)*
budget, cash	бюджет денежной наличности	*(byood-ZHET DEH-nezh-nay na-LEECH-na-stee)*
budget, investment	капиталовложения в бюджете	*(ka-pee-TAH-la-vla-ZHE-nee-ya vbyood-ZHEH-te)*
budget, marketing	бюджет маркетинга	*(byood-ZHET mar-KEH-teen-ga)*
budget, sales	коммерческий бюджет	*(kam-MEHR-ches-kee byood-ZHET)*
bulkhead	шпангоут	*(shpan-GOH-oot)*
bull	спекулянт/играющий на повышение, бык	*(spe-koo-LYAHNT eeg-RAH-yoo-shchee na pa-vee-SHEH-nee-ye, bik)*
bull market	повышение биржевого рынка	*(pa-vee-SHEH-nee-ye beer-zhe-VOH-va REEN-ka)*
bumper	буфер	*(BOO-fer)*

bunker oil	жидкое бункерное топливо	*(ZHIT-ka-ye BOON-ker-na-ya TOP-lee-va)*
burden rate	ставка накладных расходов	*(STAHF-ka nak-lad-NICH ras-KHOH-daf)*
bureaucrat	бюрократ	*(byoo-ra-KRAHT)*
business activity	коммерческая деятельность	*(kam-MEHR-ches-ka-ya DEH-ya-tel-nast)*
business card	визитная карточка	*(vee-ZEET-na-ya KAHR-tach-ka)*
business cycle	деловой цикл	*(de-la-VOY tsikl)*
business management	руководство бизнеса (менеджмент)	*(roo-ka-VOT-stva de-la-VOY DEH-ya-tel-na-styoo)*
business plan	бизнесплан	*(BEEZ-nes PLAHN)*
business policy	деловая политика	*(de-la-VAH-ya pa-LEE-tee-ka)*
business strategy	деловая стратегия	*(de-la-VAH-ya stra-TEH-ghee-ya)*
butter	масло	*(MAHS-la)*
buy at best	закупать/закупить за лучшую цену	*(za-koo-PAHT za LOOCH-choo-yoo TSEH-noo)*
buy back (v)	выкупать/выкупить	*(VEE-koo-peet)*
buy on close (v)	закупать/закупить при закрытии	*(za-koo-PAHT pree za-KREE-tee-ee)*
buy on opening (v)	закупать/закупить при открытии	*(za-koo-PAHT pree at-KREE-tee-ee)*
buyer	покупатель	*(pa-koo-PAH-tel)*
buyer, chief	главный покупатель	*(GLAHV-nee pa-koo-PAH-tel)*
buyer, credit	кредитовый покупатель	*(kre-DEE-ta-vee pa-koo-PAH-tel)*
buyer, potential	возможный покупатель	*(vaz-MOZH-nee pa-koo-PAH-tel)*
buyer's market	рынок покупателя	*(REE-nak pa-koo-PAH-te-lya)*
buyer's option	опцион за покупку	*(ap-tsee-ON za pa-KOOP-koo)*
buyer's premium	премия за покупку	*(PREH-mee-ya za pa-KOOP-koo)*

buyer's responsi-bility	ответственность покупателя	*(at-VET-stven-nast pa-koo-PAH-te-lya)*
buying power	покупательная способность	*(pa-koo-PAH-tel-na-ya spa-SOB-nast)*
buy-out (takeover)	скупка	*(SKOOP-ka)*
by-laws	устав товарищества	*(oos-TAHF ta-VAH-ree-shchest-va)*
by-product	побочный продукт	*(pa-BOCH-nee pra-DOOKT)*
byte	байт	*(bahyt)*

C

cabbage	капуста	*(ka-POOS-ta)*
cable	кабель/телекс	*(KAH-bel/TEH-leks)*
cable television	кабельное телевидение	*(KAH-bel-na-ye te-le-VEE-de-nee-ye)*
cable transfer	телеграфный перевод	*(te-le-GRAHF-nee pe-re-VOT)*
calculator	калькулятор	*(kal-koo-LYAH-tar)*
calf	телёнок	*(te-LYOH-nak)*
calfskin	телячья кожа	*(te-LYAHCH-ya KOH-zha)*
call	созвать	*(sa-ZVAHT)*
call feature	оговорка о предварительном возмещении	*(a-ga-VOHR-ka a pred-va-REE-tel-nam vaz-me-SHCHEH-nee)*
call loan	возвратная ссуда	*(vaz-VRAHT-na-ya SSOO-da)*
call money	возвратные деньги	*(vaz-VRAHT-nee-ye DEN-ghee)*
call option	опцион покупателя	*(ap-tsee-ON pa-koo-PAH-te-lya)*
call price	выкупная цена	*(vee-koop-NAH-ya tse-NAH)*
call protection	защита от опциона покупателя	*(za-SHCHEE-ta at ap-tsee-OH-na pa-koo-PAH-te-lya)*
call rate	ставка опциона	*(STAHF-ka ap-tsee-OH-na)*
call rule	правило возмещения	*(PRAH-vee-la vaz-me-SHCHEH-nee-ya)*

callback	возврат	(vaz-VRAHT)
cambium	камбий	(KAHM-bee)
campaign, advertising	рекламная кампания	(rek-LAHM-na-ya kam-PAH-nee-ya)
campaign, productivity	борьба за производительность	(bar-BAH za pra-eez-va-DEE-tel-nast)
camshaft	кулачковый вал	(koo-lach-KOH-vee val)
cancel (v)	аннулировать	(an-noo-LEE-ra-vat)
canceled check	аннулированный чек	(an-noo-LEE-ra-van-nee chek)
cancer	рак	(rahk)
canning	консервирование	(kan-ser-VEE-ra-va-nee-ye)
capacitor	конденсатор	(kan-den-SAH-tar)
capacity	полномочия	(pal-na-MOH-chee-ya)
capacity, manufacturing	производительная мощность	(pra-eez-vah-DEE-tel-na-ya MOSHCH-nast)
capacity, plant	мощность фабрики	(MOSHCH-nast FAHB-ree-kee)
capacity, utilization	уровень эксплуатации	(OO-ra-ven eks-ploo-a-TAH-tsee-ee)
capital	капитал	(ka-pee-TAHL)
capital account	счёт капитала	(shchyoht ka-pee-TAH-la)
capital allowance	ассигнование капитала	(as-seeg-na-VAH-nee-ye ka-pee-TAH-la)
capital asset	материальный актив	(ma-te-ree-AHL-nee ak-TEEF)
capital budget	бюджет капиталовложения	(byood-ZHET ka-pee-TAH-la-vla-ZHEH-nee-ya)
capital expenditure	расход из основных фондов	(ras-KHOT eez as-nav-NIKH FON-daf)
capital expenditure appraisal	оценка расхода из основных фондов	(a-TSEN-ka ras-KHOH-da eez as-nav-NIKH FON-daf)
capital exports	экспорт капитала	(EKS-part ka-pee-TAH-la)
capital gain (loss)	прирост (уменьшение) ценностей	(pree-ROST [oo-men-SHEH-nee-ye] TSEN-na-stey)
capital goods	основные производственные фонды	(as-nav-NEE-ye pra-eez-VOT-stven-nee-ye FON-dee)

capital increase	увеличение капитала	*(oo-ve-lee-CHEH-nee-ye ka-pee-TAH-la)*
capital incentive	капиталоёмкий	*(ka-pee-TAH-la-YOM-kee)*
capital letter	прописная/заглавная буква	*(pra-pees-NAH-ya BOOK-va)*
capital market	рынок капитала	*(REE-nak ka-pee-TAH-la)*
capital-output ratio	коэффициент полезного действия	*(ka-ef-fee-tsee-ENT pa-LEZ-na-va DEY-stvee-ya)*
capital, raising	мобилизация капитала	*(ma-bee-lee-ZAH-tsee-ya ka-pee-TAH-la)*
capital, return on	доходность капитала	*(da-KHOD-nast ka-pee-TAH-la)*
capital, risk	рисковый капитал	*(REES-ka-vee ka-pee-TAHL)*
capital spending	расходы капитала	*(ras-KHOH-dee ka-pee-TAH-la)*
capital stock	обыкновенная акция	*(a-bik-na-VEN-na-ya AHK-tsee-ya)*
capital structure	структура капиталовложений	*(strook-TOO-RA ka-pee-TAH-la-vla-ZHEH-neey)*
capital surplus	излишки капитала	*(eez-LEESH-kee ka-pee-TAH-la)*
capital, working	оборотный капитал	*(a-ba-ROT-nee ka-pee-TAHL)*
capitalism	капитализм	*(ka-pee-ta-LEESM)*
capitalization	капитализация	*(ka-pee-ta-lee-ZAH-tsee-ya)*
capsule	желатиновая капсула	*(zhe-la-TEE-na-va-ya KAHP-soo-la)*
car	автомобиль	*(af-ta-ma-BEEL)*
carbon	углерод	*(oog-le-ROT)*
carbon copy	машинописная копия	*(ma-shee-na-PEES-na-ya KOH-pee-ya)*
carbon steel	углеродистая сталь	*(oog-le-ROH-dees-ta-ya stahl)*
carburetor	карбюратор	*(kar-byoo-RAH-tar)*
card case	футляр для визиток	*(foot-LYAHR dlya vee-ZEE-tak)*
cargo	груз	*(groos)*
carload	вагон	*(va-GON)*
carrier	перевозчик	*(pe-re-VOZ-shcheek)*

C

carrier's risk	риск перевозчика	*(reesk pe-re-VOZ-shchee-ka)*
carrot	морковь	*(mar-KOF)*
carry-back	дополнения к отчёту за истекший период	*(da-pal-NEH-nee-ya kat-CHYOH-too za ees-TEHK-sheey pe-REE-at)*
carry-forward	перенесение	*(pe-re-ne-SEH-nee-ye)*
carrying charge	плата за провоз	*(PLAH-ta za pra-VOS)*
carrying value	стоимость груза	*(STOH-ee-mast GROO-za)*
carryover	переходящий заказ	*(pe-re-kha-DYAH-shcheey za-KAHS)*
cartel	картель	*(kar-TEL)*
cash	наличные	*(na-LEECH-nee-ye)*
cash-and-carry	розничная продажа за наличные	*(ROZ-neech-na-ya pra-DAH-zha za na-LEECH-nee-ye)*
cash-basis	за наличный расчёт	*(za na-LEECH-nee ra-SHCHYOHT)*
cash balance	баланс остатков средств в кассе	*(ba-LAHNS as-TAHT-kaf sretstf FKAHS-se)*
cash before delivery	аванс наличными	*(a-VAHNS na-LEECH-nee-mee)*
cash budget	наличный бюджет	*(na-LEECH-nee byood-ZHET)*
cash on delivery	оплачивается при доставке	*(ap-LAH-chee-va-yet-sa pree da-STAHF-ke)*
cash discount	снижение цены при платежах за наличный расчёт	*(snee-ZHEN-nee-ye tse-NEE pree pla-te-ZHAHKH za na-LEECH-nee ra-SHCHYOHT)*
cash dividend	денежный дивиденд	*(DEH-nezh-nee dee-vee-DENT)*
cash entry	инкассо	*(een-KAHS-soh)*
cash flow	размер валового дохода при самофинансировании («кэшфлоу»)	*(raz-MEHR va-la-VOH-va da-KHOH-da pree SAH-ma-fee-nan-SEE-ra-va-nee-ee ["cash flow"])*
cash flow statement	отчёт валового дохода («кэшфлоу»)	*(at-CHYOHT va-la-VOH-va da-KHOH-da ["cash flow"])*

C

cash in advance	аванс наличными	*(a-VAHNS na-LEECH-nee-mee)*
cash management	хозяйствование наличными	*(kha-ZYAHY-stva-va-nee-ye na-LEECH-nee-mee)*
cash on delivery	оплата при доставке	*(ap-LAH-ta pree da-STAHF-ke)*
cash payment	оплата наличными	*(ap-LAH-ta na-LEECH-nee-mee)*
cash surrender value	стоимость при выкупе	*(STOH-ee-mast pree VEE-koo-pe)*
cashbook	кассовая книга	*(KAHS-sa-va-ya KNEE-ga)*
cashier's check	банковский чек	*(BAHN-kaf-skee chek)*
cassette	кассета	*(kas-SEH-ta)*
cast iron	чугун	*(choo-GOON)*
casualty insurance	страхование от несчастных случаев	*(stra-kha-VAH-nee-ye at ne-SHCHAHS-nikh SLOO-cha-yef)*
catalog	прейскурант	*(preys-koo-RAHNT)*
catalyst	катализатор	*(ka-ta-lee-ZAH-tar)*
cathode	катод	*(ka-TOT)*
cattle	скот	*(skot)*
CD-ROM	неперезаписываемый компактный звукодиск	*(ne-pe-re-za-PEE-see-va-ye-mee kam-PAHKT-nee zvoo-ka-DEESK)*
cedar	кедр	*(KEDR)*
ceiling (limit)	лимит	*(lee-MEET)*
cellulose	целлюлоза	*(tse-lyoo-LOH-za)*
central bank	центральный банк	*(tsent-RAHL-nee bahnk)*
central processing unit (CPU)	процессор	*(pra-TSES-sar)*
central rate	центральная ставка	*(tsent-RAHL-na-ya STAHF-ka)*
centralization	централизация	*(tsent-ra-lee-ZAH-tsee-ya)*
certificate	свидетельство/ сертификат	*(svee-DEH-tel-stva/ser-tee-fee-KAHT)*
certificate of deposit	свидетельство о вкладе	*(svee-DEH-tel-stva a FKLAH-de)*
certificate of incorporation	свидетельство об утверждении	*(svee-DEH-tel-stva ab oot-ver-ZHDEH-nee-ee)*

C

certificate of origin	свидетельство о происхождении	*(svee-DEH-tel-stva a pra-ees-khazh-DEH-nee-ee)*
certified check	удостоверенный чек	*(oo-da-sta-VEH-ren-nee chek)*
certified public account	специалист по бухгалтерии	*(spe-tsee-a-LEEST pa bookh-gal-TEH-ree)*
chain of command	руководящая иерархия	*(roo-ka-va-DYAH-shcha-ya ee-ye-RAHR-khee-ya)*
chain store	цепной (фирменный) магазин	*(tsep-NOY [FEER-men-nee] ma-ga-ZEEN)*
chain store group	группа цепных (фирменных) магазинов	*(GROOP-pa tsep-NIKH (FEER-men-neekh] ma-ga-ZEE-naf)*
Chairman of the Board	председатель совета директоров	*(pret-se-DAH-tel sa-VEH-ta dee-rek-ta-ROF)*
chamber of commerce	торговая палата	*(tar-GOH-va-ya pa-LAH-ta)*
channel	канал	*(ka-NAHL)*
channel of distribution	распределительная сеть	*(ras-pre-de-LEE-tel-na-ya set)*
chapter	глава	*(gla-VAH)*
character	знак/символ	*(znahk/SEEM-val)*
charge account in a store	личный счёт в магазине	*(LEECH-nee shchyoht vma-ga-ZEE-ne)*
charge off	начисление за безнадёжную задолженность	*(na-chees-LEH-nee-ya za bez-na-DYOZH-noo-yoo za-DOL-zhen-nast)*
charges	расходы	*(ras-KHOH-dee)*
chart, activities	график работ	*(GRAH-feek ra-BOT)*
chart, bar	сравнительная диаграмма	*(srav-NEE-tel-na-ya dee-a-GRAHM-ma)*
chart, flow	блок-схема	*(blok-SKHEH-ma)*
chart, management	структурная схема управления	*(strook-TOOHR-na-ya SKHEH-ma oop-rav-LEH-nee-ya)*
charter	устав	*(oos-TAHF)*
chartered accountant	специалист по бухгалтерии	*(spe-tsee-a-LEEST pa bookh-gal-TEH-ree)*
chassis	шасси	*(shas-SEE)*

chattel	движимое имущество	*(DVEE-zhe-ma-ye ee-MOO-shchest-va)*
chattel mortgage	залог движимого имущества	*(za-LOK DVEE-zhe-ma-va ee-MOO-shchest-va)*
cheap	дешёвый	*(de-SHOH-vee)*
check	чек	*(chek)*
checking account	чековый счёт в банке	*(CHEH-ka-vee schyoht VBAHN-ke)*
checklist	список	*(SPEE-sak)*
chemical	химический продукт	*(khee-MEE-ches-kee pra-DOOKT)*
chemistry	химия	*(KHEE-me-ya)*
chicken	курица	*(koo-REE-tsa)*
chief accountant	главный бухгалтер	*(GLAHV-nee bookh-GAHL-ter)*
chief buyer	главный покупатель	*(GLAHV-nee pa-koo-PAH-tel)*
chief executive	главный исполнитель	*(GLAHV-nee ees-pal-NEE-tel)*
chief executive officer (C.E.O.)	исполнительный директор	*(ees-pal-NEE-tel-nee dee-REK-tar)*
chief financial officer (C.F.O.)	финансовый директор	*(fee-NAHN-sa-vee dee-REK-tar)*
chip	микросхема	*(meek-ra-SKHEH-ma)*
chloride	хлорид	*(khla-REET)*
chloroform	хлороформ	*(khla-ra-FOHRM)*
chromium	хром	*(khrom)*
cigarette case	портсигар	*(part-see-GAHR)*
circulation	тираж	*(tee-RAHSH)*
circuit	схема	*(SKHEH-ma)*
civil action	гражданский иск	*(grazh-DAHN-skee eesk)*
civil engineering	конструирование	*(kan-stroo-EE-ra-va-nee-ye)*
claim	претензия, иск	*(pre-TEN-zee-ya, eesk)*
classified advertisement	газетное объявление	*(ga-ZET-na-ye ab-yav-LEH-nee-ye)*
clean document	чистовой документ	*(chees-tah-VOY da-koo-MENT)*

C

clearinghouse	расчётная палата	*(ra-SHCHYOHT-na-ya pa-LAH-ta)*
clear-cutting	вырубаемый сплошной рубкой	*(vee-roo-BAH-ye-mee SPLAHSH-noy ROOP-kay)*
client	клиент	*(klee-YENT)*
closed account	закрытый счёт	*(za-KREE-tee shchyoht)*
closely held corporation	акционерное общество закрытого типа	*(ak-tsee-a-NEHR-na-ye OP-shchest-va za-KREE-ta-va TEE-pa)*
closing entry	заключительная статья в балансе	*(za-klyoo-CHEE-tel-na-ya sta-TYAH vba-LAHN-se)*
closing price	заключительная цена	*(za-klyoo-CHEE-tel-na-ya tse-NAH)*
cloudberry	морошка	*(ma-ROSH-ka)*
clover	клевер	*(KLEH-ver)*
clutch	сцепление	*(stse-PLEH-nee-ye)*
clutch pedal	педаль сцепления	*(pe-DAHL stse-PLEH-nee-ya)*
coal gas	угольный газ	*(OO-gal-nee gahs)*
coal gasification	газификация угля	*(ga-zee-fee-KAH-tsee-ya oog-LYAH)*
coal oil	угольная нефть	*(OO-gal-na-ya neft)*
coated paper	бумага с покрытием	*(boo-MAH-ga spa-KREE-tee-yem)*
coaxial cable	коаксиальный кабель	*(ka-ak-SEEL-nee KAH-bel)*
codicil	кодицила	*(ka-dee-TSEE-la)*
cockpit	кабина лётчика	*(ka-BEE-na LYOT-chee-ka)*
coffee break	краткий перерыв в работе	*(KRAHT-kee pe-re-RIF vra-BOH-te)*
coil	змеевик	*(zmee-ye-VEEK)*
coinsurance	совместное страхование	*(sav-MES-na-ye stra-kha-VAH-nee-ye)*
cold call	предложение товара по телефону «на авось»	*(pred-la-ZHEH-nee-ye ta-VAH-ra pa te-le-FOH-noo na avos)*
cold rolling	холодная прокатка	*(kha-LOD-na-ya pra-KAHT-ka)*
collateral	заклад	*(zak-LAHT)*

colleague	сотрудник/коллега	*(sat-ROOD-neek/kal-LEH-ga)*
collect on delivery	получать деньги по поставке	*(pa-loo-CHANT DEHN-ghee pa pas-TAHF-ke)*
collection agent	агент по взысканию	*(a-GHENT pa vzis-KAH-nee-yoo)*
collection period	срок взыскания	*(srok vzis-KAH-nee-ya)*
collective agreement	коллективное соглашение	*(kal-lek-TEEV-na-ye sag-la-SHEH-nee-ye)*
collective bargaining	выработка коллективного соглашения	*(VEE-ra-bat-la kal-lek-TEEV-na-va sag-la-SHEH-nee-ya)*
collective farm	колхоз	*(kal-KHOS)*
collector of customs	сборщик пошлин	*(ZBOHR-shcheek POSH-leen)*
colloquim	собеседование	*(sa-be-SEH-da-va-nee-ye)*
color filter	цветофильтр	*(sve-ta-VOY FEELTR)*
color printing	цветная печать	*(tsvet-NAH-ya pe-CHAHT)*
colt	жеребёнок	*(zhe-re-BYOH-nak)*
column	колонка	*(ka-LON-ka)*
combat thrust booster	ускоритель маневра	*(oos-ka-REE-tel ma-NYOV-ra)*
combination	комбинация	*(kam-bee-NAH-tsee-ya)*
combination duty	комбинированная пошлина	*(kam-bee-NEE-ra-van-na-ya POSH-lee-na)*
combine harvester	уборочная машина	*(oo-BOH-rach-na-ya ma-SHEE-na)*
combustible gas	горючий газ	*(ga-RYOO-che gahs)*
combustible shale	горючий сланец	*(ga-RYOO-che SLAH-nets)*
commerce	коммерция	*(kam-MEHR-tsee-ya)*
commercial ad	коммерческая реклама	*(kam-MEHR-ches-ka-ya rek-LAH-ma)*
commercial aviation	гражданская авиация	*(grazh-DAHN-ska-ya a-vee-AH-tsee-ya)*
commercial bank	коммерческий банк	*(kam-MEHR-ches-kee bahnk)*
commercial grade	коммерческое качество	*(kam-MEHR-ches-ka-ye KAH-chest-va)*

C

commercial invoice	коммерческий счёт	(kam-MEHR-ches-kee shchyoht)
commercially exploitable reserves	рентабельно извлекаемые запасы	(ren-TAH-bel-na eez-vle-KAH-ye-mee-ye za-PAH-see)
commission (agency)	поручение	(pa-roo-CHEH-nee-ye)
commission (fee)	комиссионные	(ka-mees-see-ON-nee-ye)
commitment	обязательство	(a-bya-ZAH-tel-stva)
commodity	товар	(ta-VAHR)
commodity exchange	товарная биржа	(ta-VAHR-na-ya BEEHR-zha)
common carrier	общественный перевозчик	(ap-SHCHEST-ven-nee pe-re-VOHZ-scheek)
common market	общий рынок	(OP-shchee REE-nak)
common stock	обыкновенная акция	(a-bik-na-VEHN-na-ya AHK-tsee-ya)
compact disk	компактный звукодиск	(kam-PAHKT-nee zvoo-ka-DEESK)
company	компания	(kam-PAH-nee-ya)
company goal	цель компании	(tsel kam-PAH-nee-ee)
company, holding	материнская компания	(ma-te-REEN-ska-ya kam-PAH-nee-ya)
company, parent	компания-учредитель	(kam-PAH-nee-ya-ooch-re-DEE-tel)
company, policy	политика компании	(pa-LEE-tee-ka kam-PAH-nee-ee)
compensating balance	компенсационный баланс	(kam-pen-sa-tsee-ON-nee ba-LAHNS)
compensation	вознаграждение, компенсация	(vaz-na-grazh-DEH-nee-ye, kam-pen-SAH-tsee-ya)
compensation trade	компенсационная торговля	(kam-pen-sa-tsee-ON-na-ya tar-GOV-lya)
competition	соревнование	(sa-rev-na-VAH-nee-ye)
competitive advantage	конкурентное преимущество	(kan-koo-RENT-na-ye pre-ee-MOO-shchest-va)
competitive edge	небольшое преимущество над конкурентом	(ne-bal-SHOH-ye pre-ee-MOO-shchest-va nat kan-koo-REN-tam)
competitive price	конкурентоспособная цена	(kan-koo-REN-ta-spa-SOHB-na-ya tse-NAH)

competitive strate-gy	стратегия конкуренции	*(stra-TEH-ghee-ya kan-koo-REN-tsee-ee)*
competitor	конкурент	*(kan-koo-RENT)*
competitor analysis	анализ конкурентов	*(a-NAH-lees kan-koo-REN-taf)*
compiler	компилятор	*(kam-PEE-lya-tar)*
complimentary copy	бесплатный экземпляр	*(bes-PLAHT-nee ek-zem-PLYAHR)*
component	компонент/составная часть	*(kam-pa-NENT/sas-tav-NAH-ya chast)*
composite index	составной показатель	*(sas-tav-NOY pa-ka-ZAH-tel)*
composition	набор	*(na-BOHR)*
composition	композиция	*(kam-pa-ZEE-tsee-ya)*
compound	химическое соединение	*(khee-MEE-ches-ka-ye sa-ye-dee-NEH-nee-ye)*
compound interest	сложные проценты	*(SLOZH-nee-ye pra-TSEN-tee)*
compounds	соединения	*(sa-ye-dee-NEH-nee-ya)*
comptroller	контролёр	*(kan-tra-LYOHR)*
computer	ЭВМ, компьютер	*(eh-veh-EM, kam-PYOO-ter)*
computer, analog	аналоговая ЭВМ	*(a-NAH-la-ga-va-ya eh-veh-EM)*
computer bank	банк компьютеров	*(bahnk kam-PYOO-te-raf)*
computer center	компьютерный центр	*(kam-PYOO-ter-nee tsentr)*
computer, digital	цифровая ЭВМ	*(tsif-ra-VAH-ya eh-veh-EM)*
computer input	компьютерный ввод	*(kam-PYOO-ter-nee vvot)*
computer language	язык компьютера	*(ya-ZIK kam-PYOO-te-ra)*
computer memory	запоминающее устройство (ЗУ)	*(za-pa-mee-NAH-yoo-shche-ye oost-ROY-stva (ZEH-OO)*
computer output	компьютерный вывод	*(kam-PYOO-ter-nee VEE-vat)*
computer program	компьютерная программа	*(kam-PYOO-ter-na-ya pra-GRAHM-ma)*
computer storage	память компьютера	*(PAH-myat [kam-PYOO-te-ra])*

C

computer terminal	компьютерный терминал	*(kam-PYOO-ter-nee ter-mee-NAHL)*
concentration	концентрирование	*(kan-tsen-TREE-ra-va-nee-ye)*
condensate	конденсат	*(kan-den-SAHT)*
condenser	конденсатор	*(kan-den-SAH-tar)*
conditional acceptance	условный акцепт	*(oos-LOV-nee ak-TSEPT)*
conditional sales contract	условный договор о продаже	*(oos-LOV-nee da-ga-VOHR a pra-DAH-zhe)*
conference room	конференц-зал	*(kan-fe-RENTS-ZAHL)*
confidential	конфиденциальный	*(kan-fee-den-tsee-AHL-nee)*
confirmation of order	подтверждение заказа	*(pat-tver-ZHDEH-nee-ye za-KAH-za)*
conflict of interest	столкновение интересов	*(stal-kna-VEH-nee-ye een-te-REH-saf)*
conglomerate	конгломерат	*(kan-gla-me-RAHT)*
conifer	хвойное дерево	*(KHVOY-na-ye DEH-re-va)*
connect (into network)	подключать	*(paht-klu-CHAHT)*
connecting rod	соединительная тяга	*(sa-ye-dee-NEE-tel-na-ya TYAH-ga)*
consideration (contract law)	встречное удовлетворение	*(FSTRECH-na-ye oo-dav-let-va-REH-nee-ye)*
consignee	консигнатор	*(kan-seeg-NAH-tar)*
consignment	консигнация	*(kan-seeg-NAH-tsee-ya)*
consolidated financial statement	сводный баланс	*(SVOD-nee ba-LAHNS)*
consolidation	укрепление	*(oo-kre-PLEH-nee-ye)*
consortium	консорциум/ концерн	*(kan-SOHR-tsee-oom/kan-TSEHRN)*
consultant	консультант	*(kan-sool-TAHNT)*
consultant, management	консультант по менеджменту	*(kan-sool-TAHNT pa MEH-nedzh-men-too)*
consumer	потребитель	*(pat-re-BEE-tel)*
consumer acceptance	принятие потребителя	*(pree-NYAH-tee-ye pat-re-BEE-te-la)*
consumer credit	потребительский кредит	*(pat-re-BEE-tel-skee kre-DEET)*

consumer goods	потребительские товары	*(pat-re-BEE-tel-skee-ye ta-VAH-ree)*
consumer price index	индекс потребительских цен	*(EEN-deks pat-re-BEE-tel-skeekh tsen)*
consumer research	потребительское исследование	*(pat-re-BEE-tel-ska-ye ees-SLEH-da-va-nee-ye)*
consumer satisfaction	удовлетворение потребителя	*(oo-dav-let-va-REH-nee-ye pat-re-BEE-te-la)*
container	контейнер	*(kan-TEY-nehr)*
content	содержание	*(sa-der-ZHAH-nee-ye)*
contingencies	непредвиденные обстоятельства	*(ne-pred-VEE-den-nee-ye ap-sta-YAH-tel-stva)*
contingent fund	фонд для непредвиденных расходов	*(fond dlya ne-pred-VEE-den-nikh ras-KHOH-daf)*
contingent liability	условное обязательство	*(oos-LOV-na-ye a-bya-ZAH-tel-stva)*
continuous mill	непрерывный прокатный стан	*(ne-pre-RIV-nee pra-KAHT0nee stahn)*
contract	договор/контракт	*(da-ga-VOHR/kan-TRAHKT)*
contract carrier	перевозчик по договору	*(pe-re-VOH-shcheek pa da-ga-VOH-roo)*
contract crude oil	контрактная нефть	*(kan-TRAHKT-na-ya neft)*
contract oil market	рынок долгосрочных сделок (на купле-продаже нефти)	*(REE-nak dal-ga-SROCH-nokh SDEH-lak [na KOOP-le pra-DAH-zhe nef-ti])*
contract month	договорный месяц	*(da-ga-var-NOY MEH-syats)*
control, cost	контроль над расходами	*(kan-TROL nad ras-KHOH-da-mee)*
control, financial	финансовый контроль	*(fee-NAHN-sa-vee kan-TROL)*
control, inventory	инвентарный контроль	*(een-ven-TAHR-nee kan-TROL)*
control, manufacturing	производственный контроль	*(pra-eez-VOT-stven-nee kan-TROL)*
control, production	управление производственным процессом	*(oop-rav-LEH-nee-ye pra-eez-VOT-stven-nim pra-TSES-sam)*
control, quality	контроль качества	*(kan-TROL KAH-chest-va)*

C

control, stock	проверка инвентаря	*(pra-VEHR-ka een-ven-ta-RYAH)*
controller	контролёр	*(kant-tra-LYOHR)*
controlling interest	контрольный пакет акций	*(kan-TROL-nee pa-KET AHK-tseey)*
convertible	автомобиль с откидным верхом	*(af-ta-ma-BEEL sat-keed-NIM VEHR-kham)*
convertible debentures	обратимая облигация	*(ab-ra-TEE-ma-ya ab-lee-GAH-tsee-ya)*
convertible preferred stock	обратимая привилегированная акция	*(ab-ra-TEE-ma-ya pree-vee-le-ghee-ROH-van-na-ya AHK-tsee-ya)*
conveyor	конвейер	*(kan-VEH-yer)*
conveyor belt	конвейерная лента	*(kan-VEH-yer-na-ya LEN-ta)*
cooperation agreement	соглашение о сотрудничестве	*(sa-gla-SHEH-nee-ye a sat-ROOD-nee-che-stve)*
cooperative	кооператив	*(ka-a-pe-ra-TEEF)*
cooperative advertising	совместная реклама	*(sav-MES-na-ya rek-LAH-ma)*
co-ownership	совместное владение	*(sav-MES-na-ye vla-DEH-nee-ye)*
copper	медь	*(met)*
copy (text)	экземпляр	*(ek-zem-PLYAHR)*
copy (reproduction)	репродукция	*(reh-pra-DOOK-tsee-ya)*
copy (v)	копировать	*(ka-PEE-ra-vat)*
copyright	авторское право	*(AHF-tar-ska-ye PRAH-va)*
cordwood	лесоматериал в кордах	*(LEH-sa-ma-te-ree-AHL FKOHR-dakh)*
corn	кукуруза	*(koo-koo-ROO-za)*
corporate growth	прирост акционерного общества	*(pree-ROST ak-tsee-a-NEHR-na-va OP-shchest-va)*
corporate image	общественное представление о компании	*(ap-SHCHEST-ven-na-ye pret-sta-VLEH-nee-ye o kam-PAH-nee-ee)*
corporate planning	планирование акционерного общества	*(pla-NEE-ra-va-nee-ye ak-tsee-a-NEHR-na-va OP-shchest-va)*

corporate struc-ture	структура акционерного общества	*(strook-TOO-ra ak-tsee-a-NEHR-na-va OP-shchest-va)*
corporation	акционерное общество	*(ak-tsee-a-NEHR-na-ye OP-shchest-va)*
corporation tax	налог на акционерные общества	*(na-LOK na ak-tsee-a-NEHR-nee-ye OP-shchest-va)*
corpus	состав	*(sas-TAHF)*
correspondence	переписка	*(pe-re-PEES-ka)*
correspondent bank	корреспондентский банк	*(kar-res-pan-DENT-skee bahnk)*
cosmodrome	космодром	*(kas-ma-DROM)*
cost (n)	стоимость	*(STOO-ee-mast)*
cost (v)	стоить	*(STOH-eet)*
cost accounting	исчисление себестоимости	*(ees-chee-SLEE-nee-ye se-be-STOH-ee-mas-tee)*
cost analysis	анализ издержек	*(a-NAH-lees eez-DEHR-zhek)*
cost, average	средняя стоимость	*(SRED-nya-ya STOH-ee-mast)*
cost and freight	КАФ (стоимость и фрахт)	*(kaf STOH-ee-mast ee frahkht)*
cost direct	непосредственная стоимость	*(ne-pa-SRET-stven-na-ya STOH-ee-mast)*
cost effective	рентабельный	*(ren-TAH-bel-neey)*
cost, factor	затраты на факторы производства	*(za-TRAH-tee na FAHK-ta-ree pra-eez-VOT-stva)*
cost, indirect	косвенные расходы	*(KOS-ven-nee-ye ras-KHOH-dee)*
cost of capital	затраты на капитал	*(za-TRAH-tee na ka-pee-TAHL)*
cost of goods sold	стоимость проданных товаров	*(STOH-ee-mast PROH-dan-neekh ta-VAH-raf)*
cost of living	прожиточный минимум	*(pra-ZHEE-tach-nee MEE-nee-moom)*
cost recovery	возмещение издержек (добычи)	*(vaz-me-SHCHE-nee-ye eez-DEHR-zhek [da-BEE-chee])*
cost reduction	экономия затрат	*(e-ka-NOH-mee-ya za-TRAHT)*

C

cost, replacement	восстановительная стоимость	*(vas-sta-na-VEE-tel-na-ya STOH-ee-mast)*
cost-benefits analysis	анализ рентабельности	*(a-NAH-lees ren-TAH-beel-na-stee)*
costs, allocation of	ассигнование расходов	*(as-seeg-na-VAH-nee-ye ras-KHOH-daf)*
costs, fixed	постоянные издержки	*(pas-ta-YAHN-nee-ye eez-DEHRSH-kee)*
costs, managed	контролируемые издержки	*(kan-tra-LEE-roo-ye-mee-ye eez-DEHRSH-kee)*
cost, production	издержки производства	*(eez-DEHRSH-kee pra-eez-VOT-stva)*
costs, set up	издержки монтажа	*(eez-DEHRSH-kee man-ta-ZHAH)*
cost, standard	нормативные издержки	*(nar-na-TEEV-nee-ye eez-DEHRSH-kee)*
cost variable	переменные издержки	*(pe-re-MEN-nee-ye eez-DEHRSH-kee)*
cotton	хлопок	*(KHLOH-pak)*
cough (v)	кашлять	*(KAHSH-lyat)*
cough drop	капли от кашля	*(KAHP-lee at KAHSH-lya)*
cough syrup	сироп от кашля	*(see-ROP at KAHSH-lya)*
count-down	отсчёт времени	*(at-SHCHYOHT VREH-me-nee)*
counterfeiting (money)	фальшивомонетчество	*(fal-SHEE-va-ma-NET-che-stvo)*
counterfeiting (goods)	контрафаксия/подделка	*(kan-tra-FAHK-see-ya)*
countervailing duty	уравнительная пошлина	*(oo-rav-NEE-tel-na-ya POSH-lee-na)*
country house	дача	*(da-CHAH)*
country of origin	страна происхождения	*(strah-NAH pra-ees-khazh-DEH-nee-ya)*
country of risk	страна риска	*(stra-NAH REES-ka)*
coupon (bond interest)	купон на дивиденд	*(koo-PON na dee-vee-DENT)*
courier service	курьерское обслуживание	*(koor-YEHR-ska-ye ap-SLOO-zhee-va-nee-ye)*
covenant (promise)	обещание в договоре	*(a-be-SHCHAH-nee-ye vda-ga-VOH-re)*

cover	обложка	*(ab-LOSH-ka)*
cover charge	плата за куверт/ предварительная оплата	*(PLAH-ta za koo-VEHRT)*
cover letter	сопроводительное письмо	*(sa-pra-va-DEE-tel-na-ye pees-MOH)*
cover ratio	коэффициент покрытия	*(ka-ef-fee-tsee-ENT pa-KREE-tee-ya)*
coverage (insurance)	страховое покрытие	*(pa-KREE-tee-ye stra-kha-VAH-nee-ya)*
cow	корова	*(ka-ROH-va)*
cowhide	воловья кожа	*(va-LOH-vya KOH-zha)*
CPU	центральный процессор	*(tsen-TRAHL-nee pra-TSES-sar)*
cracking	растрескивание	*(ras-TRES-kee-va-nee-ye)*
crankshaft	коленчатый вал	*(ka-LEN-cha-tee val)*
crash	авария	*(a-VAH-ree-ya)*
credit	кредит	*(kree-DEET)*
credit (v)	предоставлять кредит/кредитовать	*(pre-da-stav-LYAHT kree-DEET, kree-dee-ta-VAHT)*
credit balance	кредитное сальдо	*(kre-DEET-na-ye SAHL-da)*
credit bank	кредитный банк	*(kre-DEET-nee bahnk)*
credit bureau	бюро проверки кредитоспособности	*(byoo-ROH pra-VEHR-kee kree-dee-ta-spa-SOB-na-stee)*
credit card	кредитная карточка	*(kre-DEET-na-ya KAHR-tach-ka)*
credit control	кредитный контроль	*(kre-DEET-nee kan-TROL)*
credit insurance	страхование кредита	*(stra-kha-VAN-nee-ye kre-DEE-ta)*
credit line	кредитный лимит	*(kre-DEET-nee lee-MEET)*
credit management	управление кредитными операциями	*(oop-rav-LEH-nee-ye kre-DEET-nee-mee a-pe-RAH-tsee-ya-mee)*
credit note	вексельный кредит	*(VEK-sel-nee kre-DEET)*
credit rating	оценка кредитоспособности	*(a-TSEN-ka kre-DEE-ta-spa-SOB-na-stee)*
credit reference	справка для предоставления кредита	*(SPRAHF-ka dla pre-da-stav-LEH-nee-ya kree-DEE-ta)*

C

credit terms	условия кредита	*(oos-LOH-vee-ya kre-DEE-ta)*
credit union	профсоюз/ предоставляющий кредит своим членам	*(praf-sa-YOOS/pre-da-sta-VLYAH-yoo-shchee kre-DEET sva-EEM CHLEH-nam)*
creditor	кредитор	*(kree-dee-TOHR)*
crop	подрезать снимок	*(pad-REH-zat SNEEH-mak)*
crop-dusting	опыление посевов	*(a-pee-LEH-nee-ye pa-SEH-vaf)*
cross-licensing	взаимное лицензирование	*(vza-EEM-na-ye lee-tsen-ZEE-ra-va-nee-ye)*
crows	ворона	*(va-ROH-na)*
crucible	тигель	*(TEE-gel)*
crude	грубый	*(GROO-bee)*
crude oil	(сырая) нефть	*([SEE-ra-ya] neft)*
crunching (data)	сжатие	*(SZHAH-tee-ye)*
crystallisation	кристаллизация	*(krees-tal-lee-ZAH-tsee-ya)*
cucumbers	огурцы	*(a-goor-TSEE)*
cultural export permit	разрешение на экспорт культурных ценностей	*(raz-re-SHEH-nee-ye na EKS-part kool-TOOHR-nikh TSEN-na-stey)*
cultural property	культурная собственность	*(kool-TOOHR-na-ya SOP-stven-nast)*
cum dividend	добавочные дивиденды	*(da-BAH-vach-nee-ye dee-vee-DEN-dee)*
cumulative	нарастающий/ кумулятивный	*(na-ra-STAH-yoo-shchee/ koo-moo-lya-TEEV-nee)*
cumulative pre-ferred stock	кумулятивные привилегированные акции	*(koo-moo-lya-TEEV-nee pree-vee-le-ghee-ROH-van-nee-ye AHK-tsee-ee)*
cupola	вагранка	*(va-GRAHN-ka)*
currency	валюта	*(va-LYOO-ta)*
currency band	размер колебаний валюты	*(raz-MEHR ka-le-BAH-nee va-LYOO-tee)*
currency clause	валюта оговорки	*(va-LYOO-ta a-ga-VOHR-kee)*
currency conver-sion	конверсия валюты	*(kan-VEHR-see-ya va-LYOO-tee)*

currency exchange	валютная биржа	*(va-LYOOT-na-ya BEEHR-zha)*
current	ток	*(tok)*
current assets	оборотный капитал	*(a-ba-ROT-nee ka-pee-TAHL)*
current liability	текущее обязательство	*(te-KOO-shche-ye a-bya-ZAH-tel-stva)*
current ratio	коэффициент ликвидности	*(ka-ef-fee-tsee-ENT leek-VEED-na-stee)*
current yield	текущий доход	*(te-KOO-shchee da-KHOT)*
customer	покупатель	*(pa-koo-PAH-tel)*
customer service	обслуживание покупателя	*(ap-SLOO-zhee-va-nee-ye pa-koo-PAH-te-lya)*
customs	таможня	*(ta-MOZH-nya)*
customs broker	таможенный маклер	*(ta-MOH-zhen-nee MAHK-ler)*
customs duty	таможенные сборы	*(ta-MOH-zhen-nee ZBOH-ree)*
customs entry	таможенная декларация	*(ta-MOH-zhen-na-ya dek-la-RAH-tsee-ya)*
customs union	таможенный союз	*(ta-MOH-zhen-nee sa-YOOS)*
cutback	сокращение	*(sak-ra-SHCHEH-nee-ye)*
cutting angle	угол резания	*(OO-gal REH-za-nee-ya)*
cycle, business	экономический цикл	*(e-ka-na-MEE-ches-kee tsikl)*
cycle, life	жизненный цикл (продукта)	*(ZHIZ-nen-nee tsikl [pra-DOOK-ta])*
cycle, work	технологический цикл	*(tekh-na-la-GHEE-ches-kee tsikl)*
cylinder head gasket	прокладка головки цилиндра	*(prak-LAHT-ka ga-LOF-kee tsee-LEEN-dra)*
cylinder head	головка цилиндра	*(ga-LOF-ka tsee-LEEN-dra)*

D

daily	ежедневный	*(e-zhe-DNEV-nee)*
dairy farm	молочная ферма	*(ma-LOCH-na-ya FEHR-ma)*

dairy products	молочные продукты	*(ma-LOCH-nee-ye pra-DOOK-tee)*
damage	повреждение	*(pav-re-ZHDEH-nee-ye)*
data	данные	*(DAHN-nee-ye)*
data acquisition	приобретение данных	*(pree-ab-re-TEH-nee-ye DAHN-nikh)*
data bank	банк данных	*(bahnk DAHN-nikh)*
data base	база данных	*(BAH-za DAHN-nikh)*
data processing	обработка данных	*(ab-ra-BOT-ka DAHN-nikh)*
date of delivery	дата поставки	*(DAH-ta pas-TAHF-kee)*
day loan	однодневный заём	*(ad-na-DNEV-nee za-YOM)*
day order	приказ, действующий один день	*(pree-KAHS DEY-stvoo-yoo-shchee a-DEEN den)*
dead freight	мёртвый фрахт	*(MYOHRT-vee frahkht)*
dead oil	«мёртвая» (неподвижная) нефть	*(MYORT-va-ya [ne-pad-VEEZH-na-ya] neft)*
dead rent	безнадёжная задолженность	*(bez-na-DYOZH-na-ya za-DOL-zhen-nast)*
deadline	крайний срок	*(KRAHY-nee srok)*
deadlock	застой	*(za-STOY)*
deal	сделка	*(ZDEL-ka)*
deal, package	глобальный контракт	*(gla-BAHL-nee kan-TRAHKT)*
dealer	торговый агент, дилер	*(tar-GOH-vee a-GHENT, DEE-lehr)*
dealership	фирма/продающая товар данной фирмы	*(FEEHR-ma/pra-da-YOO-shcha-ya ta-VAHR DAHN-nay FEEHR-mee)*
debentures	облигации без гарантий	*(ab-lee-GAH-tsee-ee bez ga-RAHN-teey)*
debit	дебит	*(DEH-beet)*
debit entry	запись в дебит счёта	*(ZAH-pees VDEH-beet SHCHYOH-ta)*
debit note	дебит-нота	*(DEH-beet-NOH-ta)*
debt	долг	*(dolk)*
debtlessness	отсутствие задолженности	*(at-SOOT-stvee-ye za-DOL-zhen-na-stee)*

debug (v) (computers)	отлаживать программу	*(at-LAH-zhee-vat pra-GRAHM-moo)*
deductible	подлежащее вычету	*(pad-le-ZHAH-shchee-ye VEE-che-too)*
deduction	вычет	*(VEE-chet)*
DEC	компания «ДЭК»	*(kam-pa-NEE-ya dek)*
deed	акт	*(ahkt)*
deed of sale	акт продажи	*(ahkt pra-DAH-zhee)*
deed of transfer	акт передачи	*(ahkt pe-re-DAH-chee)*
deed of trust	акт в опеку	*(ahkt va-PEH-koo)*
default (n)	неуплата	*(nee-oop-LAH-ta)*
default (v)	не выполнять договор	*(ne vee-pal-NYAHT da-ga-VOHR)*
defective	дефектный	*(de-FEHKT-nee)*
defense conversion	конверсия (оборонная)	*(kan-VEHR-see-ya [a-ba-RON-na-ya])*
deferred annuities	отложенные аннуитеты	*(at-LOH-zhen-nee-ye an-noo-ee-TEH-tee)*
deferred assets	активы будущих периодов	*(ak-TEE-vee BOO-doo-shcheekh pe-REE-a-daf)*
deferred charges	расходы будущих периодов	*(ras-KHOH-dee BOO-doo-shcheekh pe-REE-a-daf)*
deferred deliveries	затягивание сроков поставки	*(za-TYAH-ghee-va-nee-ye SROH-kaf pa-STAHF-kee)*
deferred income	доходы будущих периодов	*(da-KHOH-dee BOO-doo-shcheekh pe-REE-a-daf)*
deferred liabilities	пассивы будущих периодов	*(pas-SEE-vee BOO-doo-shcheekh pe-REE-a-daf)*
deferred tax	налоги будущих периодов	*(na-LOH-ghee BOO-doo-shcheekh pe-REE-a-daf)*
deficit	дефицит	*(de-fee-TSIT)*
deficit financing	финансирование дефицита	*(fee-nan-SEE-ra-va-nee-ye de-fee-TSEE-ta)*
deficit spending	расходование при дефиците	*(ras-KHOH-da-va-nee-ye de-fee-TSEE-ta)*
deflation	дефляция	*(de-FLYAH-tsee-ya)*
defroster	обогреватель	*(a-ba-gre-VAH-tel)*
degree (general)	степень	*(STEH-pen)*

D

degree (temperature)	градус	*(GRAH-doos)*
delay	задержка	*(za-DEHRSH-ka)*
delinquent account	просроченный счёт	*(pra-SROH-che-nee shchyoht)*
delivered cost	цена с включением расходов по доставке	*(tse-NAH sfklyoo-CHEH-nee-yem ras-KHOH-pa da-STAHF-ke)*
delivered price	цена с доставкой	*(tse-NAH sda-STAHF-kay)*
delivery	доставка	*(da-STAHF-kay)*
delivery date	срок доставки	*(srok da-STAHF-kee)*
delivery notice	извещение о доставке	*(eez-ve-SHCHEH-nee-ye a da-STAHF-ke)*
delivery points	пункты доставки	*(POON-ktee da-STAHF-kee)*
delivery price	цена доставки	*(tse-NAH da-STAHF-kee)*
demand	спрос	*(spros)*
demand (v)	требовать/потребовать	*(TREH-ba-vat)*
demographic	демографический	*(de-ma-gra-FEE-ches-kee)*
demonstrated resources	подтверждённые ресурсы	*(pat-tverzh-DYOON-nee re-SOOHR-see)*
demotion	понижение в должности	*(pa-nee-ZHEH-nee-ye VDOLZH-na-stee)*
demurrage	демередж (плата за простой)	*(DEH-me-retch [PLAH-ta za pras-TOY])*
density	плотность	*(PLOT-nast)*
department	отдел	*(ad-DEL)*
department store	универмаг	*(oo-nee-ver-MAHK)*
deposit	вклад	*(fklaht)*
deposit	месторождение	*(mes-ta-razh-DEH-nee-ye)*
deposit account	вкладной счёт	*(fklahd-NOY shchyoht)*
deposit, bank	банковский счёт	*(BAHN-kaf-skee shchyoht)*
depository	хранилище	*(khra-NEE-lee-shche)*
depreciation	амортизация	*(a-mar-tee-ZAH-tsee-ya)*
depreciation, accelerated	ускоренная амортизация	*(oos-KOH-ren-na-ya a-mar-tee-ZAH-tsee-ya)*
depreciation allowance	отчисления на амортизацию	*(at-chees-LEH-nee-ya na a-mar-tee-ZAH-tsee-yoo)*

depreciation, accrued	амортизационный резерв	(a-mar-tee-za-tsee-ON-nee re-ZEHRF)
depreciation of currency	обесценивание валюты	(a-bes-TSEH-nee-va-nee-ye va-LYOO-tee)
depression	депрессия	(de-PRES-see-ya)
deputy chairman	заместитель председателя	(za-mes-TEE-tel pret-se-DAH-te-lya)
deputy manager	заместитель менеджера	(za-mes-TEE-tel MEH-ned-zhe-ra)
deregulated	разрегулированный	(raz-re-goo-LEE-ra-van-nee)
design engineering	проектирование/дизайн	(pra-yek-TEE-ra-va-nee-ye/ dee-ZAHYN)
designer	конструктор	(kan-STROOK-tar)
desktop publishing	настольные издательские средства	(nas-TOL-nee eez-DAH-tel-skee-ye SRETST-va)
desliming	обеспыливание	(a-bes-PEE-lee-va-nee-ye)
devaluation	девальвация	(de-val-VAH-tsee-ya)
developed field	освоенное месторождение	(as-VOH-en-na-ye mes-ta-razh-DEH-nee-ye)
developed drilling	эксплуатационное бурение	(eks-ploo-a-ta-tsee-ON-na-ye boo-REH-nee-ye)
development well	эксплуатационная скважина	(eks-ploo-a-ta-tsee-ON-na-ya SKVAH-zhee-na)
devonian shale	девонский сланец	(de-VON-skee SLAH-nets)
dial	номеронабиратель	(NOH-me-ra-na-bee-RAH-tel)
diesel fuel	дизельное топливо	(DEE-zel-na-ye TOP-lee-va)
differential, price	цена с надбавкой	(tse-NAH snad-BAHF-kay)
differential rent	дифференциальная рента	(deef-fe-ren-tsee-AHL-na-ya REHN-ta)
differential, tariff	надбавка к тарифу	(nad-BAHF-ka kta-REE-foo)
differential, wage	надбавка к зарплате	(nad-BAHF-ka kzar-PLAH-te)
digital	цифровой	(tsif-ra-VOY)
digital computer	цифровая ЭВМ	(tsif-ra-VAH-ya eh-veh-EM)
dilution of equity	разбавление капитала	(raz-bav-LEH-nee-ye ka-pee-TAH-la)

D

dilution of labor	обесценивание труда	*(a-bes-TSEH-nee-va-nee-ye troo-DAH)*
diode	диод	*(dee-OT)*
direct cost	прямые расходы	*(prya-MEE-ye ras-KHOH-dee)*
direct current	постоянный ток	*(pas-ta-YAHN-nee tok)*
direct expenses	прямые издержки	*(prya-MEE-ye eez-DEHRSH-kee)*
direct investment	прямые инвестиции	*(prya-MEE-ee een-ve-STEE-tsee-ee)*
direct labor (accounting)	заработная плата производственных рабочих	*(ZAH-ra-bat-na-ya PLAH-ta pra-eez-VOT-stven-nikh ra-BOH-cheekh)*
direct mail	почтовая реклама	*(pach-TOH-va-ya rek-LAH-ma)*
direct paper	непосредственные ценные бумаги	*(ne-pa-SREHT-stven-nee-ye TSEN-nee-ye boo-MAH-ghee)*
direct quotation	прямая котировка	*(pree-MAH-ya ka-TEE-rof-ka)*
direct selling	навязывание товара	*(na-VYAH-zee-va-nee-ye ta-VAH-ra)*
directional beacon	направленный радиомаяк	*(nap-RAHV-len-nee RAH-dee-a-ma-YAK)*
director	директор	*(dee-REK-tar)*
disbursement	выплата	*(VEE-pla-ta)*
discharge (v)	погашать/погасить	*(pa-ga-SHAHT/pa-ga-SEET)*
disc brake	дисковой тормоз	*(DEES-ka-vee TOHR-mazh)*
discount	скидка	*(SKEET-ka)*
discount cash flow	учётное «кэшфлоу»	*(oo-CHYOHT-na-ye "cash flow")*
discount rate	учётная ставка	*(oo-CHYOHT-na-ya STAHF-ka)*
discount securities	учётные ценные бумаги	*(oo-CHYOHT-nee-ye TSEN-nee-ye boo-MAH-ghee)*
discounting	практика предоставления скидки	*(PRAHK-tee-ka pre-da-sta-VLEH-nee-ya SKEET-kee)*
discovery bonus	«бонус» за открытие	*(BOH-noos za at-KREE-tee-ye)*

discretionary account	дискреционный счёт	*(dees-kre-tsee-ON-nee shchyoht)*
discretionary order	дискреционный заказ	*(dees-kre-tsee-ON-nee za-KAHS)*
disease	болезнь	*(ba-LEZN)*
dishonor (as a check)	опротестовать	*(a-pra-tes-ta-VAHT)*
disk	диск	*(deesk)*
disk (floppy)	гибкий диск	*(GHEEP-kee deesk)*
disk (hard)	жёсткий диск	*(ZHOST-kee deesk)*
disk (laser)	лазерный диск	*(LAH-zer-nee deesk)*
disk drive	дисковод	*(dees-ka-VOT)*
disk drive (hard)	дисковод для жёстких дисков	*(dees-ka-VOT dla ZHOST-keekh DEES-kaf)*
disk drive (floppy)	дисковод для гибких дисков	*(dees-ka-VOT dla GHEEP-keekh DEES-kaf)*
disk space	пространство на диске	*(pra-STRAHN-stva na DEES-ke)*
dispatch	отправка	*(at-PRAHF-ka)*
displacement	рабочий объём	*(ra-BOH-chee ab-YOM)*
disposable income	личный чистый доход	*(LEECH-nee CHEES-tee da-KHOT)*
dispute	спор	*(spohr)*
dispute (v)	спорить	*(SPOH-reet)*
dispute, labor	спор с профсоюзом	*(spohr spraf-sa-YOO-zam)*
distribution	распределение	*(ras-pre-de-LEE-nee-ye)*
distribution, channels of	каналы распределения	*(ka-NAH-lee ras-pre-de-LEH-nee-ya)*
distribution costs	издержки распределения	*(eez-DEHRSH-kee ras-pre-de-LEH-nee-ya)*
distribution network	распределительная сеть	*(ras-pre-de-LEH-tel-na-ya set)*
distribution policy	политика распределения	*(pa-LEE-tee-ka ras-pre-de-LEH-nee-ya)*
distributor	распределитель	*(ras-pre-de-LEH-tel)*
diuretic	мочегонное средство	*(ma-che-GON-na-ye SRET-stva)*
diversification	диверсификация	*(dee-ver-see-fee-KAH-tsee-ya)*

D

divestment	лишение	*(lee-SHEH-nee-ye)*
dividend	дивиденд	*(dee-vee-DENT)*
dividend yield	доход от дивидендов	*(da-KHOT at de-vee-DEN-taf)*
division of labor	разделение труда	*(raz-de-LEH-nee-ye troo-DAH)*
dock handling charges	пошлины причала	*(POSH-lee-nee pree-CHAH-la)*
dock (ship's receipt)	доковая накладная	*(DOK-ka-va-ya nak-lad-NAH-ya)*
document	документ	*(da-koo-MENT)*
dollar cost averaging	калькуляция себестоимости в долларах	*(kal-koo-LYAH-tsee-ya se-be-STOH-ee-ma-stee VDOL-la-rakh)*
domestic bill	внутренний вексель	*(VNOOT-ren-nee VEK-sel)*
domestic corporation	отечественное акционерное общество	*(a-TEH-chest-ven-na-ye ak-tsee-a-NEHR-na-ya OP-shchest-va)*
domestic gas	отечественный газ	*(a-TEH-chest-ven-nee gahs)*
door-to-door sales	продажа товаров на дому	*(pra-DAH-zha ta-VAH-raf na da-MOO)*
Doppler effect	эффект Допплера	*(ef-FEKT DOP-ple-ra)*
dosage	дозировка	*(da-zee-ROF-ka)*
dose	доза	*(DOH-za)*
double dealing	«двойная игра»	*(dvay-NAH-ya eeg-RAH)*
double-entry bookkeeping	двойная бухгалтерия	*(dvay-NAH-ya bookh-gal-TEH-ree-ya)*
double pricing	двойное ценообразование	*(dvay-NOH-ye TSEN-na-ab-ra-za-VAH-nee-ye)*
double taxation	двойное налогообложение	*(dvay-NOH-ye na-LOH-ga-ab-la-ZHEH-nee-ye)*
double time	в два раза быстрее	*(vdvah RAH-za bis-TREH-ye)*
down payment	аванс	*(a-VAHNS)*
down the line	подчинённый	*(pat-chee-NYON-nee)*
downswing	временный экономический спад	*(VREH-men-nee e-ka-na-MEE-ches-kee spaht)*
downtime	время простоя	*(VREH-mya pras-TOH-ya)*

downturn	экономический спад	(*e-ka-na-MEE-ches-kee spaht*)
draft (instrument)	тратта	(*TRAHT-ta*)
draft (document)	черновик	(*cher-na-VEEK*)
drawback (disad-vantage)	недостаток	(*ne-das-TAH-tak*)
drawback (money)	возврат таможенных пошлин	(*vaz-VRAHT ta-MOH-zhen-nikh POSH-leen*)
draw-down	снятие денег со счёта	(*SNYAH-tee-ye DEH-nek sa SHCHYOH-ta*)
drawee	трассат	(*tras-SAHT*)
drawer	трассант	(*tras-SAHNT*)
dressing	повязка	(*pa-VYAHZ-ka*)
drip irrigation	капельное орошение	(*KAH-pel-na-ye a-ra-SHEH-nee-ye*)
driver	водитель	(*va-DEE-tel*)
drop	капля	(*KAHP-lya*)
drop shipment	прямые грузопоставки	(*pree-MEE-ye groo-za-pas-TAHF-kee*)
drought	засуха	(*ZAH-soo-kha*)
drug	лекарственное средство/лекарство	(*le-KAHR-stven-na-ye SRET-stva*)
drugstore	аптека	(*ap-TEH-ka*)
dry cargo	сухогруз	(*soo-kha-GROOS*)
dry goods	сухой товар	(*soo-KHOY ta-VAHR*)
dry hole	непродуктивная («сухая») скважина	(*ne-pra-dook-TEEV-na-ya [soo-KHAH-ya] SKVAH-zhee-na*)
dual rotor heli-copter	двухвинтовой вертолёт	(*dvookh-vin-ta-VOY ver-ta-LYOT*)
duck	утка	(*OOT-ka*)
dummy	макет	(*MAH-ket*)
dump gas	сбросовый газ	(*ZBROH-sa-vee gahs*)
dumping (goods in trade)	демпинг	(*DEM-peenk*)
dung	кизяк	(*kee-ZYAHK*)
dunnage	подстилка	(*pat-STEEL-ka*)
duopoly	дуополия	(*doo-oh-POH-lee-ya*)

D

durable goods	товары длительного пользования	*(ta-VAH-ree DLEE-tel-na-va POL-za-va-nee-ya)*
duress	принуждение	*(pree-noozh-DEH-nee-ye)*
duty (customs)	пошлина	*(POSH-lee-na)*
duty ad valorem	адвалорные пошлины	*(ad-va-LOHR-nee-ye POSH-lee-nee)*
duty, anti-dumping	антидемпинговая пошлина	*(AHN-tee-DEHM-peen-ga-va-ya POSH-lee-na)*
duty, countervailing	компенсационная пошлина	*(kam-pen-sa-tsee-ON-na-ya POSH-lee-na)*
duty, export	вывозная пошлина	*(vee-vaz-NAH-ya POSH-lee-na)*
duty free	беспошлинный	*(bes-POSH-lee-neey)*
duty, remission	возврат пошлин	*(vaz-VRAHT POSH-leen)*
duty, specific	специфические пошлины	*(spe-tsee-FEE-ches-kee-ye POSH-lee-nee)*
dye (v)	красить	*(KRAH-seet)*
dynamics, group	групповая динамика	*(groop-pa-VAH-ya dee-NAH-mee-ka)*
dynamics, market	рыночная динамика	*(REE-nach-na-ya dee-NAH-mee-ka)*
dynamics, product	динамика продуктов	*(dee-NAH-mee-ka pra-DOOK-taf)*

E

earmark (v)	предназначать/предназначить	*pred-na-zna-CHAT/pred-na-zna-CHEET)*
early warning radar	радиолокационная станция (РЛС) дальнего обнаружения	*(RAH-dee-a-la-ka-tsee-ON-na-ya STAHN-tsee-ya [EHR-EL-ES] DAHL-ne-va ab-na-roo-ZHEH-nee-ya)*
earnings	заработок	*(ZAH-ra-ba-tak)*
earnings on assets	доход в расчёте на активы	*(da-KHOT vra-SHCHYOH-te na ak-TEE-vee)*
earnings per share	доход в расчёте на акцию	*(da-KHOT vra-SHCHYOH-te na AHK-tsee-yoo)*
earnings performance	рентабельность	*(ren-TAH-bel-nast)*

earnings/price ratio	коэффициент окупаемости капиталовложений	*(ka-ef-fee-tsee-ENT a-koo-PAH-ye-mas-tee ka-pee-TAH-la-vla-ZHEH-neey)*
earnings report	отчёт о доходах	*(at-CHYOHT a da-KHOM-dakh)*
earnings yield	реальный доход	*(re-AHL-nee da-KHOT)*
earnings, retained	нераспределённая прибыль	*(ne-ras-pre-de-LYON-na-ya PREE-beel)*
econometrics	эконометрика	*(e-ka-na-MET-ree-ka)*
economic (of the economy)	экономический	*(e-ka-na-MEE-ches-kee)*
economic indicators	экономические показатели	*(e-ka-na-MEE-ches-kee-ye pa-ka-ZAH-te-lee)*
economic life	экономическая долговечность/период рентабельной разработки месторождения	*(e-ka-na-MEE-ches-ka-ya dal-ga-VECH-nast/pe-REE-at ren-TAH-bel-nay raz-ra-BOT-kee mes-ta-razh-DEH-nee-ya)*
economize	экономить	*(e-ka-NOH-meet)*
economy	экономия	*(e-ka-NOH-mee-ya)*
edit (v)	редактировать	*(re-dak-TEE-ra-vat)*
edition	издание	*(eez-DAH-nee-ye)*
editor	редактор	*(re-DANK-tar)*
effective yield	действительный доход	*(dey-STVEE-tel-nee da-KHOT)*
efficiency	эффективность	*(ef-fe-KTEEV-nast)*
egg	яйцо	*(YAHY-tsa)*
elasticity (of supply or demand)	эластичность спроса и предложения	*(e-las-TEECH-nast SPROH-sa ee pred-la-ZHEH-nee-ya)*
electric arc furnace	электродуговая печь	*(e-LEK-tra-doo-ga-VAH-ya pech)*
electrical engineering	электротехника	*(e-lek-tra-TEKH-nee-ka)*
electricity	электричество	*(e-lek-TREE-chest-va)*
electrode	электрод	*(e-lek-TROT)*
electrolysis	электролиз	*(eh-lek-TROH-lis)*
electrolytic process	электролитический процесс	*(e-lek-tra-lee-TEE-ches-kee pra-TSES)*

E

electron	электрон	*(e-lek-TRON)*
electronic	электронный	*(e-lek-TRON-nee)*
electrostatic	электростатический	*(e-lek-tra-sta-TEE-ches-kee)*
element	элемент	*(e-le-MENT)*
elm	вяз	*(vyaz)*
embargo	запрет, эмбарго	*(zap-RET, em-BAHR-ga)*
embezzlement	присвоение чужих денежных средств	*(pree-sva-YEH-nee-ye choo-ZHIKH DEH-nezh-neekh sretstf)*
embossed paper	тиснёная бумага	*(tees-NYON-na-ya boo-MAH-ga)*
embryo	эмбрион	*(em-bree-ON)*
emergency petroleum reserves	чрезвычайные запасы жидкого топлива	*(chrez-vee-CHAHY-nee-ye za-PAH-see ZHIT-ka-va-TOP-lee-va)*
employee	служащий	*(SLOO-zha-shcheey)*
employee counseling	ориентация служащего	*(a-re-yen-TAH-tsee-ya SLOO-zha-shche-va)*
employee relations	отношения служащих с руководством	*(at-na-SHEH-nee-ya SLOO-zha-shcheekh sroo-ka-VOT-stvam)*
employment agency	биржа труда	*(BEEHR-zha troo-DAH)*
encumbrance	залог	*(za-LOK)*
end of period	конец срока	*(ka-NETS SROH-ka)*
end product	конечный продукт	*(ka-NECH-nee pra-DOOKT)*
end-use certificate	покупательский сертификат качества	*(pa-koo-PAH-tel-skee ser-tee-fee-KAHT KAH-chest-va)*
endorsee	индоссат	*(een-da-SSAHT)*
endorsement	индоссамент	*(een-da-SSAH-ment)*
endorsement (approval)	одобрение	*(a-da-BREH-nee-ye)*
endowment	дотация	*(da-TAH-tsee-ya)*
energy return ratio	коэффициент энергоотдачи	*(ka-ef-fee-tsee-ENT e-NEHR-ga-ad-DAH-chee)*
energy resources	источники энергии	*(ees-TOCH-nee-kee e-NEHR-ghee-ee)*

engine	двигатель	*(DVEE-ga-tel)*
engineer	инженер	*(een-zhe-NEER)*
engineering	техника	*(TEKH-nee-ka)*
engineering, design	инженерное проектирование	*(een-zhe-NEHR-na-ye pra-yek-TEE-ra-va-nee-ye)*
engineering, pro-duction	производственная технология	*(pra-eez-VOT-stven-na-ya tekh-na-LOH-ghee-ya)*
engrave (v)	делать клише	*(DEH-lat klee-SHEH)*
enhanced oil recov-ery	повышенное извлечение нефти	*(pa-VEE-shen-na-ye eez-vle-CHEH-nee-ye NEF-tee)*
enlarge (v)	увеличивать	*(oo-veh-LEE-chee-vat)*
enterprise	предприятие	*(pret-pree-YAH-tee-ye)*
entrepreneur	предприниматель	*(pret-pree-nee-MAH-tel)*
entry, cash	запись о поступлении наличности	*(ZAH-pees a pa-stoop-LEH-nee-ee na-LEECH-na-stee)*
entry, debit	дебетовая запись	*(DEH-be-ta-va-ya ZAH-pees)*
entry, ledger	бухгалтерская запись	*(bookh-GAHL-ter-ska-ya ZAH-pees)*
entry permit	входное разрешение	*(fkhad-NOH-ye raz-re-SHEH-nee-ye)*
enzyme	фермент	*(fer-MENT)*
equal pay for equal work	равенство заработной платы	*(RAH-ven-stva ZAH-ra-bat-nay PLAH-tee)*
equipment	оборудование	*(a-ba-ROO-da-va-nee-ye)*
equipment leasing	аренда оборудования	*(a-REN-da a-ba-ROO-da-va-nee-ya)*
equity	чистая доля в средствах	*(CHEES-ta-ya DOH-lya FSRET-stvakh)*
equity capital	собственный капитал	*(SOP-stven-nee ka-pee-TAHL)*
equity crude oil	«собственная» нефть	*(SOP-stven-na-ya neft)*
equity, dilution	разбавление чистой доли	*(raz-ba-VLEH-nee-ye CHEES-tay DOH-lee)*
equity, return on	доходы от акций	*(da-KHOH-dee at AHK-tseey)*
ergonomics	эргономика	*(ehr-ga-NOH-mee-ka)*

E

erosion	эрозия	*(e-ROH-zee-ya)*
error	ошибка	*(a-SHIP-ka)*
error message	сообщение об ошибке	*(sa-ap-SHCHEH-nee-ye a-ba-SHIP-ke)*
escalator clause	оговорка о скользящих ценах	*(a-ga-VOHR-ka a skal-ZYAH-shcheekh TSEH-nakh)*
escheat	выморочность имущества	*(VEE-ma-rach-nast ee-MOO-shchest-va)*
escrow	условно врученный документ за печатью	*(oos-LOV-na vroo-CHYON-nee da-koo-MENT za pe-CHAH-tyoo)*
estate (decedent)	имение	*(ee-MEH-nee-ye)*
estate (property)	имущество	*(ee-MOO-shchest-va)*
estate agent	агент по продаже недвижимости	*(a-GHENT pa pra-DAH-zhe ne-DVEE-zhee-ma-stee)*
estate tax	налог на имение	*(na-LOK na ee-MEH-nee-ye)*
estimate	оценка	*(a-TSEN-ka)*
estimate (v)	оценивать/оценить	*(a-TSEH-nee-vat/a-tseh-NEET)*
estimate, sales	смета оборота	*(SMEH-ta a-ba-ROH-ta)*
estimated price	сметная стоимость	*(SMET-na-ya STOH-ee-mast)*
estimated time of arrival	предполагаемое время прибытия	*(pret-pa-la-GAH-ye-ma-ye VREH-mya pree-BEE-tee-ya)*
estimated time of departure	предполагаемое время отправления	*(pret-pa-la-GAH-ye-ma-ye VREH-mya at-prav-LEH-nee-ya)*
ethane	этан	*(e-TAHN)*
ethanol	этанол	*(e-ta-NOL)*
ether	простой эфир	*(pra-STOY e-FEEHR)*
Eurobond	Евробон	*(yev-ra-BON)*
Eurocurrency	евровалюта	*(yev-ra-va-LYOO-ta)*
Eurodollar	евродоллары	*(yev-ra-DOL-la-ree)*
evaluation	оценка	*(a-TSEN-ka)*
evaluation, job	оценка работы	*(a-TSEN-ka ra-BOH-tee)*
evaporation	испарение	*(ees-pa-REH-nee-ye)*

ex dock	франко пристани	*(FRAHN-ka PREES-ta-nee)*
ex factory	франко завода	*(FRAHN-ka za-VOH-da)*
ex-gasifier price	цена франко-газогенератора	*(tse-NAH FRAHN-ka GAH-za-ghe-ne-RAH-ta-ra)*
exhaust	выхлоп	*(VIKH-lap)*
ex mill	франко фабрики	*(FRAHN-ka FAHB-ree-kee)*
ex mine	франко шахты	*(FRAHN-ka SHAHKH-tee)*
ex warehouse	франко склад	*(FRAHN-ka sklat)*
ex works	франко фабрики	*(FRAHN-ka FAHB-ree-kee)*
exchange	биржа	*(BEEHR-zha)*
exchange (v)	обменивать/обменять	*(ab-MEH-nee-vat/ab-meh-NYAHT)*
exchange control	валютный контроль	*(va-LYOOT-nee kan-TROL)*
exchange loss	валютные потери	*(va-LYOOT-nee-ye pa-TEH-ree)*
exchange rate	валютный курс	*(va-LYOOT-nee koors)*
exchange risk	риск колебания валютного курса	*(reesk ka-le-BAH-nee-ya va-LYOOT-na-va KOOHR-sa)*
excise duty	акцизная пошлина	*(ak-TSIZ-na-ya POSH-lee-na)*
excise tax	акциз	*(ak-TSIS)*
exclusive representative	исключительный представитель	*(ees-kloo-CHEE-tel-nee pret-sta-VEE-tel)*
executive	исполнитель	*(ees-pal-NEE-tel)*
executive board	президиум/совет управляющих	*(pre-ZEE-dee-oom/sa-VET oop-rav-LYAH-yoo-shcheekh)*
executive, chief	главный исполнитель	*(GLAHV-nee ees-pal-NEE-tel)*
executive committee	исполнительный комитет	*(ees-pal-NEE-tel-nee ka-mee-TET)*
executive compensation	вознаграждение исполнительного состава	*(vaz-na-gra-ZHDEH-nee-ye ees-pal-NEE-tel-na-va sa-STAH-va)*
executive director	исполнительный директор	*(ees-pal-NEE-tel-nee dee-REK-tar)*
executive, line	линейный исполнитель	*(lee-NEY-nee ees-pal-NEE-tel)*

E

executor	судебный исполнитель	(soo-DEB-nee ees-pal-NEE-tel)
exemption	освобождение	(as-va-bazh-DEH-nee-ye)
expectations, up to our	в соответствии с нашими ожиданиями	(fsa-at-VET-stvee-ee SNAH-shee-mee a-zhee-DAH-nee-ya-mee)
expenditure	издержки	(eez-DEHRSH-kee)
expenses	расходы	(ras-KHOH-dee)
experiment	эксперимент	(eks-pe-ree-MENT)
experimental	экспериментальный	(eks-pe-ree-men-TAHL-nee)
expert opinion	экспертиза	(eks-per-TEE-za)
expiry date	дата просрочки	(DAH-ta pra-SROH-chkee)
exploratory costs	затраты на проведение поисково-разведочных работ	(za-TRAH-te na pra-ve-DEH-nee-ye pa-EES-ka-va-raz-VEH-dach-neekh ra-BOT)
exploratory well	поисково-разведочная скважина	(POH-ees-ka-va-raz-VEH-dach-na-ya SKVAH-zhee-na)
export (v)	вывозить	(vee-va-ZEET)
export agent	экспортный агент	(EKS-part-nee a-GHENT)
export credit	экспортный кредит	(EKS-part-nee kre-DEET)
export duty	экспортная пошлина	(EKS-part-na-ya POSH-lee-na)
export quota	экспортная квота	(EKS-part-na-ya KVOH-ta)
export regulation	экспортные распоряжения	(EKS-part-nee-ye ras-pa-rya-ZHEN-nee-ya)
export tariff	экспортный тариф	(EKS-part-nee ta-REEF)
Export-Import bank	Экспортно-Импортный Банк (США)	(EKS-part-na-EEM-part-nee bahnk [se-sha-a])
expropriation	экспропрация	(eks-pra-pree-AH-tsee-ya)
extraction ratio	коэффициент извлечения	(ka-ef-fee-tsee-ENT eez-vle-CHEH-nee-ya)
extra-heavy oil	«сверхтяжелая» нефть	(sverkh-tya-ZHOH-la-ya neft)
ewe	овца	(af-TSAH)
eyedrop	глазные капли	(glaz-NEE-ye KAHP-lee)
eyeglass case	футляр для очков	(foot-LYAHR dlya ach-KOF)

E

F

face value	номинальная стоимость	*(na-mee-NAHL-na-ya STOH-ee-mast)*
facilities (means of production)	производственные фонды	*(pra-eez-VOT-stven-nee-ye FON-dee)*
facilities (possibilities)	производственные возможности	*(pra-eez-VOT-stven-nee-ye vaz-MOZH-na-stee)*
factor (agent)	фактор	*(FAHK-tar)*
factor (component, element)	составная часть	*(sas-tav-NAH-ya chast)*
factor analysis	фактурный анализ	*(fak-TOOHR-nee a-NAH-lees)*
factory	завод	*(za-VOT)*
factory overhead	общезаводские накладные расходы	*(OP-shche-za-vat-SKEE-ye nak-lad-NEE-ye ras-KHOH-dee)*
fail (v)	провалиться	*(pra-va-LEE-tsa)*
fail (v) (go bankrupt)	обанкротиться	*(a-bank-ROH-tee-tsa)*
failure	провал/банкротство	*(pra-VAHL/ bank-ROT-stva)*
fair market value	справедливая рыночная стоимость	*(spra-ved-LEE-va-ya REE-nach-na-ya STOH-ee-mast)*
fair return	средний доход	*(SRED-nee da-KHOT)*
fair trade	торговля на основе взаимной выгоды	*(tar-GOV-lya na as-NOH-ve vza-EEM-nay VEE-ga-dee)*
fallow-field	поле под паром	*(POH-lee pat PAH-ram)*
fan	вентилятор	*(ven-tee-LYAH-tar)*
farm	хутор	*(KHOO-tar)*
farm labor	батрак	*(bat-RAHK)*
farm out (v)	договор о субаренде (продуктивного участка)	*(da-ga-VOHR a-soob-a-REHN-de [pra-dook-TEEV-na-va oo-CHAHST-ka])*
farm-out	отдать часть работы	*(ad-DAHT chast ra-BOH-tee)*
farmer	фермер	*(FEHR-mer)*
feed	корм	*(kohrm)*

feedback	обратная связь	*(ab-RAHT-na-ya svyas)*
feed materials	сырьевые материалы	*(sihr-ye-VEE-ye ma-te-ree-YAH-lee)*
felony	фелония (уголовное преступление)	*(fe-LOH-nee-ya [oo-ga-LOHF-na-ye pres-too-PLEH-nee-ye])*
fender	крыло	*(kree-LOH)*
ferroalloys	ферросплавы	*(fehr-ra-SPLAH-vee)*
ferromanganese	ферромарганец	*(fer-ra-MAHR-ga-nets)*
ferronickel	ферроникель	*(fehr-ra-NEE-kel)*
fertilizer	удобрение	*(oo-dab-REH-nee-ye)*
fitch	хорьковый мех	*(khar-KOH-vee mekh)*
fiduciary	фидуциарный	*(fee-doo-tsee-AHR-nee)*
fiduciary loan	фидуциарная ссуда	*(fee-doo-tsee-AHR-na-ya SSOO-da)*
fiduciary relation-ship	фидуциарное отношение	*(fee-doo-tsee-AHR-na-ye at-na-SHEH-nee-ye)*
field	поле/месторождение	*(POH-le)/(mes-ta-RAZH-dee-nee-ye)*
field (data)	поле данных	*(POH-le DAHN-nikh)*
field (display)	поле индикации	*(POH-le een-dee-KAH-tsee-ye)*
field (input)	область ввода	*(OB-last VVOH-da)*
field warehousing	складирование на местах	*(skla-DEE-ra-va-nee-ye na mes-TAHKH)*
file (v)	хранить документ	*(khra-NEET da-koo-MENT)*
file (v) (submit forms)	представлять документ	*(pret-stav-LYAHT da-koo-MENT)*
file	файл	*(fahyl)*
filter	фильтр	*(feeltr)*
final oil recovery	конечная нефтеотдача	*(ka-NECH-na-ya NEF-te-ad-DAH-cha)*
finance (v)	финансировать	*(fee-nan-see-ra-VAHT)*
finance	финансы	*(fee-NAHN-see)*
finance company	финансовая компания	*(fee-NAHN-sa-va-ya kam-PAH-nee-ya)*
financial analysis	финансовый анализ	*(fee-NAHN-sa-vee a-NAH-lees)*

financial appraisal	оценка финансового состояния	*(a-TSEN-ka fee-NAHN-sa-va-va sa-sta-YAH-nee-ya)*
financial control	финансовый контроль	*(fee-NAHN-sa-vee kan-TROL)*
financial director	финансовый директор	*(fee-NAHN-sa-vee dee-REK-tar)*
financial highlights	кульминационные моменты финансового состояния	*(kool-mee-na-tsee-ON-nee ma-MEN-tee fee-NAHN-sa-va-va sa-sta-YAH-nee-ya)*
financial incentive	финансовый стимул	*(fee-NAHN-sa-vee STEE-mool)*
financial manage-ment	управление финансовой деятельностью	*(oop-rav-LEH-nee-ye fee-NAHN-sa-vay DEH-ya-tel-na-styoo)*
financial pages, newspaper	биржевой отчёт в газете	*(beer-zhe-VOY at-CHYOHT vga-ZEH-te)*
financial period	финансовый срок	*(fee-NAHN-sa-vee srok)*
financial planning	финансовое планирование	*(fee-NAHN-sa-va-ye pla-NEE-ra-va-nee-ye)*
financial services	финансовые услуги	*(fee-NAHN-sa-vee-ye oos-LOO-ghee)*
financial statement	финансовый отчёт	*(fee-NAHN-sa-vee at-CHYOHT)*
financial year	финансовый год	*(fee-NAHN-sa-vee got)*
fine (penalty)	штраф	*(strahf)*
finished goods inventory	запас готовых изделий	*(za-PAHS ga-TOH-veekh eez-DEH-leey)*
finished products	конечные продукты	*(ka-NECH-nee-ye pra-DOOK-tee)*
finishing mill	чистовой прокатный стан	*(chees-ta-VOY pra-KAHT-nee stahn)*
fir	пихта	*(PEEKH-ta)*
fire (v)	увольнять/уволить	*(oo-val-NYAHT/ oo-VOH-leet)*
fire-break	противопожарная полоса	*(pra-tee-va-pa-ZHAHR-na-ya pa-la-SAH)*
firm	фирма	*(FEEHR-ma)*
first in first out (FIFO)	первым поступил — первым продан (ФИФО)	*(PEHR-vim pa-stoo-peel PEHR-vim PROH-dan [FEE-FOH)]*

F

fiscal agent	сборщик налогов	*(ZBOHR-shcheek na-LOH-gaf)*
fiscal drag	финансовый тормоз	*(fee-NAHN-sa-vee TOHR-mas)*
fiscal year	отчётный год	*(at-CHYOHT-nee got)*
fishery	рыбный промысел	*(RIB-nee PROH-mee-sel)*
fixed assets	основные активы	*(as-nav-NEE-ye ak-TEE-vee)*
fixed capital	основной капитал	*(as-nav-NOY ka-pi-TAHL)*
fixed charges	основные издержки	*(as-nav-NEE-ye eez-DEHRSH-kee)*
fixed-commitment contract	контракт с «твёрдым обязательством»	*(kan-TRAHKT STVYOHR-dim a-bya-ZAH-tel-stvam)*
fixed costs	основные стоимости	*(as-nav-NEE-ye STOH-ee-ma-stee)*
fixed expenses	основные расходы	*(as-nav-NEE-ye ras-KHOH-dee)*
fixed frame rig/platform	стационарная буровая установка/платформа	*(sta-tsee-a-NAHR-na-ya boo-ra-VAH-ya oos-ta-NOF-ka/plat-FOHR-ma)*
fixed income	установленный доход	*(oo-STAH-nov-len-nee da-KHOT)*
fixed capital investment	вложение в основной капитал	*(vla-ZHEH-nee-ye vas-nav-NOY ka-pee-TAHL)*
fixed liability	долгосрочное обязательство	*(dal-ga-SROCH-na-ye a-bya-ZAH-tel-stva)*
fixed rate of exchange	фиксированный валютный курс	*(feek-SEE-ra-van-nee va-LYOOT-nee koors)*
fixed-rate royalty	фиксированное «роялти»	*(fee-KSEE-ra-van-na-ye ROH-yal-tee)*
fixed term	фиксированный срок	*(feek-SEE-ra-van-nee srok)*
fixture	движимость/соединенная с недвижимостью	*(DVEE-zhee-mast/sa-ye-dee-NYON-na-ya sne-DVEE-zhe-mast-yoo)*
flat bond	непроцентная облигация	*(ne-pra-TSENT-na-ya ab-lee-GAH-tsee-ya)*
flat rate	единообразная ставка	*(ye-dee-na-ab-RAHZ-na-ya STAHF-ka)*
flat yield	постоянный доход	*(pa-sta-YAHN-nee da-KHOT)*

F

flatcar	вагон-платформа	*(va-GON-plat-FOHR-ma)*
flexible tariff	непостоянная пошлина	*(ne-pa-sta-YAHN-na-ya POSH-lee-na)*
flight computer	навигационный вычислитель	*(na-vee-ga-tsee-ON-nee vee-chee-SLEE-tel)*
float	лесосплав	*(le-sa-SPLAHF)*
float (v) (issue stock)	размещать акции	*(raz-me-SHCHAHT AHK-tsee-ee)*
float (outstanding checks)	размещать чеки	*(raz-me-SHCHAHT CHEH-kee)*
floating currency	свободно плавающая валюта	*(sva-BOD-na PLAH-va-yoo-shcha-ya va-LYOO-ta)*
floater (in elections)	избиратель-гастролёр	*(eez-bee-RAH-tel-gas-tra-LYOHR)*
floating assets	оборотные средства	*(a-ba-ROT-nee-ye SRET-stva)*
floating exchange rate	плавающий валютный курс	*(PLAH-va-yoo-shchee va-LYOOT-nee koors)*
floating rate	плавающая ставка	*(PLAH-va-yoo-shcha-ya STAHF-ka)*
flock	стая	*(STAH-ya)*
floor (stock exchange)	операционный зал фондовой биржи	*(a-pe-ra-tsee-ON-nee zahl FON-da-vay BEEHR-zhe)*
floppy disk	гибкий диск	*(GHEEP-kee deesk)*
flow chart	технологическая схема	*(tekh-na-la-GHEE-ches-ka-ya SKHEH-ma)*
follow-up order	дополнительный заказ	*(da-pal-NEE-tel-nee za-KAHS)*
follow up (v)	доводить до конца	*(da-va-DEET da kan-TSAH)*
font	комплект шрифта	*(kam-PLEKT SHREEF-ta)*
foodstuffs	пищевые продукты	*(pee-shche-VEE-ye pra-DOOK-tee)*
forest	лес	*(les)*
forest fire	лесной пожар	*(les-NOY pa-ZHAHR)*
for export	назначено для экспорта	*(naz-NAH-che-na dla EKS-par-ta)*
forecast	прогноз	*(prag-NOS)*
foreign bill of exchange	иностранный вексель	*(ee-na-STRAHN-nee VEK-sel)*

F

foreign corpora-tion	иностранное акционерное общество	*(ee-na-STRAHN-na-ye ak-tsee-a-NEHR-na-ye OP-shche-stva)*
foreign currency	иностранная валюта	*(ee-na-STRAHN-na-ya va-LYOO-ta)*
foreign debt	иностранный долг	*(ee-na-STRAHN-nee dolk)*
foreign exchange	иностранная валюта	*(ee-na-STRAHN-na-ya va-LYOO-ta)*
foreign security	иностранная ценная бумага	*(ee-na-STRAHN-na-ya TSEN-na-ya boo-MAH-ga)*
foreign tax credit	иностранная налоговая скидка	*(ee-na-STRAHN-na-ya na-LOH-ga-va-ya SKEET-ka)*
foreign trade	внешняя торговля	*(VNESH-nya-ya tar-GOV-lya)*
foreman	мастер	*(MAHS-ter)*
foreword	предисловие	*(pre-dees-LOH-vee-ye)*
forgery	фальшивка-подделка	*(fal-SHIF-ka)*
form letter	стандартное письмо	*(stan-DAHRT-na-ye pees-MOH)*
format	формат	*(far-MAHT)*
formula	формула	*(FOHR-moo-la)*
forward (v)	отправлять/отправить	*(at-prav-LYAHT/at-pra-VEET)*
forward contract	запродажа будущей продукции	*(za-pra-DAH-zha BOO-doo-shchey pra-DOOK-tsee-ee)*
forward purchase	покупка на срок	*(pa-KOOP-ka na srok)*
forward shipment	груз, оплачиваемый в порту выгрузки	*(groos ap-LAH-chee-va-ye-mee FPOHR-too VEE-groos-kee)*
forwarding agent	агент/экспедитор	*(a-GHENT/esk-pe-DEE-tar)*
fossil fuels	горючие полезные ископаемые	*(ga-RYOO-chee-ye pa-LEZ-nee-ye ees-ka-PAH-ye-mee-ye)*
foul bill of lading	нечистый коносамент	*(ne-CHEES-tee ka-na-se-MENT)*
founder	учредитель	*(ooch-re-DEE-tel)*

F

foundry	литейный завод	*(lee-TEY-nee za-VOT)*
four-cylinder engine	четырёхтактный двигатель	*(chee-tee-RYOKH-TAHKT-nee DVEE-ga-tel)*
four-color	четырёхцветная печать	*(che-tee-ryokh-TSVET-na-ya pe-CHAHT)*
fowl	птица	*(PTEE-tsa)*
fox (fur)	лисий мех	*(LEE-see mekh)*
franchise	привилегия	*(pree-vee-LEH-ghee-ya)*
fraud	обман	*(ab-MAHN)*
free alongside ship	франко вдоль борта (ФАС)	*(FRAHN-ka vdol BOHR-ta)*
free and clear	необременённый	*(ne-ab-re-me-NYON-nee)*
free economic zone	свободная экономическая зона	*(sva-BOD-na-ya e-ka-na-MEE-ches-ka-ya ZOH-na)*
free enterprise	свободное предпринимательство	*(sva-BOD-na-ye pret-pree-nee-MAH-tel-stva)*
free gas	свободный газ (газ чисто газовых залежей)	*(sva-BOD-nee gahs [gahs CHEES-ta GAH-za-vikh ZAH-le-zhey])*
free list	список необлагаемых пошлиной товаров	*(SPEE-sak ne-ab-la-GAH-ye-mikh POSH-lee-nay ta-VAH-raf)*
free market	свободный рынок	*(sva-BOD-nee REE-nak)*
free of particular average	свободно от частной аварии	*(sva-BOD-na at CHAHS-nay a-VAH-ree)*
free of board (fob)	франко-борт (ФОБ)	*(FRAHN-ka-BOHRT)*
free port	порто-франко	*(POHR-ta-FRAHN-ka)*
free time	свободное время	*(sva-BOD-na-ye VREH-mya)*
free trade	беспошлинная торговля	*(bes-POSH-leen-na-ya tar-GOV-lya)*
freelance writer	писатель, работающий по найму	*(pee-SAH-tel ra-BOH-ta-yoo-shchee pa NAY-moo)*
freight	фрахт	*(frahkht)*
freight all kinds	фрахт всех видов	*(frahkht fsekh VEE-daf)*
freight collect	фрахт/оплачиваемый в порту назначения	*(frahkht/ap-LAH-chee-va-ye-mee FPAHR-too naz-na-CHEH-nee-ya)*
freight forwarder	экспедитор	*(esk-pe-DEE-tar)*

F

freight included	с фрахтом	*(SFRAHKH-tam)*
freight prepaid	фрахт/оплачиваемый предварительно	*(frahkht/ap-LAH-chee-va-yee-mee pred-va-REE-tel-na)*
frequency	частота	*(chas-ta-TAH)*
frequency curve	кривая периодичности	*(kree-VAH-ya pe-ree-a-DEECH-na-stee)*
frequency modulation (FM)	частотная модуляция	*(chas-TOT-na-ya ma-doo-LYAH-tsee-ya)*
fringe benefits	льготы и привилегии	*(LGOH-tee ee pree-vee-LEH-ghee-ee)*
fringe market	неофициальный рынок	*(ne-a-fee-tsee-AHL-nee REE-nak)*
front-end fee	внутренний взнос	*(VNOOT-ren-nee vznos)*
front-wheel drive	передний привод	*(pe-RED-nee PREE-vat)*
frost	мороз	*(ma-ROZ)*
frozen assets	замороженные активы	*(za-ma-ROH-zhen-nee-ye ak-TEE-ve)*
fruit	фрукты	*(FROOK-tee)*
fuel cycle	топливный цикл	*(TOP-leev-nee tsikl)*
fuel gas	топливный газ	*(TOP-leev-nee gahs)*
fuel oil	котельное топливо (мазут)	*(ka-TEL-na-ye TOP-lee-va [ma-ZOOT])*
fuel oil parity	мазутный паритет (цен на газ)	*(ma-ZOOT-nee pa-ree-TET [tsen na gahs])*
fuel pump	бензиновый насос	*(ben-ZEE-na-vee na-SOS)*
functional analysis	функциональный анализ	*(foonk-tsee-a-NAHL-nee a-NAH-lees)*
fund	фонд	*(font)*
fund, contingent	чрезвычайный фонд	*(chrez-vee-CHAHY-nee font)*
funds, mutual	взаимные фонды	*(vza-EEM-nee-ye FON-dee)*
fund, sinking	фонд погашения	*(font pa-ga-SHEH-nee-ya)*
funds, public	общественные фонды	*(ap-SHCHEST-ven-nee-ye FON-dee)*
funds, working	эксплуатационные фонды	*(eks-ploo-a-ta-tsee-ON-nee-ye FON-dee)*
fungible goods	заменимые товары	*(za-me-NEE-mee-ye ta-VAH-ree)*

F

furnace	печь	*(peech)*
furniture	мебель	*(MEH-bel)*
fuselage	фюзеляж	*(fyoo-ze-LYAHSH)*
futures	срочные контракты	*(SROCH-nee-ye kan-TRAHK-tee)*
futures option	опцион на срочном контракте	*(ap-tsee-ON na SROCH-nam kan-TRAHK-tee)*

G

galley proof	корректурная гранка	*(kar-rek-TOOHR-nee-ye GRAHN-kee)*
galvanizing	гальванизация	*(gal-va-nee-ZAH-tsee-ya)*
garnishment	обращение взыскания на заработную плату	*(ab-ra-SHCHEH-nee-ye vzis-KAH-nee-ya na ZAH-ra-bat-noo-yoo PLAH-too)*
gas company	газовая компания	*(GAH-za-va-ya kam-PAH-ne-ya)*
gas condensate	газовый конденсат	*(GAH-za-vee kan-den-SAHT)*
gas consumption	расход горючего	*(ras-KHOT ga-RYOO-che-va)*
gas oil	газойль	*(ga-ZOYL)*
gasoline	бензин	*(ben-ZEEN)*
gasoline tank	газгольдер	*(gaz-GOL-der)*
gas pool	газовая залежь	*(GAH-za-va-ya ZAH-lesh)*
gas well	газовая скважина	*(GAH-za-va-ya SKVAH-zhee-na)*
gas hidrate deposit	газогидратная залежь	*(GAH-za-gheed-RAHT-na-ya ZAH-lesh)*
gasohol	газохол	*(ga-za-KHOL)*
gearshift	коробка передач	*(ka-ROP-ka pe-re-DAHCH)*
general acceptance	безусловный акцепт	*(be-zoos-LOV-nee ak-TSEPT)*
general average loss	убыток от общей аварии	*(oo-BEE-tak at OP-shchey a-VAH-ree-ee)*
general manager	главный управляющий	*(GLAHV-nee oop-rav-LYAH-yoo-shchee)*

G

general meeting	общее собрание	*(OP-shchee sa-BRAH-nee-ye)*
general partner- ship	полное товарищество	*(POL-na-ye ta-VAH-ree-shchest-va)*
general strike	всеобщая забастовка	*(fse-OP-shcha-ya za-bas-TOF-ka)*
generator	генератор	*(ghe-ne-RAH-tar)*
gentleman's agree- ment	устное соглашение	*(OOS-na-ye sa-gla-SHEH-nee-ye)*
geopressured gas	газ зон геодавлений	*(gahz zon ghe-a-dav-LEH-nee-ya)*
glossy paper	глянцевая бумага	*(GLYAHN-tse-va-ya boo-MAH-ga)*
gloves	перчатки	*(per-CHAHT-kee)*
glut	насыщение рынка	*(na-see-SHCHEH-nee-ye REEN-ka)*
goat (f)	коза	*(ka-ZHA)*
goat (m)	козёл	*(ka-ZYOL)*
go around (v)	обходить/обойти	*(ap-kha-DEET/a-bay-tee)*
go public (v)	предлагать/предложить публичную подписку	*(pred-la-GAHT/pred-la-ZHEET poob-LEECH-noo-yoo pat-PEES-koo)*
go-down	падение курса	*(pa-DEH-nee-ye KOOHR-sa)*
going concern value	стоимость функционирующего предприятия	*(STOH-e-mast foonk-tsee-a-NEE-roo-yoo-shche-va pret-pree-YAH-tee-ya)*
going price	текущая цена	*(tee-KOO-shcha-ya tse-NAH)*
going rate	обычная ставка	*(a-BICH-na-ya STAHF-ka)*
gold clause	золотая оговорка	*(za-la-TAH-ya a-ga-VOHR-ka)*
gold price	цена золота	*(tse-NAH ZOH-la-ta)*
gold reserves	золотые запасы	*(za-la-TEE-ye za-PAH-see)*
good faith	добросовестность	*(da-bra-SOH-ves-nast)*
goods	товары	*(ta-VAH-ree)*
goodwill	«гудвил» — цена нематериальных активов	*(GOOD-veel – tse-NAH ne-ma-te-ree-AHL-nikh ak-TEE-vaf)*

G

goose	гусь	*(goos)*
gophers	гофры	*(GOF-ree)*
government	правительство	*(pra-VEE-tel-stva)*
government agency	государственное агентство	*(ga-soo-DAHR-stven-na-ye a-GHEHN-stva)*
government bank	государственный банк	*(ga-soo-DAHR-stven-nee bahnk)*
government bonds	государственные облигации	*(ga-soo-DAHR-stven-nee-ye ab-lee-GAH-tsee-ee)*
grace period	льготный период	*(LGOT-nee pe-REE-at)*
graft	блат	*(blaht)*
grain	зерно	*(zer-NOH)*
granary	зернохранилище	*(zer-na-khra-NEE-le-shche)*
graph	схема	*(SKHEH-ma)*
grass	трава	*(tra-VAH)*
grasshopper	кузнечик	*(kooz-NEH-cheek)*
gratuity	чаевые	*(cha-ye-VEE-ye)*
gray market	полулегальный рынок	*(POH-loo-le-GAHL-nee REE-nak)*
grazing land	выпас	*(VEE-pas)*
green house	теплица	*(tep-LEE-tsa)*
Greenwich Mean Time	Гринвичское среднее время	*(GREEN-veech-ska-ye SRED-ne-ye VREH-mya)*
grievance procedure	порядок разрешения жалоб	*(pa-RYAH-dak raz-re-SHEH-nee-ya ZHAH-lap)*
grille	решётка	*(re-SHYOT-ka)*
grinding	шлифование	*(shlee-fa-VAH-nee-ye)*
gross domestic product (GDP)	валовой внутренний продукт	*(va-la-VOY VNOOT-ren-nee pra-DOOKT)*
gross income	валовой доход	*(va-la-VOY da-KHOT)*
gross investment	валовое капиталовложение	*(va-la-VOH-ye ka-pee-TAH-la-vla-ZHEH-nee-ye)*
gross loss	валовой убыток	*(va-la-VOY oo-BEE-tak)*
gross margin	маржинальный доход	*(mar-zhee-NAHL-nee da-KHOT)*

G

gross national product	валовой общественный продукт	*(va-la-VOY ab-SHCHEST-ven-nee pra-DOOKT)*
gross price	общая цена	*(OP-shcha-ya tse-NAH)*
gross profit	валовая прибыль	*(va-la-VAH-ya PREE-bil)*
gross sales	валовой объём продажи	*(va-la-VOY ab-YOM pra-DAH-zhee)*
gross spread	валовой разрыв (между ценами)	*(va-la-VOY raz-RIF [MEZH-doo TSEH-na-mee])*
gross weight	вес брутто	*(ves BROOT-ta)*
gross yield	валовой доход	*(va-la-VOY da-KHOT)*
ground water	грунтовая вода	*(groon-TOH-va-ya va-DAH)*
group account	групповой счёт	*(groop-pa-VOY shchyoht)*
group dynamics	динамика групп	*(dee-NAH-mee-ka groop)*
group insurance	групповое страхование	*(groop-pa-VOH-ye stra-kha-VAH-nee-ye)*
growth	рост	*(rost)*
growth company	быстрорастущая компания	*(BIST-ra ras-TOO-shcha-ya kam-PAH-nee-ya)*
growth index	индекс роста	*(EEN-deks ROS-ta)*
growth rate	уровень роста	*(OO-ra-ven ROS-ta)*
guarantee	аваль	*(a-VAHL)*
guaranteed gas supplies	гарантированные поставки газа	*(ga-ran-TEE-ra-van-nee-ye pas-TAHF-kee GAH-za)*
guaranteed royalty	гарантированное «роялти»	*(ga-ran-TEE-ra-van-nee-ye ROH-yal-tee)*
guaranty bond	гарантия	*(ga-RAHN-tee-ya)*
guaranty company	авалист	*(a-va-LEEST)*
guesstimate (v)	оценивать/оценить	*(a-TSEH-nee-vat/a-tsee-NEET)*
guideline	директива	*(dee-rek-TEE-va)*

H

half-life	период полураспада	*(pe-REE-at po-loo-ras-PAH-da)*
handbag	дамская сумка	*(DAHM-ska-ya SOOM-ka)*

handicap	препятствие	*(pre-PYAHT-stvee-ye)*
hand-tooled	обработанный вручную	*(ab-ra-BOH-tan-nee vrooch-NOO-yoo)*
hangar	ангар	*(an-GAHR)*
harbor dues	портовые сборы	*(par-TOH-vee-ye ZBOH-ree)*
hard copy	твёрдая копия	*(TVYOHR-da-ya KOH-pee-ya)*
hard cover	в жёстком/твёрдом переплёте	*(VZHOST-kam pe-re-PLYOH-te)*
hard currency	твёрдая валюта	*(TVYOHR-da-ya va-LYOO-ta)*
hard energy	централизованная энергия	*(tsen-tra-lee-ZOH-van-na-ya e-NEHR-ghee-ya)*
hard sell	навязывание товаров покупателю	*(na-VYAH-zee-va-nee-ye ta-VAH-ra pa-koo-PAH-tee-lyoo)*
hardware	скобяные изделия	*(ska-bya-NEE-ye eez-DEH-lee-ya)*
hardware (computer)	аппаратные средства	*(ap-pa-RAHT-nee SRET-stva)*
hardwood	древесина лиственных пород	*(dre-ve-SEE-na LEEST-ven-nikh pa-ROT)*
harvest	урожай	*(oo-ra-ZHAHY)*
harvestable	годный на сводку	*(GOD-nee nas-VOT-koo)*
hatched larvae	вылупившиеся личинки	*(VEE-loo-peef-shee-ye-sa lee-CHEEN-ke)*
hay	сено	*(se-NAH)*
head line	заголовок/заглавие	*(za-ga-LOH-vak/za-GLAH-vee-ye)*
head office	главная контора фирмы	*(GLAHV-na-ya kan-TOH-ra FEEHR-mee)*
headhunting	подбор квалифицированных кадров	*(pad-BOHR kva-lee-fe-TSEE-ra-van-neekh KAHD-raf)*
headquarters	штаб	*(shtahp)*
heat	теплота	*(tep-la-TAH)*
heavy industry	тяжёлая промышленность	*(tee-ZHOH-la-ya pra-MISH-len-nast)*
hectare	гектар	*(gheek-TAHR)*

H

hedge (v)	хеджировать/страховаться от потери	*(khed-ZHEE-ra-vat/stra-kha-VAHT-sa at pa-TEH-ree)*
helicopter	вертолёт	*(ver-ta-LYOT)*
hen	курица	*(KOO-ree-tsa)*
herbs	кухонные травы	*(koo-KHON-nee-ye TRAH-vee)*
herbicide	гербицид	*(gher-bee-TSEE-dee)*
herd	стадо	*(STAH-da)*
hidden asset	скрытый актив	*(SKREE-tee ak-TEEF)*
high-BTU gas	высококалорийный газ	*(vee-SOH-ka-ka-la-REEY-nee gahs)*
high fidelity	с высокой точностью воспроизведения	*(SVEE-so-kay TOCH-nast-yoo vas-pra-eez-ve-DEH-nee-ya)*
highest bidder	покупщик с наилучшим предложением	*(pa-koop-SHCHEEK sna-ee-LOOCH-shim pred-la-ZHEH-nee-yem)*
hire (v)	нанимать/нанять	*(na-nee-MAHT/na-NYAHT)*
hoard (v)	припрятывать/припрятать	*(pree-PRYAH-tee-vat/pree-PRYAH-taht)*
holder	держатель	*(der-ZHAH-tel)*
holder in due course	законный держатель	*(za-KON-nee der-ZHAH-tel)*
holding company	материнская компания	*(ma-te-REEN-ska-ya kam-PAH-nee-ya)*
holster	кобура	*(ka-boo-RAH)*
home market	домашний рынок	*(da-MAHSH-nee REE-nak)*
homogeneity	гомогенность	*(ga-ma-GHEN-nast)*
hops	хмель	*(khmel)*
hormones	гормоны	*(gar-MOH-nee)*
hornbeam	граб	*(grahp)*
horse	лошадь	*(LOH-shat)*
horsepower	лошадиная сила	*(la-sha-DEE-na-ya SEE-la)*
hot money	плавающие капиталы	*(PLAH-va-yoo-shchee-ye ka-pi-TAH-lee)*
hot rolling	горячая прокатка	*(ga-RYAH-cha-ya pra-KAHT-ka)*

hourly earnings	почасовая зарплата	*(pa-cha-sa-VAH-ya zar-PLAH-ta)*
housing authority (residential)	управление жилищного фонда	*(oop-rav-LEH-nee-ye zhee-LEESHCH-na-va FON-da)*
human resources	людские ресурсы	*(lyoot-SKEE-ye re-SOOHR-see)*
hydraulic booster	гидроусилитель	*(GHEED-ra-oo-see-LEH-tel)*
hydrocarbon	углеводород	*(oog-le-va-da-ROT)*
hydrocarbon fuel	углеводородное топливо	*(oog-le-ROD-na-ye TOP-lee-va)*
hydrocarbon liquids	жидкие углеводороды (ЖУВ)	*(ZHIT-kee-ye oog-le-va-da-ROH-dee)*
hydrocarbon prospects	перспективы нефтегазоносности	*(per-spek-TEE-vee NEF-te-GAH-za-NOS-na-stee)*
hydrocloric acid	соляная кислота	*(sa-LYAH-na-ya kees-la-TAH)*
hydrolysis	гидролиз	*(gheed-ROH-lees)*
hydroponics	гидропоника	*(gheed-ra-POH-nee-ka)*
hypertension	гипертензия	*(ghee-per-TEN-zee-ya)*
hyphenate (v)	писать через дефис	*(pee-SAHT che-rez de-FEES)*
hypothecation	ипотека	*(ee-pa-TEH-ka)*

I

IBM	компания ИБМ	*(kam-PAH-nee-ya IBM)*
IBM-compatible	ИБМ-совместимый	*(AHY-BEE-EM-sav-me-STEE-mee)*
icon	образ (пиктограмма)	*(OB-ras [pik-ta-GRAHM-ma)*
idle capacity	резервная мощность	*re-ZHERV-na-ya MOSHCH-nast)*
ignition	зажигание	*(za-shee-GAH-nee-ye)*
illegal	незаконный	*(ne-za-KON-nee)*
illegal shipments	незаконные грузы	*(ne-za-KON-nee-ye GROO-zee)*
imitation	подделка	*(pad-DEL-ka)*

implication (con-clusion)	значение	*(zna-CHEH-nee-ye)*
implication (involvement)	вовлечение	*(va-vle-CHEH-nee-ye)*
implied agreement	подразумеваемое соглашение	*(pad-ra-zoo-me-VAH-ye-ma-ye sag-la-SHEH-nee-ye)*
import	импорт	*(EEM-part)*
import (v)	ввозить/ввезти	*(vva-ZEET/vve-ZTEE)*
import declaration	ввозное заявление	*(vvaz-NOH-ye za-yav-LEH-nee-ye)*
import deposits	импортный взнос	*(EEM-part-nee vznos)*
import duty	импортная пошлина	*(EEM-part-na-ya POSH-lee-na)*
import license	импортная лицензия	*(EEM-part-na-ya lee-TSEN-zee-ya)*
import quota	импортная квота	*(EEM-part-na-ya KVOH-ta)*
import regulations	импортные распоряжения	*(EEM-part-nee-ye ras-pa-rya-ZHEH-nee-ya)*
import tariff	импортный тариф	*(EEM-part-nee ta-REEF)*
impound (v)	наложить арест	*(na-la-ZHEET a-REST)*
improve upon (v)	улучшать/улучшить	*(oo-looch-SHAHT/oo-LOOCH-sheet)*
improvement	улучшение	*(oo-looch-SHEH-nee-ye)*
impulse purchase	покупка от импульса	*(pa-KOOP-ka at EEM-pool-sa)*
impurity	примесь	*(PREE-mes)*
imputed	презюмируемый	*(pre-zyoo-MEE-roo-ye-mee)*
in the red	быть в долгу	*(beet vdal-GOO)*
in transit	в пути	*(fpoo-TEE)*
inadequate	недостаточный, неадекватный	*(ne-da-STAH-tach-nee/ne-ad-e-KVAHT-nee)*
incentive	стимул	*(STEE-mool)*
inch	дюйм	*(dyoom)*
inchoate interest	интерес/не оформленный окончательно	*(een-te-RES/ne-a-FOHR-mlen-nee a-kan-CHAH-tel-na)*
incidental expenses	побочные расходы	*(pa-BOCH-nee ras-KHOH-dee)*

income	доход	*(da-KHOT)*
income account	счёт доходов	*(shchyoht da-KHOH-daf)*
income bonds	процентные облигации	*(pra-TSENT-nee-ye ab-lee-GAH-tsee-ee)*
income bracket	рамка доходов	*(RAHM-ka da-KOH-dakh)*
income statement	отчёт о доходах	*(at-CHYOHT a da-KHO-daf)*
income tax	подоходный налог	*(pa-da-KHOD-nee na-LOK)*
income, gross	валовой доход	*(va-la-VOY da-KHOT)*
income, net	чистый доход	*(CHEES-tee da-KHOT)*
incorporate (v)	учреждать акционерное общество	*(ooch-rezh-DAHT ak-tsee-a-NEHR-na-ye OP-shchest-va)*
increase	прирост	*(pree-ROST)*
increase (v)	увеличивать/увеличить	*(oo-ve-LEE-chee-vat/oo-ve-lee-CHEET)*
increased costs	дополнительные расходы	*(da-pal-NEE-tel-nee-ye ras-KHOH-dee)*
incremental cash flow	приростное «кэшфлоу»	*(pree-ROST-na-ye "cash flow")*
incremental cash costs	приростные расходы	*(pree-ROST-nee-ye ras-KHOH-dee)*
indebtedness	задолженность	*(za-DOL-zhen-nast)*
indemnity	индемнитет (гарантия от убытков)	*(een-dem-nee-TET [ga-RAHN-tee-ya at oo-BIT-kaf])*
indenture	договор ученичества	*(da-ga-VOHR oo-che-NEE-chest-va)*
index	индекс	*(een-DEKS)*
index (v)	снабжать/снабдить	*(snab-ZHAHT/snab-DEET)*
indexing	индексация	*(een-dek-SAH-tsee-ya)*
indirect claim	непосредственная претензия	*(ne-pa-SRET-stven-na-ya pre-TEN-zee-ya)*
indirect costs	косвенные издержки	*(KOS-ven-nee-ye eez-DEHRSH-kee)*
indirect expenses	косвенные затраты	*(KOS-ven-nee-ye za-TRAH-tee)*
indirect labor expenses	косвенные трудовые расходы	*(KOS-ven-nee-ye troo-da-VEE-ye ras-KHOH-dee)*

I

indirect taxes	косвенные налоги	*(KOS-ven-nee-ye na-LOH-ghee)*
induction	индукция	*(een-DOOK-tsee-ya)*
induction furnace	индукционная печь	*(een-dook-tsee-ON-na-ya pech)*
industrial accident	промышленное аварийное происшествие	*(pra-MISH-len-na-ye a-va-REEY-na-ye pra-ees-SHEST-vee-ye)*
industrial arbitration	промышленный арбитраж	*(pra-MISH-len-nee ar-beet-RAHSH)*
industrial direct heating	прямое промышленное использование топлива	*(pre-MOH-ye pra-MISH-len-na-ye ees-pol-za-va-nee-ye TOP-lee-va)*
industrial engineering	промышленный инжиниринг	*(pra-MISH-len-nee een-zhe-NEE-reenk)*
industrial gas	промышленный природный газ	*(pra-MISH-len-nee pree-ROD-nee gahs)*
industrial goods	промышленные товары	*(pra-MISH-len-nee-ye ta-VAH-ree)*
industrial insurance	производственное страхование	*(pra-eez-VOT-stven-na-ye stra-kha-VAH-nee-ye)*
industrial planning	промышленное проектирование	*(pra-MISH-len-na-ye pra-yek-TEE-ra-va-nee-ye)*
industrial relations	отношения между администрацией и рабочими	*(at-na-SHEH-nee-ya mezh-doo ad-mee-nee-STRAH-tsee-yey ee ra-BOH-chee-mee)*
industrial union	промышленное объединение	*(pra-MISH-len-na-ye ab-ye-dee-NEH-nee-ye)*
industry	промышленность	*(pra-MISH-len-nast)*
industry-wide	по всей отрасли (промышленности)	*(pa fsey OT-ras-lee [pra-MISH-len-na-stee])*
inefficient	непроизводительный	*(ne-pra-eez-VAH-dee-tel-nee)*
inelastic demand	неэластичный спрос	*(ne-e-la-STEECH-nee spros)*
inelastic supply	неэластичное предложение	*(ne-e-la-STEECH-na-ye pred-la-ZHEH-nee-ye)*
infant industry	молодая отрасль промышленности	*(ma-la-DAH-ya OT-rasl pra-MISH-len-na-stee)*
inferred reserves	подразумеваемые запасы	*(pad-ra-zoo-me-VAH-ye-mee-ye za-PAH-see)*

inflation	инфляция	*(een-FLYAH-tsee-ya)*
inflationary	инфляционный	*(een-fla-tsee-ON-nee)*
infrastructure	инфраструктура	*(een-fra-strook-TOO-ra)*
ingot mold	изложница	*(eez-LOZH-nee-tsa)*
ingots	слитки	*(SLEET-kee)*
inheritance tax	налог на наследство	*(na-LOK na nas-LET-stva)*
injector	инжектор	*(een-ZHEK-tar)*
injunction	судебный запрет	*(soo-DEB-nee zap-RET)*
initial reserves	начальные разведанные запасы	*(na-CHAHL-nee-ye raz-VEH-dan-nee-ye za-PAH-see)*
ink	чернила	*(cher-NEE-la)*
inland bill of lading	внутренний коносамент	*(VNOOT-ren-nee ka-na-sa-MENT)*
in-line booster	последовательно расположенный ускоритель	*(pas-LEH-da-va-tel-na ras-pa-LOH-zhen-nee oos-ka-REE-tel)*
innovation	новшество/нововведение	*(NOF-she-stva/no-vo-VVE-de-nee-ye)*
inorganic chemistry	неорганическая химия	*(ne-ar-ga-NEE-ches-ka-ya KHEE-mee-ya)*
input	ввод	*(vvot)*
insecticide	инсектицид	*(een-sek-tee-TSIT)*
insert	вкладыш	*(FKLAH-deesh)*
insects	насекомые	*(na-se-KOH-mee-ye)*
insolvent	несостоятельный должник	*(ne-sa-sta-YAH-tel-nee dal-ZHNEEK)*
inspection	осмотр	*(as-MOTR)*
inspector	ревизор/инспектор	*(re-vee-ZOHR/een-SPEK-tar)*
instability	нестабильность	*(ne-sta-BEEL-nast)*
installment credit	кредит с погашением в рассрочку	*(kre-DEET spa-ga-SHEH-nee-em vras-SROCH-koo)*
installment plan	погашение долга в рассрочку	*(pa-ga-SHEH-nee-ee DOL-GA vras-SROCH-koo)*
institutional advertising	учреждённая реклама	*(ooch-rezh-DYON-na-ya rek-LAH-ma)*
institutional investor	инвестор-учреждение	*(een-VES-tar-ooch-rezh-DEH-nee-ye)*

I

instruct (v) (order)	давать/дать указания	*(da-VAHT/dat oo-ka-ZAH-nee-ya)*
instruct (v) (teach)	обучать/обучить	*(a-boo-CHAT/a-boo-CHEET)*
instrument (document)	правовой акт (документ)	*(pra-va-VOY ahkt [da-koo-MENT])*
instrumental capital	производительный капитал	*(pra-eez-va-DEE-tel-nee ka-pee-TAHL)*
insulator	инсулятор	*(een-soo-LYAH-tar)*
insurance	страхование	*(stra-kha-VAH-nee-ye)*
insurance broker	страховой маклер	*(stra-kha-VOY MAHK-ler)*
insurance company	страховая компания	*(stra-kha-VAH-ya kam-PAH-nee-ya)*
insurance fund	страховой фонд	*(stra-kha-VOY font)*
insurance policy	страховой полис	*(stra-kha-VOY POH-lees)*
insurance premium	страховой взнос	*(stra-kha-VOY vznos)*
insurance underwriter	страховой поручитель-гарант	*(stra-kha-VOY pa-roo-CHAH-tel-ga-RAHNT)*
intangible assets	нематериальные активы	*(ne-ma-te-ree-AHL-nee ak-TEE-vee)*
integrated circuit (IC)	интегральная схема (ИС)	*(een-te-GRAHL-na-ya SKHEH-ma [EE-ES])*
integrated management system	комплексная система управления	*(KOM-pleks-na-ya sees-TEH-ma oop-rav-LEH-nee-ya)*
Intel	компания «Интель»	*(kam-PAH-nee-ya EEN-tel)*
Intel-based	Интеловский	*(EEN-te-lof-skee)*
interact (v)	взаимодействовать	*(vza-ee-ma-DEY-stva-vat)*
interbank	межбанковский	*(mezh-BAHN-kaf-skee)*
interest	проценты	*(pra-TSEN-tee)*
interest (return on capital)	проценты на капитал	*(pra-TSEN na ka-pee-TAHL)*
interest (share)	имущественное право (доля)	*(ee-MOO-shchest-ven-na-ye PRAH-va [DOH-lya])*
interest arbitrage	процентный арбитраж	*(pra-TSEN-nee ar-beet-RAHSH)*
interest expenses	расходы по уплате процентов	*(ras-KHOH-dee pa oop-LAH-te pra-TSEN-taf)*

interest income	процентный доход	*(pra-TSEN-nee da-KHOT)*
interest parity	процентный паритет	*(pra-TSEN-nee pa-ree-TET)*
interest period	срок интереса	*(srok een-te-REH-sa)*
interest rate	процентная ставка	*(pra-TSEN-na-ya STAHF-ka)*
interim	промежуточный	*(pra-me-ZHOO-tach-nee)*
interim budget	промежуточный бюджет	*(pra-me-ZHOO-tach-nee byood-ZHET)*
interim statement	промежуточный финансовый отчёт	*(pra-me-ZHOO-tach-nee fee-NAHN-sa-vee at-CHYOHT)*
interlocking directorate	советы директоров с взаимными членами	*(sa-VEH-tee dee-rek-ta-ROF zvza-EEM-nee-mee CHLEH-na-mee)*
intermediary	посредник	*(pa-SRED-neek)*
intermediary goods	полуфабрикаты	*(poh-loo-fab-ree-KAH-tee)*
internal	внутренний	*(VNOOT-ren-nee)*
internal audit	внутренняя ревизия	*(VNOOT-ren-nya-ya re-VEE-zee-ya)*
internal funding	внутреннее финансирование	*(VNOOT-ren-ne-ye fee-nan-SEE-ra-va-nee-ye)*
internal rate of return	внутренняя ставка рентабельности	*(VNOOT-ren-nya-ya STAHF-ka ren-TAH-bel-na-stee)*
Internal Revenue Service	Служба Налогообложения (США)	*(SLOOZH-ba na-LOH-ga-ab-la-ZHEH-nee-ya)*
International Date Line	линия перемены дат	*(LEE-nee-ya pe-re-MEH-nee dat)*
International Energy Agency	Международное Энергетическое Агентство	*(mezh-doo-na-ROD-na-ye e-ner-ghe-TEE-ches-ka-ye a-GHENT-stva)*
International Gas Union	Международный Газовый Союз	*(mezh-doo-na-ROD-nee GAH-za-vee sa-YOOS)*
International Geological Congress	Международный Геологический Конгресс	*(mezh-doo-na-ROD-nee ghe-a-la-GHEE-ches-kee kan-GRES)*
interstate commerce	межштатная торговля	*(mezh-doo-SHTAHT-na-ya TAHR-gov-lya)*
intervene (v)	вмешиваться/вмешаться	*(VMEH-shee-vat-sa/vme-SHAH-tsa*
interview (media)	интервью	*(een-tehr-VYOO)*

I

intestate	умерший без завещания	*(oo-MEHR-sheey bez za-ve-SHCHAH-nee-ya)*
in the red	быть в долгу	*(beet vdal-GOO)*
in transit	в пути	*(fpoo-TEE)*
intrinsic value	присущая стоимость	*(pree-SOO-shcha-ya STOH-ee-mast)*
invalidate (v)	лишать законной силы	*(lee-SHAHT za-KON-nay SEE-lee)*
inventory	запас	*(za-PAHS)*
inventory control	запасной контроль	*(za-pas-NOY kan-TROL)*
inventory turnover	движение запасов	*(dvee-ZHEH-nee-ye za-PAH-saf)*
inverted market	оборотный рынок	*(a-ba-ROT-nee REE-nak)*
invest (v)	вкладывать/вложить капитал	*(FKLAH-dee-vat/vla-ZHEET ka-pee-TAHL)*
invested capital	инвестированный капитал	*(een-ves-TEE-ra-van-nee ka-pee-TAHL)*
investment	капиталовложение	*(ka-pee-TAH-la-vla-ZHEH-nee-ye)*
investment adviser	финансовый советник	*(fee-NAHN-sa-vee sa-VET-neek)*
investment analysis	анализ капиталовложения	*(a-NAH-lees ka-pee-TAH-la-vla-ZHEH-neey)*
investment bank	инвестиционный банк	*(een-ve-stee-tsee-ON-nee bahnk)*
investment budget	капиталовложение в бюджете	*(ka-pee-TAH-la-vla-ZHEH-nee-ye vbyood-ZHEH-te)*
investment company	инвестиционная компания	*(een-ve-stee-tsee-ON-na-ya kam-PAH-nee-ya)*
investment credit	инвестиционный кредит	*(een-ve-stee-tsee-ON-nee kre-DEET)*
investment criteria	критерии капиталовложения	*(kree-TEH-ree-ee ka-pee-TAH-la-vla-ZHEH-nee-ya)*
investment grade	инвестиционное качество	*(een-ve-stee-tsee-ON-na-ye KAH-chest-va)*
investment policy	политика капиталовложения	*(pa-lee-tee-KAH ka-pee-TAH-la-vla-ZHEH-nee-ya)*
investment program	программа капиталовложения	*(pra-GRAHM-ma ka-pee-TAH-la-vla-ZHEH-nee-ya)*

I

investment strate-gy	стратегия капиталовложения	*(stra-TEH-ghee-ya ka-pee-TAH-la-vla-ZHEH-nee-ya)*
investment trust	инвестиционный траст	*(een-ve-stee-tsee-ON-nee trahst)*
investor relations	отношения с инвесторами	*(at-na-SHEH-nee-ya sin-VES-ta-ra-mee)*
invisible exports	невидимый экспорт	*(ne-VEE-dee-mee EKS-part)*
invisible imports	невидимый импорт	*(ne-VEE-dee-mee EEM-part)*
invitation to bid	конкурс на выполнение работ	*(KON-koors na vee-pal-NEH-nee-ya ra-BOT)*
invoice	счёт-фактура	*(shchyoht-fak-TOO-ra)*
invoice cost	фактурная стоимость	*(fak-TOOHR-na-ya STOH-ee-mast)*
iron	железо	*(zhe-LEH-za)*
iron ore	железная руда	*(zhe-LEZ-na-ya roo-DAH)*
irrigate (v)	орошать	*(o-ra-SHAHT)*
isotope	изотоп	*(ee-za-TOP)*
issue (v)	выпускать/выпустить в обращение	*(vee-poos-KAHT/VEE-poo-steetvab-ra-SHCHEH-nee-ye)*
issue price	цена эмиссии	*(tse-NAH e-MEES-see-ee)*
issue (stock)	выпуск акций	*(VEE-poosk AHK-tseey)*
issued shares	выпускаемые акции	*(vee-poos-KAH-ye-mee-ye AHK-tsee-ee)*
italic	курсив	*(koor-SEEF)*
item (balance sheet)	статья	*(sta-TYAH)*
item (product)	изделие	*(eez-DEH-lee-ye)*
itemize (v)	перечислять/перечислить	*(pe-re-chees-LYAHT/pe-re-chees-LEET)*
itemized account	перечисленный счёт	*(pe-re-CHEES-len-nee shchot)*

J

jacket	суперобложка	*(SOO-per-ab-LOSH-ka)*
Jason clause	оговорка Язона	*(a-ga-VOHR-ka ya-ZOH-na)*

jawbone (v)	упорно уговаривать	*(oo-POHR-na oo-ga-VAH-ree-vat)*
jenny	подвижной кран	*(pad-veezh-NOY krahn)*
jet fighter	реактивный истребитель	*(re-ak-TEEV-nee ees-tre-BEE-tel)*
jet fuel	топливо для реактивных самолётов	*(TOP-lee-va dlya re-ak-TEEV-nikh sa-ma-LYOH-taf)*
jet lag	нарушение суточного ритма	*(na-ROO-she-nee-ye SOO-tach-na-va REET-ma)*
jet plane	реактивный самолёт	*(re-ak-TEEV-nee sa-ma-LYOT)*
job	задание, работа	*(za-DAH-nee-ye, ra-BOH-ta)*
job analysis	анализ работ	*(a-NAH-lees ra-BOHT)*
job description	должностная инструкция	*(DOHLZH-nast-na-ya een-STROOK-tsee-ya)*
job evaluation	оценка работы	*(a-TSEN-ka ra-BOH-tee)*
job hopper	тот, кто часто меняет место работы («летун»)	*(tot, ktoh CHAHS-ta me-NYAH-yet MES-ta ra-BOH-tee [le-TOON])*
job lot	отдельная партия	*(at-DEHL-na-ya PAHR-tee-ya)*
job performance	выполнение работы	*(vee-pal-NEH-nee-ee ra-BOH-tee)*
job security	гарантия занятости	*(ga-RAHN-tee-ya ZAH-nya-ta-stee)*
job shop	предприятие/производящее по заказу	*(pret-pree-YAH-tee-ye/pra-eez-va-DYAH-shcheye pa za-KAH-zoo)*
jobber	маклер на бирже	*(MAHK-ler na BEEHR-zhe)*
joint account	общий счёт	*(OP-shchee shchyoht)*
joint cost	совместная стоимость	*(sav-MES-na-ya STOH-ee-mast)*
joint estate	совместное имущество	*(sav-MES-na-ye ee-MOO-shchest-va)*
joint liability	совместная ответственность	*(sav-MES-na-ya at-VET-stven-nast)*
joint owner	совладелец	*(sa-vla-DEH-lets)*

J

joint stock company	совместное акционерное общество	*(sav-MES-na-ye ak-tsee-a-NEHR-na-ye OP-shche-stva)*
joint venture	совместное предприятие	*(sav-MES-na-ye pret-pree-YAH-tee-ye)*
journal	журнал/дневник	*(zhoor-NAHL/DNEV-nikh)*
journeyman	квалифицированный рабочий	*(kva-lee-fee-TSEE-ra-van-nee ra-BOH-chee)*
joystick	джойстик (рычаг)	*(DZHOY-steek [ree-CHAHK])*
junior partner	младший партнер	*(MLAHT-shee part-NYOHR)*
junior security	младшие ценные бумаги	*(MLAHT-shee-ye TSEN-nee-ye boo-MAH-ghee)*
jurisdiction	юрисдикция	*(yoo-rees-DEEK-tsee-ya)*
justify (v)	выключать (строку)	*(vee-kloo-CHAHT [stra-KOO])*

K

keep posted (v)	информировать	*(een-far-MEE-ra-vat)*
key	клавиша	*(KLAH-vee-sha)*
key case	футляр для ключей	*(foot-LYAHR dlya kloo-CHEY)*
key exports	ключевые вывозы	*(klyoo-che-VEE-ye VEE-va-zee)*
key man insurance	страхование от потери ключевого исполнителя	*(stra-kha-VAH-nee-ye at pa-TEH-ree klyoo-che-VOH-va ees-pal-NEE-te-lya)*
keyboard	клавиатура	*(kla-vee-a-TOO-ra)*
Keynesian economics	экономические принципы Кэйнса	*(e-ka-na-MEE-ches-kee-ye PREEN-tsee-pe KEYN-sa)*
kickback	магарыч	*(ma-ga-RICH)*
kidskin	шевро	*(shev-ROH)*
kiln	печь	*(pech)*
kilobyte	килобайт	*(kee-la-BAHYT)*
kilowatt	киловатт	*(kee-la-VAHT)*
kiting	выписка чеков против неинкасированных сумм	*(VEE-pees-ka CHEH-kaf PROH-teef ne-een-kas-SEE-ra-van-neekh soomm)*

K

knot	сучок, узел	*(soo-CHOK, OO-zel)*
know-how	«ноу-хау»	*(NOH-oo-KHAH-oo)*

L

labor	труд	*(troot)*
labor code	кодекс законов о труде	*(KOH-deks za-KOH-naf a troo-DEH)*
labor dispute	трудовой спор	*(troo-da-VOY spohr)*
labor force	рабочий коллектив	*(ra-BOH-chee kal-lek-TEEF)*
labor-intensive	трудоёмкий	*(troo-da-YOM-kee)*
labor law	закон о труде	*(za-KON a troo-DEH)*
labor leader	руководитель профсоюза	*(roo-ka-va-DEE-tel praf-sa-YOO-za)*
labor market	рынок труда	*(REE-nak troo-DAH)*
labor relations	отношения с рабочими	*(at-na-SHEH-nee-ya sra-BOH-chee-mee)*
labor-saving	рационализаторский	*(ra-tsee-a-na-lee-ZAH-tar-skee)*
labor turnover	оборот труда	*(a-ba-ROT troo-DAH)*
labor union	профсоюз	*(praf-sa-YOOS)*
laboratory	лаборатория	*(la-ba-ra-TOH-ree-ya)*
laboratory technician	лаборант	*(la-ba-RAHNT)*
laborer	рабочий	*(ra-BOH-chee)*
lacquer	лак	*(lahk)*
lagging indicator	показатель отставания	*(pa-ka-ZAH-tel at-sta-VAH-nee-ya)*
laissez-faire	невмешательство	*(ne-vme-SHAH-tel-stva)*
lamb	мерлушка	*(mer-LOOSH-ka)*
lamb	ягнёнок	*(yag-NYOH-nak)*
LAN (local area network)	локальная сеть	*(la-KAHL-na-ya set)*
land	земля	*(zem-LYAH)*
land grant	предоставление земли	*(pre-da-stav-LEH-nee-ye zem-LEE)*

land reform	земельная реформа	*(ze-MEL-na-ya re-FOHR-ma)*
land tax	поземельный налог	*(pa-ze-MEL-nee na-LOK)*
landed cost	стоимость с выгрузкой на берег	*(STOH-ee-mast SVEEG-roos-kay na BEH-rek)*
landing charges	сборы по выгрузке	*(ZBOH-ree pa VEEG-roos-ke)*
landing costs	расходы по выгрузке	*(ras-KHOH-dee pa VEEG-roos-ke)*
landing gear	шасси	*(shas-SEE)*
landowner	землевладелец	*(zem-le-vla-DEH-lets)*
laptop	дорожная ЭВМ	*(da-ROZH-na-ya eh-veh-EM)*
larch	лиственница	*(LEEST-ven-nee-tsa)*
large-scale	крупный масштаб	*(KROOP-nee ma-SHTAHP)*
laser	лазер	*(LAH-ser)*
last in – first out (LIFO)	«последним поступил — первым продан» (ЛИФО)	*(pas-LED-neem pas-too-PEEL – PEHR-veem PROH-dan [LEE-FOH])*
launch pad	пусковой стол	*(poos-ka-VOY stol)*
launcher	пусковая установка	*(poos-ka-VAH-ya oos-ta-NOF-ka)*
law	закон	*(za-KON)*
law of diminishing returns	закон сокращающихся доходов	*(za-KON sa-kra-SHCHAH-yoo-shcheekh-sa da-KHOH-daf)*
lawsuit	судебный иск	*(soo-DEB-nee eesk)*
lawyer	адвокат	*(ad-va-KAHT)*
laxative	слабительное средство	*(sla-BEE-tel-na-ye SRET-stva)*
lay off (v)	временно увольнять рабочих	*(VRE-men-na oo-val-NYAHT ra-BOH-cheekh)*
lay out	расположение	*(ras-pa-la-ZHEH-nee-ye)*
lay time	срок задержки судна в порту	*(srok za-DEHRSH-kee SOOD-na fpar-TOO)*
lay up (v)	выводить/вывести из строя	*(vee-va-DEET/vee-ves-TEE ees STROH-ya)*
laydays	сталийные дни	*(sta-LEEY-nee dnee)*

layout	схема расположения	*(SKHEH-ma ras-pa-la-ZHEH-nee-ya)*
leader	глава	*(gla-VAH)*
leading indicator	ведущий экономический показатель	*(ve-DOO-shchee e-ka-na-MEE-ches-kee pa-ka-ZAH-tel)*
leads and lags	контемпоризация	*(kan-tem-pa-ree-ZAH-tsee-ya)*
leaf	лист	*(leest)*
leaf-eating insects	листоеды	*(lees-ta-YEH-dee)*
leakage	утечка	*(oo-TECH-ka)*
lean gas	тощий газ	*(TOH-shchee gahs)*
lease (v) (as lessee)	брать/взять в аренду	*(brat/vzyat va-REHN-doo)*
lease (v) (as lessor)	сдавать/сдать в аренду	*(zda-VAHT/zdat va-REHN-doo)*
lease bonus	арендный бонус	*(a-REND-nee BOH-noos)*
leather	кожа	*(ko-ZHA)*
leather goods	кожевенный товар	*(ka-ZHEH-ven-nee ta-VAHR)*
leather jacket	кожаная куртка	*(KOH-zha-na-ya KOOHRT-ka)*
leave of absence	отпуск	*(OT-poosk)*
LED display	светодиодный индикатор	*(sve-ta-dee-OD-nee een-dee-KAH-tar)*
ledger	бухгалтерская книга	*(bookh-GAHL-ter-ska-ya KNEE-ga)*
ledger account	счёт в бухгалтерской книге	*(shchyoht vbookh-GAHL-ter-skay KNEE-ghe)*
ledger entry	бухгалтерская запись	*(bookh-GAHL-ter-ska-ya ZAH-pees)*
legacy	легат (наследство)	*(le-GAHT [na-SLEHD-stva])*
legal entity	юридическое лицо	*(yoo-ree-DEE-ches-ka-ye lee-TSOH)*
legal holiday	официальный выходной	*(a-fee-tsee-AHL-nee vee-khad-NOY)*
legal list (fiduciary investment)	список подписчиков (на ценные бумаги)	*(SPEE-sak pad-PEE-shchee-kaf [na TSEN-nee-ye boo-MAH-ghee])*

legal monopoly	регулируемая монополия	*(re-goo-LEE-roo-ye-ma-ya ma-na-POH-lee-ya)*
legal tender	законное платежное средство	*(za-KON-na-ye pla-TYOZH-na-ye SRET-stva)*
legislation	законодательство	*(za-ka-na-DAH-tel-stva)*
lessee	арендатор	*(a-ren-DAH-tar)*
lessor	арендодатель	*(a-REN-da-DAH-tel)*
letter	письмо/буква	*(pees-MOH/BOOK-va)*
letter of credit	аккредитив	*(ak-kre-dee-TEEF)*
letter of guaranty	гарантийное письмо	*(ga-ran-TEEY-nba-ye pees-MOH)*
letter of indemnity	поручительство	*(pa-roo-CHEE-tel-stva)*
letter of introduction	рекомендательное письмо	*(re-ka-men-DAH-tel-na-ye pees-MOH)*
lettuce	салат	*(sa-LAHT)*
level out (v)	выравнивать	*(vee-RAHV-nee-vat)*
leverage	средство для достижения цели	*(SRET-stva dla da-stee-ZHEH-nee-ya TSEH-lee)*
levy taxes (v)	взимать налоги	*(vzee-MAHT na-LOH-ghee)*
liability (legal)	ответственность	*(at-VEHT-stven-nast)*
liability (accounting)	статья пассива	*(sta-TYAH pas-SEE-va)*
liability, actual	фактическая ответственность	*(fak-TEE-ches-ka-ya at-VEHT-stven-nast)*
liability, assumption of	принятие ответственности	*(pree-NYAH-tee-ye at-VEHT-stven-nas-tee)*
liability, contingent	условное обязательство	*(oos-LOV-na-ye a-bya-ZAH-tel-stva)*
liability, current	текущее обязательство	*(te-KOO-shche-ye a-bya-ZAH-tel-stva)*
liability, fixed	долгосрочное обязательство	*(dal-ga-SROCH-na-ye a-bya-ZAH-tel-stva)*
liability, insurance	полис страхования ответственности	*(POH-lees stra-kha-VAH-nee-ya at-VEHT-stven-nas-tee)*
liability, secured	обязательство/ обеспеченное закладом	*(a-bya-ZAH-tel-stva /a-bes-PEH-chen-na-ye za-KLAH-dam)*

L

liability, unsecured	обязательство/не обеспеченное закладом	*(a-bya-ZAH-tel-stva /ne-a-bes-PEH-chen-na-ye za-KLAH-dam)*
liable for tax	подлежащий обложению налогами	*(pad-le-ZHAH-shchee ab-la-ZHEH-nee-yoo na-LOH-ga-mee)*
liable to (responsible)	ответственный	*(at-VEHT-stven-nee)*
libel	пасквиль	*(PAHSK-veel)*
license	лицензия	*(lee-TSEN-zee-ya)*
license fees	лицензионные сборы	*(lee-tsen-zee-ON-nee-ye ZBOH-ree)*
licensed warehouse	лицензированный склад	*(lee-tsen-ZEE-ra-van-nee sklat)*
lichen	лишайник	*(lee-SHAYH-neek)*
lien	залоговое право	*(za-LOH-ga-va-ye PRAH-va)*
life cycle	жизненный цикл (продукта)	*(ZHIZ-nen-nee tsikl [pra-DOOK-ta])*
life insurance policy	полис страхования жизни	*(POH-lees stra-kha-VAH-nee-ya ZHIZ-nee)*
life member	пожизненный член	*(pa-ZHIZ-nen-nee chlen)*
life of a patent	срок действия патента	*(srok DEY-stvee-ya pa-TEN-ta)*
lift	подъёмная сила	*(pad-YOM-na-ya SEE-la)*
light (crude) oil	лёгкая нефть	*(LYOKH-ka-ya neft)*
lime (linden tree)	липа	*(LEE-pa)*
lime (soil)	известь	*(EEZ-vest)*
limestone	известняк	*(eez-vest-NYAK)*
limited order (stock market)	лимитированное указание	*(lee-mee-TEE-ra-van-na-ye oo-ka-ZAH-nee-ye)*
limited liability	ограниченная ответственность	*(ag-ra-NEE-chen-na-ya at-VEHT-stven-nast)*
limited partnership	товарищество с ограниченной ответственностью	*(ta-VAH-ree-shchest-va sag-ra-NEE-chen-nay at-VEHT-stven-na-styoo)*
line	строка	*(stra-KHA)*
line drawing	штриховой оригинал	*(shtree-kha-VOY a-ree-ghee-NAHL)*

line executive	линейный исполнитель	*(lee-NEY-nee ees-pal-NEE-tel)*
line of business	отрасль торговли	*(OT-rasl tar-GOV-lee)*
linear	прямолинейный	*(prya-ma-lee-NEY-nee)*
lingonberry	брусника	*(broos-NEE-ka)*
liquid assets	ликвидные активы	*(leek-VEED-nee-ye ak-TEE-vee)*
liquid fuel	жидкое топливо	*(ZHIT-ka-ye TOP-lee-va)*
liquidation	ликвидация	*(leek-ve-DAH-tsee-ya)*
liquidation value	стоимость при ликвидации	*(STOH-ee-mast pree leek-ve-DAH-tsee-ee)*
liquidity	ликвидность	*(leek-VEED-nast)*
liquidity preference	предпочтение ликвидности	*(pret-PAHCH-te-nee-ye leek-VEED-nas-tee)*
liquidity ratio	коэффициент ликвидности	*(ka-ef-fee-tsee-ENT leek-VEED-nas-tee)*
liquified gases	сжиженные газы	*(ZHZHEE-zhen-nee-ye GAH-see)*
liquified natural gas	сжиженный природный газ	*(ZHZHEE-zhen-nee pree-ROD-nee gahs)*
liquified natural gas carrier	танкер-метановоз	*(TAHN-ker me-ta-na-VOS)*
list price	прейскурантная цена	*(preys-koo-RAHNT-na-ya tse-NAH)*
listed securities	ценные бумаги зарегистрированные на биржу	*(TSEN-nee-ye boo-MAH-ghee, za-re-ghees-TREE-ra-van-nee-ye na BEEHR-zhe)*
listing	допуск ценных бумаг на бирже	*(DOH-poosk TSEN-nikh boo-MAHK na BEEHR-zhoo)*
litigation	тяжба	*(TYAHZH-ba)*
lithographic paper	литографская бумага	*(lee-ta-GRAHF-ska-ya boo-MAH-ga)*
living trust	пожизненная собственность	*(pa-ZHIZ-nen-na-ya SOHB-stven-nast)*
lizard (skin)	кожа ящерицы	*(KOH-zha YAH-shche-ree-tsee)*

loan	ссуда	*(SSOO-da)*
lobbying	агитация в кулуарах	*(a-ghee-TAH-tsee-ya fkoo-loo-AH-rakh)*
local	локальный	*(la-KAHL-nee)*
local customs	местные обычаи	*(MES-nee-ye a-BEE-cha-ee)*
local tax	местный сбор	*(MES-nee zbohr)*
lock out (v)	локаут (массовый расчёт рабочих)	*(la-KAH-oot [MAHS-sa-vee ra-SHCHYOHT ra-BOH-cheekh])*
locust (insect)	саранча	*(sa-ran-CHA)*
logistics	стратегии	*(la-GHEES-tee-ka)*
logo	эмблема	*(em-BLEH-ma)*
long hedge	хеджирование в ожидании понижения	*(khed-ZHEE-ra-va-nee-ye va-zhee-DAH-nee-ee pa-nee-ZHEH-nee-ya)*
long-range planning	перспективное планирование	*(per-spek-TEEV-na-ye pla-NEE-ra-va-nee-ye)*
long-term capital account	долгосрочный счёт капитала	*(dal-ga-SROCH-nee shchyoht ka-pee-TAH-la)*
long-term debt	долгосрочный долг	*(dal-ga-SROCH-nee dolk)*
loss	убыток	*(oo-BEE-tak)*
loss, gross	валовой убыток	*(va-la-VOY oo-BEE-tak)*
loss leader	товар, продаваемый в убыток (для привлечения покупателя)	*(ta-VAHR pra-da-VAH-ye-mee voo-BEE-tak [dlya pree-vle-CHEH-nee-ya pa-koo-PAH-te-lya])*
loss, net	чистый убыток	*(CHEES-tee oo-BEE-tak)*
lot	партия, удел	*(PAHR-tee-ya, OO-del)*
low-BTU gas	низкокалорийный газ	*(NEES-ka-ka-la-REEY-nee gahs)*
low income	низкий доход	*(NEES-kee da-KHOT)*
low-interest loans	ссуды на льготных условиях	*(SSOO-dee na LGOT-nikh oos-LOH-vee-yakh)*
low-yield bonds	облигации низкого дохода	*(ab-lee-GAH-tsee-ee NEES-ka-va da-KHOH-da)*
lower case	строчная буква	*(strach-NAH-ya BOOK-va)*
lubrication	смазывание	*(SMA-zee-vah-nee-ye)*
lump sum	паушальная сумма	*(pa-oo-SHAHL-na-ya SOOM-ma)*

luxury goods	товары роскоши	*(ta-VAH-ree ROS-ka-shee)*
luxury tax	сбор на товары роскоши	*(zbohr na ta-VAH-ree ROS-ka-shee)*
lynx	рысь	*(ris)*

M

mach speed	сверхзвуковая скорость (сверх Маха)	*(SVEHRKH-zvoo-ka-VAH-ya SKOH-rast [sverkh MAH-kha])*
machinery	оборудование	*(a-ba-ROO-da-va-nee-ye)*
macroeconomics	макроэкономика	*(MAHK-ra-e-ka-NOH-mee-ka)*
magnetic tape	магнитная лента	*(mag-NEET-na-ya LEN-ta)*
mail order	торгующий по почтовым заказам	*(tar-GOO-yoo-shchee pa pach-TOH-vim za-KAH-zam)*
mailing list	список адресатов	*(SPEE-sak ad-re-SAH-taf)*
mainframe	универсальная ЭВМ	*(oo-nee-ver-SAHL-na-ya eh-veh-EM)*
maintenance	техническое обслуживание	*(teck-NEE-ches-ka-ye ap-SLOO-zhee-va-nee-ye)*
maintenance contract	договор о техническом обслуживании	*(da-ga-VOHR a teck-NEE-ches-kam ap-SLOO-zhee-va-nee-ee)*
majority interest	бóльшая часть (акции и т.д.)	*(BOL-sha-ya chast [AHK-tsee-ee ee-TEH-DEH])*
make available (v)	предоставлять/ предоставить	*(pre-da-sta-VLYAHT/pre-da-STAH-veet)*
makeup case	коробка для косметики/ косметичка	*(ka-ROP-ka dla kas-MEH-tee-ke/kas-meh-TEECH-ka)*
make-or-buy decision	решение о производстве или закупке	*(re-SHEH-nee-ye a pra-eez-VOT-stve ee za-KOOP-ke)*
maker (of check, etc.)	трассант	*(tras-SAHNT)*
makeshift	временное приспособление	*(VREH-men-na-ye prees-pa-sab-LEH-nee-ye)*
malleability	ковкость	*(KOF-kast)*

man (gal) Friday	«Пятница» (верный помощник)	*(PYAHT-nee-tsa [VEHR-nee pa-MOSH-neek])*
man hours	человеко-часы	*(che-la-VEH-ka-cha-SEE)*
manage (v)	руководить	*(roo-ka-va-DEET)*
manage costs	контролируемые расходы	*(kant-ra-LEE-roo-ye-mee-ye ras-KHOH-dee)*
management	управление	*(oop-rav-LEH-nee-ye)*
management accounting	оперативный отчёт	*(a-pe-ra-TEEV-nee at-CHYOHT)*
management buy-out	«МБО» (скупка менеджментом)	*(EM-BEH-OH [SKOOP-ka MEH-ned-zhmen-tam])*
management chart	схема управленческой структуры	*(SKHEH-ma oop-rav-LEN-ches-kay strook-TOO-ree)*
management consultant	консультант по менеджменту	*(kan-sool-TAHNT pa MEH-ned-zhmen-too)*
management fee	зарплата управленческого персонала	*(zar-PLAH-ta oop-rav-LEN-ches-ka-va per-sa-NAH-la)*
management group	управленческая группа	*(oop-rav-LEN-ches-ka-ys GROOP-pa)*
management team	управленческая команда	*(oop-rav-LEN-ches-ka-ya ka-MAHN-da)*
management, business	управление коммерческими предприятиями	*(oop-rav-LEH-nee-ye kam-MEHR-ches-kee-mee pret-pree-YAH-tee-ya-mee)*
management, credit	управление кредитными операциями	*(oop-rav-LEH-nee-ye kre-DEET-nee-mee a-pe-RAH-tsee-ya-mee)*
management, financial	управление финансовой деятельностью	*(oop-rav-LEH-nee-ye fee-NAHN-sa-vay DEH-ya-tel-nas-tyoo)*
management, line	передовое управление	*(pe-re-da-VOH-ye oop-rav-LEH-nee-ye)*
management, market	управление рынком	*(oop-rav-LEH-nee-ye REEN-kam)*
management, office	управление офисом	*(oop-rav-LEH-nee-ye OF-fee-sam)*
management, personnel	управление кадрами	*(oop-rav-LEH-nee-ye KAHD-ra-mee)*

M

management, product	управление продукцией	*(oop-rav-LEH-nee-ye pra-DOOK-tsee-yey)*
management, sales	управление сбытом	*(oop-rav-LEH-nee-ye SBEE-tam)*
management, systems	управление системами	*(oop-rav-LEH-nee-ye sees-TEH-ma-mee)*
management, top	высшее руководство	*(VISH-she-ee roo-ka-VOT-stva)*
management-volume inventory	изучение запаса прироста и отпада насаждений	*(ee-zoo-CHEH-nee-ye za-PAH-sa, pree-ROS-ta ee at-PAH-da na-sazh-DEH-neey)*
manager	менеджер	*(MEH-ned-zher)*
mandate	мандат	*(man-DAHT)*
mandatory redemption	принудительный выкуп	*(pree-noo-DEE-tel-nee VEE-koop)*
manganese ore	марганцевая руда	*(MAHR-gan-tse-va-ya roo-DAH)*
manifest	манифест	*(ma-nee-FEST)*
manmade fibers	искусственные волокна	*(ees-KOOS-tven-nee-ye va-LOK-na)*
manpower	рабочая сила	*(ra-BOH-cha-ya SEE-la)*
manual	справочное руководство	*(SPRAH-vach-na-ye roo-ka-VOT-stva)*
manual worker	работник физического труда	*(ra-BOT-neek fee-ZEE-ches-ka-va troo-DAH)*
manufacturer	производитель	*(pra-eez-va-DEE-tel)*
manufacturer's agent	агент производителя	*(a-GHENT pra-eez-va-DEE-te-la)*
manufacturer's representative	представитель производителя	*(pret-sta-VEE-tel pra-eez-va-DEE-te-la)*
manufacturing	производство	*(pra-eez-VOTS-tva)*
manufacturing capacity	производственная мощность	*(pra-eez-VOTS-tven-na-ya MOSHCH-nast)*
manufacturing control	производственный контроль	*(pra-eez-VOTS-tven-nee kan-TROL)*
manure	навоз	*(na-VOS)*
maple	клён	*(klyon)*

mare	кобыла	*(ka-BEE-la)*
margin	маржа	*(MAHR-zha)*
margin, fixed	твердая наценка	*(TVYOHR-da-ya na-TSEN-ka)*
margin, gross	валовая прибыль	*(VAH-la-va-ya PREE-bil)*
margin net	чистая прибыль	*(CHEES-ta-ya PREE-bil)*
margin of safety	коэффициент безопасности	*(ka-ef-fee-tsee-ENT be-za-PAHS-na-stee)*
margin, profit	маржинальная прибыль	*(mar-zhee-NAHL-na-ya PREE-bil)*
marginal cost	предельная стоимость	*(pre-DEL-na-ya STOH-ee-mast)*
marginal costs	предельные издержки производства	*(pre-DEL-nee eez-DEHRSH-kee pra-eez-VOT-stva)*
marginal field	«маржинальное» (экономически граничное) месторождение	*(mar-ZHEE-nal-na-ye [e-ka-na-MEE-ches-kee gra-NEECH-na-ye] mes-ta-razh-DEH-nee-ye)*
marginal prices	крайние цены	*(KRAHY-nee-ye TSEH-nee)*
marginal producer well	«маржинальная» (экономически граничная) скважина	*(mar-ZHEE-nal-na-ya [e-ka-na-MEE-ches-kee gra-NEECH-na-ye] SKVAH-zhee-na)*
marginal productivity	маржинальная производительность	*(mar-zhee-NAHL-na-ya pra-eez-va-DEE-tel-nast)*
marginal reserve	«маржинальные» (экономически граничные) запасы	*(mar-ZHEE-nal-nee-ye [e-ka-na-MEE-ches-kee gra-NEECH-nee-ye] za-PAH-see)*
marginal revenue	маржинальный доход	*(mar-zhee-NAHL-nee da-KHOT)*
marine cargo insurance	страхование морских грузов	*(stra-kha-VAH-nee-ye mar-SKEEKH GROO-saf)*
marine underwriter	страхователь морских грузов	*(stra-kha-VAH-tel mar-SKEEKH GROO-saf)*
markdown	скидка	*(SKEET-ka)*
marker (crude) oil	«эталонная» нефть	*(e-ta-LON-na-ya neft)*
market	рынок	*(REE-nak)*

market (v)	находить рынок сбыта	*(na-kha-DEET REE-nak ZBEE-ta)*
market access	доступ в рынок	*(DOS-toop VREE-nak)*
market appraisal	оценка рынка	*(a-TSEN-ka RIN-ka)*
market dynamics	рыночная динамика	*(REE-nach-na-ya dee-NAH-mee-ka)*
market forces	рыночные силы	*(REE-nach-nee-ye SEE-lee)*
market index	индекс рынка	*(EEN-deks RIN-ka)*
market management	управление рынком	*(oop-rav-LEH-nee-ye RIN-kam)*
market penetration	проникновение рынка	*(pra-neek-na-VEH-nee-ye RIN-ka)*
market plan	рыночный план	*(REE-nach-nee plahn)*
market position	рыночная конкурентоспособность	*(REE-nach-na-ya kan-koo-REN-ta-spa-SOB-nast)*
market potential	возможности рынка	*(vaz-MOZH-na-stee RIN-ka)*
market price	рыночная цена	*(REE-nach-na-ya tse-NAH)*
market rating	рыночная оценка	*(REE-nach-na-ya a-TSEN-ka)*
market report	рыночный отчёт	*(REE-nach-nee at-CHYOHT)*
market research	изучение возможностей рынка	*(ee-zoo-CHEH-nee-ye vaz-MOZH-na-stey RIN-ka)*
market saturation	насыщение рынка	*(na-see-SHCHEH-nee-ye RIN-ka)*
market survey	опрос потребителей	*(ap-ROS pa-tre-BEE-te-ley)*
market trend	тенденция рынка	*(ten-DEN-tsee-ya RIN-ka)*
market value (general)	рыночная стоимость	*(REE-nach-na-ya STOH-ee-mast)*
market value (stocks)	меновая стоимость	*(MEH-na-va-ya STOH-ee-mast)*
marketable gas	товарный газ	*(ta-VAHR-nee gahs)*
marketable securities	ценные бумаги, легко реализуемые	*(TSEN-nee-ye boo-MAH-ghee, lekh-KOH re-a-lee-ZOO-ye-mee-ye)*
marketing	маркетинг	*(mar-KEH-teenk [also: MAHR-ke-teenk])*

M

marketing budget	бюджет маркетинга	(*byood-ZHET mar-KEH-teen-ga*)
marketing concept	идея маркетинга	(*ee-DEH-ya mar-KEH-teen-ga*)
marketing plan	план маркетинга	(*plahn mar-KEH-teen-ga*)
market place	базарная площадь	(*ba-ZAHR-na-ya PLOH-shchat*)
markup	повышение цен	(*pa-vee-SHEH-nee-ye tsen*)
marmot	сурок	(*soo-ROK*)
marsh gas	болотный газ	(*ba-LOT-nee gahs*)
mass marketing	массовый маркетинг	(*MAHS-sa-vee mar-KEH-teenk*)
mass media	средства массовой информации	(*SRET-stva MAHS-sa-vay een-far-MAH-ee*)
mass production	поточно-массовое производство	(*pa-TOCH-na-MAHS-sa-va-ye pra-eez-VOT-stva*)
matched samples	комплект образцов	(*kam-PLEKT ab-ras-TSOF*)
materials	материалы	(*ma-te-ree-YAH-lee*)
maternity leave	отпуск по беременности и родам	(*OT-poosk pa-be-REH-men-nas-tee ee ROH-dam*)
mathematical model	математическая модель	(*ma-te-ma-TEE-ches-ka-ya ma-DEL*)
matrix	матрица	(*MAH-tree-tsa*)
maturity date	срок наступления	(*srok na-stoo-PLEH-nee-ya*)
maximize (v)	увеличивать до предела	(*oo-ve-LEE-chee-vat da pre-DEH-la*)
mean (average)	средний	(*SRED-nee*)
measure (v)	измерять/измерить	(*eez-me-RYAHT/eez-MEH-reet*)
mechanical engineering	машиностроение	(*ma-SHEE-na-stra-YAEH-nee-ye*)
media	средства	(*SRET-stva*)
median	медиана	(*mee-dee-AH-na*)
mediation	посредничество	(*pa-SRED-nee-che-stva*)
medication	медикамент	(*me-dee-ka-MENT*)
medicine	медицина	(*mee-dee-TSEE-na*)

M

medium of exchange	средство международных отчётов	*(SRET-stva mezh-doo-na-ROD-neekh at-CHYOH-taf)*
medium term	среднесрочно	*(SRED-ne-SROCH-na)*
meet the price (v)	заплатить цену	*(zap-la-TEET TSEH-noo)*
meeting	собрание	*(sab-RAH-nee-ye)*
megabyte	мегабайт	*(me-ga-BAHYT)*
member-firm	фирма-член	*(FEEHR-ma-chlen)*
memorandum	меморандум	*(me-ma-RAHN-doom)*
memory	запоминающее устройство (ЗУ)	*(za-pa-mee-NAH-yoo-shche-ye oos-TROY-stva) [ZEH-OO]*
memory resident	находящийся постоянно в ЗУ	*(na-kha-DYAH-shcheey-sa pas-ta-YAHN-na VZEH-OO)*
menu-driven	управляемый в режиме меню	*(oop-rav-LYAH-ye-mee vre-ZHEE-me me-NYOO)*
mercantile	торговый	*(tar-GOH-vee)*
mercantile agency	торговое агентство	*(tar-GOH-va-ye a-GHENT-stva)*
mercantile law (in general)	торговое право	*(tar-GOH-va-ye PRAH-va)*
mercantile law (a specific law)	торговый закон	*(tar-GOH-vee za-KON)*
merchandise	товар	*(ta-VAHR)*
merchandising	розничная продажа	*(ROZ-neech-na-ya pra-DAH-zha)*
merchant	коммерсант	*(ka-mer-SANT)*
merchant bank	торговый банк	*(tar-GOH-vee bahnk)*
merchant guild	торговая ассоциация	*(tar-GOH-va-ya as-sa-tsee-AH-tsee-ya)*
merger	слияние	*(slee-YAH-nee-ye)*
metals	металлы	*(me-TAHL-lee)*
method	метод	*(MEH-tat)*
metrification	введение метрической системы	*(vve-DEH-nee-ye met-REE-ches-kay see-STEH-mee)*
mice	мыши	*(MEE-she)*
microchip	микросхема	*(meek-ra-SKHEH-ma)*

microcomputer	микроЭВМ	*(meek-ra-eh-veh-EM)*
microfiche	микрофиша	*(meek-ra-FEE-sha)*
microfilm	микрофильм	*(meek-ra-FEELM)*
microphone	микрофон	*(mek-ra-FON)*
microprocessor	микропроцессор	*(meek-ra-pra-TSES-sar)*
microwave	микроволновый	*(meek-ra-val-NOH-vee)*
middle management	средний слой управления	*(SRED-nee sloy oo-prav-LEH-nee-ya)*
middleman	посредник	*(pa-SRED-neek)*
Mig fighter	истребитель «МиГ»	*(ees-tre-BEE-tel Mig)*
mileage	расстояние в милях на галлон топлива	*(ras-sta-YAH-nee-ye VMEE-lyakh na gal-LON TOP-lee-va)*
milk	молоко	*(ma-la-KOH)*
milking machine	доильная машина	*(da-EEL-na-ya ma-SHEE-na)*
milling allowance	допуск на обработку	*(DOH-poosk na-ab-ra-BOT-koo)*
minicomputer	миниЭВМ	*(mee-nee-eh-veh-EM)*
minimum reserves	минимальный резерв	*(mee-nee-MAHL-nee re-ZEHRF)*
minimum wage	минимальная зарплата	*(mee-nee-MAHL-na-ya zar-PLAH-ta)*
mink	норковый	*(NOHR-ka-vee)*
minority interest	меньшая часть акции	*(MEN-sha-ya chahst AHK-tsee)*
mint	монетный двор	*(ma-NET-nee dvor)*
miscalculation	просчёт	*(pra-SHCHYOHT)*
miscellaneous	разнообразный	*(raz-na-ab-RAHZ-nee)*
misleading	вводящий в заблуждение	*(vva-DYAH-shchee vzab-loozh-DEH-nee-ye)*
misunderstanding	недоразумение	*(ne-da-ra-zoo-MEH-nee-ye)*
mixed costs	смешанные стоимости	*(SMEH-shan-nee-ye STOH-ee-ma-stee)*
mixed fuel	смешанное топливо	*(SMEH-shan-nee-ye TOP-lee-va)*
mixed sampling	выборочный контроль	*(SMEH-shan-nee-ye VEE-ba-rach-nee kant-ROL)*

mobile launcher	передвижная пусковая установка	*(pe-re-dveezh-NAH-ya poos-ka-VAH-ya oos-ta-NOF-ka)*
mobility of labor	мобильность рабочей силы	*(ma-BEEL-nast ra-BOH-chey SEE-lee)*
mock-up	макет	*(ma-KET)*
mode	способ	*(SPOH-sap)*
model	модель	*(ma-DEL)*
modem	модем	*(ma-DEM)*
modular production	комплектное производство	*(kam-PLEKT-na-ye pra-eez-VOT-stva)*
mole	грамм-молекула	*(GRAHM-ma-LEH-koo-la)*
molybdenum	молибден	*(ma-LEEB-den)*
monetary base	валютный базис	*(va-LYOOT-nee BAH-zees)*
monetary credits	денежные кредиты	*(DEH-nezh-nee-ye kre-DEE-tee)*
monetary policy	монетарная политика	*(ma-ne-TAHR-na-ya pa-LEE-tee-ka)*
money	деньги	*(DEN-ghee)*
money market	валютный рынок	*(va-LYOOT-nee REE-nak)*
money order	денежный почтовый перевод	*(DEH-nezh-nee pach-TOH-vee pe-re-VOT)*
money supply	запас денег	*(za-PAHS DEH-nek)*
monitor	монитор	*(ma-nee-TOHR)*
monopoly	монополия	*(ma-na-POH-lee-ya)*
monopsony	монопсония (рынок с одним покупателем)	*(ma-na-PSOH-nee-ya (REE-nak sad-NEEM pa-koo-PAH-te-lem)*
moonlighting	халтура	*(khal-TOO-ra)*
morale	моральный дух	*(ma-RAHL-nee dookh)*
moratorium	отсрочка	*(at-SROCH-ka)*
Morocco leather	сафьян	*(saf-YAHN)*
morphine	морфин	*(mar-FEEN)*
mortgage	ипотека	*(ee-pa-TEH-ka)*
mortgage bank	ипотечный банк	*(ee-pa-TECH-nee bahnk)*
mortgage bond	закладная	*(za-klad-NAH-ya)*

M

mortgage deben-ture	долговое обязательство под залог	*(dal-ga-VOH-ye a-bya-ZAH-tel-stva pad za-LOK)*
most-favored nation	наиболее благоприятствуемая нация	*(na-ee-BOH-leye bla-ga-pree-YAHT-stvoo-ye-ma-ya NAH-tsee-ya)*
mother board	объединительная плата	*(ab-ye-de-NEE-tel-na-ya PLAH-ta)*
motion (legal)	ходатайство	*(kha-DAH-tay-stvo)*
motion (parliamen-tary)	предложение	*(pred-la-ZHEH-nee-ye)*
motivation study	изучение мотивировки	*(ee-zoo-CHEH-nee-ye ma-tee-VEE-rov-kee)*
mouse	манипулятор «мышь»	*(ma-nee-poo-LYAH-tar mish)*
movement of goods	перегрузка товаров	*(pe-re-GROOS-ka ta-VAH-raf)*
moving expenses	расходы на переезд	*(ras-KHOH-dee na pe-re-YEZD)*
multicurrency	многовалютный	*(mna-ga-va-LYOOT-nee)*
multilateral agree-ment	многостороннее соглашение	*(mna-ga-sta-RON-ne-ye sa-gla-SHEH-nee-ye)*
multilateral trade	многосторонняя торговля	*(mna-ga-sta-RON-nya-ya tar-GOV-lya)*
multinational cor-poration	многонациональное акционерное общество	*(mna-ga-na-tsee-a-NAHL-na-ye ak-tsee-a-NEHR-na-ye OP-shchest-va)*
multinational oil company	транснациональная нефтяная компания	*(TRAHNS-na-tsee-a-NAHL-na-ya nef-tee-NAH-ya kam-PAH-nee-ya)*
multi-user	многоабонентский	*(MNOH-ga-a-ba-NENT-skee)*
multiple exchange rates	множественные валютные курсы	*(MNOH-zhest-ven-nee-ye va-LYOOT-nee-ye KOOHR-see)*
multiple taxation	множественное налогообложение	*(MNOH-zhest-ven-na-ye na-LOH-ga-ab-la-ZHEH-nee-ye)*
multiple	кратное число	*(KRAHT-na-ye chees-LOH)*
multiplier	множитель	*(MNOH-zhee-tel)*

N

multiprogramming	мультипрограммирование	*(MOOL-tee-pra-gra-MEE-ra-va-nee-ye)*
municipal bond	облигация муниципальной корпорации	*(ab-lee-GAH-tsee-ya moo-nee-tsee-PAHL-nay kar-pa-RAH-tsee)*
mushrooms	грибы	*(GREE-be)*
mutual	взаимный	*(vza-EEM-nee)*
mutual funds	взаимные фонды	*(vza-EEM-nee-ye FON-dee)*
mutual savings bank	взаимо-сберегательный банк	*(vza-EEM-a-zbe-re-GAH-tel-nee bahnk)*
mutually exclusive classes	взаимо-исключающие классы	*(vza-EEM-a-ees-kloo-CHEH-tel-nee-ye KLAHS-see)*

N

named point of destination	названный пункт назначения	*(NAHZ-van-nee poonkt naz-na-CHEH-nee-ya)*
named point of exportation	названный пункт выезда	*(NAHZ-van-nee poonkt VEE-yez-da)*
named point of origin	названный пункт происхождения	*(NAHZ-van-nee poonkt pra-ees-kha-ZHDEH-nee-ya)*
named port of importation	названный порт ввоза	*(NAHZ-van-nee poonkt VVOH-za)*
named port of shipment	названный порт отгрузки	*(NAHZ-van-nee poonkt at-GROOS-kee)*
narcotic	наркотик	*(nar-KOH-teek)*
national bank	национальный банк	*(na-tsee-a-NAHL-nee bahnk)*
national debt	государственный долг	*(ga-soo-DAHR-stven-nee dolk)*
nationalism	национализм	*(na-tsee-a-na-LEEZM)*
nationalization	национализация	*(na-tsee-a-na-lee-ZAH-tsee-ya)*
native produce	местные продукты	*(MEST-nee-ye pra-DOOK-tee)*
natural gas	природный газ	*(pree-ROD-nee gahs)*
natural resources	природные богатства	*(pree-ROD-nee-ye ba-GAHT-stva)*

near money	«квази-деньги» (почти деньги)	*(KVAH-zee DEN-ghee (pach-TEE DEN-ghee)*
negative	негатив	*(ne-ga-TEEF)*
negative cash flow	отрицательное «кэшфлоу»	*(at-ree-TSAH-tel-na-ye "cash flow")*
negative pledge	договорное обязательство о воздержании от действия	*(da-ga-vor-NOH-ye a-bya-ZAH-tel-stva a vaz-der-ZHAH-nee-ee at DYE-stvee-ya)*
negligent	небрежный	*(ne-BREZH-nee)*
negotiable (transferable)	оборотный	*(a-ba-ROT-nee)*
negotiable securities	оборотные ценные бумаги	*(a-ba-ROT-nee-ye TSEN-nee-ye boo-MAH-ghee)*
negotiable (subject to discussion)	подлежащий переуступке	*(pad-le-ZHAH-shchee pe-re-oo-STOOP-ke)*
negotiated sale	договоренная продажа	*(da-ga-va-RYON-na-ya pra-DAH-zha)*
negotiation	переговоры	*(pe-re-ga-VOH-ree)*
net asset value	номинальная стоимость чистой суммы	*(na-mee-NAHL-na-ya STOH-ee-mast CHEES-tay SOOM-mee)*
net asset worth	ценность чистой суммы активов	*(TSEN-nast CHEES-tay SOOM-mee ak-TEE-vaf)*
net assets	чистые активы	*(CHEES-tee-ye ak-TEE-vee)*
net borrowed reserves	чистые наёмные резервы	*(CHEES-tee-ye na-YOM-nee-ye re-ZEHR-vee)*
net cash flow	чистое «кэшфлоу»	*(CHEES-ta-ye "cash flow")*
net change	чистое изменение	*(CHEES-ta-ye eez-me-NEH-nee-ye)*
net equity assets	чистые активы собственного капитала	*(CHEES-tee-ye ak-TEE-vee SOP-stven-na-va ka-pee-TAH-la)*
net income	чистый доход	*(CHEES-tee da-KHOT)*
net investment	чистое капиталовложение	*(CHEES-ta-ye ka-pee-TAH-la-vla-ZHEH-nee-ye)*
net loss	чистый убыток	*(CHEES-tee oo-BEE-tak)*
net margin	чистая прибыль	*(CHEES-ta-ya PREE-bil)*
net profit	чистая прибыль	*(CHEES-ta-ya PREE-bil)*

N

net refinery output	чистое производство нефтепродуктов	*(CHEES-ta-ye pra-eez-VOT-stva NEF-te-pra-DOOK-taf)*
net sales	чистая сумма продаж	*(CHEES-ta-ya SOOM-ma pra-DAHSH)*
net working capital	чистый функционирующий капитал	*(CHEES-tee foonk-tsee-a-NEE-roo-yoo-shchee ka-pee-TAHL)*
net worth	чистая ценность	*(CHEES-ta-ya TSEN-nast)*
network	сеть	*(set)*
new field wildcat	поисковая скважина на новое месторождение	*(pa-ees-KOH-va-ya SKVAH-zhee-na na NOH-va-ye mes-ta-razh-DEE-nee-ye)*
new issue	новый выпуск	*(NOH-vee VEE-poosk)*
new money	новые деньги	*(NOH-vee-ye DEN-ghee)*
new pool test	поисковая скважина на новую залежь (новый горизонт)	*(pa-ees-KOH-va-ya SKVAH-zhee-na na NOH-voo-yoo ZAH-lesh [NOH-vee ga-ree-ZONT])*
new product development	развитие новых продуктов	*(raz-VEE-tee-ye NOH-vikh pra-DOOK-taf)*
newsletter	информационный бюллетень	*(een-far-ma-tsee-ON-nee byoo-le-TEN)*
newspaper	газета	*(ga-ZHEH-ta)*
newsprint	газетная бумага	*(ga-ZEHT-na-ya boo-MAH-ga)*
newsstand	газетный киоск	*(ga-ZEHT-nee kee-OSK)*
nickel	никель	*(NEE-kel)*
night depository	ночное хранение	*(nach-NOH-ye khra-NEH-nee-ye)*
nitric acid	азотная кислота	*(a-ZOT-na-ya kees-la-TAH)*
nitrogen	азот	*(a-ZOT)*
non-recoverable reserve	неизвлекаемые запасы	*(ne-eez-vle-KAH-ye-mee-ye za-PAH-see)*
no par value	без номинальной цены	*(bez na-mee-NAHL-nay TSEH-nee)*
no problem(s)	нет проблем	*(nyet pra-BLEM)*
nominal price	номинальная цена	*(na-mee-NAHL-na-ya TSEH-na)*

N

nominal yield	номинальный доход	*(na-mee-NAHL-nee da-KHOT)*
noncumulative preferred stock	не кумулятивные привилегированные акции	*(ne-koo-moo-la-TEEV-nee-ye pree-vee-le-ghee-ROH-van-nee-ye AHK-tsee-ee)*
noncurrent assets	нетекущие активы	*(ne-te-KOO-shchee-ye ak-TEE-vee)*
nondurable goods	товары кратковременного пользования	*(ta-VAH-ree krat-ka-VREH-men-ma-va POL-za-va-nee-ya)*
nonfeasance	невыполнение обязанностей	*(ne-vee-pal-NEH-nee-ye a-BYAH-zan-nas-tey)*
nonmember	нечлен	*(ne-CHLEN)*
nonprofit	некоммерческий	*(ne-kam-MEHR-ches-kee)*
nonresident	непостоянный житель	*(ne pas-ta-YAHN-nee ZHEE-tel)*
norm	норма	*(NOHR-ma)*
notary	нотариус	*(na-TAH-ree-oos)*
note, credit	вексельный кредит	*(VEK-sel-nee kre-DEET)*
note, debit	дебит-нота	*(DEH-beet NOH-ta)*
note, promissory	долговое обязательство	*(dal-ga-VOH-ye a-bya-ZAH-tel-stva)*
note receivable	вексель к получению	*(VEK-sel kpa-loo-CHEH-nee-yoo)*
novation	новация (перевод долга)	*(na-VAH-tsee-ya [pe-re-VOT DOL-ga])*
null	нуль	*(nool)*
null and void	не имеющий юридической силы	*(ne ee-MEH-yoo-shchee yoo-ree-DEE-ches-kay SEE-lee)*
nullify (v)	аннулировать	*(an-noo-LEE-ra-vat)*
numerical control	цифровой контроль	*(tsif-ra-VOY kan-TROL)*
nutria	нутрия	*(NOOT-ree-ya)*

O

| oak | дуб | *(doop)* |
| obligation | обязательство | *(a-bya-ZAH-tel-stva)* |

obligatory (oil) stocks	обязательные товарные запасы	*(a-bee-ZAH-tel-nee ta-VAHR-nee za-PAH-see)*
obsolescence	устаревание	*(oos-ta-re-VAH-nee-ye)*
occupation	занятие	*(za-NYAH-tee-ye)*
occupational hazard	профессиональный риск	*(pra-fes-see-a-NAHL-nee reesk)*
odd lot	разрозненная партия	*(raz-ROZ-nen-na-ya PAHR-tee-ya)*
odd lot broker	маклер разрозненных комплектов	*(MAHK-ler raz-ROZ-nen-nikh kam-PLEK-taf)*
odometer	одометр	*(o-DOH-metr)*
offline	автономный от системы (компьютер)	*(af-ta-NOM-nee at see-STEH-mee [kam-PYOO-ter])*
off-the-books	вне баланса	*(vne ba-LAHN-sa)*
offer (v)	предлагать/предложить	*(pred-la-GAHT/pred-la-ZHEET)*
offer for sale	выставлять на продажу	*(vee-stav-LYAHT na pra-DAH-zhoo)*
offered price	предложенная цена	*(pred-LOH-zhen-na-ya TSEH-na)*
offered rate	предложенная ставка	*(pred-LOH-zhen-na-ya STAHF-ka)*
office	офис	*(OH-fees)*
office, branch	филиал	*(fee-lee-AHL)*
office, head	штаб	*(shtahp)*
office management	управление офисом	*(oo-prav-LEH-nee-ye OH-fee-sam)*
offset printing	офсетная печать	*(af-SET-na-ya pe-CHANT)*
offshore company	офшорная компания	*(OF-SHOHR-na-ya kam-PAH-nee-ya)*
oil	нефть	*(neft)*
oil bitumen	нефтяной (технический) битум	*(nef-tee-NOY [tekh-NEE-ches-kee] BEE-toom)*
oil bonus	натуральный (нефтяной) бонус	*(na-too-RAHL-nee [nef-tee-NOY] BOH-noos)*
oil (stocks) afloat/at sea	«нефть на плаву»	*(neft na pla-VOO)*
oil well	нефтяная скважина	*(nef-tee-NAH-ya SKVAH-zhee-na)*

oil-well gas	газ нефтяных скважин	*(gahs nef-tee-NIKH SKVAH-zheen)*
oil yield	выход нефти (сланцевой смолы)	*(VEE-khat NEF-tee [SLAHN-tse-vay sma-LEE])*
ointment	мазь	*(mas)*
oligopoly	олигополия (рынок немногих продавцов)	*(a-lee-ga-POH-lee-ya [REE-nak nem-NOH-gheekh pra-daf-TSOF])*
oligopsony	олигопсония (рынок немногих покупателей)	*(a-lee-ga-PSOH-nee-ya [REE-nak nem-NOH-gheekh pa-koo-PAH-te-ley])*
omit (v)	пропускать/пропустить	*(pra-poos-KAHT/pra-poos-TEET)*
on account	в счёт	*(fshchyoht)*
on consignment	на консигнации	*(na kan-seeg-NAH-tsee-ee)*
on demand	по предъявлении	*(pa pred-yav-LEH-nee-yoo)*
on line (computer)	оперативный (компьютер)	*(a-pe-ra-TEEV-nee [kam-PYOO-ter])*
on-the-job training	обучение по месту работы	*(a-boo-CHEH-nee-ye pa MES-too ra-BOH-tee)*
open account	открытый счёт	*(at-KREE-tee shchot)*
open cover	генеральный полис	*(ghe-ne-RAHL-nee POH-lees)*
open door policy	политика «открытых дверей»	*(pa-LEE-tee-ka "at-KREE-tikh dve-REY")*
open market	открытый рынок	*(at-KREE-tee REE-nak)*
open order	открытый заказ	*(at-KREE-tee za-KAHS)*
open shop	предприятие, принимающее членов и нечленов профсоюзов	*(pret-pree-YAH-tee-ye pree-nee-MAH-yoo-shche-ye CHLEH-naf ee ne-CHLEH-naf praf-sa-YOO-saf)*
opening balance	начальный баланс	*(na-CHAHL-nee ba-LAHNS)*
opening price	первоначальная цена	*(per-va-na-CHAHL-na-ya tse-NAH)*
operating budget	операционный бюджет	*(a-pe-ra-tsee-ON-nee byood-ZHET)*

operating expenses	эксплуатационные расходы	*(eks-ploo-a-ta-tsee-ON-nee-ye ras-KHOH-dee)*
operating income	доход от операций	*(da-KHOT aht a-pe-RAH-tseey)*
operating profit	прибыль от операций	*(PREE--bil aht a-pe-RAH-tseey)*
operating statement	операционный отчёт	*(a-pe-ra-tsee-ON-nee at-CHYOHT)*
operations audit	ревизия операций	*(re-VEE-zee-ya a-pe-RAH-tseey)*
operations headquarters	штаб операций	*(shtahp a-pe-RAH-tseey)*
operations management	операционное управление	*(a-pe-ra-tsee-ON-na-ye oop-rav-LEH-nee-ye)*
opium	опиум	*(OH-pee-oom)*
opossum	опоссум	*(a-POS-soom)*
optical	оптический	*(ap-TEE-ches-kee)*
optical character recognition	оптическое распознание знаков	*(ap-TEE-ches-ka-ye ras-pa-zna-VAH-nee-ye ZNAH-kaf)*
option (put or call options)	опцион	*(ap-TSEE-on)*
orbit	орбита	*(ar-BEE-ta)*
orbital refueling base	орбитальная заправочная станция	*(ar-bee-TAHL-na-ya zap-RAH-vach-na-ya STAHN-tsee-ya)*
orchard farming	плодоводство	*(pla-da-VOT-stva)*
order	заказ	*(za-KAHS)*
order form	бланк заказа	*(blahnk za-KAH-za)*
order number	номер заказа	*(NOH-mer za-KAH-za)*
order of the day	распорядок дня	*(ras-pa-RYAH-dak dnyah)*
order, to place an (v)	заказывать/заказать	*(za-KAH-zy-vat/za-ka-ZAHT)*
ordinary capital	обыкновенный капитал	*(a-bik-na-VEHN-nee ka-pee-TAHL)*
ore	руда	*(roo-DAH)*
organic	органический	*(ar-ga-NEE-ches-kee)*
organic chemistry	органическая химия	*(ar-ga-NEE-ches-ka-ya KHEE-mee-ya)*

organization	организация	*(ar-ga-nee-ZAH-tsee-ya)*
organization chart	схема организации	*(SKHEH-ma ar-ga-nee-ZAH-tsee-ee)*
Organization of Petroleum Exporting-Countries (OPEC)	Организация Стран Экспортёров Нефти (ОПЕК)	*(ar-ga-nee-ZAH-tsee-ya strahn eks-par-TYOH-raf NEF-tee [oh-PEK])*
original cost	первоначальная стоимость	*(per-va-na-CHAHL-na-ya STOH-ee-mast)*
original entry	первоначальная запись	*(per-va-na-CHAHL-na-ya ZAH-pees)*
original maturity	первоначальный срок наступления	*(per-va-na-CHAHL-nee srok nas-too-PLEH-nee-ya)*
OS	ОС	*(os)*
oscillator	осциллятор	*(at-tsil-LYAH-tar)*
ostrich (skin)	страусовая кожа	*(STRAH-oo-sa-va-ya KOH-zha)*
other assets	прочие активы	*(PROH-chee-ye ak-TEE-vee)*
other liabilities	прочие пассивы	*(PROH-chee-ye pas-SEE-vee)*
otter	выдра	*(VID-ra)*
out-of-pocket expenses	побочные расходы	*(pa-BOCH-nee-ye ras-KHOH-dee)*
outbid (v)	предложить более выгодную цену	*(pred-la-ZHIT BOH-lee VEE-gad-noo-yoo TSEH-noo)*
outlay	затрата	*(za-TRAH-ta)*
outlet	возможности сбыта	*(vaz-MOZH-na-stee ZBEE-ta)*
outlook (prediction)	перспектива	*(per-spek-TEE-va)*
outlook (philosophy)	кругозор	*(kroo-ga-ZOHR)*
output	выпуск	*(VEE-poosk)*
outsized articles	нестандартные предметы	*(ne-stan-DAHRT-nee-ye pred-MEH-tee)*
outstanding contract	невыполненный контракт	*(ne-VEE-pal-nen-nee kan-TRAHKT)*

outstanding debt	недоплаченные долги	*(ne-da-PLAH-chen-nee-ye dal-GHEE)*
outstanding stock	акции/выпущенные в обращение	*(AHK-tsee/VEE-poo-shchen-nee-ye vab-ra-SHCHEH-nee-ye)*
out-turn	действительные результаты	*(dey-STVEE-tel-nee-ye re-zool-TAH-tee)*
over-the-counter guotation	котировка вторичного рынка	*(ka-tee-ROF-ka FTAH-reech-na-va REEN-ka)*
overage	излишек	*(eez-LEE-shek)*
overbought	купленный не по средствам	*(KOOP-len-nee ne pa SRETS-vam)*
overcapitalized	имея больший капитал/ чем нужно	*(ee-MEH-ya BOL-shee ka-pee-TAHL/chem NOOZH-na)*
overcharge	завышенная цена	*(za-VEE-shen-na-ya tse-NAH)*
overcharge (v)	назначать завышенную цену	*(naz-na-CHANT za-VEE-shen-noo-yoo TSEH-noo)*
overdraft	овердрафт (превышение кредита)	*(OH-vehr-DRAHFT [pre-vee-SHEH-nee-ye kre-DEE-ta])*
overdue	просроченный	*(pra-SROH-chen-nee)*
overhang	выступ	*(VIS-toop)*
overhead	накладные расходы	*(na-klad-NEE-ye ras-KHOH-dee)*
overlap	частичное совладение	*(chas-TEECH-na-ye sa-vla-DEH-nee-ye)*
overnight	за ночь	*zah-noch)*
overpayment	переплата	*(pe-re-PLAH-ta)*
oversold	продано сверх запасов	*(PROH-da-na sverkh za-PAH-saf)*
overstock	излишний запас	*(eez-LEESH-nee za-PAHS)*
oversubscribe (v)	превышать по подписке акций	*(pree-vee-SHAHT pa pat-PEES-ke AHK-tseey)*
oversupply	избыточное снабжение	*(eez-BEE-tach-na-ye snab-ZHEH-nee-ye)*
overtime	сверхурочный	*(SVEHRKH-oo-ROCH-nee)*
overvalue (v)	переоценивать/ переоценить	*(pe-re-a-TSEH-nee-vat/pe-re-a-tse-NEET)*

owl	сова	*(sa-VAH)*
owner	владелец	*(vla-DEH-lets)*
owner's equity	доля владельца	*(DOH-lya vla-DEHL-tsa)*
ownership	право собственности	*(PRAH-va SOP-stven-na-stee)*

P

package deal	глобальный контракт	*(gla-BAHL-nee kan-TRAHKT)*
packaging	упаковка	*(oo-pa-KOF-ka)*
packing case	ящик для упаковки	*(YAH-shcheek dla oo-pa-KOF-kee)*
page	страница	*(stra-NEE-tsa)*
page makeup	расположение страницы	*(ras-pa-la-ZHEH-nee-ye stra-NEE-tsee)*
pagination	пагинация	*(pa-ghee-NAH-tsee-ya)*
paid holiday	оплаченный выходной	*(ap-LAH-chen-nee vee-khad-NOY)*
paid in full	полностью оплаченный	*(POL-na-styoo ap-LAH-chen-nee)*
paid up capital	оплаченный капитал	*(ap-LAH-chen-nee ka-pee-TAHL)*
paid up shares	полностью оплаченные акции	*(POL-na-styoo ap-LAH-chen-nee-ye AHK-tsee-ee)*
paint	краска	*(KRAHS-ka)*
pallet	паллет	*(PAHL-let)*
palletized freight	груз на паллетах	*(groos na PAHL-le-takh)*
pamphlet	памфлет	*(pam-FLET)*
panel	щит	*(shcheet)*
paper	бумага	*(boo-MAH-ga)*
paperback	в бумажном переплёте	*(vboo-MAHZH-nam pe-re-PLYOH-te)*
paper mill	бумажная фабрика	*(boo-MAHZH-na-ya FAHB-ree-ka)*
paper profit	доходы, имеющиеся лишь на бумаге	*(da-KHOH-dee ee-MEH-yoo-shchee-ye-sa leesh na boo-MAH-ghe)*

parallel circuit	параллельная схема	*(pa-ra-LEL-na-ya SKHEH-ma)*
par value	номинальная стоимость	*(na-mee-NAHL-na-ya STOH-ee-mast)*
par, above	выше номинальной цены	*(VEE-she na-mee-NAHL-nay tse-NEE)*
par, below	ниже номинальной цены	*(NEE-zhe na-mee-NAHL-nay tse-NEE)*
parcel post	посылка по почте	*(pa-SIL-ka pa POCH-te)*
parent company	компания-учредитель	*(kam-PAH-nee-ya-ooch-re-DEE-tel)*
parity	паритет	*(pa-ree-TET)*
parity crude	«паритетный» (базисный) сорт	*(pa-ree-TET-nee [BAH-zees-nee] sohrt)*
parity price	эквивалентная цена	*(ek-vee-va-LENT-na-ya tse-NAH)*
part cargo	частичный груз	*(chas-TEECH-nee groos)*
partial payment	частичный платёж	*(chas-TEECH-nee pla-TYOSH)*
particle board	древесностружечная плита (ДСП)	*(dre-VES-na-STROO-zhech-na-ya plee-TAH [DEH-ES-PEH])*
participation crude	«нефть партнера»	*(neft part-NYOH-ra)*
participation fee	расходы по участию	*(ras-KHO-dee pa oo-CHAHS-tee-yoo)*
particular average loss	убыток от частичной аварии	*(oo-BEE-tak aht chas-TEECH-nay a-VAH-ree-ee)*
partner	партнер	*(part-NYOHR)*
partnership	товарищество	*(ta-VAH-ree-shche-stva)*
passbook	банковская расчётная книга	*(BAHN-kaf-ska-ya ra-SHCHYOHT-na-ya KNEE-ga)*
passed dividend	необъявленный дивиденд	*(ne-ab-YAHV-len-nee dee-vee-DENT)*
passport case	футляр для паспорта	*(foot-LYAHR dlya PAHS-par-ta)*
past due	просроченный	*(pra-SROH-chen-nee)*
pasteurizer	пастеризатор	*(pas-te-ree-ZAH-tar)*
patent	патент	*(pa-TENT)*

P

patent application	заявка на патент	*(za-YAHF-ka na pa-TENT)*
patent law	закон о патентах	*(za-KON a pa-TEN-takh)*
patent leather	лакированная кожа/лак	*(la-kee-ROH-van-na-ya KOH-zha/lak)*
patent pending	нерешённый патент	*(ne-re-SHON-nee pa-TENT)*
patent royalty	патентное роялти	*(pa-TENT-na-ye ROH-yal-tee)*
patented process	запатентованный процесс	*(za-pa-ten-TOH-van-nee pra-TSESS)*
pattern	пример	*(pree-MEHR)*
pay (v)	платить/заплатить	*(pla-TEET/za-pla-TEET)*
pay off (v)	рассчитываться/ рассчитаться	*(ra-SHCHEE-tee-vat-sa) ras-schee-TAHT-sya)*
pay up (v)	выплачивать	*(vee-PLAH-chee-vat)*
payable on demand	подлежащий уплате при требовании	*(pad-le-ZHAH-shchee oop-LAH-te pree TREH-ba-va-nee-ye)*
payable to bearer	подлежащий уплате предъявителю	*(pad-le-ZHAH-shchee oop-LAH-te pret-ya-VEE-te-lyoo)*
payable to order	подлежащий уплате по распоряжению	*(pad-le-ZHAH-shchee oop-LAH-te pa ras-par-ya-ZHE-nee-yoo)*
payback period	срок погашения долга	*(srok pa-ga-SHEH-nee-ya DOL-ga)*
payee	лицо, получающее платёж	*(lee-TSOH pa-loo-CHAH-yoo-shchee pla-TYOSH)*
payer	плательщик	*(pla-TEL-shcheek)*
payload	полезный груз	*(pa-LEZ-nee groos)*
paymaster	кассир	*(kas-SEEHR)*
payment	уплата	*(oop-LAH-ta)*
payment in full	полная уплата	*(POL-na-ya oop-LAH-ta)*
payment in kind	оплата натурой	*(ap-LAH-ta na-TOO-ray)*
payment, refused	отвергнутая оплата	*(at-VEHR-gnoo-ta-ya ap-LAH-ta)*
payout period	период выплаты	*(pe-REE-at VIP-la-tee)*
payroll	платежная ведомость	*(pla-TYOZH-na-ya VEH-da-mast)*
payroll tax	налог на зарплату	*(na-LOK na zar-PLAH-too)*

PC	персональная ЭВМ	*(per-sa-NAHL-na-ya eh-veh-EM)*
peach	персик	*(PEHR-seek)*
peak load	максимальное бремя	*(mak-see-MAHL-na-ye BREH-mya)*
pear	груша	*(GROO-sha)*
pegged price	искусственно поддерживаемая цена	*(ees-KOO-stven-na pad-DEHR-zhee-va-ye-ma-ya tse-NAH)*
pegging	искусственное поддержание цены	*(ees-KOO-stven-na-ye pad-DEHR-zha-nee-ye tse-NEE)*
pellet	пилюля	*(pee-LYOO-lya)*
penalty clause	штрафная оговорка	*(strahf-NAY-ya a-ga-VOHR-ka)*
penalty-fraud action	иск о мошенничестве	*(eesk a ma-SHEH-nee-chest-ve)*
penicillin	пенициллин	*(pe-nee-tsee-LEEN)*
penny stock	«пенни сток»/недорогие спекулятивные акции	*(PEN-nee stok/ne-da-ra-GHEE-ye spe-koo-la-TEEV-nee-ye AHK-tsee-ee)*
pension fund	пенсионный фонд	*(pen-see-ON-nee font)*
per capita	на душу населения	*(na DOO-shoo na-se-LEH-nee-ya)*
per diem	в день	*(vden)*
peripheral	периферийное устройство	*(pe-re-fe-REEY-na-ye oos-TROYST-va)*
peripherals	периферийное оборудование	*(pe-re-fe-REEY-na-ye a-ba-ROO-da-va-nee-ye)*
per share	на акцию	*(na AHK-tsee-yoo)*
percentage earnings	процентный доход	*(pra-TSENT-nee da-KHOT)*
percentage of profit	процент прибыли	*(pra-TSENT PREE-bee-lee)*
percentage point	процент	*(pra-TSENT)*
periodic inventory	периодическая инвентаризация	*(pe-ree-a-DEE-ches-ka-ya een-ven-ta-ree-ZAH-tsee-ya)*
perks	побочные преимущества	*(pa-boch-NEE-ye pre-ee-MOO-shche-stva)*

permit	разрешение	*(raz-re-SHEH-nee-ye)*
perpetual inventory	постоянная инвентаризация	*(pa-sta-YAHN-na-ya een-ven-ta-ree-ZAH-tsee-ya)*
personal deduction	персональный вычет (с налогов)	*(per-sa-NAHL-nee VEE-chet [sna-LOH-gaf])*
personal exemption	персональное освобождение (от налогов)	*(per-sa-NAHL-na-ye as-va-bazh-DEH-nee-ye at na-LOH-gaf])*
personal income tax	подоходный налог с физических лиц	*(pa-da-KHOD-nee na-LOK sfee-ZEE-ches-keekh leets)*
personal liability	личная ответственность	*(LEECH-na-ya at-VET-stven-nast)*
personal property	движимое имущество	*(DVEE-zhee-ma-ye ee-MOO-shchest-va)*
personality test	психологический тест	*(psee-kha-la-GHEE-ches-kee test)*
personnel department	отдел кадров	*(at-DEL KAHD-raf)*
personnel management	управление кадрами	*(oop-rav-LEH-nee-ye KAHD-ra-mee)*
petrochemical	нефтехимический	*(NEF-te-khee-MEE-ches-kee)*
petrodollars	«нефтяные доллары»	*(nef-te-NEH-ye DOL-la-ree)*
petroleum	нефть/нефть и газ	*(neft/neft ee gahs)*
petroliferous	нефтегазоносный	*(nef-te-ga-za-NOS-nee)*
pharmaceutical	фармацевтический	*(far-ma-tsef-TEE-ches-kee)*
pharmacist	фармацевт	*(far-ma-TSEFT)*
phase in (v)	вводить по этапам	*(vva-DEET pa e-TAH-pam)*
phase out (v)	снимать/снять по этапам	*(snee-MAHT/snyat pa e-TAH-pam)*
phosphate	соль фосфорной кислоты	*(sol FOS-fahr-nay kees-la-TEE)*
physician	врач	*(vrahch)*
pica	цицеро	*(TSEE-tse-roo)*
picket line	пикет	*(pee-KET)*
pickling	травление	*(trav-LEH-nee-ye)*
pickup and delivery	заезд и доставка	*(za-YEST ee da-STAHF-ka)*

pie chart	круговая схема пропорциональности	*(kroo-ga-VAH-ya SKHEH-ma pra-par-tsee-a-NAHL-na-stee)*
piecework	штучная работа	*(SHTOOCH-na-ya ra-BOH-ta)*
piggyback service	контрейлерные услуги	*(kan-TREY-ler-nee-ye oos-LOO-ghee)*
pig iron	чушковый чугун	*(CHOOSH-ka-vee choo-GOON)*
pigment	пигмент	*(peeg-MENT)*
pigskin	свиная кожа	*(svee-NAH-ya KOH-zha)*
pilferage	мелкая кража	*(MEL-ka-ya KRAH-zha)*
pill	таблетка	*(tab-LET-ka)*
pilotage	лоцманская проводка	*(LOTS-man-ska-ya pra-VOT-ka)*
pine	сосна	*(sas-NAH)*
pinion	шестерня	*(shes-ter-NYAH)*
pipage	перекачка по трубопроводу	*(pe-re-KAHCH-ka pa troo-ba-pra-VOH-doo)*
pipe line fill	«наполнение трубопровода»	*(na-pal-NEH-nee-ye troo-ba-pra-VOH-da)*
piston	поршень	*(POHR-shen)*
place on order (v)	поместить заказ	*(pa-mes-TEET za-KAHS)*
place of business	деловое помещение	*(de-la-VOH-ye pa-me-SHCHEH-nee-ye)*
plan	план	*(plahn)*
plan, market	рыночный план	*(REE-nach-nee plahn)*
planned obsolescence	запланированное устаревание	*(za-plah-NEE-ra-van-na-ye oo-sta-re-VAH-nee-ye)*
plant (v)	сеять	*(SEH-yat)*
plant	растение	*(ras-TEH-nee-ye)*
plants	растения	*(ras-TEH-nee-ya)*
plant capacity	мощность фабрики	*(MOSHCH-nast FAHB-ree-kee)*
plant location	местонахождение фабрики	*(mesta-na-khazh-DEH-nee-ye FAHB-ree-kee*
plant manager	руководитель/директор фабрики	*(roo-ka-va-DEE-tel/dee-REK-tar FAHB-ree-kee)*

P

plate   288

plate	стереотип/толстый лист	*(ste-re-a-TEEP/(TOL-stee leest)*
pledge	залог	*(za-LOK)*
plenary meeting	пленарное совещание	*(ple-NAHR-na-ye sa-ve-SHCHAH-nee-ye)*
plough	плуг	*(plook)*
plow back earnings (v)	превращаться в капитал	*(pre-VRAH-shchat fka-pee-TAHL)*
plum	слива	*(SLEE-va)*
plywood	фанера	*(fa-NEH-ra)*
pocketbook	записная книжка	*(za-pees-NAH-ya KNEEZH-ka)*
point of order	порядок ведения заседания	*(pa-RYAH-dak ve-DEH-nee-ya za-se-DAH-nee-ya)*
point, percentage	процент	*(pra-TSENT)*
policy	политика	*(pa-LEE-tee-ka)*
policy (insurance)	полис страхования/ страховой полис	*(POH-lees stra-kha-VAH-nee-ya/stra-kha-VOY POH-lees)*
policyholder	держатель полиса	*(der-ZHAH-tel POH-lee-sa)*
pollination	опыление	*(a-pee-LEH-nee-ye)*
polymer	полимер	*(pa-lee-MEHR)*
pond	пруд	*(proot)*
pool (v)	объединять в общий фонд	*(ab-ye-dee-NYAHT VOP-shchee font)*
pool of funds	объединение фондов	*(ab-ye-dee-NEH-nee-ye FON-daf)*
pooling of interests	объединение интересов	*(ab-ye-dee-NEH-nee-ye een-te-REH-saf)*
port	порт	*(pohrt)*
portable	мобильный	*(ma-BEEL-nee)*
portfolio	портфель капиталовложений	*(part-FEL ka-pee-ta-la-vla-ZHEH-neey)*
portfolio management	руководство портфеля	*(roo-ka-VOT-stva part-FEH-lya)*
positive	позитивный	*(pa-see-TEEV-nee)*
positive cash flow	активное «кэшфлоу»	*(ak-TEEV-na-ye "cash flow")*

post (v) (bookkeeping)	делать проводку	*(DEH-lat pra-VOT-koo)*
postdate (n)	пометка задним числом	*(pa-MET-ka ZAHD-neem chees-LOM)*
postpone (v)	отсрочивать/откладывать	*(at-SROH-chee-vat/at-KLAH-dee-vat)*
potato (es)	картофель	*(kar-TOH-fel)*
potential buyers	возможные покупатели	*(vaz-MOZH-nee-ye pa-koo-PAH-te-lee)*
potential sales	возможная продажа	*(vaz-MOZH-na-ya pra-DAH-zha)*
powder	порошок	*(pa-ra-SHOK)*
power	энергия	*(e-NEHR-gee-ya)*
power steering	рулевое управление с усилителем	*(roo-lee-VOH-ye oop-rav-LEH-nee-ye soo-see-LEE-te-lem)*
practical	практический	*(prak-TEE-ches-kee)*
preemptive right	преимущественное право	*(pree-ee-MOO-shchest-ven-na-ye PRAH-va)*
prefabricated	заранее изготовленный	*(za-RAH-nee-ye eez-ga-TOV-len-nee)*
preface	предисловие	*(pree-dee-SLOH-vee-ye)*
preferential crude	«преференциальная» (льготная) нефть	*(pre-fe-ren-tsee-AHL-na-ya [LGOT-na-ya] neft)*
preferential debts	первоочередные долги	*(per-va-a-che-red-NEE-ye dal-GHEE)*
preferential tariff	таможенный тариф	*(pre-fe-ren-tsee-AHL-nee ta-MOH-zhen-nee ta-REEF)*
preferred stock	привилегированная акция	*(pree-vee-le-ghee-ROH-van-na-ya AHK-tsee-ya)*
preliminary prospectus	предварительный проспект	*(pred-va-REE-tel-nee pras-PEKT)*
premises	помещения	*(pa-me-SHCHEH-nee-ya)*
premium, insurance	страховой взнос	*(stra-kha-VOY vznos)*
premium offer	особо выгодное предложение	*(a-SOH-ba VEE-gad-na-ye pred-la-ZHEH-nee-ye)*
premium price	цена с надбавкой	*(tse-NAH snad-BAHF-kay)*
prepaid expenses (balance sheet)	оплаченные заранее расходы	*(ap-LAH-chen-nee-ye za-RAH-ne-ye ras-KHOH-dee)*

prepay (v)	уплачивать/уплатить заранее	*(oop-LAH-chee-vat /oop-la-TEET za-RAH-ne-ye)*
president	президент	*(pre-zee-DENT)*
prescription	рецепт	*(re-TSEPT)*
press clipping	газетная вырезка	*(ga-ZET-na-ya VEE-res-ka)*
pressure	давление	*(dav-LEH-nee-ye)*
preventive maintenance	профилактический ремонт	*(pra-fee-lak-TEE-ches-kee re-MONT)*
price	цена	*(tse-NAH)*
price (v)	назначить цену	*(naz-na-CHAHT TSEH-noo)*
price cutting	снижение цены	*(snee-ZHEE-nee-ye tse-NEE)*
price differential	дифференцированные цены	*(deef-fe-ren-TSEE-ra-van-ne-ye TSEH-nee)*
price/earnings (p/e) ratio	соотношение дохода и цены (акции)	*(sa-at-na-SHEH-nee-ye da-KHOH-da ee tse-NEE [AKH-tsee-ee])*
price elasticity	эластичность цены	*(e-las-TEECH-nast tse-NEE)*
price fixing	фиксирование цен	*(feek-SEE-ra-va-nee-ye tsen)*
price index	индекс цен	*(EEN-deks tsen)*
price limit	предельная цена	*(pre-DEHL-na-ya tse-NAH)*
price list	прейскурант	*(preys-koo-RAHNT)*
price range	диапазон цен	*(dee-a-pa-ZON tsen)*
price support	поддержание цен	*(pad-der-ZHAH-nee-ye tsen)*
price tag	ярлык с указанием цены	*(yar-LIK soo-ka-ZAH-nee-yem tse-NEE)*
price war	«война цен» (конкуренция)	*(vay-NAH tsen [kan-koo-REN-tsee-ya])*
primary market	основной рынок	*(as-nav-NOY REE-nak)*
primary reserves	основные резервы/запасы, извлекаемые первичными методами разработки месторождения	*(as-nav-NEE-ye re-ZEHR-vee/za-PAH-see eez-vle-KAH-ye-mee-ye per-VEECH-nee-mee MEH-ta-da-mee raz-ra-BOT-kee mes-ta-razh-DEH-nee-ya])*
prime costs	себестоимость	*(se-be-STOH-ee-mast)*

prime rate	привилегированная ставка	*(pre-vee-le-ghee-ROH-van-na-ya STAHF-ka)*
principal (capital)	капитал	*(ka-pee-TAHL)*
principal (employer of an agent)	доверитель	*(da-ve-REE-tel)*
print run	тираж	*(tee-RAHSH)*
printed circuit	печатная схема	*(pe-CHAHNT-na-ya SKHEH-ma)*
printed matter	печатный материал	*(pe-CHAHT-nee ma-te-ree-YAHL)*
printer	принтер	*(PREEN-ter)*
printing	печатание	*(pe-CHAH-ta-nee-ye)*
printout (computer)	распечатка (компьютера)	*(ras-pe-CHAHT-ka [kam-PYOO-te-ra])*
priority	приоритет	*(pree-a-ree-TET)*
private farm	частный хутор	*(CHAHS-nee KHOO-tar)*
private fleet	частный парк (машин)	*(CHAHS-nee pahrk [ma-SHIN])*
private label (or brand)	фирменный знак	*(FEEHR-men-nee znahk)*
private placement (finance)	частные капиталовложения	*(CHAHS-nee-ye ka-pee-TAH-la-vla-ZHEH-nee-ya)*
pro forma statement	примерная ведомость	*(pree-MEHR-na-ya VEH-da-mast)*
probate	дела о наследстве	*(de-LAH a na-SLET-stve)*
probe	космический зонд	*(kas-MEE-ches-kee zont)*
problem	проблема	*(pra-BLEH-ma)*
problem solving	решение проблемы	*(re-SHEH-nee-ye pra-BLEH-mee)*
proceeds	выручка	*(VEE-rooch-ka)*
process (v)	оформлять/оформить	*(a-farm-LYAHT/a-FOHR-meet)*
process	процесс	*(pra-TSES)*
process gas	технологический газ	*(tekh-na-la-GHEE-ches-kee gahs)*
processing error	ошибка в обработке (данных)	*(a-SHIP-ka vab-ra-BOT-ke [DAHN-neekh])*
processor	процессор	*(pra-TSES-sar)*

P

procurement	снабжение	*(snab-ZHEH-nee-ye)*
producer gas	генераторный газ	*(ghe-ne-RAH-tar-nee gahs)*
product	продукт	*(pra-DOOKT)*
product analysis	анализ качества продукции	*(a-NAH-lees KAH-chest-va pra-DOOK-tsee-ee)*
product design	дизайн продукта	*(dee-ZAHYN pra-DOOK-ta)*
product development	развитие продукта	*(raz-VEE-tee-ye pro-DOOK-ta)*
product dynamics	динамика продукта	*(dee-NAH-mee-ka pra-DOOK-ta)*
product group	группа продуктов	*(GROOP-pa pra-DOOK-taf)*
product life	долговечность изделия	*(dal-ga-VECH-nast eez-DEH-lee-ya)*
product management	управление продукцией	*(oop-rav-LEH-nee-ye pra-DOOK-tsee-yey)*
product profitability	рентабельность	*(ren-TAH-bel-nast)*
production	производство	*(pra-eez-VOT-stva)*
production control	управление производственным процессом	*(oop-rav-LEH-nee-ye pra-eez-VOT-stven-nim pra-TSES-sam)*
production costs	издержки производства	*(eez-DEHRSH-kee pra-eez-VOT-stva)*
production length	стандартная длина заготовки	*(stan-DAHRT-na-ya dlee-NAH za-go-TOF-kee)*
production life	период эксплуатации месторождения	*(pee-REE-at eks-ploo-a-TAH-tsee-ee mes-ta-razh-DEH-nee-ya)*
production line	конвейер	*(kan-VEH-YEHR)*
production process	производственный процесс	*(pra-eez-VOT-stven-nee pra-TSES)*
production schedule	производственный график	*(pra-eez-VOT-stven-nee GRAH-feek)*
productivity	производительность	*(pra-eez-va-DEE-tel-nast)*
profession	профессия	*(pra-FES-see-ya)*
profit	прибыль	*(PREE-bil)*
profit-and-loss account	счёт прибылей и убытков	*(shchyoht PREE-bee-ley ee oo-BIT-kaf)*

profit-and-loss statement	отчёт прибылей и убытков	*(at-CHYOHT PREE-bee-ley ee oo-BIT-kaf)*
profit factor	коэффициент рентабельности	*(ka-ef-fee-tsee-ENT ren-TAH-bel-na-stee)*
profit, gross	валовая прибыль	*(VAH-la-va-ya PREE-bil)*
profit impact	влияние на рентабельность	*(vlee-YAH-nee-ye na ren-TAH-bel-nast)*
profit margin	коэффициент рентабельности	*(ka-ef-fee-tsee-ENT ren-TAH-bel-na-stee)*
profit, net	чистая прибыль	*(CHEES-ta-ya PREE-bil)*
profit projection	плановая прибыль	*(PLAH-na-va-ya PREE-bil)*
profit sharing	участие в прибылях	*(oo-CHAHS-tee-ye FPREE-bee-lyakh)*
profit-taking	прибыльная операция	*(PREE-bil-na-ya a-pe-RAH-tsee-ya)*
profitability	рентабельность	*(ren-TAH-bel-nast)*
profitability analysis	анализ рентабельности	*(a-NAH-lees ren-TAH-bel-na-stee)*
pro forma invoice	примерная фактура	*(pree-MEHR-na-ya fak-TOO-ra)*
program	программа	*(pra-GRAHM-ma)*
program (v)	программировать	*(pra-gram-MEE-ra-vat)*
programming	программирование	*(pra-gram-MEE-ra-va-nee-ye)*
prohibited goods	запрещённые товары	*(za-pre-SHCHYON-nee-ye ta-VAH-ree)*
project	проект	*(pra-YEKT)*
project (v)	проектировать	*(pra-yek-TEE-ra-vat)*
project planning	проектирование	*(pra-yek-TEE-ra-va-nee-ye)*
promissory note	долговое обязательство	*(dal-ga-VOH-ye a-bya-ZAH-tel-stva)*
promotion (position)	продвижение по службе	*(pra-dvee-ZHEH-nee-ee pa SLOOZH-be)*
promotion, (sales)	стимулирование сбыта	*(stee-moo-LEE-ra-va-nee-ye ZBEE-ta)*
proof of loss	доказательство потери	*(da-ka-ZAH-tel-stva pa-TEH-ree)*
proofreading	корректурное чтение	*(kar-rek-TOOHR-na-ye CHTEH-nee-ye)*

property	собственность	*(SOP-stven-nast)*
proprietary	собственнический	*(SOP-stven-nee-ches-kee)*
proprietor	собственник	*(SOP-stven-neek)*
prospectus	проспект	*(pras-PEKT)*
protectionism	протекционизм	*(pra-tek-tsee-a-NEEZM)*
protest (banking, law)	протест	*(pra-TEST)*
proxy	доверенность	*(da-VER-ren-nast)*
proxy statement	ведомость доверенности	*(VEH-da-mast da-VEH-ren-nas-tee)*
public auction	аукцион	*(a-ook-tsee-ON)*
public company	акционерное общество открытого типа	*(ak-tsee-a-NEHR-na-ye OP-shchest-va at-KREE-ta-va- TEE-pa)*
public domain	всеобщее достояние	*(fse-OP-shche-ye da-sta-YAH-nee-ye)*
public funds	общественные фонды	*(ap-SHCHEST-ven-nee-ye FOHN-dee)*
public offering	публичное предложение (ценных бумаг)	*(poob-LEECH-na-ye pred-la-ZHEH-nee-ye [TSEN-nikh boo-MAHK])*
public opinion poll	опрос общественного мнения	*(ap-ROS ap-SHCHEST-ven-na-va MNE-nee-ya)*
public property	общественная собственность	*(ap-SHCHEST-ven-na-ya SOPST-ven-nast)*
public sale	публичные торги	*(poob-LEECH-nee-ye TOHR-ghee)*
public sector	государственный сектор	*(ga-soo-DAHR-stven-nee SEK-tar)*
public utility	предприятие общественного пользования	*(pret-pree-YAH-tee-ya ap-SHCHEST-ven-na-va POL-za-va-nee-ya)*
public works	общественные сооружения	*(ap-SHCHEST-ven-nee-ye sa-a-roo-ZHEH-nee-ya)*
publicity	известность	*(eez-VEST-nast)*
publisher	издатель	*(eez-DAH-tel)*
publishing house	издательство	*(eez-DAH-tel-stva)*
pulp	волокнистый полуфабрикат	*(va-lak-NEES-tee poh-loo-fab-ree-KAHT)*

pump price	цена франко-бензоколонки	*(tse-NAH FRAHN-ka-ben-za-ka-LON-kee)*
pump priming	государственное стимулирование экономики	*(ga-soo-DAHR-stven-na-ye stee-moo-LEE-ra-va-nee-ye e-ka-NOH-mee-kee)*
purchase (v)	покупать/купить	*(pa-koo-PAHT)*
purchase money mortgage	ипотека за покупку	*(ee-pa-TEH-ka za pa-KOOP-koo)*
purchase order	заказ на поставку	*(za-KAHS na pas-TAHF-koo)*
purchase price	покупная цена	*(pa-KOOP-na-ya tse-NAH)*
purchasing agent	агент по закупкам	*(a-GHENT pa za-KOOP-kam)*
purchasing manager	начальник по закупкам	*(na-CHAHL-neek pa za-KOOP-kam)*
purchasing power	покупательная способность	*(pa-koo-PAH-tel-na-ya spa-SOB-nast)*
pure risk	чистый риск	*(CHEES-tee reesk)*
purgative	очистительное средство	*(a-cheees-TEE-tel-nee)*
purification	очистка	*(a-CHEEST-ka)*
purse	сумочка	*(SOO-mach-ka)*
put and call	двойной опцион	*(dvay-NOY ap-tsee-ON)*
put in a bid (v)	сделать заявку цены	*(ZDEH-lat za-YAHF-koo tse-NEE)*
put option	опцион на продажу	*(ap-tsee-ON na pra-DAH-zhoo)*
pyramid selling	продажа акций по методике «пирамида»	*(pra-DAH-zha AHK-tseey pa me-TOH-dee-ke "pee-ra-MEE-da")*
piramiding	методика «пирамида»	*(me-TOH-dee-ka "pee-ra-MEE-da")*

Q

qualification	квалификация	*(kva-lee-fee-KAH-tsee-ya)*
qualified acceptance endorsement	условный акцептный индоссамент	*(oos-LOV-nee ak-TSEPT-nee een-da-sa-MENT)*
quality control	контроль качества	*(kant-ROL KAH-chest-va)*

quality goods	качественные товары	*(KAH-chest-ven-nee-ye ta-VAH-ree)*
quantity	количество	*(ka-LEE-chest-va)*
quantity discount	скидка за количество	*(SKEET-ka za ka-LEE-chest-va)*
quasi-public company	корпорация по оказанию общественных услуг	*(kar-pa-RAH-tsee-ya pa a-ka-ZAH-nee-yoo ap-SHCHEST-ven-nikh oos-LOOK)*
quick assets	быстро реализуемые активы	*(BIST-ra re-a-lee-ZOO-ye-mee-ye ak-TEE-vee)*
quit claim deed	акт отказа от права	*(ahkt at-KAH-za at PRAH-va)*
quorum	кворум	*(KVOH-room)*
quota	квота	*(KVOH-ta)*
quota (export)	экспортная квота	*(EKS-part-na-ya KVOH-ta)*
quota (import)	импортная квота	*(EEM-part-na-ya KVOH-ta)*
quota (sales)	продажная квота	*(pra-DAHZH-na-ya KVOH-ta)*
quota system	система квот	*(sees-TEH-ma kvot)*
quotation (stock exchange)	котировка	*(ka-tee-ROF-ka)*

R

rabbit	кролик	*(KROH-leek)*
raccoon	енот	*(ye-NOT)*
rack jobber	оптовик	*(ap-ta-VEEK)*
radial tire	радиальная шина	*(ra-dee-AHL-na-ya SHEE-na)*
radiator	радиатор	*(ra-dee-AH-tar)*
radish	редиска	*(re-DEES-ka)*
rail shipment	вагонная погрузка	*(va-GON-na-ya pa-GROOS-ka)*
rain check	обещание принять приглашение в следующий раз	*(a-be-SHCHAH-nee-ye pree-NYAHT pree-gla-SHEH-nee-ye FSLEH-doo-yoo-shchee rahs)*

raising capital	мобилизация капитала	*(ma-bee-lee-ZAH-tsee-ya ka-pee-TAH-la)*
rally	оживление (курса на бирже)	*(a-zhiv-LEH-nee-ye [KOOHR-sa na BEEHR-zhe])*
rally (v)	оживляться/оживиться	*(a-zhiv-LYAHT-sa/a-zhi-VEET-sa)*
ram	баран	*(ba-RAHN)*
random access memory (RAM)	ЗУ с произвольным порядком выборки	*(ZEE-OO spra-eez-VOL-nim pa-RYAHT-kam VEE-bar-kee)*
random sample	случайная выборка	*(sloo-CHAHY-na-ya VEE-bar-ka)*
range	диапазон	*(dee-a-PAH-son)*
rate	ставка	*(STAHF-ka)*
rate of growth	уровень роста	*(OO-ra-ven ROH-sta)*
rate of increase	ставка увеличения	*(STAHF-ka oo-ve-lee-CHEH-nee-ya)*
rate of interest	процентная ставка	*(pra-TSENT-na-ya STAHF-ka)*
rate of return	норма рентабельности	*(NOHR-ma ren-TAH-bel-na-stee)*
rating (credit)	оценка рентабельности	*(a-TSEN-ka ren-TAH-bel-na-stee)*
rating (market)	рыночная оценка	*(REE-nach-na-ya a-TSEN-ka)*
ratio	коэффициент	*(ka-ef-fee-tsee-ENT)*
rationing	рационирование	*(ra-tsee-a-NEE-ra-va-nee-ye)*
rats	крысы	*(KREE-see)*
raw gas	неочищенный газ	*(ne-a-CHEE-shchen-nee gahs)*
raw materials	сырье	*(sihr-YOH)*
reactant	реагент	*(re-a-GHENT)*
ready cash	наличные деньги	*(na-LEECH-nee-ye DEN-ghee)*
real assets	реальные активы	*(re-AHL-nee-ye ak-TEE-vee)*
real estate	недвижимость	*(ne-DVEE-zhee-mast)*
real income	реальный доход	*(re-AHL-nee da-KHOT)*

R

real investment	чистые инвестиции	(CHEES-tee-ye een-ve-STEE-tsee-ee)
real price	действительные цены	(deyst-VEE-tel-nee-ye TSEH-nee)
real time	действительное время	(deyst-VEE-tel-na-ye VREH-mya)
real wages	реальная зарплата	(re-AHL-na-ya zar-PLAH-ta)
ream	стопа	(sta-PAH)
reaper	жатвенная машина	(ZHAT-ven-na-ya ma-SHEE-na)
rear axle	задний мост/задняя ось	(ZAHD-nee most/ZAHD-nya-ya os)
reasonable care	достаточная забота	(da-STAH-tach-na-ya za-BOH-ta)
rebate	возврат определенного процента стоимости	(vaz-VRAHT ap-re-de-LYON-na-va pra-TSEN-ta STOH-ee-mas-tee)
reboot (v)	повторять начальную загрузку	(paf-ta-RYAHT na-CHAHL-noo-yoo za-GROOS-koo)
recapitalization	перекапитализация	(pe-re-ka-pee-ta-lee-ZAH-tsee-ya)
receipt (paper)	квитанция	(kvee-TAHN-tsee-ya)
receiver	приемник	(pree-YOM-neek)
recession	рецессия	(re-TSES-see-ya)
reciprocal training	взаимное обучение	(vza-EEM-na-ye a-boo-CHEH-nee-ye)
record	запись	(ZAH-pees)
recourse	регресс	(re-GRES)
recoverable booster	ускоритель многократного действия	(oos-ka-REE-tel mna-ga-KRAHT-na-va DEY-stvee-ya)
recoverable reserves	извлекаемые запасы	(eez-vle-LAH-ye-mee-ye za-PAH-see)
recovery	возмещение	(vaz-me-SHCHEH-nee-ye)
recovery of expenses	возмещение расходов	(vaz-me-SHCHEH-nee-ye ras-KHOH-daf)
red tape	волокита	(va-la-KEE-ta)
redeemable bond	выкупаемая облигация	(vee-koo-PAH-ye-ma-ya ab-lee-GAH-tsee-ya)

redemption allowance	ассигнование погашения	*(as-seeg-na-VAH-nee-ye pa-ga-SHEH-nee-ya)*
redemption fund	фонд погашения	*(font pa-ga-SHEH-nee-ya)*
redemption premium	эмиссионная премия	*(e-mees-see-ON-na-ya PREH-mee-ya)*
rediscount rate	ставка переучёта	*(STAHF-ka pe-re-oo-CHYOH-ta)*
reduction (chemical)	восстановление	*(vas-sta-nav-LEH-nee-ye)*
re-entry	вход в плотные слои атмосферы	*(fkhot FPLOT-nee-ye sla-EE at-mas-FEH-ree)*
reference, credit	справка для предоставления кредита	*(SPRAHF-ka dlya pre-da-stav-LEH-nee-ya kre-DEE-ta)*
reference number	регистрационный номер	*(re-ghee-stra-tsee-ON-nee NOH-mer)*
refinancing	перефинансирование	*(pe-re-fee-nan-SEE-ra-va-nee-ye)*
refine (v)	очищать	*(a-chee-SHCHAHT)*
refinery	нефтеочистительный завод	*(NEF-te-a-chees-TEE-tel-nee za-VOT)*
refinery feed stock	нефтезаводское сырье	*(NEF-te-za-vat-SKOH-ye sihr-YOH)*
refinery fuel	нефтезаводское топливо	*(NEF-te-za-vat-SKOH-ye TOP-lee-va)*
reflation	рефляция	*(re-FLYAH-tsee-ya)*
reforestation	лесовосстановление	*(LEH-sa-vas-sta-nav-LEH-nee-ye)*
refund	возврат денег	*(vaz-VRAHT DEH-neg)*
refuse acceptance (v)	отказаться от акцепта	*(at-ka-ZAH-tsa at ak-TSEP-ta)*
refuse payment (v)	отказаться от уплаты	*(at-ka-ZAH-tsa aht oo-PLAH-tee)*
registered check	зарегистрированный чек	*(za-re-ghee-STREE-ra-van-nee check)*
registered mail	заказная корреспонденция	*(za-kaz-NAH-ya kar-res-pan-DEHN-tsee-ya)*
registered representative	зарегистрированный представитель	*(za-re-ghee-STREE-ra-van-nee pret-sta-VEE-tel)*
registered securities	именные ценные бумаги	*(ee-men-NEE-ye TSEN-nee-ye boo-MAH-ghee)*

registered trade-mark	зарегистрированная торговая марка	*(za-re-ghee-STREE-ra-van-na-ya tar-GOH-va-ya MAHR-ka)*
regression analysis	анализ регрессии	*(a-NAH-lees re-GRES-see-ee)*
regressive tax	регрессивный налог	*(re-gres-SEEV-nee na-LOK)*
regular warehouse	товарный склад	*(ta-VAHR-nee sklat)*
regulation	распоряжение	*(ras-pa-rya-ZHEH-nee-ye)*
reimburse (v)	возмещать/возместить	*(vaz-me-SHCHAHT/vaz-mes-TEET)*
reinsurer	перестраховщик	*(pe-re-stra-KHOV-shcheek)*
relational data base	реляционная база данных	*(re-la-tsee-ON-na-ya BAH-za DAHN-nikh)*
reliable source	надёжный источник	*(na-DYOZH-nee ees-TOCH-neek)*
remainder	оставшаяся часть	*(as-TAHF-sha-ya-sa chahst)*
remedies	лечебные средства	*(le-CHEB-nee-ye SRET-stva)*
remedy (law)	средство судебной защиты	*(SRET-stva soo-DEB-nay za-SHCHEE-tee)*
remission of a customs duty	освобождение от уплаты таможенной пошлины	*(as-va-bazh-DEH-nee-ye at oop-LAH-tee ta-MOH-zhen-nay POSH-lee-nee)*
remission of a tax	освобождение от уплаты налога	*(as-va-bazh-DEH-nee-ye at oop-LAH-tee na-LOH-ga)*
remuneration	вознаграждение	*(vaz-na-grazh-DEH-nee-ye)*
renegotiate (v)	пересмотреть договор	*(pe-re-smat-RET)*
renew (v)	обновлять/обновить	*(ab-nav-LYAHT/ab-na-VEET)*
rent	арендная плата	*(a-REND-na-ya PLAH-ta)*
rent (v) (rent from)	брать/взять в аренду	*(braht /vzyat va-REN-doo)*
rent (v) (rent to)	сдавать/сдать в аренду	*(sda-VAHT/sdat va-REN-doo)*
reorder (v)	сделать повторный заказ	*(ZDEH-lat paf-TOHR-nee za-KAHS)*
reorganization	реорганизация	*(re-ar-ga-nee-ZAH-tsee-ya)*
repay (v)	уплачивать/уплатить	*(oo-PLAH-chee-vat/oo-pla-TEET)*
repeat order	вторичный заказ	*(fta-REECH-nee za-KAHS)*

replacement cost	восстановительная стоимость	*(vas-sta-na-VEE-tel-na-ya STOH-ee-mast)*
replacement parts	запчасти	*(zap-CHAHS-tee)*
reply (v)	отвечать/ответить	*(at-VEH-chat/at-VEH-teet)*
report	сообщение	*(sa-ap-SHCHEH-nee-ye)*
repossession	изъятие имущества	*(eez-YAH-tee-ye ee-MOO-shche-stva)*
representative	представитель	*(pret-sta-VEE-tel)*
request for bid	объявление о принятии предложений	*(ab-yav-LEH-nee-ye a pree-NYAH-tee-ee pred-la-ZHEH-neey)*
requirement	потребность	*(pa-TREB-nast)*
resale	перепродажа	*(pe-re-pra-DAH-zha)*
research	исследование	*(ees-SLEH-da-va-nee-ye)*
research and development	проектно-исследовательская работа	*(pra-YEKT-na-ees-SLEH-da-va-tel-ska-ya ra-BOH-ta)*
reserve	резерв	*(re-ZEHRF)*
resistance	сопротивление	*(sap-ra-teev-LEH-nee-ye)*
resolution	резолюция	*(re-za-LYOO-tsee-ya)*
resonance	резонанс	*(re-za-NAHNS)*
resource allocation	ассигнование ресурсов	*(as-seeg-na-VAH-nee-ye re-SOOHR-saf)*
restrictions on export (import)	ограничение на экспорт (импорт)	*(ag-ra-nee-CHEH-nee-ye na EKS-part [EEM-part])*
restructuring	перестройка	*(pe-re-STROY-ka)*
resume (v)	продолжать/продолжить (производство и т.п.)	*(pra-dal-ZHAHT/pra-DOHL-zheet [pra-eez-VOT-stva ee tahk PROH-she)*
retail	розничный	*(ROZ-neech-nee)*
retail bank	розничный банк	*(ROZ-neech-nee bahnk)*
retail merchandise	розничные товары	*(ROZ-neech-nee-ye ta-VAH-ree)*
retail outlet	розничный магазин	*(ROZ-neech-nee ma-ga-ZEEN)*
retail price	розничная цена	*(ROZ-neech-na-ya tse-NAH)*
retail sales tax	налог с розничного оборота	*(na-LOK SROZ-neech-na-va a-ba-ROH-ta)*

R

retail trade	розничная продажа	*(ROZ-neech-na-ya pra-DAH-zha)*
retained earnings	нераспределённый доход	*(ne-ras-pre-de-LYON-nee da-KHOT)*
retained profits	нераспределённая прибыль	*(ne-ras-pre-de-LYON-na-ya PREE-bil)*
retirement	выход на пенсию	*(VEE-khat na PEN-see-yoo)*
retirement (debt)	погашение долгов	*(pa-ga-SHEH-nee-ye dal-GOF)*
retractories	огнеупорные материалы	*(ag-ne-oo-POHR-nee-ye ma-te-ree-YAH-lee)*
retroactive	имеющий обратную силу	*(ee-MEH-yoo-shchee ab-RAHT-noo-yoo SEE-loo)*
return on capital	процент на капитал	*(pra-TSENT na ka-pee-TAHL)*
return on investment	процент на инвестиции	*(pra-TSENT naeen-ve-STEE-tsee-ee)*
return on sales	доход от продажи	*(da-KHOT at pra-DAH-zhee)*
return, rate of	норма прибыли	*(NOHR-ma PREE-bee-lee)*
revaluation	переоценка	*(pe-re-a-TSEN-ka)*
revenue	доход	*(da-KHOT)*
revenue bond	процентная облигация	*(pra-TSENT-na-ya ab-lee-GAH-tsee-ya)*
reverse stock split	перегруппировка акций	*(pe-re-groop-pee-ROF-ka AHK-tseey)*
revocable trust	отзывная доверительная собственность	*(at-ziv-NAH-ya da-ve-REE-tel-na-ya SOP-stven-nast)*
revolving credit	револьверный кредит	*(re-val-VEHR-nee kre-DEET)*
revolving fund	револьверный фонд	*(re-val-VEHR-nee font)*
reward	вознаграждение	*(vaz-nag-razh-DEH-nee-ye)*
rider (contracts)	дополнительный пункт (к договору)	*(da-pal-NEE-tel-nee poonkt [gda-ga-VOH-roo])*
right of resource	право регресса	*(PRAH-va re-GRES-sa)*
right of way	право прохода	*(PRAH-va pra-KHOH-da)*
rings	кольца	*(KOL-tsa)*
risk	риск	*(reesk)*
risk analysis	анализ риска	*(a-NAH-lees REES-ka)*

R

risk assessment	оценка риска	*(a-TSEN-ka REES-ka)*
risk capital	рискованный капитал	*(res-KOH-van-nee ka-pee-TAHL)*
rocket	ракета	*(ra-KEH-ta)*
rod	стержень	*(STEHR-zhen)*
rollback	понижение рыночных цен (до прежнего уровня)	*(pa-nee-ZHEH-nee-ye REE-nach-nikh tsen [da PREZH-ne-va- OO-rav-nya])*
rolling mill	прокатный стан	*(pra-KAHT-nee stahn)*
rolling stock	подвижной состав	*(pad-veezh-NOY sa-STAHF)*
rollover	налоговый кредит «рол-овер»	*(na-LOH-ga-vee kre-DEET ROL-OH-vehr)*
ROM	постоянное запоминающее устройство (ПЗУ)	*(pas-ta-YAHN-na-ye za-pa-mee-NAH-yoo-shchee-ye oos-TROYST-va)*
rooster	петух	*(pe-TOOKH)*
rough draft	черновик	*(cher-na-VEEK)*
rough estimate	приблизительная смета	*(pree-blee-ZEE-tel-na-ya SMEH-ta)*
round lot	круговая партия	*(kroo-ga-VAH-ya PAHR-tee-ya)*
routine (computers)	рутинная операция	*(roo-TEEN-na-ya a-pe-RAH-tsee-ya)*
row	строка	*(stra-KAH)*
royalty	роялти	*(ROH-yal-tee)*
royalty (book)	авторский гонорар (книга)	*(AHF-tar-skee ga-na-RAHR [KNEE-ga])*
royalty (patent)	авторский гонорар (патент)	*(AHF-tar-skee ga-na-RAHR [pa-TENT])*
run-time	период прогона	*(pe-REE-at pra-GOH-na)*
running expenses	эксплуатационные расходы	*(eks-ploo-a-ta-tsee-ON-nee-ye ras-KHOH-dee)*
rural	деревенский	*(de-re-VEN-skee)*
rush order	срочный заказ	*(SROCH-nee za-KAHS)*
rust (plant disease)	ржавчина	*(RZHAHF-chee-na)*
rye	рожь	*(rozh)*

R

S

sable	соболь	*(SOH-bal)*
saddle	седло	*(sed-LOH)*
saddler	шорник	*(SHOHR-neek)*
safe deposit box	банковское хранилище	*(BAHN-kaf-ska-ye khra-NEE-le-shche)*
safeguard (v)	охранять	*(a-khra-NYAHT)*
salary	жалованье	*(ZHAH-la-va-nee-ye)*
sales	сбыт/продажа	*(zbit/pra-DAH-zha)*
sales analysis	анализ доходов от продажи	*(a-NAH-lees da-KHOH-daf at pra-DAH-zhee)*
sales budget	коммерческий бюджет	*(kam-MEHR-ches-kee byood-ZHET)*
sales estimate	оценка доходов от продажи	*(a-TSEN-ka da-KHOH-daf at pra-DAH-zhee)*
sales force	состав продавцов	*(sas-TAHF pra-daf-TSOF)*
sales forecast	прогноз доходов от продажи	*(prag-NOS da-KHOH-daf at pra-DAH-zhee)*
sales management	управление сбытом	*(oo-prav-LEH-nee-ye ZBEE-tam)*
sales promotion	стимулирование сбыта	*(stee-moo-LEE-ra-va-nee-ye ZBEE-ta)*
sales quota	продажная квота	*(pra-DAHZH-na-ya KVOH-ta)*
sales tax	налог с оборота	*(na-LOK sa-ba-ROH-ta)*
sales turnover	товарооборот	*(ta-VAH-ra-a-ba-ROH-t)*
sales volume	объем продажи	*(ab-YOM pra-DAH-zhee)*
salt	соль	*(sol)*
salts	соли	*(SOH-lee)*
salvage (v)	спасать имущество	*(spa-SAHT ee-MOO-shchest-va)*
salvage charges	расходы по спасению	*(ras-KHOH-dee pa spa-SEH-nee-yoo)*
salvage value	оценка спасенного имущества	*(a-TSEN-ka spa-SYON-na-va ee-MOO-shchest-va)*
salve	мазь	*(mahs)*
sample	образец	*(a-bra-ZETS)*

sample (v)	отбирать/отобрать образцы	*(ad-bee-RAHT/a-tab-RAHT a-braz-TSEE)*
sample line	выборочная партия	*(VEE-ba-rach-na-ya PAHR-tee-ya)*
sample size	размер образца	*(raz-MEHR a-braz-TSAH)*
saponification	омыление	*(a-mee-LEH-nee-ye)*
satellite	спутник	*(SPOOT-neek)*
save	сохранять	*(sakh-ra-NYAHT)*
savings	сбережения	*(zbe-re-ZHEH-nee-ya)*
savings account	сберегательный счёт	*(zbe-re-GAH-tel-nee shchyoht)*
savings bank	банковская сберегательная касса	*(BAHN-kaf-ska-ya zbe-re-GAH-tel-na-ya KAHS-sa)*
savings bond	сберегательные облигации (США)	*(zbe-re-GAH-tel-nee-ye ab-lee-GAH-tsee-ee)*
saw	пила	*(pee-LAH)*
saw-mill	лесопильный	*(le-sa-PEEL-nee)*
sawdust	опилки	*(a-PEEL-ke)*
scale	окалина	*(a-KAH-lee-na)*
scanner	сканнер	*(SKAHN-ner)*
scanning	развёртка	*(raz-VYORT-ka)*
schedule	график	*(GRAH-feek)*
schedule (v)	составлять график	*(sa-stav-LYAHT GRAH-feek)*
scissor case	футляр для ножниц	*(foot-LYAHR dla NOZH-neets)*
scrape	(металлический) лом	*([me-tal-LEE-ches-kee] lom)*
screen (v)	проверять/проверить (кандидата и т.п.)	*(at-va-DEET [kan-dee-DAH-ta na DOLZH-nast ee TEH-PEH])*
screen	экран	*(ek-RAHN)*
script (document)	подлинник	*(POD-leen-neek)*
scythe	коса	*(ka-SAH)*
sealed bid	предложение в запечатанном конверте	*(pred-la-ZHEH-nee-ye vza-pe-CHAH-tan-nam kan-VEHR-te)*

S

sealskin	тюленья шкура	*(tyoo-LEN-ya SHKOO-ra)*
seasonal	сезонный	*(se-ZON-nee)*
seat	сиденье	*(see-DEN-ye)*
second mortgage	вторичная ипотека	*(fta-REECH-na-ya ee-pa-TEH-ka)*
second position	вторичная позиция	*(fta-REECH-na-ya pa-ZEE-tsee-ya)*
secondary (crude) oil	вторичная нефть	*(fta-REECH-na-ya neft)*
secondary fuel	вторичное топливо	*(fta-REECH-na-ye TOP-lee-va)*
secondary market (securities)	второстепенный рынок (ценных бумаг)	*(fta-ra-ste-PEN-nee REE-nak [TSEN-nikh boo-MAHG])*
secondary reserves	вторичные запасы	*(fta-REECH-nee-ye za-PAH-see)*
secretary	секретарь	*(se-kre-TAHR)*
secured accounts	гарантированные счета	*(ga-ran-TEE-ra-van-nee-ye shche-TAH)*
securities	ценные бумаги	*(TSEN-nee-ye boo-MAH-ghee)*
security	гарантия	*(ga-RAHN-tee-ya)*
security oil stocks	сверхнормативные коммерческие запасы (жидкого топлива)	*(SVEHRKH-nar-ma-TEEV-nee-ye kam-MEHR-ches-kee-ye za-PAH-see [ZHIT-ka-va TOP-lee-va])*
sedative	седативное средство	*(se-da-TEEV-na-ye SRET-stva)*
seeder	сеялка	*(SEH-yal-ka)*
seedling	сеянец	*(SEH-ya-nets)*
seeds	семена	*(se-me-NAH)*
self-appraisal	самооценка	*(sa-ma-a-TSEN-ka)*
self-employed	работающий по найму	*(ra-BOH-ta-yoo-shchee pa NAHY-moo)*
self-service	самообслуживание	*(sa-ma-ap-SLOO-zhee-va-nee-ye)*
sell (v)	продавать/продать	*(pra-DAHT)*
sell direct (v)	продавать/продать непосредственно	*(pra-DAHT ne-pa-SRET-stven-na)*

semiconductor	полупроводник	*(POH-loo-pra-vad-NEEK)*
semivariable costs	полупеременные издержки	*(POH-loo-pe-re-MEN-nee-ye eez-DEHRSH-kee)*
senior lien	первое залоговое право	*(PEHR-va-ye za-LOH-ga-va-ye PRAH-va)*
seniority	старшинство/выслуга лет	*(star-shin-STVOH)*
separated gas	сепарированный газ	*(se-pa-REE-ra-van-nee gahs)*
separation	разделение	*(raz-de-LEH-nee-ye)*
serial	серийный	*(se-REEY-nee)*
serial bonds	серийные облигации	*(se-REEY-nee-ye ab-lee-GAH-tsee-ee)*
serial storage (computer)	серийное ЗУ (компьютер)	*(se-REEY-na-ye ZEH-OO [kam-PYOO-ter])*
serum	сыворотка	*(SEE-va-rat-ka)*
server	сервер	*(SEHR-ver)*
service (v)	обслуживать/обслужить	*(ap-SLOO-zhee-vat/ab-sloo-ZHEET)*
service, advisory	совещательное обслуживание	*(sa-ve-SHCHAH-tel-na-ye ap-SLOO-zhee-va-nee-ye)*
service contract	договор об обслуживании, подрядный контракт	*(da-ga-VOHR ab ap-SLOO-zhee-va-nee-ee, (pad-RYAHD-nee kan-TRAHKT)*
service, customer	обслуживание покупателя	*(ap-SLOO-zhee-va-nee-ye pa-koo-PAH-te-lya)*
set-up costs	издержки монтажа	*(eez-DEHRSH-kee man-ta-ZHAH)*
settlement	урегулирование претензий	*(oo-re-goo-LEE-ra-va-nee-ye pre-TEN-zeey)*
settlement in full	полное урегулирование претензий	*(POL-na-ye oo-re-goo-LEE-ra-va-nee-ye pre-TEN-zeey)*
"Seven Sisters", the	«Семь Сестёр» (монополии-участники нефтяного картеля)	*("sem ses-TYOHR" [ma-na-POH-lee-ee oo-CHAST-nee-kee nef-tee-NOH-va kar-TEH-lya])*
severance pay	выходное пособие	*(vee-khad-NOH-ye pa-SOH-bee-ye)*
sewing kit	швейный комплект	*(SHVEY-nee kamp-LEKT)*

S

sewn cover	тканевый переплёт	*(TKAH-nee-vee pe-re-PLYOT)*
shaft	вал	*(val)*
shale oil	сланцевая нефть	*(SLAHN-tse-va-ya neft)*
shareholder	акционер	*(ak-tsee-a-NEHR)*
shareholder's equity	чистая доля акционеров	*(CHEES-ta-ya DOH-lya ak-tsee-a-NEH-raf)*
shareholder's meeting	собрание акционеров	*(sa-BRAH-nee-ye ak-tsee-a-NEH-raf)*
shares	акции	*(AHK-tsee)*
sheep	овца	*(af-TSAH)*
sheet	оттиск/лист	*(OT-teesk/leest)*
shelf life	срок годности при хранении	*(srok GOD-na-stee pree khra-NEH-nee-ee)*
shift (working hours)	срок годности при хранении	*(SMEH-na)*
shipment	погрузка	*(pa-GROOS-ka)*
shipper	грузоотправитель	*(GROO-za-at-pra-VEE-tel)*
shipping agent	экспедиторский агент	*(eks-pe-DEE-tar-skee a-GHENT)*
shipping charges	расходы на погрузку	*(ras-KHOH-dee na pa-GROOS-koo)*
shipping expenses	издержки на погрузку	*(eez-DEHRSH-kee na pa-GROOS-koo)*
shipping instructions	погрузочные инструкции	*(pa-GROO-zach-nee-ye een-STROOK-tsee-ee)*
shock absorber	амортизатор	*(a-mar-tee-ZAAH-tar)*
shopping center	торговый центр	*(tar-GOH-vee tsentr)*
short delivery	недостача при доставке	*(ne-da-STAH-cha pree da-STAHF-ke)*
short of cash	нехватка наличных	*(ne-KHVAHT-ka na-LEECH-nikh)*
short position	короткая позиция	*(ka-ROT-ka-ya pa-ZEE-tsee-ya)*
short sale	продажа без покрытия на срок	*(pra-DAH-zha bes pa-KREE-tee-ya na srok)*
short supply	недостаточное количество	*(ne-da-STAH-tach-na-ye ka-LEE-chest-va)*

short-term capital account	краткосрочный капитальный счёт	*(krat-ka-SROCH-nee ka-pee-TAHL-nee shchyoht)*
short-term debt	краткосрочный долг	*(krat-ka-SROCH-nee dolk)*
short-term financing	краткосрочное финансирование	*(krat-ka-SROCH-na-ye fee-nan-SEE-ra-va-nee-ye)*
short waves	короткие волны	*(ka-ROT-kee VOL-nee)*
shortage	дефицит	*(de-fee-TSEET)*
sick leave	отпуск по болезни	*(OT-poosk pa ba-LEZ-nee)*
sickle	серп	*(serp)*
sight draft	вексель на предъявителя	*(VEK-sel na pred-ya-VEE-te-lya)*
signature	подпись	*(POT-pees)*
signature bonus	первоначальный бонус	*(per-va-na-CHAHL-nee BOH-noos)*
silent partner	пассивный партнер	*(pas-SEEV-nee part-NYOHR)*
silicon	кремний	*(KREM-nee)*
silo	силос зерновой	*(SEE-las zer-na-VOY)*
sinking fund	фонд погашения облигации	*(font pa-ga-SHEH-nee-ya ab-lee-GAH-tseey)*
sinus	синус	*(see-NOOS)*
six-cylinder engine	шеститактный двигатель	*(shes-tee-TAHKT-nee DVEE-ga-tel)*
size	размер	*(raz-MEHR)*
skilled labor	квалифицированный труд	*(kva-lee-fee-TSEE-ra-van-nee troot)*
slabs	плоская заготовка	*(PLOS-ka-ya za-ga-TOF-ka)*
slaughter house	скотобойня	*(ska-ta-BOY-nya)*
sleeping pill	снотворная таблетка/снотворное	*(sna-TVOR-na-ya tab-LET-ka/sna-TVOR-na-ye)*
sliding parity	скользящий паритет	*(skal-ZYAH-shchee pa-ree-TET)*
sliding price scale	скользящая шкала цен	*(skal-ZYAH-shcha-ya shka-LAH tsen)*
slippers	туфли/тапочки	*(TOOF-lee/TAH-pach-kee)*
sludge gas	отстойный газ	*(at-STOY-nee gahs)*
slump	спад	*(spaht)*
small business	малый бизнес	*(MAH-lee BEEZ-nes)*

S

small capital	капитель	*(ka-pee-TEL)*
snakeskin	змеиная кожа	*(zme-EE-na-ya KOH-zha)*
sneeze (v)	чихать	*(chee-KHAHT)*
soft currency	неконвертируемая валюта	*(ne-kan-ver-TEE-roo-ye-ma-ya va-LYOO-ta)*
soft goods	текстиль	*(tek-STEEL)*
soft loan	льготный заём	*(LGOT-nee za-YOM)*
soft sell	тонкое рекламирование	*(TON-ka-ye re-kla-MEE-ra-va-nee-ye)*
software	«программное обеспечение, «софтвер»	*(pra-GRAHM-na-ye a-bes-pe-CHEH-nee-ye, "soft-VEHR"*
sole agent	исключительный агент	*(ees-kloo-CHEE-tel-nee a-GHENT)*
sole proprietorship	единоличная собственность	*(ye-dee-na-LEECH-na-ya SOP-stven-nast)*
sole rights	исключительные права	*(ees-kloo-CHEE-tel-nee-ye pra-VAH)*
solid fuel	твёрдое топливо	*(TVYOHR-da-ye TOP-lee-va)*
solubility	растворимость	*(ras-tva-REE-mast)*
solute	растворённое вещество	*(ras-tva-RYON-na-ye ve-shche-STVOH)*
solution	раствор	*(ras-TVOHR)*
solvency	платежеспособность	*(pla-te-zhe-spa-SOB-nast)*
solvent	растворитель	*(ras-tva-REE-tel)*
sound	звук	*(zvook)*
sour gas	кислый (высокосернистый) газ	*(KEES-lee [vee-SOH-ka-ser-NEES-tee] gahs)*
sour grade oil	кислая (высокосернистая) нефть	*(KEES-la-ya [vee-SOH-ka-ser-NEES-ta-ya] neft)*
sow	свиноматка	*(svee-na-MAHT-ka)*
soybeans	соевые бобы	*(SOH-ye-vee-ye ba-BEE)*
space	космос	*(KOS-mas)*
space-bar	клавиша пробела	*(KLAH-vee-sha pra-BEH-la)*
space walk	передвижение в открытом космосе	*(pe-re-dvee-ZHEH-nee-ye vat-KREE-tam KOS-ma-se)*

S

space shuttle	многоразовый воздушно-космический аппарат (МВКА)	*(mna-ga-RAH-za-vee vaz-DOOSH-na-kas-MEE-ches-kee a-pa-RAHT; EM-VEH-KAH-AH)*
space station	орбитальная станция (ОС)	*(ar-bee-TAHL-na-ya STAHN-tsee-ya; OH-ES)*
space-plane	воздушно-космический самолёт	*(vaz-DOOSH-na-kas-MEE-ches-kee sa-ma-LYOT)*
space-suit	космический скафандр	*(kas-MEE-ches-kee ska-FAHNDR)*
spacecraft	космический аппарат (КА)	*(kas-MEE-ches-kee a-pa-RAHT: KAH-AH)*
spare tire	запасная шина	*(za-pas-NAH-ya SHEE-na)*
spark plug	запальная свеча	*(za-PAHL-na-ya sve-CHAH)*
speaker	акустическая система	*(a-koos-TEE-ches-ka-ya sees-TEH-ma)*
specialist (stock exchange)	постоянный биржевой маклер	*(pa-sta-YAHN-nee beer-zhe-VOY MAHK-ler)*
specialty goods	обособленные товары	*(a-ba-SOB-len-nee-ye ta-VAH-ree)*
specialty steels	специальные стали	*(spe-tsee-AHL-nee-ye STAH-lee)*
specific duty	специфические пошлины	*(spe-tsee-FEE-ches-kee-ye POSH-lee-nee)*
speculator	спекулянт	*(spe-koo-LYAHNT)*
speedometer	спидометр	*(spee-DOH-metr)*
speed up (v)	ускорять/ускорить	*(oo-ska-RYAT/oo-SKOH-reet)*
spin off	побочный результат	*(pa-BOCH-nee re-zool-TAHT)*
spine	переплёт	*(pe-re-PLYOT)*
split, stock	перегруппировка акций	*(pe-re-groop-pee-ROF-ka AHK-tseey)*
spoilage	брак	*(brahk)*
sponsor (of a fund or partnership)	спонсор	*(SPON-sar)*
spot delivery	доставка с немедленной оплатой	*(da-STAHF-ka sne-MED-len-nay ap-LAH-tay)*
spot market	рынок «спот» (наличного товара)	*(REE-nak "spot" [na-LEECH-na-va ta-VAH-ra)*

S

spot price	цена рынка «спот»	*(tse-NAH RIN-ka "spot"*
spread	разница	*(RAHZ-nee-tsa)*
spreadsheet	динамическая электронная таблица	*(dee-na-MEE-ches-ka-ya e-lek-TRON-na-ya tab-LEE-tsa)*
spring	весна/рессоры	*(ves-NAH/res-SOH-ree)*
spring wheat	яровая пшеница	*(ya-ra-VAH-ya pshe-NEE-tsa)*
spruce	ель	*(yel)*
stable	стойло	*(STOY-la)*
staff	персонал/кадры	*(per-sa-NAHL/ka-DREE)*
staff organization	организационная структура персонала	*(ar-ga-nee-za-tsee-ON-na-ya strook-TOO-ra per-sa-NAH-la)*
stainless steel	нержавеющая сталь	*(ne-rzha-VEH-yoo-shcha-ya stahl)*
stale check	просроченный чек	*(pra-SROH-chen-nee chek)*
stand-alone word processor	автономный текстообразный процессор	*(af-ta-NOM-nee teks-ta-ab-RAHZ-nee pra-TSES-sar)*
stand-alone work-station	автономная рабочая станция	*(af-ta-NOM-na-ya ra-BOH-cha-ya STAHN-tsee-ya)*
stand in line (v)	стоять в очереди	*(sta-YAHT VOH-che-re-dee)*
standard costs	нормативные издержки	*(nar-ma-TEEV-nee-ye eez-DEHRSH-kee)*
standard deviation	среднее квадратичное отклонение	*(SRED-ne-ye kvad-ra-TEECH-na-ye at-kla-NEH-nee-ye)*
standard of living	жизненный уровень	*(ZHIZ-nen-nee OO-ra-ven)*
standard practice	общепринятая практика	*(OP-shche-PREE-nya-ta-ya PRAHK-tee-ka)*
standard time	стандартное время	*(stan-DAHRT-na-ye VREH-mya)*
standardization	нормализация	*(nar-ma-lee-ZAH-tsee-ya)*
standing charges	нормативные затраты	*(nar-ma-TEEV-nee-ye za-TRAH-tee)*
standing costs	нормативные расходы	*(nar-ma-TEEV-nee-ye ras-KHOH-dee)*
standing order	регламент	*(reg-LAH-ment)*

S

starch	крахмал	*(krakh-MAHL)*
starlings	скворцы	*(skvar-TSEE)*
start-up costs	первоначальные расходы	*(per-va-na-CHAHL-nee-ye ras-KHOH-dee)*
starter	стартер	*(STAHR-ter)*
statement	ведомость	*(VEH-da-mast)*
statement, finan-cial	финансовый отчёт	*(fee-NAHN-sa-vee at-CHYOHT)*
statement of account	выписка банковского счёта	*(VEE-pees-ka BAHN-kaf-ska-va SHCHYOH-ta)*
statement, pro forma	примерная ведомость	*(pree-MEHR-na-ya VEH-da-mast)*
statement, profit-and-loss	отчёт прибылей и убытков	*(at-CHYOHT PREE-bee-ley ee oo-BIT-kaf)*
statistics	статистика	*(sta-TEES-tee-ka)*
stature	законодательный акт	*(za-ka-na-DAH-tel-nee ahkt)*
stature of limita-tions	закон об исковой давности	*(za-KON ab ees-ka-VOY DAHV-na-stee)*
steel mill	сталеплавильный завод	*(sta-le-pla-VEEL-nee za-VOT)*
steering	рулевое управление	*(roo-le-VOH-ye oop-rav-LEH-nee-ye)*
steering column	колонка руля	*(ka-LON-ka roo-LYA)*
steering wheel	руль	*(rool)*
stereophonic	стереофонический	*(ste-re-a-fa-NEE-ches-kee)*
stimulant	стимулятор	*(stee-moo-LYAH-tar)*
stimulate	стимулировать	*(stee-moo-LEE-ra-vat)*
stock (inventory)	запасы	*(za-PAH-see)*
stock (share)	акция	*(AHK-tsee-ya)*
stock-in-trade	запас товаров	*(za-PAHS ta-VAH-raf)*
stock certificate	свидетельство на акцию	*(svee-DEH-tel-stva na AHK-tsee-yoo)*
stock exchange	фондовая биржа	*(FON-da-va-ya BEEHR-zha)*
stock index	индекс курсов акций	*(EEN-deks KOOHR-saf AHK-tseey)*
stock issue	выпуск акций	*(VEE-poosk AHK-tseey)*

S

stock market	фондовая биржа	*(FON-da-va-ya BEEHR-zha)*
stock option	опцион на акции	*(ap-tsee-ON na AHK-tsee-ee)*
stock power	акционерное полномочие	*(ak-tsee-a-NEHR-na-ye pal-na-MOH-chee-ye)*
stock profit	акционерная прибыль	*(ak-tsee-a-NEHR-na-ya PREE-bil)*
stock purchase	покупка акций	*(pa-KOOP-ka AHK-tseey)*
stock split	перегруппировка акций	*(pe-re-groop-pee-ROF-ka AHK-tseey)*
stock takeover	приобретение контрольного пакета акций	*(pree-a-bre-TEH-nee-ye kan-TROL-na-va pa-KEH-ta AHK-tseey)*
stock-tank oil	резервуарная нефть	*(re-zer-voo-AHR-na-ya neft)*
stock turnover	оборот акций	*(a-ba-ROT AHK-tseey)*
stockbroker	биржевой маклер	*(beer-zhe-VOY MAHK-ler)*
stockholder	акционер	*(ak-tsee-a-NEHR)*
stockholder's equity	доля акционера	*(DOH-lya ak-tsee-a-NEH-ra)*
storage	хранение	*(khra-NEH-nee-ye)*
storage (computer)	запоминающее устройство (ЗУ)	*(za-pa-mee-NAH-yoo-shche-ye oos-TROY-stva [ZEH-OO])*
storage facility	хранилище	*(khra-NEE-le-shchee)*
store	магазин	*(ma-ga-ZEEN)*
store (v)	складировать	*(skla-DEE-ra-vat)*
store (computer)	запоминать/запомнить	*(za-pa-mee-NAHT/za-POM-neet)*
stowage	укладка	*(ook-LAHT-ka)*
stowage charges	расходы по укладке	*(ras-KHOH-dee pa ook-LAHT-ke)*
straddle	страдл (двойной опцион)	*(strahdl [dvay-NOY ap-tsee-ON])*
strapping	смешанная операция	*(SMEH-shan-na-ya a-pe-RAH-tsee-ya)*
strategic reserves	стратегические запасы	*(stra-te-GHEE-ches-kee-ye za-PAH-see)*
streamline (v)	упростить (процесс, работу)	*(oo-pras-TEET [pra-TSES, ra-BOH-too])*

stress management	контроль стресса	*(kan-TROL STRES-sa)*
strike	забастовка	*(za-bas-TOF-ka)*
strike, wildcat	«дикая» забастовка	*(DEE-ka-ya za-bas-TOF-ka)*
strikebreaker	штрейкбрехер	*(shtreyk-BREH-kher)*
stripper (well)	малодебитная скважина	*(MAH-la-DEH-beet-na-ya SKVAH-zhee-na)*
structural shapes	профили	*(PROH-fee-lee)*
subcontract	субподряд	*(soop-pad-RYANT)*
sublease	субаренда	*(soo-ba-REN-da)*
subscription price (periodicals)	подписная цена	*(pat-pees-NAH-ya tse-NAH)*
subscription price (securities)	вклад по подписке	*(fklaht pa pat-PEES-ke)*
subsidiary	дочерняя компания	*(da-CHEHR-nya-ya kam-PAH-nee-ya)*
subsidy	дотация/субсидия	*(da-TAH-tsee-ya)/soop-SEE-dee-ya)*
substandard	нестандартный	*(ne-stan-DAHRT-nee)*
substitute fuel	заменяющее топливо	*(za-me-NYAH-yoo-shche-ye TOP-lee-va)*
sucess ratio	коэффициент результативности	*(ka-ef-fee-tsee-ENT re-zool-ta-TEEV-na-stee)*
suede	замша	*(ZAHM-sha)*
suede jacket	замшевая куртка	*(ZAHM-she-va-ya KOOHRT-ka)*
suitcase	чемодан	*(che-ma-DAHN)*
sulfuric acid	серная кислота	*(SEHR-na-ya kees-la-TAH)*
sulphamide	сульфамид	*(sool-fa-MEET)*
summer	лето	*(LEH-ta)*
super alloys	жаропрочный сплав	*(zha-ra-PROCH-nee splahf)*
supersede (v)	сменять	*(sme-NYAHT)*
supersonics	аэродинамика сверхзвуковых скоростей	*(AH-eh-ra-dee-NAH-mee-ka sverkh-zvoo-ka-VIKH ska-ra-STEY)*
supervisor	начальник	*(na-CHAHL-neek)*
supplier	поставщик	*(pas-taf-SHCHEEK)*
supply and demand	спрос и предложение	*(spros ee pred-la-ZHEH-nee-ye)*

S

support	поддержка	*(pad-DEHRSH-ka)*
surplus capital	излишки капитала	*(eez-LEESH-kee ka-pee-TAH-la)*
surplus goods	излишние товары	*(eez-LEESH-nee-ye ta-VAH-ree)*
surtax	добавочный подоходный налог	*(da-BAH-vach-nee pa-da-KHOD-nee na-LOK)*
suspend payment (v)	приостановлять платежи	*(pree-as-ta-NAHV-lee-vat pla-te-ZHEE)*
suspension	подвеска	*(pad-VES-ka)*
swine	свинья	*(sveen-YAH)*
sweet crude	сладкая (малосернистая) нефть	*(SLAHT-ka-ya [MAH-la-ser-NEES-ta-ya] neft)*
sweet gas	сладкий (малосернистый) газ	*(SLAHT-kee [MAH-la-ser-NEES-tee] gahs)*
switch	переключатель	*(pe-re-klyoo-CHAH-tel)*
syndicate	синдикат	*(seen-dee-KAHT)*
system crash	полный отказ системы	*(POL-nee at-KAHS sees-TEH-mee)*
systems analysis	системный анализ	*(sees-TEM-nee a-NAH-lees)*
systems design	дизайн систем	*(dee-ZAHYN sees-TEM)*
systems engineering	проектирование систем	*(pra-yek-TEE-ra-va-nee-ye sees-TEM)*
systems management	управление системами	*(oop-rav-LEH-nee-ye sees-TEH-ma-mee)*
synthesis	синтез	*(SEEN-tes)*
synthetic crude (oil)	синтетическая нефть	*(seen-te-TEE-ches-ka-ya neft)*
synthetic liquid fuels (SLF)	синтетические жидкие топлива	*(seen-te-TEE-ches-kee-ye ZHIT-kee-ye TOP-lee-va)*
synthetic natural gas (SNG)	синтетический природный газ	*(seen-te-TEE-ches-kee pree-ROD-nee gahs)*
syringe	шприц	*(shpreets)*

T

table	таблица	*(tab-LEE-tsa)*
table of contents	оглавление	*(a-glav-LEH-nee-ye)*

tablet	таблетка	*(tab-LET-ka)*
take down (v)	снимать	*(snee-MAHT)*
take-home pay	чистая зарплата/зарплата после вычетов	*(CHEES-ta-ya zar-PLAH-ta)*
take off	скидка	*(SKEET-ka)*
take out (v)	вынимать/вынуть	*(vee-nee-MAHT/VEE-noot)*
take out (v) (insur-ance)	получить страховой полис	*(pa-loo-CHEET stra-kha-VOY POH-lees)*
take out (v) (patent)	брать/взять патент	*(brat/vsyaht pa-TENT)*
takeover	приобретение контрольного пакета акций	*(pree-ab-re-TEH-nee-ye kan-TROL-na-va pa-KEH-ta AK-tseey)*
takeover bid	«опа» (публичное предложение о приобретении акций)	*(OH-pa [poob-LEECH-na-ye pred-la-ZHEH-nee-ye a pree-ab-re-TEH-nee AK-tseey])*
tangible assets	материальные активы	*(ma-te-ree-AHL-nee-ye ak-TEE-vee)*
tan (v)	дубить	*(doo-BEET)*
tanker	танкер	*(TAHN-ker)*
tanner	дубильщик	*(doo-BEEL-shcheek)*
tannery	кожевенный завод	*(ka-ZHEH-ven-nee za-VOT)*
tannin	танин	*(ta-NEEN)*
tape	лента	*(LEN-ta)*
tape recorder	магнитофон	*(mag-nee-ta-FON)*
tariff	тариф	*(ta-REEF)*
tariff barriers	тарифные барьеры	*(ta-REEF-nee-ye bar-YEH-ree)*
tariff charge	тарифные расходы	*(ta-REEF-nee-ye ras-KHOH-dee)*
tariff classification	тарифная классификация	*(ta-REEF-na-ya klas-see-fee-KAH-tsee-ya)*
tariff commodity	товар, подлежащий тарификации	*(ta-VAHR pad-le-ZHAH-shchee ta-ree-fee-KAH-tsee-ee)*
tariff differential	надбавка к тарифу	*(nad-BAHF-ka kta-REEF-foo)*
tariff war	таможенная война	*(ta-MOH-zhen-na-ya vay-NAH)*

T

task force	оперативная группа	*(a-pe-ra-TEEV-na-ya GROOP-pa)*
tax	налог	*(na-LOK)*
tax allowance	льгота на налог	*(LGOH-ta na na-LOK)*
tax base	база налогообложения	*(BAH-za na-LOH-ga-ab-la-ZHEH-nee-ya)*
tax burden	бремя налогов	*(BREH-mya na-LOH-gaf)*
tax collector	сборщик налогов	*(ZBOHR-shcheek na-LOH-gaf)*
tax deduction	вычет с налогов	*(VEE-chet sna-LOH-gaf)*
tax evasion	уклонение от уплаты налогов	*(ook-la-NEH-nee-ye at oo-PLAH-tee na-LOH-gaf)*
tax, excise	акциз	*(ak-TSIS)*
tax-free	освобожденный от уплаты налогов	*(as-va-bazh-DYON-nee at oo-PLAH-tee na-LOH-gaf)*
tax-free income	доход/освобождённый от уплаты налогов	*(da-KHOT/as-va-bazh-DYON-nee at oo-PLAH-tee na-LOH-gaf)*
tax havens	налоговые гавани	*(na-LOH-ga-vee-ye GAH-va-nee)*
tax-payer	налогоплательщик	*(na-LOH-ga-pla-TEL-shcheek)*
tax relief	скидка с налога	*(SKEET-ka sna-LOH-ga)*
tax, sales	налог с оборота	*(na-LOK sa-ba-ROH-ta)*
tax shelter	приём для уклонения от налогов	*(pree-YOM dlya ook-la-NEH-nee-ya at na-LOH-gaf)*
taxation	налогообложение	*(na-LOH-ga-ab-la-ZHEH-nee-ye)*
telecommunications	телесвязь	*(TEH-le-SVYAHS)*
telemarketing	продажа по телефону	*(pra-DAH-zha pa te-le-FOH-noo)*
teller	кассир	*(kas-SEEHR)*
tender offer	оферта	*(a-FEHR-ta)*
term bond	облигация по срочному займу	*(ab-lee-GAH-tsee-ya pa SROCH-na-moo ZAHY-moo)*

term insurance	страхование на определённое время	*(stra-kha-VAH-nee-ye na ap-re-de-LYON-na-ye VREH-mya)*
terminal	терминал	*(ter-mee-NAHL)*
terminate (v)	прекращать/прекратить	*(pre-kra-SHCHAHT/pre-kra-TEET)*
terminate (v) (employment)	увольнять/уволить	*(oo-val-NYAHT/oo-VOH-leet)*
terms of sale	условия продажи	*(oos-LOH-vee-ya pra-DAH-zhee)*
terms of trade	внешнеторговый товарооборот	*(VNESH-ne-tar-GOH-vee ta-VAH-ra-a-ba-ROT)*
territorial waters	территориальные воды	*(ter-ree-ta-ree-AHL-nee-ye VOH-dee)*
territory	территория	*(ter-ree-TOH-ree-ya)*
tertiary (crude) oil	третичная нефть	*(tre-TEECH-na-ya neft)*
tertiary (oil) inventory	третичные товарные запасы	*(tre-TEECH-nee ta-VAHR-nee-ye za-PAH-see)*
tertiary reserves	третичные запасы	*(tre-TEECH-nee za-PAH-see)*
test tube	пробирка	*(pra-BEEHR-ka)*
thermal lift	подъемная сила восходящих потоков воздуха	*(pad-YOM-na-ya SEE-la vas-kha-DYAH-shcheekh pa-TOH-kaf VOZ-doo-kha)*
thermometer	термометр/градусник	*(ter-MOH-metr/GRAH-doos-neek)*
thin market	сокращенный рынок	*(sa-kra-SHCHYON-nee REE-nak)*
thresher	молотилка	*(ma-la-TEEL-ka)*
through bill of lading	сквозной коносамент	*(skvaz-NOY ka-na-sa-MENT)*
throughput	пропускная способность	*(pra-poosk-NAH-ya spa-SOB-nast)*
ticker (stock prices)	биржевой телеграфный аппарат	*(beer-zhe-VOY te-le-GRAHF-nee ap-pa-RAHT)*
ticker tape	серпантин из тиккерной ленты	*(ser-pan-TEEN eez TEEK-ker-nay LEHN-tee)*
tied aid	связанная помощь	*(SVYAH-zan-na-ya POH-mashch)*

T

tied loan	связанная ссуда	*(SVYAH-zan-na-ya SSOO-da)*
tight gas	газ в плотных породах	*(gahs FPLOT-nikh pa-ROH-dakh)*
tight market	тесный рынок	*(TES-nee REE-nak)*
timberland	лесная площадь	*(les-NAH-ya PLOH-shchat)*
time bill of exchange	долгосрочный вексель	*(dal-ga-SROCH-nee VEK-sel)*
time deposit	срочный вклад	*(SROCH-nee fklaht)*
time sharing	разделение использования недвижимости по срокам	*(raz-de-LEH-nee-ye ees-POL-za-va-nee-ya ne-DVEE-zhee-ma-stee pa SROH-kam)*
time zone	поясное время	*(pa-yas-NOH-ye VREH-mya)*
timetable (schedule)	график	*(GRAH-feek)*
timetable (transport)	расписание	*(ras-pee-SAH-nee-ye)*
tip (inside information)	намёк	*(na-MYOK)*
tire	шина	*(SHEE-na)*
titanium	титан	*(tee-TAHN)*
title (to property)	правовой титул	*(pra-va-VOY TEE-tool)*
title (position)	название	*(naz-VAH-nee-ye)*
title insurance	страхование против дефектов правового титула	*(stra-kha-VAH-nee-ye PROH-teef de-FEHK-taf pra-va-VOH-va TEE-too-la)*
titration	титрирование	*(tee-tra-VAH-nee-ye)*
tomato	помидоры	*(pa-mee-DOH-ree)*
tone	тон	*(ton)*
tonnage	тоннаж	*(tan-NAHSH)*
tools of one's trade	орудие труда	*(a-ROO-dee-ye TROO-da)*
top management	высшее руководство	*(VISH-shee-ye roo-ka-VOT-stva)*
top price	лучшая цена	*(LOOCH-sha-ya tse-NAH)*
top quality	лучшее качество	*(LOOCH-shee-ye KAH-chest-va)*

torque	крутящий момент	*(kroo-TYAH-shchee ma-MENT)*
tort	деликт	*(de-LEEKT)*
tote bag	мешок	*(me-SHOK)*
toughness	вязкость	*(VYAHS-kast)*
town gas	коммунальный газ	*(kam-moo-NAHL-nee gahs)*
toxicology	токсикология	*(tak-see-ka-LOH-gee-ya)*
toxin	токсин	*(tak-SEEN)*
tractor	трактор	*(TRAHK-tar)*
trade	торговля	*(tar-GOV-lya)*
trade (v)	торговать	*(tar-ga-VAHT)*
trade acceptance	акцентированная коммерческая тратта	*(ak-tsen-TEE-ra-van-na-ya kam-MEHR-ches-ka-ya TRAH-ta)*
trade agreement	торговое соглашение	*(tar-GOH-va-ye sag-la-SHEH-nee-ye)*
trade association	торговая ассоциация	*(tar-GOH-va-ya as-sa-tsee-AH-tsee-ya)*
trade barrier	торговый барьер	*(tar-GOH-vee bar-YEHR)*
trade commission	торговая комиссия	*(tar-GOH-va-ya ka-MEES-see-ya)*
trade credit	торговый кредит	*(tar-GOH-vee kre-DEET)*
trade date	дата операции	*(DAH-ta a-pe-RAH-tsee-ee)*
trade discount	торговая скидка	*(tar-GOH-va-ya SKEET-ka)*
trade fair	ярмарка	*(YAHR-mar-ka)*
trade house	торговый дом	*(tar-GOH-vee dom)*
trade union	профсоюз	*(praf-sa-YOOS)*
trademark	товарный знак	*(ta-VAHR-nee znahk)*
trader	торговец	*(tar-GOH-vets)*
trader (stocks)	маклер	*(MAHK-ler)*
trading company	торговая компания	*(tar-GOH-va-ya kam-PAH-nee-ya)*
trainee	стажёр	*(sta-ZHOHR)*
tranquilizer	транквилизатор	*(trank-vee-le-ZAH-tar)*
transaction	операция	*(a-pe-RAH-tsee-ya)*
transfer	перевод	*(pe-re-VOT)*

T

transfer (v)	переводить	*(pe-re-va-DEET)*
transformer	трансформатор	*(trans-far-MAH-tar)*
transistor	транзистор	*(tran-ZEES-tar)*
transit, mass	общественный транспорт	*(ap-SHCHEST-ven-nee TRAHNS-part)*
translator	переводчик	*(pe-re-VOT-cheek)*
transmitter	передатчик	*(pe-re-DAHT-cheek)*
traveler's check	туристский чек	*(too-REEST-skee chek)*
traveling salesman	коммивояжер	*(koh-mee-va-ya-ZHOHR)*
treasurer	казначей	*(kaz-na-CHEY)*
treasury bills	казначейские векселя	*(kaz-na-CHEY-skee-ye vek-seh-LYAH)*
treasury bonds	казначейские облигации	*(kaz-na-CHEY-skee-ye ab-lee-GAH-tsee-ee)*
treasury notes	казначейские ноты	*(kaz-na-CHEY-skee-ye NOH-tee)*
treasury stock	собственные акции в портфеле	*(SOP-stven-nee-ye AHK-tsee fpart-FEH-le)*
treaty	международный договор	*(mezh-doo-na-ROD-nee da-ga-VOHR)*
tree	дерево	*(DEH-re-va)*
tree gene bank	лесосеменная плантация	*(LEH-sa-se-men-NAH-ya plan-TAH-tsee-ya)*
tree ring analysis	анализ годичных слоев	*(a-NAH-lees ga-DEECH-nikh sla-YOF)*
trend	тенденция	*(ten-DEHN-tsee-ya)*
trial balance	пробный баланс	*(PROB-nee ba-LAHNS)*
troubleshoot (v)	улаживать/уладить конфликты	*(oo-LAH-zhee-vat/oo-LAH-deet kan-FLEEK-tee)*
trouble-shooter	щуп для поиска неисправностей	*(shchoop dla POH-ees-ka ne-ees-PRAHV-na-stey)*
true in situ recovery of shale oil (TIS)	обычная внутрипластовая перегонка (горючих сланцев)	*(a-BICH-na-ya vnoot-ree-plas-ta-VAH-ya pe-re-GON-ka [ga-RYOO-cheekh SLAHN-tsef])*
truck	грузовик	*(groo-za-VEEK)*
truck farming	промышленное огородничество	*(pra-MISH-len-na-ye a-ga-ROD-nee-chest-va)*
trunk	сундук	*(soon-DOOK)*

T

trust	трест	*(trehst)*
trust company	трест-компания	*(TREHST-kam-PAH-nee-ya)*
trust deed	акт учреждения доверительной собственности	*(ahkt ooch-re-ZHDEH-nee-ya da-ve-REE-tel-nay SOP-stven-na-stee)*
trust receipt	сохранная расписка	*(sa-KHRAHN-na-ya ras-PEES-ka)*
trustee	доверенное лицо	*(da-VEH-ren-na-ye lee-TSOH)*
turbine	турбина	*(toor-BEE-na)*
turbo-jet	турбореактивный двигатель	*(TOOHR-ba-re-ak-TEEV-nee DVEE-ga-tel)*
turbulence	турбулентность	*(toor-boo-LENT-nast)*
tungsten	вольфрам	*(val-FRAHM)*
turn-key	сдаваемый под ключ	*(zda-VAH-ye-mee pat klyooch)*
turnover	оборот	*(a-ba-ROT)*
two-tiered market	двухэтапный рынок	*(dvookh-eh-TAHP-nee REE-nak)*

U

ultimate recover- able reserves	максимально извлекаемые запасы	*(mak-see-MAHL-nee-ye eez-vle-KAH-ye-mee-ye za-PAH-see)*
ultra vires act	акт вне компетенции	*(ahkt vne kam-pe-TEHN-tsee-ee)*
uncollectible accounts	безнадёжная задолженность	*(bez-na-DYOZH-na-ya za-DOL-zhen-nast)*
uncrunching (data)	развёртывание (сжатого файла)	*(RAHZ-vyor-tee-va-nee-ye [ZHCHAH-ta-va FAHY-la])*
undercapitalized	сбивать цены	*(zbee-VAHT TSEH-nee)*
undercut	слаборазвитые страны	*(sla-ba-RAHZ-vee-tee-ye STRAH-nee)*
underdeveloped	недостаточно капитализированный	*(ne-da-STAH-tach-na ka-pee-ta-lee-ZEE-ra-van-nee)*
underestimate (v)	недооценивать/ недооценить	*(ne-da-a-TSEH-nee-vat)/ ne-da-a-TSEH-neet)*

underpaid	низкооплачиваемые	(NEES-ka-ap-LAH-chee-va-ye-mee-ye)
undersigned	нижеподписавшийся	(NEE-zhe-pat-pee-SAHF-shee-ye-sa)
understanding (agreement)	договорённость	(da-ga-va-RYON-nast)
undertake (v)	предпринимать/ предпринять	(pret-pree-nee-MAHT/ pret-pree-NYAHT)
undervalue (v)	обесценивать/обесценить	(a-bes-TSEH-nee-vat/ a-bes-TSEEH-neet)
underwriter	поручитель-гарант	(pa-roo-CHEE-tel-ga-RAHNT)
underwriter (securities)	гарант размещения	(ga-RAHNT raz-me-SHCHEH-nee-ya)
undeveloped nations	неразвитые страны	(nee-RAHZ-vee-tee-ye) STRAH-nee)
undeveloped proved reserves	неосвоенные доказанные запасы	(ne-as-VOH-yen-nee-ye da-KAH-zan-nee-yee za-PAH-see)
undiscovered potential resources	неоткрытые ресурсы	(ne-at-KREE-tee-ye re-SOOHR-see)
undrilled proved reserves	неразбуренные доказанные запасы	(ne-raz-BOO-ren-nee-ye da-KAH-zan-nee-ye za-PAH-see)
unearned increment	незаработанный прирост	(ne-za-ra-BOH-tan-nee pree-ROST)
unearned revenue	незаработанный доход	(ne-za-ra-BOH-tan-nee da-KHOT)
unemployment	безработица	(bez-ra-BOH-tee-tsa)
unemployment compensation	пособие по безработице	(pa-SOH-bee-ye pa bez-ra-BOH-tee-tse)
unfavorable	неблагоприятный	(ne-bla-ga-pree-YAHT-nee)
unfeasible	неосуществимый	(nee-a-soo-shchest-VEE-mee)
union, labor	профсоюз	(praf-sa-YOOS)
unit costs	издержки производства на единицу	(eez-DEHRSH-kee pra-eez-VOT-stva na ye-dee-NEE-tsoo)
Unit Energy cost	удельные энергетические затраты	(oo-DEL-nee e-ner-ghe-TEE-ches-kee-ye zat-RAH-tee)

U

unit price	цена на единицу	*(TSEH-na na ye-dee-NEE-tsoo)*
Univac	система «Юнивак»	*(sees-TEH-ma oo-nee-VAHK)*
unlisted	не котирующийся (на бирже)	*(ne-ka-TEE-roo-yoo-shcheey-sa [na BEEHR-zhe])*
unload (v)	выгружать/выгрузить	*(vee-groo-ZHAHT/VEE-groo-zeet)*
"unpumpables"	перерабатываемая нефть	*(pe-re-ra-BAH-tee-va-ye-ma-ya neft)*
unsecured loan	необеспеченная ссуда	*(ne-a-bes-PEH-chen-na-ya SSOO-da)*
unskilled labor	неквалифицированный труд	*(ne-kva-lee-fee-TSEE-ra-van-nee troot)*
up to our expectations	в соответствии с нашими ожиданиями	*(fsa-at-VET-stvee SNAH-shee-mee a-zhee-DAH-nee-ya-mee)*
up-market	выше среднего уровня	*(VEE-she SRED-ne-va OO-rav-nya)*
upturn	подъём	*(pad-YOM)*
urea	мочевина	*(ma-che-VEE-na)*
use tax	налог на пользование	*(na-LOK na POL-za-va-nee-ye)*
useable commercial inventories	коммерческие запасы	*(kam-MEHR-ches-kee-ye za-PAH-see)*
useful life	срок службы	*(srok SLOOZH-bee)*
user	пользователь	*(POL-za-va-tel)*
user-friendly	дружелюбный к пользователю	*(droo-zhe-LYOOB-nee KPOL-za-va-te-lyoo)*
usury	ростовщичество	*(ras-ta-FSHCHEE-che-stva)*
utility	коммунальные услуги	*(kam-moo-NAHL-nee-ye oos-LOO-ghee)*

V

V8 engine	двигатель с восемью клапанами	*(DVEE-ga-tel sva-se-MYOO KLAH-pa-na-mee)*
vaccine	вакцина	*(vak-TSEE-na)*

vacuum melting furnace	вакуумированная плавильная печь	*(va-koo-oo-MEE-ra-van-na-ya pla-VEEL-na-ya peech)*
valid	действительный	*(dey-STVEE-tel-nee)*
validate (v)	утверждать	*(oo-tverzh-DAHT)*
valuation	оценка	*(a-TSEN-ka)*
value	стоимость/ценность	*(STOH-ee-mast/TSEHN-nast)*
value of a field	оценочная стоимость (запасов) месторождения	*(a-TSEH-nach-na-ya STOH-ee-mast [za-PAH-saf] mes-ta-razh-DEH-nee-ya)*
value-added tax (VAT)	налог на добавленную стоимость	*(na-LOK na da-BAHV-len-noo-yoo STOH-ee-mast)*
value, asset	номинальная стоимость активов	*(na-mee-NAHL-na-ya STOH-ee-mast ak-TEE-vaf)*
value, book	балансовая стоимость	*(ba-LAHN-sa-va-ya STOH-ee-mast)*
value, face	номинальная стоимость	*(no-mee-NAHL-na-ya STOH-ee-mast)*
value for duty	таможенная оценка	*(ta-MOH-zhen-na-ya a-TSEHN-ka)*
value, market (general)	рыночная стоимость	*(REE-nach-na-ya STOH-ee-mast)*
value, market (stocks)	меновая стоимость	*(MEH-na-va-ya STOH-ee-mast)*
valve	клапан	*(KLAH-pan)*
vanadium	ванадий	*(va-NAH-deey)*
variable annuity	переменный аннуитет	*(pe-re-MEHN-nee an-noo-ee-TET)*
variable costs	переменные издержки	*(pe-re-MEHN-nee-ye eez-DEHRSH-kee)*
variable import levy	переменные импортные сборы	*(pe-re-MEHN-nee-ye EEM-part-nee ZBOH-ree)*
variable rate	переменная ставка	*(pe-re-MEHN-na-ya STAHF-ka)*
variable rate mortgage	закладная с изменяющейся ставкой процента	*(zak-lad-NAH-ya siz-me-NYAH-yoo-shchey-sa STAHF-kay pra-TSEN-ta)*

variance	отклонение (валютного курса и т.д.)	*(at-kla-NEH-nee-ye [va-LYOOT-na-va- KOOHR-sa ee te-DEH])*
vegetables	овощи	*(OH-va-shchee)*
velocity of money	скорость обращения	*(SKOH-rast ab-ra-SHCHEH-nee-ya)*
vendor	продавец	*(pra-da-VETS)*
vendor's lien	залоговое право продавца	*(za-LOH-ga-va-ye PRAH-va pra-daf-TSAH)*
venture capital	рисковый капитал	*(rees-KOH-vee ka-pee-TAHL)*
vertical integration	вертикальная интеграция	*(ver-tee-KAHL-na-ya een-te-GRAH-tsee-ya)*
vested interests	признанные имущественные права	*(PREEZ-nan-nee-ye ee-MOO-shchest-ven-nee pra-VAH)*
vested rights	признанные права	*(PREEZ-nan-nee-ye pra-VAH)*
veterinarian	ветеринар	*(ve-te-ree-NAHR)*
veto	вето	*(VEH-ta)*
vice-president	вице-президент	*(VEE-tse-pre-zee-DENT)*
videocassette player	видеомагнитофон	*(VEE-de-a-mag-nee-ta-FON)*
village	село	*(se-LOH)*
vitamin	витамин	*(vee-ta-MEEN)*
viticulture	виноградарство	*(vee-na-GRAH-dar-stva)*
voided check	аннулированный чек	*(an-noo-LEE-ra-van-nee chek)*
void	недействительный	*(ne-dey-STVEE-tel-nee)*
volatile market	изменчивый рынок	*(eez-MEHN-chee-vee REE-nak)*
voltage	напряжение	*(na-pre-ZHEH-nee-ye)*
volume	объём	*(ab-YOM)*
volume discount	скидка за большой объём	*(SKEET-ka za bal-SHOY ab-YOM)*
voting right	право голоса	*(PRAH-va GOH-la-sa)*
voucher	ваучер	*(VAH-oo-cher)*

W

wage	заработная плата	*(ZAH-ra-bat-na-ya PLAH-ta)*
wage differential	надбавка к зарплате	*(nad-BAHF-ka gzar-PLAH-te)*
wage dispute	спор о зарплате	*(spohr a zar-PLAH-te)*
wage earner	кормилец семьи	*(kar-MEE-lets se-MEE)*
wage freeze	замораживание зарплаты	*(za-ma-RAH-zhee-va-nee-ye zar-PLAH-tee)*
wage level	уровень заработной платы	*(OO-ra-ven ZAH-ra-bat-nay PLAH-tee)*
wage scale	шкала заработной платы	*(shka-LAH ZAH-ra-bat-nay PLAH-tee)*
wage structure	структура заработной платы	*(strook-TOO-ra ZAH-ra-bat-nay PLAH-tee)*
wages	зарплата	*(zar-PLAH-ta)*
waiver clause	оговорка об отказе от права	*(a-ga-VOHR-ka ab at-KAH-ze at PRAH-va)*
walkout	стачка	*(STAHCH-ka)*
want-ad	объявление в газете	*(ab-yav-LEH-nee-ye vga-ZEH-te)*
warehouse	товарный склад	*(ta-VAHR-nee sklaht)*
warehouseman	владелец склада	*(vla-DEH-lets SKLAH-da)*
warrant (guarantee)	гарантия	*(ga-RAHN-tee-ya)*
warranty	гарантия	*(ga-RAHN-tee-ya)*
wasting assets	растрата имущества	*(ras-TRAH-ta ee-MOO-shchest-va)*
watch band	ремешок для часов	*(re-me-SHOK dlya cha-SOF)*
water pump	водяной насос	*(va-dya-NOY na-SOS)*
wave	волна	*(val-NAH)*
waybill	накладная	*(nak-lad-NAH-ya)*
wealth	богатство	*(ba-GAHT-stva)*
wear and tear	нормальная убыль и нормальный износ	*(nar-MAHL-na-ya OO-bil ee nar-MAHL-nee eez-NOS)*
weeds	сорняки	*(sar-nya-KEE)*

weight	вес	*(ves)*
weighted average	средняя взвешенная	*(SRED-nya-ya VZVEH-shen-na-ya)*
well	скважина/колодец	*(SKVAH-zhee-na/(ka-LOH-dets)*
well density	плотность бурения	*(PLOT-nast boo-REH-nee-ya)*
well permit	лицензия на бурение скважины	*(lee-TSEN-zee-ya na boo-REH-nee-ye SKVAH-zhee-nee)*
well tangibles	амортизируемые расходы на строительство скважин	*(a-mar-tee-ZEE-roo-ye-mee-ye ras-KHOH-dee na stra-EE-tel-stva SKVAH-zheen)*
well head price	цена франко-скважины	*(tse-NAH FRAHN-ka-SKVAH-zhee-nee)*
well head value	выручка на устье скважины	*(VEE-rooch-ka na OOST-ye SKVAH-zhee-nee)*
wharfage charges	причальный сбор	*(pree-CHAHL-nee zbohr)*
wheat	пшеница	*(pshe-NEE-tsa)*
wheel	колесо	*(ka-le-SOH)*
when issued	по выпуску	*(pa VEE-poos-koo)*
whip	плётка	*(PLYOT-ka)*
white-collar work-er	«белый воротничок» (высокооплачиваемый работник)	*(BEH-lee va-rat-nee-CHOK [vee-sa-KOH ap-LAH-chee-va-ye-mee ra-BOT-neek])*
wholesale market	оптовый рынок	*(OP-ta-vee REE-nak)*
wholesale price	оптовая цена	*(OP-ta-va-ya tse-NAH)*
wholesale trade	оптовая торговля	*(OP-ta-va-ya tar-GOV-lya)*
wholesaler	оптовый торговец/оптовик	*(OP-ta-vee tar-GOH-vets/ap-ta-VEEK)*
wild cat	поисковая скважина	*(pa-ees-KOH-va-ya SKVAH-zhee-na)*
wild cat drilling	поисковое бурение	*(pa-ees-KOH-va-ye boo-REH-nee-ye)*
wildcat strike	«дикая» забастовка	*(DEE-ka-ya za-bas-TOF-ka)*
will	завещание	*(za-ve-SHCHAH-nee-ye)*
wind-break	защитная лесополоса	*(za-SHCHEET-na-ya LEH-sa-pa-la-sa)*

W

windfall profit	непредвиденная прибыль	*(ne-pred-VEE-den-na-ya PREE-bil)*
windmill	ветряная мельница	*(vet-rya-NAH-ya MEL-nee-tsa)*
windshield	ветровое стекло	*(vet-ra-VOH-ye stek-LOH)*
window dressing	«приукрашивание» (баланса)	*(pre-ook-RAH-shee-va-nee-ye [ba-LAHN-sa])*
window-based	основанный на применении окон	*(as-NOH-van-nee na-pree-me-NEH-nee-ee OH-kan)*
wing	крыло	*(kree-LOH)*
winter	зима	*(zee-MAH)*
winter wheat	озимая пшеница	*(a-ZEE-ma-ya pshe-NEE-tsa)*
wire	проволока	*(PROH-va-la-ka)*
wire transfer (v)	переводить/перевести по телеграфу	*(pe-re-va-DEET/pe-re-veh-STEE pa te-le-GRAH-foo)*
withholding tax	удержание налогов	*(oo-der-ZHAH-nee-ye na-LOH-gaf)*
witness	свидетель	*(svee-DEH-tel)*
witness (v)	свидетельствовать	*(svee-DEH-tel-stva-vat)*
wood	древесина	*(dre-ve-SEE-na)*
word-processing	текстообработка	*(teks-ta-ab-ra-BOT-ka)*
word processor	текстовой процессор	*(TEKS-ta-voy pra-TSES-sar)*
work (v)	работать	*(ra-BOH-tat)*
work by contract	работать по договору	*(ra-BOH-tat pa da-ga-VOH-roo)*
work cycle	цикл работы	*(tsikl ra-BOH-tee)*
work day	рабочий день	*(ra-BOH-chee den)*
work in progress	незавершённое производство	*(ne-za-ver-SHON-na-ye pra-eez-VOT-stva)*
work load	рабочая нагрузка	*(ra-BOH-cha-ya na-GROOS-ka)*
work permit	разрешение на право работы	*(raz-re-SHEH-nee-ye na PRAH-va ra-BOH-tee)*
workforce	рабочая сила	*(ra-BOH-cha-ya SEE-la)*
working assets	оборотные средства	*(a-ba-ROT-nee SRETS-tva)*
working balance	оборотный баланс	*(a-ba-ROT-nee ba-LAHNS)*

W

working capital	оборотный капитал	*(a-ba-ROT-nee ka-pee-TAHL)*
working class	рабочий класс	*(ra-BOH-chee klahs)*
working funds	оборотные фонды	*(a-ba-ROT-nee-ye FON-dee)*
working hours	часы работы	*(cha-SEE ra-BOH-tee)*
working interest	деятельное долевое участие на основе аренды	*(DEH-ya-tel-na-ye da-le-VOH-ye oo-CHAHS-tee-ye na as-NOH-ve a-REN-dee)*
working tools	эксплуатационные приборы	*(eks-ploo-a-ta-tsee-ON-nee pree-BOH-ree)*
workplace	место работы	*(MES-ta ra-BOH-tee)*
workshop	мастерская	*(mas-ter-SKAH-ya)*
workstation	рабочая станция	*(ra-BOH-cha-ya STAHN-tsee-ya)*
World Bank	Мировой Банк	*(mee-ra-VOY bahnk)*
worm	червь	*(chehrf)*
worth, net	чистая ценность	*(CHEES-ta-ya TSEN-nast)*
worthless	ничтожный	*(neech-TOZH-nee)*
writ	судебный приказ	*(soo-DEB-nee pree-KAHS)*
write off (v)	списывать/списать со счета	*(SPEE-see-vat/spee-SAHT sa SHCHYOH-ta)*
write-off	суммы, списанные со счета	*(SOOM-mee SPEE-san-nee-ye sa SHCHYOH-ta)*
write-down	снижение оплачиваемой суммы	*(snee-ZHEH-nee-ye ap-LAH-chee-va-ye-may SOOM-mee)*
write-protected	защищённый от записи	*(za-shchee-SHCHYON-nee at ZAH-pee-see)*
written agreement	письменное соглашение	*(PEES-men-na-ye sa-gla-SHEH-nee-ye)*

Y

yardstick	аршин («ярд»)	*(ar-SHIN ["yard"])*
year	год	*(got)*
year-end	конец года	*(ka-NETS GOH-da)*

year, fiscal	отчётный год	*(at-CHYOHT-nee got)*
yield	доход	*(da-KHOT)*
yield (v) (give into)	подаваться	*(pa-da-VAHT-sa)*
yield to maturity	доход до наступления	*(da-KHOT da nas-toop-LEH-nee-ya)*

Z

zero coupon	облигация «зеро»	*(ab-LEE-gar-tsee-ya "zeh-ROH)*
zero gravity	невесомость	*(ne-ve-SOH-mast)*
zinc	цинк	*(tsink)*
ZIP code	почтовый индекс (США)	*(pach-TOH-vee een-DEKS)*
zone	зона	*(ZOH-na)*
zoning law	закон о районировании	*(za-KON a ray-a-NEE-ra-va-nee-ee)*

Y

A

абандон	*(a-ban-DON)*	abandonment
абсентеизм	*(ap-sen-te-EEZM)*	absenteeism
авалист	*(a-va-LEEST)*	guaranty company
аваль	*(a-VAHL)*	guarantee
аваль и регистрация	*(a-VAHL ee re-ghees-TRAH-tsee-ya)*	back and filing
аванс	*(a-VAHNS)*	down payment
аванс наличными	*(a-VAHNS na-LEECH-nee-mee)*	cash in advance
аванс фрахта	*(a-VAHNS FRAHKH-ta)*	advance freight
авансировать	*(a-van-SEE-ra-vat)*	advance (v) (money)
аварийное повреждение	*(a-va-REEY-na-ye pav-re-ZHDEH-nee-ye)*	accident damage
авария	*(a-VAH-ree-ya)*	crash
авиаперевозка	*(AH-vee-a-pe-re-VOS-ka)*	air shipment
авиафрахт	*(AH-vee-a-FRAHKHT)*	air freight
авиация	*(a-vee-AH-tsee-ya)*	aviation
авиаэлектроника	*(AH-vee-a-e-lek-TROH-nee-ka)*	avionics
авизо	*(a-VEE-za)*	advise note
авизовать	*(a-vee-za-VAHT)*	advise (v)
автаркия	*(af-TAHR-kee-ya)*	autarchy
автоматизация	*(af-ta-ma-tee-ZAH-tsee-ya)*	automation
автоматическая коробка передач	*(af-ta-ma-TEE-ches-ka-ya ka-ROP-ka pe-re-DAHCH)*	automatic gearshift
автоматический	*(af-ta-ma-TEE-ches-kee)*	automatic
автомобиль	*(af-ta-ma-BEEL)*	automobile, car
автомобиль с откидным верхом	*(af-ta-ma-BEEL sat-keed-NOM VEHR-kham)*	convertible
автономная рабочая станция	*(af-ta-NOM-na-ya ra-BOH-cha-ya STAHN-tsee-ya)*	stand-alone workstation
автономный	*(af-ta-NOM-nee)*	autonomous

автономный от системы (компьютер)	*(af-ta-NOM-nee at see-STEH-mee [kam-PYOO-ter])*	offline
автономный текстообразный процессор	*(af-ta-NOM-nee teksta-ab-RAHZ-nee pra-TSES-sar)*	stand-alone word processor
автопилот	*(AHF-ta-pee-LOT)*	auto-pilot
авторский гонорар (книга)	*(AHF-tar-skee ga-na-RAHR [KNEE-ga])*	royalty (book)
авторский гонорар (патент)	*(AHF-tar-skee ga-na-RAHR [pa-TENT])*	royalty (patent)
авторское право	*(AHF-tar-ska-ye PRAH-va)*	copyright
агент	*(a-GHENT)*	agent
агент по взысканию	*(a-GHENT pa vzis-KAH-nee-yoo)*	collection agent
агент по закупкам	*(a-GHENT pa za-KOOP-kam)*	purchasing agent
агент по продаже недвижимости	*(a-GHENT pa pra-DAH-zhe ne-DVEE-zhee-ma-stee)*	estate agent
агент производителя	*(a-GHENT pra-eez-va-DEE-te-la)*	manufacturer's agent
агент, экспедитор	*(a-GHENT, eek-spa-dee-TOR)*	forwarding agent
агентство	*(a-GHENT-stva)*	agency
агитация в кулуарах	*(a-ghee-TAH-tsee-ya fkoo-loo-AH-rakh)*	lobbying
агротехника	*(ag-ra-TEKH-nee-ka)*	agricultural engineering
адвалорная пошлина	*(ad-va-LOHR-na-ya POSH-lee-na)*	ad valorem duty
адвокат	*(ad-va-KAHT)*	attorney, lawyer
адвокатура	*(ad-va-ka-TOO-ra)*	Bar (legal profession)
адендум	*(a-DEN-doom)*	addendum
административные расходы	*(ad-mee-nee-stra-TEEV-nee-ye ras-KHOH-dee)*	administrative expenses
административный	*(ad-mee-nee-stra-TEEV-nee)*	administrative
администратор	*(ad-mee-nee-STRAH-tar)*	administrator
администрация	*(ad-mee-nee-STRAH-tsee-ya)*	administration
адрес	*(AHD-res)*	address

азот	*(a-ZOT)*	nitrogen
азотная кислота	*(a-ZOT-na-ya kees-la-TAH)*	nitric acid
аккредитив	*(ak-kree-dee-TEEF)*	letter of credit
аккумулятор	*(ak-koo-moo-LYAH-tar)*	battery
аккумуляторная жидкость	*(ak-koo-moo-LYAH-tar-na-ya ZHIT-kast)*	battery fluid
акр	*(ahkr)*	acre
акроним	*(ak-ROH-neem)*	acronym
акт	*(ahkt)*	deed
акт в опеку	*(ahkt va-PEH-koo)*	deed of trust
акт вне компетенции	*(ahkt vne kam-pe-TEHN-tsee-ee)*	ultra vires act
акт отказа от права	*(ahkt at-KAH-za at PRAH-va)*	quit claim deed
акт передачи	*(ahkt pe-re-DAH-chee)*	deed of transfer
акт продажи	*(ahkt pra-DAH-zhee)*	deed of sale
акт учреждения доверительной собственности	*(ahkt ooch-re-ZHDEH-nee-ya da-ve-REE-tel-nay SOP-stven-na-stee)*	trust deed
актив	*(ak-TEEF)*	asset
активное «кэш-флоу»	*(ak-TEEV-na-ye "cash flow")*	positive cash flow
активные запасы	*(ak-TEEV-nee-ye za-PAH-see)*	active reserves
активный газ (подземного газохранилища)	*(ak-TEEV-nee gahs [pad-ZEM-na-va ga-za-khra-NEE-lee-shcha])*	active gas
активы будущих периодов	*(ak-TEE-vee BOO-doo-shcheekh pe-REE-a-daf)*	deferred assets
актуарий	*(ak-too-AH-reey)*	actuary
акустическая муфта	*(a-koos-TEE-ches-ka-ya MOOF-ta)*	acoustic coupler
акустическая система	*(a-koos-TEE-ches-ka-ya sees-TEH-ma)*	speaker
акцентированная коммерческая тратта	*(ak-tsen-TEE-ra-va-na-ya kam-MEHR-ches-ka-ya TRAHT-ta)*	trade acceptance
акцепт	*(ak-TSEPT)*	acceptance (bill of agreement)

акцептант	*(ak-tsep-TAHNT)*	acceptor
акцептованный вексель	*(ak-tsep-TOH-va-nee VEK-sel)*	acceptance bill
акциз	*(ak-TSIS)*	excise tax
акцизная пошлина	*(ak-TSIZ-na-ya POSH-lee-na)*	excise duty
акции	*(AKH-tsee-ee)*	shares
акции, выпущенные в обращение	*(AKH-tsee-ee, VEE-poo-shchen-nee-ye vab-ra-SHCHEH-nee-ye)*	outstanding stock
акционер	*ak-tsee-a-NEHR)*	shareholder, stockholder
акционерная прибыль	*(ak-tsee-a-NEHR-na-ya PREE-bil)*	stock profit
акционерное общество	*(ak-tsee-a-NEHR-na-ye OP-shchest-va)*	corporation
акционерное общество закрытого типа	*(ak-tsee-a-NEHR-na-ye OP-shchest-va za-KREE-ta-va TEE-pa)*	closely held corporation
акционерное общество открытого типа	*(ak-tsee-a-NEHR-na-ye OP-shchest-va at-KREE-ta-va TEE-pa)*	public company
акционерное полномочие	*(ak-tsee-a-NEHR-na-ye pal-na-MOH-chee-ye)*	stock power
акция	*(AKH-tsee-ya)*	stock (share)
акция на предъявителя	*(AKH-tsee-ya na pred-ya-VEE-te-lya)*	bearer security
алгоритм	*(al-ga-REETM)*	algorithm
аллонж	*(al-LONSH)*	allonge
алюминий	*(a-lyoo-MEE-neey)*	aluminum
альпари	*(al-pa-REE)*	at par
альтернативный заказ	*(al-ter-na-TEEV-nee za-KAHS)*	alternative order
аммиак	*(am-mee-AHK)*	ammonia
амортизатор	*(a-mar-tee-ZAH-tar)*	stock absorber
амортизационный резерв	*(a-mar-tee-za-tsee-ON-nee re-ZEHRF)*	depreciation, accrued
амортизация	*(a-mar-tee-ZAH-tsee-ya)*	depreciation
амортизируемые расходы на строительство скважин	*(a-mar-tee-ZEE-roo-ye-mee-ye ras-KHOH-dee na stra-EE-tel-stva SKVAH-zhin)*	well tangibles

амплитудная модуляция	*(am-plee-TOOD-na-ya ma-doo-LYAH-tsee-ya)*	amplitude modulation (AU)
анализ	*(a-NAH-lees)*	analysis
анализ безубыточ-ности	*(a-NAH-lees be-zoo-BEE-tach-na-stee)*	break-even analysis
анализ годичных слоев	*(a-NAH-lees ga-DEECH-nikh sla-YOF)*	tree ring analysis
анализ деятельно-сти	*(a-NAH-lees DEH-ya-tel-na-stee)*	analysis, functional
анализ доходов и расходов	*(a-NAH-lees da-KHOH-daf ee ras-KHOH-daf)*	input-output analysis
анализ доходов от продажи	*(a-NAH-lees da-KHOH-daf at pra-DAH-zhee)*	sales analysis
анализ издержек	*(a-NAH-lees eez-DEHR-zhek)*	cost analysis
анализ капитало-вложения	*(a-NAH-lees ka-pee-TAH-la-vla-ZHEH-neey)*	investment analysis
анализ качества продукции	*(a-NAH-lees KAH-chest-va pra-DOOK-tsee-ye)*	product analysis
анализ конкурен-тов	*(a-NAH-lees kan-koo-REN-taf)*	competition analysis
анализ прибыль-ности	*(a-NAH-lees PREE-bil-na-stee)*	profitability analysis
анализ работ	*(a-NAH-lees ra-BOT)*	job analysis
анализ регрессии	*(a-NAH-lees re-GRES-see-ee)*	regression analysis
анализ рентабель-ности	*(a-NAH-lees ren-TAH-bel-na-stee)*	cost-benefit (profit) analysis
анализ риска	*(a-NAH-lees REES-ka)*	risk analysis
анализ соперни-ков	*(a-NAH-lees sa-PEHR-nee-kaf)*	competitor analysis
анализ требова-ний	*(a-NAH-lees TREH-ba-va-neey)*	analysis needs
анализ финансо-вого состояния	*(a-NAH-lees fee-NAHN-sa-va-va sa-sta-YAH-nee-ya)*	financial analysis
анализ экосистемы леса	*(a-NAH-lees e-ka-sees-TEH-mee LEH-sa)*	analysis of forest ecosystem
аналитик	*(a-na-LEE-teek)*	analyst
аналитическая химия	*(a-na-lee-TEE-ches-ka-ya KHEE-mee-ya)*	analytic chemistry
аналоговая ЭВМ	*(a-NAH-la-ga-va-ya eh-veh-EM)*	analog computer

A

анаэробный микроорганизм	*(a-na-e-ROB-nee meek-ra-ar-ga-NEEZM)*	anaerobe
анестезирующее средство	*(a-ne-stee-ZEE-roo-yoo-shchee-ye SRET-stva)*	anaesthetic
анкета	*(an-KEH-ta)*	application form
аннуитет (ежегодная рента)	*(an-noo-ee-TET [ye-zhe-GOD-na-ya REN-ta])*	annuity
аннулирование	*(an-noo-LEE-ra-va-nee-ye)*	abatement (suspension)
аннулированный чек	*(an-noo-LEE-ra-van-nee chek)*	canceled, voided check
аннулировать	*(an-noo-LEE-ra-vat)*	cancel, nullify (v)
антационное средство	*(an-ta-tsee-ON-na-ya SRET-stva)*	antacid
антибиотик	*(an-tee-bee-OH-teek)*	antibiotic
антидатировать	*(an-tee-da-TEE-ra-vat)*	back date (v)
антидемпинговая пошлина	*(AHN-tee-DEM-peen-ga-va-ya POSH-lee-na)*	anti-dumping duty
антидепрессант	*(an-tee-de-pres-SAHNT)*	antidepressant
антикоагулянт	*(an-tee-koh-a-goo-LYAHNT)*	anticoagulant
антимонопольное законодательство	*(AHN-tee-ma-na-POL-na-ye za-ka-na-DAH-tel-stva)*	antitrust laws
антисептическое средство	*(an-tee-sep-TEE-ches-ka-ye SRET-stva)*	antiseptic
аппаратные средства	*(ap-pa-RAHT-nee-ye SRET-stva)*	hardware
аппаратура	*(ap-pa-ra-TOO-ra)*	hardware (computer)
аптека	*(ap-TEH-ka)*	drugstore
арбитр	*(ar-BEETR)*	arbitrator
арбитраж	*(ar-beet-RASH)*	arbitrage, arbitration
аренда оборудования	*(a-REN-da a-ba-ROO-da-va-nee-ya)*	equipment leasing
арендатор	*(a-ren-DAH-tar)*	lessee
арендная плата	*(a-REND-na-ya PLAH-ta)*	rent
арендодатель	*(a-REN-da-DAH-tel)*	lessor
арендный бонус	*(a-REND-nee BOH-noos)*	lease bonus

арестовывать/аре-стовать	*(a-res-TOH-vee-vat/a-res-toh-VAHT)*	attach (v) (seize)
аршин («ярд»)	*(ar-SHIN ["yard'"])*	yardstick
ассигнование	*(as-seeg-na-VAH-nee-ye)*	(budget) appropriation
ассигнование капитала	*(as-seeg-na-VAH-nee-ye ka-pee-TAH-la)*	capital allowance
ассигнование ответственно-стей	*(as-seeg-na-VAH-nee-ye at-VET-stven-na-stee)*	allocation of responsibilities
ассигнование погашения	*(as-seeg-na-VAH-nee-ye pa-ga-SHEH-nee-ya)*	redemption allowance
ассигнование рас-ходов	*(as-seeg-na-VAH-nee-ye ras-KHOH-daf)*	allocation of costs
ассигнование ресурсов	*(as-seeg-na-VAH-nee-ye re-SOOHR-saf)*	resource allocation
ассигновывать/ ассигновать	*(as-seeg-NOH-vee-vat/as-seeg-na-VAHT)*	assign (v)
асфальт	*(as-FAHLT)*	asphalt
атом	*(AH-tam)*	atom
атомный	*(AH-tam-nee)*	atomic
атташе (кэйс)	*(at-ta-SHEH [kehys])*	briefcase
аттестация	*(a-tes-TAH-tsee-ya)*	attestation
аукцион	*(a-ook-tsee-ON)*	public auction
аэрация	*(a-eh-RAH-tsee-ya)*	aeration
аэродинамика	*(AH-e-ra-dee-NAH-mee-ka)*	aerodynamics
аэродинамика сверхзвуковых скоростей	*(AH-e-ra-dee-NAH-mee-ka sverkh-zvoo-ka-VIKH ska-ra-STEY)*	supersonic
аэродинамические весы	*(AH-e-ra-dee-na-MEE-ches-kee-ye ve-SEE)*	aerodynamic balance
аэронавигация	*(AH-e-ra-na-vee-GAH-tsee-ya)*	air navigation
аэронавтика	*(AH-e-ra-NAHF-tee-ka)*	aeronautics
аэропорт	*(ah-e-ra-POHRT)*	airport

Б

база данных	*(BAH-za DAHN-nikh)*	database

база налогообло- жения	*(BAH-za na-LOH-ga-ab-la- ZHEH-nee-ya)*	tax base
базарная площадь	*(ba-ZAHRna-ya PLOH- shchat)*	marketplace
базисная валюта	*(BAH-zees-na-ya va-LYOO- ta)*	base currency
базисная ставка	*(BAH-zees-na-ya STAHF- ka)*	base rate
базисная цена	*(BAH-zees-na-ya tse-NAH)*	base price
базисная цена на «эталонную» нефть	*(BAH-zees-na-ya tse-NAH na e-ta-LON-noo-yoo neft)*	benchmark price (of crude oil)
базисный год	*(BAH-zees-nee got)*	base year
базисный процент	*(BAH-zees-nee pra-TSENT)*	basis point
базовая контракт- ная цена (на природный газ)	*(BAH-za-va-ya kan- TRAHKT-na-ya tse-NAH [na pree-ROD-nee gahs])*	base price (for natural gas)
байт	*(bahyt)*	byte
баланс	*(ba-LAHNS)*	balance, balance sheet
баланс остатков средств в кассе	*(ba-LAHNS as-TAHT-kaf sretstf FKAHS-se)*	cash balance
баланс текущих расчётов	*(ba-LAHNS tee-KOO- shcheekh ra-SHCHYOH- taf)*	account balance
балансовая стои- мость	*(ba-LAHN-sa-va-ya STOH- ee-mast)*	book value
балансовый срок	*(ba-LAHN-sa-vee srok)*	accounting period
балка	*(BAHL-ka)*	beam
балласт	*(bal-LAHST)*	ballast
баллистический	*(bal-lee-STEE-ches-kee)*	ballistic
бальза заячья	*(BAHL-za ZAH-yach-ya)*	balsa
банк	*(bahnk)*	bank
банк-акцептант	*(bahnk-ak-tsep-TAHNT)*	acceptance house
банк данных	*(bahnk DAHN-nikh)*	data bank
банк компьюте- ров	*(bahnk kam-PYOO-te-raf)*	computer bank
банкнота	*(bahnk-NOH-ta)*	banknote, bill (currency)
банковская ведо- мость	*(BAHN-kaf-ska-ya VEH-da- mast)*	bank statement

банковская расчётная книга	(BAHN-kaf-ska-ya ra-SHCHOT-na-ya KNEE-ga)	pass book
банковская сберегательная касса	(BAHN-kaf-ska-ya zbe-re-GAH-tel-na-ya KAHS-sa)	savings bank
банковская ссуда	(BAHN-kaf-ska-ya SSOO-da)	bank loan
банковская ставка	(BAHN-kaf-ska-ya STAHF-ka)	bank rate
банковские сборы	(BAHN-kaf-skee-ye ZBOH-ree)	bank charges
банковский аккредитив	(BAHN-kaf-skee a-kre-dee-TEEF)	bank letter of credit
банковский акцепт	(BAHN-kaf-skee ak-TSEPT)	bank acceptance
банковский баланс	(BAHN-kaf-skee ba-LAHNS)	bank balance
банковский вексель	(BAHN-kaf-skee VEK-sel)	bank draft
банковский вклад	(BAHN-kaf-skee fklaht)	bank deposit
банковский обмен	(BAHN-kaf-skee ab-MEN)	bank exchange
банковский ордерный чек	(BAHN-kaf-skee OHR-der-nee chek)	bank money order
банковский ревизор	(BAHN-kaf-skee re-vee-ZOHR)	bank examiner
банковский счёт	(BAHN-kaf-skee shchyot)	deposit, bank
банковский чек	(BAHN-kaf-skee chek)	(bank) cashier's check
банковское оправдание	(BAHN-kaf-ska-ye ap-rav-DAH-nee-ye)	bank release
банковское хранилище	(BAHN-kaf-ska-ye khra-NEE-lee-shche)	safe deposit box
банкротство	(BAHN-kroot-stva)	bankruptcy, failure
баран	(ba-RAHN)	ram
баржа	(BAHR-zha)	barge transportation
баратрия	(ba-RAHT-ree-ya)	barratry
баррель	(BAHR-rel)	barrel
барсук	(bar-SOOK)	badger
батрак	(bat-RAHK)	farm labor

Б

без номинальной цены	*(bez na-mee-NAHL-nay TSEH-nee)*	no par value
безнадёжная задолженность	*(bez-na-DYOZH-na-ya za-DOL-zhen-nast)*	uncollectibles, bad debts
безработица	*(bez-ra-BOH-tee-tsa)*	unemployment
безусловный акцепт	*(be-zoos-LOV-nee ak-TSEPT)*	general acceptance
«белый воротни-чок» (рабочий)	*(BEH-lee va-rat-nee-CHOK [ra-BOH-chee])*	white-collar worker
бенефициар	*(be-ne-fee-tsee-AHR)*	beneficiary
бензин	*(ben-ZEEN)*	gasoline
бензиновый насос	*(ben-ZEE-na-vee na-SOS)*	fuel pump
бензол	*(ben-ZOL)*	benzene
берёза	*(be-RYOH-za)*	birch
бесплатный экземпляр	*(bes-PLAHT-nee ek-zem-PLYAHR)*	complimentary copy
беспошлинная торговля	*(bes-POSH-leen-na-ya tar-GOV-lya)*	free trade
беспошлинный	*(bes-POSH-leen-nee)*	duty free
бизнесплан	*(BEEZ-nes-PLAHN)*	business plan
биолог	*(bee-OH-lak)*	biologist
биология	*(bee-a-LOH-ghee-ya)*	biology
биохимия	*(bee-a-KHEE-mee-ya)*	biochemistry
биржа	*(BEEHR-zha)*	exchange
биржа труда	*(BEEHR-zha troo-DAH)*	employment agency
биржевой маклер	*(beer-zhe-VOY MAHK-ler)*	stockbroker
биржевой отчёт в газете	*(beer-zhe-VOY at-CHYOHT vga-ZEH-te)*	financial pages, newspaper
биржевой теле-графный аппа-рат	*(beer-zhe-VOY te-le-GRAHF-nee ap-pa-RAHT)*	ticker (stock prices)
бит	*(beet)*	bit
битум	*(bee-TOOM)*	bitumen
бланк заказа	*(blahnk za-KAH-za)*	order form
блат	*(blaht)*	graft
блок	*(blok)*	block
блок-схема	*(blok-SKHEH-ma)*	chart, flow

блокированная валюта	*(bla-KEE-ra-van-na-ya va-LYOO-ta)*	blocked currency
бобёр	*(bobyer)*	beaver
богатство	*(ba-GAHT-stva)*	wealth
бойкот	*(bay-KOT)*	boycott
болезнь	*(ba-LEZN)*	disease
болеутоляющий	*(BOH-le-oo-ta-LYAH-yoo-shchee)*	analgesic
болотный газ	*(ba-LOT-nee gahs)*	marsh gas
бо́льшая часть (акции и т.д.)	*(BOL-sha-ya chast [AHK-tsee ee TEH-DEH])*	majority interest
большое увеличе-ние	*(bal-SHOH-ye oo-ve-lee-CHEH-nee-ye)*	blowup
бонд	*(bond)*	bond
бондовая транс-портная компа-ния	*(BON-da-va-ya TRAHNS-part-na-ya kam-PAH-nee-ya)*	bonded carrier
«бонус« за откры-тие	*(BOH-noos za at-KREE-tee-ye)*	discovery bonus
борьба за произ-водительность	*(bar-BAH za pra-eez-va-DEE-tel-nast)*	campaign, productivity
ботаническое средство	*(ba-ta-NEE-ches-ka-ye SRET-stva)*	botanic
ботинки	*(ba-TEEN-kee)*	ankle boots
ботулизм	*(ba-too-LEEZM)*	botulism
брак	*(brahk)*	spoilage
бракераж	*(bra-ke-RAHSH)*	broken stowage
брать/взять в аренду	*(brat/vsaht va-REHN-doo)*	lease, rent (v) (as lessee)
брать/взять в долг	*(brat/vsaht vdolk)*	borrow (v)
брать/взять патент	*(brat/vsaht pa-TENT)*	take out (v) (patent)
бремя налогов	*(BREH-mya na-LOH-gaf)*	tax burden
Британская Тепловая Единица (БТЕ)	*(bree-TAHN-ska-ya tep-la-VAH-ya e-dee-NEE-tsa [BEH-TEH-YEH])*	British Termal Unit (BTU)
брошюра	*(bra-SHOO-ra)*	brochure
брусника	*(broos-NEE-ka)*	lingonberry
бук	*(book)*	beech

буква	(BOOK-va)	letter
бум	(boom)	boom
бумага	(boo-MAH-ga)	paper
бумага с покрыти-ем	(boo-MAH-ga spa-KREE-tee-yem)	coated paper
бумажная фабри-ка	(boo-MAHZH-na-ya FAHB-ree-ka)	paper mill
бумажник	(boo-MAHZH-neek)	billfold
буфер	(BOO-fer)	bumper
бухгалтер	(bookh-GHAL-ter)	accountant
бухгалтерия	(bookh-gal-TEH-ree-ya)	bookkeeping
бухгалтерская запись	(bookh-GAHL-ter-ska-ya ZAH-pees)	ledger entry
бухгалтерская книга	(bookh-GAHL-ter-ska-ya KNEE-ga)	ledger
бухгалтерская опись	(bookh-GAHL-ter-ska-ya OH-pees)	boon inventory
бухгалтерская стоимость	(bookh-GAHL-ter-ska-ya STOH-ee-mast)	boon value
бухгалтерская стоимость по акции	(bookh-GAHL-ter-ska-ya STOH-ee-mast pa AHK-tsee-ee)	boon value per share
бухгалтерский отдел	(bookh-GAHL-ter-skee at-DEL)	accounting department
бык	(bik)	bull
быстро растущая компания	(BIST-ra ras-TOO-shcha-ya kam-PAH-nee-ya)	growth company
быстро реализуе-мые активы	(BIST-ra re-a-lee-ZOO-ye-mee-ye ak-TEE-vee)	quick assets
быть в долгу	(beet vdal-GOO)	in the red
бэрбоут-чартер	(behr-BOH-OOT CHAHR-ter)	bareboat charter
бювар	(byoo-VAHR)	blotter
бюджет	(byood-ZHET)	budget
бюджет денежной наличности	(byood-ZHET DEH-nezh-nay na-LEECH-na-stee)	budget, cash
бюджет капита-ловложения	(byood-ZHET ka-pee-TAH-la-vla-ZHEH-neey)	capital budget

бюджет маркетинга	*(byood-ZHET mar-KEH-teen-ga)*	marketing budget
бюро проверки кредитоспособности	*(byoo-ROH pra-VEHR-kee kre-dee-ta-spa-SOB-na-stee)*	credit bureau
бюрократ	*(byoo-ra-KRAHT)*	bureaucrat

В

в бумажном переплёте	*(vboo-MAHZH-nam pe-re-PLYOH-te)*	paperback
в два раза быстрее	*(vdvah RAH-za bis-TREH-ye)*	double time
в день	*(vden)*	per diem
в жёстком переплёте	*(VZHOST-kam pe-re-PLYOH-te)*	hardcover
в лучшем случае	*(VLOOCH-shem SLOO-cha-ye)*	at best
в обращении	*(vab-ra-SHCHEH-nee-ee)*	afloat (in circulation)
в пути	*(fpoo-TEE)*	in transit
в соответствии с нашими ожиданиями	*(fsa-at-VET-stvee-ee SNAH-shee-mee a-zhee-DAH-nee-ya-mee)*	up to our expectations
в счёт	*(fshchyoht)*	on account
вагон	*(va-GON)*	carload
вагон-платформа	*(va-GON-plat-FOHR-ma)*	flatcar
вагонная погрузка	*(va-GON-na-ya pa-GROOS-ka)*	rail shipment
вагранка	*(va-GRAHN-ka)*	cupola
вакуумированная плавильная печь	*(va-koo-oo-MEE-ra-van-na-ya pla-VEEL-na-ya pech)*	vacuum melting furnace
вакцина	*(vak-TSEE-na)*	vaccine
вал	*(vahl)*	shaft
валовая прибыль	*(va-la-VAH-ya PREE-bil)*	gross profit, margin
валовое капиталовложение	*(va-la-VOH-ye ka-pee-TAH-la-vla-ZHEH-nee-ye)*	gross investment
валовой внутренний продукт	*(va-la-VOY VNOOT-ren-nee pra-DOOKT)*	gross domestic product (GDP)

валовой доход	(va-la-VOY da-KHOT)	gross income, yield
валовой обще- ственный про- дукт	(va-la-VOY ap-SHCHEST- ven-nee pra-DOOKT)	gross national product
валовой объём продажи	(va-la-VOY ab-YOM pra- DAH-zhee)	gross sales
валовой разрыв (между ценами)	(va-la-VOY raz-RIF [me- zhdoo TSE-na-mee])	gross spread
валовой убыток	(va-la-VOY oo-BEE-tak)	gross loss
валюта	(va-LYOO-ta)	currency
валюта оговорки	(va-LYOO-ta a-ga-VOHR- kee)	currency clause
валютная биржа	(va-LYOOT-na-ya BEEHR- zha)	currency exchange
валютные потери	(va-LYOOT-nee-ye pa-TEH- ree)	exchange loss
валютный базис	(va-LYOOT-nee BAH-zees)	monetary base
валютный кон- троль	(va-LYOOT-nee kan-TROL)	exchange control
валютный курс	(va-LYOOT-nee koors)	exchange rate
валютный рынок	(va-LYOOT-nee REE-nak)	money market
ванадий	(va-NAH-deey)	vanadium
ваучер	(VAH-oo-cher)	voucher
введение метриче- ской системы	(vve-DEH-nee-ye met-REE- ches-kay see-STEH-mee)	metrification
введение	(vve-DEH-nee-ye)	introduction
ввод	(vvot)	input
вводить/ввести по этапам	(vva-DEET/vves-TEE pa e- TAH-pam)	phase in (v)
вводящий в заблуждение	(vva-DYAH-shchee vzab- loozh-DEH-nee-ye)	misleading
ввозить/ввезти	(vva-ZEET/vve-ZTEE)	import (v)
ввозное заявление	(vvaz-NOH-ye za-yav-LEH- nee-ye)	import declaration
вдоль	(vdol)	alongside
ведомость	(VEH-da-mast)	statement
ведомость дове- ренности	(VEH-da-mast da-VEH-ren- nas-tee)	proxy statement

ведущий экономический показатель	*(ve-DOO-shchee e-ka-na-MEE-ches-kee pa-ka-ZAH-tel)*	leading indicator
вексель	*(VEK-sel)*	bill
вексель к получению	*(VEK-sel kpa-loo-CHEH-nee-yoo)*	note receivable
вексель на предъявителя	*(VEK-sel na pred-ya-VEE-te-lya)*	sight draft
вексельный кредит	*(VEK-sel-nee kre-DEET)*	credit note
вексельный маклер	*(VEK-sel-nee MAHK-ler)*	bill broker
вентилятор	*(ven-tee-LYAH-tar)*	fan
вертикальная интеграция	*(ver-tee-KAHL-na-ya een-te-GRAH-tsee-ya)*	vertical integration
вертолёт	*(ver-ta-LYOT)*	helicopter
вес	*(ves)*	weight
вес брутто	*(ves BROOT-ta)*	gross weight
весна	*(ves-NAH)*	spring
ветеринар	*(ve-te-ree-NAHR)*	veterinarian
вето	*(VEH-ta)*	veto
ветровое стекло	*(vet-ra-VOH-ye stek-LOH)*	windshield
ветряная мельница	*(vet-rya-NAH-ya MEL-nee-tsa)*	windmill
взаимно-сберегательный банк	*(vza-EEM-na-zbe-re-GAH-tel-nee bahnk)*	mutual savings bank
взаимное лицензирование	*(vza-EEM-na-ye lee-tsen-ZEE-ra-va-nee-ye)*	cross-licensing
взаимное обучение	*(vza-EEM-na-ye a-boo-CHEH-nee-ye)*	reciprocal training
взаимные фонды	*(vza-EEM-nee-ye FON-dee)*	mutual funds
взаимный	*(vza-EEM-nee)*	mutual
взаимодействовать	*(vza-ee-ma-DEY-stva-vat)*	interact (v)
взаимо-исключающие классы	*(vza-EEM-a-ees-kloo-CHAH-yoo-shche-ye KLAHS-see)*	mutually exclusive classes
вздорожание	*(vzda-ra-ZHAH-nee-ye)*	appreciation
взимать налоги	*(vzee-MAHT na-LOH-ghee)*	levy taxes (v)

видеомагнитофон	(VEE-de-a-mag-nee-ta-FON)	ideocassette player
визитная карточ-ка	(vee-ZEET-na-ya KAHR-tach-ka)	business card
виноградарство	(vee-na-GRAH-dar-stva)	viticulture
витамин	(vee-ta-MEEN)	vitamin
вице-президент	(VEE-tse-pre-zee-DENT)	vice-president
вклад	(fklaht)	deposit
вклад по подписке	(fklaht pa pat-PEES-ke)	subscription price (securities)
вкладной счёт	(fklahd-NOY shchyoht)	deposit account
вкладывать/вло-жить капитал	(FKLAH-dee-vat/VLO-zheet ka-pee-TAHL)	invest (v)
вкладыш	(FKLAH-deesh)	insert
владелец	(vla-DEH-lets)	owner
владелец склада	(vla-DEH-lets SKLAH-da)	warehouseman
влияние на рента-бельность	(vlee-YAH-nee-ye na ren-TAH-bel-nast)	profit impact
вложение в основ-ной капитал	(vla-ZHEH-nee-ye vas-nav-NOY ka-pee-TAHL)	fixed capital investment
вмешиваться/вме-шаться	(VMEH-shee-vat-sa/vme-SHAH-tsa)	intervene (v)
вне баланса	(vne ba-LAHN-sa)	off-the-books
внешнеторговый товарооборот	(VNESH-ne-tar-GOH-vee ta-VAH-ra-a-ba-ROT)	terms of trade
внешняя ревизия	(VNESH-nya-ya re-VEE-zee-ya)	audit, outside
внешняя торговля	(VNESH-nya-ya tar-GOV-lya)	foreign trade
внутреннее финансирова-ние	(VNOOT-ren-ne-ye fee-nan-SEE-ra-va-nee-ye)	internal funding
внутренний	(VNOOT-ren-nee)	internal
внутренний век-сель	(VNOOT-ren-nee VEK-sel)	domestic bill
внутренний взнос	(VNOOT-ren-nee vznos)	front-end fee
внутренний коно-самент	(VNOOT-ren-nee ka-na-sa-MENT)	inland bill of lading

внутренняя ревизия	*(VNOOT-ren-nya-ya re-VEE-zee-ya)*	internal audit
внутренняя ставка рентабельности	*(VNOOT-ren-nya-ya STAHF-ka ren-TAH-bel-na-stee)*	internal rate of return
вовлечение	*(va-vle-CHEH-nee-ye)*	implication (involvement)
водитель	*(va-DEE-tel)*	driver
водяной газ	*(va-dya-NOY gahs)*	blue gas
водяной насос	*(va-dya-NOY na-SOS)*	water pump
военно- воздушные силы (ВВС)	*(va-YEN-na-vaz-DOOSH-nee-ye SEE-lee (VEH-VEH-ES)*	air force
возврат	*(vaz-VRAHT)*	callback, refund
возврат определённого процента стоимости	*(vaz-VRAHT a-pree-de-LYON-na-va pra-TSEN-ta STOH-ee-mas-tee)*	rebate
возврат пошлин	*(vaz-VRAHT POSH-leen)*	remission of duty
возврат таможенных пошлин	*(vaz-VRAHT ta-MOH-zhen-nikh POSH-leen)*	drawback (money)
возвратная ссуда	*(vaz-VRAHT-na-ya SSOO-da)*	call loan
возвратные деньги	*(vaz-VRAHT-nee-ye DEN-ghee)*	call money
воздушно-космический самолёт	*(vaz-DOOSH-na-kas-MEE-ches-kee sa-ma-LYOT)*	space plane
воздушно-сухой	*(vaz-DOOSH-na-so-KHOY)*	air-seasoned
воздушный фильтр	*(vaz-DOOSH-nee feeltr)*	air filter
возместить/возмещать	*(vaz-mes-TEET/vaz-me-SHCHAHT)*	reimburse (v)
возмещение	*(vaz-me-SHCHEH-nee-ye)*	recovery
возмещение издержек (добычи)	*(vaz-me-SHCHEH-nee-ye eez-DEHR-zhek [da-BEE-chee])*	cost recovery
возмещение расходов	*(vaz-me-SHCHEH-nee-ye ras-KHOH-daf)*	recovery of expenses
возможная продажа	*(vaz-MOZH-na-ya pra-DAH-zha)*	potential sales
возможности рынка	*(vaz-MOZH-na-stee RIN-ka)*	market potential

B

возможности сбыта	(va-MOZH-na-stee ZBEE-ta)	outlet
возможные поку-патели	(vaz-MOZH-nee-ye pa-koo-PAH-te-lee)	potential buyers
вознаграждение	(vaz-na-grazh-DEH-nee-ye)	remuneration, reward
вознаграждение агентства	(vaz-na-grazh-DEH-nee-ye a-GHENT-stva)	agency fee
вознаграждение исполнительно-го состава	(vaz-na-grazh-DEH-nee-ye ees-pal-NEE-tel-na-va sa-STAH-va)	executive compensation
война цен (конку-ренция)	(vay-NAH tsen [kan-koo-REN-tsee-ya])	price war
волна	(val-NAH)	wave
воловья кожа	(va-LOH-vya KOH-zha)	cowhide
волокита	(va-la-KEE-ta)	red tape
волокнистый полуфабрикат	(va-lak-NEES-tee poh-loo-fab-ree-KAHT)	pulp
вольфрам	(val-FRAHM)	tungsten
ворона	(va-ROH-na)	crows
восстановитель-ная стоимость	(vas-sta-na-VEE-tel-na-ya STOH-ee-mast)	replacement cost
восстановление	(vas-sta-nav-LEH-nee-ye)	reduction (chemical)
врач	(vrahch)	physician
временно уволь-нять рабочих	(VREH-men-na oo-vol-NYAHT ra-BOH-cheekh)	lay off (v)
временное закры-тие банков	(VREH-men-na-ye za-KREE-tee-ye BAHN-kaf)	bank holiday
временное при-способление	(VREH-men-na-ye prees-pa-sab-LEH-nee-ye)	makeshift
временный век-сель	(VREH-men-nee VEK-sel)	bill of sight
временный эконо-мический спад	(VREH-men-nee e-ka-na-MEE-ches-kee spaht)	downswing
время простоя	(VREH-mya pras-TOH-ya)	downtime
всеобщая заба-стовка	(fse-OP-shcha-ya za-bas-TOF-ka)	general strike
всеобщее достоя-ние	(fse-OP-shche-ye da-sta-YAH-nee-ye)	public domain
вспомогательная деятельность	(fspa-ma-GAH-tel-na-ya DEH-ya-tel-nast)	ancillary operation

встреча	*(FSTREH-cha)*	appointment (engagement)
встречное удо-влетворение	*(FSTRECH-na-ye oo-dav-let-va-REH-nee-ye)*	consideration (contract law)
вторичная ипоте-ка	*(fta-REECH-na-ya ee-pa-TEH-ka)*	second mortgage
вторичная нефть	*(fta-REECH-na-ya neft)*	secondary (crude) oil
вторичная пози-ция	*(fta-REECH-na-ya pa-ZEE-tsee-ya)*	second position
вторичное топли-во	*(fta-REECH-na-ye TOP-lee-va)*	secondary fuel
вторичные запасы	*(fta-REECH-nee-ye za-PAH-see)*	secondary reserves
вторичный заказ	*(fta-REECH-nee za-KAHS)*	repeat order
второстепенный рынок (ценных бумаг)	*(fta-ra-ste-PEN-nee REE-nak [TSEN-nikh boo-MAHK])*	secondary market (securities)
вход в плотные слои атмосфе-ры	*(fkhot FPLOT-nee-ye sla-EE at-mas-FEH-ree)*	re-entry
входное разреше-ние	*(fkhad-NOH-ye raz-re-SHEH-nee-ye)*	entry permit
вяз	*(vyas)*	elm
вязкость	*(VYAHS-kast)*	toughness
выборочная пар-тия	*(VEE-ba-rach-na-ya PAHR-tee-ya)*	sample line
выборочный кон-троль	*(VEE-ba-rach-nee KANT-rol)*	mixed sampling
выведение	*(vee-ve-DEH-nee-ye)*	breeding
выводить/вывести из строя	*(vee-va-DEET/VEE-ve-stee ees STROH-ya)*	lay up (v)
вывозить/вывезти	*(vee-va-ZEET/VEE-ves-tee)*	export (v)
вывозная пошли-на	*(vee-vaz-NAH-ya POSH-lee-na)*	export duty
выгружать/выгрузить	*(vee-groo-ZHAHT/VEE-groo-zeet)*	unload (v)
выдра	*(VID-ra)*	otter
выключать (стро-ку)	*(vee-klyoo-CHANT [stra-KOO])*	justify (v)
выкупаемая обли-гация	*(vee-koo-PAH-ye-ma-ya ab-lee-GAH-tsee-ya)*	redeemable bond

выкупить	*(VEE-koo-peet)*	buy back (v)
выкупная цена	*(vee-koop-NAH-ya tse-NAH)*	call price
вылупившиеся личинки	*(VEE-loo-peef-shee-ye-sa lee-CHEEN-kee)*	hatched larvae
выморочность имущества	*(VEE-ma-rach-nast ee-MOO-shchest-va)*	escheat
вынимать/вынуть	*(vee-nee-MAHT/VEE-noot)*	take out (v)
выпас	*(VEE-pas)*	grazing land
выписка банковского счёта	*(VEE-pees-ka BAHN-kaf-ska-va SHCHOH-ta)*	statement of account
выписка чеков против неинкассированных сумм	*(VEE-pees-ka CHEH-kaf PROH-teef ne-een-kas-SEE-ra-van-neekh soom)*	kiting
выплата	*(VEE-pla-ta)*	disbursement
выплачивать/ выплатить	*(vee-PLAH-chee-vat/VEE-pla-teet)*	pay up (v)
выполнение работы	*(vee-pal-NEH-nee-ye ra-BOH-tee)*	job performance
выпуск	*(VEE-poosk)*	output
выпуск акций	*(VEE-poosk AHK-tseey)*	stock issue
выпуск облигаций	*(VEE-poosk ab-lee-GAH-tseey)*	bond issue
выпускаемые акции	*(vee-poos-KAH-ye-mee-ye AHK-tsee-ee)*	issued shares
выпускать/выпустить в обращение	*(vee-poos-KAHT/VEE-poos-teet vab-ra-SHCHEH-nee-ye)*	issue (v)
выработка коллективного соглашения	*(VEE-ra-bat-ka kal-lek-TEEV-na-va sag-la-SHEH-nee-ya)*	collective bargaining
выравнивать	*(vee-RAHV-nee-vat)*	level out (v)
вырубаемый сплошной рубкой	*(vee-roo-BAH-ye-mee SPLASHSH-noy ROOP-kay)*	clear-cutting
выручка	*(VEE-rooch-ka)*	proceeds
выручка на устье скважины	*(VEE-rooch-ka na OOST-ye SKVAH-zhee-nee)*	well head value
выслуга лет	*(VEE-sloo-ga lyet)*	seniority

высококалорий- ный газ	*(vee-SOH-ka-ka-la-REEY- nee gahs)*	high-BTU gas
высококвалифи- цированный бухгалтер	*(vee-SOH-ka-kva-lee-fee- TSEE-ra-van-nee bookh- GAHL-ter)*	accountant (CPA)
высота	*(vee-sa-TAH)*	altitude
выставлять/ выставить на продажу	*(vee-stav-LYAHT/VEE-sta- veet na pra-DAH-zhoo)*	offer for sale
выступ	*(VIS-toop)*	overhang
высшее руковод- ство	*(VISH-she-ye roo-ka-VOT- stva)*	top management
выхлоп	*(VIKH-lap)*	exhaust
выход на пенсию	*(VEE-khat na PEN-see-yoo)*	retirement
выход нефти (сланцевой смолы)	*(VEE-khat NEF-tee [SLAHN-tse-vahy sma- LEE])*	oil yield
выходное пособие	*(vee-khad-NOH-ye pa-SOH- bee-ye)*	severance pay
вычет	*(VEE-chet)*	deduction
вычет с налогов	*(VEE-chet sna-LOH-gaf)*	tax deduction
выше номиналь- ной цены	*(VEE-she na-mee-NAHL- nay tse-NEE)*	above par
выше нормы	*(VEE-she NOHR-mee)*	above-the-line
выше среднего уровня	*(VEE-she SRED-ne-va- OO- rav-nya)*	up-market
вышеупомянутый	*(VEE-she-oo-pa-MYAH- noo-tee)*	above mentioned

Г

газ нефтяных скважин	*(gahs nef-tee-NIKH SKVAH- zhin)*	oil-well gas
газ зон геодавле- ний	*(gahs zon ghe-a-dav-LEH- ney)*	geopressured gas
газ в плотных породах	*(gahs FPLOT-nikh pa-ROH- dakh)*	tight gas
газгольдер	*(gaz-GOL-der)*	gasoline tank

газета	(ga-ZEH-ta)	newspaper
газетная бумага	(ga-ZET-na-ya boo-MAH-ga)	newsprint
газетная вырезка	(ga-ZET-na-ya VEE-res-ka)	press clipping
газетное объявление	(ga-ZET-na-ye ab-yav-LEH-nee-ye)	classified advertisement
газетный киоск	(ga-ZET-nee kee-OSK)	newsstand
газификация угля	(ga-zee-fee-KAH-tsee-ya oog-LYAH)	coal gasification
газовая залежь	(GAH-za-va-ya ZAH-lesh)	gas pool
газовая скважина	(GAH-za-va-ya SKVAH-zhee-na)	gas well
газовая компания	(GAH-za-va-ya kam-PAH-nee-ya)	gas company
газовый конденсат	(GAH-za-vee kan-den-SAHT)	gas condensate
газогидратная залежь	(GAH-za-gheed-RAHT-na-ya ZAH-lesh)	gas hidrate deposit
газойль	(ga-ZOYL)	gas oil
газохол	(ga-za-KHOL)	gasohol
гальванизация	(gal-va-nee-ZAH-tsee-ya)	galvanizing
гарант размещения	(ga-RAHNT raz-me-SHCHEH-nee-ya)	underwriter (securities)
гарантийное письмо	(ga-ran-TEEY-na-ye pees-MOH)	letter of guaranty
гарантийный вексель	(ga-ran-TEEY-nee VEK-sel)	back note
гарантированное «роялти»	(ga-ran-TEH-ra-van-na-ye ROH-yal-tee)	guaranteed royalty
гарантированные поставки газа	(ga-ran-TEH-ra-van-nee-ye pas-TAHF-kee GAH-za)	guaranteed gas supplies
гарантированные счета	(ga-ran-TEH-ra-van-nee-ye shche-TAH)	secured accounts
гарантия	(ga-RAHN-tee-ya)	guaranty bond, security, warrant, warranty
гарантия занятости	(ga-RAHN-tee-ya ZAH-nya-ta-stee)	job security
гектар	(ghek-TAHR)	hectare
генеральный полис	(ghe-ne-RAHL-nee POH-lees)	open cover

генератор	*(ghe-ne-RAH-tar)*	generator
генераторный газ	*(ghe-ne-RAH-tar-nee gahs)*	producer gas
гербицид	*(gher-bee-TSEE-dee)*	herbicide
гибкий диск	*(GHEEP-kee deesk)*	floppy disk
гидролиз	*(gheed-ROH-lees)*	hydrolysis
гидропоника	*(gheed-ra-POH-nee-ka)*	hydroponics
гидроусилитель	*(GHEED-ra-oo-see-LEE-tel)*	hydraulic booster
гипертензия	*(ghee-per-TEN-zee-ya)*	hypertension
глава	*(gla-VAH)*	leader
глава	*(gla-VAH)*	chapter
главная контора фирмы	*(GLAHV-na-ya kan-TOH-ra FEEHR-mee)*	head office
главный бухгал-тер	*(GLAHV-nee bookh-GAHL-ter)*	chief accountant
главный исполни-тель	*(GLAHV-nee ees-pal-NEE-tel)*	chief executive
главный покупа-тель	*(GLAHV-nee pa-koo-PAH-tel)*	chief buyer
главный управля-ющий	*(GLAHV-nee oop-rav-LYAH-yoo-shchee)*	general manager
глазные капли	*(glaz-NEE-ye KAHP-lee)*	eyedrop
глобальная стра-ховка	*(gla-BAHL-na-ya stra-KHOF-ka)*	blanket insurance
глобальный бонд	*(gla-BAHL-nee bond)*	blanket bond
глобальный заказ	*(gla-BAHL-nee za-KAHS)*	blanket order
глобальный контракт	*(gla-BAHL-nee kan-TRAHKT)*	package deal
глянцевая бумага	*(GLYAHN-tsee-va-ya boo-MAH-ga)*	glossy paper
год	*(got)*	year
годный на сводку	*(GOD-nee nas-VOT-koo)*	harvestable
годовая ревизор-ская проверка	*(ga-da-VAH-ya re-vee-ZOHR-ska-ya pra-VEHR-ka)*	annual audit
годовой	*(ga-da-VOY)*	annual
годовой отчёт	*(ga-da-VOY at-CHOT)*	annual report

Г

годовые счета	(ga-da-VEE-ye shche-TAH)	annual accounts
головка цилиндра	(ga-LOF-ka tsee-LEEN-dra)	cylinder heat
голубика	(ga-loo-BEE-ka)	blueberry
гомогенность	(ga-ma-GHEN-nast)	homogeneity
гормоны	(gar-MOH-nee)	hormones
горючие полезные ископаемые	(ga-RYOO-chee-ye pa-LEZ-nee-ye ees-ka-PAH-ye-mee-ye)	fossil fuels
горючий газ	(ga-RYOO-chee gahs)	combustible gas
горючий сланец	(ga-RYOO-chee SLAH-nets)	combustible shale
горячая прокатка	(ga-RYAH-cha-ya pra-KAHT-ka)	hot rolling
государственное агентство	(ga-soo-DAHR-stven-na-ye a-GHEN-stva)	government agency
государственное стимулирование экономики	(ga-soo-DAHR-stven-na-ye stee-moo-LEE-ra-va-nee-ye e-ka-NOH-mee-kee)	pump priming
государственные облигации	(ga-soo-DAHR-stven-nee-ye ab-lee-GAH-tsee-ee)	government bonds
государственный банк	(ga-soo-DAHR-stven-nee bahnk)	government bank
государственный долг	(ga-soo-DAHR-stven-nee dolk)	national debt
государственный сектор	(ga-soo-DAHR-stven-nee SEK-tar)	public sector
гофры	(GOF-ree)	gophers
граб	(grahp)	hornbeam
градус	(GRAH-doos)	degree (temperature)
градусник	(GRAH-doos-nikh)	thermometer
гражданская авиация	(grazh-DAHN-ska-ya a-vee-AH-tsee-ya)	commercial aviation
гражданский иск	(grazh-DAHN-skee eesk)	civil action
грамм-молекула	(GRAHM-ma-LEH-koo-la)	mole
граница	(gra-NEE-tsa)	border
график	(GRAH-feek)	schedule, timetable
график работ	(GRAH-feek ra-BOT)	activities chart
грибы	(gree-BEE)	mushrooms

Г

Гринвичское среднее время	*(GREEN-veech-ska-ye SRED-ne-ye VREH-mya)*	Greenwich Mean Time
грубый	*(GROO-bee)*	crude
груз	*(groos)*	cargo
груз на паллетах	*(groos na PAHL-le-takh)*	palletized freight
груз, оплачиваемый в порту выгрузки	*(groos ap-LAH-chee-va-yemee FPOHR-too VEE-groos-ke)*	forward shipment
грузовик	*(groo-za-VEEK)*	truck
грузоотправитель	*(GROO-za-at-pra-VEE-tel)*	shipper
грунтовая вода	*(groon-TOH-va-ya va-DAH)*	ground water
группа продуктов	*(GROOP-pa pra-DOOK-taf)*	product group
группа (фирменных) цепных магазинов	*(GROOP-pa [FEER-menneekh] tsep-NIKH ma-ga-ZEE-naf)*	chain store group
групповая динамика	*(groop-pa-VAH-ya dee-NAH-mee-ka)*	dynamics group
групповое страхование	*(groop-pa-VOH-ye stra-kha-VAH-nee-ye)*	group insurance
групповой счёт	*(groop-pa-VOY shchyoht)*	group account
груша	*(GROO-sha)*	pear
гудвил — цена нематериальных активов	*(GOOD-veel tse-NAH nema-te-ree-AHL-nikh ak-TEE-vaf)*	goodwill
гусь	*(goos)*	goose

Д

давать/дать указания	*(da-VAHT/daht oo-ka-ZAH-nee-ya)*	instruct (v) (order)
давление	*(dav-LEH-nee-ye)*	pressure
дамская сумка	*(DAHM-ska-ya SOOM-ka)*	handbag
данные	*(DAHN-nee-ye)*	data
дата операции	*(DAH-ta a-pe-RAH-tsee-ee)*	trade date
дата поставки	*(DAH-ta pas-TAHF-kee)*	date of delivery
дата просрочки	*(DAH-ta pra-SROH-chkee)*	expiry date
дача	*(DAH-cha)*	country house

двигатель	*(DVEE-ga-tel)*	engine
двигатель с восе-мью клапанами	*(DVEE-ga-tel sva-se-MYOO KLAH-pa-na-mee)*	V8 engine
движение запасов	*(dvee-ZHEH-nee-ye za-PAH-saf)*	inventory turnover
движимое имуще-ство	*(DVEE-zhe-ma-ye ee-MOO-shchest-va)*	chattel, personal property
движимость, соединённая с недвижимостью	*(DVEE-zhee-mast sa-ye-dee-NYON-na-ya sne-DVEE-zhee-mast-yoo)*	fixture
двойная бухгалте-рия	*(dvay-NAH-ya bookh-gal-TEH-ree-ya)*	double-entry bookeeping
«двойная игра»	*(dvay-NAH-ya eeg-RAH)*	double dealing
двойное налогоо-бложение	*(dvay-NOH-ye na-LOH-ga-ab-la-ZHEH-nee-ye)*	double taxation
двойное ценообра-зование	*(dvay-NOH-ye TSEN-na-ab-ra-za-VAH-nee-ye)*	double pricing
двойной код	*(dvay-NOY KOT)*	binary code
двойной опцион	*(dvay-NOY ap-tsee-ON)*	put and call
двухвинтовой вер-толёт	*(dvookh-vin-ta-VOY ver-ta-LYOT)*	dual rotor helicopter
двухэтапный рынок	*(dvookh-eh-TAHP-nee REE-nak)*	two-tiered market
дебетовая запись	*(DEH-be-ta-va-ya ZAH-pees)*	entry, debit
дебит	*(DEH-beet)*	debit
дебит-нота	*(DEH-beet-NOH-ta)*	debit note
девальвация	*(de-val-VAH-tsee-ya)*	devaluation
девонский сланец	*(de-VON-skee SLAH-nets)*	devonian shale
действительное время	*(deyst-VEE-tel-na-ye VREH-mya)*	real time
действительные активы	*(dey-STVEE-tel-nee-ye ak-TEE-vee)*	active assets
действительные долги	*(dey-STVEE-tel-nee-ye dol-GHEE)*	active debts
действительные результаты	*(dey-STVEE-tel-nee-ye re-zool-TAH-tee)*	out-turn
действительные цены	*(dey-STVEE-tel-nee-ye TSEH-nee)*	real price

действительный	*(dey-STVEE-tel-nee)*	valid
действительный доход	*(dey-STVEE-tel-nee da-KHOT)*	effective yield
действительный счёт	*(dey-STVEE-tel-nee shchyoht)*	active account
дела о наследстве	*(de-LAH a na-SLET-stve)*	probate
делать клише	*(DEH-lat klee-SHEH)*	engrave (v)
делать/сделать проводку	*(DEH-lat/ZDEH-lat pra-VOT-koo)*	post (v) (bookkeeping)
деликт	*(de-LEEKT)*	tort
деловая политика	*(de-la-VAH-ya pa-LEE-tee-ka)*	business policy
деловая стратегия	*(de-la-VAH-ya stra-TEH-ghee-ya)*	business strategy
деловое помещение	*(de-la-VOH-ye pa-me-SHCHEH-nee-ye)*	place of business
деловой цикл	*(de-la-VOY tsikl)*	business cycle
демередж (плата за простой)	*(DEH-me-retsh [PLAH-ta za pras-TOY])*	demurrage
демографический	*(de-ma-gra-FEE-ches-kee)*	demographic
демпинг	*(DEM-peenk)*	dumping (goods in trade)
денежные кредиты	*(DEH-nezh-nee-ye kre-DEE-tee)*	monetary credits
денежный вексель	*(DEH-nezh-nee VEK-sel)*	accommodation paper
денежный дивиденд	*(DEH-nezh-nee dee-vee-DENT)*	cash dividend
денежный почтовый перевод	*(DEH-nezh-nee pach-TOH-vee pe-re-VOT)*	money order
день расчёта	*(den ra-SHCHYOH-ta)*	account day
деньги	*(DEN-ghee)*	money
депорт	*(de-POHRT)*	backwardation
депрессия	*(de-PRES-see-ya)*	depression
дерево	*(DEE-re-va)*	tree
деревенский	*(de-re-VEN-skee)*	rural
держатель	*(der-ZHAH-tel)*	bearer, holder
держатель полиса	*(der-ZHAH-tel POH-lee-sa)*	policyholder

дефектный	*(de-FEHKT-nee)*	defective
дефицит	*(de-fee-TSIT)*	deficit, shortage
дефляция	*(de-FLYAH-tsee-ya)*	deflation
дешёвый	*(de-SHOH-vee)*	cheap
деятельное долевое участие на основе аренды	*(DEH-ya-tel-na-ye da-le-VOH-ye oo-CHAHS-tee-ye na as-NOH-ve a-REN-dee)*	working interest
джойстик (рычаг)	*(DZHOY-steek [ree-CHAHK])*	joystick
диапазон	*(dee-a-pa-ZON)*	range
диапазон цен	*(dee-a-pa-ZON tsen)*	price range
диверсификация	*(dee-ver-see-fee-KAH-tsee-ya)*	diversification
дивиденд	*(dee-vee-DENT)*	dividend
дизайн продукта	*(dee-ZAHYN pra-DOOK-ta)*	product design
дизайн систем	*(dee-ZAHYN sees-TEM)*	systems design
дизельное топливо	*(DEE-zel-na-ye TOP-lee-va)*	diesel fuel
«дикая» забастовка	*(DEE-ka-ya za-bas-TOF-ka)*	wildcat strike
дилер	*(dee-LER)*	dealer
динамика групп	*(dee-NAH-mee-ka groop)*	group dynamics
динамика продукта	*(dee-NAH-mee-ka pra-DOOK-ta)*	product dynamics
динамическая электронная таблица	*(dee-na-MEE-ches-ka-ya e-lek-TRON-na-ya tab-LEE-tsa)*	spreadsheet
диод	*(dee-OT)*	diode
директива	*(dee-rek-TEE-va)*	guideline
директор	*(dee-REK-tar)*	director
диск	*(deesk)*	disk
дисковод	*(dees-ka-VOT)*	disk drive
дисковод для гибких дисков	*(dees-ka-vot dla GHEEP-keekh DEES-kaf)*	disk drive (floppy)
дисковод для жёстких дисков	*(dees-ka-vot dla ZHOST-keekh DEES-kaf)*	disk drive (hard)
дисковый тормоз	*(DEES-ka-vee TOHR-mas)*	disc brake

Д

дискреционный заказ	*(dees-kre-tsee-ON-nee za-KAHS)*	discretionary order
дискреционный счёт	*(dees-kre-tsee-ON-nee shchyoht)*	discretionary account
дифференциаль-ная рента	*(deef-fe-ren-tsee-AHL-na-ya REHN-ta)*	differential rent
дифференциро-ванные цены	*(deef-fe-ren-TSEE-ra-van-nee-ye TSEH-nee)*	price differential
дневник	*(DNEV-nikh)*	journal
добавочные диви-денды	*(da-BAH-vach-nee-ye dee-vee-DEN-tee)*	cum dividend
добавочные про-дажи	*(da-BAH-vach-nee-ye pra-DAH-zhee)*	add-on sales
добавочный подо-ходный налог	*(da-BAH-vach-nee pa-da-KHOD-nee na-LOK)*	surtex
добросовестность	*(da-bra-SOH-ves-nast)*	good faith
доверенное лицо	*(da-VEH-ren-na-ye lee-TSOH)*	trustee
доверенность	*(da-VEH-ren-nast)*	power of attorney, proxy
доверитель	*(da-ve-REE-tel)*	principal (employer of an agent)
доводить/довести до конца	*(da-va-DEET/da-vee-STEE da kan-TSAH)*	follow up (v)
договор	*(da-ga-VOHR)*	contract
договор о распре-делении	*(da-ga-VOHR a ras-pre-de-LEH-nee-ee)*	allotment letter
договор о субарен-де (продуктив-ного участка)	*(da-ga-VOHR a-soob-a-REHN-de [pra-dook-TEEV-na-va oo-CHAHST-ka])*	farm-out
договор о техниче-ском обслужи-вании	*(da-ga-VOHR a tekh-NEE-ches-kam ap-SLOO-zhee-va-nee-ee)*	maintenance contract
договор об акцеп-те	*(da-ga-VOHR ab ak-TSEP-te)*	acceptance agreement
договор об арби-траже	*(da-ga-VOHR ab ar-beet-RAH-zhe)*	arbitration agreement
договор об обслу-живании	*(da-ga-VOHR ab ap-SLOO-zhee-va-nee-ee)*	service contract
договор учениче-ства	*(da-ga-VOHR oo-che-NEE-chest-va)*	indenture

Д

договорённая про-дажа	(da-ga-va-RYON-na-ya pra-DAH-zha)	negotiated sale
договорённость	(da-ga-va-RYON-nast)	understanding (agreement)
договорное обяза-тельство о воз-держании от действия	(da-ga-var-NOH-ye a-bya-ZAH-tel-stva a vaz-der-ZHAH-nee-ee at DEY-stvee-ya)	negative pledge
договорный месяц	(da-ga-var-NOY MEH-syats)	contract month
доза	(DOH-za)	dose
дозировка	(da-zee-ROF-ka)	dosage
доильная машина	(da-EEL-na-ya ma-SHEE-na)	milking machine
доказательство потери	(da-ka-ZAH-tel-stva pa-TEH-ree)	proof of loss
доковая наклад-ная	(DOH-ka-va-ya nak-lad-NAH-ya)	dock (ship's receipt)
документ	(da-koo-MENT)	document
долг	(dolk)	debt
долговечность изделия	(dal-ga-VECH-nast eez-DEH-leey)	product life
долговое обяза-тельство	(dal-ga-VOH-ye a-bya-ZAH-tel-stva)	promissory note
долговое обяза-тельство под залог	(dal-ga-VOH-ye a-bya-ZAH-tel-stva pad za-LOK)	mortgage debenture
долгосрочное обя-зательство	(dal-ga-SROCH-na-ye a-bya-ZAH-tel-stva)	fixed liability
долгосрочный вексель	(dal-ga-SROCH-nee VEK-sel)	time bill of exchange
долгосрочный долг	(dal-ga-SROCH-nee dolk)	long-term debt
долгосрочный счёт капитала	(dal-ga-SROCH-nee shchyoht ka-pee-TAH-la)	long-term capital account
должностная инструкция	(DOLZH-nast-na-ya een-STROOK-tsee-ya)	job description
доля акционера	(DOH-lya ak-tsee-a-NEH-ra)	stockholder's equity
доля владельца	(DOH-lya vla-DEHL-tsa)	owner's equity
домашний рынок	(da-MAHSH-nee REE-nak)	home market

домна	(DOM-na)	blast furnace
дополнения к отчёту за истекший период	(da-pal-NEH-nee-ya kat-CHYOH-too za ees-TEK-sheey pe-REE-at)	carry-back
дополнительные расходы	(da-pal-NEE-tel-nee-ye ras-KHOH-dee)	increased costs
дополнительный заказ	(da-pal-NEE-tel-nee za-KAHS)	follow-up order
дополнительный налог	(da-pal-NEE-tel-nee na-LOK)	back taxes
дополнительный пункт (к договору)	(da-pal-NEE-tel-nee poonkt [gda-ga-VOH-roo])	rider (contracts)
допуск на обработку	(DOH-poosk na-ab-ra-BOT-koo)	milling allowance
допуск ценных бумаг на биржу	(DOH-poosk TSEN-nikh boo-MAHK na BEEHR-zhoo)	listing
дорожная ЭВМ	(da-ROZH-na-ya eh-veh-EM)	laptop
доска	(das-KAH)	board
досковый фут	(das-ka-VOY foot)	board foot
доставка	(da-STAHF-ka)	delivery
доставка с немедленное оплатой	(da-STAHF-ka sne-MED-len-nay ap-LAH-tay)	spot delivery
достаточная забота	(da-STAH-tach-na-ya za-BOH-ta)	reasonable care
достичь предела рентабельности	(da-STEECH pre-DEH-la ren-TAH-bel-na-stee)	break-even (v)
доступ в рынок	(DOS-toop VREE-nak)	market access
дотация	(da-TAH-tsee-ya)	endowment
дотация	(da-TAH-tsee-ya)	subsidy
доход	(da-KHOT)	income, revenue, yield
доход в расчёте на активы	(da-KHOT vra-SHCHYOH-te na ak-TEE-vee)	earnings on assets
доход в расчёте на акцию	(da-KHOT vra-SHCHYOH-te na AHK-tsee-yoo)	earnings per share
доход до наступления	(da-KHOT da nas-toop-LEH-nee-ya)	yield to maturity

Д

доход, освобож- дённый от упла- ты налогов	*(da-KHOT as-va-bazh- DYON-nee at oo-PLAH- tee na-LOH-gaf)*	tax-free income
доход от дивиден- дов	*(da-KHOT aht dee-vee- DEN-taf)*	dividend yield
доход от операций	*(da-KHOT aht a-pe-RAH- tseey)*	operating income
доход от продажи	*(da-KHOT aht pra-DAH- zhee)*	return on sales
доходность капи- тала	*(da-KHOD-nast ka-pee- TAH-la)*	capital, return on
доходы будущих периодов	*(da-KHON-dee BOO-doo- shcheekh pe-REE-a-daf)*	deferred income
доходы, имеющие- ся лишь на бумаге	*(da-KHON-dee ee-MEE- yoo-shchee-ye-sa leesh na boo-MAH-ghe)*	paper profit
доходы от акций	*(da-KHON-dee at AHK- tseey)*	return on equity
дочерняя компа- ния	*(da-CHEHR-nya-ya kam- PAH-nee-ya)*	affiliate, subsidiary
древесина	*(dre-ve-SEE-na)*	wood
древесина лиственных пород	*(dre-ve-SEE-na LEEST-ven- nikh pa-ROT)*	hardwood
древесно-стружеч- ная плита (ДСП)	*(dre-VES-na-STROO-zhech- na-ya plee-TAH [DEH- ES-PEH])*	particle board
дружелюбный к пользователю	*(droo-zhe-LYOOB-nee KPOL-za-va-te-lyoo)*	user-friendly
дружеский акцепт	*(DROO-zhes-kee ak-TSEPT)*	accommodation bill
дружеский кредит	*(DROO-zhes-kee kre-DEET)*	accommodation credit
дружеское жиро	*(DROO-zhes-ka-ye zhee- ROH)*	accommodation endorsement (v)
дружественный паритет	*(DROO-zhes-tven-nee pa- ree-TET)*	accommodation parity
дуб	*(doop)*	oak
дубильщик	*(doo-BEEL-shcheek)*	tanner
дубить	*(doo-BEET)*	tan (v)
дуополия	*(doo-oh-POH-lee-ya)*	duopoly
дюйм	*(dyooym)*	inch

Е

Евробон	*(yev-ra-BON)*	Eurobond
евровалюта	*(yev-ra-va-LYOO-ta)*	Euro currency
евродоллары	*(yev-ra-DOL-la-ree)*	Eurodollar
единоличная собственность	*(ye-dee-na-LEECH-na-ya SOP-stven-nast)*	sole proprietorship
единообразная ставка	*(ye-dee-na-ab-RAHZ-na-ya STAHF-ka)*	flat rate
ежедневный	*(e-zhe-DNEV-nee)*	daily
ель	*(yel)*	spruce
енот	*(ye-NOT)*	raccoon

Ж

Ж

жалованье	*(ZHAH-la-va-nee-ye)*	salary
жаропрочный сплав	*(zha-ra-PROCH-nee splahf)*	supper alloys
жатвенная машина	*(ZHAHT-ven-na-ya ma-SHEE-na)*	reaper
желатиновая капсула	*(zhe-la-TEE-na-va-ya KAHP-soo-la)*	capsule
железная руда	*(zhe-LEZ-na-ya roo-DAH)*	iron ore
железо	*(zhe-LEH-za)*	iron
жеребёнок	*(zhe-re-BYOH-nak)*	colt
жёсткий диск	*(ZHOST-kee deesk)*	disk (hard)
жидкие углеводороды (ЖУВ)	*(ZHIT-kee-ye oog-le-va-da-ROH-dee [zhoof])*	hydrocarbon liquids
жидкое бункерное топливо	*(ZHIT-ka-ye BOON-ker-na-ye TOP-lee-va)*	bunker oil
жидкое топливо	*(ZHIT-ka-ye TOP-lee-va)*	liquid fuel
жизненный уровень	*(ZHIZ-nen-nee OO-ra-ven)*	standard of living
жизненный цикл (продукта)	*(ZHIZ-nen-nee tsikl [pra-DOOK-ta])*	life cycle (of a product)
жирный шрифт	*(ZHIR-nee shrift)*	bold face

жук	*(zhook)*	beetle
журнал	*(zhoor-NAHL)*	journal

З

забастовка	*(za-bas-TOF-ka)*	strike
завещание	*(za-ve-SHCHAH-nee-ye)*	will
завод	*(za-VOT)*	factory
завышенная цена	*(za-VEE-shen-na-ya tse-NAH)*	overcharge
заголовок/ заглавие	*(za-ga-LOH-vak)/za-GLAH-vee-ye)*	headline
заглавная буква	*(za-GLAHV-na-ya BOOK-va)*	capital letter
задание	*(za-DAH-nee-ye)*	job
задержка	*(za-DEHRSH-ka)*	delay
задний мост	*(ZAHD-nee most)*	rear axle
задолженность	*(za-DOL-zhen-nast)*	indebtedness
заезд и доставка	*(za-YEST ee da-STAHF-ka)*	pickup and delivery
зажигание	*(za-zhee-GAH-nee-ye)*	ignition
заказ	*(za-KAHS)*	order
заказ на поставку	*(za-KAHS na pas-TAHF-koo)*	purchase order
заказать	*(za-ka-ZAHT)*	orer, to place an (v)
заказная корре- спонденция	*(za-kaz-NAH-ya kar-res-pan-DEHN-tsee-ya)*	registered mail
заклад	*(zak-LAHT)*	collateral
закладная	*(za-klad-NAH-ya)*	bill of sale, mortgage bond
закладная с изме- няющейся став- кой процента	*(za-klad-NAH-ya siz-me-NYAH-yoo-shchey-sa STAHF-kay pra-TSEN-ta)*	variable rate mortgage
заключительная статья в балан- се	*(za-klyoo-CHEE-tel-na-ya sta-TYAH vba-LAHN-se)*	closing entry
заключительная цена	*(za-klyoo-CHEE-tel-na-ya tse-NAH)*	closing price
закон	*(za-KON)*	law
закон о патентах	*(za-KON a pa-TEN-takh)*	patent law

закон о районировании	*(za-KON a ray-a-NEE-ra-va-nee-ye)*	zoning law
закон о труде	*(za-KON a troo-DEH)*	labor law
закон об исковой давности	*(za-KON ab ees-ka-VOY DAHV-na-stee)*	statute of limitations
закон сокращающихся доходов	*(za-KON sa-kra-SHCHAH-yoo-shcheekh-sa da-KHOH-daf)*	law of diminishing returns
законное платёжное средство	*(za-KON-na-ye pla-TYOZH-na-ye SRET-stva)*	legal tender
законный держатель	*(za-KON-nee der-ZHAH-tel)*	holder in due course
законодательный акт	*(za-ka-na-DAH-tel-nee ahkt)*	statute
законодательство	*(za-ka-na-DAH-tel-stva)*	legislation
закрытый счёт	*(za-KREE-tee shchyoht)*	closed account
закупать/закупить за лучшую цену	*(za-koo-PAHT/za-koo-PEEHT za LOOCH-shoo-yoo TSEH-noo)*	buy at best (v)
закупать/закупить при закрытии	*(za-koo-PAHT/za-koo-PEEHT pree za-KREE-tee-ee)*	buy on close (v)
закупать/закупить при открытии	*(za-koo-PAHT/za-koo-PEEHT pree at-KREE-tee-ee)*	buy on opening (v)
зал для совещаний	*(zahl dla sa-ve-SHCHAH-neey)*	boardroom
залог	*(za-LOK)*	encumbrance, pledge
залог движимого имущества	*(za-LOK DVEE-zhe-ma-va ee-MOO-shchest-va)*	chattel mortgage
залоговая поддержка	*(za-LOH-ga-va-ya pad-DEHRSH-ka)*	backup bonds
залоговое право	*(za-LOH-ga-va-ye PRAH-va)*	lien
залоговое право продавца	*(za-LOH-ga-va-ye PRAH-va pra-daf-TSAH)*	vendor's lien
заменимые товары	*(za-me-NEE-mee-ye ta-VAH-ree)*	fungible goods
заменяющее топливо	*(za-me-NYAH-yoo-shchee-ye TOP-lee-va)*	substitute fuel

3

заместитель менеджера	*(za-mes-TEE-tel MEH-ned-zhe-ra)*	deputy manager
заместитель председателя	*(za-mes-TEE-tel pret-se-DAH-te-lya)*	deputy chairman
замораживание зарплаты	*(za-ma-RAH-zhee-va-nee-ye zar-PLAH-tee)*	wage freeze
замораживание фондов	*(za-ma-RAH-zhee-va-nee-ye FON-daf)*	blockage of funds
замороженные активы	*(za-ma-ROH-zhen-nee-ye ak-TEE-vee)*	frozen assets
замша	*(ZAHM-sha)*	suede
замшевая куртка	*(ZAHM-she-va-ya KOOHRT-ka)*	suede jacket
за наличный расчет	*(za na-LEECH-nee ra-SHCHYOHT)*	cash-flow
за ночь	*(za noch)*	overnight
занятие	*(za-NYAH-tee-ye)*	occupation
запальная свеча	*(za-PAHL-na-ya sve-CHAH)*	spark plug
запас	*(za-PAHS)*	inventory
запас готовых изделий	*(za-PAHS ga-TOH-veekh eez-DEH-leey)*	finished goods inventory
запас денег	*(za-PAHS DEH-nek)*	money supply
запас товаров	*(za-PAHS ta-VAH-raf)*	stock-in-trade
запасная шина	*(za-pas-NAH-ya SHEE-na)*	spare tire
запасной контроль	*(za-pas-NOY kan-TROL)*	inventory control
запасы	*(za-PAH-see)*	stock (inventory)
запасы, извлекаемые первичными методами разработки месторождения	*(za-PAH-see eez-vle-KAH-ye-mee-ye per-VEECH-nee-mee MEH-ta-da-mee raz-ra-BOT-kee mes-ta-razh-DEH-nee-ya)*	primary reserves
запатентованный процесс	*(za-pa-ten-TOH-van-nee pra-TSESS)*	patented process
записная книжка	*(za-pees-NAH-ya KNEEZH-ka)*	pocketbook
запись	*(ZAH-pees)*	record
запись в дебет счёта	*(ZAH-pees VDEH-beet SHCHYOH-ta)*	debit entry

3

запись о поступлении наличности	*(ZAH-pees a pa-stoop-LEH-nee-ye na-LEECH-na-stee)*	entry, cash
запланированное устаревание	*(za-plah-NEE-ra-van-na-ye oo-sta-re-VAH-nee-ye)*	planned obsolescence
заплатить цену	*(za-PLAH-teet tse-NOO)*	meet the price (v)
запоминать/ запомнить	*(za-pa-mee-NAHT/za-POM-neet)*	store (computer)
запоминающее устройство (ЗУ)	*(za-pa-mee-NAH-yoo-shchee-ye oost-ROY-stva [ZEH-OO])*	computer memory (storage)
запоминающее устройство (ЗУ)	*(za-pa-mee-NAH-yoo-shchee-ye oost-ROY-stva (ZEH-OO)*	memory
запрашиваемая цена	*(za-PRAH-shee-va-ye-ma-ya tse-NAH)*	asked price
запрет	*(zap-RET)*	embargo
запрещённые товары	*(za-pre-SHCHYOH-nee-ye ta-VAH-ree)*	prohibited goods
запродажа будущей продукции	*(za-pra-DAH-zha BOO-doo-shchey pra-DOOK-tsee-ee)*	forward contract
запрос	*(zap-ROS)*	inquiry
запчасти	*(zap-CHAHS-tee)*	replacement parts
заработная плата	*(ZAH-ra-bat-na-ya PLAH-ta)*	wage
заработная плата производственных рабочих	*(ZAH-ra-bat-na-ya PLAH-ta pra-eez-VOT-stven-nikh ra-BOH-chekh)*	direct labor (accounting)
заработок	*(ZAH-ra-ba-tak)*	earnings
заранее изготовленный	*(za-RAH-nee-ye eez-ga-TOV-len-nee)*	prefabricated
зарегистрированная торговая марка	*(za-re-ghee-STREE-ra-van-na-ya tar-GOH-va-ya MAHR-ka)*	registered trade mark
зарегистрированный представитель	*(za-re-ghee-STREE-ra-van-nnee pret-sta-VEE-tel)*	registered representative
зарегистрированный чек	*(za-re-ghee-STREE-ra-van-nee chek)*	registered check
зарплата	*(zar-PLAH-ta)*	wages

зарплата после вычетов	*(zar-PLAH-ta POS-le VEE-shchee-taf)*	take-home pay
зарплата управленческого персонала	*(zar-PLAH-ta oop-rav-LEN-ches-ka-ga per-sa-NAH-la)*	management fee
засоление	*(za-sa-LEH-nee-ye)*	alkalization
застой	*(za-STOY)*	deadlock
засуха	*(ZAH-soo-kha)*	drought
затрата	*(za-TRAH-ta)*	outlay
затраты на капитал	*(za-TRAH-tee na ka-pee-TAHL)*	cost of capital
затраты на проведение поисково-разведочных работ	*(za-TRAH-tee na pra-ve-DEH-nee-ye POH-ees-ka-va-raz-VEH-dach-nikh ra-BOT)*	exploratory costs
затраты на факторы производства	*(za-TRAH-tee na FAHK-ta-ree pra-eez-VOT-stva)*	cost, factor
затягивание сроков поставки	*(za-TYAH-ghee-va-nee-ye SROH-kaf pa-STAHF-kee)*	deferred deliveries
защита от опциона покупателя	*(za-SHCHEE-ta at ap-tsee-OH-na pa-koo-PAH-te-lya)*	call protection
защитная лесополоса	*(za-SHCHEET-na-ya LEH-sa-pa-la-SAH)*	wind-break
защищённый от записи	*(za-shchee-SHCHYON-nee ad-ZAH-pee-see)*	write-protected
заявка на патент	*(za-YAHF-ka na pa-TENT)*	patent application
звук	*(zvook)*	sound
земельная реформа	*(ze-MEHL-na-ya re-FOHR-ma)*	land reform
земельный участок	*(ze-MEHL-nee oo-CHAHS-tak)*	acreage allotment
землевладелец	*(zem-le-vla-DEH-lets)*	landowner
земля	*(zem-LYAH)*	land
зерно	*(zer-NOH)*	grain
зернохранилище	*(zer-na-khra-NEE-lee-shche)*	granary
зима	*(zee-MAH)*	winter

змеевик	*(zme-ye-VEEK)*	coil
змеиная кожа	*(zme-EE-na-ya KOH-zha)*	snakeskin
знак, символ	*(znahk, SEEM-val)*	character
значение	*(zna-CHEH-nee-ye)*	implication (conclusion)
зола	*(za-LAH)*	ash (residue)
золотая оговорка	*(za-la-TAH-ya a-ga-VOHR-ka)*	gold clause
золотые запасы	*(za-la-TEE-ye za-PAH-see)*	gold reserves
зольность	*(ZOL-nast)*	ash content
зона	*(ZOH-na)*	zone
зона таможенного досмотра	*(ZOH-na tea-MOH-zhen-na-va da-SMOT-ra)*	bond areas
ЗУ с произволь-ным порядком выборки	*(ZEH-OO spra-eez-VOL-nim pa-RYAHT-kam VEE-bar-kee)*	random access memory (RAM)

И

ИБМ-совмести-мый	*(AHY-BEE-EM-sav-me-STEE-mee)*	IBM compatible
идея маркетинга	*(ee-DEH-ya mar-KEH-teen-ga)*	marketing concept
избиратель-гастролёр	*(eez-bee-RAH-tel-gas-tra-LYOHR)*	floater (in elections)
избыточное снаб-жение	*(eez-BEE-tach-na-ye snab-ZHEH-nee-ye)*	oversupply
известность	*(eez-VEST-nast)*	publicity
известняк	*(eez-ves-NYAHK)*	limestone
известь	*(EEZ-vest)*	lime (soil)
извещение о доставке	*(eez-ve-SHCHEH-nee-ye a da-STAHF-ke)*	delivery notice
извлекаемые запасы	*(eez-vle-KAH-ye-mee-ye za-PAH-see)*	recoverable reserves
издание	*(eez-DAH-nee-ye)*	edition
издатель	*(eez-DAH-tel)*	publisher
издательство	*(eez-DAH-tel-stva)*	publishing house
изделие	*(eez-DEH-lee-ye)*	item (product)
издержки	*(eez-DEHRSH-kee)*	expenditure

издержки монта-жа	*(eez-DEHRSH-kee man-ta-ZHA)*	set-up costs
издержки на погрузку	*(eez-DEHRSH-kee na pa-GROOS-koo)*	shipping expenses
издержки произ-водства	*(eez-DEHRSH-kee pra-eez-VOT-stva)*	production costs
издержки произ-водства на еди-ницу	*(eez-DEHRSH-kee pra-eez-VOT-stva na ye-dee-NEE-tsoo)*	unit costs
издержки распре-деления	*(eez-DEHRSH-kee ras-pre-de-LEH-nee-ya)*	distribution costs
излишек	*(eez-LEE-shek)*	overage
излишки капитала	*(eez-LEESH-kee ka-pee-TAH-la)*	capital surplus
излишние товары	*(eez-LEESH-nee-ye ta-VAH-ree)*	surplus goods
излишний запас	*(eez-LEESH-nee za-PAHS)*	overstock
изложница	*(eez-LOZH-nee-tsa)*	ingot mold
изменение	*(eez-me-NEH-nee-ye)*	amendment, alteration
изменение погра-ничных пошлин	*(eez-me-NEH-nee-ye pa-gra-NEECH-nikh POSH-leen)*	border tax adjustment
изменчивый рынок	*(eez-MEHN-chee-vee REE-nak)*	volatile market
изменять/изме-нить	*(eez-me-NYAHT/eez-me-NEET)*	adjust, amend (v)
измерять/изме-рить	*(eez-me-RYAHT/eez-MEH-reet)*	measure (v)
изолятор	*(ee-za-LYAH-tar)*	insulator
изотоп	*(ee-za-TOP)*	isotope
изучение возмож-ностей рынка	*(ee-zoo-CHEH-nee-ye vaz-MOZH-na-stey RIN-ka)*	market research
изучение мотиви-ровки	*(ee-zoo-CHEH-nee-ye ma-tee-VEE-rav-kee)*	motivation study
изучение запаса, прироста и отпада насаж-дений	*(ee-zoo-CHEH-nee-ye za-PAH-sa, pree-ROS-ta ee at-PAH-da na-sazh-DEH-neey)*	management-volume inventory
изъятие имуще-ства	*(eez-YAH-tee-ye ee-MOO-shche-stva)*	repossession
имение	*(ee-MEH-nee-ye)*	estate (decedent)

именные ценные бумаги	*(ee-men-NEE-ye TSEN-nee-ye boo-MAH-ghee)*	registered securities
иметь полномочие	*(ee-MET pal-na-MOH-chee-ye)*	authority, to have (v)
имеющий обратную силу	*(ee-MEH-yoo-shchee ab-RAHT-noo-yoo SEE-loo)*	retroactive
имея больший капитал, чем нужно	*(ee-MEH-ya BOL-shee ka-pee-TAHL chem NOOZH-na)*	overcapitalization
импорт	*(EEM-part)*	import
импортная квота	*(EEM-part-na-ya KVOH-ta)*	import quota
импортная лицензия	*(EEM-part-na-ya lee-TSEN-zee-ya)*	import license
импортная пошлина	*(EEM-part-na-ya POSH-lee-na)*	import duty
импортные распоряжения	*(EEM-part-nee-ye ras-pa-rya-ZHEH-nee-ya)*	import regulations
импортный взнос	*(EEM-part-nee vznos)*	import deposits
импортный тариф	*(EEM-part-nee ta-REEF)*	import tariff
имущественное право (доля)	*(ee-MOO-shchest-ven-na-ye PRAH-va [DOH-lya])*	interest (share)
имущество	*(ee-MOO-shchest-va)*	estate (property)
инвентарный контроль	*(een-ven-TAHR-nee kan-TROL)*	inventory control
инвестированный капитал	*(een-ves-TEE-ra-van-nee ka-pee-TAHL)*	invested capital
инвестиционная компания	*(een-ve-stee-tsee-ON-na-ya kam-PAH-nee-ya)*	investment company
инвестиционное качество	*(een-ve-stee-tsee-ON-na-ye KAH-chest-va)*	investment grade
инвестиционный банк	*(een-ve-stee-tsee-ON-nee bahnk)*	investment bank
инвестиционный кредит	*(een-ve-stee-tsee-ON-nee kre-DEET)*	investment credit
инвестиционный траст	*(een-ve-stee-tsee-ON-nee trahst)*	investment trust
инвестор-учреждение	*(een-VES-tar-ooch-rezh-DEH-nee-ye)*	institutional investor
индекс	*(EEN-deks)*	index
индекс курсов акций	*(EEN-deks KOOHR-saf AHK-tseey)*	stock index

И

индекс потреби-тельских цен	*(EEN-deks pat-re-BEE-tel-skeekh tsen)*	consumer price index
индекс роста	*(EEN-deks ROS-ta)*	growth index
индекс рынка	*(EEN-deks RIN-ka)*	market index
индекс цен	*(EEN-deks tsen)*	price index
индексация	*(een-dek-SAH-tsee-ya)*	indexing
индемнитет (гарантия от убытков)	*(een-dem-nee-TET [ga-RAHN-tee-ya at oo-BIT-kaf])*	indemnity
индоссамент	*(een-da-SSAH-ment)*	endorsement
индоссат	*(een-da-SSAHT)*	endorsee
индукционная печь	*(een-dook-tsee-ON-na-ya pech)*	induction furnace
индукция	*(een-DOOK-tsee-ya)*	induction
инжектор	*(een-ZHEK-tar)*	injector
инженер	*(een-zhe-NEHR)*	engineer
инженерное про-ектирование	*(een-zhe-NEHR-na-ye pra-yek-TEE-ra-va-nee-ye)*	design engineering
инкассо	*(een-KAHS-soh)*	cash entry
иностранная валюта	*(ee-na-STRAHN-na-ya va-LYOO-ta)*	foreign currency (exchange)
иностранная налоговая скид-ка	*(ee-na-STRAHN-na-ya na-LOH-ga-va-ya SKEET-ka)*	foreign tax credit
иностранная цен-ная бумага	*(ee-na-STRAHN-na-ya TSEN-na-ya boo-MAH-ga)*	foreign security
иностранное акционерное общество	*(ee-na-STRAHN-na-ye ak-tsee-a-NEHR-na-ye OP-shche-stva)*	foreign corporation
иностранное общество акци-онеров	*(ee-na-STRAHN-na-ye OP-shche-stva ak-tsee-a-NEH-raf)*	alien corporation
иностранный век-сель	*(ee-na-STRAHN-nee VEK-sel)*	foreign bill of exchange
иностранный долг	*(ee-na-STRAHN-nee dolk)*	foreign debt
инспектор	*(een-SPEK-tar)*	inspector
инсектицид	*(een-sek-tee-TSIT)*	insecticide
интегральная схема (ИС)	*(een-te-GRAHL-na-ya SKHEH-ma [EES])*	integrated circuit (IC)

Интеловский	*(EEN-te-lof-skee)*	Intel-base
интервью	*(een-tehr-VYOO)*	interview (media)
интерес, не оформленный окончательно	*(een-te-RES ne-a-FOHR-mlen-nee a-kan-CHAH-tel-na)*	inchoate interest
инфляционный	*(een-fla-tsee-ON-nee)*	inflationary
инфляция	*(een-FLYAH-tsee-ya)*	inflation
информационный бюллетень	*(een-far-ma-tsee-ON-nee byoo-le-TEN)*	newsletter
информировать	*(een-far-MEE-ra-vat)*	keep posted (v)
инфраструктура	*(een-fra-strook-TOO-ra)*	infrastructure
инъекция	*(een-YEK-tsee-ya)*	injection
ипотека	*(ee-pa-TEH-ka)*	hypothecation, mortgage
ипотека за покупку	*(ee-pa-TEH-ka za pa-KOOP-koo)*	purchase money mortgage
ипотечный банк	*(ee-pa-TECH-nee bahnk)*	mortgage bank
иск о мошенничестве	*(eesk a ma-SHEN-nee-chest-ve)*	penalty-fraud action
исключительные права	*(ees-kloo-CHEE-tel-nee-ye pra-VAH)*	sole rights
исключительный агент	*(ees-kloo-CHEE-tel-nee a-GHENT)*	sole agent
исключительный представитель	*(ees-kloo-CHEE-tel-nee pret-sta-VEE-tel)*	exclusive representative
искусственно поддерживаемая цена	*(ees-KOOS-stven-na pad-DEHR-zhee-va-ye-ma-ya tse-NAH)*	pegged price
искусственное поддержание цены	*(ees-KOOS-stven-na-ye pad-DEHR-zha-nee-ye tse-NEE)*	pegging
искусственные волокна	*(ees-KOOS-stven-nee-ye va-LOK-na)*	manmade fibers
искусственный интеллект	*(ees-KOOS-stven-nee een-tel-LEKT)*	artificial intelligence
искусство	*(ees-KOOS-stva)*	art
испарение	*(ees-pa-REH-nee-ye)*	evaporation
исполнитель	*(ees-pal-NEE-tel)*	executive
исполнитель на счету	*(ees-pal-NEE-tel na shche-TOO)*	account executive

И

исполнительный директор	*(ees-pal-NEE-tel-nee dee-REK-tar)*	chief executive officer (CEO), executive director
исполнительный комитет	*(ees-pal-NEE-tel-nee ka-mee-TET)*	executive committee
исправленная ставка	*(ees-PRAHV-len-na-ya STAHF-ka)*	adjusted rate
исправленная статья в балансе	*(ees-PRAHV-len-na-ya sta-TYAH vba-LAHN-se)*	adjusted entry
исправленная цена СИФ	*(ees-PRAHV-len-na-ya tse-NAH seef)*	adjusted CIF price
исправленный валовой доход	*(ees-PRAHV-len-nee va-la-VOY da-KHOT)*	adjusted gross income
исправлять/ исправить	*(ees-prav-LYAHT/ees-PRAH-veet)*	adjust (v) (correct)
испытание	*(ees-pee-TAH-nee-ye)*	assay
испытывать/ испытать	*(ees-PEE-tee-vat/ees-pee-TAHT)*	assay (v)
исследование	*(ees-SLEH-da-va-nee-ye)*	research
исследование по рекламе	*(ees-SLEH-da-va-nee-ye pa rek-LAH-me)*	advertising research
истекать кровью	*(ees-te-KAHT KROH-vyoo)*	bleed (v)
источники энергии	*(ees-TOCH-nee-kee e-NEHR-ghee-ee)*	energy resources
истощение	*(ees-ta-SHCHEH-nee-ye)*	attrition
истребитель «МиГ»	*(ees-tre-BEE-tel mig)*	Mig fighter
исчисление себестоимости	*(ees-chee-SLEE-nee-ye se-be-STOH-ee-mas-tee)*	cost accounting

---

Й

йод	*(yot)*	iodine

К

кабель	*(KAH-bel)*	cable
кабельное телевидение	*(KAH-bel-na-ye te-le-VEE-de-nee-ye)*	cable television

кабина летчика	*(ka-BEE-na LYOT-chee-ka)*	cockpit
кадры	*(ka-DREE)*	personnel, staff
казначей	*(kaz-na-CHEY)*	treasurer
казначейские векселя	*(kaz-na-CHEY-skee-ye vek-seh-LYAH)*	treasury bills
казначейские ноты	*(kaz-na-CHEY-skee-ye NOH-tee)*	treasury notes
казначейские облигации	*(kaz-na-CHEY-skee-ye ab-lee-GAH-tsee-ee)*	treasury bonds
как можно скорее	*(kak MOZH-na ska-REH-ye)*	as soon as possible
калькулятор	*(kal-koo-LYAH-tar)*	calculator
калькуляция издержек производства	*(kal-koo-LYAH-tsee-ya eez-DEHR-zhek pra-eez-VOT-stva)*	accounting, cost
калькуляция себестоимости в долларах	*(kal-koo-LYAH-tsee-ya se-be-STOH-ee-ma-stee VDOL-la-rakh)*	dollar cost averaging
калькуляция стоимости с учётом убытков	*(kal-koo-LYAH-tsee-ya STOH-ee-ma-stee soo-CHYOH-tam oo-BEET-kaf)*	absorption costing
камбий	*(KAHM-bee)*	cambium
канал	*(ka-NAHL)*	channel
каналы распределения	*(ka-NAH-lee ras-pre-de-LEH-nee-ya)*	distribution, channels of
капельное орошение	*(KAH-pel-na-ye a-ra-SHEH-nee-ye)*	drip irrigation
капитал	*(ka-pee-TAHL)*	principal (capital)
капитализация	*(ka-pee-ta-lee-ZAH-tsee-ya)*	capitalization
капитализм	*(ka-pee-ta-LEEZM)*	capitalism
капиталовложение	*(ka-pee-TAH-la-vla-ZHEH-nee-ye)*	investment
капиталовложение в бюджете	*(ka-pee-TAH-la-vla-ZHEH-nee-ya vbyood-ZHEH-te)*	investment budget
капиталоёмкий	*(ka-pee-TAH-la-YOM-kee)*	capital-intensive
капитальный бюджет	*(ka-pee-TAHL-nee byood-ZHET)*	budget, capital
капитель	*(ka-pee-TEL)*	small capital
капли от кашля	*(KAHP-lee at KAHSH-lya)*	cough drop
капля	*(KAHP-lya)*	drop

капуста	(ka-POOS-ta)	cabbage
каракуль	(ka-RAH-kool)	astrakhan
карбюратор	(kar-byoo-RAH-tar)	carburetor
картель	(kar-TEL)	cartel
картофель	(kar-TOH-fel)	potato (es)
кассета	(kas-SEH-ta)	cassette
кассир	(kas-SEEHR)	paymaster, teller
кассовая книга	(KAHS-sa-va-ya KNEE-ga)	cash book
катализатор	(ka-ta-lee-ZAH-tar)	catalyst
катод	(ka-TOT)	cathode
КАФ (стоимость и фрахт)	(kaf [STOH-ee-mast ee frahkht])	cost and freight
качественные товары	(KAH-chest-ven-nee-ye ta-VAH-ree)	quality goods
кашлять	(KAHSH-lyat)	cough (v)
квази-деньги (почти деньги)	(KVAH-zee-DEN-ghee [pach-TEE DEN-ghee])	near money
квалификация	(kva-lee-fee-KAH-tsee-ya)	qualification
квалифицирован-ный рабочий	(kva-lee-fee-TSEE-ra-van-nee ra-BOH-chee)	journeyman
квалифицирован-ный труд	(kva-lee-fee-TSEE-ra-van-nee troot)	skilled labor
квитанция	(kvee-TAHN-tsee-ya)	receipt (paper)
кворум	(KVOH-room)	quorum
квота	(KVOH-ta)	quota
кедр	(KEDR)	cedar
кизяк	(kee-ZYAHK)	dung
киловатт	(kee-la-VAHT)	kilowatt
килобайт	(kee-la-BAHYT)	kilobyte
кипа	(KEE-pa)	bale
кислая (высоко-сернистая) нефть	(KEES-la-ya [vee-SOH-ka-ser-NEES-ta-ya] neft)	sour crude oil
кислая почва	(KEES-la-ya POCH-va)	acidic (soil)
кислота	(kees-la-TAH)	acid
кислотоустойчи-вый	(kees-LOH-ta-oos-TOY-che-vee)	acid-tolerant

К

кислые отходы	*(KEES-lee-ye at-KHOH-dee)*	acid spoil
кислый (высоко-сернистый) газ	*(KEES-lee [vee-SOH-ka-ser-NEES-tee] gahs)*	sour gas
клавиатура	*(kla-vee-a-TOO-ra)*	keyboard
клавиша	*(KLAH-vee-sha)*	key
клавиша пробела	*(KLAH-vee-sha pra-BEH-la)*	space-bar
клапан	*(KLAH-pan)*	valve
классификация облигаций	*(klas-see-fee-KAH-tsee-ya ab-lee-GAH-tseey)*	bond rating
клевер	*(KLEH-ver)*	clover
клён	*(klyon)*	maple
клиент	*(klee-YENT)*	client
ключевые вывозы	*(klyoo-che-VEE-ye VEE-va-zee)*	key exports
книга	*(KNEE-ga)*	book
коаксиальный кабель	*(ka-ak-see-AHL-nee KAH-bel)*	coaxial cable
кобура	*(ka-boo-RAH)*	holster
кобыла	*(ka-BEE-la)*	mare
ковкость	*(KOF-kast)*	mallability
кодекс законов о труде	*(KOH-deks za-KOH-naf a troo-DEH)*	labor code
кодицила	*(ka-dee-TSEE-la)*	codicil
кожа	*(KOH-zha)*	leather
кожа ящерицы	*(KOH-zha YAH-shche-ree-tsee)*	lizard (skin)
кожаная куртка	*(KOH-zha-na-ya KOOHRT-ka)*	leather jacket
кожаный ручной чемоданчик (кейс)	*(KOH-zha-nee rooch-NOY che-ma-DAHN-cheek [keis])*	attache case
кожевенный завод	*(ka-ZHEH-ven-nee za-VOT)*	tannery
кожевенный товар	*(ka-ZHEH-ven-nee ta-VAHR)*	leather goods
коза	*(ka-ZAH)*	goat (f)
козёл	*(ka-ZYOL)*	goat (m)
коленчатый вал	*(ka-LEN-cha-tee val)*	crankshaft

К

колесо	*(ka-le-SOH)*	wheel
количество	*(ka-LEE-chest-va)*	quantity
коллективное соглашение	*(kal-lek-TEEV-na-ye sag-la-SHEH-nee-ye)*	collective agreement
колодец	*(ka-LOH-dets)*	well
колонка	*(ka-LON-ka)*	column
колонка руля	*(ka-LON-ka roo-LYAH)*	steering column
колхоз	*(kal-KHOS)*	collective farm
кольца	*(KOL-tsa)*	rings
комбинация	*(kam-bee-NAH-tsee-ya)*	combination
комбинированная пошлина	*(kam-bee-NEE-ra-van-na-ya POSH-lee-na)*	combination duty
комиссионные	*(ka-mees-see-ON-nee-ye)*	commission (fee)
коммерсант	*(ka-mer-SANT)*	merchant
коммерция	*(kam-MEHR-tsee-ya)*	commerce
коммерческая деятельность	*(kam-MEHR-ches-ka-ya DEH-ya-tel-nast)*	business activity
коммерческая реклама	*(kam-MEHR-ches-ka-ya rek-LAH-ma)*	commercial ad
коммерческие запасы	*(kam-MEHR-ches-kee-ye za-PAH-see)*	useable commercial inventories
коммерческий банк	*(kam-MEHR-ches-kee bahnk)*	commercial bank
коммерческий бюджет	*(kam-MEHR-ches-kee byood-ZHET)*	sales budget
коммерческий счёт	*(kam-MEHR-ches-kee shchyoht)*	commercial invoice
коммерческое качество	*(kam-MEHR-ches-ka-ye KAH-chest-va)*	commercial grade
коммивояжер	*(koh-mee-va-ya-ZHOHR)*	traveling salesman
коммунальный газ	*(kam-moo-NAHL-nee gahs)*	town gas
коммунальные услуги	*(kam-moo-NAHL-nee-ye oos-LOO-ghee)*	utility
компактный зву-кодиск	*(kam-PAHKT-nee zvoo-ka-DEESK)*	compact disk
компания	*(kam-PAH-nee-ya)*	company

K

компания «Интел»	*(kam-PAH-nee-ya EEN-tel)*	Intel
компания «ИБМ»	*(kam-PAH-nee-ya AY-BEE-EM)*	IBM
компания «Аппэл»	*(kam-PAH-nee-ya apple)*	Apple
компания «ДЭК»	*(kam-PAH-nee-ya dek)*	DEC
компания-учредитель	*(kam-PAH-nee-ya-ooch-re-DEE-tel)*	parent company
компенсационная пошлина	*(kam-pen-sa-tsee-ON-na-ya POSH-lee-na)*	countervailing duty
компенсационная торговля	*(kam-pen-sa-tsee-ON-na-ya tar-GOV-la)*	compensation trade
компенсационный баланс	*(kam-pen-sa-tsee-ON-nee ba-LAHNS)*	compensating balance
компенсация	*(kam-pen-SAH-tsee-ya)*	compensation
компилятор	*(kam-PEE-lya-tar)*	compiler
комплексная система управления	*(KOM-pleks-na-ya sees-TEH-ma oop-rav-LEH-nee-ya)*	integrated management system
комплект образцов	*(kam-PLEKT ab-ras-TSOF)*	matched samples
комплект шрифта	*(kam-PLEKT SHREEF-ta)*	font
комплектное производство	*(kam-PLEKT-na-ye pra-eez-VOT-stva)*	modular production
композиция	*(kam-pa-ZEE-tsee-ya)*	composition
компонент	*(kam-pa-NENT)*	component
компьютер	*(kam-PYOO-ter)*	computer
компьютерная программа	*(kam-PYOO-ter-na-ya pra-GRAHM-ma)*	computer program
компьютерный ввод	*(kam-PYOO-ter-nee vvot)*	computer input
компьютерный вывод	*(kam-PYOO-ter-nee VEE-vat)*	computer output
компьютерный терминал	*(kam-PYOO-ter-nee ter-mee-NAHL)*	computer terminal
компьютерный центр	*(kam-PYOO-ter-nee tsentr)*	computer center
конвейер	*(kan-VEH-yer)*	assembly/production line, conveyor

К

конвейерная лента	*(kan-VEH-yehr-na-ya LEN-ta)*	conveyor belt
конверсия валюты	*(kan-VEHR-see-ya va-LYOO-tee)*	currency conversion
конверсия (оборонная)	*(kan-VEHR-see-ya [a-ba-RON-na-ya])*	defense conversion
конгломерат	*(kan-gla-me-RAHT)*	conglomerate
конденсат	*(kan-den-SAHT)*	condensate
конденсатор	*(kan-den-SAH-tar)*	capacitor
конденсатор	*(kan-den-SAH-tar)*	condenser
конец года	*(ka-NETS GOH-da)*	year-end
конец срока	*(ka-NETS SROH-ka)*	end of period
конечная нефтеотдача	*(ka-NECH-na-ya NEF-te-at-DAH-cha)*	final oil recovery
конечный продукт	*(ka-NECH-nee pra-DOOKT)*	end product
конечные продукты	*(ka-NECH-nee-ye pra-DOOK-tee)*	finished products
конкурент	*(kan-koo-RENT)*	competitor
конкурентное преимущество	*(kan-koo-RENT-na-ye pre-ee-MOO-shchest-va)*	competitive advantage
конкурентоспособная цена	*(kan-koo-REN-ta-spa-SOHB-na-ya tse-NAH)*	competitive price
конкурс на выполнение работ	*(KON-koors na vee-pal-NEH-nee-ye ra-BOT)*	invitation to bid
коносамент	*(ka-na-sa-MENT)*	bill of lading
консигнатор	*(kan-seeg-NAH-tar)*	consignee
консигнация	*(kan-seeg-NAH-tsee-ya)*	consignment
консервирование	*(kan-ser-VEE-ra-va-nee-ye)*	canning
консорциум	*(kan-SOHR-tsee-oom)*	consortium
конструирование	*(kan-stroo-EE-ra-va-nee-ye)*	civil engineering
конструктор	*(kan-STROOK-tar)*	designer
консультант	*(kan-sool-TAHNT)*	consultant
консультант по менеджменту	*(kan-sool-TAHNT pa MEH-nedzh-men-too)*	management consultant
контейнер	*(kan-TEY-nehr)*	container
контемпоризация	*(kan-tem-pa-ree-ZAH-tsee-ya)*	leads and lags

К

контракт с «твер-дым обязатель-ством»	*(kan-TRAHKT STVYOHR-dim a-bya-ZAH-tel-stvam)*	fixed-commitment contract
контрактная нефть	*(kan-TRAHKT-na-ya neft)*	contract crude oil
контрафаксия	*(kan-tra-FAHK-see-ya)*	counterfeiting (goods)
контрейлерные услуги	*(kan-TREY-ler-nee-ye oos-LOO-ghee)*	piggyback service
контролёр	*(kan-tra-LYOHR)*	comptroller, controller
контролируемые расходы	*(kant-ra-LEE-roo-ye-mee-ye ras-KHOH-dee)*	managed costs
контроль качества	*(kan-TROL KAH-chest-va)*	quality control
контроль над рас-ходами	*(kan-TROL nad ras-KHOH-da-mee)*	cost control
контроль стресса	*(kan-TROL STRES-sa)*	stress management
контрольный пакет акций	*(kan-TROL-nee pa-KET AHK-tseey)*	controlling interest
конференц-зал	*(kan-fe-RENTS-ZAHL)*	conference room
конфиденциаль-ный	*(kan-fee-den-tsee-AHL-nee)*	confidential
концерн	*(kan-TSEHRN)*	concern (business), consortium
концентрирование	*(kan-tsen-TREE-ra-va-nee-ye)*	concentration
кооператив	*(ka-a-pe-ra-TEEF)*	cooperative
копировать	*(ka-PEE-ra-vat)*	copy (v)
кора	*(ka-RAH)*	bark
корм	*(kohrm)*	feed
кормилец семьи	*(kohr-MEE-lets se-MEE)*	wage corner
коробка для кос-метики	*(ka-ROP-ka dla kas-MEH-tee-kee)*	makeup case
коробка передач	*(ka-ROP-ka pe-re-DAHCH)*	gearshift
корова	*(ka-ROH-va)*	cow
короткая позиция	*(ka-ROT-ka-ya pa-ZEE-tsee-ya)*	short position
короткие волны	*(ka-ROT-kee-ye VOL-nee)*	short waves

корпорация по оказанию общественных услуг	*(kar-pa-RAH-tsee-ya pa a-ka-ZAH-nee-yoo ap-SHCHEST-ven-nikh oos-LOOK)*	quasi-public company
корректурная гранка	*(kar-rek-TOOHR-na-ya GRAHN-ka)*	galley proof
корректурное чтение	*(kar-rek-TOOHR-na-ye CHTEH-nee-ye)*	proofreading
корреспондентский банк	*(kar-res-pan-DENT-skee bahnk)*	correspondent bank
коса	*(ka-SAH)*	scythe
косвенные затраты	*(KOS-ven-nee-ye za-TRAH-tee)*	indirect expenses
косвенные издержки	*(KOS-ven-nee-ye eez-DEHRSH-kee)*	indirect costs
косвенные налоги	*(KOS-ven-nee-ye na-LOH-ghee)*	indirect taxes
косвенные расходы	*(KOS-ven-nee-ye ras-KHOH-dee)*	cost, indirect
косвенные трудовые расходы	*(KOS-ven-nee-ye troo-da-VEE-ye ras-KHOH-dee)*	indirect labor expenses
космический аппарат (КА)	*(kas-MEE-ches-kee ap-pa-RAHT [KAH-AH])*	spacecraft
космический зонд	*(kas-MEE-ches-kee zont)*	probe
космический скафандр	*(kas-MEE-ches-kee ska-FAHNDR)*	space-suit
космодром	*(kas-ma-DROM)*	cosmodrome
космос	*(KOS-mas)*	space
котельное топливо, мазут	*(ka-TEL-na-ye TOP-lee-va, ma-ZOOT)*	fuel oil
котировка	*(ka-tee-ROF-ka)*	quotation (stock market)
котировка вторичного сырья	*(ka-tee-ROF-ka fta-REECH-na-va SIHR-ya)*	over-the-counter quotation
коэффициент	*(ka-ef-fee-tsee-ENT)*	ratio
коэффициент безопасности	*(ka-ef-fee-tsee-ENT be-za-PAHS-na-stee)*	margin of safety
коэффициент извлечения	*(ka-ef-fee-tsee-ENT eez-vle-CHEH-nee-ya)*	extraction ratio
коэффициент ликвидности	*(ka-ef-fee-tsee-ENT leek-VEED-na-stee)*	acid-test (liquidity) ratio

К

коэффициент окупаемости капиталовложений	*(ka-ef-fee-tsee-ENT a-koo-PAH-ee-mas-tee ka-pee-TAH-la-vla-ZHEH-neey)*	earnings/price ratio
коэффициент покрытия	*(ka-ef-fee-tsee-ENT pa-KREE-tee-ya)*	cover ratio
коэффициент полезного действия	*(ka-ef-fee-tsee-ENT pa-LEZ-na-va DEY-stvee-ya)*	capital-output ratio
коэффициент результативности	*(ka-ef-fee-tsee-ENT re-zool-ta-TEEV-na-stee)*	success ratio
коэффициент рентабельности	*(ka-ef-fee-tsee-ENT ren-TAH-bel-na-stee)*	profit margin (factor)
коэффициент энергоотдачи	*(ka-ef-fee-tsee-ENT e-NEHR-ga-ad-DAH-chee)*	energy return ratio
коэффициенты баланса	*(ka-ef-fee-tsee-EN-tee ba-LAHN-sa)*	balance ratios
крайние цены	*(KRAHY-nee-ye TSEH-nee)*	marginal price
крайний срок	*(KRAHY-nee srok)*	deadline
красить	*(KRAH-seet)*	dye (v)
краска	*(KRAHS-ka)*	paint
краткий перерыв в работе	*(KRAHT-kee pe-re-RIF vra-BOH-te)*	coffee break
краткосрочно выше нормы	*(krat-ka-SROCH-na VEE-she NOHR-mee)*	above-the-line (short term)
краткосрочное финансирование	*(krat-ka-SROCH-na-ye fee-nan-SEE-ra-va-nee-ye)*	short-term financing
краткосрочный долг	*(krat-ka-SROCH-nee dolk)*	short-term debt
краткосрочный капитальный счёт	*(krat-ka-SROCH-nee ka-pee-TAHL-nee shchyoht)*	short-term capital account
кратное число	*(KRAHT-na-ye chees-LOH)*	multiple
крахмал	*(krakh-MAHL)*	starch
кредит	*(kre-DEET)*	credit
кредит с погашением в рассрочку	*(kre-DEET spa-ga-SHEH-nee-em vras-SROCH-koo)*	installment credit
кредитная карточка	*(kre-DEET-na-ya KAHR-tach-ka)*	credit card

К

кредитное сальдо	*(kre-DEET-na-ye SAHL-da)*	credit balance
кредитный	*(kre-DEET-nee)*	acceptance credit
кредитный баланс	*(kree-DEE-ta-vee ba-LAHNS)*	credit balance
кредитный банк	*(kre-DEET-nee bahnk)*	credit bank
кредитный контроль	*(kre-DEET-nee kan-TROL)*	credit control
кредитный лимит	*(kre-DEET-nee lee-MEET)*	credit line
кредитный покупатель	*(kre-DEET-nee pa-koo-PAH-tel)*	credit buyer
кредитор	*(kre-dee-TOHR)*	creditor
кремний	*(KREM-nee)*	silicon
кривая в форме колокола	*(kree-VAH-ya FFOHR-me KOH-la-ka-la)*	bell-shaped curve
кривая периодичности	*(kree-VAH-ya pe-ree-a-DEECH-na-stee)*	frequency curve
кристаллизация	*(krees-tal-lee-ZAH-tsee-ya)*	crystallization
критерии капиталовложения	*(kree-TEH-ree-ee ka-pee-TAH-la-vla-ZHEH-nee-ya)*	investment criteria
кровь	*(krof)*	blood
кролик	*(KROH-leek)*	rabbit
круглая схема пропорциональности	*(KROOG-la-ya SKHEH-ma pra-par-tsee-a-NAHL-na-stee)*	pie chart
круглосуточные биржевые операции	*(kroog-la-SOO-tach-nee-ye beer-zhe-VEE-ye a-pe-RAH-tsee-ee)*	after-hours trading
круговая партия	*(kroo-ga-VAH-ya PAHR-tee-ya)*	round lot
кругозор	*(kroo-ga-ZOHR)*	outlook (philosophy)
крупный масштаб	*(KROOP-nee ma-SHTAHP)*	large-scale
крутящий момент	*(kroo-TYAH-shchee ma-MENT)*	torque
крыло	*(kree-LOH)*	fender
крыло	*(kree-LOH)*	wing
крысы	*(KREE-see)*	rats
кузнечик	*(kooz-NEH-cheek)*	grasshopper
кузов	*(KOO-zaf)*	body

К

кукуруза	*(koo-koo-ROO-za)*	corn
кулачковый вал	*(koo-lach-KOH-vee val)*	camshaft
кульминационные моменты финансового состояния	*(kool-me-na-tsee-ON-nee-ye ma-MEN-tee fee-NAHN-sa-va-va sa-sta-YAH-nee-ya)*	financial highlights
культурная соб-ственность	*(kool-TOOHR-na-ya SOP-stven-nast)*	cultural property
кумулятивный	*(koo-moo-lya-TEEV-nee)*	cumulative
кумулятивные привилегиро-ванные акции	*(koo-moo-lya-TEEV-nee-ye pree-vee-le-ghee-ROH-van-nee-ye AHK-tsee-ee)*	cumulative preferred stock
купленный не по средствам	*(KOOP-len-nee ne pa SRETS-vam)*	overbought
купон на дивиденд	*(koo-PON na dee-vee-DENT)*	coupon (bond interest)
курица	*(KOO-ree-tsa)*	hen
куры	*(KOO-ree)*	chickens
курсив	*(koor-SEEF)*	italic
курьерское обслу-живание	*(koor-YEHR-ska-ye apb-SLOO-zhee-va-nee-ye)*	courier service
кухонные травы	*(koo-KHOH-nee-ye TRAH-vee)*	herbs

Л

лаборант	*(la-ba-RAHNT)*	laboratory technician
лаборатория	*(la-ba-ra-TOH-ree-ya)*	laboratory
лазер	*(LAH-zehr)*	laser
лазерный диск	*(LAH-zehr-nee deesk)*	disk (laser)
лак	*(lahk)*	lacquer, patent leather
лакированная кожа/лак	*(ka-lee-ROH-van-na-ya KOH-zha/lahk)*	patent leather
легат	*(le-GAHT)*	legacy
легированная сталь	*(le-GHEE-ra-van-na-ya stahl)*	alloy steel
легкая нефть	*(LYOKH-ka-ya neft)*	light (crude) oil
лекарственное средство	*(le-KAHR-stven-na-ye SRET-stva)*	drug, medication

Л

лента	*(LEN-ta)*	tape
лес	*(les)*	forest
лесная площадь	*(les-NAH-ya PLOH-shchat)*	timberland
лесной пожар	*(les-NOY pa-ZHAHR)*	forest fire
лесовосстановле-ние	*(LEH-sa-vas-sta-nav-LEH-nee-ye)*	reforestation
лесоматериал в кордах	*(LEH-sa-ma-te-ree-AHL FKOHR-dakh)*	cordwood
лесопильный	*(le-sa-PEEL-nee)*	saw-mill
лесосеменная плантация	*(LEH-sa-se-men-NAH-ya plan-TAH-tsee-ya)*	tree gene bank
лесосплав	*(le-sa-SPLAHF)*	float
лето	*(LEH-ta)*	summer
летун	*(le-TOON)*	job-hopper
лечебные средства	*(le-CHEB-nee-ye SRET-stva)*	remedies
ликвидация	*(leek-ve-DAH-tsee-ya)*	liquidation
ликвидность	*(leek-VEED-nast)*	liquidity
ликвидные акти-вы	*(leek-VEED-nee-ye ak-TEE-vee)*	liquid assets
лимит	*(lee-MEET)*	ceiling
лимитированное указание	*(lee-mee-TEE-ra-van-na-ye oo-ka-ZAH-nee-ye)*	limited order (stock market)
линейный испол-нитель	*(lee-NEY-nee ees-pal-NEE-tel)*	line executive
линия перемены дат	*(LEE-nee-ya pe-re-MEH-nee dat)*	International Date Line
липа	*(LEE-pa)*	lime (linden tree)
лисий мех	*(LEE-see mekh)*	fox (fur)
лист	*(leest)*	leaf, sheet
лиственница	*(LEEST-ven-nee-tsa)*	larch
листоеды	*(lees-ta-YEH-dee)*	leaf-eating insects
литейный завод	*(lee-TEY-nee za-VOT)*	foundry
литографская бумага	*(lee-ta-GRAHF-ska-ya boo-MAH-ga)*	litographic paper
лицензионные сборы	*(lee-tsen-zee-ON-nee-ye ZBOH-ree)*	license fees

Л

лицензированный склад	*(lee-tsen-ZEE-ra-van-nee sklat)*	licensed warehouse
лизензия	*(lee-TSEN-zee-ya)*	license
лицензия на бурение скважины	*(lee-TSEN-zee-ya na boo-REH-nee-ye SKVAH-zhee-nee)*	well permit
лицо, получающее платеж	*(lee-TSOH pa-loo-CHAH-yoo-shchee-ye pla-TYOSH)*	payee
личная ответственность	*(LEECH-na-ya at-VET-stven-nast)*	personal liability
личный счёт в магазине	*(LEECH-nee shchyoht vma-ga-ZEE-ne)*	charge account in a store
личный чистый доход	*(LEECH-nee CHEES-tee da-KHOT)*	disposable income
лишайник	*(lee-SHAHY-neek)*	lichen
лишать законной силы	*(lee-SHAHT za-KON-nay SEE-lee)*	invalidate (v)
лишение	*(lee-SHEH-nee-ye)*	divestment
локальная сеть	*(la-KAHL-na-ya set)*	LAN (local area network)
локальный	*(la-KAHL-nee)*	local
локаут (массовый расчёт рабочих)	*(la-KAH-oot [MAHS-sa-vee ra-SHCHYOHT ra-BOH-cheekh])*	lock out (v)
лом (металлический)	*(lom [me-tal-LEE-ches-kee])*	scrap
лоцманская проводка	*(LOTS-man-ska-ya pra-VOT-ka)*	pilotage
лошадиная сила	*(la-sha-DEE-na-ya SEE-la)*	horsepower
лошадь	*(LOH-shat)*	horse
луч	*(looch)*	beam
лучшая цена	*(LOOCH-sha-ya tse-NAH)*	top price
лучшее качество	*(LOOCH-shee-ye KAH-chest-va)*	top quality
льгота на налог	*(LGOH-ta na na-LOK)*	tax allowance
льготный заём	*(LGOT-nee za-YOM)*	soft loan
льготный период	*(LGOT-nee pe-REE-at)*	grace period
льготы и привилегии	*(LGOH-tee ee pree-vee-LEH-ghee-ee)*	fringe benefits

| людские ресурсы | (lyoot-SKEE-ye re-SOOHR-see) | human resources |
| люцерна | (lyoo-TSEHR-na) | alfalfa |

М

магазин	(ma-ga-ZEEN)	store
магарыч	(ma-ga-RICH)	kickback
магнитная лента	(mag-NEET-na-ya LEN-ta)	magnetic tape
магнитофон	(mag-nee-ta-FON)	tape recorder
мазутный паритет (цен на газ)	(ma-ZOOT-nee pa-ree-TET [tsen na gahs])	fuel oil parity
мазь	(mas)	ointment
мазь	(mas)	salve
макет	(ma-KET)	mock-up
макет	(ma-KET)	dummy
маклер	(MAHK-ler)	broker, stocktrader
маклер на бирже	(MAHK-ler na BEEHR-zhe)	jobber
маклер разрозненных комплектов	(MAHK-ler raz-ROZ-nen-nikh kam-PLEK-taf)	odd lot broker
маклер софтвера	(MAHK-ler saft-VEH-ra)	software broker
макроэкономика	(MAHK-ra-e-ka-NOH-mee-ka)	macroeconomics
максимальное бремя	(mak-see-MAHL-na-ye BREH-mya)	peak load
максимальные извлекаемые запасы	(mak-see-MAHL-nee-ye eez-vle-KAH-ye-mee-ye za-PAH-see)	ultimate recoverable reserves
малодебитная скважина	(MAH-la DEH-beet-na-ya SKVAH-zhee-na)	stripper (well)
мандат	(man-DAHT)	mandate
манипулятор «мышь»	(ma-nee-poo-LYAH-tar mish)	mouse
манифест	(ma-nee-FEST)	manifest
марганцевая руда	(MAHR-gan-tse-va-ya roo-DAH)	manganese ore
маржа	(MAHR-zha)	margin

Л

маржинальная прибыль	*(mar-zhee-NAHL-na-ya PREE-bil)*	margin, profit
маржинальная производитель- ность	*(mar-zhee-NAHL-na-ya pra- eez-va-DEE-tel-nast)*	marginal productivity
«маржинальная» (экономически граничная) скважина	*(mar-zhee-NAHL-na-ya [e- ka-na-MEE-ches-kee gra- NEECH-na-ya] SKVAH- zhee-na)*	marginal producer well
«маржинальное» (экономически граничное) месторождение	*(mar-zhee-NAHL-na-ye [e- ka-na-MEE-ches-kee gra- NEECH-na-ye] mes-ta- razh-DEH-nee-ye)*	marginal field
«маржинальные» (экономически граничные) запасы	*(mar-zhee-NAHL-nee-ye [e- ka-na-MEE-ches-kee gra- NEECH-nee-ye] za-PAH- see)*	marginal reserve
маржинальный доход	*(mar-zhee-NAHL-nee da- KHOT)*	gross margin, marginal revenue
маркетинг	*(mar-KEH-teenk)*	marketing
масло	*(MAHS-la)*	butter
массив	*(mas-SEEF)*	array
массовый марке- тинг	*(MAS-sa-vee mar-KEH- teenk)*	mass marketing
мастер	*(MAHS-ter)*	foreman
мастерская	*(mas-ter-SKAH-ya)*	workshop
математическая модель	*(ma-te-ma-TEE-ches-ka-ya ma-DEL)*	mathematical model
материалы	*(ma-te-ree-YAH-lee)*	materials
материальные активы	*(ma-te-ree-AHL-nee-ye ahk- TEE-vee)*	tangible assets
материальный актив	*(ma-te-ree-AHL-nee ak- TEEF)*	capital asset
материнская ком- пания	*(ma-te-REEN-ska-ya kam- PAH-nee-ya)*	holding company
матрица	*(MAH-tree-tsa)*	matrix
машинописная копия	*(ma-shee-na-PEES-na-ya KOH-pee-ya)*	carbon copy
машиностроение	*(ma-SHEE-na-stra-YEH- nee-ye)*	mechanical engineering
МБО (скупка менеджментом)	*(EM-BEH-OH [SKOOP-ka MEH-ned-zhmen-tom])*	management buy-out

М

мебель	*(MEH-bel)*	furniture
мегабайт	*(me-ga-BAHYT)*	megabyte
медиана	*(me-dee-AH-na)*	median
медикамент	*(me-dee-ka-MENT)*	medication
медицина	*(me-dee-TSEE-na)*	medicine
медь	*(met)*	copper
межбанковский	*(mezh-BAHN-kaf-skee)*	interbank
Международное Энергетическое Агентство	*(mezh-doo-na-ROD-na-ye e-ner-ghe-TEE-ches-ka-ye a-GHENT-stva)*	International Energy Agency
Международный Газовый Союз	*(mezh-doo-na-ROD-nee GAH-za-vee sa-YOOS)*	International Gas Union
Международный Геологический Конгресс	*(mezh-doo-na-ROD-nee ghe-a-la-GHEE-ches-kee kan-GRES)*	International Geological Congress
международный договор	*(mezh-doo-na-ROD-nee da-ga-VOHR)*	treaty
междуштатная торговля	*(mezh-doo-SHTAHT-na-ya TAHR-gov-lya)*	interstate commerce
мелкая кража	*(MEL-ka-ya KRAH-zha)*	pilferage
меморандум	*(me-ma-RAHN-doom)*	memorandum
менеджер	*(MEH-ned-zher)*	manager
менеджер данного фирменного знака	*(MEH-ned-zher DAHN-na-va FEEHR-men-na-va ZNAH-ka)*	brand manager
менеджер района	*(MEH-ned-zher ra-YOH-na)*	area manager
меновая стои-мость	*(MEH-na-va-ya STOH-ee-mast)*	market value (stocks)
меньшая часть акции	*(MEN-sha-ya chahst AHK-tsee-ee)*	minority interest
менять/обменять товары	*(me-NYAHT/ab-me-NYAHT ta-VAH-ree)*	barter (v)
мерлушка	*(mer-LOOSH-ka)*	lamb
местные обычаи	*(MES-nee-ye a-BEE-cha-ee)*	local customs
местные продук-ты	*(MEST-nee-ye pra-DOOK-tee)*	native produce
местный сбор	*(MES-nee zbohr)*	local tax
местонахождение фабрики	*(mesta-na-khazh-DEH-nee-ye FAHB-ree-kee))*	plant location

M

место работы	*(MES-ta ra-BOH-tee)*	workplace
месторождение	*(mes-ta-razh-DEH-nee-ye)*	field
месторождение	*(mes-ta-razh-DEH-nee-ye)*	deposit
металлы	*(me-TAHL-lee)*	metals
метод	*(MEH-tat)*	method
методика «пира- **мида»**	*(me-TOH-dee-ka pee-ra-MEE-da)*	pyramiding
«мертвая» (непод- **вижная нефть)**	*(MYOHRT-va-ya [ne-pad-VEEZH-na-ya neft])*	dead oil
мёртвый фрахт	*(MYOHRT-vee frahkht)*	dead freight
мешок	*(me-SHOK)*	tote bag
микроволновый	*(meek-ra-val-NOH-vee)*	microwave
микропроцессор	*(meek-ra-pra-TSES-ar)*	microprocessor
микросхема	*(meek-ra-SKHEH-ma)*	(micro)-chip
микросхема	*(meek-ra-SKHEH-ma)*	microcomputer
микрофильм	*(meek-ra-FEELM)*	microfilm
микрофиша	*(meek-ra-FEE-sha)*	microfiche
микрофон	*(meek-ra-FON)*	microphone
микроЭВМ	*(MEEK-ra-eh-veh-EM)*	microcomputer
минимальная зар- **плата**	*(mee-nee-MAHL-na-ya zar-PLAH-ta)*	minimum wage
минимальный **резерв**	*(mee-nee-MAHL-nee re-ZEHRF)*	minimum reserves
миниЭВМ	*(MEE-nee-eh-veh-EM)*	minicomputer
мировой банк	*(mee-ra-VOY bahnk)*	World Bank
младшие ценные **бумаги**	*(MLAHT-shee-ye TSEN-nee-ye boo-MAH-ghee)*	junior security
младший партнер	*(MLAHT-shee part-NYOHR)*	junior partner
многоабонентский	*(MNOH-ga-a-ba-NENT-skee)*	multi-user
многовалютный	*(mna-ga-va-LYOOT-nee)*	multicurrency
многоразовый **воздушно-кос-** **мический аппа-** **рат (МВКА)**	*(mna-ga-RAH-za-vee vaz-DOOSH-na-kas-MEE-ches-kee a-pa-RAHT [EM-VEH-KAH-AH])*	space shuttle
многонациональ- **ное акционер-** **ное общество**	*(mna-ga-na-tsee-a-NAHL-na-ye ak-tsee-a-NEHR-na-ye OP-shchest-va)*	multinational corporation

многостороннее соглашение	*(mna-ga-sta-RON-nee-ye sa-gla-SHEH-nee-ye)*	multilateral agreement
многосторонняя торговля	*(mna-ga-sta-RON-nya-ya tar-GOV-la)*	multilateral trade
множественное налогообложение	*(MNOH-zhest-ven-na-ye na-LOH-ga-ab-la-ZHEH-nee-ye)*	multiple taxation
множественные валютные курсы	*(MNOH-zhest-ven-nee-ye va-LYOOT-nee-ye KOOHR-see)*	multiple exchange rates
множитель	*(MNOH-zhee-tel)*	multiplier
мобилизация капитала	*(ma-bee-lee-ZAH-tsee-ya ka-pee-TAH-la)*	mobility of labor
мобильность рабочей силы	*(ma-BEEL-nast ra-BOH-cheey SEE-lee)*	rasing capital
мобильный	*(ma-BEEL-nee)*	portable
модем	*(ma-DEM)*	modem
мозговой штурм	*(maz-ga-VOY shtoorm)*	brainstorm
молибден	*(ma-leeb-DEN)*	molybderum
молодая отрасль промышленности	*(ma-la-DAH-ya OT-rasl pr-MISH-len-na-stee)*	infant industry
молоко	*(ma-la-KOH)*	milk
молотильщик	*(ma-la-TEEL-shcheek)*	thresher
молочная ферма	*(ma-LOCH-na-ya FEHR-ma)*	dairy farm
молочные продукты	*(ma-LOCH-nee-ye pra-DOOK-tee)*	dairy products
монетарная политика	*(ma-ne-TAHR-na-ya pa-LEE-tee-ka)*	monetary policy
монетный двор	*(ma-NET-nee dvor)*	mint
монитор	*(ma-nee-TOHR)*	monitor
монополия	*(ma-na-POH-lee-ya)*	monopoly
монопсония (рынок с одним покупателем)	*(ma-na-PSOH-nee-ya [REE-nak sad-NEEM pa-koo-PAH-te-lem])*	monopsony
моральный дух	*(ma-RAHL-nee dookh)*	morale
морковь	*(mar-KOF)*	carrot
мороз	*(ma-ROZ)*	frost

морошка	*(ma-ROSH-ka)*	cloudberry
морфин	*(mar-FEEN)*	morphine
мочевина	*(ma-che-VEE-na)*	urea
мочегонное средство	*(ma-che-GON-na-ye SRET-stva)*	diuretic
мощность фабрики	*(MOSHCH-nast FAHB-ree-kee)*	plant capacity
мультипрограммирование	*(MOOL-tee-pra-gra-MEE-ra-va-nee-ye)*	multiprogramming
мыши	*(MEE-shee)*	mice

Н

на акцию	*(na AHK-tsee-yoo)*	per share
на душу населения	*(na DOO-shoo na-se-LEH-nee-ya)*	per capita
на предъявителя	*(na pred-ya-VEE-te-la)*	at sight
на рынке	*(na REEN-ke)*	at the market
наблюдательный совет	*(na-blyoo-DAH-tel-nee sa-VET)*	board of supervisors
набор	*(na-BOHR)*	composition
набор стандартных формулировок	*(na-BOHR stan-DAHRT-nikh for-moo-lee-ROH-vak)*	boiler-plate
навигационный вычислитель	*(na-vee-ga-tsee-ON-nee ve-chee-SLEE-tel)*	flight computer
навоз	*(na-VOS)*	manure
навязывание товара	*(na-VYAH-zee-va-nee-ye ta-VAH-ra)*	direct selling
навязывание товаров покупателю	*(na-VYAH-zee-va-nee-ye ta-VAH-raf pa-koo-PAH-te-lyoo)*	hard sell
надбавка	*(nad-BAHF-ka)*	allowance (subsidy)
надбавка к зарплате	*(nad-BAHF-ka gzar-PLAH-te)*	wage differential
надбавка к тарифу	*(nad-BAHF-ka kta-REE-foo)*	differential, tariff
надёжный источник	*(na-DYOHZH-nee ees-TOCH-neek)*	reliable source

Н

название	*(naz-VAH-nee-ye)*	title
названный порт отгрузки	*(NAHZ-van-nee pohrt at-GROOS-kee)*	named port of shipment
названный пункт ввоза	*(NAHZ-van-nee poonkt VVOH-za)*	named point of importation
названный пункт выезда	*(NAHZ-van-nee poonkt VEE-yez-da)*	named point of exportation
названный пункт назначения	*(NAHZ-van-nee poonkt naz-na-CHEH-nee-ya)*	named point of destination
названный пункт происхождения	*(NAHZ-van-nee poonkt pra-ees-kha-ZHDEH-nee-ya)*	named point of origin
наземная перегон- ка	*(na-ZEM-na-ya pe-re-GON-ka)*	above-ground retorting
назначать/назна- чить завышен- ную цену	*(naz-na-CHAT/naz-na-CHEET za-VEE-shen-noo-yoo TSEH-noo)*	overcharge (v)
назначать/назна- чить цену	*(naz-na-CHAT/naz-na-CHEET TSEH-noo)*	price (v)
назначение	*(na-zna-CHEH-nee-ye)*	appointment (nomination)
назначено для экспорта	*(naz-NAH-che-na dla EKS-par-ta)*	for export
наиболее благо- приятствуемая нация	*(na-ee-BOH-le-ye bla-ga-pree-YAHT-stvoo-ye-ma-ya NAH-tsee-ya)*	most-favored nation
накладная	*(nak-lad-NAH-ya)*	waybill
накладные расходы	*(na-klad-NEE-ye ras-KHOH-dee)*	overhead
накопление	*(na-ka-PLEH-nee-ye)*	accumulation
накопленная амортизация	*(na-KOP-len-na-ya a-mar-tee-ZAH-tsee-ya)*	accumulated depreciation
наличные	*(na-LEECH-nee-ye)*	cash
наличные деньги	*(na-LEECH-nee-ye DEN-ghee)*	ready cash
наличный бюджет	*(na-LEECH-nee byood-ZHET)*	cash budget
налог	*(na-LOK)*	tax
налог на акцио- нерные обще- ства	*(na-LOK na ak-tsee-a-NEHR-nee-ye OP-shchest-va)*	corporation tax

налог на добавленную стоимость	(na-LOK na da-BAHV-len-noo-yoo STOH-ee-mast)	value-added tax (VAT)
налог на зарплату	(na-LOK na zar-PLAH-too)	payroll tax
налог на имение	(na-LOK na ee-MEH-nee-ye)	estate tax
налог на наследство	(na-LOK na nas-LET-stva)	inheritance tax
налог на пользование	(na-LOK na POL-za-va-nee-ye)	use tax
налог с оборота	(na-LOK sa-ba-ROH-ta)	sales tax
налог с розничного оборота	(na-LOK SROZ-neech-na-va a-ba-ROH-ta)	retail sales tax
налоги будущих периодов	(na-LOH-ghee BOO-doo-shcheekh pe-REE-a-daf)	deferred tax
налоговые гавани	(na-LOH-ga-vee-ye GAH-va-nee)	tax havens
налоговый кредит («рол-овер»)	(na-LOH-ga-vee kre-DEET [ROL-OH-vehr])	rollover
налогообложение	(na-LOH-ga-ab-la-ZHEH-nee-ye)	taxation
налогоплательщик	(na-LOH-ga-pla-TEL-shcheek)	tax-payer
наложить арест	(na-la-ZHEET a-REST)	impound (v)
намёк	(na-MYOK)	tip (inside information)
нанимать/нанять	(na-nee-MAHT/na-NYAHT)	hire (v)
наполнение трубопровода	(na-pol-NEH-nee-ye troo-ba-pra-VOH-da)	pipe line fill
направленный радиомаяк	(nap-RAHV-len-nee RAH-dee-a-ma-YAHK)	directional beacon
напряжение	(na-pre-ZHEH-nee-ye)	voltage
нарастание	(na-ras-TAH-nee-ye)	accrual
нарастать	(na-ras-TAHT)	accrue (v)
нарастающий	(na-ra-STAH-yoo-shchee)	cumulative
наркотик	(nar-KOH-teek)	narcotic
наросшая амортизация	(na-ROSH-sha-ya a-mar-tee-ZAH-tsee-ya)	accrued depreciation
наросшие активы	(na-ROSH-shee-ye ak-TEE-vee)	accrued assets

наросшие налоги	(na-ROSH-shee-ye na-LOH-ghee)	accrued taxes
наросшие проценты	(na-ROSH-shee-ye pra-TSEN-tee)	accrued interest
наросшие расходы	(na-ROSH-shee-ye ras-KHOH-dee)	accrued expenses
наросший доход	(na-ROSH-shee da-KHOT)	accrued revenue
нарушение суточного ритма	(na-ROO-shee-nee-ye SOO-tach-na-va REET-ma)	jet lag
насекомые	(na-se-KOH-mee-ye)	insects
настольные издательские средства	(nas-TOL-nee-ye eez-DAH-tel-skee-ye SRETST-va)	desktop publishing
насыщение	(na-see-SHCHEH-nee-ye)	glut
насыщение рынка	(na-see-SHCHEH-nee-ye RIN-ka)	market saturation
натуральный (нефтяной) бонус	(na-too-RAHL-nee [nef-tee-NOY] BOH-noos)	oil bonus
находить/найти рынок сбыта	(na-kha-DEET/na-EYTEE REE-nak ZBEE-ta)	market (v)
находящийся постоянно в ЗУ	(na-kha-DYAH-shcheey-sa pas-ta-YAHN-na VZEH-OO)	memory resident
национализация	(na-tsee-a-na-lee-ZAH-tsee-ya)	nationalization
национализм	(na-tsee-a-na-LEEZM)	nationalism
национальный банк	(na-tsee-a-NAHL-nee bahnk)	national bank
начальник	(na-CHAHL-neek)	supervisor
начальник по закупкам	(na-CHAHL-neek pa za-KOOP-kam)	purchasing manager
начальный баланс	(na-CHAHL-nee ba-LAHNS)	opening balance
начальные разведанные запасы	(na-CHAHL-nee-ye raz-VEH-dan-nee-ye za-PAH-see)	initial reserves
начисление за безнадёжную задолженность	(na-chees-LEH-nee-ye za bez-na-DYOZH-noo-yoo za-DOL-zhen-nast)	charge off

не выполнить/не выполнять договор	*(/ne VEE-pal-neet/ne vee-pal-NYAHT da-ga-VOHR)*	default (v)
не имеющий юридической силы	*(ne ee-MEH-yoo-shchee yoo-ree-DEE-ches-kay SEE-lee)*	null and void
не коммерческий	*(ne kam-MEHR-ches-kee)*	nonprofit
не котирующийся (на бирже)	*(ne ka-TEE-roo-yoo-shcheey-sa [na BEEHR-zhe])*	unlisted
не кумулятивные привилегированные акции	*(ne koo-moo-la-TEEV-nee-ye pre-vee-le-ghee-ROH-van-nee-ye AHK-tsee-ee)*	noncumulative preferred stock
не постоянный житель	*(ne pas-ta-YAHN-nee ZHEE-tel)*	nonresident
неблагоприятный	*(ne-bla-ga-pree-YAHT-nee)*	unfavorable
небольшое преимущество над конкурентом	*(ne-bal-SHOH-ye pree-ee-MOO-shchest-va nat kan-koo-REN-tam)*	competitive edge
небрежный	*(ne-BREZH-nee)*	negligent
невесомость	*(ne-ve-SOH-mast)*	zero gravity
невидимый импорт	*(ne-VEE-dee-mee EEM-part)*	invisible imports
невидимый экспорт	*(ne-VEE-dee-mee EKS-part)*	invisible exports
невмешательство	*(ne-vme-SHAH-tel-stva)*	laissez-faire
невыполнение обязанностей	*(ne-vee-pal-NEH-nee-ye a-BYAH-zan-nas-tey)*	nonfeasance
невыполненные заказы	*(ne-VEE-pal-nen-nee-ye za-KAH-zee)*	back log
невыполненный заказ	*(ne-VEE-pal-nen-nee za-KAHZ)*	back order
невыполненный контракт	*(ne-VEE-pal-nen-nee kan-TRAHKT)*	outstanding contract
негатив	*(ne-ga-TEEF)*	negative
недвижимость	*(ne-DVEE-zhee-mast)*	real estate
недействительный	*(ne-dey-STVEE-tel-nee)*	void
недооценивать	*(ne-da-a-TSEH-nee-vat)*	underestimate (v)
недоплаченные долги	*(ne-da-PLAH-chen-nee-ye dal-GHEE)*	outstanding debt

Н

недоразумение	*(ne-da-ra-zoo-MEH-nee-ye)*	misunderstanding
недостаток	*(ne-das-TAH-tak)*	drawback (disadvantage)
недостаточно капитализиро- ванный	*(ne-da-STAH-tach-na ka- pee-ta-lee-ZEH-ra-van- nee)*	undercapitalized
недостаточное количество	*(ne-da-STAH-tach-na-ye ka- LEE-chest-va)*	short supply
недостаточный	*(ne-da-STAH-tach-nee)*	inadequate
недостача при доставке	*(ne-da-STAH-cha pree da- STAHF-ke)*	short delivery
незавершенное производство	*(ne-za-ver-SHON-na-ye pra- eez-VOT-stva)*	work in progress
незаконные грузы	*(ne-za-KON-nee-ye GROO- zee)*	illegal shipments
незаконный	*(ne-za-KON-nee)*	illegal
незаработанный доход	*(ne-za-ra-BOH-tan-nee da- KHOT)*	unearned revenue
незаработанный прирост	*(ne-za-ra-BOH-tan-nee pree-ROST)*	unearned increment
неизвлекаемые запасы	*(ne-eez-vle-KAH-ye-mee-ye za-PAH-see)*	non-recoverable reserve
неквалифициро- ванный труд	*(ne-kva-lee-fee-TSEE-ra- van-nee troot)*	unskilled labor
неконвертируемая валюта	*(ne-kan-ver-TEE-roo-ye-ma- ya va-LYOO-ta)*	soft currency
нематериальные активы	*(ne-ma-ter-YAHL-nee-ye ak- TEE-vee)*	intangible assets
необеспеченная ссуда	*(ne-a-bes-PEH-chen-na-ya SSOO-da)*	unsecured loan
необременённый	*(ne-ab-re-me-NYON-nee)*	free and clear
необъявленный дивиденд	*(ne-ab-YAV-len-nee dee-vee- DENT)*	passed dividend
неорганическая химия	*(ne-ar-ga-NEE-ches-ka-ya KHEE-mee-ya)*	inorganic chemistry
неосвоенные дока- занные запасы	*(ne-as-VOH-yen-nee-ye da- KAH-zan-nee-ye za-PAH- see)*	undeveloped proved reserves
неосуществимый	*(ne-a-soo-shchest-VEE-mee)*	unfeasible
неоткрытые ресурсы	*(ne-at-KREE-tee-ye re- SOOHR-see)*	undiscovered potential resources

неофициальный рынок	*(ne-a-fee-tsee-AHL-nee REE-nak)*	fringe market
неочищенный газ	*(ne-a-CHEE-shchen-nee gahs)*	raw gas
неперезаписывае-мый компакт-ный звукодиск	*(ne-pe-re-za-PEE-see-va-ye-mee kam-PAHKT-nee zvoo-ka-DEESK)*	CD ROM
непосредственная претензия	*(ne-pa-SRET-stven-na-ya pre-TEN-zee-ya)*	indirect claim
непосредственная стоимость	*(ne-pa-SRET-stven-na-ya STOH-ee-mast)*	cost direct
непосредственные ценные бумаги	*(ne-pa-SRET-stven-nee-ye TSEN-nee-ye boo-MAH-ghee)*	direct paper
непостоянная пошлина	*(ne-pas-ta-YAHN-na-ya POSH-lee-na)*	flexible tariff
непредвиденная прибыль	*(ne-pred-VEE-den-na-ya PREE-bil)*	windfall profit
непредвиденные обстоятельства	*(ne-pred-VEE-den-nee-ye apb-sta-YAH-tel-stva)*	contingencies
непрерывный прокатный стан	*(ne-pre-RIV-nee pra-KAHT-nee stahn)*	continuous mill
непродуктивная («сухая») сква-жина	*(ne-pra-dook-TEEV-na-ya [soo-KHAH-ya] SKVAH-zhee-na)*	dry hole
непроизводитель-ный	*(ne-pra-eez-va-DEE-tel-nee)*	inefficient
непроцентная облигация	*(ne-pra-TSENT-na-ya ab-lee-GAH-tsee-ya)*	flat bond
неразбуренные доказанные запасы	*(ne-raz-BOO-ren-nee-ye da-KAH-san-nee-ye za-PAH-see)*	undrilled proved reserves
неразвитые страны	*(ne-RAHZX-vee-tee-ye STRAH-nee)*	undeveloped nations
нераспределённая прибыль	*(ne-ras-pre-de-LYON-na-ya PREE-beel)*	retained profits
нераспределённый доход	*(ne-ras-pre-de-LYON-nee da-KHOT)*	retained earnings
нерешённый патент	*(ne-re-SHON-nee pa-TENT)*	patent pending
нержавеющая сталь	*(ne-rzha-VEH-yoo-shcha-ya stahl)*	stainless steel

несостоятельный должник	*(ne-sa-sta-YAH-tel-nee dal-ZHNEEK)*	insolvent
нестабильность	*(ne-sta-BEEL-nast)*	instability
нестандартные предметы	*(ne-stan-DAHRT-nee-ye pred-MEH-tee)*	outsized articles
нестандартный	*(ne-stan-DAHRT-nee)*	substandard
нет проблем	*(nyet prah-BLEM)*	no problem(s)
нетекущие активы	*(ne-te-KOO-shchee-ye ak-TEE-vee)*	noncurrent assets
неуплата	*(nee-oop-LAH-ta)*	default (n)
нефтегазоносный	*(nef-te-ga-za-NOS-nee)*	petroliferous
нефтезаводское сырье	*(NEF-te-za-vat-SKOH-ye sihr-YOH)*	refinery feed stock
нефтезаводское топливо	*(NEF-te-za-vat-SKOH-ye TOP-lee-va)*	refinery fuel
нефтеочистительный завод	*(NEF-te-a-chees-TEE-tel-nee za-VOT)*	refinery
нефтехимический	*(NEF-te-khee-MEE-ches-kee)*	petrochemical
нефть	*(neft)*	oil, petroleum
«нефть партнёра»	*(neft part-NYOH-ra)*	participation crude
«нефть на плаву»	*(neft na pla-VOO)*	oil (stocks) afloat/at sea
нефть (сырая)	*(neft) [see-RAH-ya])*	crude oil
нефтяная скважина	*(nef-tee-NAH-ya SKVAH-zhee-na)*	oil well
нефтяной (технический) битум	*(nef-tee-NOY [tekh-NEE-ches-kee) BEE-toom)*	oil bitumen
«нефтяные доллары»	*(nef-tee-NEH-ye DOL-la-ree)*	petrodollars
нехватка наличных	*(ne-KHVAHT-ka na-LEECH-nikh)*	short of cash
нечистый коносамент	*(ne-CHEES-tee ka-na-sa-MENT)*	foul bill of lading
нечлен	*(ne-CHLEN)*	nonmember
неэластичное предложение	*(ne-e-la-STEECH-na-ye pred-la-ZHEH-nee-ye)*	inelastic supply
неэластичный спрос	*(ne-e-la-STEECH-nee spros)*	inelastic demand

Н

ниже номиналь- ной цены	*(NEE-zhe na-mee-NAHL- nay tse-NEE)*	below par
ниже номиналь- ной цены	*(NEE-zhe na-mee-NAHL- nay tse-NEE)*	par, below
ниже нормы	*(NEE-zhe NOHR-mee)*	below the line
нижеподписав- шийся	*(NEE-zhe-pad-pee-SAHF- shee-ye-sa)*	undersigned
низкий доход	*(NEES-kee da-KHOT)*	low income
низкокалорийный газ	*(NEES-ka-ka-lo-REEY-nee gahs)*	low-BTU gas
низкооплачивае- мые	*(NEES-ka-ap-LAH-chee-va- ye-mee-ye)*	underpaid
никель	*(NEE-kel)*	nickel
ничтожный	*(neech-TOZH-nee)*	worthless
новация (перевод долга)	*(na-VAH-tsee-ya [pe-re- VOT DOL-ga])*	novation
нововведение	*(no-vo-VVE-de-nee-ye)*	innovation
новшество	*(NOF-she-stva)*	innovation
новые деньги	*(NOH-vee-ye DEN-ghee)*	new money
новый выпуск	*(NOH-vee VEE-poosk)*	new issue
номер заказа	*(NOH-mer za-KAH-za)*	order number
номер счёта	*(NOH-mer SHCHYOH-ta)*	account number
номеронабиратель	*(NOH-me-ra-na-bee-RAH- tel)*	dial
номинальная сто- имость	*(na-mee-NAHL-na-ya STOH-ee-mast)*	face (par) value
номинальная сто- имость активов	*(na-mee-NAHL-na-ya STOH-ee-mast ak-TEE- vaf)*	asset value
номинальная сто- имость чистой суммы	*(na-mee-NAHL-na-ya STOH-ee-mast CHEES- tay SOOM-mee)*	net asset value
номинальная цена	*(na-mee-NAHL-na-ya tse- NAH)*	nominal price
номинальный доход	*(na-mee-NAHL-nee da- KHOT)*	nominal yield
норковый	*(NOHR-ka-vee)*	mink
норма	*(NOHR-ma)*	norm
норма прибыли	*(NOHR-ma PREE-bee-lee)*	return, rate of

норма рентабель-ности	(NOHR-ma ren-TAH-bel-na-stee)	rate of return
нормализация	(nar-ma-lee-ZAH-tsee-ya)	standardization
нормальная убыль и нор-мальный износ	(nar-MAHL-na-ya OO-bil ee nar-MAHL-nee eez-NOS)	wear and tear
нормативные затраты	(nar-ma-TEEV-nee-ye za-TRAH-tee)	standing charges
нормативные издержки	(nar-ma-TEEV-nee-ye eez-DEHRSH-kee)	standard costs
нормативные рас-ходы	(nar-ma-TEEV-nee-ye ras-KHOH-dee)	standing costs
нотариус	(na-TAH-ree-oos)	notary
ноу-хау	(NOH-oo-KHAH-oo)	know-how
ночное хранение	(nach-NOH-ye khra-NEH-nee-ye)	night depository
нуль	(nool)	null
нутрия	(NOOT-ree-ya)	nutria

О

обанкротиться	(a-bank-ROH-tee-tsa)	fail (v) (go bankrupt)
обеспыливание	(a-bes-PEE-lee-va-nee-ye)	desliming
обесценивание валюты	(a-bes-TSEH-nee-va-nee-ye va-LYOO-tee)	depreciation of currency
обесценивание труда	(a-bes-TSEH-nee-va-nee-ye troo-DAH)	dilution of labor
обесценивать/обе-сценить	(a-bes-TSEH-nee-vat/a-bes-TSEEH-neet)	undervalue (v)
обещание в дого-воре	(a-be-SHCHAH-nee-ye vda-ga-VOH-re)	covenant (promise)
обещание принять приглашение в следующий раз	(a-be-SHCHAH-nee-ye pree-NYAHT pree-gla-SHEH-nee-ye FSLEH-doo-yoo-shchee rahs)	rain check
область ввода	(OB-last VVOH-da)	field (input)
облигации без гарантий	(ab-lee-GAH-tsee-ee bez ga-RAHN-teey)	debentures
облигации низко-го дохода	(ab-lee-GAH-tsee-ee NEES-kha-va da-KHOH-da)	low-yield bonds

Н

облигация	*(ab-lee-GAH-tsee-ya)*	bond, debenture
облигация «зеро»	*(ab-lee-GAH-tsee-ya zeh-ROH)*	zero coupon
облигация муни-ципальной кор-порации	*(ab-lee-GAH-tsee-ya moo-nee-tsee-PAHL-nay kar-pa-RAH-tsee-ee)*	municipal bond
облигация на предъявителя	*(ab-lee-GAH-tsee-ya na pred-ya-VEE-te-lya)*	bearer bond
облигация по срочному займу	*(ab-lee-GAH-tsee-ya pa SROCH-na-moo ZAHY-moo)*	term bond
обложка	*(ab-LOSH-ka)*	cover
обман	*(ab-MAHN)*	fraud
обмен товаров	*(ab-MEHN ta-VAH-raf)*	barter
обменивать/обме-нять	*(ab-MEH-nee-vat/ab-meh-NYAHT)*	exchange (v)
обновлять/обно-вить	*(ab-nav-LYAHT/ab-na-VEET)*	renew (v)
обогреватель	*(a-ba-gre-VAH-tel)*	defroster
оборот активов	*(a-ba-ROT ak-TEE-vaf)*	asset turnover
оборот акций	*(a-ba-ROT AHK-tseey)*	stock turnover
оборот труда	*(a-ba-ROT troo-DAH)*	labor turnover
оборотные сред-ства	*(a-ba-ROT-nee-ye SRET-stva)*	floating (working) assets
оборотные фонды	*(a-ba-ROT-nee-ye FON-dee)*	working funds
оборотные цен-ные бумаги	*(a-ba-ROT-nee-ye TSEN-nee-ye boo-MAH-ghee)*	negotiable securities
оборотный	*(a-ba-ROT-nee)*	negotiable (transferable)
оборотный баланс	*(a-ba-ROT-nee ba-LAHNS)*	working balance
оборотный капи-тал	*(a-ba-ROT-nee ka-pee-TAHL)*	current assets, working capital
оборотный рынок	*(a-ba-ROT-nee REE-nak)*	inverted market
оборудование	*(a-ba-ROO-da-va-nee-ye)*	machinery
обособленные товары	*(a-ba-SOB-len-nee-ye ta-VAH-ree)*	specialty goods
обоюдное согла-сие и взаимоу-довлетворение	*(a-ba-YOOD-na-ye sa-GLAH-see-ye ee vza-EE-ma-oo-dav-let-va-REH-nee-ye)*	accord and satisfaction

O

обработанный вручную	*(ab-ra-BOH-tan-nee vrooch-NOO-yoo)*	hand-tooled
обработка данных	*(ab-ra-BOT-ka DAHN-nikh)*	data processing
образ (пиктограмма)	*(AB-raz [peek-ta-GRAHM-ma])*	icon
образец	*(a-bra-ZETS)*	sample
обратимая облигация	*(ab-ra-TEE-ma-ya ab-lee-GAH-tsee-ya)*	convertible debentures
обратимая привилегированная акция	*(ab-ra-TEE-ma-ya pree-vee-lee-ghee-ROH-van-na-ya AHK-tsee-ya)*	convertible preferred stock
обратная связь	*(ab-RAHT-na-ya svyas)*	feedback
обратный фрахт	*(ab-RAHT-nee frahkht)*	back haul
обращение взыскания на заработную плату	*(ab-ra-SHCHEH-nee-ye vzis-KAH-nee-ya na ZAH-ra-bat-noo-yoo PLAH-too)*	garnishment
обрезать страницу в край	*(ab-REH-zat stra-NEE-tsoo fkrahy)*	bleed
обслуживание покупателя	*(ap-SLOO-zhee-va-nee-ye pa-koo-PAH-te-lya)*	customer service
обслуживание после продажи товара	*(ap-SLOO-zhee-va-nee-ye POS-le pra-DAH-zhee ta-VAH-ra)*	after-sales service
обслуживать/обслужить	*(ap-SLOO-zhee-vat/ap-sloo-ZHEET)*	service (v)
обучать/обучить	*(a-boo-CHAT/a-boo-CHEET)*	instruct (v) (teach)
обучение по месту работы	*(a-boo-CHEH-nee-ye pa MES-too ra-BOH-tee)*	on-the-job training
обходить/обойти	*(ap-kha-DEET/a-BOY-tee)*	go around (v)
общая	*(OP-shcha-ya)*	across the board
общая аварийная стоимость	*(OP-shcha-ya a-va-REEY-na-ya STOH-ee-mast)*	average cost
общая цена	*(OP-shcha-ya tse-NAH)*	gross price
общее предложение	*(OP-shche-ye pred-la-ZHEH-nee-ye)*	aggregate supply
общее собрание	*(OP-shche-ye sa-BRAH-nee-ye)*	general meeting

общезаводские накладные расходы	(OP-shche-za-vat-SKEE-ye nak-lad-NEE-ye ras-KHOH-dee)	factory overhead
общепринятая практика	(OP-shche-PREE-nya-ta-ya PRAHK-tee-ka)	standard practice
общественная собственность	(ap-SHCHEST-ven-na-ya SOPST-ven-nast)	public property
общественное представление о компании	(ap-SHCHEST-ven-na-ye pret-sta-VLEH-nee-ye o kam-PAH-nee-ee)	corporate image
общественные сооружения	(ap-SHCHEST-ven-nee-ye sa-a-roo-ZHEH-nee-ya)	public works
общественные фонды	(ap-SHCHEST-ven-nee-ye FON-dee)	public funds
общественный перевозчик	(ap-SHCHEST-ven-nee pe-re-VOH-shcheek)	common carrier
общественный транспорт	(ap-SHCHEST-ven-nee TRAHNS-part)	mass transit
общий риск	(OP-shchee reesk)	aggregate risk
общий рынок	(OP-shchee REE-nak)	common market
общий спрос	(OP-shchee spros)	aggregate demand
общий счёт	(OP-shchee shchyoht)	joint account
объединение	(ab-ye-dee-NEH-nee-ye)	amalgamation
объединение интересов	(ab-ye-dee-NEH-nee-ye een-te-REH-saf)	pooling of interests
объединение фондов	(ab-ye-dee-NEH-nee-ye FON-daf)	pool of funds
объединительная плата	(ab-ye-dee-NEH-nee-tel-na-ya PLAH-ta)	mother board
объединять в общий фонд	(ab-ye-dee-NYAHT VOP-shchee font)	pool (v)
объём	(ab-YOM)	volume
объём продажи	(ab-YOM pra-DAH-zhe)	sales volume
объявление в газете	(ab-yav-LEH-nee-ye vga-ZEH-te)	want-ad
объявление о принятии предложений	(ab-yav-LEH-nee-ye a pree-NYAH-tee-ee pred-la-ZHEH-neey)	request for bid
обыкновенная акция	(a-bik-na-VEN-na-ya AHK-tsee-ya)	capital (common) stock

0

обыкновенный капитал	*(a-bik-na-VEN-nee ka-pee-TAHL)*	ordinary capital
обычная внутри-пластовая пере-гонка (горючих сланцев)	*(a-BICH-na-ya vnoot-ree-plas-ta-VAH-ya pe-re-GON-ka [ga-RYOO-cheekh SLAHN-tsef])*	true in situ recovery of shale oil
обычная ставка	*(a-BICH-na-ya STAHF-ka)*	going rate
обязательные товарные запа-сы	*(a-bee-ZAH-tel-nee-ye ta-VAHR-nee-ye za-PAH-see)*	obligatory (oil) stocks
обязательство	*(a-bya-ZAH-tel-stva)*	commitment, obligation
обязательство, не обеспеченное закладом	*(a-bya-ZAH-tel-stva ne-a-bes-PEH-chen-na-ye za-KLAH-dam)*	unsecured liability
обязательство, обеспеченное закладом	*(a-bya-ZAH-tel-stva a-bes-PEH-chen-na-ye za-KLAH-dam)*	secured liability
овердрафт (пре-вышение креди-та)	*(OH-vehr-DRAHFT [pre-vee-SHEH-nee-ye kre-DEE-ta])*	overdraft
овец	*(a-VETS)*	sheep
овощи	*(OH-va-shchee)*	vegetables
овца	*(af-TSAH)*	ewe
оглавление	*(a-glav-LEH-nee-ye)*	table of contents
огнеупорные материалы	*(ag-ne-oo-POHR-nee-ye ma-te-ree-YAH-lee)*	refractories
оговорка о пред-варительном возмещении	*(a-ga-VOHR-ka a pred-va-REE-tel-nam vaz-me-SHCHEH-nee-ee)*	call feature
оговорка о прича-ле	*(a-ga-VOHR-ka a pree-CHAH-le)*	berth terms
оговорка о сколь-зящих ценах	*(a-ga-VOHR-ka a skal-ZYAH-shchekh TSEH-nakh)*	escalator clause
оговорка об отка-зе от права	*(a-ga-VOHR-ka ab at-KAH-ze at PRAH-va)*	waiter clause
оговорка об уско-рении	*(a-ga-VOHR-ka ab oos-ka-REH-nee-ee)*	acceleration clause
оговорка Язона	*(a-ga-VOHR-ka ya-ZOH-na)*	Jason clause
ограничение на экспорт (импорт)	*(ag-ra-nee-CHEH-nee-ye na EKS-part [EEM-part])*	restrictions on export (import)

ограниченная ответствен- ность	*(ag-ra-NEE-chen-na-ya at-VEHT-stven-nast)*	limited liability
огурец	*(a-goo-RETS)*	cucumber
одежда	*(a-DEZH-da)*	apparel
однодневный заём	*(ad-na-DNEV-nee za-YOM)*	day loan
одобрение	*(a-da-BREH-nee-ye)*	approval
одобрение	*(a-da-BREH-nee-ye)*	endorsement (approval)
одобрять/одо- брить	*(a-da-BRYAHT/a-DOH-breet)*	approve (v)
одометр	*(a-DOH-metr)*	odometer
оживление (курса на бирже)	*(a-zhiv-LEH-nee-ye [KOOHR-sa na BEEHR-zhe])*	rally
оживляться/ожи- виться	*(a-zhiv-LYAHT-sa/a-zhi-VEET-sa)*	rally (v)
озимая пшеница	*(a-ZEE-ma-ya pshe-NEE-tsa)*	winter wheat
окалина	*(a-KAH-lee-na)*	scale
окорочный станок	*(OH-ka-rach-nee sta-NOK)*	barker
олигополия (рынок немно- гих продавцов)	*(a-lee-ga-POH-lee-ya [REE-nak nem-NOH-gheekh pra-daf-TSOF])*	oligopoly
олигопсония (рынок немно- гих покупате- лей)	*(a-lee-ga-PSOH-nee-ya [REE-nak nem-NOH-gheekh pa-koo-PAH-te-ley])*	oligopsomy
ольха	*(al-KHAN)*	alder
омыление	*(a-mee-LEH-nee-ye)*	saporification
опа (публичное предложение о приобретении акций)	*(OH-pa [poob-LEECH-na-ye pred-la-ZHEH-nee-ye a pree-ab-re-TEH-nee-ee AHK-tseey])*	takeover bid
оперативная груп- па	*(a-pe-ra-TEEV-na-ya GROOP-pa)*	task force
оперативный (компьютер)	*(a-pe-ra-TEEV-nee [kam-PYOO-ter])*	on line (computer)
оперативный отчёт	*(a-pe-ra-TEEV-nee at-CHYOHT)*	management accounting

0

операционное управление	*(a-pe-ra-tsee-ON-na-ye oop-rav-LEH-nee-ye)*	operations management
операционный бюджет	*(a-pe-ra-tsee-ON-nee byood-ZHET)*	operating budget
операционный зал фондовой биржи	*(a-pe-ra-tsee-ON-nee zahl FON-da-vay BEEHR-zhee)*	floor (stock exchange)
операционный отчёт	*(a-pe-ra-tsee-ON-nee at-CHYOHT)*	operating statement
операция	*(a-pe-RAH-tsee-ya)*	transaction
опилки	*(a-PEEL-kee)*	sawdust
описание рабочих обязанностей	*(a-pee-SAH-nee-ye ra-BOH-chikh a-BYAH-zan-na-stey)*	job description
описание приобретения	*(a-pee-SAH-nee-ye pre-ab-re-TEH-nee-ya)*	acquisition profile
опиум	*(OH-pee-oom)*	opium
оплата наличными	*(ap-LAH-ta na-LEECH-nee-mee)*	cash payment
оплата натурой	*(ap-LAH-ta na-TOO-ray)*	payment in kind
оплата при доставке	*(ap-LAH-ta pree da-STAHF-ke)*	cash on delivery
оплаченные заранее расходы	*(ap-LAH-chen-nee-ye za-RAH-ne-ye ras-KHOH-dee)*	prepaid expenses (balance sheet)
оплаченный выходной	*(ap-LAH-chen-nee vee-khad-NOY)*	paid holiday
оплаченный капитал	*(ap-LAH-chen-nee ka-pee-TAHL)*	paid up capital
оплачивается при доставке	*(ap-LAH-chee-va-yet-sa pree da-STAHF-ke)*	cash on delivery
опоссум	*(a-POS-soom)*	opossum
опрос общественного мнения	*(ap-ROS ap-SHCHEST-ven-na-va MNE-nee-ya)*	public opinion poll
опрос потребителей	*(ap-ROS pa-tre-BEE-te-ley)*	market survey
опротестовать	*(a-pra-tes-ta-VAHT)*	dishonor (as a check)
оптический	*(ap-TEE-ches-kee)*	optical
оптическое распознавание знаков	*(ap-TEE-ches-ka-ye ras-pa-zna-VAH-nee-ye ZNAH-kaf)*	optical character recognition

0

оптовая торговля	*(OP-ta-va-ya tar-GOV-lya)*	wholesale trade
оптовая цена	*(OP-ta-va-ya tse-NAH)*	wholesale price
оптовик	*(ap-ta-VEEK)*	rack jobber, wholesaler
оптовый рынок	*(OP-ta-vee REE-nak)*	wholesale market
оптовый торговец	*(OP-ta-vee tar-GOH-vets)*	wholesaler
опцион	*(ap-tsee-ON)*	option (put or call options)
опцион на акции	*(ap-tsee-ON na AHK-tsee-ee)*	stock option
опцион за покупку	*(ap-tsee-ON za pa-KOOP-koo)*	buyer's option
опцион на прода-жу	*(ap-tsee-ON na pra-DAH-zhoo)*	put option
опцион на сроч-ном контракте	*(ap-tsee-ON na SROCH-nam kan-TRAHK-te)*	futures option
опцион покупате-ля	*(ap-tsee-ON pa-koo-PAH-te-lya)*	call option
опыление	*(a-pee-LEH-nee-ye)*	pollination
опыление посевов	*(a-pee-LEH-nee-ye pa-SEH-vaf)*	crop-dusting
орбита	*(ar-BEE-ta)*	orbit
орбитальная заправочная станция	*(ar-bee-TAHL-na-ya zap-RAH-vach-na-ya STAHN-tsee-ya)*	orbital refueling base
орбитальная стан-ция (ОС)	*(ar-bee-TAHL-na-ya STAHN-tsee-ya [OH-ES])*	space station
организационная структура пер-сонала	*(ar-ga-nee-za-tsee-ON-na-ya strook-TOO-ra per-sa-NAH-la)*	staff organization
организация	*(ar-ga-nee-ZAH-tsee-ya)*	organization
Организация Стран-Экспортёров Нефти (ОПЕК)	*(ar-ga-nee-ZAH-tsee-ya strahn eks-par-TYOH-raf NEF-tee [oh-PEK])*	Organization of Petroleum Exporting Countries (OPEC)
органическая химия	*(ar-ga-NEE-ches-ka-ya KHEE-mee-ya)*	organic chemistry
органический	*(ar-ga-NEE-ches-kee)*	organic
ориентация слу-жащего	*(a-ree-yen-TAH-tsee-ya SLOO-zha-shche-va)*	employee counseiling
орошать	*(a-ra-SHAHT)*	irrigate (v)

0

орудие труда	(a-ROO-dee-ye TROO-da)	tools of one's trade
оружие	(a-ROO-zhee-ye)	armaments
ОС	(os)	OS
освобождение	(as-va-bazh-DEH-nee-ye)	exemption
освобождение от уплаты налога	(as-va-bazh-DEH-nee-ye at oop-LAH-tee na-LOH-ga)	remission of a tax
освобождение от уплаты таможенной пошлины	(as-va-bazh-DEH-nee-ye at oop-LAH-tee ta-MOH-zhen-nay POSH-lee-nee)	remission of a customs duty
освобождённый от уплаты налогов	(as-va-bazh-DEH-nee-ye at oop-LAH-tee na-LOH-gaf)	tax-free
освоенное месторождение	(as-VOH-yen-na-ye mes-ta-razh-DEH-nee-ye)	developed field
осень	(OH-sen)	autumn
осмотр	(as-MOTR)	inspection
основание	(as-na-VAH-nee-ye)	base
основанный на применении окон	(as-NOH-van-nee na pree-mee-NEH-nee-ee OH-kan)	window-based
основной капитал	(as-nav-NOY ka-pee-TAHL)	fixed capital
основной рынок	(as-nav-NOY REE-nak)	primary market
основные активы	(as-nav-NEE-ye ak-TEE-vee)	fixed assets
основные издержки	(as-nav-NEE-ye eez-DEHRSH-kee)	fixed charges
основные производственные фонды	(as-nav-NEE-ye pra-eez-VOT-stven-nee-ye FON-dee)	capital goods
основные расходы	(as-nav-NEE-ye ras-KHOH-dee)	fixed expenses
основные резервы	(as-nav-NEE-ye re-ZEHR-vee)	primary reserves
основные средства	(as-nav-NEE-ye SRET-stva)	assets, fixed
основные стоимости	(as-nav-NEE-ye STOH-ee-ma-stee)	fixed costs
особо выгодное предложение	(a-SOH-ba VEE-gad-na-ye pred-la-ZHEH-nee-ye)	premium offer

оставшаяся часть	*(as-TAHF-sha-ya-sa chahst)*	remainder
осциллятор	*(as-tsil-LYAH-tar)*	oscillator
отбирать/ото- брать образцы	*(ad-BEE-rat/a-tab-RAHT a- braz-TSEE)*	sample (v)
отбор	*(at-BOHR)*	acceptance, sampling
отвергнутая опла- та	*(at-VEHR-gnoo-ta-ya ap- LAH-ta)*	payments, refused
ответственность	*(at-VEHT-stven-nast)*	liability
ответственность покупателя	*(at-VEHT-stven-nast pa- KOO-pa-te-lya)*	buyer's responsibility
ответственный	*(at-VEHT-stven-nee)*	accountable, liable
отвечать/ответить	*(at-VEH-chat/at-VEH-teet)*	reply (v)
отводить /отвести (кандидата на должность и т.п.)	*(at-va-DEET/at-ves-TEE [kan-dee-DAH-ta na DOLZH-nast ee TEH- PEH])*	screen (v)
отдать часть рабо- ты	*(at-DAHT chahst ra-BOH- tee)*	farm out (v)
отдел	*(at-DEL)*	department
отдел кадров	*(at-DEL KAHD-raf)*	personnel department
отдельная партия	*(at-DEHL-na-ya PAHR-tee- ya)*	job lot
отечественное акционерное общество	*(a-TEH-chest-ven-na-ye ak- tsee-a-NEHR-na-ye OP- shchest-va)*	domestic corporation
отечественный газ	*(a-TEH-chest-ven-nee gahs)*	domestic gas
отжиг	*(OT-zhik)*	annealing
отзывная довери- тельная соб- ственность	*(at-ziv-NAH-ya da-ve-REE- tel-na-ya SOP-stven-nast)*	recovable trust
отказаться от акцепта	*(at-ka-ZAH-tsa at ak-TSEP- ta)*	refuse acceptance (v)
отказаться от претензий	*(at-ka-ZAH-tsa at pre- TEHN-zeey)*	abandon (v)
отказаться от уплаты	*(at-ka-ZAH-tsa aht oo- PLAH-tee)*	refuse payment (v)
откладывать/ отложить	*(at-KLAH-dee-vat/at-la- ZHEET)*	postpone (v)

0

отклонение (валютного курса и т.д.)	*(at-kla-NEH-nee-ye [va-LYOOT-na-va KOOR-sa ee te-DEH])*	variance
открытый заказ	*(at-KREE-tee za-KAHZ)*	open order
открытый рынок	*(at-KREE-tee REE-nak)*	open market
открытый счёт	*(at-KREE-tee shchyoht)*	open account
отлаживать/отладить программу	*(at-LAH-zhee-vat/at-LAH-deet pra-GRAHM-moo)*	debug (v) (computers)
отложенные аннуитеты	*(at-LOH-zhen-nee-ye an-noo-ee-TEH-tee)*	deferred annuities
отношения между администрацией и рабочими	*(at-na-SHEH-nee-ya MEZH-doo ad-mee-nee-STRAH-tsee-yey ee ra-BOH-chee-mee)*	industrial relations
отношения с инвесторами	*(at-na-SHEH-nee-ya sin-VES-ta-ra-mee)*	investor relations
отношения с рабочими	*(at-na-SHEH-nee-ya sra-BOH-chee-mee)*	labor relations
отношения служащих с руководством	*(at-na-SHEH-nee-ya SLOO-zha-shcheekh sroo-ka-VOT-stvam)*	employee relations
отправка	*(at-PRAHF-ka)*	dispatch
отправлять/ отправить	*(at-prav-LYAHT/at-PRAH-veet)*	forward (v)
отпуск	*(OT-poosk)*	leave of absence
отпуск по беременности и родам	*(OT-poosk pa be-REH-men-nas-tee ee ROH-dam)*	maternity leave
отпуск по болезни	*(OT-poosk pa ba-LEZ-nee)*	sick leave
отрасль торговли	*(OT-rasl tar-GOV-lee)*	line of business
отрицательное «кэшфлоу»	*(at-ree-TSAH-tel-na-ye "cash flow")*	negative cash flow
отсрочивать/ отсрочить	*(at-SROH-chee-vat/at-SROH-cheet)*	postpone (v)
отсрочка	*(at-SROCH-ka)*	moratorium
отставание	*(at-sta-VAH-nee-ye)*	arrears
отстойный газ	*(at-STOY-nee gahs)*	sludge gas
отсутствие задолженности	*(at-SOOT-stvee-ye za-DOL-zhen-na-stee)*	debtlessness

0

отсчёт времени	*(at-SHCHYOHT VREH-me-nee)*	count-down
оттиск	*(OT-teesk)*	sheet
отчёт о валовом доходе «кэш-флоу»	*(at-CHYOHT o va-la-VOM da-KHOH-de ["cash flow"])*	cash flow statement
отчёт о доходах	*(at-CHYOHT a da-KHOH-dakh)*	profit-and-loss statement
отчёт о доходах	*(at-CHYOHT a da-KHOH-dakh)*	statement, profit-and-loss
отчёт прибылей и убытков	*(at-CHYOHT PREE-bee-ley ee oo-BIT-kaf)*	earnings report
отчёт прибылей и убытков	*(at-CHYOHT PREE-bee-ley ee oo-BIT-kaf)*	income statement
отчётный год	*(at-CHYOHT-nee got)*	fiscal year
отчисления на амортизацию	*(at-chees-LEH-nee-ya na a-mar-tee-ZAH-tsee-yoo)*	depreciation allowance
оферта	*(a-FEHR-ta)*	tender office
офис	*(OH-fees)*	office
официальный выходной	*(a-fee-tsee-AHL-nee vee-khad-NOY)*	legal holiday
оформлять/оформить	*(a-farm-LYAHT/a-FOHR-meet)*	process (v)
офсетная печать	*(af-SET-na-ya pe-CHAHT)*	offset printing
офшорная компания	*(af-SHOHR-na-ya kam-PAH-nee-ya)*	offshore company
охранять/охранить	*(a-khra-NYAT/a-khra-NEET)*	safeguard (v)
оценивать/оценить	*(a-TSEH-nee-vat/a-tsee-NEET)*	appraise, estimate (v)
оценивать/оценить имущество	*(a-TSEH-nee-vat/a-tsee-NEET ee-MOO-shche-stva)*	assess (v)
оценка	*(a-TSEN-ka)*	appraisal, assessment, estimate, valuation
оценка доходов от продажи	*(a-TSEN-ka da-KHOH-daf at pra-DAH-zhee)*	sales estimate
оценка имущества для обложения налогом	*(a-TSEN-ka ee-MOO-shchest-va dla ab-la-ZHEH-nee-ya na-LOH-gam)*	assessed valuation

оценка кредито-способности	*(a-TSEN-ka kree-DEE-ta-spa-SOB-na-stee)*	credit rating
оценка работы	*(a-TSEN-ka ra-BOH-tee)*	job evaluation
оценка расхода из основных фон-дов	*(a-TSEN-ka ras-KHOH-da eez as-nav-NIKH FON-daf)*	capital expenditure appraisal
оценка рентабель-ности	*(a-TSEN-ka ren-TAH-bel-na-stee)*	rating (credit)
оценка риска	*(a-TSEN-ka REES-ka)*	risk assessment
оценка рынка	*(a-TSEN-ka RIN-ka)*	market appraisal
оценка спасённого имущества	*(a-TSEN-ka spa-SYON-na-va ee-MOO-shchest-va)*	salvage value
оценка финансо-вого состояния	*(a-TSEN-ka fee-NAHN-sa-va-va sa-sta-YAH-nee-ya)*	financial appraisal
оценочная стои-мость (запасов) месторождения	*(a-TSEN-nach-na-ya STOO-ee-mast [za-PAH-saf] mes-ta-razh-DEH-nee-ya)*	value of a field
оценочная сква-жина	*(a-TSEN-nach-na-ya SKVAH-zhee-na)*	appraisal well
очистка	*(a-CHEEST-ka)*	purification
очистительный	*(a-chees-TEE-tel-nee)*	purgative
очищать	*(a-chee-SHCHAHT)*	refine (v)
ошибка	*(a-SHIP-ka)*	error
ошибка в обработ-ке (данных)	*(a-SHIP-ka vab-ra-BOT-ke [DAHN-neekh])*	processing error

П

пагинация	*(pa-ghee-NAH-tsee-ya)*	pagination
падение курса	*(pa-DEH-nee-ye KOOR-sa)*	go-down
падение на бирже-вом рынке	*(pa-DEH-nee-ye na beer-zhe-VOM REEN-ke)*	bear market
пакетные задания	*(pa-ket-NEE-ye za-DAH-nee-ya)*	batched jobs
паллет	*(PAHL-let)*	pallet
памфлет	*(pam-FLET)*	pamphlet
память компьюте-ра	*(PAH-myat kam-PYOO-te-ra)*	computer storage

0

папка	(PAHP-ka)	binder
параллельная схема	(pa-ral-LEL-na-ya SKHEH-ma)	parallel circuit
паритет	(pa-ree-TET)	parity
«паритетный» (базисный) сорт	(pa-ree-TET-nee [BAH-zees-nee] sohrt)	parity crude
партия	(par-TEE-ya)	lot
партнёр	(part-NYOHR)	partner
пасека	(PAH-se-ka)	apiary
пасквиль	(PAHSK-veel)	libel
пассивный баланс	(pas-SEEV-nee ba-LAHNS)	adverse balance
пассивный партнёр	(pas-SEEV-nee part-NYOR)	silent partner
пассивы будущих периодов	(pas-SEE-vee BOO-doo-shcheekh pe-REE-a-daf)	deferred liabilities
пастеризатор	(pas-te-ree-ZAH-tar)	pasteurizer
патент	(pa-TENT)	patent
патентное роялти	(pa-TENT-na-ye ROH-yal-tee)	patent royalty
паушальная сумма	(pa-oo-SHAHL-na-ya SOOM-ma)	lump sum
пахотная земля	(PAH-khat-na-ya zem-LYAH)	arable land
педаль сцепления	(pe-DAHL stse-PLEH-nee-ya)	clutch pedal
пенициллин	(pe-nee-tsee-LEEN)	penicillin
пенни сток: недорогие спекулятивные акции	(PEN-nee stok: ne-da-ra-GHEE-ye spe-koo-la-TEEV-nee-ye AHK-tsee-ee)	penny stock
пенсионный фонд	(pen-see-ON-nee font)	pension fund
первое залоговое право	(PEHR-va-ye za-LOH-ga-va-ye PRAH-va)	senior lien
первоклассная акция	(per-va-KLAHS-na-ya AHK-tsee-ya)	blue-chip stock
первоначальная запись	(per-va-na-CHAHL-na-ya ZAH-pees)	original entry
первоначальная стоимость	(per-va-na-CHAHL-na-ya STOH-ee-mast)	original cost

первоначальная цена	*(per-va-na-CHAHL-na-ya tse-NAH)*	opening price
первоначальный бонус	*(per-va-na-CHAHL-nee BOH-noos)*	signature bonus
первоначальный срок наступления	*(per-va-na-CHAHL-nee srok nas-too-PLEH-nee-ya)*	original maturity
первоначальные расходы	*(per-va-na-CHAHL-nee-ye ras-KHOH-dee)*	start-up costs
первоочередные долги	*(per-va-a-che-red-NEE-ye dal-GHEE)*	preferential debts
первый заместитель менеджера	*(PEHR-vee za-mes-TEE-tel MEH-ned-zhe-ra)*	assistant general manager
первым поступил — первым продан **(ФИФО)**	*(PEHR-vim pa-stoo-PEEL PEHR-vim PROH-dan [FEE-FOH])*	first in-first out (FIFO)
перевод	*(pe-re-VOT)*	transfer
переводить/перевести	*(pe-re-vah-DEET/pe-re-veh-STEE)*	transfer (v)
переводить/перевести по телеграфу	*(pe-re-vah-DEET/pe-re-veh-STEE pa te-le-GRAH-foo)*	wire transfer (v)
переводчик	*(pe-re-VOT-cheek)*	translator
перевозчик	*(pe-re-VOH-shcheek)*	carrier
перевозчик по договору	*(pe-re-VOH-shcheek pa da-ga-VOH-roo)*	contract carrier
переговоры	*(pe-re-ga-VOH-ree)*	negotiation
перегонка (горючих сланцев)	*(pe-re-GOHN-ka [ga-RYOO-chikh SLAHN-tsef])*	(TIS)
перегрузка товаров	*(pe-re-GROOS-ka ta-VAH-raf)*	movement of goods
перегруппировка акций	*(pe-re-groop-pee-ROF-ka AHK-tseey)*	(reverse) stock split
передаточный механизм	*(pe-re-DAH-tach-nee me-kha-NEEZM)*	gearing
передатчик	*(pe-re-DAHT-cheek)*	transmitter
передвижение в открытом космосе	*(pe-re-DVEE-zhe-nee-ye vat-KREE-tam KOS-ma-se)*	space walk

передвижная пусковая установка	*(pe-re-dveezh-NAH-ya poos-ka-VAH-ya oos-ta-NOF-ka)*	mobile launcher
передний привод	*(pe-RED-nee PREE-vat)*	front-wheel drive
передовое управление	*(pe-re-da-VOH-ye oop-rav-LEH-nee-ye)*	line management
перекапитализация	*(pe-re-ka-pee-tah-lee-ZAH-tsee-ya)*	recapitalization
перекачка по трубопроводу	*(pe-re-KAHCH-ka pa troo-ba-pra-VOH-doo)*	pipage
переключатель	*(pe-re-kloo-CHAH-tel)*	switch
переменная ставка	*(pe-re-MEHN-na-ya STAHF-ka)*	variable rate
переменные издержки	*(pe-re-MEHN-nee-ye eez-DEHRSH-kee)*	variable costs
переменные импортные сборы	*(pe-re-MEHN-nee-ye EEM-part-nee ZBOH-ree)*	variable import levy
переменный аннуитет	*(pe-re-MEHN-nee an-noo-ee-TET)*	variable annuity
переменный ток	*(pe-re-MEHN-nee tok)*	alternating current
перенесение	*(pe-re-ne-SEH-nee-ye)*	carry-forward
переоценивать	*(pe-re-a-TSEH-nee-vat)*	overvalue (v)
переоценка	*(pe-re-a-TSEN-ka)*	revaluation
переписка	*(pe-re-PEES-ka)*	correspondence
переплата	*(pe-re-PLAH-ta)*	overpayment
переплёт	*(pe-re-PLYOT)*	binding, spine
переплётный пресс	*(pe-re-PLYOT-nee press)*	bookbinding press
переплётчик	*(pe-re-PLYOT-cheek)*	bookbinder
перепродажа	*(pe-re-pra-DAH-zha)*	back selling, resale
перерабатываемая нефть	*(pe-re-ra-BAH-tee-va-ye-ma-ya neft)*	inpumpables (inventory)
переработка по наделам	*(pe-re-ra-BOT-ka pa na-DEH-lam)*	batch processing
пересмотреть договор	*(pe-re-smat-RET da-ga-VOHR)*	renegotiate (v)
перестраховщик	*(pe-re-stra-KHOF-shcheek)*	reinsurer
перестройка	*(pe-re-STROY-ka)*	restructuring

перефинансирова- ние	*(pe-re-fee-nan-SEE-ra-va- nee-ye)*	refinancing
переходящий заказ	*(pe-re-kha-DYAH-shcheey za-KAHS)*	carryover
перечисленный счёт	*(pe-re-CHEES-len-nee shchot)*	itemized account
перечислять/пере- числить	*(pe-re-chees-LYAHT/pe-re- chees-LEET)*	itemize (v)
период выплаты	*(pe-REE-at VIP-la-tee)*	payout period
период полураспа- да	*(pe-REE-at poh-loo-ras- PAH-da)*	half-life
период прогона	*(pe-REE-at pra-GOH-na)*	run-time
период рентабель- ной разработки месторождения	*(pe-REE-at ren-TAH-bel- nay raz-ra-BOT-kee mes- ta-razh-DEH-nee-ya)*	economic life
период эксплуата- ции месторож- дения	*(pe-REE-at eks-ploo-a-TAH- tsee-ee mes-ta-razh-DEH- nee-ya)*	production life
периодическая инвентаризация	*(pe-ree-a-DEE-ches-ka-ya een-ven-ta-ree-ZAH-tsee- ya)*	periodic inventory
периферийное оборудование	*(pe-ree-fe-REEY-na-ye a-ba- ROO-da-va-nee-ye)*	peripherals
периферийное устройство	*(pe-ree-fe-REEY-na-ye oos- TROYST-va)*	peripheral
персик	*(PEHR-seek)*	peach
персонал	*(per-sa-NAHL)*	staff
персональная ЭВМ	*(per-sa-NAHL-na-ya eh-veh- EM)*	PC
персональное освобождение (от налогов)	*(per-sa-NAHL-na-ye as-va- bazh-DEH-nee-ye at na- LOH-gaf)*	personal exemption
персональный вычет (с нало- гов)	*(per-sa-NAHL-nee VEE-chet [sna-LOH-gaf])*	personal deduction
перспектива	*(per-spek-TEE-va)*	outlook (prediction)
перспективное планирование	*(per-spek-TEEV-na-ye pla- NEE-ra-va-nee-ye)*	long range planning
перспективы нефтегазонос- ности	*(per-spek-TEEV-ee NEF-te- GAH-za-NOS-na-stee)*	hydrocarbon prospects

перчатки	(per-CHAHT-kee)	gloves
петродоллары	(pet-ra-DOL-la-ree)	petrodollars
петух	(pe-TOOKH)	rooster
печатание	(pe-CHAH-ta-nee-ye)	printing
печатная схема	(pe-CHAHT-na-ye SKHEH-ma)	printed circuit
печатный матери-ал	(pe-CHAHT-nee ma-te-ree-YAHL)	printed matter
печь	(pech)	furnace
печь	(pech)	kiln
пигмент	(peeg-MENT)	pigment
пикет	(pee-KET)	picket line
пила	(pee-LAH)	saw
пилюля	(pee-LYOO-lya)	pellet
пильное полотно	(PEEL-na-ye pa-lat-NOH)	blade
писатель, работа-ющий по дого-вору	(pee-SAH-tel ra-BOH-ta-yoo-shchee pa da-ga-VOH-roo)	freelance writer
писать через дефис	(pee-SAHT che-rez de-FEES)	hyphenate (v)
письменное согла-шение	(PEES-men-na-ye sa-gla-SHEH-nee-ye)	written agreement
письменные пока-зания под при-сягой	(PEES-men-nee-ye pa-ka-ZAH-nee-ya pat pree-SYAH-gay)	affidavit
письмо	(pees-MOH)	letter
пихта	(PEEKH-ta)	fir
пищевые продук-ты	(pee-shchee-VEE-ye pra-DOOK-tee)	foodstuffs
плавающая став-ка	(PLAH-va-yoo-shcha-ya STAHF-ka)	floating rate
плавающие капи-талы	(PLAH-va-yoo-shchee-ye ka-pee-TAH-lee)	hot money
плавающий валютный курс	(PLAH-va-yoo-shchee va-LYOOT-nee koors)	floating exchange rate
план	(plahn)	plan
план маркетинга	(plahn mar-KEH-teen-ga)	marketing plan

планирование акционерного общества	(pla-NEE-ra-va-nee-ye ak-tsee-a-NEHR-na-va OP-shchest-va)	corporate planning
плановая прибыль	(PLAH-na-va-ya PREE-bil)	profit projection
плата за провоз	(PLAH-ta za pra-VOS)	carrying charge
платежеспособность	(pla-te-zhe-spa-SOB-nast)	solvency
платежеспособный	(pla-te-zhe-spa-SOB-nee)	afloat (debt-free)
платежная ведомость	(pla-TYOZH-na-ya VEH-da-mast)	payroll
плательщик	(pla-TEL-shcheek)	payer
платёж авансом	(pla-TYOZH a-VAHN-sam)	advance payment
платёжный баланс	(pla-TYOZH-nee ba-LAHNS)	balance of payments
платить	(pla-TEET)	pay (v)
племенной скот	(ple-men-NOY skot)	breeding stock
пленарное совещание	(ple-NAHR-na-ye sa-ve-SHCHAH-nee-ye)	plenary meeting
плётка	(PLYOT-ka)	whip
плодоводство	(pla-da-VOT-stva)	orchard farming
плоская заготовка	(PLOS-ka-ya za-ga-TOF-ka)	slabs
плотность	(PLOT-nast)	density
плотность бурения	(PLOT-nast boo-REH-nee-ya)	well density
плуг	(plook)	plough
по всей отрасли (промышленности)	(pa fsey OT-ras-lee [pra-MISH-len-na-stee])	industry-wide
по выпуску	(pa VEE-poos-koo)	when issued
по извещению	(pa eez-ve-SHCHEH-nee-yoo)	as per advice
по предъявлении	(pa pred-yav-LEH-nee-ee)	on demand
побочный продукт	(pa-BOCH-nee pra-DOOKT)	by-product
побочный результат	(pa-BOCH-nee re-SOOL-tat)	spin off
побочные расходы	(pa-BOCH-nee-ye ras-KHOH-dee)	incidental expenses

побочные расходы	*(pa-BOCH-nee-ye ras-KHOH-dee)*	out-of-pocket expenses
побочные преимущества	*(pa-BOCH-nee-ye pre-ee-MOO-shche-stva)*	perks
повестка дня	*(pa-VEST-ka dnya)*	agenda
повреждение	*(pav-re-ZHDEH-nee-ye)*	damage
повторять начальную загрузку	*(paf-ta-RYANT na-CHAHL-noo-yoo za-GROOS-koo)*	reboot (v)
повязка	*(pa-VYAHZ-ka)*	dressing
повышать/повысить	*(pa-vee-SHAHT/pa-vee-SEET)*	advance (v) (promote)
повышение биржевого рынка	*(pa-vee-SHEH-nee-ye beer-zhe-VOH-va REEN-ka)*	bull market
повышение цен	*(pa-vee-SHEH-nee-ye tsen)*	markup
повышенное извлечение нефти	*(pa-VEE-shen-na-ye eez-vle-CHEH-nee-ye NEF-tee)*	enhanced oil recovery
погашать/погасить	*(pa-ga-SHAHT/pa-ga-SEET)*	discharge (v)
погашение в рассрочку	*(pa-ga-SHEH-nee-ye vras-SROCH-koo)*	amortization
погашение долга в рассрочку	*(pa-ga-SHEH-nee-ye DOL-ga vras-SROCH-koo)*	installment plan
погашение долгов	*(pa-ga-SHEH-nee-ye dal-GOF)*	retirement (debt)
погрузка	*(pa-GROOS-ka)*	shipment
погрузочные инструкции	*(pa-GROO-zach-nee-ye een-STROOK-tsee-ee)*	shipping instructions
подаваться	*(pa-da-VAHT-sa)*	yield (v) (give into)
подбор квалифицированных кадров	*(pad-BOHR kva-lee-fee-TSEE-ra-van-neekh KAHD-raf)*	headhunting
подвеска	*(pad-VES-ka)*	suspension
подвижной кран	*(pad-veezh-NOY krahn)*	jenny
подвижной состав	*(pad-veezh-NOY sa-STAHF)*	rolling stock
подделка	*(pad-DEL-ka)*	imitation, counterfeit
поддержание цен	*(pad-der-ZHAH-nee-ye tsen)*	price support
поддержка	*(pad-DEHRSH-ka)*	backing, support
подкисление	*(pat-kee-SLEH-nee-ye)*	acidifcation

подключать	(pat-kloo-CHAHT)	connect (into network)
подлежащее вычету	(pad-le-ZHAH-shchee-ye VEE-che-too)	deductible
подлежащий обложению налогами	(pad-le-ZHAH-shchee ab-la-ZHEH-nee-yoo na-LOH-ga-mee)	liable for tax
подлежащий уплате по распоряжению	(pad-le-ZHAH-shchee oop-LAH-te pa ras-par-ya-ZHEH-nee-yoo)	payable to order
подлежащий уплате предъявителю	(pad-le-ZHAH-shchee oop-LAH-te pred-ya-VEE-te-lyoo)	payable to bearer
подлежащий уплате при требовании	(pad-le-ZHAH-shchee oop-LAH-te pree TREH-ba-va-nee-yee)	payable to demand
подлинник	(POD-leen-neek)	script (document)
подмастерье	(pad-mas-TEH-rye)	apprentice
подоходный налог	(pa-da-KHOD-nee na-LOK)	income tax
подоходный налог с физических лиц	(pa-da-KHOD-nee na-LOK sfee-ZEE-ches-keekh leets)	personal income tax
подписная цена	(pat-pees-NAH-ya tse-NAH)	subscription price (periodicals)
подпись	(POT-pees)	signature
подразумеваемое соглашение	(pad-ra-zoo-me-VAH-ye-ma-ye sag-la-SHEH-nee-ye)	implied agreement
подразумеваемые запасы	(pad-ra-zoo-me-VAH-ye-mee-ye za-PAH-see)	inferred reserves
подрезать снимок	(pad-REH-sat SNEEH-mak)	crop
подрядный контракт	(pad-RYAHD-nee kan-TRAHKT)	service contract
подстилка	(pat-STEEL-ka)	dunnage
подтверждение акцепта	(pat-tver-ZHDEH-nee-ye ak-TSEP-ta)	acknowledgement of payment
подтверждение заказа	(pat-tver-ZHDEH-nee-ye za-KAH-za)	confirmation of order
подтверждённые ресурсы	(pat-tverzh-DYON-nee-ye re-SOOHR-see)	demonstrated resources
подчинённый	(pat-chee-NYON-nee)	down the line
подшипник	(pat-SHIP-neek)	bearings

П

подъём	(pad-YOM)	upturn
подъёмная сила	(pad-YOM-na-ya SEE-la)	lift
подъёмная сила восходящих потоков воздуха	(pad-YOM-na-ya SEE-la vas-kha-DYAH-shcheekh pa-TOH-kaf VOZ-doo-kha)	thermal lift
пожизненная собственность	(pa-ZHIZ-nen-na-ya SOHP-stven-nast)	living trust
пожизненный член	(pa-ZHIZ-nen-nee chlen)	life member
поземельный налог	(pa-ze-MEHL-nee na-LOK)	land tax
позитивный	(pa-zee-TEEV-nee)	positive
поисково-разведочная скважина	(POH-ees-ka-va-raz-VEH-dach-na-ya SKVAH-zhee-na)	exploratory well
поисковая скважина	(POH-ees-ka-va-ya SKVAH-zhee-na)	wild cat
поисковая скважина на новое месторождение	(POH-ees-ka-va-ya SKVAH-zhee-na na NOH-va-ye mes-ta-razh-DEH-nee-ye)	new field wildcat
поисковая скважина на новую залежь (новый горизонт)	(POH-ees-ka-va-ya SKVAH-zhee-na na NOH-voo-yoo ZAH-lesh [NOH-vee ga-ree-ZONT])	new pool test
поисковое бурение	(POH-ees-ka-va-ye boo-REH-nee-ye)	wild cat drilling
показатель отставания	(pa-ka-ZAH-tel at-sta-VAH-nee-ya)	lagging indicator
покрывать/-покрыть	(pa-kree-VAHT/pa-KREET)	absorb (v)
покрывать/-покрыть убыток	(pa-kree-VAHT/pa-KREET oo-BEE-tak)	absorb the loss (v)
покрытие страхования	(pa-KREE-tee-ye stra-kha-VAH-nee-ya)	coverage (insurance)
покупатель	(pa-KOO-pa-tel)	buyer, costumer
покупательная способность	(pa-koo-PAH-tel-na-ya spa-SOB-nast)	buyer (purchasing) power
покупательский сертификат качества	(pa-koo-PAH-tel-skee ser-tee-fee-KAHT KAH-chest-va)	end-use certificate

покупать	(pa-koo-PAHT)	purchase (v)
покупка акций	(pa-KOOP-ka AHK-tseey)	stock purchase
покупка на срок	(pa-KOOP-ka na srok)	forward purchase
покупка от импульса	(pa-KOOP-ka at EEM-pool-sa)	impulse purchase
покупная цена	(pa-koop-NAH-ya tse-NAH)	purchase price
покупщик с наилучшим предложением	(pa-koop-SHCHEEK sna-ee-LOOCH-shim pred-la-ZHEH-nee-yem)	highest bidder
поле	(POH-le)	field
поле данных	(POH-le DAHN-nikh)	field (data)
поле индикации	(POH-le een-dee-KAH-tsee-ee)	field (display)
поле под паром	(POH-le pad PAH-ram)	fallow-field
полезный груз	(pa-LEZ-nee groos)	payload
полимер	(pa-lee-MEHR)	polymer
полис страхования	(POH-lees stra-kha-VAH-nee-ya)	policy (insurance)
полис страхования жизни	(POH-lees stra-kha-VAH-nee-ya ZHIZ-nee)	life insurance policy
полис страхования ответственности	(POH-lees stra-kha-VAH-nee-ya at-VEHT-stven-nas-tee)	liability insurance
политика	(pa-LEE-tee-ka)	policy
политика капиталовложения	(pa-LEE-tee-ka ka-pee-TAH-la-vla-ZHEH-nee-ya)	investment policy
политика компании	(pa-LEE-tee-ka kam-PAH-nee-ee)	company policy
политика «открытых дверей»	(pa-LEE-tee-ka "at-KREE-tikh dve-REY")	open door policy
политика распределения	(pa-LEE-tee-ka ras-pre-de-LEH-nee-ya)	distribution policy
полная уплата	(POL-na-ya oop-LAH-ta)	payment in full
полное товарищество	(POL-na-ye ta-VAH-ree-shchest-va)	general partnership
полное урегулирование претензий	(POL-na-ye oo-re-goo-LEE-ra-va-nee-ye pre-TEN-zeey)	settlement in full

полномочия	*(pal-na-MOH-chee-ya)*	capacity
полностью опла-ченные акции	*(POL-na-styoo ap-LAH-chen-nee-ye AHK-tsee-ee)*	paid up shares
полностью опла-ченный	*(POL-na-styoo ap-LAH-chen-nee)*	paid in full
полный отказ системы	*(POL-nee at-KAHS sees-TEH-mee)*	system crash
полупеременные издержки	*(POH-loo-pe-re-MEN-nee-ye eez-DEHRSH-kee)*	semivariable costs
полулегальный рынок	*(POH-loo-le-GAHL-nee REE-nak)*	gray market
полупроводник	*(POH-loo-pra-vad-NEEK)*	semiconductor
полуфабрикаты	*(POH-loo-fab-ree-KAH-tee)*	intermediary goods
получающий еже-годную ренту	*(pa-loo-CHAH-yoo-shchee ye-zhe-GOD-noo-yoo REN-too)*	annuitant
получить/полу-чать деньги по поставке	*(pa-loo-CHEET/pa-loo-CHANT DEHN-ghee pa pas-TAHF-ke)*	collect on delivery
получить страхо-вой полис	*(pa-loo-CHEET stka-kha-VOY POH-lees)*	take out (v) (insurance)
пользователь	*(POL-za-va-tel)*	user
поместить заказ	*(pa-mes-TEET za-KAHS)*	place on order (v)
пометка задним числом	*(pa-MEHT-ka ZAHD-nim chees-LOM)*	back date (n)
помещения	*(pa-me-SHCHEH-nee-ya)*	premises
помидоры	*(pa-mee-DOH-ree)*	tomatoes
помощник	*(pa-MOSH-neek)*	assistant
помощник менед-жера	*(pa-MOSH-neek MEH-ned-zhe-ra)*	assistant manager
понижение в должности	*(pa-nee-ZHEH-nee-ye VDOLZH-na-stee)*	demotion
понижение рыноч-ных цен (до прежнего уров-ня)	*(pa-nee-ZHEH-nee-ye REE-nach-nikh tsen [da PREZH-ne-va OO-rav-nya])*	rollback
порошок	*(pa-ra-SHOK)*	powder
порт	*(port)*	port
порто-франко	*(POHR-ta-FRAHN-ka)*	free port

портовые сборы	*(par-TOH-vee-ye ZBOH-ree)*	harbor dues
портфель капиталовложений	*(part-FEL ka-pee-ta-la-vla-ZHEH-neey)*	portfolio
портсигар	*(part-see-GAHR)*	cigarette case
поручение	*(pa-roo-CHEH-nee-ye)*	commission (agency)
поручитель-гарант	*(pa-roo-CHEE-tel-ga-RAHNT)*	underwriter
поручительство	*(pa-roo-CHEE-tel-stva)*	letter of indemnity
поршень	*(POHR-shen)*	piston
порядок ведения заседания	*(pa-RYAH-dak ve-DEH-nee-ya za-se-DAH-nee-ya)*	point of order
порядок разрешения жалоб	*(pa-RYAH-dak raz-re-SHEH-nee-ya ZHAH-lap)*	grievance procedure
порядок учёта	*(pa-RYAH-dak oo-CHYOH-ta)*	accounting method
последним поступил — первым продан (ЛИФО)	*(pas-LED-neem pas-too-PEEL-PEHR-veem PROH-dan [LEE-FOH])*	last in-first out (LIFO)
последовательно расположенный ускоритель	*(pas-LEH-da-va-tel-na ras-pa-LOH-zhen-nee oos-ka-REE-tel)*	in-line booster
посмертный дар	*(pa-SMEHRT-nee dar)*	bequest
пособие по безработице	*(pa-SOH-bee-ye pa bez-ra-BOH-tee-tse)*	unemployment compensation
посредник	*(pa-SRED-neek)*	intermediary, middleman
посредничество	*(pa-SRED-nee-che-stva)*	mediation
поставщик	*(pas-taf-SHCHEEK)*	supplier
постоянная инвентаризация	*(pa-sta-YAHN-na-ya een-ven-ta-ree-ZAH-tsee-ya)*	perpetual inventory
постоянное запоминающее устройство (ПЗУ)	*(pa-sta-YAHN-na-ye za-pa-mee-NAH-yoo-shche-ye oos-TROYST-va)*	ROM
постоянные издержки	*(pa-sta-YAHN-nee-ye eez-DEHRSH-kee)*	costs, fixed
постоянный биржевой маклер	*(pa-sta-YAHN-nee beer-zhe-VOY MAHK-ler)*	specialist (stock exchange)
постоянный доход	*(pa-sta-YAHN-nee da-KHOT)*	flat yield

постоянный ток	*(pa-sta-YAHN-nee tok)*	direct current
посылка по почте	*(pa-SIL-ka pa POCH-te)*	parcel post
поточно-массовое производство	*(pa-TOCH-na-MAHS-sa-va-ye pra-eez-VOT-stva)*	mass production
потребитель	*(pat-re-BEE-tel)*	consumer
потребительские товары	*(pat-re-BEE-tel-skee-ye ta-VAH-ree)*	consumer goods
потребительский кредит	*(pat-re-BEE-tel-skee kre-DEET)*	consumer credit
потребительское исследование	*(pat-re-BEE-tel-ska-ye ees-SLEH-da-va-nee-ye)*	consumer research
потребность	*(pa-TREB-nast)*	requirement
почасовая зарплата	*(pa-cha-sa-VAH-ya zar-PLAH-ta)*	hourly earnings
почтовая реклама	*(pach-TOH-va-ya rek-LAH-ma)*	direct mail
почтовый индекс (США)	*(pach-TOH-vee een-DEKS)*	ZIP code
пошлина	*(POSH-lee-na)*	duty (customs)
пошлины причала	*(POSH-lee-nee pree-CHAH-la)*	dock handling charges
пояс	*(POH-yas)*	belt
поясное время	*(pa-yas-NOH-ye VREH-mya)*	time zone
правило возмещения	*(PRAH-vee-la vaz-me-SHCHEH-nee-ya)*	call rule
правительство	*(pra-VEE-tel-stva)*	government
право выпускать облигации	*(PRAH-va vee-poos-KAHT ab-lee-GAH-tsee-ee)*	bond power
право голоса	*(PRAH-va GOH-la-sa)*	voting right
право прохода	*(PRAH-va pra-KHOH-da)*	right of way
право регресса	*(PRAH-va re-GRES-sa)*	right of resource
право собственности	*(PRAH-va SOP-stven-na-stee)*	ownership
правовой акт (документ)	*(pra-va-VOY ahkt [da-koo-MENT])*	instrument (document)
правовой акт	*(pra-va-YOY akht)*	action, legal
правовой титул	*(pra-va-YOY TEE-tool)*	title

правопередатель	*(PRAH-va-pe-re-DAH-tel)*	assignor
правопреемник	*(PRAH-va-pre-YEM-neek)*	assignee
практика предоставления скидки	*(PRAHK-tee-ka pre-da-sta-VLEH-nee-ya SKEET-kee)*	discounting
практический	*(prak-TEE-ches-kee)*	practical
превращать/превратить в капитал	*(pre-VRAH-shchat/pre-vra-TEET fka-pee-TAHL)*	plow back earnings (v)
превышать/превысить по подписке акций	*(pre-vee-SHAHT/pre-vee-SEET pa pat-PEES-ke AHK-tseey)*	oversubscribe (v)
предварительная плата	*(pred-va-REE-tel-na-ya PLAH-ta)*	cover charge
предварительное возмещение	*(pred-va-REE-tel-na-ye vaz-me-SHCHEH-nee-ye)*	advance refunding
предварительное извещение	*(pred-va-REE-tel-na-ye eez-ve-SHCHEH-nee-ye)*	advance notice
предварительный проспект	*(pred-va-REE-tel-nee pras-PEKT)*	preliminary prospectus
предел безубыточности	*(pre-DEHL be-soo-BEE-tach-na-stee)*	break-even point
предельная стоимость	*(pre-DEHL-na-ya STOH-ee-mast)*	marginal cost
предельная цена	*(pre-DEHL-na-ya tse-NAH)*	price limit
предельные издержки производства	*(pre-DEHL-nee-ye eez-DEHRSH-kee pra-eez-VOT-stva)*	marginal costs
предисловие	*(pre-dees-LOH-vee-ye)*	foreword, preface
предлагать/предложить	*(pred-LAH-gat/pred-la-ZHEET)*	offer (v)
предлагать/предложить публичную подписку	*(pred-LAH-gat/pred-la-ZHEET poob-LEECH-noo-yoo pat-PEES-koo)*	go public (v)
предложение	*(pred-la-ZHEH-nee-ye)*	motion (parliamentary)
предложение в запечатанном конверте	*(pred-la-ZHEH-nee-ye vza-pe-CHAH-tan-nam kan-VEHR-te)*	sealed bid
предложение за покупку контрольного пакета акций	*(pred-la-ZHEH-nee-ye za pa-KOOP-koo kan-TROL-na-va pa-KEH-ta AHK-tseey)*	bid (takeover)

Ⅱ

предложение товара по телефону (на авось)	*(pred-la-ZHEH-nee-ye ta-VAH-ra pa te-le-FOH-noo [na a-VOS])*	cold call
предложенная ставка	*(pred-LOH-zhen-na-ya STAHF-ka)*	offered rate
предложенная цена	*(pred-LOH-zhen-na-ya tse-NAH)*	offered price
предложить более выгодную цену	*(pred-la-ZHIT BOH-lee VEE-gad-noo-yoo TSEH-noo)*	outbid (v)
предназначать/ предназначить	*(pred-naz-NAH-chat/pred-na-zna-CHEET)*	earmark (v)
предоставление земли	*(pre-da-stav-LEH-nee-ye zem-LEE)*	land grant
предоставлять/ предоставить	*(pre-da-sta-VLYAHT/pre-da-STAH-veet)*	make available (v)
предоставлять/ предоставить кредит, кредитовать	*(pre-da-sta-VLYAHT/pre-da-STAH-veet kre-DEET, kre-dee-ta-VAHT)*	credit (v)
предполагаемое время отправления	*(pred-pa-la-GAH-ye-ma-ye VREH-mya at-prav-LEH-nee-ya)*	estimated time of departure
предполагаемое время прибытия	*(pred-pa-la-GAH-ye-ma-ye VREH-mya pree-BEE-tee-ya)*	estimated time of arrival
предпочтение ликвидности	*(pret-PAHCH-te-nee-ye leek-VEED-nas-tee)*	liquidity preference
предприниматель	*(pret-pree-nee-MAH-tel)*	entrepreneur
предпринимать/предпринять	*(pret-pree-nee-MAHT/pret-pree-NYAHT)*	undertake (v)
предприятие	*(pret-pree-YAH-tee-ye)*	enterprise
предприятие общественного пользования	*(pret-pree-YAH-tee-ye ap-SHCHEST-ven-na-va POL-za-va-nee-ya)*	public utility
предприятие, принимающее членов и нечленов профсоюзов	*(pret-pree-YAH-tee-ye pree-nee-MAH-yoo-shche-ye CHLEH-naf ee ne-CHLEH-naf praf-sa-YOO-zaf)*	open shop
предприятие, производящее по заказу	*(pret-pree-YAH-tee-ye pra-eez-va-DYAH-shchee-ye pa za-KAH-zoo)*	job shop

председатель сове-та директоров	*(pret-se-DAH-tel sa-VEH-ta dee-rek-ta-ROF)*	Chairmen of the Board
представитель	*(pret-sta-VEE-tel)*	representative
представитель производителя	*(pret-sta-VEE-tel pra-eez-va-DEE-te-la)*	manufacturer's representative
представлять/ представить документ	*(pret-stav-LYAHT/pret-sta-VEET da-koo-MENT)*	file (v) (submit forms)
предусматривать/ предусмотреть в смете	*(pre-doos-MAHT-ree-vat/pre-doos-maht-REET FSMEH-te)*	account for (v)
президент	*(pre-zee-DENT)*	president
президиум	*(pre-ZEE-de-oom)*	executive board
презюмируемый	*(pre-zyoo-MEE-roo-ye-mee)*	imputed
преимуществен-ное право	*(pre-ee-MOO-shchest-ven-na-ye PRAH-va)*	preemptive right
прейскурант	*(preys-koo-RAHNT)*	catalog, price list
прейскурантная цена	*(preys-koo-RAHNT-na-ya tse-NAH)*	list price
прекращать/пре-кратить	*(pre-kra-SHCHAHT/pre-kra-TEET)*	terminate (v)
премия	*(PREH-mee-ya)*	bonus (premium)
премия за покуп-ку	*(PREH-mee-ya za pa-KOOP-koo)*	buyer's premium
препятствие	*(pre-PYAHT-stvee-ye)*	handicap
претензия, иск	*(pre-TEN-zee-ya, eesk)*	claim
преференциаль-ная (льготная) нефть	*(pre-fe-ren-tsee-AHL-na-ya [LGOT-na-ya] neft)*	preferential crude
преференциаль-ный таможен-ный тариф	*(pre-fe-ren-tsee-AHL-nee ta-MOH-zhen-nee ta-REEF)*	preferential tariff
при закрытии	*(pree za-KREE-tee-ee)*	at the close
при открытии	*(pree at-KREE-tee-ee)*	at the opening
приблизительная смета	*(pree-blee-ZEE-tel-na-ya SMEH-ta)*	rough estimate
прибыль	*(PREE-bil)*	profit
прибыль от опера-ций	*(PREE-bil at a-pe-RAH-tseey)*	operating profit

прибыльная операция	*(PREE-bil-na-ya a-pe-RAH-tsee-ya)*	profit-taking
приверженность к данной марке	*(pree-VEHR-zhen-nast GDAHN-nay MAHR-ke)*	brand loyalty
привилегированная акция	*(pree-vee-le-ghee-ROH-van-na-ya AHK-tsee-ya)*	preferred stock
привилегированная ставка	*(pree-vee-le-ghee-ROH-van-na-ya STAHF-ka)*	prime rate
привилегия	*(pree-vee-LEH-ghee-ya)*	franchise
приём для уклонения от налогов	*(pree-YOM dlya ook-la-NEH-nee-ya at na-LOH-gaf)*	tax shelter
приёмник	*(pree-YOM-neek)*	receiver
признание фирменного знака	*(pree-ZNAH-nee-ye FEEHR-men-na-va ZNAH-ka)*	brand recognition
признанные имущественные права	*(PREEZ-nan-nee-ye ee-MOO-shchest-ven-nee-ye pra-VAH)*	vested interests
признанные права	*(PREEZ-nan-nee-ye pra-VAH)*	vested rights
признавать/признать	*(preez-na-VAHT/preez-NAHT)*	acknowledge (v)
приказ, действующий один день	*(pree-KAHS DEY-stvoo-yoo-shchee a-DEEN den)*	day order
прикреплять/прикрепить	*(pree-krep-LYAHT/pree-kree-PEET)*	attach (v) (affix, adhere)
приложение	*(pree-la-ZHEH-nee-ye)*	attachment (contract)
пример	*(pree-MEHR)*	pattern
примерная ведомость	*(pree-MEHR-na-ya VEH-da-mast)*	pro forma statement
примерная фактура	*(pree-MEHR-na-ya fak-TOO-ra)*	pro forma invoice
примесь	*(PREE-mes)*	impurity
принимать/принять	*(pree-nee-MAHT/pree-NYAHT)*	accept (v)
принудительный выкуп	*(pree-noo-DEE-tel-nee VEE-koop)*	mandatory redemption
принуждение	*(pree-nooz-DEH-nee-ye)*	duress

П

принципы бухгал- терского дела	*(PREEN-tsee-pee bookh- GAHL-ter-ska-va DEH- la)*	accounting principles
принятие ответ- ственности	*(pree-NYAH-tee-ye at-VET- stven-na-stee)*	assumption of liability
принятие потре- бителя	*(pree-NYAH-tee-ye pat-re- BEE-te-la)*	consumer acceptance
принятие фирмен- ного знака	*(pree-NYAH-tee-ye FEEHR- men-na-va ZNAH-ka)*	brand acceptance
принтер	*(PREEN-tehr)*	printer
приобретение	*(pree-ab-re-TEH-nee-ye)*	acquisition
приобретение дан- ных	*(pree-ab-re-TEH-nee-ye DAHN-nikh)*	data acquisition
приобретение кон- трольного паке- та акций	*(pree-ab-re-TEH-nee-ye kan-TROL-na-va pa- KEH-ta AHK-tseey)*	stock takeover
приобретённые права	*(pre-ab-re-TYON-nee-ye pra-VAH)*	acquired rights
приобретать/при- обрести	*(pree-ab-re-TAHT/pree-ab- re-STEE)*	acquire (v)
приоритет	*(pree-a-ree-TET)*	priority
приостановлять/ приостановить платежи	*(pree-as-ta-NAHV-lyat/pree- as-ta-nah-VEET pla-te- ZHEE)*	suspend payment (v)
припрятывать/ припрятать	*(pree-PRYAH-tee-vat/pree- PRYAH-taht)*	hoard (v)
природный газ	*(pree-ROD-nee gahs)*	natural gas
природные богат- ства	*(pree-ROD-nee-ye ba- GAHT-stva)*	natural resources
прирост	*(pree-ROST)*	accretion, increase
прирост акцио- нерного обще- ства	*(pree-ROST ak-tsee-a- NEHR-na-va OP-shchest- va)*	corporate growth
прирост запасов	*(pree-ROST za-PAH-saf)*	additions to reserves
прирост (умень- шение) ценно- стей	*(pree-ROST [oo-men- SHEH-nee-ye] TSEN-na- stey)*	capital gain (loss)
приростное «кэш- флоу»	*(pree-ROST-na-ye "cash flow")*	incremental cash flow
приростные рас- ходы	*(pree-ROST-nee-ye ras- KHOH-dee)*	incremental costs

присвоение чужих денежных средств	*(pree-sva-YEH-nee-ye choo-ZHIKH DEH-nezh-nikh sretstf)*	embezzlement
присущая стоимость	*(pree-SOO-shcha-ya STOH-ee-mast)*	intrinsic value
приукрашивание баланса	*(pree-ook-RAH-shee-va-nee-ye ba-LAHN-sa)*	window dressing
причальный сбор	*(pree-CHAHL-nee zbohr)*	wharfage charges
пробирка	*(pra-BEEHR-ka)*	test tube
проблема	*(pra-BLEH-ma)*	problem
пробный баланс	*(PROB-nee ba-LAHNS)*	trial balance
провал	*(pra-VAHL)*	failure
провалиться	*(pra-va-LEE-tsa)*	fail (v)
проверка инвентаря	*(pra-VEHR-ka een-ven-ta-RYAH)*	control, stock
проволока	*(PROH-va-la-ka)*	wire
прогноз	*(prag-NOS)*	forecast
прогноз доходов от продажи	*(prag-NOS da-KHOH-daf at pra-DAH-zhee)*	sales forecast
программа	*(pra-GRAHM-ma)*	program
программа	*(pra-GRAHM-ma)*	computer program
программа капиталовложения	*(pra-GRAHM-ma ka-pee-TAH-la-vla-ZHEH-nee-ya)*	investment program
программирование	*(pra-gram-MEE-ra-va-nee-ye)*	programming
программировать	*(pra-gram-MEE-ra-vat)*	program (v)
программное обеспечение	*(pra-GRAHM-na-ye a-bes-pe-CHEH-nee-ye)*	software
продавец	*(pra-da-VETS)*	vendor
продажа	*(pra-DAH-zha)*	sales
продажа акций по методике пирамида	*(pra-DAH-zha AHK-tseey pa me-TOH-dee-ke pee-ra-MEE-da)*	pyramid selling
продажа без покрытия на срок	*(pra-DAH-zha bes pa-KREE-tee-ya na srok)*	short sale
продажа по телефону	*(pra-DAH-zha pa te-le-FOH-noo)*	telemarketing

продажа товаров на дому	*(pra-DAH-zha ta-VAH-raf na da-MOO)*	door-to-door sales
продажная квота	*(pra-DAHZH-na-ya KVOH-ta)*	sales quota
продано сверх запасов	*(PROH-da-na sverkh za-PAH-saf)*	oversold
продавать/про-дать	*(pra-da-VAHT/pra-DAHT)*	sell (v)
продавать/про-дать непосред-ственно	*(pra-da-VAHT/pra-DAHT ne-pa-SRET-stven-na)*	sell direct (v)
продвижение по службе	*(pra-dvee-ZHEH-nee-ye pa SLOOZH-be)*	promotion (position)
продолжать/про-должить	*(pra-dal-ZHAHT/pra-DOHL-zheet)*	resume (v)
продукт	*(pra-DOOKT)*	product
проект	*(pra-YEKT)*	blueprint, project
проектирование	*(pra-yek-TEE-ra-va-nee-ye)*	project planning
проектирование, дизайн	*(pra-yek-TEE-ra-va-nee-ye, dee-ZAHYN)*	design engineering
проектирование систем	*(pra-yek-TEE-ra-va-nee-ye sees-TEM)*	systems engineering
проектировать	*(pra-yek-TEE-ra-vat)*	project (v)
проектно-исследо-вательская работа	*(pra-YEKT-na-ees-LEH-da-va-tel-ska-ya ra-BOH-ta)*	research and development
прожиточный минимум	*(pra-ZHEE-tach-nee MEE-nee-moom)*	cost of living
производитель	*(pra-eez-va-DEE-tel)*	manufacturer
производительная мощность	*(pra-eez-va-DEE-tel-na-ya MOSHCH-nast)*	capacity, manufacturing
производитель-ность	*(pra-eez-va-DEE-tel-nast)*	productivity
производитель-ный капитал	*(pra-eez-va-DEE-tel-nee ka-pee-TAHL)*	instrumental capital
производитель-ный контроль	*(pra-eez-va-DEE-tel-nee kan-TROL)*	manufacturing control
производственная мощность	*(pra-eez-VOT-stven-na-ya MOSHCH-nast)*	manufacturing capacity
производственная технология	*(pra-eez-VOT-stven-na-ya tekh-na-LOH-ghee-ya)*	engineering, production

производственное страхование	(pra-eez-VOT-stven-na-ye stra-kha-VAH-nee-ye)	industrial insurance
производственные возможности	(pra-eez-VOT-stven-nee-ye vaz-MOZH-na-stee)	facilities (possibilities)
производственные фонды	(pra-eez-VOT-stven-nee-ye FON-dee)	facilities (means of production)
производствен-ный график	(pra-eez-VOT-stven-nee GRAH-feek)	production schedule
производствен-ный контроль	(pra-eez-VOT-stven-nee kan-TROL)	control, manufacturing
производствен-ный процесс	(pra-eez-VOT-stven-nee pra-TSES)	production process
производство	(pra-eez-VOT-stva)	manufacturing production
производство по наделам	(pra-eez-VOT-stva pa na-DEH-lam)	batch production
прокатный стан	(pra-KAHT-nee stahn)	rolling mill
прокладка голов-ки цилиндра	(prak-LAHT-ka ga-LOF-kee tsee-LEEN-dra)	cylinder heat gasket
промежуточный	(pra-me-ZHOO-tach-nee)	interim
промежуточный бюджет	(pra-me-ZHOO-tach-nee byood-ZHET)	interim budget
промежуточный финансовый отчёт	(pra-me-ZHOO-tach-nee fee-NAHN-sa-vee at-CHYOHT)	interim statement
промышленное аварийное про-исшествие	(pra-MISH-len-na-ye a-va-REEY-na-ye pra-ees-SHEST-vee-ye)	industrial accident
промышленное огородничество	(pra-MISH-len-na-ye a-ga-ROD-nee-chest-va)	truck farming
промышленное объединение	(pra-MISH-len-na-ye ab-ye-dee-NEH-nee-ye)	industrial union
промышленное проектирование	(pra-MISH-len-na-ye pra-yek-TEE-ra-va-nee-ye)	industrial planning
промышленность	(pra-MISH-len-nast)	industry
промышленный арбитраж	(pra-MISH-len-nee ar-beet-RAHSH)	industrial arbitration
промышленный природный газ	(pra-MISH-len-nee pree-ROD-nee gahs)	industrial gas
промышленный инжиниринг	(pra-MISH-len-nee een-zhe-NEE-reenk)	industrial engineering

промышленные товары	*(pra-MISH-len-nee-ye ta-VAH-ree)*	industrial goods
проникновение рынка	*(pra-neek-na-VEH-nee-ye RIN-ka)*	market penetration
прописная буква	*(pra-pees-NAH-ya BOOK-va)*	capital letter
пропускать/пропустить	*(pra-poos-KAHT/pra-poos-TEET)*	omit (v)
пропускная способность	*(pra-poosk-NAH-ya spa-SOB-nast)*	throughout
проспект	*(pras-PEKT)*	prospectus
просроченный	*(pra-SROH-chen-nee)*	overdue, past due
просроченный счёт	*(pra-SROH-chen-nee shchyoht)*	delinquent account
просроченный чек	*(pra-SROH-chen-nee chek)*	stale check
простой эфир	*(pras-TOY e-FEEHR)*	ether
пространство на диске	*(pro-STRAHN-stva na DEES-ke)*	disk space
просчёт	*(pra-SHCHYOHT)*	miscalculation
протекционизм	*(pra-tek-tsee-a-NEEZM)*	protectionism
протест	*(pra-TEST)*	protest (banking, law)
против всех рисков	*(PROH-teev fsekh REES-kaf)*	against all risks
противовоспалительный	*(PROH-te-va-vas-pa-LEE-tel-nee)*	anti-inflammatory
противопожарная полоса	*(pra-te-va-pa-ZAHR-na-ya pa-la-SAH)*	fire-break
профессиональный риск	*(pra-fees-see-a-NAHL-nee reesk)*	occupational hazard
профессия	*(pra-FES-see-ya)*	profession
профилактический ремонт	*(pra-fee-lak-TEE-ches-kee re-MONT)*	preventive maintenance
профили	*(PROH-fee-lee)*	structural shapes
профсоюз	*(praf-sa-YOOS)*	labor union, trade union
профсоюз, предоставляющий кредит своим членам	*(praf-sa-YOOS pre-da-sta-VLYAH-yoo-shchee kre-DEET sva-EEM CHLEH-nam)*	credit union
процент	*(pra-TSENT)*	percentage point

процент на инвестиции	*(pra-TSENT na een-ve-STEE-tsee-ee)*	return on investment
процент на капитал	*(pra-TSENT na ka-pee-TAHL)*	return on capital
процент прибыли	*(pra-TSENT PREE-bee-lee)*	percentage of profit
процентная облигация	*(pra-TSENT-na-ya ab-lee-GAH-tsee-ya)*	revenue bond
процентная ставка	*(pra-TSENT-na-ya STAHF-ka)*	interest rate
процентные облигации	*(pra-TSENT-nee-ye ab-lee-GAH-tsee-ee)*	income bonds
процентный арбитраж	*(pra-TSENT-nee ar-beet-RAHSH)*	interest arbitrage
процентный доход	*(pra-TSENT-nee da-KHOT)*	interest income
процентный паритет	*(pra-TSENT-nee pa-ree-TET)*	interest parity
проценты	*(pra-TSENT-tee)*	interest
процесс	*(pra-TSES)*	process
процессор	*(pra-TSES-sar)*	central processing unit (CPU), processor
прочие активы	*((PROH-chee-ye ahk-TEE-vee)*	other assets
прочие пассивы	*(PROH-chee-ye pas-SEE-vee)*	other liabilities
пруд	*(proot)*	pond
прямая котировка	*(pree-MAH-ya ka-TEE-rof-ka)*	direct quotation
прямое промышленное использование топлива	*(pree-MOH-ye pra-MISH-len-na-ye ees-POHL-za-va-nee-ye TOP-lee-va)*	industrial direct heating
прямолинейный	*(prya-ma-lee-NEY-nee)*	linear
прямые грузопоставки	*(pree-MEE-ye groo-za-pas-TAHF-kee)*	drop shipment
прямые издержки	*(pree-MEE-ye eez-DEHRSH-kee)*	direct expenses
прямые инвестиции	*(pree-MEE-ye een-ve-STEE-tsee-ee)*	direct investment
прямые расходы	*(pree-MEE-ye ras-KHOH-dee)*	direct cost

психологический тест	*(psee-kha-la-GHEE-ches-kee test)*	personality test
птица	*(PTEE-tsa)*	fowl
публичное предло-жение (ценных бумаг)	*(poob-LEECH-na-ye pred-la-ZHEH-nee-ye [TSEN-nikh boo-MAHK])*	public offering
публичные торги	*(poob-LEECH-nee-ye TOHR-ghee)*	public sale
пункты доставки	*(POON-ktee da-STAHF-kee)*	delivery points
пусковая установ-ка	*(poos-ka-VAH-ya oos-ta-NOF-ka)*	launcher
пусковой стол	*(poos-ka-VOY stol)*	launch pad
пшеница	*(pshe-NEE-tsa)*	wheat
«Пятница» (вер-ный помощник)	*(PYAHT-nee-tsa [VEHR-nee pa-MOSH-neek])*	man (gal) Friday

Р

работа	*(ra-BOH-ta)*	job
работать	*(ra-BOH-tat)*	work (v)
работать по дого-вору	*(ra-BOH-tat pa da-ga-VOH-roo)*	work by contract
работающий по найму	*(ra-BOH-ta-yoo-shchee pa NAHY-moo)*	self-employed
работник физиче-ского труда	*(ra-BOT-neek fee-ZEE-ches-ka-va troo-DAH)*	manual worker
рабочая нагрузка	*(ra-BOH-cha-ya na-GROOS-ka)*	work load
рабочая сила	*(ra-BOH-cha-ya SEE-la)*	manpower, workforce
рабочая станция	*(ra-BOH-cha-ya STAHN-tsee-ya)*	workstation
рабочий	*(ra-BOH-chee)*	laborer
рабочий день	*(ra-BOH-chee den)*	work day
рабочий класс	*(ra-BOH-chee klahs)*	working class
рабочий коллек-тив	*(ra-BOH-chee kal-lek-TEEF)*	labor force
рабочий объём	*(ra-BOH-chee ab-YOM)*	displacement
равенство зара-ботной платы	*(RAH-ven-stva ZAH-ra-bat-nay PLAH-tee)*	equal pay for equal work

радиальная шина	(ra-dee-AHL-na-ya SHEE-na)	radial tire
радиатор	(ra-dee-AH-tar)	radiator
радиовещание	(RAH-dee-a-ve-SHCHAH-nee-ye)	broadcasting
радиолокацион-ная станция (РЛС) дальнего обнаружения	(RAH-dee-a-la-ka-tsee-ON-na-ya STAHN-tsee-ya [EHR-EL-ES] DAHL-ne-va ab-na-roo-ZHEH-nee-ya)	early warning radar
разбавка к тари-фу	(raz-BAHF-ka kta-REEF-foo)	tariff differential
разбавление капи-тала	(raz-bav-LEH-nee-ye ka-pee-TAH-la)	dilution of equity
разбавление чистой доли	(raz-ba-VLEH-nee-ye CHEES-tay DOH-lee)	equity, dilution
развёртка	(raz-VYOHRT-ka)	scanning
развёртывание (сжатого файла)	(RAHZ-vyor-tee-va-nee-ye [ZHZHAH-ta-va FAHY-la])	uncrunching (data)
развитие новых продуктов	(raz-VEE-tee-ye NOH-vikh pra-DOOK-taf)	new product development
развитие продук-та	(raz-VEE-tee-ye pra-DOOK-ta)	product development
разделение	(raz-de-LEH-nee-ye)	separation
разделение использования недвижимости по срокам	(raz-de-LEH-nee-ye ees-POL-za-va-nee-ya ne-DVEE-zhee-ma-stee pa SROH-kam)	time sharing
разделение труда	(raz-de-LEH-nee-ye troo-DAH)	division of labor
размер	(raz-MEHR)	size
размер валового дохода при самофинанси-ровании («кэш-флоу»)	(raz-MEHR va-la-VOH-va da-KHOH-da pree SAH-ma-fee-nan-SEE-ra-va-nee-ee ["cash flow"])	cash flow
размер колебаний валюты	(raz-MEHR ka-le-BAH-nee va-LYOO-tee)	currency band
размер образца	(raz-MEHR a-braz-TSAH)	sample size
размещать акции	(raz-me-SHCHAHT AHK-tsee-ee)	float (v) (issue stock)

размещать чеки	*(raz-me-SHCHAHT CHEH-kee)*	float (outstanding checks)
разница	*(RAHZ-nee-tsa)*	spread
разнообразный	*(raz-na-ab-RAHZ-nee)*	miscellaneous
разрегулирован-ный	*(raz-re-goo-LEE-ra-van-nee)*	deregulated
разрешать/разре-шить	*(raz-re-SHAHT/ras-re-SHEET)*	allow (v)
разрешение	*(raz-re-SHEH-nee-ye)*	permit
разрешение на право работы	*(raz-re-SHEH-nee-ye na PRAH-va ra-BOH-tee)*	work permit
разрешение на экспорт куль-турных ценно-стей	*(raz-re-SHEH-nee-ye na EKS-part kool-TOOHR-nikh TSEN-na-stey)*	cultural export permit
разрозненная пар-тия	*(raz-ROZ-nen-na-ya PAHR-tee-ya)*	odd lot
рак	*(rahk)*	cancer
ракета	*(ra-KEH-ta)*	rocket
ракетоплан	*(ra-ke-ta-PLAHN)*	boost-glide aircraft
рамка доходов	*(RAHM-ka da-KHOH-daf)*	income bracket
распечатка (ком-пьютера)	*(ras-pe-CHAHT-ka [kam-PYOO-te-ra])*	printout (computer)
расписание	*(ras-pee-SAH-nee-ye)*	timetable (transport)
расположение	*(ras-pa-la-ZHEH-nee-ye)*	layout
расположение страницы	*(ras-pa-la-ZHEH-nee-ye stra-NEE-tsee)*	page makeup
распорядок дня	*(ras-pa-RYAH-dak dnyah)*	order of the day
распоряжение	*(ras-pa-rya-ZHEH-nee-ye)*	regulation
распределение	*(ras-pre-de-LEH-nee-ye)*	allotment, distribution
распределитель	*(ras-pre-de-LEE-tel)*	distributor
распределитель-ная сеть	*(ras-pre-de-LEE-tel-na-ya set)*	distribution network
распределять/рас-пределить	*(ras-pre-de-LYAHT/ras-pre-de-LEET)*	allot (v)
расстояние в милях на галлон горючего	*(ras-sta-YAH-nee-ye VMEE-lyakh na gal-LON TOP-lee-va)*	mileage

рассчитывать/ рассчитаться	*(ras-SHCHEE-tee-vat-sa/ras-SHCHEE-ta-tsya)*	pay off (v)
раствор	*(ras-TVOHR)*	solution
растворённое вещество	*(ras-tva-RYON-na-ye ve-shche-STVOH)*	salute
растворимость	*(ras-tva-REE-mast)*	solubility
растворитель	*(ras-tva-REE-tel)*	solvent
растение	*(ras-TEH-nee-ye)*	plant
растения	*(ras-TEH-nee-ya)*	plants
растрата имущества	*(ras-TRAH-ta ee-MOO-shchest-va)*	wasting assets
растрескивание	*(ras-TRES-kee-va-nee-ye)*	cracking
расход горючего	*(ras-KHOT ga-RYOO-che-va)*	gas consumption
расход из основных фондов	*(ras-KHOT eez as-nav-NIKH FON-daf)*	capital expenditure
расходование при дефиците	*(ras-KHOH-da-va-nee-ye pree de-fe-TSEE-te)*	deficit spending
расходы	*(ras-KHOH-dee)*	charges, expenses
расходы будущих периодов	*(ras-KHOH-dee BOO-doo-shcheekh pe-REE-a-daf)*	deferred charges
расходы капитала	*(ras-KHOH-dee ka-pee-TAH-la)*	capital spending
расходы на переезд	*(ras-KHOH-dee na pe-re-YEZD)*	moving expenses
расходы на погрузку	*(ras-KHOH-dee na pa-GROOS-koo)*	shipping charges
расходы по выгрузке	*(ras-KHOH-dee pa VEEG-roos-ke)*	landing costs
расходы по спасению	*(ras-KHOH-dee pa spa-SEH-nee-yoo)*	salvage charges
расходы по укладке	*(ras-KHOH-dee pa ook-LAHT-ke)*	stowage charges
расходы по уплате процентов	*(ras-KHOH-dee pa oop-LAH-te pra-TSEN-taf)*	interest expenses
расходы по участию	*(ras-KHOH-dee pa oo-CHAHS-tee-yoo)*	participation fee
расчётная палата	*(ra-SHCHYOT-na-ya pa-LAH-ta)*	clearinghouse

P

рационализатор- ский	(ra-tsee-a-na-lee-ZAH-tar- skee)	labor-saving
рационирование	(ra-tsee-a-NEE-ra-va-nee- ye)	rationing
реагент	(re-a-GHENT)	reactant
реактивный истребитель	(re-ak-TEEV-nee ees-tre- BEE-tel)	jet fighter
реактивный само- лёт	(re-ak-TEEV-nee sa-ma- LYOT)	jet plane
реальная зарпла- та	(re-AHL-na-ya zar-PLAH- ta)	real wages
реальные активы	(re-AHL-nee-ye ak-TEE-vee)	real assets
реальный доход	(re-AHL-nee da-KHOT)	real income, real earnings yield
реальный доход после вычета налогов	(re-AHL-nee da-KHOT POS-le VEE-che-ta na- LOH-gaf)	after-tax real rate of return
реальный общий убыток	(re-AHL-nee OP-shchee oo- BEE-tak)	actual total loss
ревизия баланса	(re-VEE-zee-ya ba-LAHN- sa)	auditing balance sheet
ревизия операций	(re-VEE-zee-ya a-pe-RAH- tseey)	operations audit
ревизовать	(ree-vee-za-VAHT)	audit (v)
ревизор	(re-vee-ZOHR)	auditor, inspector
револьверный кредит	(re-val-VEHR-nee kre- DEET)	revolving credit
револьверный фонд	(re-val-VEHR-nee font)	revolving fund
регистрационный номер	(re-ghee-stra-tsee-ON-nee NOH-mer)	reference number
регламент	(reg-LAH-ment)	standing order
регресс	(re-GRES)	recourse
регрессивный налог	(re-gres-SEEV-nee na-LOK)	regressive tax
регулируемая монополия	(re-goo-LEE-roo-ye-ma-ya ma-na-POH-lee-ya)	legal monopoly
редактировать	(re-dak-TEE-ra-vat)	edit (v)
редактор	(re-DAHK-tar)	editor

редиска	(re-DEES-ka)	radish (es)
резерв	(re-ZEHRF)	reserve
резервная мощность	(re-ZEHRV-na-ya MOSHCH-nast)	idle capacity
резервное устройство	(re-ZEHRV-na-ye oos-TROY-stva)	backup
резервуарная нефть	(re-zer-voo-AHR-na-ya neft)	stock-tank oil
резолюция	(re-za-LYOO-tsee-ya)	resolution
резонанс	(re-za-NAHNS)	resonance
рейтинг фирменного знака	(REY-teenk FEEHR-men-na-va ZNAH-ka)	brand image
реклама	(rek-LAH-ma)	advertisement
рекламная кампания	(rek-LAHM-na-ya kam-PAH-nee-ya)	campaign, advertising
рекламная компания	(rek-LAHM-na-ya kam-PAH-nee-ya)	advertising campaign
рекламное агентство	(rek-LAHM-na-ye a-GHENT-stva)	advertising agency
рекламные расходы	(rek-LAHM-nee-ye ras-KHOH-dee)	advertising expenses
рекламные средства	(rek-LAHM-nee-ye SRET-stva)	advertising media
рекламный бюджет	(rek-LAHM-nee byood-ZHET)	advertising budget
рекламный менеджер	(rek-LAHM-nee MEH-ned-zhehr)	advertising manager
рекламный стенд	(rek-LAHM-nee stend)	billboard
рекомендательное письмо	(re-ka-men-DAH-tel-na-ye pees-MOH)	letter of introduction
реляционная база данных	(re-la-tsee-ON-na-ya BAH-za DAHN-nikh)	relational data base
ремешок для часов	(re-me-SHOK dlya cha-SOF)	watch band
рентабельно извлекаемые запасы	(ren-TAH-bel-na eez-vle-KAH-ye-mee-ye za-PAH-see)	commercially exploitable reserves
рентабельность	(ren-TAH-bel-nast)	earnings, profitability
рентабельный	(ren-TAH-bel-nee)	cost effective

реорганизация	*(re-ar-ga-nee-ZAH-tsee-ya)*	reorganization
репродукция	*(re-prah-DOOK-tsee-ya)*	copy (reproduction)
эрессоры	*(res-SOH-ree)*	spring
рефляция	*(re-FLAH-tsee-ya)*	reflection
рецепт	*(re-TSEPT)*	prescription
рецессия	*(re-TSES-see-ya)*	recession
решать/решить	*(re-SHAHT/re-SHEET)*	adjudge (v)
решение	*(re-SHEH-nee-ye)*	adjudication
решение о произ- водстве или закупке	*(re-SHEH-nee-ye a pra-eez- VOT-stve ee za-KOOP- ke)*	make-or-buy decision
решение пробле- мы	*(re-SHEH-nee-ye pra- BLEH-mee)*	problem solving
решётка	*(re-SHYOHT-ka)*	grille
ржавчина	*(RHZAHF-chee-na)*	rust (plant disease)
риск	*(reesk)*	risk
риск колебания валютного курса	*(reesk ka-le-BAH-nee-ya va- LYOOT-na-va- KOOHR- sa)*	exchange risk
риск перевозчика	*(reesk pe-re-VOZ-shchee- ka)*	carrier's risk
рисковый капитал	*(rees-KOH-vee ka-pee- TAHL)*	risk, venture capital
рожь	*(rozh)*	rye
розничная прода- жа	*(ROZ-neech-na-ya pra- DAH-zha)*	merchandising retail trade
розничная прода- жа за наличные	*(ROZ-neech-na-ya pra- DAH-zha za na-LEECH- nee-ye)*	cash-and-carry
розничная цена	*(ROZ-neech-na-ya tse-NAH)*	retail price
розничные това- ры	*(ROZ-neech-nee-ye ta-VAH- ree)*	retail merchandise
розничный	*(ROZ-neech-nee)*	retail
розничный банк	*(ROZ-neech-nee bahnk)*	retail bank
розничный мага- зин	*(ROZ-neech-nee ma-ga- ZEEN)*	retail outlet
рост	*(rost)*	growth
ростовщичество	*(ras-ta-FSHCHEE-che-stva)*	usury

роялти	*(ROH-yal-tee)*	royalty
руда	*(roo-DAH)*	ore
руководитель профсоюза	*(roo-ka-va-DEE-tel praf-sa-YOO-za)*	labor leader
руководитель фабрики	*(roo-ka-va-DEE-tel FAHB-ree-kee)*	plant manager
руководить	*(roo-ka-va-DEET)*	manage (v)
руководство бизнеса (менеджмент)	*(roo-ka-VOT-stva de-la-VOY DEH-ya-tel-na-styoo)*	business management
руководство портфеля	*(roo-ka-VOT-stva part-FEH-lya)*	portfolio management
руководящая иерархия	*(roo-ka-va-DYAH-shcha-ya ee-ye-RAHR-khee-ya)*	chain of command
руководящий комитет	*(roo-ka-va-DYAH-shchee ka-mee-TET)*	board, executive
рулевое управление	*(roo-le-VOH-ye oop-rav-LEH-nee-ye)*	steering
рулевое управление с усилителем	*(roo-le-VOH-ye oop-rav-LEH-nee-ye soo-see LEE-te-lem)*	power steering
руль	*(rool)*	steering wheel
рутинная операция	*(roo-TEEN-na-ya a-pe-RAH-tsee-ya)*	routine (computers)
рыбный промысел	*(RIB-nee PROH-mee-sel)*	fishery
рынок	*(REE-nak)*	market
рынок долгосрочных сделок (на купле-продаже нефти)	*(REE-nak dal-ga-SROCH-nikh ZDEH-lak [na KOOP-le-pra-DAH-zhe NEF-tee])*	contract oil market
рынок капитала	*(REE-nak ka-pee-TAH-la)*	capital market
рынок наличного товара	*(REE-nak na-LEECH-na-va-ta-VAH-ra)*	spot market
рынок «спот» (наличного товара)	*(REE-nak spot [na-LEECH-na-va- ta-VAH-ra])*	spot market
рынок покупателя	*(REE-nak pa-koo-PAH-te-lya)*	buyer's market
рынок труда	*(REE-nak TROO-da)*	labor market
рыночная динамика	*(REE-nach-na-ya dee-NAH-mee-ka)*	market dynamics

P

рыночная конку- рентоспособ- ность	(REE-nach-na-ya kan-koo- REN-ta-spa-SOB-nast)	market position
рыночная оценка	(REE-nach-na-ya a-TSEN- ka)	market rating
рыночная оценка	(REE-nach-na-ya a-TSEN- ka)	rating (market)
рыночная стои- мость	(REE-nach-na-ya STOH-ee- mast)	market value (general)
рыночная цена	(REE-nach-na-ya tse-NAH)	market price
рыночные силы	(REE-nach-nee-ye SEE-lee)	market forces
рыночный отчёт	(REE-nach-nee at- CHYOHT)	market report
рыночный план	(REE-nach-nee plahn)	market plan
рысь	(ris)	lynx

С

с высокой точнос- тью воспроиз- ведения	(SVEE-so-kay TOCH-nast- yoo vas-pra-eez-ve-DEH- nee-ya)	high fidelity
с фрахтом	(SFRAHKH-tam)	freight included
салат	(sa-LAHT)	lettuce
самолёт	(sa-ma-LYOT)	airplane
самообслужива- ние	(sa-ma-ap-SLOO-zhee-va- nee-ye)	self-service
самооценка	(sa-ma-a-TSEN-ka)	self-appraisal
сапоги	(sa-pa-GHEE)	boots
сапожная мастер- ская	(sa-POZH-na-ya mas-ter- SKAH-ya)	shoe repair shop
сарай	(sa-RAHY)	barn
саранча	(sa-ran-CHAH)	locust (insect)
сафьян	(saf-YAHN)	Morocco leather
сберегательные облигации (США)	(zbe-re-GAH-tel-nee-ye ab- lee-GAH-tsee-ee)	savings bond
сберегательный счёт	(zbe-re-GAH-tel-nee shchyoht)	savings account
сбережения	(zve-re-ZHEH-nee-ya)	savings

сбивать цены	*(zbee-VAHT TSEH-nee)*	undercut (v)
сбор на товары роскоши	*(zbohr na ta-VAH-ree ROS-ka-shee)*	luxury tax
сборщик	*(ZBOHR-shcheek)*	tax collector
сборщик налогов	*(ZBOHR-shcheek na-LOH-gaf)*	fiscal agent
сборщик пошлин	*(ZBOHR-shcheek POSH-leen)*	collector of customs
сборы по выгрузке	*(ZBOH-ree pa VEEG-roos-ke)*	landing charges
сбросовый газ	*(ZBROH-sa-vee gahs)*	dump gas
сбыт	*(zbit)*	sales
свекловичный сахар	*(svek-la-VEECH-nee SAH-khar)*	beet sugar
свёкла	*(SVYOK-la)*	beet
сверхзвуковая скорость (сверх Маха)	*(SVEHRKH-zvoo-ka-va-ya SKOH-rast [sverkh MAH-kha])*	mach speed
сверхнормативные коммерческие запасы (жидкого топлива)	*(SVEHRKH-nar-ma-TEEV-nee-ye kam-MEHR-ches-kee-ye za-PAH-see [ZHIT-ka-va TOP-lee-va])*	security oil stocks
«сверхтяжелая» нефть	*(sverkh-tya-ZHOH-la-ya neft)*	extra-heavy oil
сверхурочный	*(SVEHRKH-oo-ROCH-nee)*	overtime
светодиодный индикатор	*(sve-ta-dee-OD-nee een-dee-KAH-tar)*	LED display
свидетель	*(svee-DEH-tel)*	witness
свидетельство на акцию	*(svee-DEH-tel-stva na AHK-tsee-yoo)*	stock certificate
свидетельство о вкладе	*(svee-DEH-tel-stva a FKLAH-dee)*	certificate of deposit
свидетельство о происхождении	*(svee-DEH-tel-stva a pra-ees-khazh-DEH-nee-ee)*	certificate of origin
свидетельство об утверждении	*(svee-DEH-tel-stva ab oot-ver-ZHDEH-nee-ee)*	certificate of incorporation
свидетельство, сертификат	*(svee-DEH-tel-stva , ser-tee-fee-KAHT)*	certificate
свидетельствовать	*(svee-DEH-tel-stva-vat)*	witness (v)

свиная кожа	(svee-NAH-ya KOH-zha)	pigskin
свиноматка	(svee-na-MAHT-ka)	sow
свинья	(sveen-YAH)	swine
свободная эконо-мическая зона	(sva-BOD-na-ya e-ka-na-MEE-ches-ka-ya ZOH-na)	free economic zone
свободно от част-ной аварии	(sva-BOD-na at CHAHS-nay a-VAH-ree-ee)	free of particular average
свободно плаваю-щая валюта	(sva-BOD-na PLAH-va-yoo-shcha-ya va-LYOO-ta)	floating currency
свободное время	(sva-BOD-na-ye VREH-mya)	free time
свободное пред-приниматель-ство	(sva-BOD-na-ye pret-pree-nee-MAH-tel-stva)	free enterprise
свободный газ (газ чисто газо-вых залежей)	(sva-BOD-nee gahs [gahs CHEES-ta GAH-za-vikh ZAH-le-zhey])	free gas
свободный рынок	(sva-BOD-nee REE-nak)	free market
сводный баланс	(SVOD-nee ba-LAHNS)	consolidated financial statement
связанная помощь	(SVYAH-zan-na-ya POH-mashch)	tied aid
связанная ссуда	(SVYAH-zan-na-ya SSOO-da)	tied loan
сдаваемый под ключ	(zda-VAH-ye-mee pat klyooch)	turn-key
сдавать/сдать в аренду	(zda-VAHT/ZDAHT va-REHN-doo)	lease (v) (as lessor)
сдавать/сдать в аренду	(zda-VAHT/ZDAHT va-REHN-doo)	rent (v) (rent to)
сделать заявку цены	(ZDEH-lat za-YAHF-koo tse-NEE)	put in a bid (v)
сделать повтор-ный заказ	(ZDEH-lat paf-TOHR-nee za-KAHS)	reorders (v)
сделка	(ZDEL-ka)	deal
себестоимость	(se-be-STOH-ee-mast)	prime costs
седативное сред-ство	(se-da-TEEV-na-ye SRET-stva)	sedative
седло	(sed-LOH)	saddle

сезонный	(se-ZON-nee)	seasonal
секретарь	(se-kre-TAHR)	secretary
село	(se-LOH)	village
сельское хозяй-ство	(SEL-ska-ye kha-ZYAHY-stva)	agriculture
сельскохозяй-ственный бюл-летень	(sel-ska-kha-ZYAHY-stven-nee byool-le-TEN)	agricultural paper
сельскохозяй-ственные това-ры	(sel-ska-kha-ZYAHY-stven-nee-ye ta-VAH-ree)	agricultural products
семена	(se-me-NAH)	seeds
«Семь Сестёр» (монополии-участники нефтяного кар-теля)	(sem ses-TYOHR [ma-na-POH-lee-ee oo-CHAHST-nee-ke nef-tee-NOH-va kar-TEH-la])	the Seven Sisters
сено	(SEH-na)	hay
сепарированный газ	(se-pa-REE-ra-van-nee gahs)	separated gas
сервер	(SEHR-ver)	server
серийное ЗУ (ком-пьютер)	(se-REEY-na-ye ZEH-OO [kam-PYOO-ter])	serial storage (computer)
серийный	(se-REEY-nee)	serial
серийные облига-ции	(se-REEY-nee-ye ab-lee-GAH-tsee-ee)	serial bonds
серная кислота	(SEHR-na-ya kees-la-TAH)	sulfuric acid
серп	(sehrp)	sickle
серпантин из тик-керной ленты	(ser-pan-TEEN eez TEEK-ker-nay LEHN-tee)	ticker tape
сертификат	(ser-tee-FEE-kat)	certificate
сеть	(set)	network
сеялка	(SEH-yal-ka)	seeder
сеянец	(SEH-ya-nets)	seedling
сеять	(SEH-yat)	plant (v)
сжатие	(ZHZHAH-tee-ye)	crunching (data)
сжиженные газы	(ZHZHEE-zhen-nee-ye GAH-zee)	liquified gases

сжиженный при- родный газ	(ZHZHEE-zhen-nee pree- ROD-nee gahs)	liquified natural gas
сиденье	(see-DEN-ye)	seat
силос зерновой	(SEE-las zer-na-VOY)	silo
синдикат	(seen-dee-KAHT)	syndicate
синий воротничок (простой рабо- чий)	(SEE-nee va-rat-nee-CHOK [pra-STOY ra-BOH- chee])	blue-collar worker
синтез	(SEEN-tes)	synthesis
синтетическая нефть	(seen-te-TEE-ches-ka-ya neft)	synthetic crude (oil)
синтетические жидкие топлива	(seen-te-TEE-ches-kee-ye ZHIT-kee-ye TOP-lee-va)	synthetic liquid fuels (SLF)
синтетический природный газ	(seen-te-TEE-ches-kee pree- ROD-nee gahs)	synthetic natural gas (SNG)
синус	(see-NOOS)	sinus
синхронный гене- ратор	(seen-KHRON-nee ghe-ne- RAH-tar)	alternator
синька	(SEEN-ka)	blueprint
сироп от кашля	(see-ROP at KAHSH-lya)	cough syrup
система квот	(sees-TEH-ma kvot)	quota system
система «Юнивак»	(sees-TEH-ma oo-nee- VAHK)	Univac
системный анализ	(sees-TEHM-nee a-NAH- lees)	systems analysis
сканнер	(SKAHN-nehr)	scanner
скважина	(SKVAH-zhee-na)	well
сквозной коноса- мент	(skvaz-NOY ka-na-sa- MENT)	through bill of lading
скворцы	(skvar-TSEE)	starlings
скидка	(SKEET-ka)	allowance, discount, markdown
скидка за боль- шой объём	(SKEET-ka za bal-SHOY ab- YOM)	volume discount
скидка за количе- ство	(SKEET-ka za ka-LEE- chest-va)	quantity discount
скидка с налога	(SKEET-ka sna-LOH-ga)	tax relief
складирование на местах	(skla-DEE-ra-va-nee-ye na mes-TAHKH)	field waterhousing

складировать	(skla-DEE-ra-vat)	store (v)
скобяные изделия	(ska-bya-NEE-ye eez-DEH-lee-ya)	hardware
скользящая шкала цен	(skal-ZYAH-shcha-ya shka-LAH tsen)	sliding price scale
скользящий паритет	(skal-ZYAH-shchee pa-ree-TET)	sliding parity
скорость обращения	(SKOH-rast ab-ra-SHCHEH-nee-ya)	velocity of money
скот	(skot)	cattle
скотобойня	(ska-ta-BOY-nya)	slaughter house
скрытый актив	(SKREE-teey ak-TEEF)	hidden asset
скупка	(SKOOP-ka)	buy-out (takeover)
слабительное средство	(sla-BEE-tel-na-ye SRET-stva)	laxative
слаборазвитые страны	(sla-ba-RAHZ-vee-tee-ye STRAH-nee)	underdeveloped nations
сладкая (малосернистая) нефть	(SLAHT-ka-ya [MAH-la-ser-NEES-ta-ya] neft)	sweet crude
сладкий (малосернистый) газ	(SLAHT-kee [MAH-la-ser-NEES-tee] gahs)	sweet gas
сланцевая нефть	(SLAHN-tsee-va-ya neft)	shale oil
слива	(SLEE-va)	plum
слитки	(SLEET-kee)	ingots
слияние	(slee-YAH-nee-ye)	merger
сложные проценты	(SLOZH-nee-ye pra-TSEN-tee)	compound interest
служащий	(SLOO-zha-shchee)	employee
Служба Налогообложения (США)	(SLOOZH-ba na-LOH-ga-ab-la-ZHEH-nee-ya)	Internal Revenue Service
случайная выборка	(sloo-CHAHY-na-ya VEE-bar-ka)	tandom sample
смазывание	(SMAH-zee-va-nee-ye)	lubrication
смена	(SMEH-na)	shift (working hours)
сменять	(sme-NYAHT)	supersede (v)
смета оборота	(SMEH-ta a-ba-ROH-ta)	estimate, sales
сметная стоимость	(SMET-na-ya STOH-ee-mast)	estimated price

С

смешанная опера-ция	(SMEH-shan-na-ya a-pe-RAH-tsee-ya)	strapping
смешанное топли-во	(SMEH-shan-na-ye TOP-lee-va)	mixed fuel
смешанные стои-мости	(SMEH-shan-nee-ye STOH-ee-ma-stee)	mixed costs
снабжать/снаб-дить	(snab-ZHAHT/snab-DEET)	index (v)
снабжение	(snab-ZHEH-nee-ye)	procurement
снижение оплачи-ваемой суммы	(snee-ZHEH-nee-ye ap-LAH-chee-va-ye-may SOOM-mee)	write-down
снижение цены	(sznee-ZHEH-nee-ye tse-NEE)	price cutting
снижение цены при платежах за наличный расчёт	(snee-ZHEH-nee-ye tse-NEE pree pla-te-ZHAHKH za na-LEECH-nee ra-SHCHYOHT)	cash discount
снимать/снять	(snee-MAHT/snyaht)	take down (v)
снимать/снять по этапам	(snee-MAHT/snyaht pa e-TAH-pam)	phase out (v)
снотворная таблетка	(sna-TVOHR-na-ya tab-LET-ka)	sleeping pill
снятие денег со счёта	(SNYAH-tee-ye DEH-nek sa SHCHYOH-ta)	draw-down
собеседование	(sa-be-SEH-da-va-nee-ye)	colloquium
собирать/собрать	(sa-bee-RAHT/sa-BRAHT)	assemble (v)
соболь	(SOH-bal)	sable
собрание	(sab-RAH-nee-ye)	assembly
собрание	(sab-RAH-nee-ye)	meeting
собрание акционе-ров	(sab-RAH-nee-ye ak-tsee-a-NEH-raf)	shareholder's meeting
«собственная» нефть	(SOP-stven-na-ya neft)	equity crude oil
собственник	(SOP-stven-neek)	proprietor
собственник абсентеист	(SOP-stven-neek ap-sen-te-EEST)	absentee owner
собственнический	(SOP-stven-nee-ches-kee)	proprietary
собственность	(SOP-stven-nast)	property

собственные акции в порт- феле	*(SOP-stven-nee-ye AHK- tsee-ee fpart-FEH-le)*	treasury stock
собственный капитал	*(SOP-stven-nee ka-pee- TAHL)*	equity capital
сова	*(sa-VAH)*	owl
совет директоров	*(sa-VET dee-rek-ta-ROF)*	board of directors
совет управляю- щих	*(sa-VET oop-rav-LYAH-yoo- shcheekh)*	executive board
советы директо- ров с взаимны- ми членами	*(sa-VEH-tee dee-rek-ta-ROF zvza-EEM-nee-mee CHLEH-na-mee)*	interlocking directorate
совещание дирек- торов	*(sa-ve-SHCHAH-nee-ye dee- rek-ta-ROF)*	board meeting
совещательное обслуживание	*(sa-ve-SHCHAH-tel-na-ye ap-SLOO-zhee-va-nee-ye)*	advisory service
совещательный совет	*(sa-ve-SHCHAH-tel-nee sa- VEHT)*	advisory counsel
совладелец	*(sa-vla-DEH-lets)*	joint owner
совместимый назад	*(sav-mes-TEE-mee na- ZAHT)*	backward compatible
совместная ответ- ственность	*(sav-MES-na-ya at-VET- stven-nast)*	joint liability
совместная рекла- ма	*(sav-MES-na-ya rek-LAH- ma)*	cooperative advertising
совместная стои- мость	*(sav-MES-na-ya STOH-ee- mast)*	joint cost
совместное акцио- нерное обще- ство	*(sav-MES-na-ye ak-tsee-a- NEHR-na-ye OP-shche- stva)*	joint stock company
совместное владе- ние	*(sav-MES-na-ye vla-DEH- nee-ye)*	co-ownership
совместное иму- щество	*(sav-MES-na-ye ee-MOO- shchest-va)*	joint estate
совместное пред- приятие	*(sav-MES-na-ye pret-pree- YAH-tee-ye)*	joint venture
совместное стра- хование	*(sav-MES-na-ye stra-kha- VAH-nee-ye)*	coinsurance
согласительная платформа	*(sag-la-SEE-tel-na-ya plat- FOHR-ma)*	accommodation platform
соглашение	*(sa-gla-SHEH-nee-ye)*	agreement

соглашение о сотрудничестве	(sa-gla-SHEH-nee-ye a sat-ROOD-nee-che-stve)	cooperation agreement
содержание	(sa-der-ZHAH-nee-ye)	content
соевые бобы	(SOH-ye-vee-ye ba-BEE)	soybeans
соединения	(sa-ye-dee-NEH-nee-ya)	compounds
соединительная тяга	(sa-ye-dee-NEE-tel-na-ya TYAH-ga)	connecting rod
созвать	(sa-ZVAHT)	call (v)
сокращение	(sak-ra-SHCHEH-nee-ye)	cutback
сокращённый рынок	(sa-kra-SHCHYOH-nee REE-nak)	thin market
соли	(SOH-lee)	salts
соль	(sol)	salt
соль фосфорной кислоты	(sol FOS-far-nay kees-la-TEE)	phosphate
соляная кислота	(sa-LYAH-na-ya kees-la-TAH)	hydrochloric acid
сообщение	(sa-ap-SHCHEH-nee-ye)	report
сообщение об ошибке	(sa-ap-SHCHEH-nee-ye a-ba-SHIP-ke)	error message
соотношение дохода и цены (акции)	(sa-at-na-SHEH-nee-ye da-KHOH-da ee tse-NEE)	price/earnings (p/e) ratio
сопроводительное письмо	(sa-pra-va-DEE-tel-na-ye pees-MOH)	cover letter
сопровождающие товары	(sa-pra-vazh-DAH-yoo-shchee-ye ta-VAH-ree)	accompanied goods
сопротивление	(sap-ra-teev-LEH-nee-ye)	resistance
соревнование	(sa-rev-na-VAH-nee-ye)	competition
сорняки	(sar-nya-KEE)	weeds
сосна	(sas-NAH)	pine
состав	(sas-TAHF)	corpus
состав продавцов	(sas-TAHF pra-daf-TSOF)	sales force
составлять график	(sa-stav-LYAHT GRAH-feek)	schedule (v)
составная часть	(sas-tav-NAH-ya chast)	component
составная часть	(sas-tav-NAH-ya chast)	factor (component, element)

составной показатель	(sas-tav-NOY pa-ka-ZAH-tel)	composite index
сотрудник, коллега	(sat-ROOD-neek, kal-LEH-ga)	colleague
софтвер (программное обеспечение)	(soft-VEHR [pra-GRAHM-na-ye a-bes-pe-CHEH-nee-ye])	software
сохранная расписка	(sa-KHRAHN-na-ya ras-PEES-ka)	trust receipt
сохранять	(sakh-ra-NYAHT)	save
спад	(spaht)	slump
спасать имущество	(spa-SAHT ee-MOO-shchest-va)	salvage (v)
спекулянт	(spe-koo-LYAHNT)	speculator
спекулянт, играющий на повышение	(spe-koo-LYANT eeg-RAH-yoo-shchee na pa-vee-SHEH-nee-ye)	bull
спекулянт, играющий на понижение	(spe-koo-LYANT eeg-RAH-yoo-shchee na pa-nee-ZHEH-nee-ye)	bear
специалист по бухгалтерии	(spe-tsee-a-LEEST pa bookh-gal-TEH-ree)	chartered accountant, CPA
специфические пошлины	(spe-tsee-FEE-ches-kee-ye POSH-lee-nee)	specific duty
СПИД	(speet)	AIDS
спидометр	(spee-DOH-metr)	speedometer
список	(SPEE-sak)	checklist
список адресатов	(SPEE-sak ad-re-SAH-taf)	mailing list
список необлагаемых пошлиной товаров	(SPEE-sak ne-ab-la-GAH-ye-mikh POSH-lee-nay ta-VAH-raf)	free list
список подписчиков (на ценные бумаги)	(SPEE-sak pad-PEE-shchee-kaf [na TSEN-nee-ye boo-MAH-ghee])	legal list (fiduciary investments)
списывать/списать со счёта	(SPEE-see-vat/spee-SAHT sa SHCHYOH-ta)	write off (v)
спонсор	(SPON-sar)	sponsor (of a friend or partnership)
спор	(spohr)	dispute
спор о зарплате	(spohr a zar-PLAH-te)	wage dispute

спор с профсою-зом	*(spohr spraf-sa-YOO-zam)*	dispute, labor
спорить	*(SPOH-reet)*	dispute (v)
способ	*(SPOH-sap)*	mode
справедливая рыночная стоимость	*(spra-ved-LEE-vay-ya REE-nach-na-ya STOH-ee-mast)*	fair market value
справка для предоставления кредита	*(SPRAHF-ka dla pre-da-stav-LEH-nee-ya kre-DEE-ta)*	credit reference
справочное руководство	*(SPRAH-vach-na-ye roo-ka-VOT-stva)*	manual
спрос	*(spros)*	demand
спрос и предложение	*(spros ee pred-la-ZHEN-nee-ye)*	supply and demand
спутник	*(SPOOT-neek)*	satellite
сравнительная диаграмма	*(srav-NEE-tel-na-ya dee-a-GRAHM-ma)*	chart, bar
среднее арифметическое	*(SRED-nee-ye a-reef-me-TEE-ches-ka-ye)*	arithmetic mean
среднее квадратичное отклонение	*(SRED-nee-ye kvad-ra-TEECH-na-ye at-kla-NEH-nee-ye)*	standard deviation
среднесрочно	*(SRED-ne-SROCH-na)*	medium term
средние издержки на единицу	*(SRED-nee-ye eez-DEHRZH-kee na ye-dee-NEE-tsoo)*	average unit cost
средний	*(SRED-nee)*	mean (average)
средний доход	*(SRED-nee da-KHOT)*	fair return
средний слой управления	*(SRED-nee sloy oo-prav-LEH-nee-ya)*	middle management
средняя взвешенная	*(SRED-nya-ya VZVEH-shen-na-ya)*	weighted average
средняя стоимость	*(SRED-nya-ya STOH-ee-mast)*	average cost
средняя удельная продуктивность	*(SRED-nya-ya oo-DEL-na-ya pra-dook-TEEV-nast)*	average productivity per unit vol.
средняя цена	*(SRED-nya-ya tse-NAH)*	average price
средства массовой информации	*(SRET-stva MAHS-sa-vay een-far-MAH-tsee-ee)*	mass media

средство для достижения цели	*(SRET-stva dla da-stee-ZHEH-nee-ya TSEH-lee)*	leverage
средство международных отчётов	*(SRET-stva mezh-doo-na-ROD-neekh at-CHYOH-taf)*	medium of exchange
средство судебной защиты	*(SRET-stva soo-DEB-nay za-SHCHEE-tee)*	remedy (law)
срок взыскания	*(srok vzis-KAH-nee-ya)*	collection period
срок годности при хранении	*(srok GOD-na-stee pree khra-NEH-nee-ee)*	shelf life
срок действия патента	*(srok DEY-stvee-ya pa-TEN-ta)*	life of a patent
срок доставки	*(srok da-STAHF-kee)*	delivery date
срок задержки судна в порту	*(srok za-DEHRSH-kee SOOD-na fpar-TOO)*	lay time
срок интереса	*(srok een-te-REH-sa)*	interest period
срок наступления	*(srok na-stoop-LEH-nee-ya)*	maturity date
срок погашения долга	*(srok pa-ga-SHEH-nee-ya DOL-ga)*	payback period
срок службы	*(srok SLOOZH-bee)*	useful life
срочная авиаперевозка	*(SROCH-na-ya AH-vee-a-pe-re-VOS-ka)*	air express
срочные контракты	*(SROCH-nee-ye kan-TRAHK-tee)*	futures
срочный вклад	*(SROCH-nee fklaht)*	time deposit
срочный заказ	*(SROCH-nee za-KAHS)*	rush order
ссуда	*(SSOO-da)*	loan
ссуды на льготных условиях	*(SSOO-dee na LGOT-nikh oos-LOH-vee-yakh)*	low-interest loans
ставка	*(STAHF-ka)*	rate
ставка допустимой амортизации	*(STAHF-ka da-poos-TEE-may a-mar-tee-ZAH-tsee-ee)*	allowance, depreciation
ставка накладных расходов	*(STAHF-ka nak-lad-NIKH ras-KHOH-daf)*	burden rate
ставка опциона	*(STAHF-ka ap-tsee-OH-na)*	call rate
ставка переучёта	*(STAHF-ka pe-re-oo-CHYOH-ta)*	rediscount rate

ставка присоеди- нения	*(STAHF-ka pree-sa-e-dee- NEH-nee-ya)*	accession rate
ставка платы за рекламу	*(STAHF-ka PLAH-ty za rek- LAH-moo)*	advertising rate
ставка увеличения	*(STAHF-ka oo-ve-lee- CHEH-nee-ya)*	rate of increase
стадо	*(STAH-da)*	herd
стажёр	*(sta-ZHYOHR)*	trainee
сталеплавильный завод	*(sta-le-pla-VEEL-nee za- VOT)*	steel mill
сталийные дни	*(sta-LEEY-nee-ye dnee)*	laydays
стандартная длина заготов- ки	*(stan-DAHRT-na-ya dlee- NAH za-ga-TOF-kee)*	production length
стандартное время	*(stan-DAHRT-na-ye VREH- mya)*	standard time
стандартное пись- мо	*(stan-DAHRT-na-ye pees- MOH)*	form letter
старшинство	*(star-shin-STVOH)*	seniority
стартер	*(STAHR-ter)*	starter
статистика	*(sta-TEES-tee-ka)*	statistics
статья	*(sta-TYAH)*	item (balance sheet)
статья актива	*(sta-TYAH ak-TEE-va)*	asset (balance sheet)
статья пассива	*(sta-TYAH pas-SEE-va)*	liability (balance sheet)
стационарная буровая уста- новка/платфор- ма	*(sta-tsee-a-NAHR-na-ya boo-ra-VAH-ya oos-ta- NOF-ka/plat-FOHR-ma)*	fixed fram rig/platform
стачка	*(STAHCH-ka)*	walkout
стая	*(STAH-ya)*	flock
степень	*(STEH-pen)*	degree (general)
стереофонический	*(ste-re-a-fa-NEE-ches-kee)*	stereophonic
стереотип	*(ste-re-a-TEEP)*	plate
стержень	*(STEHR-zhen)*	rod
стимул	*(STEE-mool)*	incentive
стимулирование сбыта	*(stee-moo-LEE-ra-va-nee-ye ZBEE-ta)*	sales promotion
стимулировать	*(stee-moo-LEE-ra-vat)*	stimulate

стимулятор	(stee-moo-LAH-tar)	stimulant
стихийное бед-ствие	(stee-KHEEY-na-ye BET-stvee-ye)	act of God
стоимость	(STOH-ee-mast)	cost, value
стоимость акти-вов	(STOH-ee-mast ak-TEE-vaf)	asset value
стоимость груза	(STOH-ee-mast GROO-za)	carrying value
стоимость при выкупе	(STOH-ee-mast pree VEE-koo-pe)	cash surrender value
стоимость при ликвидации	(STOH-ee-mast pree leek-vee-DAH-tsee-ee)	liquidation value
стоимость подго-товки запасов	(STOH-ee-mast pad-ta-TOF-kee za-PAH-saf)	below ground value
стоимость продан-ных товаров	(STOH-ee-mast PROH-dan-nikh ta-VAH-raf)	cost of goods sold
стоимость с выгрузкой на берег	(STOH-ee-mast SVEEG-roos-kay na BEH-rek)	landed cost
стоимость функ-ционирующего предприятия	(STOH-ee-mast foonk-tsee-a-NEE-roo-yoo-shche-va pret-pree-YAH-tee-ya)	going concern value
стоить	(STOH-eet)	cost (v)
стойло	(STOY-la)	stable
столкновение интересов	(stalk-na-VEH-nee-ye een-te-REH-saf)	conflict of interest
стопа	(sta-PAH)	ream
стоять в очереди	(sta-YAHT VOH-che-re-dee)	stand in line (v)\
страдл (двойной опцион)	(strahdl [dvay-NOY ap-tsee-ON])	straddle
страна происхож-дения	(stra-NAH pra-ees-khazh-DEH-nee-ya)	country of origin
страна риска	(stra-NAH REES-ka)	country of risk
страница	(stra-NEE-tsa)	page
стратегические запасы	(stra-te-GHEE-ches-kee-ye za-PAH-see)	strategic reserves
стратегия капита-ловложения	(stra-TEH-ghee-ya ka-pee-TAH-la-vla-ZHEH-nee-ya)	investment strategy
стратегия конку-ренции	(stra-TEH-ghee-ya kan-koo-REN-tsee-ee)	competitive strategy

страусовая кожа	*(STRAH-oo-sa-va-ya KOH-zha)*	ostrich (skin)
страхование	*(stra-kha-VAH-nee-ye)*	insurance
страхование кредита	*(stra-kha-VAH-nee-ye kree-DEE-ta)*	credit insurance
страхование морских грузов	*(stra-kha-VAH-nee-ye mar-SKEEKH GROO-zaf)*	marine cargo insurance
страхование на определенное время	*(stra-kha-VAH-nee-ye na ap-re-de-LYON-na-ye VREH-mya)*	term insurance
страхование от несчастных случаев	*(stra-kha-VAH-nee-ye at ne-SHCHAHS-nikh SLOO-cha-yef)*	casualty insurance
страхование от потери ключевого исполнителя	*(stra-kha-VAH-nee-ye at pa-TEH-ree klyoo-che-VOH-va ees-pal-NEE-te-lya)*	key man insurance
страхование против дефектов правового титула	*(stra-kha-VAH-nee-ye PROH-teef de-FEHK-taf pra-va-VOH-va TEE-too-la)*	title insurance
страхователь морских грузов	*(stra-kha-VAH-tel mahr-SKEEKH GROO-zaf)*	marine underwriter
страховаться от потери	*(stra-kha-VAHT-sa at pa-TEH-ree)*	hedge (v)
страховая компания	*(stra-kha-VAH-ya kam-PAH-nee-ya)*	insurance company
страховой взнос	*(stra-kha-VOY vznos)*	insurance premium
страховой взнос	*(stra-kha-VOY vznos)*	premium, insurance
страховой маклер	*(stra-kha-VOY MAHK-ler)*	insurance broker
страховой полис	*(stra-kha-VOY POH-lees)*	insurance policy
страховой поручитель-гарант	*(stra-kha-VOY pa-roo-CHEE-tel-ga-RAHNT)*	insurance underwriter
страховой фонд	*(stra-kha-VOY font)*	insurance fund
строка	*(stra-KAH)*	line
строка	*(stra-KAH)*	row
строчная буква	*(strach-NAH-ya BOOK-va)*	lower case
структура акционерного общества	*(strook-TOO-ra ak-tsee-a-NEHR-na-va OP-shchest-va)*	corporate structure

структура заработной платы	*(strook-TOO-ra ZAH-ra-bat-nay PLAH-tee)*	wage structure
структура капиталовложений	*(strook-TOO-ra ka-pee-TAH-la-vla-ZHEH-neey)*	capital structure
структурная схема управления	*(strook-TOOHR-na-ya SKHEH-ma oop-rav-LEH-nee-ya)*	chart, management
субаренда	*(soo-ba-REN-da)*	sublease
субподряд	*(soop-pad-RYAHT)*	subcontract
субсидия	*(soop-SEE-dee-ya)*	subsidy
судебный запрет	*(soo-DEB-nee zap-RET)*	injunction
судебный иск	*(soo-DEB-nee eesk)*	lawsuit
судебный исполнитель	*(soo-DEB-nee ees-pal-NEE-tel)*	executor
судебный приказ	*(soo-DEB-nee pree-KAHS)*	writ
сульфамид	*(sool-fa-MEET)*	sulphamide
сумма	*(SOOM-ma)*	amount
суммы, списанные со счёта	*(SOOM-mee SPEE-san-nee-ye sa SHCHYOH-ta)*	write-off
сумочка	*(SOO-mach-ka)*	purse
сундук	*(soon-DOOK)*	trunk
суперобложка	*(SOO-per-ab-LOSH-ka)*	jacket
сурок	*(soo-ROK)*	marmot
сутунки	*(soo-TOON-kee)*	billets
сухогруз	*(soo-kha-GROOS)*	dry cargo
сухой товар	*(soo-KHOY ta-VAHR)*	dry goods
сучок	*(soo-CHOK)*	knot
схема	*(SKHEH-ma)*	graph
схема	*(SKHEH-ma)*	circuit
схема организации	*(SKHEH-ma ar-ga-nee-ZAH-tsee-ee)*	organization chart
схема расположения	*(SKHEH-ma ras-pa-la-ZHEH-nee-ya)*	layout
схема управленческой структуры	*(SKHEH-ma oop-rav-LEN-ches-kay strook-TOO-ree)*	management chart
сцепление	*(stse-PLEH-nee-ye)*	clutch
счета дебиторов	*(shche-TAH dee-BEE-ta-raf)*	accounts receivable

C

счета, подлежащие оплате	(sche-TAH pad-le-ZHAH-shchee-ye ap-LAH-te)	accounts payable
счёт	(shchyoht)	account
счёт в банке	(shchyoht VBAHN-ke)	bank account
счёт в бухгалтерской книге	(shchyoht vbookh-GAHL-ter-skay KNEE-ghe)	ledger account
счёт доходов	(shchyoht da-KHOH-daf)	income account
счёт капитала	(shchyoht ka-pee-TAH-la)	capital account
счёт прибылей и убытков	(shchyoht PREE-bee-ley ee oo-BIT-kaf)	profit-loss account
счёт-фактура	(shchyoht-fak-TOO-ra)	invoice
сыворотка	(SEE-va-rat-ka)	serum
сырье	(sihr-YOH)	raw materials
сырьевые материалы	(sihr-ye-VEE-ye ma-te-ree-YAH-lee)	feed materials

Т

таблетка	(tab-LET-ka)	pill
таблетка	(tab-LET-ka)	tablet
таблица	(tab-LEE-tsa)	table
тавро	(tav-ROH)	brand (on cattle)
таможенная война	(ta-MOH-zhen-na-ya vay-NAH)	tariff war
таможенная декларация	(ta-MOH-zhen-na-ya dek-la-RAH-tsee-ya)	customs entry
таможенная оценка	(ta-MOH-zhen-na-ya a-TSEHN-ka)	value for duty
таможенные сборы	(ta-MOH-zhen-nee-ye ZBOH-ree)	customs duty
таможенный маклер	(ta-MOH-zhen-nee MAHK-ler)	customs broker
таможенный склад	(ta-MOH-zhen-nee sklaht)	bonded warehouse
таможенный союз	(ta-MOH-zhen-nee sa-YOOS)	customs union
таможня	(ta-MOZH-nya)	customs
танин	(ta-NEEN)	tannin

танкер	*(TAHN-ker)*	tanker
танкер-метановоз	*(TAHN-ker-me-ta-na-VOS)*	liquified natural gas carrier
тапочки	*(TAH-pach-kee)*	slippers
тариф	*(ta-REEF)*	tariff
тарифная класси-фикация	*(ta-REEF-na-ya klas-see-fee-KAH-tsee-ya)*	tariff classification
тарифные барье-ры	*(ta-REEF-nee-ye bar-YEH-ree)*	tariff barriers
тарифные рас-ходы	*(ta-REEF-nee-ye ras-KHOH-dee)*	tariff charge
твёрдая наценка	*(TVYOHR-da-ya na-TSEN-ka)*	margin, fixed
твёрдая валюта	*(TVYOHR-da-ya va-LYOO-ta)*	hard currency
твёрдая копия	*(TVYOHR-da-ya KOH-pee-ya)*	hard copy
твёрдое топливо	*(TVYOHR-da-ye TOP-lee-va)*	solid fuel
текстиль	*(tek-STEEL)*	soft goods
текстовой процес-сор	*(TEKS-ta-vee pra-TSES-sar)*	word processor
текстообработка	*(tesks-ta-ab-ra-BOT-ka)*	word processing
текущая цена	*(tee-KOO-shcha-ya tse-NAH)*	going price
текущее обяза-тельство	*(tee-KOO-shche-ye a-bya-ZAH-tel-stva)*	current liability
текущее обяза-тельство	*(tee-KOO-shche-ye a-bya-ZAH-tel-stva)*	liability, current
текущие активы	*(tee-KOO-shchee-ye ak-TEE-vee)*	assets, current
текущий доход	*(tee-KOO-shchee da-KHOT)*	current yield
телеграфный перевод	*(te-le-GRAHF-nee pe-re-VOT)*	cable transfer
телекс	*(TEH-leks)*	cable
телёнок	*(te-LYOH-nak)*	calf
телесвязь	*(TEH-le-SVYAHS)*	telecommunication
телячья кожа	*(te-LYAHCH-ya KOH-zha)*	calfskin
тенденция	*(ten-DEHN-tsee-ee)*	trend

T

тенденция рынка	*(ten-DEHN-tsee-ya RIN-ka)*	market trend
теплица	*(tep-LEE-tsa)*	green house
теплота	*(tep-la-TAH)*	heat
терминал	*(ter-mee-NAHL)*	terminal
термометр	*(ter-MOH-metr)*	thermometer
территориальные воды	*(ter-ree-ta-ree-AHL-nee-ye VOH-dee)*	territorial waters
территория	*(ter-ree-TOH-ree-ya)*	territory
тесный рынок	*(TES-nee REE-nak)*	tight market
техника	*(TEKH-nee-ka)*	engineering
техническое обслуживание	*(tekh-NEE-ches-ka-ye ap-SLOO-zhee-va-nee-ye)*	maintenance
технологическая схема	*(tekh-na-la-GHEE-ches-ka-ya SKHEH-ma)*	flow chart
технологический газ	*(tekh-na-la-GHEE-ches-kee gahs)*	process gas
технологический цикл	*(tekh-na-la-GHEE-ches-kee tsikl)*	cycle, work
тигель	*(TEE-ghel)*	crucible
тираж	*(tee-RAHSH)*	circulation, print run
тиснёная бумага	*(tees-NYOH-na-ya boo-MAH-ga)*	embossed paper
титан	*(tee-TAHN)*	titanium
титрование	*(tee-tra-VAH-nee-ye)*	titration
тканевый пере-плёт	*(TKAH-ne-vee pe-re-PLYOT)*	sewn
тля	*(tlyah)*	aphid
товар	*(ta-VAHR)*	commodity, merchandise
товар в кипах	*(ta-VAHR FKEE-pakh)*	bale cargo
товар, подлежа-щий тарифу	*(ta-VAHR pad-le-ZHAH-shchee ta-REE-foo)*	tariff commodity
товар, продавае-мый в убыток (для привлече-ния покупате-ля)	*(ta-VAHR pra-da-VAH-ye-mee voo-BEE-tak [dla pree-vle-CHEN-nee-ya pa-koo-PAH-te-lya])*	loss leader
товарищество	*(ta-VAH-ree-shche-stva)*	partnership

товарищество с ограниченной ответственностью	*(ta-VAH-ree-shche-stva sag-ra-NEE-chen-nay at-VEHT-stven-na-styoo)*	limited partnership
товарная биржа	*(ta-VAHR-na-ya BEEHR-zha)*	commodity exchange
товарный газ	*(ta-VAHR-nee gahs)*	marketable gas
товарный знак	*(ta-VAHR-nee znahk)*	trademark
товарный склад	*(ta-VAHR-nee sklat)*	regular warehouse
товарооборот	*(ta-VAHR-ra-a-ba-ROT)*	sales turnover
товары	*(ta-VAHR-ree)*	goods
товары длительного пользования	*(ta-VAHR-ree DLEE-tel-na-va POL-za-va-nee-ya)*	durable goods
товары кратковременного пользования	*(ta-VAHR-ree krat-ka-VREH-men-na-va POL-za-va-nee-ya)*	unendurable goods
товары, пломбированные таможней	*(ta-VAHR-ree plam-BEE-ra-van-nee-ye ta-MOZH-ney)*	bonded goods
товары роскоши	*(ta-VAHR-ree ROS-ka-shee)*	luxury goods
ток	*(tok)*	current
токсикология	*(tak-see-ka-LOH-ghee-ya)*	toxicology
токсин	*(tak-SEEN)*	toxin
толстый лист	*(TOL-stee leest)*	plate
тон	*(ton)*	tone
тонкое рекламирование	*(TON-ka-ye re-kla-MEE-ra-va-nee-ye)*	soft sell
тоннаж	*(tan-NAHSH)*	tonnage
топливный газ	*(TOP-leev-nee gahs)*	fuel gas
топливный цикл	*(TOP-leev-nee tsikl)*	fuel cycle
топливо для реактивных самолётов	*(TOP-lee-va dla re-ak-TEEV-nikh sa-ma-LYOH-taf)*	jet fuel
торговать	*(tar-ga-VAHT)*	trade (v)
торговая ассоциация	*(tar-GOH-va-ya as-sa-tsee-AH-tsee-ya)*	merchant guild, trade association
торговая комиссия	*(tar-GOH-va-ya ka-MEES-see-ya)*	trade commission

T

торговая компания	*(tar-GOH-va-ya kam-PAH-nee-ya)*	trading company
торговая палата	*(tar-GOH-va-ya pa-LAH-ta)*	chamber of commerce
торговая скидка	*(tar-GOH-va-ya SKEET-ka)*	trade discount
торговец	*(tar-GOH-vets)*	trader
торговля	*(tar-GOV-lya)*	trade
торговля на основе взаимной выгоды	*(tar-GOV-lya na as-NOH-ve vza-EEM-nay VEE-ga-dee)*	fair trade
торговое агентство	*(tar-GOH-va-ye a-GHEHNT-stva)*	mercantile agency
торговое право	*(tar-GOH-va-ye PRAH-va)*	mercantile law (in general)
торговое соглашение	*(tar-GOH-va-ye sag-la-SHEH-nee-ye)*	trade agreement
торговый	*(tar-GOH-vee)*	mercantile
торговый агент	*(tar-GOH-vee a-GHENT, DEE-lehr)*	dealer
торговый банк	*(tar-GOH-vee bahnk)*	merchant bank
торговый барьер	*(tar-GOH-vee bar-YEHR)*	trade barrier
торговый дом	*(tar-GOH-vee dom)*	trade house
торговый закон	*(tar-GOH-vee za-KON)*	mercantile law (a specific law)
торговый кредит	*(tar-GOH-vee kree-DEET)*	trade credit
торговый центр	*(tar-GOH-vee tsentr)*	shopping center
торгующий по почтовым заказам	*(tar-GOO-yoo-shchee pa pach-TOH-vim za-KAH-zam)*	mail order
тормоз	*(TOHR-mas)*	brake
тормозная педаль	*(tar-maz-NAH-ya pe-DAHL)*	brake pedal
тот, кто часто меняет место работы («летун»)	*(tot, ktoh CHAHS-ta me-NYAH-yet MES-ta ra-BOH-tee ["le-TOON"])*	job hopper
тощий газ	*(TOH-shchee gahs)*	lean gas
трава	*(tra-VAH)*	grass
травление	*(trav-LEH-nee-ye)*	pickling
трактор	*(TRAHK-tar)*	tractor
транзистор	*(tran-ZEES-tar)*	transistor

транквилизатор	*(trank-vee-lee-ZAH-tar)*	tranquilizer
транснациональ-ная нефтяная компания	*(TRAHNS-na-tsee-a-NAHL-na-ya nef-tee-NAH-ya kam-PAH-nee-ya)*	multi-national oil company
трансформатор	*(trans-far-MAH-tar)*	transformer
трассант	*(tras-SAHNT)*	drawer, maker (of check, etc.)
трассат	*(tras-SAHT)*	drawee
тратта	*(TRAHT-ta)*	bill of exchange, draft
требовать/потре-бовать	*(TREH-ba-vat/pa-TREH-ba-vat)*	demand (v)
трест	*(TREHST)*	trust
трест-компания	*(TREHST-kam-PAH-nee-ya)*	trust company
третичная нефть	*(tre-TEECH-na-ya neft)*	tertiary (crude) oil
третичные запасы	*(tre-TEECH-nee-ye za-PAH-see)*	tertiary reserves
третичные товар-ные запасы	*(tre-TEECH-nee-ye ta-VAHR-nee-ye za-PAH-see)*	tertiary (oil) inventory
труд	*(troot)*	labor
трудовой спор	*(troo-da-VOY spohr)*	labor dispute
трудоёмкий	*(troo-da-YOM-kee)*	labor intensive
турбина	*(toor-BEE-na)*	turbine
турбореактивный двигатель	*(TOOHR-ba-re-ak-TEEV-nee DVEE-ga-tel)*	turbojet
турбулентность	*(toor-boo-LENT-nast)*	turbulence
туристский чек	*(too-REEST-skee chek)*	traveller's check
туфли	*(TOOF-lee)*	slippers
тюленья шкура	*(tyoo-LEN-ya SHKOO-ra)*	sealskin
тяжба	*(TYAHZH-ba)*	litigation
тяжёлая промыш-ленность	*(tee-ZHOH-la-ya pra-MISH-len-nast)*	heavy industry

У

| уборочная маши-на | *(oo-BOH-rach-na-ya ma-SHEE-na)* | combine harvester |
| убыток | *(oo-BEE-tak)* | loss |

убыток от общей аварии	(oo-BEE-tak at OP-shchey a-VAH-ree-ee)	general average loss
убыток от частичной аварии	(oo-BEE-tak at chas-TEECH-nay a-VAH-ree-ee)	particular average loss
увеличение капитала	(oo-veh-lee-CHEH-nee-ye ka-pee-TAH-la)	capital increase
увеличивать	(oo-veh-LEE-chee-vat)	enlarge, increase
увеличивать до предела	(oo-veh-LEE-chee-vat da pre-DEH-la)	maximize (v)
увольнять/уволить	(oo-val-NYAHT/oo-VOH-leet)	fire, terminate
углеводород	(oog-le-va-da-ROT)	hydrocarbon
углеводородное топливо	(oog-le-va-da-ROD-na-ye TOP-lee-va)	hydrocarbon fuel
углерод	(oog-le-ROT)	carbon
углеродистая сталь	(oog-le-ROH-dees-ta-ya stahl)	carbon steel
угол резания	(OO-gal REH-za-nee-ya)	cutting angle
угольная нефть	(OO-gal-na-ya neft)	coal oil
угольный газ	(OO-gal-nee gahs)	coal gas
удел	(oo-DEL)	lot
удельные энергетические затраты	(oo-DEL-nee-ee e-ner-ghe-tee-ches-kee-ye zat-RAH-tee)	Unit Energy cost
удержание налогов	(oo-der-ZHAH-nee-ee na-LOH-gaf)	withholding tax
удобрение	(oo-da-BREH-nee-ye)	fertilizer
удовлетворение потребителя	(oo-dav-let-va-REH-nee-ye pat-re-BEE-te-la)	consumer satisfaction
удовлетворительный уровень качества	(oo-dav-le-tva-REE-tel-nee OO-ra-ven KAH-chest-va)	acceptable quality level
удостоверенный чек	(oo-da-sta-VEH-ren-nee chek)	certified check
узел	(OO-zel)	knot
укладка	(ook-LAHT-ka)	stowage
уклонение от уплаты налогов	(ook-la-NEH-nee-ye at oo-PLAH-tee na-LOH-gaf)	tax evasion

укрепление	*(oo-kre-PLEH-nee-ye)*	consolidation
уксусная кислота	*(OOK-soos-na-ya kees-la-TAH)*	acetic acid
улаживать/уладить конфликты	*(oo-LAH-zhee-vat/oo-LAH-deet kan-FLEEK-tee)*	troubleshoot (v)
улучшать/улучшить	*(oo-looch-SHAHT/oo-LOOCH-sheet)*	improve upon (v)
улучшение	*(oo-looch-SHEH-nee-ye)*	improvement
уменьшение	*(oo-men-SHEH-nee-ye)*	abatement (reduction)
умерший без завещания	*(oo-MEHR-shee bez za-ve-SHCHAH-nee-ya)*	interstate
универмаг	*(oo-nee-ver-MAHK)*	department store
универсальная ЭВМ	*(oo-nee-vehr-SAHL-na-ya eh-veh-EM)*	mainframe computer
универсальная ЭВМ	*(oo-nee-vehr-SAHL-na-ya eh-veh-EM)*	mainframe
упаковка	*(oo-pa-KOF-ka)*	packaging
уплата	*(oop-LAH-ta)*	payment
уплачивать/уплатить	*(oop-LAH-chee-vat/oo-PLAH-teet)*	repay (v)
уплачивать/уплатить заранее	*(oop-LAH-chee-vat/oo-PLAH-teet za-RAH-nee-ye)*	prepay (v)
уполномоченная подпись	*(oo-pal-na-MOH-chen-na-ya POT-pees)*	authorized signature
уполномоченные акции	*(oo-pal-na-MOH-chen-nee-ye AHK-tsee-ee)*	authorized shares
уполномоченный представитель фирмы	*(oo-pal-na-MOH-chen-nee pret-sta-VEE-tel FEEHR-mee)*	authorized dealer
уполномочить	*(oo-pal-na-MOH-cheet)*	authorize (v)
упорно уговаривать	*(oo-POHR-na oo-ga-VAH-ree-vat)*	jawbone (v)
управление	*(oop-rav-LEH-nee-ye)*	management
управление жилищного фонда	*(oop-rav-LEH-nee-ye zhee-LEESHCH-na-va FON-da)*	housing authority (residential)
управление кадрами	*(oop-rav-LEH-nee-ye KAHD-ra-mee)*	personnel management

у

управление ком- мерческими предприятиями	*(oop-rav-LEH-nee-ye kam- MEHR-ches-kee-mee pret-pree-YAH-tee-ya- mee)*	business management
управление кре- дитными опера- циями	*(oop-rav-LEH-nee-ye kre- DEET-nee-mee a-pe- RAH-tsee-ya-mee)*	credit management
управление офи- сом	*(oop-rav-LEH-nee-ye OF- fee-sam)*	office management
управление про- дукцией	*(oop-rav-LEH-nee-ye pra- DOOK-tsee-yey)*	product management
управление произ- водственным процессом	*(oop-rav-LEH-nee-ye pra- eez-VOT-stven-nim pra- TSES-sam)*	production control
управление рын- ком	*(oop-rav-LEH-nee-ye REEN-kam)*	market management
управление сбы- том	*(oop-rav-LEH-nee-ye ZBEE- tam)*	sales management
управление систе- мами	*(oop-rav-LEH-nee-ye sees- TEH-ma-mee)*	systems management
управление финансовой деятельностью	*(oop-rav-LEH-nee-ye fee- NAHN-sa-vay DEH-ya- tel-na-styoo)*	financial management
управленческая группа	*(oop-rav-LEN-ches-ka-ya GROOP-pa)*	management group
управленческая команда	*(oop-rav-LEN-ches-ka-ya ka-MAHN-da)*	management team
управляемый в режиме меню	*(oop-rav-LYAH-ye-mee vre- ZHEE-me me-NYOO)*	menu-driven
упростить (про- цесс, работу)	*(oop-ras-TEET [pra-TSES, ra-BOH-too])*	streamline (v)
уравнительная пошлина	*(oo-rav-NEE-tel-na-ya POSH-lee-na)*	countervailing duty
урегулирование претензий	*(oo-re-goo-LEE-ra-va-nee- ye pre-TEN-zeey)*	settlement
уровень заработ- ной платы	*(OO-ra-ven ZAH-ra-bat-nay PLAH-tee)*	wage level
уровень роста	*(OO-ra-ven ROH-sta)*	growth rate
уровень роста	*(OO-ra-ven ROH-sta)*	rate of growth
уровень эксплуа- тации	*(OO-ra-ven eks-ploo-a- TAH-tsee-ee)*	capacity of utilization
урожай	*(oo-ra-ZHAHY)*	harvest

усилитель	*(oo-see-LEE-tel)*	amplifier
усокоренная амор-тизация	*(oos-KOH-ren-na-ya a-mar-tee-ZAH-tsee-ya)*	accelerated depreciation
ускоренная пре-мия	*(oos-KOH-ren-na-ya PREH-mee-ya)*	accelerating premium
ускоритель манев-ра	*(oos-ka-REE-tel ma-NYOV-ra)*	combat thrust booster
ускоритель много-кратного дей-ствия	*(oos-ka-REE-tel mna-ga-KRAHT-na-va- DEY-stvee-ya)*	recoverable booster
ускорить/ускорять	*(oo-SKOH-reet/oo-ska-RYAHT)*	speed up (v)
условия кредита	*(oos-LOH-vee-ya kre-DEE-ta)*	credit terms
условия продажи	*(oos-LOH-vee-ya pra-DAH-zhee)*	terms of sale
условно вручен-ный документ за печатью	*(oos-LOV-na vroo-CHYON-nee da-koo-MENT za pe-CHAH-tyoo)*	escrow
условное обяза-тельство	*(oos-LOV-na-ye a-bya-ZAH-tel-stva)*	contingent liability
условный акцепт	*(oos-LOV-nee ak-TSEPT)*	conditional acceptance
условный акцепт-ный индосса-мент	*(oos-LOV-nee ak-TSEPT-nee een-da-sa-MENT)*	qualified acceptance endorsement
условный договор о продаже	*(oos-LOV-nee da-ga-VOHR a pra-DAH-zhe)*	conditional sales contract
устав	*(oos-TAHF)*	charter
устав товарище-ства	*(oos-TAHF ta-VAH-ree-shchest-va)*	by-laws
установленный доход	*(oo-STAH-nov-len-nee da-KHOT)*	fixed income
устаревание	*(oos-ta-re-VAH-nee-ye)*	obsolescence
устное соглаше-ние	*(OOS-na-ye sa-gla-SHEH-nee-ye)*	gentleman's agreement
утвердительное действие	*(oo-tver-DEE-tel-na-ye DEY-stvee-ye)*	affirmative action
утверж-дать/утвердить	*(oo-tverzh-DAHT/oo-tver-DEET)*	validate (v)
утечка	*(oo-TECH-ka)*	leakage
утка	*(OOT-ka)*	duck

участие в прибы- лях	(oo-CHAHS-tee-ye FPREE- bee-lyakh)	profit sharing
учётная ставка	(oo-CHOT-na-ya STAHF- ka)	discount rate
учётное «кэш- флоу»	(oo-CHYOHT-na-ye "cash flow")	discount cash flow
учётные ценные бумаги	(oo-CHYOHT-nee-ye TSEN- nee-ye boo-MAH-ghee)	discount securities
учредитель	(ooch-re-DEE-tel)	founder
учреждать акцио- нерное обще- ство	(ooch-rezh-DAHT ak-tsee-a- NEHR-na-ye OP-shchest- va)	incorporate (v)
учреждённая реклама	(ooch-rezh-DYON-na-ya rek-LAH-ma)	institutional advertising

У

Ф

файл	(fahyl)	file
фактическая ответствен- ность	(fak-TEE-ches-ka-ya at- VET-stven-nast)	actual liability
фактическая сто- имость в нали- чии	(fak-TEE-ches-ka-ya STOH- ee-mast vna-LEE-chee- ee)	actual cash value
фактические рас- ходы	(fak-TEE-ches-kee-ye ras- KHOH-dee)	actual costs
фактор	(FAHK-tar)	factor (agent)
фактура	(fak-TOO-ra)	bill (invoice)
фактурная стои- мость	(fak-TOOR-na-ya STOH-ee- mast)	invoice cost
фактурный ана- лиз	(fak-TOOR-nee a-NAH-lees)	factor analysis
фальшивка	(fal-SHIF-ka)	forgery
фальшивомонет- ничество	(fal-SHEE-va-ma-NET-nee- che-stva)	counterfeiting (money)
фанера	(fa-NEH-ra)	plywood
фармацевт	(far-ma-TSEFT)	pharmacist
фармацевтиче- ский	(far-ma-tsef-TEE-ches-kee)	pharmaceutical
фасоль	(fa-SOL)	bean

фелония (уголов-ное преступ-ление)	*(fe-LOH-nee-ya [oo-ga-LOHF-na-ye pres-too-PLEH-nee-ye])*	felony
фермент	*(fer-MENT)*	enzyme
фермер	*(FEHR-mer)*	farmer
ферромарганец	*(fehr-ra-MAHR-ga-nets)*	ferromanganese
ферроникель	*(fehr-ra-NEE-kel)*	ferronickel
ферросплавы	*(fehr-ra-SPLAH-vee)*	ferroalloys
фидуциарная ссуда	*(fee-doo-tsee-AHR-na-ya SSOO-da)*	fiduciary loan
фидуциарное отношение	*(fee-doo-tsee-AHR-na-ye at-na-SHEH-nee-ye)*	fiduciary relationship
фидуциарный	*(fee-doo-tsee-AHR-nee)*	fiduciary
фиксирование цен	*(feek-SEE-ra-va-nee-ye tsen)*	price fixing
фиксированное «роялти»	*(feek-SEE-ra-va-na-ye ROH-yal-tee)*	fixed-rate royalty
фиксированный валютный курс	*(feek-SEE-ra-va-nee va-LYOOT-nee koors)*	fixed rate of exchange
фиксированный срок	*(feek-SEE-ra-va-nee srok)*	fixed term
филиал	*(fee-lee-AHL)*	branch office
фильтр	*(feeltr)*	filter
финансирование дефицита	*(fee-nan-SEE-ra-va-nee-ye de-fee-TSEE-ta)*	deficit financing
финансировать	*(fee-nan-SEE-ra-vaht)*	finance (v)
финансовая ком-пания	*(fee-NAHN-sa-va-ya kam-PAH-nee-ya)*	finance company
финансовое пла-нирование	*(fee-NAHN-sa-va-ye pla-NEE-ra-va-nee-ye)*	financial planning
финансовые услу-ги	*(fee-NAHN-sa-vee-ye oos-LOO-ghee)*	financial services
финансовый ана-лиз	*(fee-NAHN-sa-vee a-NAH-lees)*	financial analysis
финансовый год	*(fee-NAHN-sa-vee got)*	financial year
финансовый директор	*(fee-NAHN-sa-vee dee-REK-tar)*	chief financial officer (C.F.O.)
финансовый кон-троль	*(fee-NAHN-sa-vee kan-TROL)*	financial control
финансовый отчёт	*(fee-NAHN-sa-vee at-CHYOHT)*	financial statement

Ф

финансовый советник	(fee-NAHN-sa-vee sa-VET-neek)	investment advise
финансовый срок	(fee-NAHN-sa-vee srok)	financial period
финансовый стимул	(fee-NAHN-sa-vee STEE-mool)	financial incentive
финансовый тормоз	(fee-NAHN-sa-vee TOHR-mas)	fiscal drag
финансы	(fee-NAHN-see)	finance
фирма	(FEEHR-ma)	firm
фирма-член	(FEEHR-ma-chlen)	member-firm
фирма, продающая товар данной фирмы	(FEEHR-ma pra-da-YOO-shcha-ya ta-VAHR DAHN-nay FEEHR-mee)	dealership
фирменный знак	(FEEHR-men-nee znahk)	brand, private label
фонд	(font)	fund
фонд для непредвиденных расходов	(font dlya ne-pred-VEE-den-nikh ras-KHOH-daf)	contingent fund
фонд погашения	(font pa-ga-SHEH-nee-ya)	redemption fund
фонд погашения облигации	(font pa-ga-SHEH-nee-ya ab-lee-GAH-tseey)	sinking fund
фондовая биржа	(FON-da-va-ye BEEHR-zha)	stock exchange, market
форзацная бумага	(far-ZAHTS-na-ya boo-MAH-ga)	boom-end paper
формат	(far-MAHT)	format
формула	(FOHR-moo-la)	formula
формула кредитоспособности	(FOHR-moo-la kre-dee-ta-spa-SOB-na-stee)	ability-to-pay concept
форсажная камера	(far-SAHZH-na-ya ka-MEH-ra)	alter-burner
франко-борт (ФОБ)	(FRAHN-ka BOHRT)	free on board (fob)
франко вдоль борта (ФАС)	(FRAHN-ka vdol BOHR-ta)	free alongside ship
франко завода	(FRAHN-ka za-VOH-da)	ex factory
франко пристани	(FRAHN-ka PREES-ta-nee)	ex dock
франко склад	(FRAHN-ka sklat)	ex warehouse
франко фабрики	(FRAHN-ka FAHB-ree-kee)	ex mill, works
франко шахты	(FRAHN-ka SHAHKH-tee)	ex mine

Ф

фрахт	*(frahkht)*	freight
фрахт всех видов	*(frahkht fsekh VEE-daf)*	freight all kinds
фрахт, оплачивае-мый в порту назначения	*(frahkht ap-LAH-chee-va-ye-mee FPAHR-too naz-na-CHEH-nee-ya)*	freight collect
фрахт, оплачивае-мый предвари-тельно	*(frahkht ap-LAH-chee-va-ye-mee pred-va-REE-tel-na)*	freight prepaid
фрахтование	*(frahkh-ta-VAH-nee-ye)*	affreightment
фрукты	*(FROOK-tee)*	fruit
функциональный анализ	*(foonk-tsee-a-NAHL-nee a-NAH-lees)*	functional analysis
футляр для визи-ток	*(foot-LYAHR dlya vee-ZEE-tak)*	card case
футляр для клю-чей	*(foot-LYAHR dlya kloo-CHEY)*	key case
футляр для нож-ниц	*(foot-LYAHR dlya NOZH-neets)*	scissor case
футляр для очков	*(foot-LYAHR dlya ach-KOF)*	eyeglass case
футляр для паспорта	*(foot-LYAHR dlya PAHS-par-ta)*	passport case
фюзеляж	*(fyoo-ze-LYAHSH)*	fuselage

X

халтура	*(khal-TOO-ra)*	moonlighting
хвойное дерево	*(KHVOY-na-ye DEH-re-va)*	conifer
хеджирование в ожидании пони-жения	*(khed-ZHEE-ra-va-nee-ye va-zhee-DAH-nee-ee pa-nee-SHEH-nee-ya)*	long hedge
хеджировать	*(khed-ZHEE-ra-vat)*	hedge (v
химический про-дукт	*(khee-MEE-ches-kee pra-DOOKT)*	chemical
химическое соеди-нение	*(khee-MEE-ches-ka-ye sa-ye dee-NEH-nee-ye)*	compound
химия	*(KHEE-mee-ya)*	chemistry
хлеб	*(khlep)*	bread
хлопок	*(KHLOH-pak)*	cotton
хлорид	*(khla-REET)*	chloride

хлороформ	*(khla-ra-FOHRM)*	chloroform
хмель	*(khmel)*	hops
ходатайство	*(kha-DAH-tay-stva)*	motion (legal)
хозяйствование наличными	*(kha-ZYAHY-stva-va-nee-ye na-LEECH-nee-mee)*	cash management
хорошая сделка	*(kha-ROH-sha-ya ZDEL-ka)*	bargain
хорьковый мех	*(khar-KOH-vee mekh)*	fitch
хранение	*(khra-NEH-nee-ye)*	storage
хранилище	*(khra-NEE-lee-shche)*	depository
хранилище	*(khra-NEE-lee-shche)*	storage facility
хранить документ	*(khra-NEET da-koo-MENT)*	file (v)
хром	*(khrom)*	chromium
хутор	*(KHOO-tar)*	farm

Ц

X

цветная печать	*(tsvet-NAH-ya pe-CHANT)*	color printing
цветофильтр	*(tsve-ta-FEELTR)*	color filter
целлюлоза	*(tse-lyoo-LOH-za)*	cellulose
цель компании	*(tsel kam-PAH-nee-yee)*	company goal
цена	*(tse-NAH)*	price
цена доставки	*(tse-NAH da-STAHF-kee)*	delivery price
цена золота	*(tse-NAH ZOH-la-ta)*	gold price
цена на единицу	*(tse-NAH na ye-dee-NEE-tsoo)*	unit price
цена покупателя и продавца	*(tse-NAH pa-koo-PAH-te-lya ee pra-daf-TSAH)*	bid and asked
цена с включением расходов по доставке	*(tse-NAH sfklyoo-CHEH-nee-yem ras-KHOH-daf pa das-TAHF-ke)*	delivered cost
цена с доставкой	*(tse-NAH zda-STAHF-kay)*	delivered price
цена с надбавкой	*(tse-NAH snad-BAHF-kay)*	premium price (differential)
цена рынка «спот»	*(tse-NAH RIN-ka spot)*	spot price
цена франко-бензоколонки	*(tse-NAH FRAHN-ka-ben-za-ka-LON-kee)*	pump price

цена франко-газо-генератора	*(tse-NAH FRAHN-ka-GAH-za-ghe-ne-RAH-ta-ra)*	ex-gasifier price
цена франко-скважины	*(tse-NAH FRAHN-ka-SKVAH-zhee-nee)*	well head price
цена эмиссии	*(tse-NAH e-MEES-see-ee)*	issue price
ценность	*(TSEN-nast)*	value
ценность чистой суммы активов	*(TSEN-nast CHEES-tay SOOM-mee ak-TEE-vaf)*	net asset worth
ценные бумаги	*(TSEN-nee-ye boo-MAH-ghee)*	securities
ценные бумаги, зарегистриро-ванные на бирже	*(TSEN-nee-ye boo-MAH-ghee za-re-ghees-TREE-ra-van-nee-ye na BEEHR-zhe)*	listed securities
ценные бумаги, легко реализуе-мые	*(TSEN-nee-ye boo-MAH-ghee lekh-KOH re-a-lee-ZOO-ye-mee-ye)*	marketable securities
централизация	*(tsen-tra-lee-ZAH-tsee-ya)*	centralization
централизованная энергия	*(tsen-tra-lee-ZOH-van-na-ya e-NEHR-ghee-ya)*	hard energy
центральная став-ка	*(tsent-RAHL-na-ya STAHF-ka)*	central rate
центральный банк	*(tsent-RAHL-nee bahnk)*	central bank
центральный про-цессор	*(tsent-RAHL-nee pra-TSES-sar)*	CPU
цепной (фирмен-ный) магазин	*(tsep-NOY [FEER0men-nee] ma-ga-ZEEN)*	chain store
цикл работы	*(tsikl ra-BOH-tee)*	work cycle
цинк	*(tsink)*	zinc
цифровая ЭВМ	*(tsif-ra-VAH-ya eh-veh-EM)*	digital computer
цифровой	*(tsif-ra-VOY)*	digital
цифровой кон-троль	*(trif-ra-VOY kan-TROL)*	numerical control
цицеро	*(TSEE-tse-roh)*	pica

Ч

чаевые	*(cha-ye-VEE-ye)*	gratuity
частичное совла-дение	*(chas-TEECH-na-ye sa-va-DEH-nee-ye)*	overlap

частичный груз	(chas-TEECH-nee groos)	part cargo
частичный платёж	(chas-TEECH-nee pla-TYOSH)	partial payment
частные капиталовложения	(CHAHS-nee-ye ka-pee-TAH-la-vla-ZHEH-nee-ya)	private placement (finance)
частный парк (машин)	(CHAHS-nee pahrk [ma-SHIN])	private fleet
частный хутор	(CHAHS-nee KHOO-tar)	private farm
частота	(chas-ta-TAH)	frequency
частотная модуляция	(chas-TOT-na-ya ma-doo-LYAH-tsee-ya)	frequency modulation (FM)
часы работы	(cha-SEE ra-BOH-tee)	working hours
чек	(chek)	check
чековый счёт в банке	(CHEH-ka-vee schyoht VBAHN-ke)	checking account
человеко-часы	(che-la-VEH-ka-cha-SEE)	man hours
чемодан	(che-ma-DAHN)	suitcase
червь	(chehrf)	worm
черника	(cher-NEE-ka)	bilberry
чернила	(cher-NEE-la)	inn
чёрно-белый	(CHYOHR-na-BEH-lee)	black and white
черновик	(cher-na-VEEK)	draft (document)
чёрный рынок	(CHYOHR-nee REE-nak)	black market
четырёхтактный двигатель	(che-tee-RYOKH-TAHKT-nee DVEE-ga-tel)	four-cylinder engine
четырёхцветная печать	(che-tee-RYOKH-TSVET-na-ya pe-CHANT)	four color
чистая доля акционеров	(CHEES-ta-ya DOH-lya ak-tsee-a-NEH-raf)	shareholder's equity
чистая доля в средствах	(CHEES-ta-ya DOH-lya FSRET-stvakh)	equity
чистая зарплата	(CHEES-ta-ya zar-PLAH-ta)	take-home pay
чистая прибыль	(CHEES-ta-ya PREE-bel)	net margin, profit
чистая сумма продаж	(CHEES-ta-ya SOOM-ma pra-DAHSH)	net sales
чистая ценность	(CHEES-ta-ya TSEN-nast)	net worth

Ч

чистовой доку- мент	(chees-ta-VOY da-koo- MENT)	clean document
чистовой прокат- ный стан	(chees-ta-VOY pra-KAHT- nee stahn)	finishing mill
чистое капиталов- ложение	(CHEES-ta-ye ka-pee-TAH- la-vla-ZHEH-nee-ye)	net investment
чистое «кэшфлоу»	(CHEES-ta-ye "cash flow")	net cash flow
чистое производ- ство нефтепро- дуктов	(CHEES-ta-ye pra-eez-VOT- stva NEF-te-pra-DOOK- taf)	net refinery output
чистые активы	(CHEES-tee-ye ak-TEE-vee)	net assets
чистые активы собственного капитала	(CHEES-tee-ye ak-TEE-vee SOP-stven-na-va ka-pee- TAH-la)	net equity assets
чистые инвести- ции	(CHEES-tee-ye een-ve- STEE-tsee-ee)	real investment
чистые наёмные резервы	(CHEES-tee-ye na-YOM-nee re-ZEHR-vee)	net borrowed reserves
чистый доход	(CHEES-tee da-KHOT)	net income
чистый риск	(CHEES-tee reesk)	pure risk
чистый убыток	(CHEES-tee oo-BEE-tak)	net loss
чистый функцио- нирующий капитал	(CHEES-tee foonk-tsee-a- NEE-roo-yoo-shchee ka- pee-TAHL)	net working capital
чихать	(chee-KHANT)	sneeze (v)
член фирмы	(chlen FEEHR-mee)	member of a firm
чрезвычайные запасы жидкого топлива	(chrez-vee-CHAHY-nee-ye za-PAH-see ZHIT-ka-va TOP-lee-va)	emergency petroleum reserves
чрезвычайный фонд	(chrez-vee-CHAHY-nee font)	contingent fund
чугун	(choo-GOON)	cast iron
чушковый чугун	(CHOOSH-ka-vee choo- GOON)	pig iron

Ш

| шасси | (shas-SEE) | chassis, landing gear |
| швейный ком-
плект | (SHVEY-nee kamp-LEKT) | sewing kit |

шевро	*(shev-ROH)*	kidskin
шестерня	*(shes-ter-NYAH)*	pinion
шеститактный двигатель	*(shes-tee-TAHKT-nee DVEE-ga-tel)*	six-cylinder engine
шина	*(SHEE-na)*	tire
шкала заработной платы	*(shka-LAH ZAH-ra-bat-nay PLAH-tee)*	wage scale
шлифование	*(shlee-fa-VAH-nee-ye)*	grinding
шорник	*(SHOHR-neek)*	saddler
шпангоут	*(shpan-GOH-oot)*	bulkhead
шприц	*(shpreets)*	syringe
штаб	*(shtahp)*	headquarters, head office
штаб операций	*(shtahp a-pe-RA-tsey)*	operations headquarters
штраф	*(shtrahf)*	fine (penalty)
штрафная оговор-ка	*(shtrahf-NAH-ya a-ga-VOHR-ka)*	penalty clause
штрейкбрехер	*(shtreyk-BREH-kher)*	strikebreaker
штриховой ориги-нал	*(shtree-kha-VOY a-ree-ghee-nal)*	line drawing
штучная работа	*(SHTOOCH-na-ya ra-BOH-ta)*	piecework

Ш

Щ

щелочная почва	*(shche-lach-NAH-ya POCH-va)*	alkaline (soil)
щит	*(shcheet)*	panel
щуп для поиска неисправностей	*(shchoop dla POH-ees-ka ne-ees-PRAHV-na-stey)*	troubleshooter

Э

ЭВМ	*(eh-veh-EM)*	computer
эквивалентная цена	*(ek-vee-va-LENT-na-ya tse-NAH)*	parity price
экземпляр	*(ek-zem-PLYAHR)*	copy (text)

эконометрика	(e-ka-na-MET-ree-ka)	econometrics
эконо́мить	(e-ka-NOH-meet)	economize (v)
экономическая долговечность	(e-ka-na-MEE-ches-ka-ya dal-ga-VECH-nast)	economic life
экономические показатели	(e-ka-na-MEE-ches-kee-ye pa-ka-ZAH-te-lee)	economic indicators
экономические принципы Кэйнса	(e-ka-na-MEE-ches-kee-ye PREEN-tsee-pe KEYN-sa)	keynesian economics
экономический	(e-ka-na-MEE-ches-kee)	economic
экономический спад	(e-ka-na-MEE-ches-kee spat)	downturn
экономический цикл	(e-ka-na-MEE-ches-kee tsikl)	cycle, business
экономия	(e-ka-NOH-mee-ya)	economy
экономия затрат	(e-ka-NOH-mee-ya za-TRAHT)	cost reduction
экран	(ek-RAHN)	screen
экспедитор	(eks-pe-DEE-tar)	freight forwarder, forwarding agent
экспедиторский агент	(eks-pe-DEE-tar-skee a-GHENT)	shipping agent
эксперимент	(eks-pe-ree-MENT)	experiment
эксперименталь-ный	(eks-pe-ree-men-TAHL-nee)	experimental
экспертиза	(eks-per-TEE-za)	expert opinion
эксплуатационная скважина	(eks-ploo-a-ta-tsee-ON-na-ya SKVAH-zhee-na)	development well
эксплуатационное бурение	(eks-ploo-a-ta-tsee-ON-na-ye boo-REH-nee-ye)	developed drilling
эксплуатацион-ные приборы	(eks-ploo-a-ta-tsee-ON-nee-ye pree-BOH-ree)	working tools
эксплуатацион-ные расходы	(eks-ploo-a-ta-tsee-ON-nee-ye ras-KHOH-dee)	operating expenses
эксплуатацион-ные фонды	(eks-ploo-a-ta-tsee-ON-nee-ye FON-dee)	working funds
экспорт капитала	(EKS-part ka-pee-TAH-la)	capital exports
экспортная квота	(EKS-part-na-ya KVOH-ta)	export quota
экспортная пошлина	(EKS-part-na-ya POSH-lee-na)	export duty

Э

Экспортно-Импортный Банк (США)	*(EKS-part-na-EEM-part-nee bahnk [se-sha-a])*	Export Import Bank (USA)
экспортные распоряжения	*(EKS-part-nee-ye ras-pa-rya-ZHEH-nee-ya)*	export regulation
экспортный агент	*(EKS-part-nee a-GHENT)*	export agent
экспортный кредит	*(EKS-part-nee kre-DEET)*	export credit
экспортный тариф	*(EKS-part-nee ta-REEF)*	export tariff
экспроприация	*(eks-pra-pree-AH-tsee-ya)*	expropriation
эластичность спроса и предложения	*(e-las-TEECH-nast SPROH-sa ee pred-la-ZHEH-nee-ya)*	elasticity (of supply or demand)
эластичность цены	*(e-las-TEECH-nast tse-NEE)*	price elasticity
электричество	*(e-lek-TREE-chest-va)*	electricity
электрод	*(e-lek-TROT)*	electrode
электродуговая печь	*(e-LEK-tra-doo-ga-VAH-ya pech)*	electric arc furnace
электролиз	*(e-lek-TROH-lis)*	electrolysis
электролитический процесс	*(e-lek-tra-lee-TEE-ches-kee pra-TSES)*	electrolytic process
электрон	*(e-lek-TRON)*	electron
электронный	*(e-lek-TRON-nee)*	electronic
электростатический	*(e-lek-tra-sta-TEE-ches-kee)*	electrostatic
электротехника	*(e-lek-tra-TEKH-nee-ka)*	electrical engineering
элемент	*(e-le-MENT)*	element
эмбарго	*(em-BAHR-ga)*	embargo
эмблема	*(em-BLEH-ma)*	logo
эмбрион	*(em-bree-OHN)*	embryo
эмиссионная премия	*(e-mees-see-ON-na-ya PREH-mee-ya)*	redemption premium
энергия	*(e-NEHR-ghee-ya)*	power
эргономика	*(ehr-ga-NOH-mee-ka)*	ergonomics
эрозия	*(e-ROH-zee-ya)*	erosion

Э

«эталонная» нефть	*(e-ta-LON-na-ya neft)*	marker (crude) oil
этан	*(e-TAHN)*	ethane
этанол	*(e-ta-NOL)*	ethanol
эффект Допплера	*(ef-FEKT DOP-ple-ra)*	Doppler effect
эффективность	*(ef-fe-KTEEV-nast)*	efficiency

Ю

юридическое лицо	*(yoo-ree-DEE-ches-ka-ye lee-TSOH)*	legal entity
юрисдикция	*(yoo-rees-DEEK-tsee-ya)*	jurisdiction

Я

яблоко	*(YAHB-la-ka)*	apple
ягнёнок	*(yag-NYOH-nak)*	lamb
язык компьютера	*(ya-ZIK kam-PYOO-te-ra)*	computer language
яйцо	*(YAHY-tsa)*	egg
якорная пошлина	*(YAH-kar-na-ya POSH-lee-na)*	anchorage dues
ярлык с указани- ем цены	*(yar-LIK soo-ka-ZAH-nee-yem tse-NEE)*	price tag
ярмарка	*(YAHR-mar-ka)*	trade fair
яровая пшеница	*(ya-ra-VAH-ya pshe-NEE-tsa)*	spring wheat
ясень	*(YAH-sen)*	ash (tree)
ячмень	*(yach-MEN)*	barley
ящик для упаков- ки	*(YAH-shcheek dla oo-pa-KOF-kee)*	packing case

Я

VIII. MAPS

These maps of the NIS will be helpful in doing business in those areas.

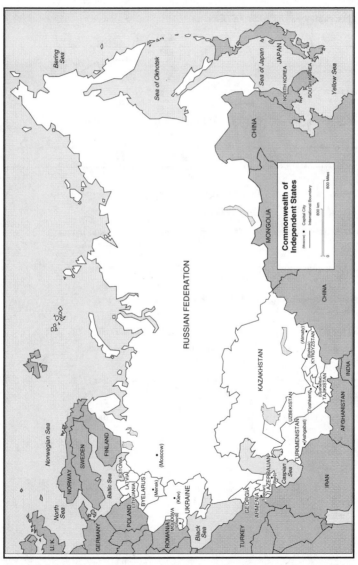

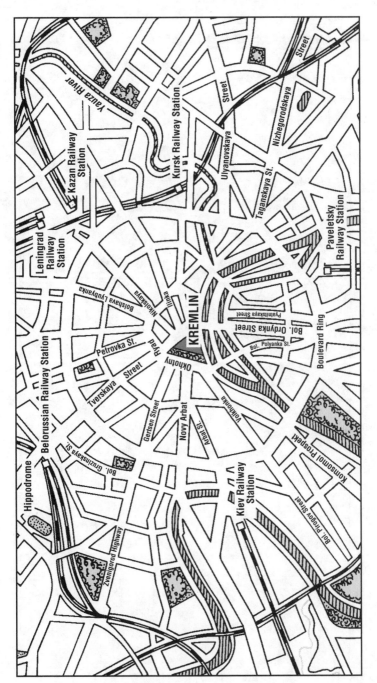

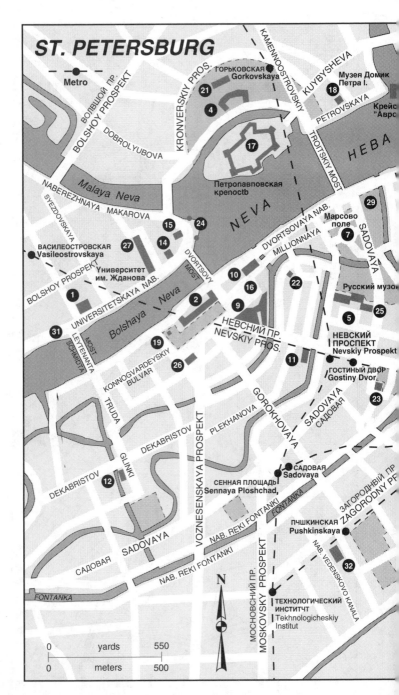

ST. PETERSBURG

Metro

ВОЛЬШОЙ ПР.
BOLSHOY PROSPEKT

DOBROLYUBOVA

KRONVERSKIY PROS.

ТОРЬКОВСКАЯ
Gorkovskaya

KAMENNOOSTROVSKIY

KUYBYSHEVA

Музея Домик
Петра I.

PETROVSKAYA

Крейс
"Авро

НЕВА

Петропавловская
крепостb

TROITSKIY MOST

NABEREZHNAYA MAKAROVA

Malaya Neva

SVEZDOVSKAYA

NEVA

DVORTSOVAYA NAB.

Марсово
поле

SADOVAYA

ВАСИЛЕОСТРОВСКАЯ
Vasileostrovskaya

MILLIONNAYA

Русский музо

Университет
им. Жданова

BOLSHOY PROSPEKT

DVORTSOVY MOST

UNIVERSITETSKAYA NAB.

Bolshaya Neva

НЕВСНИЙ ПР.
NEVSKIY PROS.

НЕВСКИЙ
ПРОСПЕКТ
Nevskiy Prospekt

MOST LEYTENANTA SCHMIDTA

KONNOGVARDEYSKIY BULVAR

ГОСТИНЫЙ ДВОР
Gostiny Dvor

TRUDA

GLINKI

DEKABRISTOV

PLEKHANOVA

GOROKHOVAYA

SADOVAYA
САДОВАЯ

DEKABRISTOV

VOZNESENSKAYA PROSPEKT

САДОВАЯ
Sadovaya

ЗАГОРОДНЫЙ ПР
ZAGORODNY PR

СЕННАЯ ПЛОЩАДЬ
Sennaya Ploshchad,

FONTANKA

ПЧШКИНСКАЯ
Pushkinskaya

NAB. VEDENSKOVO KANALA

SADOVAYA

NAB. REKI FONTANKI

NAB. REKI FONTANKI

САДОВАЯ

FONTANKA

N

МОСОВНСИЙ ПР.
MOSKOVSKY PROSPEKT

ТЕХНОЛОГИЧЕСКИЙ
ИНСТИТЧТ
Tekhnnologicheskiy
Institut

| 0 | yards | 550 |
| 0 | meters | 500 |

1 Academy of Arts
2 Admiralty
3 Alexander Nevsky Monastery
4 Artillery Museum
5 Arts Square
6 Aurora Cruiser
7 Field of Mars
8 Finland Station
9 Former General Staff Bldg.
10 Hermitage
11 Kazan Cathedral
12 Marinskiy Theater
13 Moscow Station
14 Museum of Anthroplogy
   and Ethnography
15 Naval Museum
16 Palace Square
17 Peter and Paul Fortress
18 Peter's Cottage
19 Peter the Great Monument
   and Decembrists' Square
20 Piskarevky Cemetery
21 Planetarium
22 Pushkin House
23 Pushkin Theater
24 Rostral Column
25 Russian Museum
26 St. Isaac's Cathedral
27 St. Petersburg State
   University
28 Smolny
29 Summer Garden
30 Tavricheskiy Palace
31 University Embankment
32 Vitebsk Station

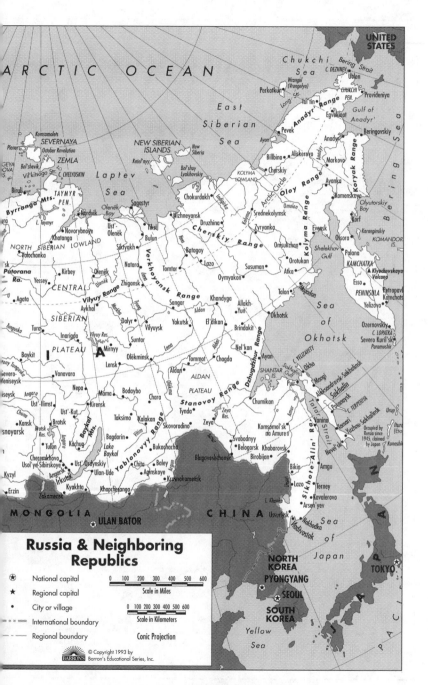

ARCTIC OCEAN

UNITED STATES

Chukchi Sea

Bering Strait

C. DEZHNEV

Uelen

Wrangel (Wrangelya)

Perkatkun

Provideniya

CHUKCHI PEN.

Iul'tin

Egvekinot

Gulf of Anadyr'

East Siberian Sea

Ayon

Pevek

Anadyr

Beringovskiy

Billbino

Aliskerovo

Markovo

Komsomolets

SEVERNAYA

Pioner

October Revolution

ZEMLA

Bol'shevik

Vil'kitsogo St.

C. CHELYUSKIN

NEW SIBERIAN ISLANDS

New Siberia

Kotel'nyy

Bol'shoy Lyakhovskiy

KOLYMA LOWLAND

Cherskiy

Arctic Circle

Oloy Range

Ayanka

Kamenskoye

Olyutorskiy Bay

Biruli

TAYMYR PEN.

Chokurdakh

Indigirka

Srednekolymsk

Omolon

Korf

Karaginskiy I.

KOMANDOR IS.

Byrranga Mts.

Nordvik

Olenëk Bay

Sagastyr

Nizhneyansk

Druzhina

Zyryanka

Omsukchan

Evensk

Oscora

Palana

KAMCHATKA

L. Taymyr

Novorybnoye

Khatanga

Ust'-Olenëk

Tiksi

Cherskiy Range

Orotukan

Shelekhov Gulf

Klyuchevskaya Volcano

NORTH SIBERIAN LOWLAND

Volochanka

Bulun

Batagay

Lazo

Susuman

Atka

PENINSULA

Esso

Petropavl Kamchats

'sk

Pútorana Ra.

Yessey

Kirbey

Olenëk

Siktyakh

Natara

Tomtor

Oymyakon

Talon

Magadan

Sea of Okhotsk

Yelizovo

Agata

CENTRAL

Olenëk

Zhigansk

Khandyga

Allakh-Yun'

Ozernovskiy

C. LOPATKA

Tura

Vilyuy Range

Aykhal

Sangar

El'dikan

Brindakit

Okhotsk

Severo Kuril'sk

Paramushir

Tunguska

Inarigda

Dalyr

Yakutsk

SIBERIAN

Vilyuysk

Nel'kan

Baykit

Suntar

Tommot

Chagda

Ayan

Vanavara

PLATEAU

Mirnyy

Olëkminsk

Aldan

SHANTAR IS.

Nepa

Máma

Bodaybo

Chara

ALDAN

PLATEAU

Chumikan

Urup

iseysk

Ust'-Ilimst

Taksimo

Kalakan

Tynda

Stanovoy Range

C. TERPENIYA

Uzhno-Sakhalinsk

Ituru (Eto

Chuna

Kansk

Bratsk

Ust'-Kut

Kirensk

Bagdarin

Vitim

Skovorodino

Zeya

Zeya Res.

Komsomol'sk na Amure

Vanino

Sovetskaya Gavan'

snoyarsk

Bratsk Res.

Tulun

Kachug

Baley

Svobodnyy

Belogorsk

Khabarovsk

Cheremkhovo

Usol'ye-Sibirskoye

Angarsk

Irkutsk

Ust'-Ordynskiy

Ulan-Ude

Chita

Aginskoye

Bukachacha

Blagoveshchensk

Birobijan

Bikin

Amgu

Kyzyl

Zakamensk

Kyakhta

Khapcheranga

Lazo

Terney

Kavalerovo

Arsen'yev

Erzin

MONGOLIA

★ **ULAN BATOR**

CHINA

Ussuriysk

Nakhodka

Vladivostok

Sea of Japan

NORTH KOREA

PYONGYANG

SEOUL

SOUTH KOREA

TOKYO

Yellow Sea

Russia & Neighboring Republics

⬟ National capital

★ Regional capital

• City or village

▪ ▪ ▪ International boundary

--- Regional boundary

0 100 200 300 400 500 600

Scale in Miles

0 100 200 300 400 500 600

Scale in Kilometers

Conic Projection

© Copyright 1993 by
BARRON'S Barron's Educational Series, Inc.

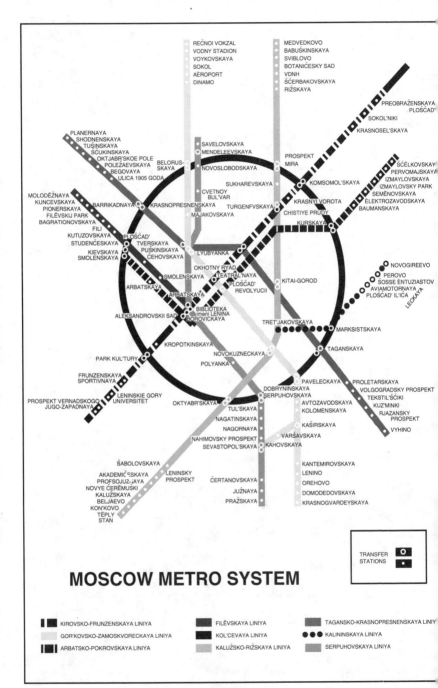

MOSCOW METRO SYSTEM

TRANSFER
STATIONS

- KIROVSKO-FRUNZENSKAYA LINIYA
- GOR'KOVSKO-ZAMOSKVORECKAYA LINIYA
- ARBATSKO-POKROVSKAYA LINIYA
- FILÊVSKAYA LINIYA
- KOL'CEVAYA LINIYA
- KALUŽSKO-RIŽSKAYA LINIYA
- TAGANSKO-KRASNOPRESNENSKAYA LINIY
- KALININSKAYA LINIYA
- SERPUHOVSKAYA LINIYA